Victorian Glass Novelties

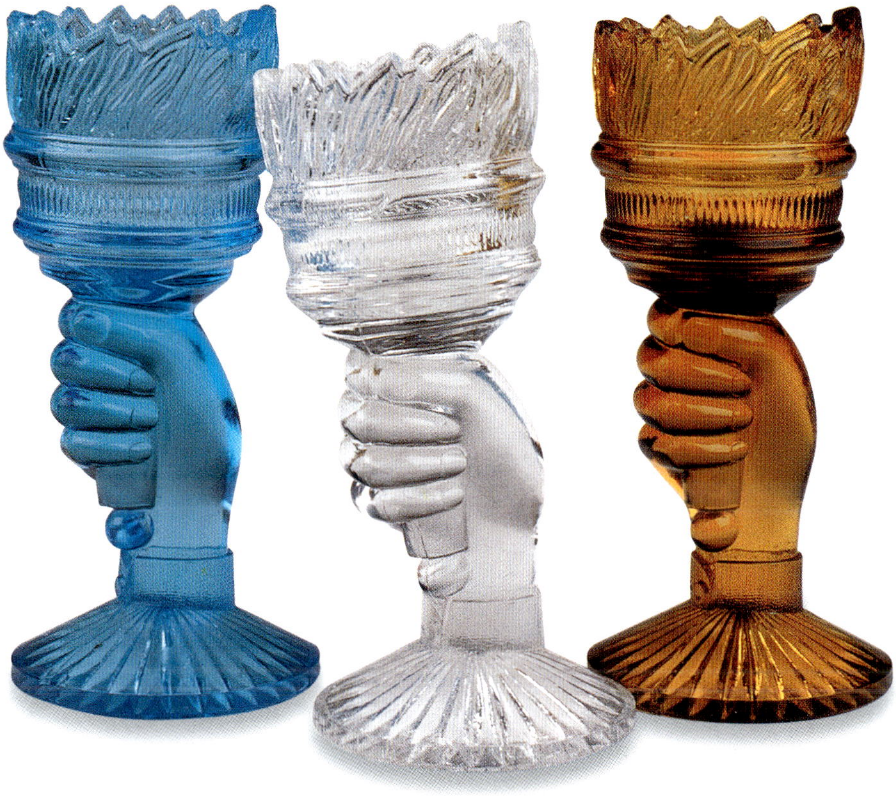

Jo & Bob Sanford

Schiffer Publishing Ltd

4880 Lower Valley Road, Atglen, PA 19310 USA

Dedication

To Pat and Bob Costa

About the Values

The values placed on these items were gathered from dealers who exhibit at major antiques shows in the United States and from collectors who have specialized collections. These values will vary in different sections of the country and values will fluctuate, as dealers usually must pay higher prices as they replenish their stock and they in turn must make a small profit. This is strictly an estimated value guide and must not be used as a buying guide. The best guide to buying when starting to collect these items is to know and trust the dealer that you are buying from.

Library of Congress Control Number: 2002112424

Designed by Kevin Kelly
Cover by Bruce Waters
Type set in Zaph Chancery Bd BT/Souvenir Lt BT

ISBN: 0-7643-1703-2
Printed in China
1 2 3 4

Published by Schiffer Publishing Ltd.
4880 Lower Valley Road
Atglen, PA 19310
Phone: (610) 593-1777; Fax: (610) 593-2002
E-mail: Schifferbk@aol.com
Please visit our web site catalog at
www.schifferbooks.com
We are always looking for people to write books on new and related subjects. If you have an idea for a book please contact us at the above address.

This book may be purchased from the publisher.
Include $3.95 for shipping.
Please try your bookstore first.
You may write for a free catalog.

In Europe, Schiffer books are distributed by
Bushwood Books
6 Marksbury Ave.
Kew Gardens
Surrey TW9 4JF England
Phone: 44 (0)20-8392-8585
Fax: 44 (0)20-8392-9876
E-mail: Bushwd@aol.com
Free postage in the UK. Europe: air mail at cost

Acknowledgments

We thank the collectors and dealers who contributed to the making of this book. Without them this book would not have been possible. Some wished to remain anonymous and we respected their wishes. We are grateful to the following people and their contributions.

Walt Adams for his photo of the Lion lamp.
Neila & Tom Bredehoft for photos of their collection and Tom for the photography of their collection.
Pat & Bob Costa for allowing us to photograph their collection.
Larry Dosier for allowing photos of his collection.
Alice Hatch for allowing photos of her collection and also for the photography of her collection and the Larry Dosier collection.
Barbara & Lowell Jones for allowing me to photograph rarities from their collection.
Shaun Kotlarsky for the photos of the Hemingray factory glassware.
Dave Peterson for his vaseline glass.
The staff of The Rakow Library, the Corning Museum of Glass, Corning, New York.
The staff of the Delaware County District Library, Delaware, Ohio.
The staff of the Volusia County Public Library, Deland, Florida.

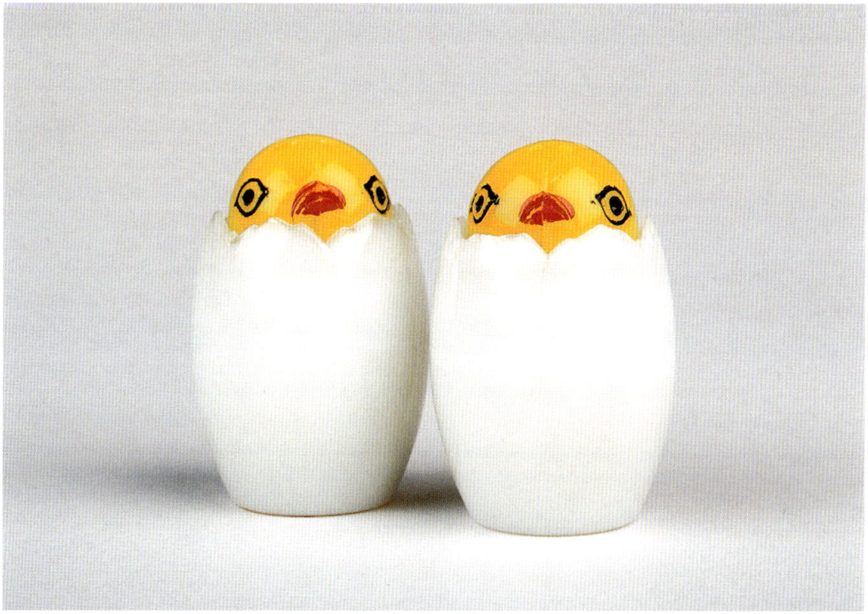

Preface

Among the many things made of glass that are collected today probably the most diversified are the novelties, which consist of candy containers, perfume bottles, decanters, paperweights, toothpick holders, salt cellars, saltshakers, butter dishes, celeries, table settings, mustard and/or horse-radish jars, packer's goods, and figurals. Packer's goods are containers for such items as mustard, spices, and candy to be marketed in. Almost all tableware factories and many specialty glass factories from the mid-1880s period manufactured novelties of various kinds. We have attempted to illustrate as many as possible in this volume.

One very large problem that we encountered in writing this book was the gathering of facts. While the trade journals had included a great deal of information and illustrations about the patterns of the tableware factories, very little was written about or illustrations printed of the novelties unless they were part of a set. We have accepted the attributions of other authors when proof was offered.

Items similar to the ones illustrated in this book have appeared in other reference books such as those containing opaque glass, historical glass, candy containers, saltshakers and toothpick holders, and others. Our objective is to cover this field as broadly as possible because we feel that the wide variety makes an outstanding collection.

You may have a novelty that isn't listed or pictured in this book. If you have anything different we would like for you to contact us through the publishing house so that we can document them.

Contents

Acknowledgments 3
Preface 4
Introduction 6
Getting Acquainted with Novelties 7
The Manufacturers 8
Bibliography 192

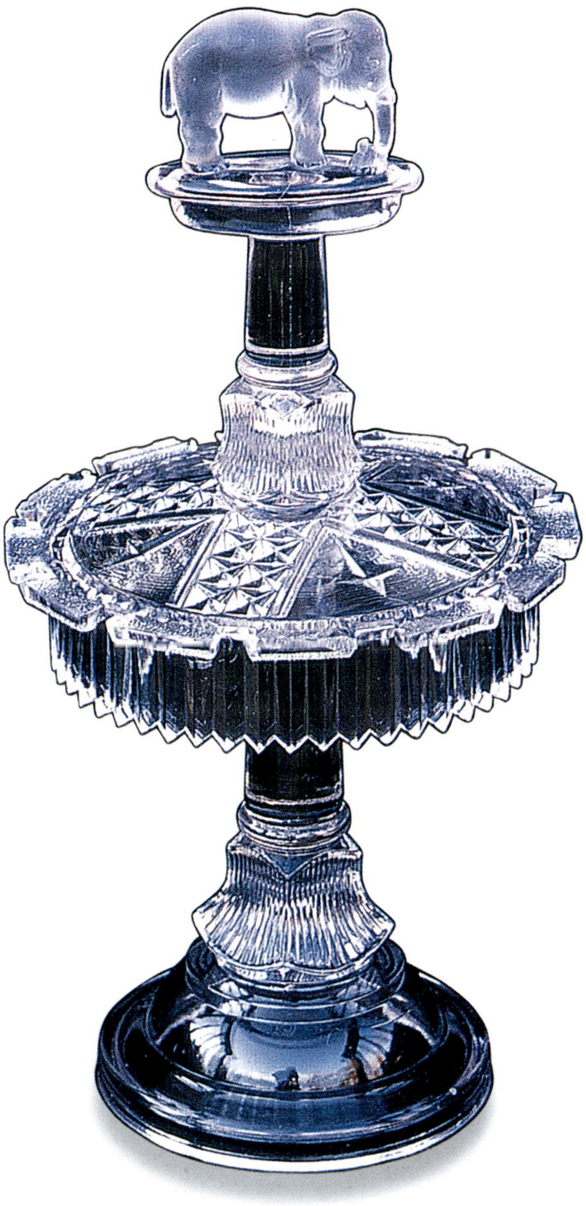

Introduction

The glass industry has been a vital part of the growth and development of our country. The people who worked this business and furnished us with so many items have probably never been properly appreciated. Most of the owners and operators experienced fires, floods, strikes, lockouts, bankruptcies, dissolutions, and financial crunches due to economic slowdowns and recessions.

The workers faced layoffs, lockouts, and terrible working conditions at times.

The salesmen who took to the road selling, taking orders for their merchandise, exposed themselves to various health risks, the most common being pneumonia. Some died at an early age.

Many young boys were employed at the glass works and most were about twelve years old. The minimum age in the 1880s was twelve years of age. When Congress tried to raise it to fourteen, the manufacturers' lobbyists succeeded in getting the measure defeated.

Two of the more important workers in the tableware factories were the chemists and the mold makers. The chemist had the formulas for the various types and colors of glassware. These formulae he kept as a carefully guarded secret and usually passed them down to his son and he to his son. The mold maker chipped the molds for the glass items.

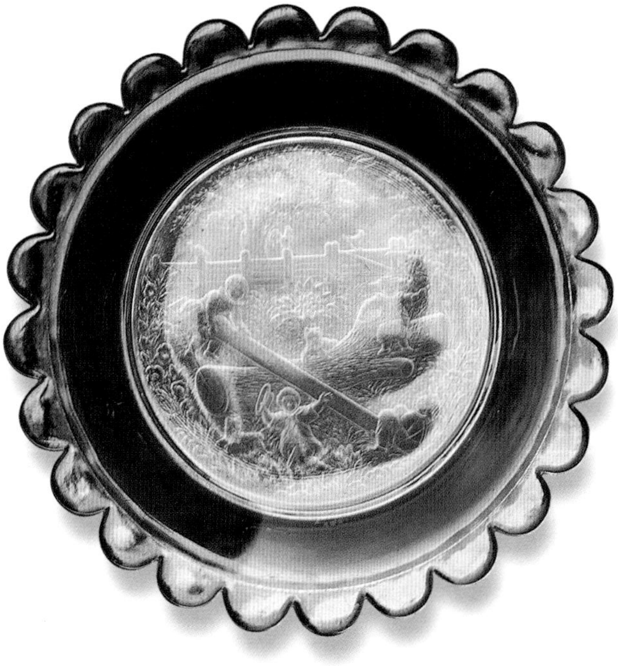

Getting Acquainted with Novelties

The best sources of information as to what was being manufactured are the trade journals and manufacturers catalogs of the time. While researching the trade journals of the time it is necessary to know that the writers sometimes used the name of the glassworks when referring to a factory, and this glassworks might have a different name than the factory. Another problem encountered is that some of these factories had nicknames. The well known names of glassworks were *White House, Ft. Pitt, Jenny Lind, South Wheeling, and East End Works.* In the trade journal *China, Glass and Lamps* of February 1906, an interesting article appeared, titled *Bellaire as a Glass City.* This article also mentions nicknames. Here is the article in its entirety:

> *The first glass factory erected in Bellaire was the Belmont. It was built on Central Avenue on the site now occupied by the Novelty Stamping Co. This factory was built in the latter part of the 60s and started with one furnace. Afterward an additional furnace was built. The Belmont was built by former employees of the old Hobbs plant in Wheeling, and among these were John Robinson, Henry Over, Jacob Crimmel, Henry Crimmel, and others. The next plant built was the National Glass Works, now Rodefer's. It was erected by the late Capt. John Fink, brother-in-law of Senator N. B. Scott, of Wheeling, and others. Here is where the Senator made his start in the glass business. This plant was built about 1870.*
>
> *Then came the small bottle plant erected just opposite what was known as Ned Monahan's saloon. This plant was operated by Mr. Arbogast and sons, Christopher, James, and Alexander. This firm afterwards built a large factory on what is known as the Jackley farm, about one mile west of Bellaire. Next came the Ohio Glass Co., nicknamed "The Cassell." It was built by Levi Cassell and others. This plant was erected at the mouth of the Heatherington coalmine. The next was the Star Glass Works, nicknamed the "Dolly Varden," built and operated by Col. Sullivan and sons, Theodore and John. This plant stood near the site now occupied by the Bellaire Brewing Co.*
>
> *Another was a small plant built by Benjamin Powers and sons for the manufacture of bottles. This factory was erected near where Berrysteed's ice plant stands today. Then came the Bellaire Goblet Co.'s works, nicknamed the "Circus." This plant stood at what is known as Morgan's coal works. Next in line was the Bellaire Bottle Co.'s plant, situated on the site now occupied by them. Then came the Aetna Glass Co., now known as the "Century." All of the above were flint factories except the Arbogast and Powers plants. Bellaire reached her zenith as a manufacturing city in 1880. At that time the glass industries in operation were: Belmont Glass Co., two furnaces on tableware; Aetna Glass Co., one furnace on tableware; Bellaire Goblet Co., two furnaces on goblets and novelties; Rodefer Bros., one furnace on a variety of ware; Bellaire Bottle Co., one furnace on bottles, and the Bellaire Lantern Globe Co., one furnace on lantern globes.*

With this in mind let's start by looking at some of the factories and a little that is known of their products.

The Manufacturers

Adams and Company were organized in 1861 at Pittsburgh and continued in operation until 1891 when they became factory A of the United States Glass Company. They were known to have made many novelties and many more that have not been documented. In October of 1880 this firm was *turning out beautiful glass mugs bearing the portrait of General Garfield.* These mugs were distributed along the route of a big parade in honor of his election. For a short period of time in 1885, the Adams factory was producing a Grant plate; but, when Adams and Company was advised by Bryce, Higbee & Company that Adams was infringing on their rights, the Adams Company ceased production. It is unknown how many of the Adams plates are in existence.

From an illustrated advertisement we find that the Adams Company produced the Shoe Brush Match, Clothes Brush Toilet Box, Tomato Butter, Grape Wall Match, Barrow Salt, and Hair Brush Toilet Box.

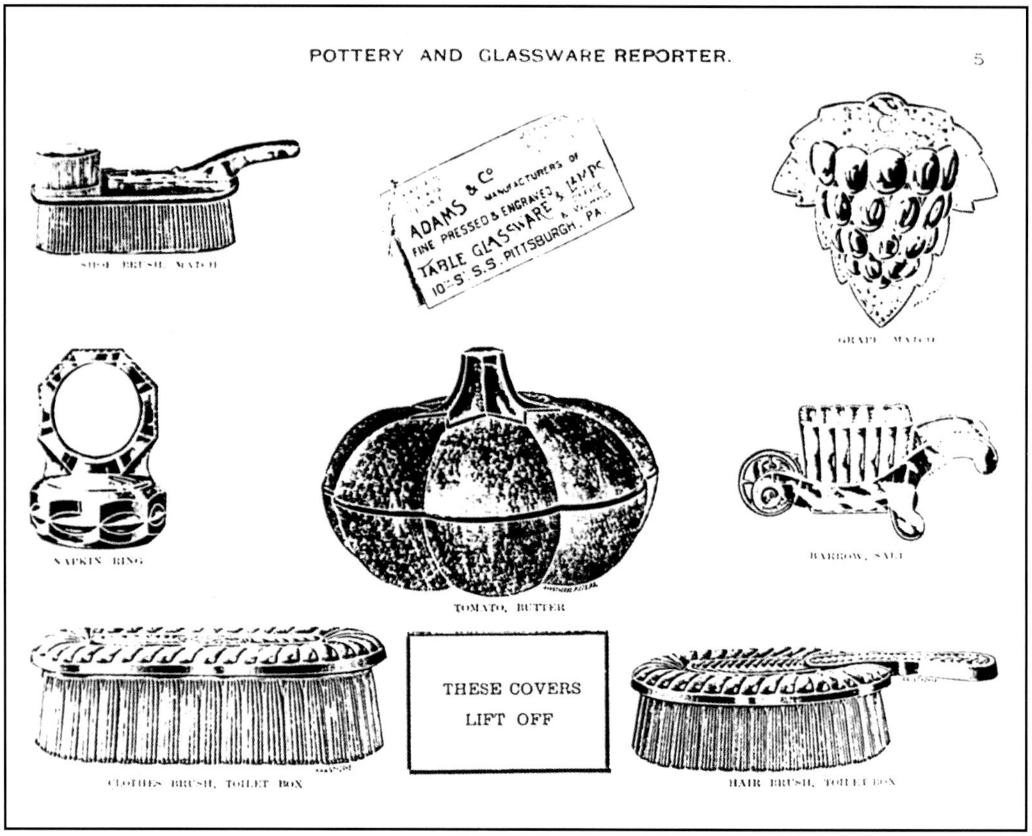

Other items known to be made by the Adams & Company are the Book Match or Toothpick Holder in clear, amber, blue, opal, and opaque blue; a Kettle in clear, amber, blue, and canary; and the Coal Skuttle in clear, apple green, aqua, blue, and canary.

The **Aetna Glass and Manufacturing Company** of Bellaire, Ohio, were organized in 1880 and continued producing glassware until 1889. During this time they made some novelties that stirred the imagination. Although they described most of their products in advertisements, they did not illustrate them. In 1880, their first year of production, they were *producing a goblet with steamboats and hotels on them and when orders were placed they would add the name of the hotel or boat.*

In 1882 Aetna were turning out *goblets and punch tumblers with Garfield's profile on them.* The following year the Aetna Works were busy producing a popular novelty, the Rebecca jug. It is not known whether other novelties were being produced at this time; however, a few months later the announcement was made that they were now producing a new butter dish with a lion couchant as a lid and that other goods would be out in a short time. True to their word, the Aetna Works introduced a large bowl called the "Jumbo" the following month. This *large fruit bowl measures twelve inches high.*

In 1884 the Aetna started the year off strong with a very handsome salver and bowl, the *Epergne* style, a cabbage egg dish, the Jumbo fruit bowl, and chicken butter dishes. A few months into the year 1884, the firm was introducing *butter patties in canary and topaz called the Butterfly. In etched ware they were making a design representing two old men drinking to each others health, a dog lying at their feet denoting faithfulness, and a horse signifying the flight of time.* The design is called *Old Lang Syne.* Another design was the *Old Oaken Bucket* but no description was given.

The Aetna, as most glass manufacturers, also did private mold and manufacturing work as was in evidence with a novelty produced for the Western Shot Manufacturing Company. It was a tall glass fashioned after a tower, nearly a foot high and filled with shot, to be given to the customers of the Shot Company.

Perhaps one of the most interesting tableware sets made was manufactured by the Aetna Company and introduced in December of 1884. It was their Number 300 set. It was also known as their *White House* set. *The pieces are convex instead of concave, — Among the novelties is a butter of a novel shape with an elevated cover. A combined sugar and spoonholder, shaped like an old castle with ivy trained very gracefully over the towers and windows, is the neatest thing that the Aetna has turned out in years. There was also a butter dish, an exact facsimile of the nation's capitol, the dome, and upper portion forming the cover.* (*Crockery & Glass Journal* 1884.)

It appears that the Aetna Company always had good selling novelties on the market. In January of 1886 they introduced a receptacle for tobacco and cigars in the shape of a knobby castle.

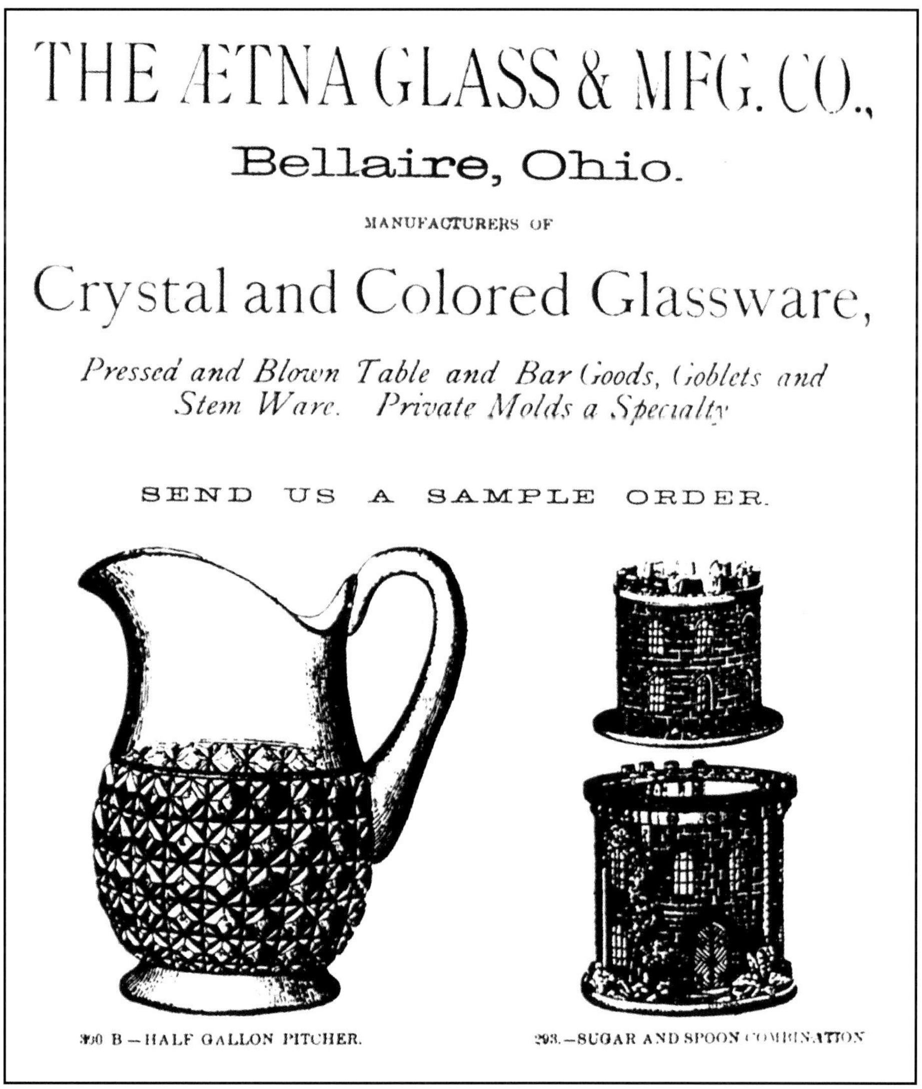

The Aetna Company had an enterprising Secretary by the name of E. B. Bowie who designed a most novel toothpick holder or match holder. It has three human figures adorning the *Egyptian Pillars.* A photo of this holder appears elsewhere in this book.

Although it is not a novelty we feel that this last bit of information should be added about the Aetna Glass products. An article appeared in the trade journals on October 27, 1887, which tells about their new ware — *the latest is their — Snowflake water sets — a new opal night light and a snowflake breakfast set in assorted opalescent colors are also very attractive.*

Not all novel items are novelties to be collected, but the information should be made available; therefore, we must report that the **Agnew & Company** of Pittsburgh were manufacturing glass balls for rifle practice in February of 1880. Although this is not a significant bit of news, it does help bring into focus the fact that it was not always the large tableware factory that was producing everything. By the end of the year the factory name had been changed to **Agnew & Brown** and they were making glass balls at the rate of 50,000 per week.

Atterbury and Company, of Pittsburgh, Pennsylvania, came into existence in 1865 and were owned and operated by James S. and Thomas B. Atterbury, who held numerous patents for glassware. The Atterburys were well known for their opal novelties. Among these were the Fish relish, Rabbit covered dish, Duck covered dish, Boar's Head and Bull's Head covered dishes, Reclining Cat covered dish, Reclining Fox covered dish, and the Reclining Lion covered dish. These are only a few of the many novel items manufactured by Atterbury and Company.

Now lets look at some of the items that Atterbury manufactured that are not novelties to be collected and are not items that you would expect from this firm. In 1880, Mr. J. S. Atterbury announced that they were busy making opal knife handles and shutters of colored glass for the inside of windows.

In the year 1880, Mr. Thomas Atterbury secured a patent for his *cloth and fabric*. A quote from the *Crockery and Glass Journal* is *Messrs. Atterbury and Co., of the South side, are turning out large quantities of iridescent glass, and samples of the cloth fabric ...* The firm then proceeded to manufacture a dress for Sarah Bernhardt and an exhibit of items including glass shawls, glass neckties, and glass feathers, all of which were made of their glass cloth. Although Mr. Atterbury was more or less ridiculed for proceeding with his glass cloth, he continued by making a glass tablecloth and napkins and a childs dress and received a request from Fannie Davenport for a dress. Of course the Atterburys were delighted when the government asked for samples of the glass cloth. The government believed that the glass cloth could be used for fish hatching in place of wire cloth.

In 1882 Atterbury and Company received a patent for glass roofing shingles.

Although the above-mentioned items are not novelty collectibles, they provide insight into the ability of the glass men to have many novel ideas.

Another small glass factory started business in 1882. Hartford P. Brown and a Mr. Maxwell leased the Beaver Glass House at Pittsburgh where they manufactured paperweights, for which Mr. Maxwell held patents.

The larger factories were also making paperweights in 1882 and it is noted in the trade journals that the **Bellaire Goblet Company** was making a very pretty paperweight, a miniature replica of Plymouth Rock. The Bellaire Goblet Company made many other novelties at Bellaire, Ohio, and later at Findlay, Ohio. Some of their most popular items include the famous Coach Fruit Bowl, Cigar Lighter, Celery flat RR car, master salt RR car, and salt RR car, all being made in the Number 600 Stars and Bars pattern. They also manufactured the Pig on a flat car, Pig paperweight, the Clock match holder, the Corset perfume holder, the high button shoe, and the turtle salt dip.

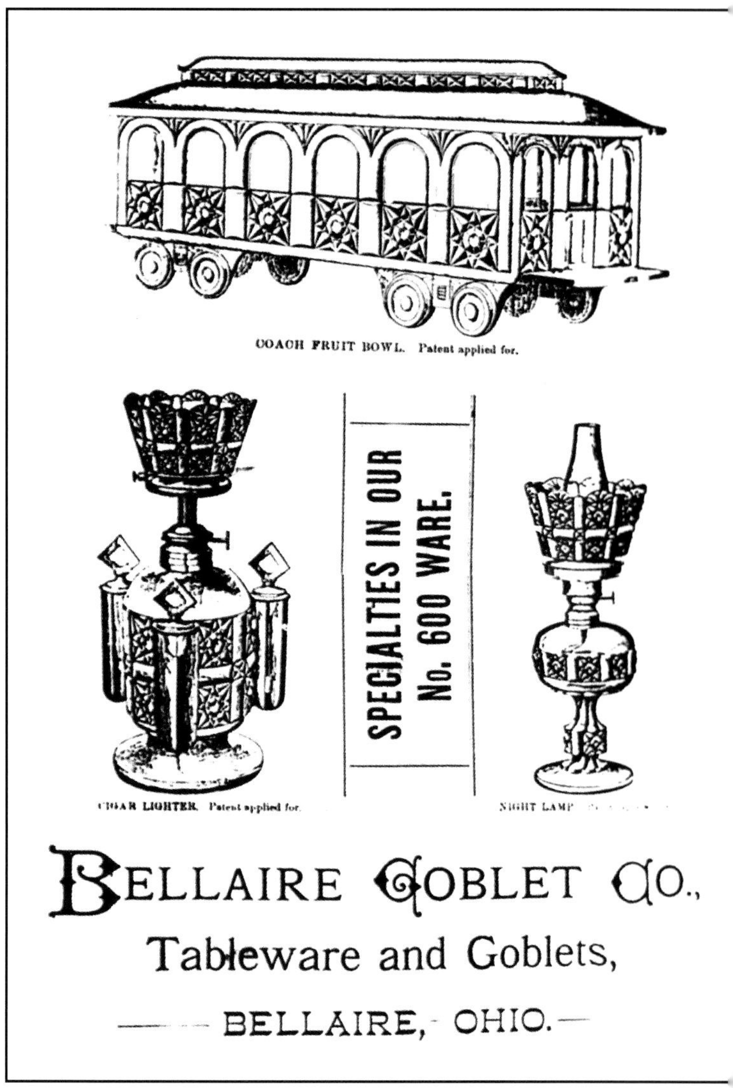

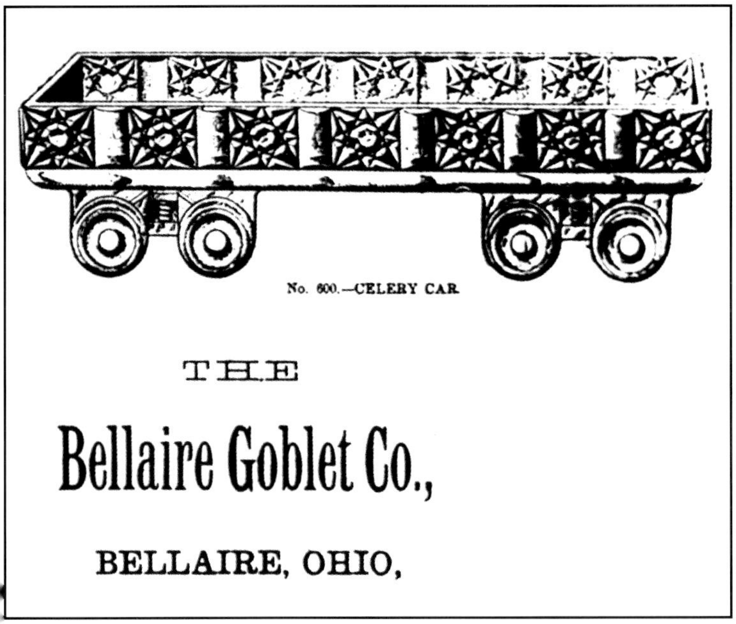

The **Belmont Glass Company** of Bellaire, Ohio, made some very nice tableware and novelties in pressed glass; but, as they did not advertise as much as the other tableware factories, there is little known about their novelties. We do know from an article in the *Crockery and Glass Journal* in 1887 that one item they were manufacturing was — *the dog-tearing-the-hat toothpick or match holder.* The Belmont Glass Company manufactured glassware from 1866 to 1890 and undoubtedly made many undocumented novelties.

The **Bonita Glass Company** of Cicero, Indiana, which were organized in 1897 and manufactured glassware until its demise in 1900, was a factory whose products have always remained a mystery. Although we have found no illustrations of their work, we do have advertisements and their history to keep us interested. Their advertisements give us the information that they produced novelties in white and black opaque glass. The organizers of the Bonita Glass Co. were Otto Jaeger, John Hobbs, and his son Charles Hobbs. These men had all been associated with the Hobbs Company at Wheeling and were well known for their talents in making glassware. Also located at Cicero, Indiana, was the **Arduser Mould Shop**, which had moved from Findlay, Ohio. The Arduser Mould Co. was known for their fine mould work, as they were responsible for the famous Lord's Supper bread tray that was manufactured by the Model Flint Glass Company.

As we stated at the beginning of this book, it is not possible to correctly determine the factory where some novelties were made. To give credibility to this statement we are presenting this article that was printed in *China, Glass, and Lamps* on November of 1901.

> ***August Bosson**, one of the skilled glassworkers at the Consolidated Lamp and Glass Co.'s Coraopolis, Pa., factory, has built a small glass furnace in his yard and this winter will make a line of fancy glassware and novelties, such as paperweights, etc, —.*

It is impossible to know how many glassworkers were doing the same.

Another of the older firms to manufacture novelties was **Bryce Brothers.** One of their most popular novelties, and the one which was probably copied by others, was their water pail. The miniature was for *juveniles* and was true to the original with the graining of the sides, the rivets in the hoops, and the knots in the wood. In 1885 they were manufacturing a toy tea set in this pattern. The pattern was continued for many years and items were added including various sizes, with tin lids, that were sold for packers' goods.

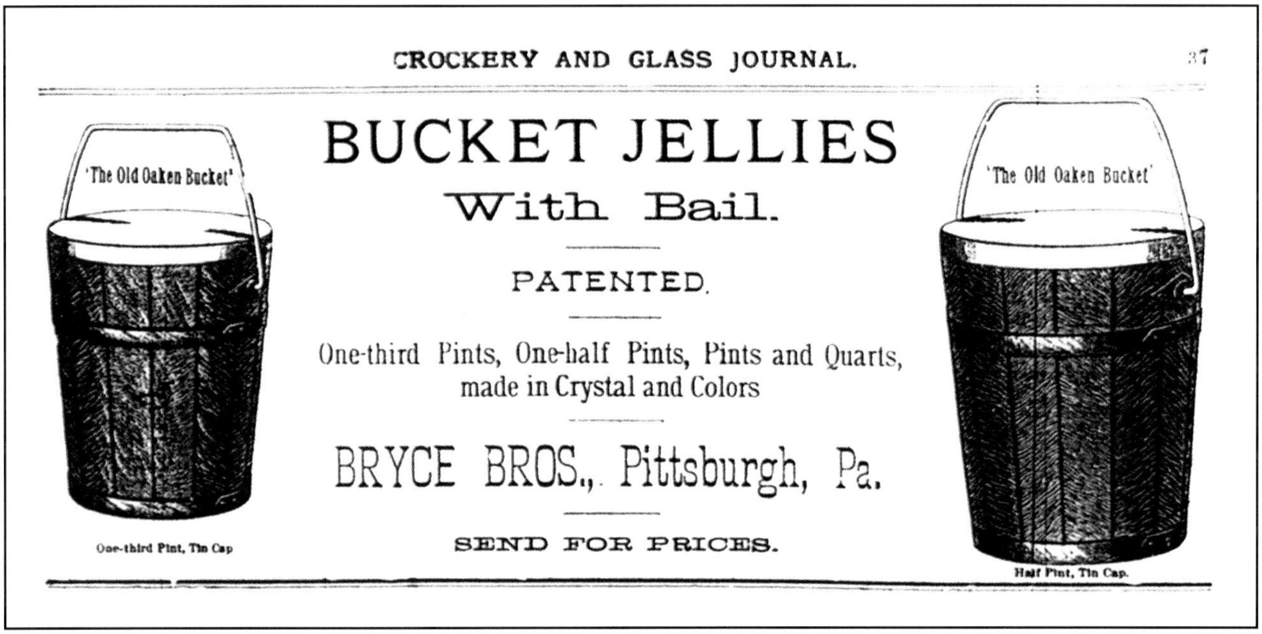

In the *Crockery and Glass Journal* of December 1890, it was noted that the Bryce Brothers were working at full capacity and that among the items that they were manufacturing were *an immense number of knick-knacks and miscellaneous articles* and that to list them would take several pages.

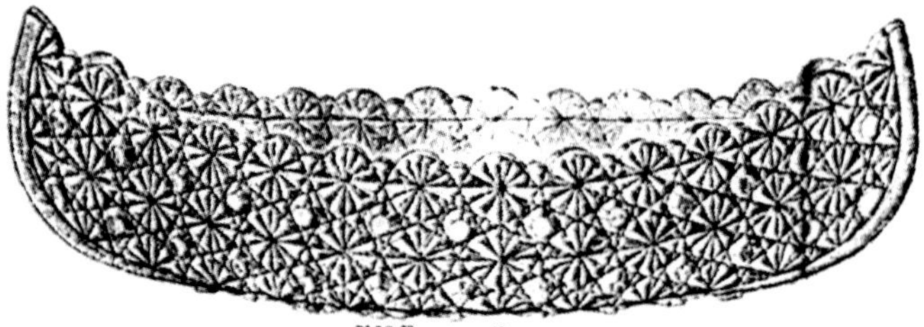

3109 Puritan Boat

In 1907 it is interesting to discover that this firm was making fine lead blown bar and table glassware including tumblers and stemware, finger bowls, sherbets, nappies, wine and water sets; however, equally interesting is the fact that they were also adding an iridescent effect on some of their lines. Were they making their own version of carnival glass?

From the American Glassworker of 1885 it was noted that *Henry Hand, engraver at* ***Bryce, Higbee & Company****, of Homestead, Pennsylvania, excelled himself by engraving the word Laurel on a beautiful glass horn made by the Piltier boys at the* ***McKee Brothers****, and presented by the Homestead Fire Company, to George Metzel, of the Laurel Fire Engine Company, of York, Pennsylvania.* As you can see, many novelties are one of a kind. The Grant bread plate manufactured by Bryce, Higbee and Co. was described and accepted as such a beautiful work of art that a *Diamond alley Italian artist has taken plaster paris casts from the reverse side, and is retailing the diamond surrounded bust of the 'soldier and patriot' at 25 cents a piece.*

Bryce, Walker and Company were busy in the late months of 1880 making items for the approaching holiday season. Included in these were their perfumery bottles, toilet bottles, etc. It was written in the trade papers that they were experiencing an unusual demand for these products. This is another company about which very little was written in the trade journals of the time.

An article did appear in the *Crockery and Glass Journal* in June of 1881. This article describes a novel use of glass that Bryce, Walker and Company was manufacturing. *Bryce, Walker & Co. are now making for a Southern tobacco grower large numbers of a white glass imitation of a flower which is to be used as a trap to catch the tobacco fly. It looks very much like a miniature smokebell, and the bottom having been covered with a poisonous mixture it is suspended among the tobacco plants. The unsuspecting fly, supposing it to be a real flower, crawls in and imbibes some of the artificial honey, which is the means of its final destruction.*

There is a very evident reason why some of the factories were covered very well in the trade journals and others were almost completely ignored. The journals naturally gave more coverage to the companies who gave them the most advertising dollars. In short, it was economics.

There has been very little information documented about the **Buckeye Glass Company** at Martins Ferry, Ohio. In 1881, it was written that a number of blowers and fitters found that they had some leisure time to fill. To fill this time they started making mantle ornaments, each in the shape of a richly colored and pictorial ball attached to a stand. The company sold them by the pair for $1.25 to $2.00 a pair. Although there was no description given, the Buckeye was producing a novelty in the shape of a night lamp in 1882. It is a shame that the writers for the various trade journals did not give descriptions of the various items that the glass factories placed on display. This is especially true when in 1887 the only description given for the new items from the Buckeye was *salts, peppers, toothpick and match holders in endless variety, some in the shape of butterflies and every other shape imaginable, and all decorated by hand.* (*Crockery & Glass Journal* 1887)

The **Cambridge Glass Company** at Cambridge, Ohio, was organized by the National Glass Company and began production in 1902. It was completely independent from the National combine. A Cambridge catalog was published in 1903 and illustrated several novelties. Most of the items that were illustrated in this catalog were items that were made from molds that had been transferred from other National factories. We feel that for this reason these products should be listed and credited to the original factories.

The Cambridge advertised a *new cigar jar* in 1907 and an illustrated advertisement appeared in *China, Glass and Lamps* in an October issue.

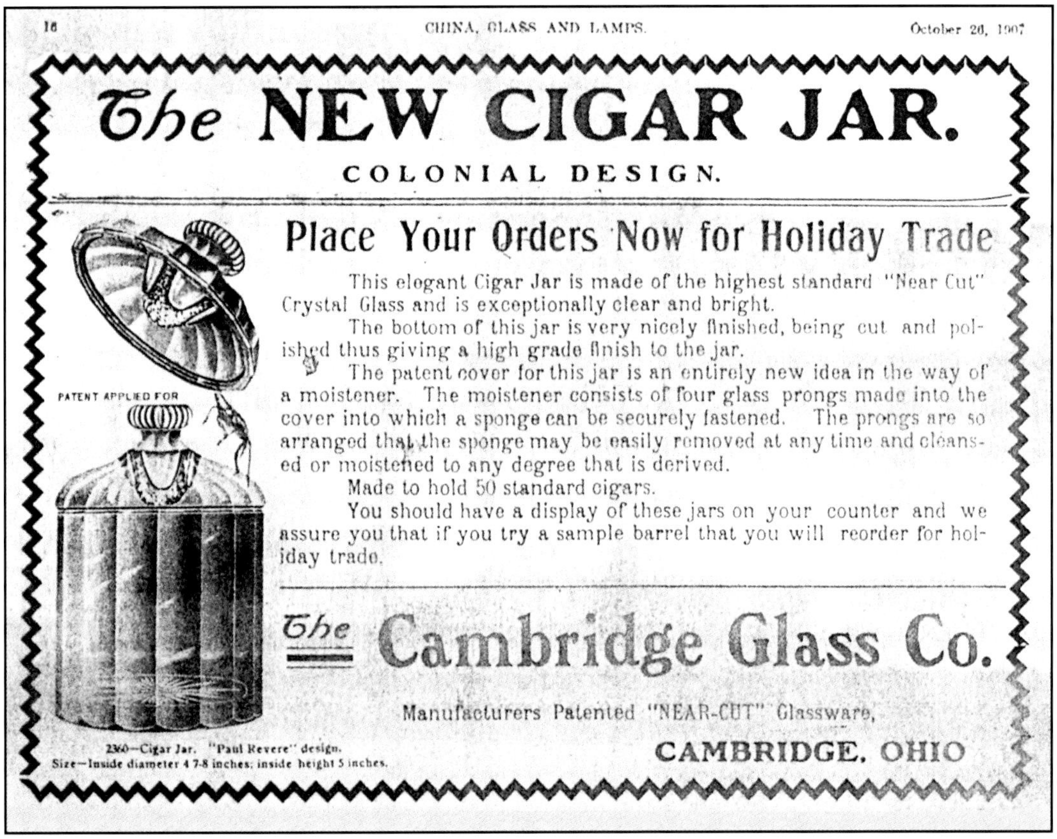

The Cambridge was also making a new glass rolling pin in 1907. The pin was a hollow glass cylinder into which a wooden piece was fitted, the wood protruding at both ends to form handles.

The Canton Glass Company of Canton, Ohio, and later of Marion, Indiana, started producing glassware of all types in 1883. Perhaps their best-known tableware, which also could be considered a novelty, is their Jumbo pattern. As it was not a best selling item on the market, it became known as Barker's white elephant; this name was bestowed, of course, because David Barker was the designer. One item made by this firm has caused some confusion as to who manufactured it. When a fire destroyed their factory at Canton, they leased a plant at Beaver Falls, Pennsylvania. While at Beaver Falls, the Canton manufactured the *Railroad* platter.

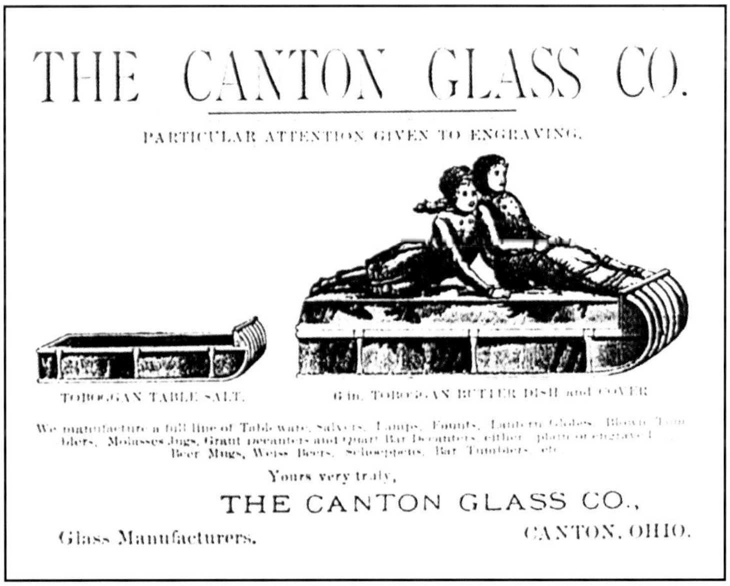

In 1896 the Canton was making packing goods and novelties in flint, opal, turquoise, and black glass. One of the items that they were manufacturing was pressed glass coffins, which were warranted to be airtight and weighing from forty-two to sixty pounds each. They were advertising that they were ready to fill orders for infant sizes at short notice.

The Canton continued making the Columbus plate in plain and opal ware and added candy containers and paperweights to their large list of products.

In 1897 the Canton advertised novelties in opal, turquoise, blue, and jet; an open edge stamp plate in opal, turquoise and jet; a hen and egg; paperweights; and packer's goods in blue and opal. It is also known that they manufactured a five-inch bonton slipper, a six-inch toboggan butter dish with a lid, and a toboggan table salt.

It was said throughout the industry that if you wanted something made that was difficult, then take it to the Canton; if they couldn't make it then it couldn't be made. This was a high compliment from their peers. Two of their novelties are inkwells in the shapes of chairs. The larger of the two has a square based cover with a kitten on it. The smaller has a round lid, which is a better fit as the inkwell openings are both round.

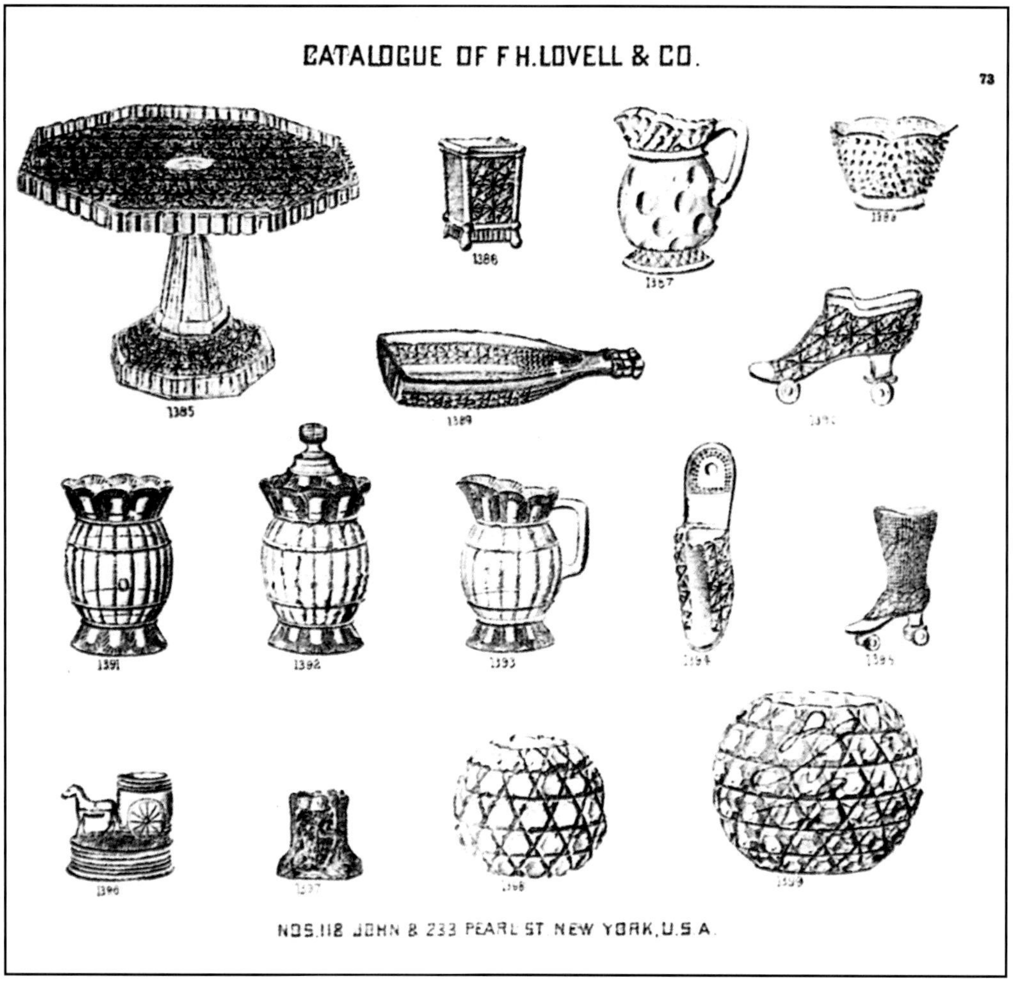

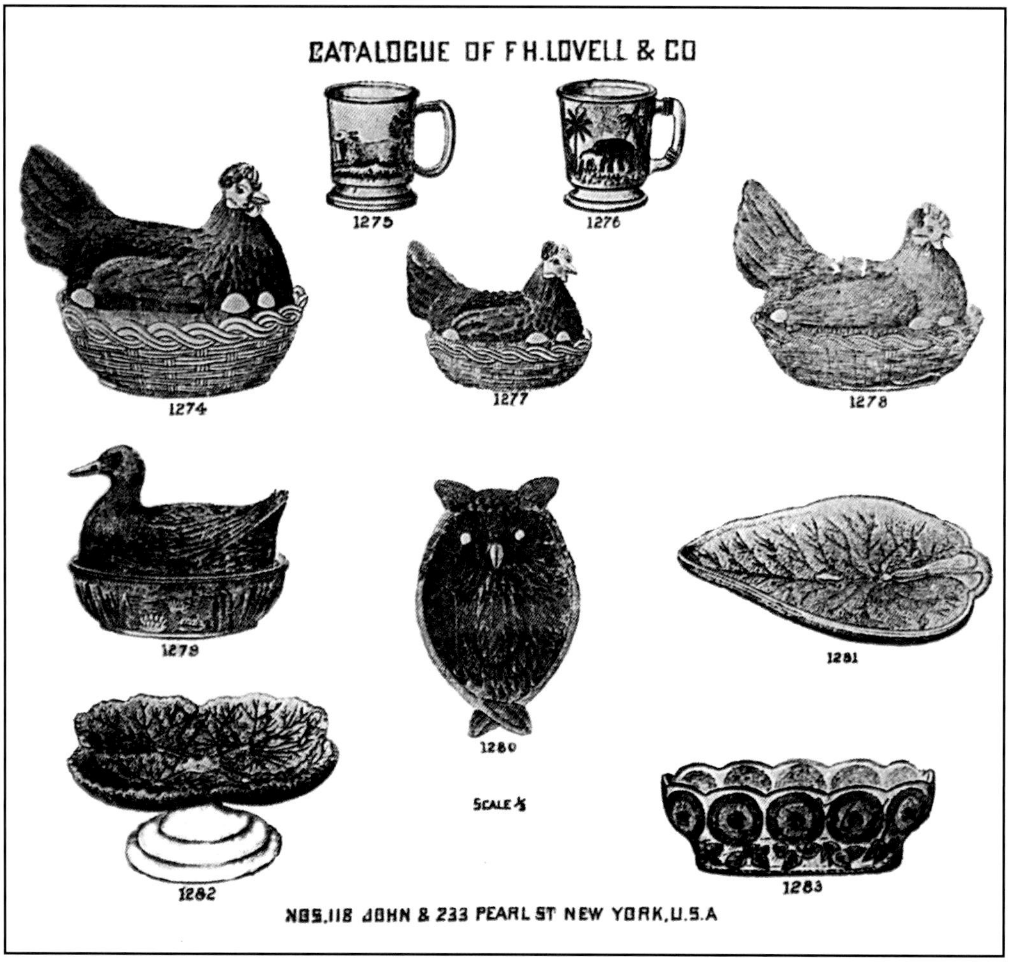

The **Central Glass Company** (sometimes referred to in the trade journals as the **East End Glass Works**) of Wheeling, West Virginia, made a glass tableware set in a pattern that could be described as a novelty, the Log Cabin pattern. The pieces in this pattern all resemble log buildings and are so well detailed that the reproductions can be easily detected. As an example, items in the original pattern have door handles but the reproductions don't. Another of their very popular patterns was not so popular with the Treasury Department of the United States Government. This was the Silver Age or U. S. Coin pattern. The coins that appeared on the various pieces so closely resembled the real coins of the day that the molds were destroyed under the supervision of the Treasury Department. Other novelties manufactured by the Central were the Owl in Stump toothpick holder, Horse with Cart toothpick holder, and *an inkstand of curious design, the leading feature of which is a recumbent horse of exquisite formation.*

Challinor, Taylor & Company of Tarentum, Pennsylvania, manufactured some outstanding novelties. Some of the finest were the company's salt and pepper shakers, toothpick holders, sugar shakers, and syrup pitchers, each in the form of an acorn and made in black, opal, and rose blush colors. They also manufactured covered dishes in a hen, a duck, a swan, and an eagle. This firm produced a pickle dish in the shape of a fish, a boot perfume in a slag glass, butterfly wall match holders which were decorated opal glass, an owl pitcher, an Indian head match safe, a bull's head covered dish, and more. The Challinor was well known for its quality products.

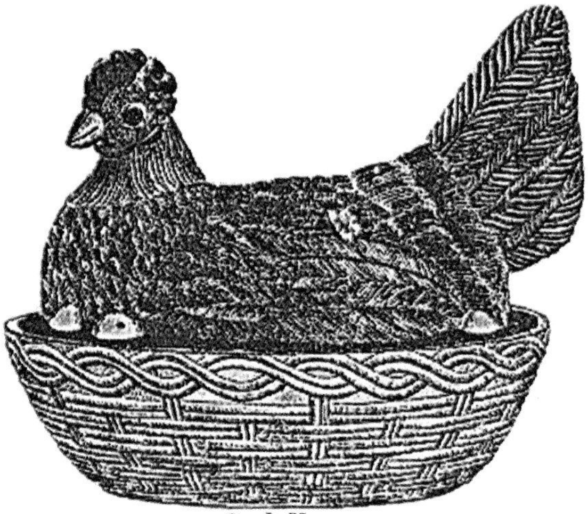

Opal Hen
Decoration A

The **Columbia Glass Company** of Findlay, Ohio, produced several highly prized novelties including the Kitten in Slipper (which was an inkwell, although sometimes found in toothpick holder collections), the Dog vase, the Early Bird (which was made in toothpick holder and salt and pepper shaker), the boy and girl cup and saucer, the dog head plate, and the cat head plate. These items can be found in clear and some in blue, amber, and canary. The Columbia became the first tableware factory to be established at Findlay, Ohio, in 1886 and continued producing glassware until being closed by the United States Glass Company in 1892. They had become a part of the large concern in 1891.

Although not necessarily known for their novelty production, the **Consolidated Lamp and Glass Company** of Coraopolis, Pennsylvania, made several items that must be considered such. In 1906 they were manufacturing a gas light globe in the form of a bunch of grapes. It was manufactured in green. Novelty collectors and lamp collectors collect two of the favorites as well. The first is a beautiful Santa Claus night lamp which is avidly sought. The second is the Columbus night lamp, one of the most difficult to find. There are probably many other novelties made by this firm but no proof has been found.

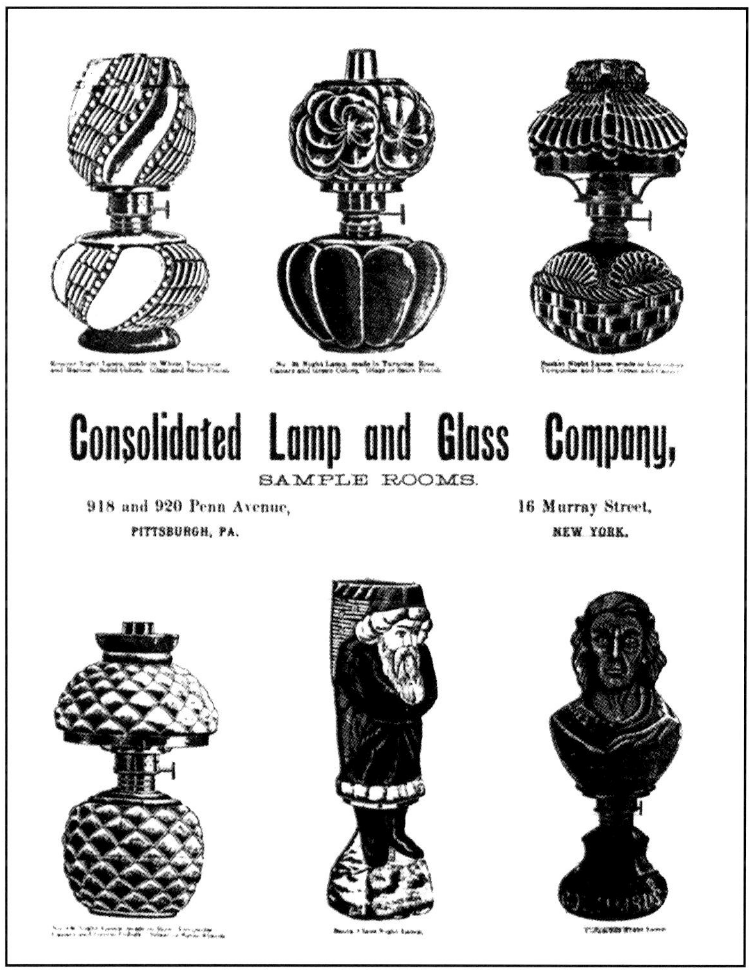

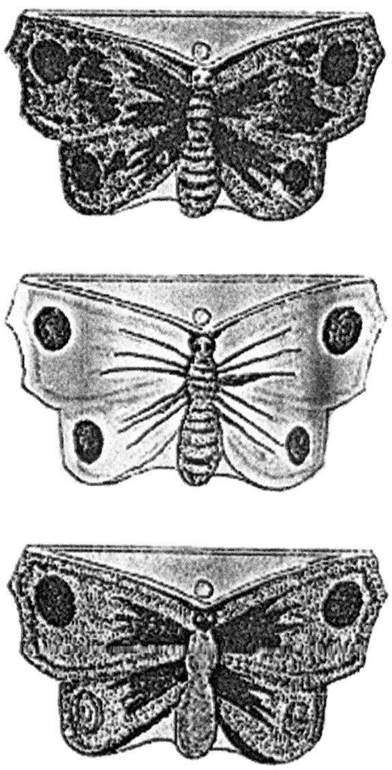

27 Hanging Match Safes
Decorated

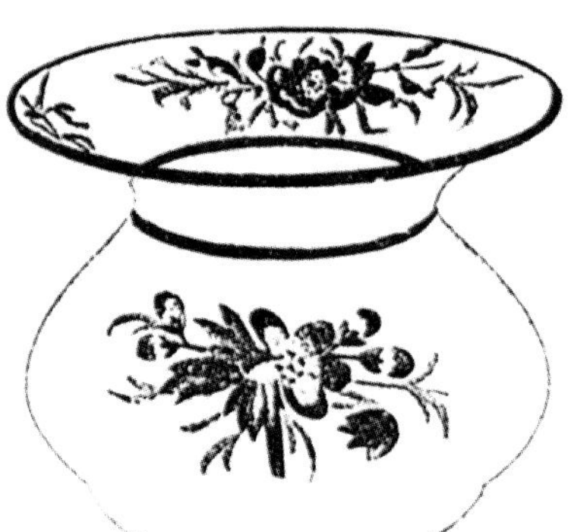

Cuspidore
Assorted Decorations

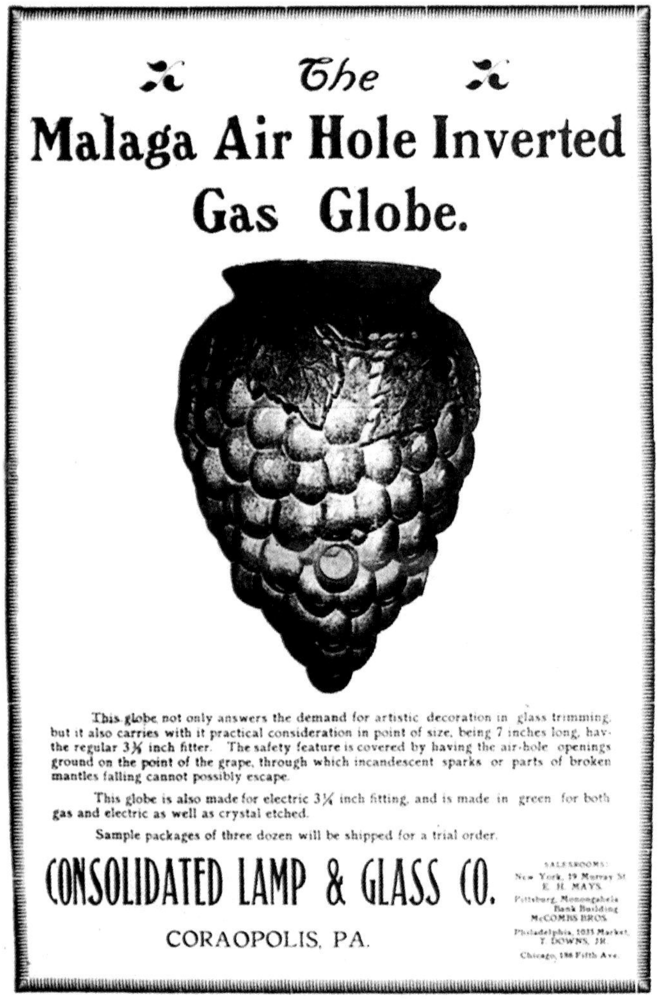

Many novelties can be attributed to the **Co-operative Flint Glass Company** of Beaver Falls, Pennsylvania. In the *Crockery & Glass Journal* of 1887 is an interesting item about a butter dish that this company were manufacturing. *They have out this spring a butter dish with a cover in the form of a glass bell – a real bell with metal clapper, and emitting a clear and sonorous sound...* Also in *China, Glass & Lamps* we find that one of their novelties in 1893 was a Columbus plate, with the figure of Columbus impressed upon it. Fortunately there are also illustrations available from catalogs of this firm. One of their products is the *Lillie* pickle dish. It is nearly heart shaped and has the name Lillie impressed in it. They made a tray that pictures the Old Statehouse at Philadelphia, which was erected in 1735. In novelty salts they manufactured a Tub with the design of a tub made of wood and another in the form of a cradle. The Co-operative made a toothpick holder or match holder in the form of an anvil and in at least five different colors. A mustard jar was made in the form of a beehive, and one of the most unusual novelties was a covered, patented, flytrap. This novel piece of glass was made to attract the fly by having a sweet mixture inside. The fly, entering through a hole in the bottom, couldn't escape after gaining entry. Another of their popular novelties was a toothpick holder in the form of a frog on a lily pad. This was a flourishing company because of the many items that they made, including some very popular tableware patterns.

Sundries

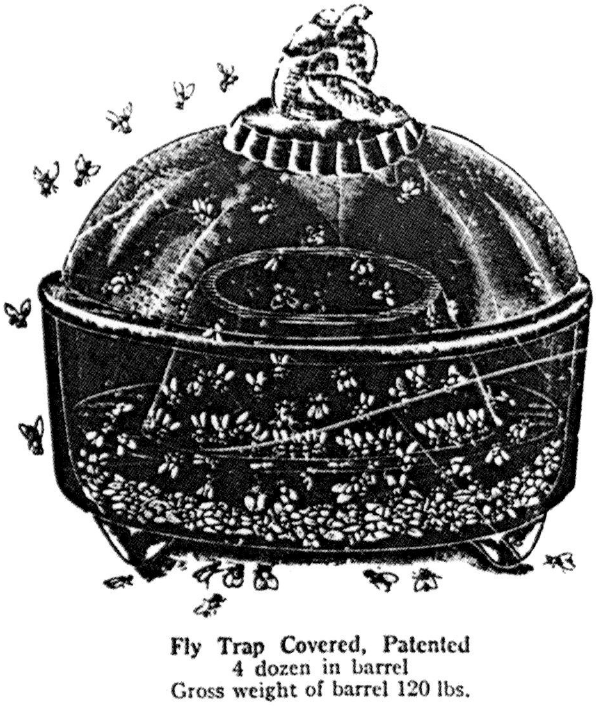

Fly Trap Covered, Patented
4 dozen in barrel
Gross weight of barrel 120 lbs.

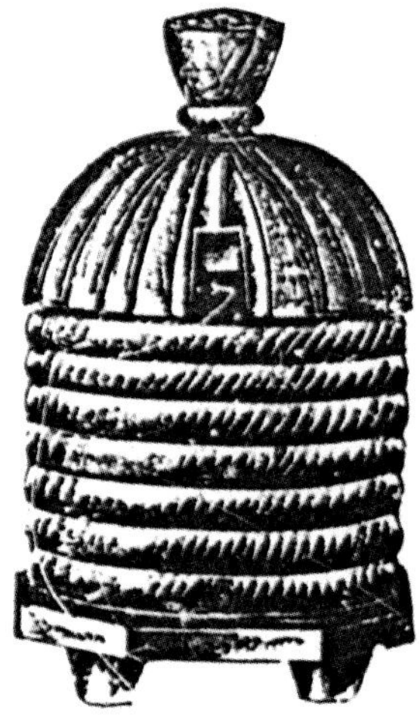

Beehive Mustard and Cover
18 dozen in barrel
Gross weight of barrel 160 lbs.

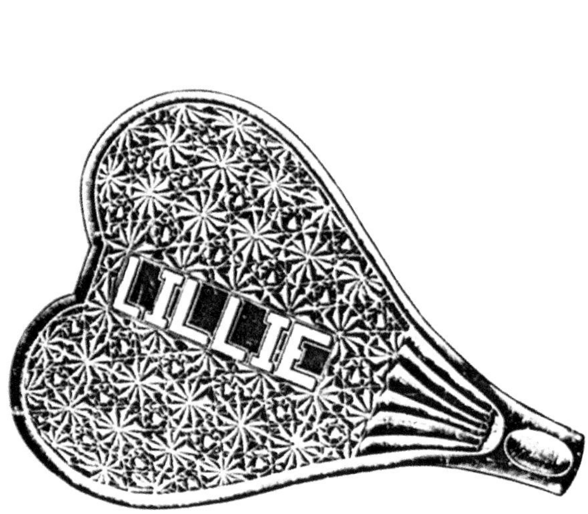

Lillie Pickle
15 dozen in barrel
Gross weight of barrel 160 lbs.

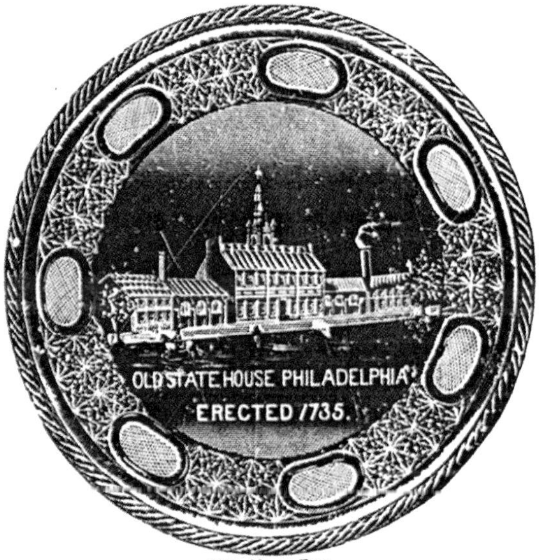

State House Tray
3½ dozen in barrel
Gross weight of barrel 195 lbs.

The Crystal Glass Company are referred to many times in the trade journals; but, it is never made specifically clear which factory they are talking about. There were several firms bearing the name of Crystal. The factory we are referring to is the factory at Pittsburgh, Pennsylvania. In 1880 it was reported that the Crystal Glass Company was making a Christmas mug intended to captivate the children. Sadly enough, there was no description or illustration. For a New York wholesale house a novelty was made in the shape of a boat in acid etched glass for holding flowers and arranged to be suspended in a window by means of ribbons.

Although the **Dalzell, Gilmore and Leighton Co.** of Findlay, Ohio, were probably best known for the production of their Onyx, Floradine, and Klondike wares in tableware, this firm made some outstanding novelties. In 1889 it was reported that *a special production in the shape of a gentleman of Ethiopian descent, accoutred in elegant costume and equipped with a brass tray containing decanter and glasses* was made, but that there was only one such masterpiece and it was unknown whether or not it was for sale. This was evidently an attractive item because it is later confirmed that it was being produced and that it was listed as the Mr. Snowball wine set and that a Mrs. Snowball would be added. At this same time other novelties were introduced by the firm such as a flask in the form of an old German Pipe, a decanter in the form of a German Gentleman, a Clown decanter, a decanter in the shape of a dagger, and figural colognes.

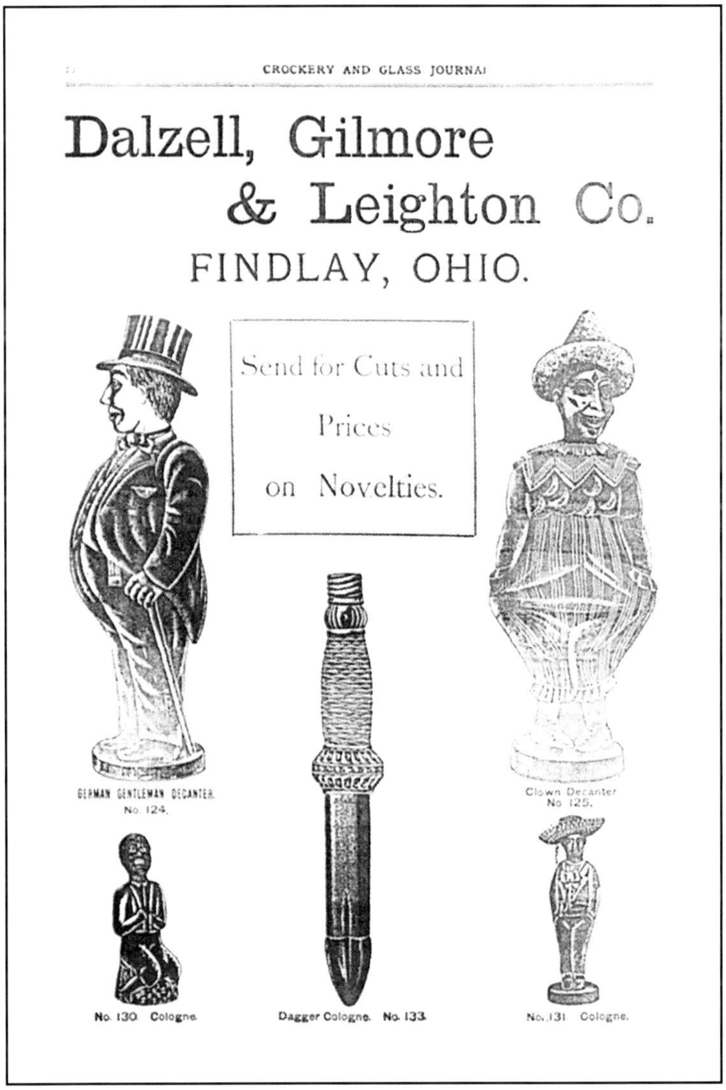

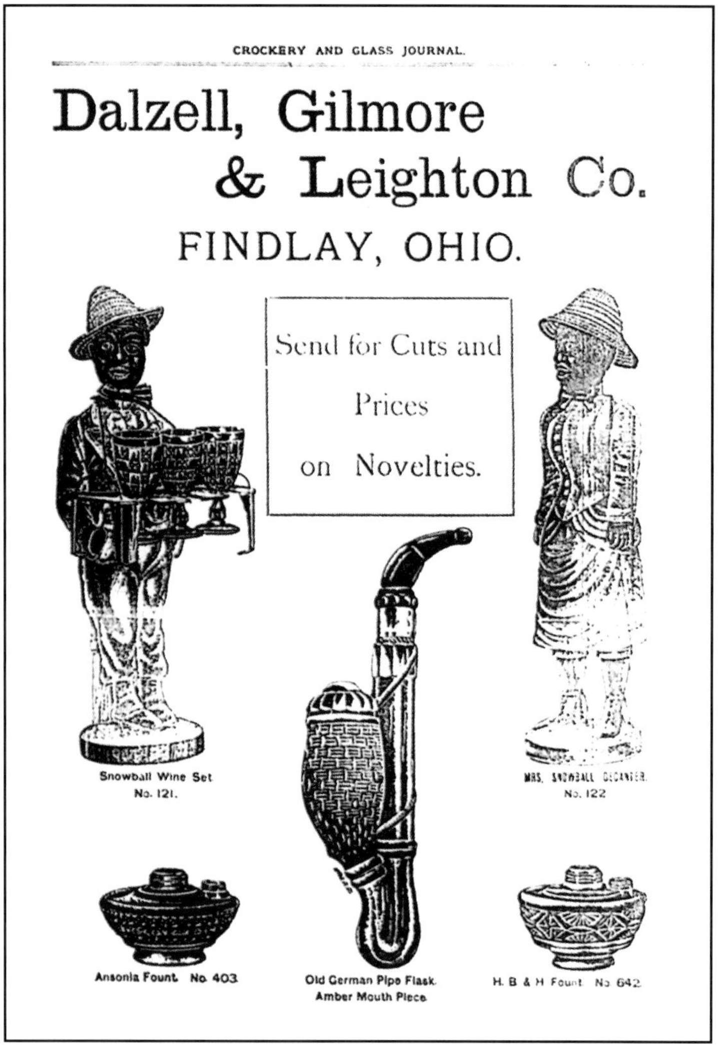

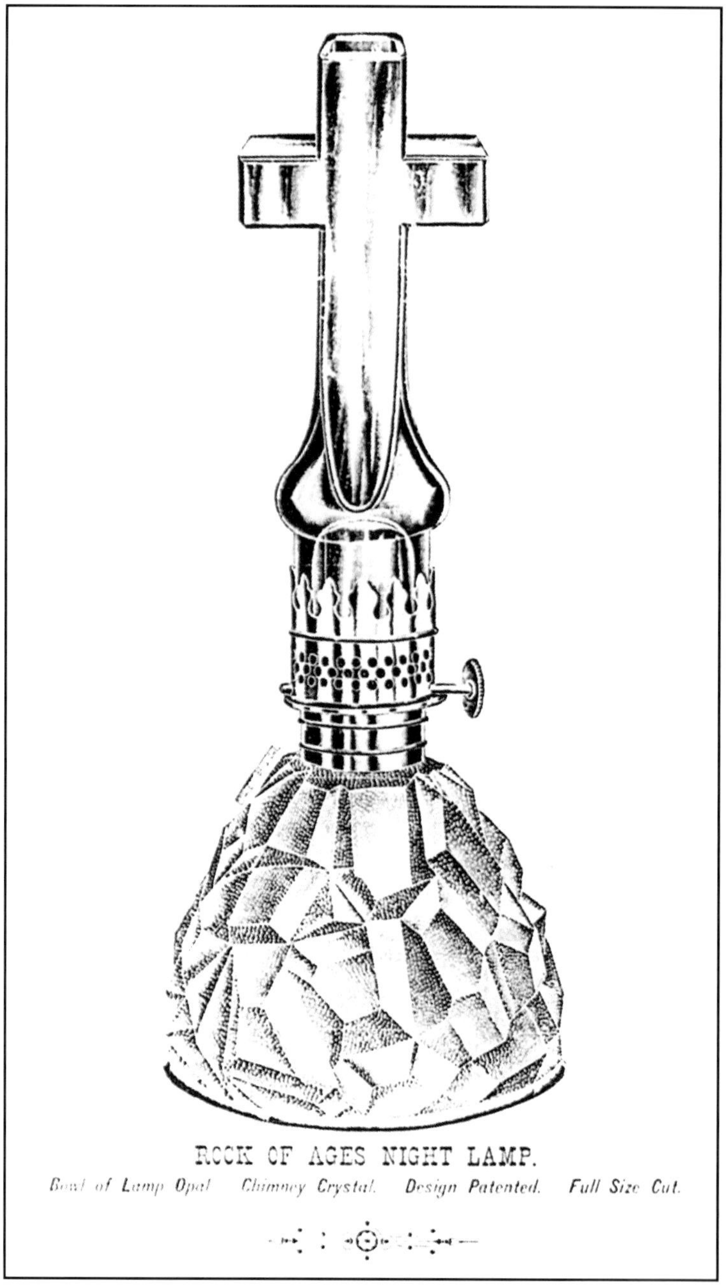

Two novelties were introduced in 1892. One of these has been illustrated in a trade journal but we could not locate an example of the lamp itself. It is the Rock of Ages night lamp. The bowl is shaped in the form of a rock and made of opal glass and surmounted by a cruciform chimney of crystal. The second is a political campaign flask with an etched mirror on one side. Dalzell is also known to have made another campaign item in the shape of a horn with no other description given.

A gentleman named August Spurber held several patents, including a hinged glass box, which he assigned to Dalzell, Gilmore and Leighton for production.

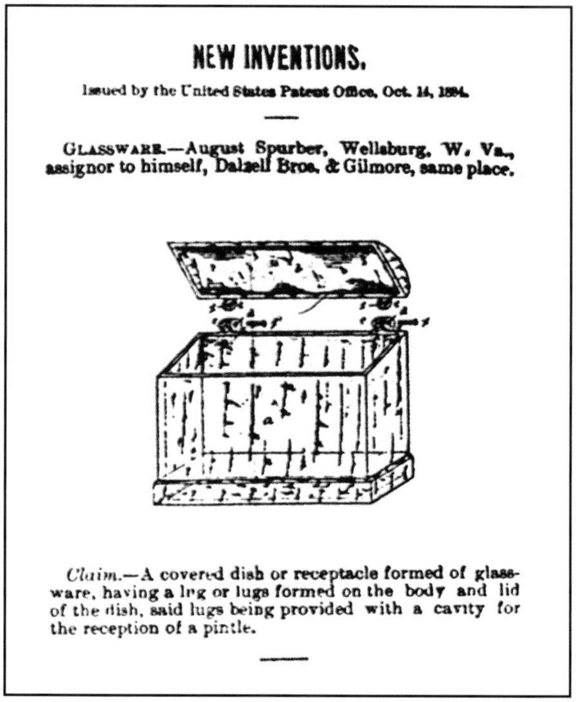

NEW INVENTIONS.

Issued by the United States Patent Office, Oct. 16, 1894.

GLASSWARE.—August Spurber, Wellsburg, W. Va., assignor to himself, Dalzell Bros. & Gilmore, same place.

Claim.—A covered dish or receptacle formed of glassware, having a lug or lugs formed on the body and lid of the dish, said lugs being provided with a cavity for the reception of a pintle.

A stamp rack was an unusual item and would be a welcome addition to any collection. The Dalzell stamp rack is a stand with a bowl on top and an Owl in the bowl. Another unusual and attractive novelty is a pitcher in the form of a parrot. The details are outstanding, with the top of the head forming a hinged spout and the feet being made of pot metal on which, along with the tail, it rests. The glass is of course green.

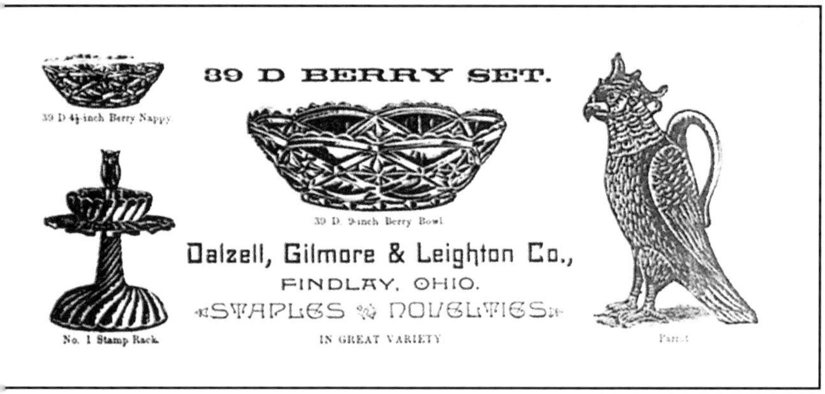

The **Dithridge & Co.** of Pittsburgh, Pennsylvania, was noted for their lamps and globes and also their toothpick holders and saltshakers in many beautiful colors of opaque glass. One of their best selling night lamps was the Mother Goose. Opaque novelties were another product type for which they were noted. Three of their finest were the Chicken on a Sleigh, the Easter Easel (both of which were manufactured in 1901), and the Easter Rabbit covered figural made in 1900. They also made countless novelties that are still undocumented.

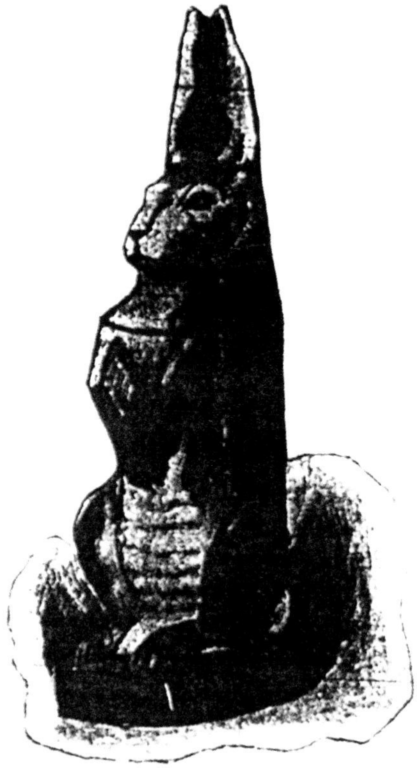

EASTER RABBIT.—DITHRIDGE & CO.

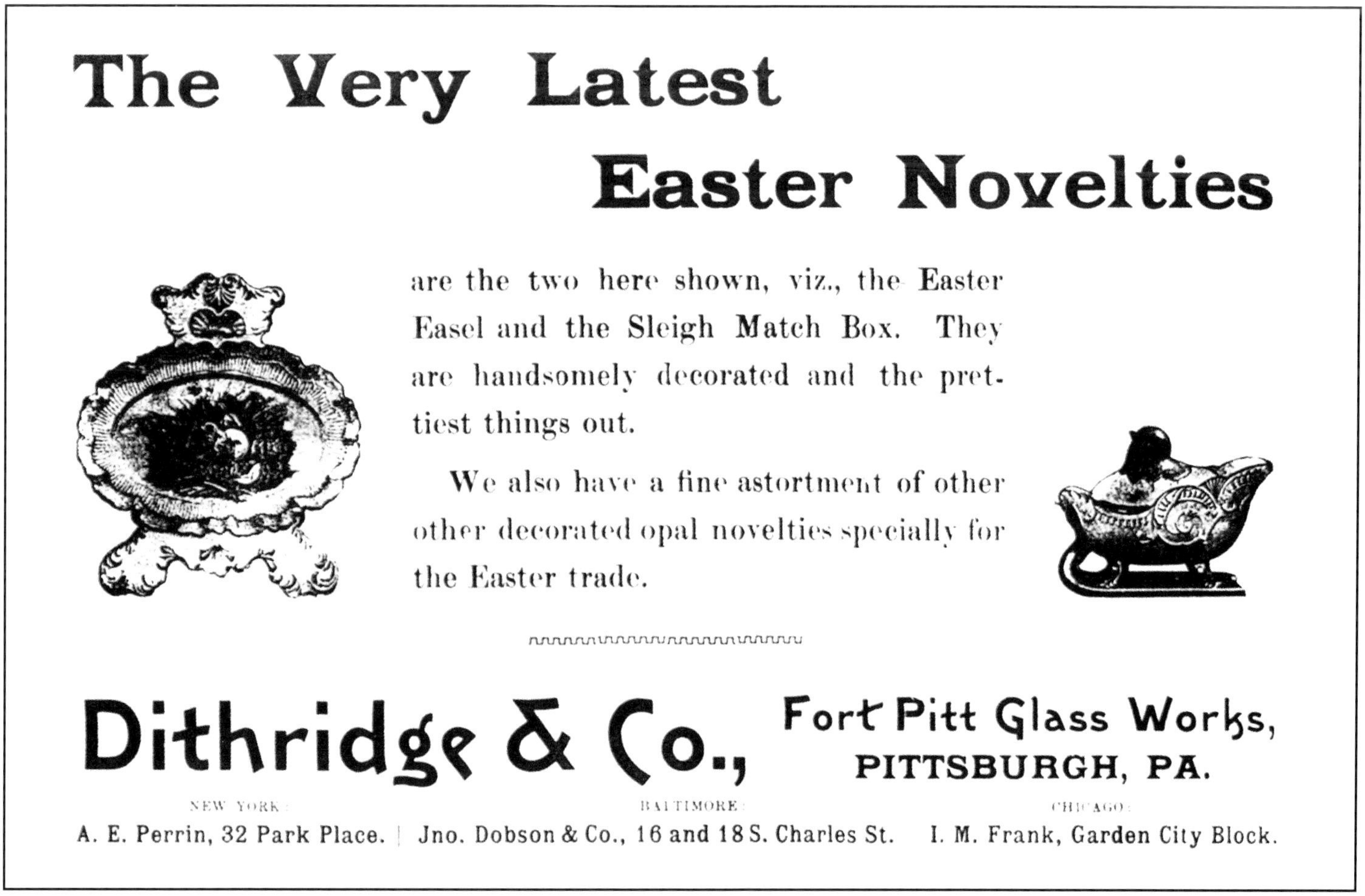

A different type of novelty was manufactured by the **Dithridge Bros. Lead Glass Co.** of Marion, Indiana. For the Columbian World's Fair in 1892 they offered engraved tumblers to commemorate the occasion. All of the etchings pertained to the discovery of America by Columbus.

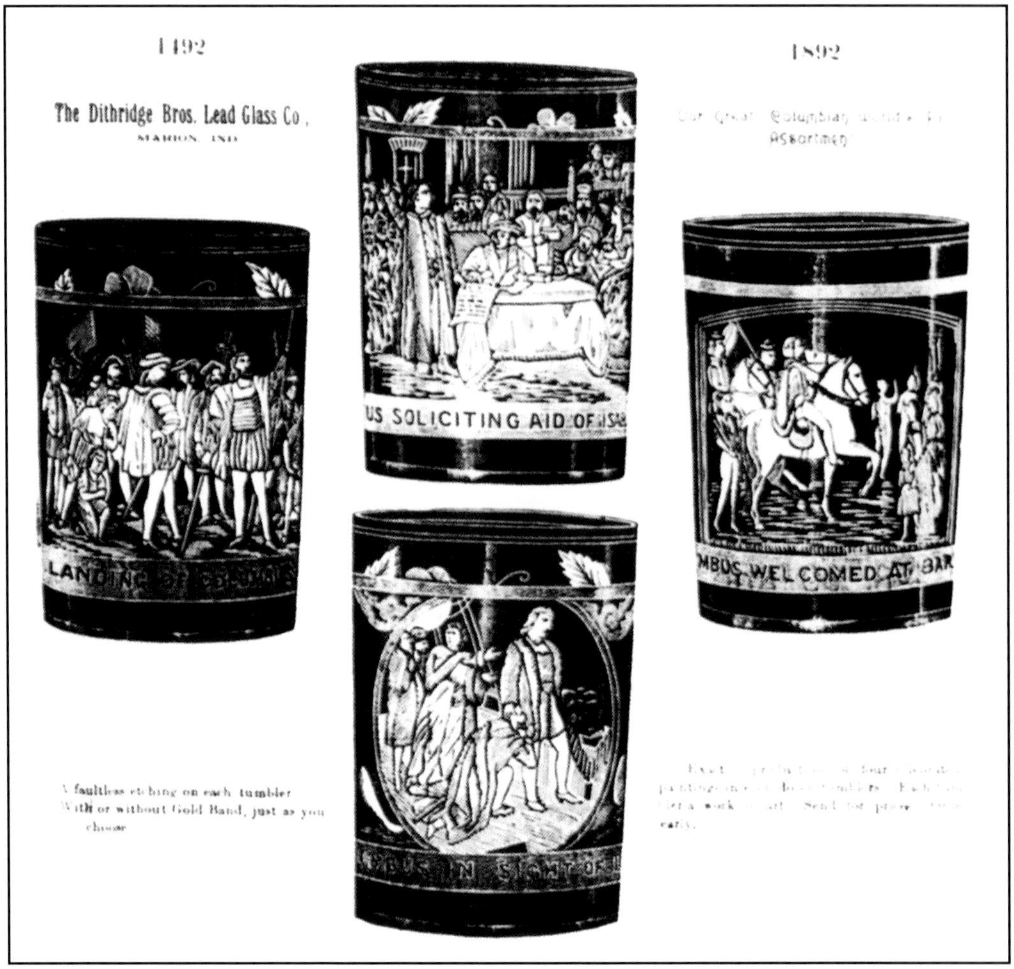

Doyle & Company was organized in 1855 and produced tableware and novelties until 1891 when the company became a part of the United States Glass Co. as factory P. We have been able to positively attribute only one of their many novelties and that is the Acorn dish, which is illustrated here and in the photo section. It is known to exist in clear, amber, and blue. This attribution is based on an illustration found in a wholesale catalog in which the entire page includes nothing but known Doyle & Co. products. The remainder of the page includes their No. 150 or Hobnail with Thumbprint Base pattern.

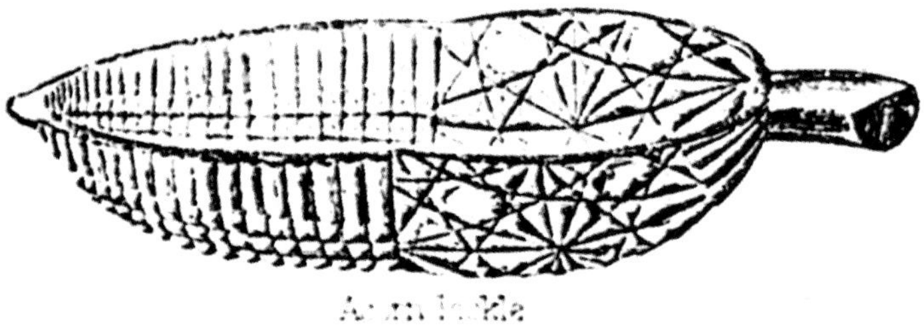

The **Geo. Duncan & Sons** glass company at Pittsburgh, Pennsylvania, began operations in 1874 when Mr. Duncan bought out the widows and remaining heirs of the D. C. Ripley Company. The factory was located on Pittsburgh's Southside. In charge of the operations of the firm were his son, James E., and his son-in-law, A. H. Heisey. They made many desirable tableware patterns and novelties, but in this book we are focusing strictly on the novelties. An 1884 item was a polka dot hat made in clear, amber, old gold, blue, and canary. The following year they produced a hobnail-patterned hat, the pattern is known today as Daisy and Button. These hats came in four sizes: the salt, toothpick holder, spoon holder, and celery. The colors were clear, amber, old gold, canary, blue, and clear with amber stain around the top. Following these in production were a sitz bath type chair, a solid seat chair (which helps to distinguish it from the Canton product), a Gypsy Kettle, a little German Bandmaster cap, slippers, a whisk broom shape pickle dish, a pickle dish in the shape of a boat in the Maltese pattern, and a glass vase in the shape of an umbrella. A. H. Heisey designed this umbrella. Most of these items were offered in the previously mentioned colors.

GLASS VASE.

AUGUSTUS H. HEISEY, Pittsburgh, Pa.

Claim.—1. The combination of a conical glass body which is longitudinally swelled or corrugated, a central stem passing through and fitting closely in an opening in the smaller end of the body and having a collar bearing against the inside thereof, and an external nut engaging a thread on the same.

2. The combination of a conical glass body which is longitudinally swelled or corrugated, a series of ledges or shoulders located upon the inside of the swells of the body, and a central stem connected to the smaller end of the body.

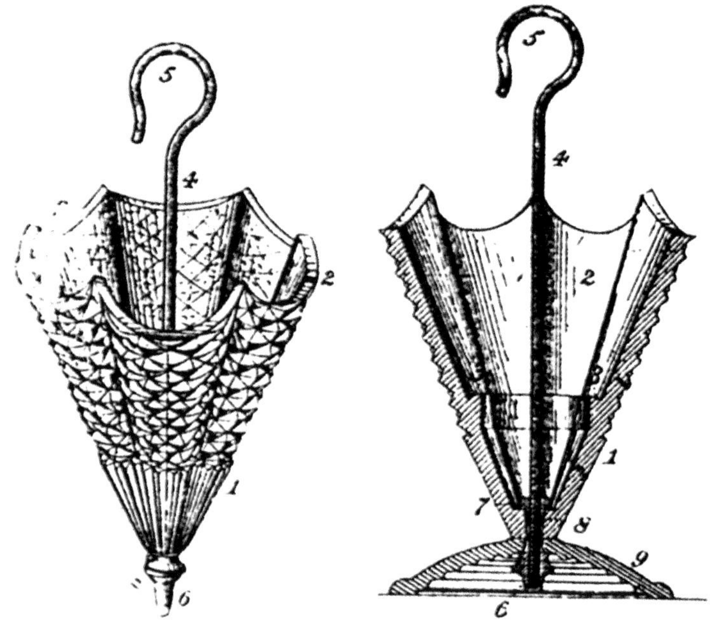

3. The combination of a conical glass body which is longitudinally swelled or corrugated and provided with a tapered or conical opening in the centre of its smaller end, a stem having a conical enlargement fitting a corresponding opening in the smaller end of the body, engaging a thread on the stem below said enlargement and bearing against the outside of the smaller end of the body.

4. The combination of a conical glass body which is longitudinally swelled or corrugated, a base or foot abutting against the smaller end of the body, a stem passing through and fitting closely in central openings in the body and base and having a collar bearing against the inside of the body, and a nut engaging a stem and bearing against the lower surface of the base.

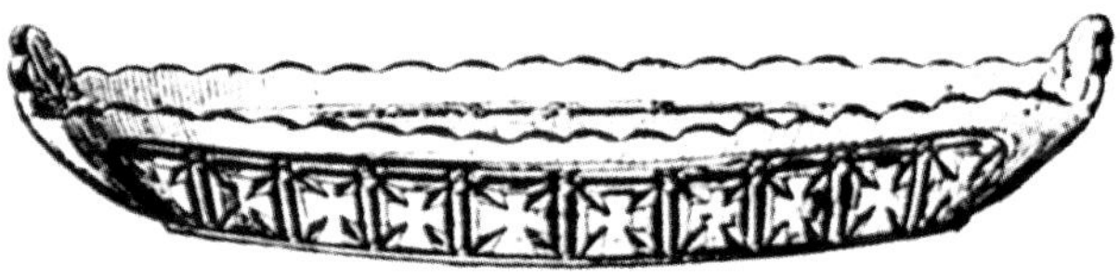

PICKLE BOAT.

Special attention called to the

Maltese, or No. 1003 Set.

For Sale by all the leading Jobbers in the country.

GEO. DUNCAN & SONS, Pittsburgh, Pa.

Cheaper than the Cheapest.

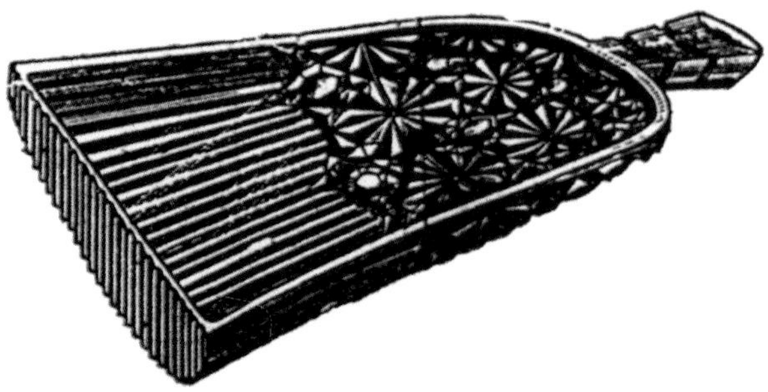

C. & J. WHISK PICKLE.

(CUT HALF SIZE.)

Price 25 cents per dozen in assorted colors. Cuts and prices of other sizes will follow as soon as molds are completed, rated at corresponding value.

——GEO. DUNCAN & SONS,——

Pittsburgh, Pa.

The **Eagle Glass and Manufacturing Company**, of Wellsburg, West Virginia, started producing glassware in 1895. Much of their wares were novelties made in opal glass. In 1897 *China, Glass & Lamps* reported that they were exhibiting opal goods: *The novelties consist of hanging baskets, about two by four inches, lugged and corded, figured, with a rabbit and chicken on alternate sides, a spray being thrown over the figures, in relief, which is decorated in gold, making a showy, neat and handsome ornament for mantle, window, chandelier, panel or china board. — In match safes they make a boot, in opal and blue, and an opal vase shaped safe.*

EAGLE GLASS & MFG. CO.

No. 40 Match Box

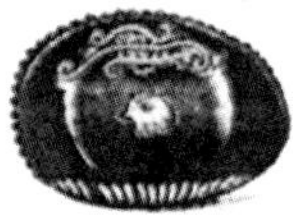

No. 18 Easter Egg.

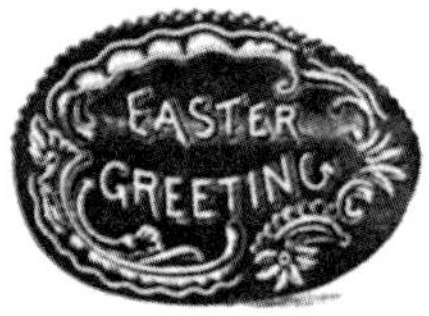

No. 10 Easter Egg.

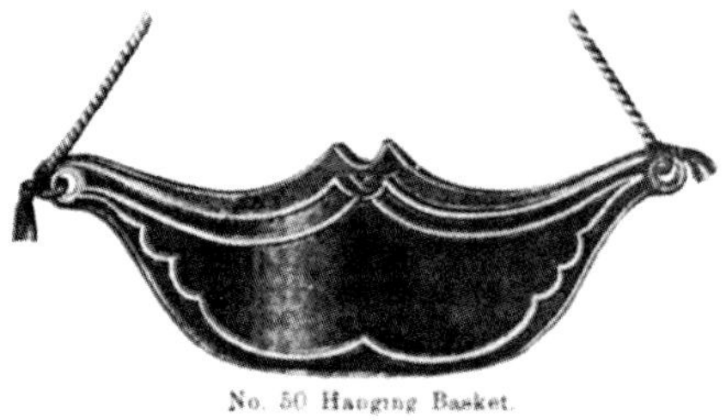

No. 50 Hanging Basket.

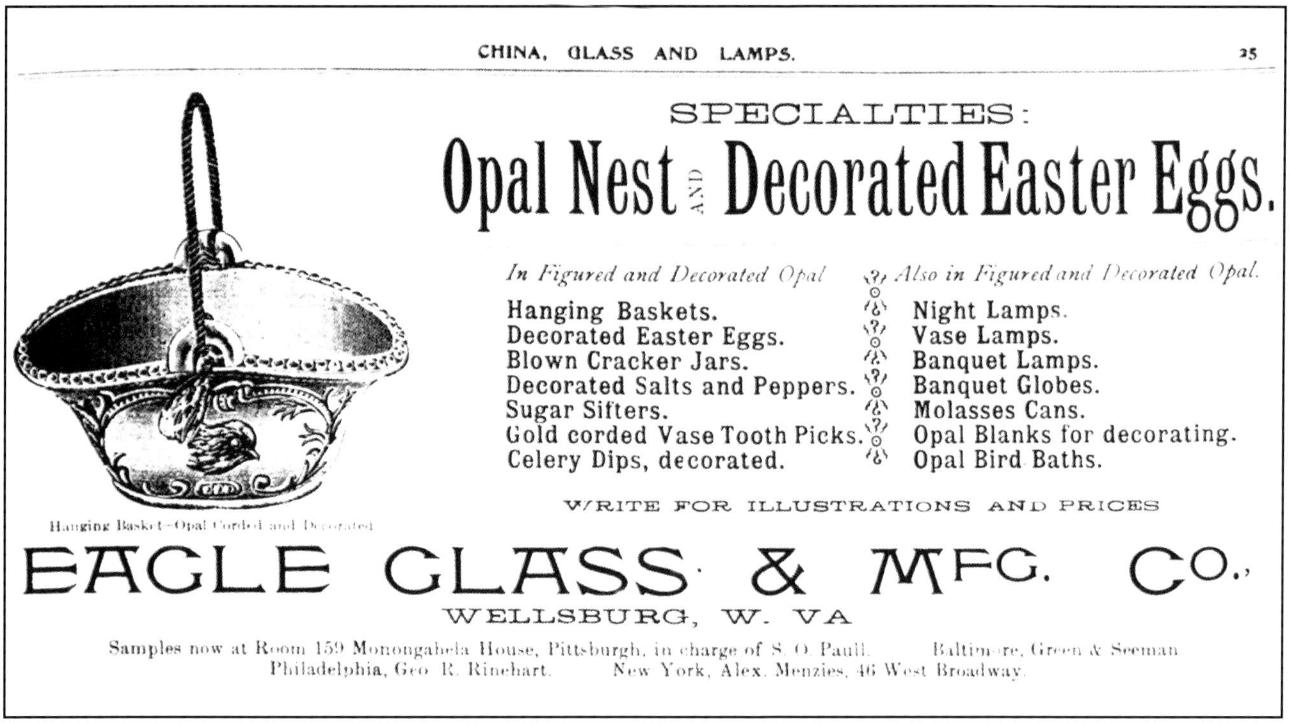

In their illustrated advertisements we find the hanging basket, butterfly match box, a match safe in the form of a smokers pipe, a bonbon dish in the form of a sitz bath, toothpick holder in the form of a bundle of cigars, a wall match box, a gondola shape hanging basket, and several Easter eggs. They are also known to have made a toothpick holder called fiber bundle.

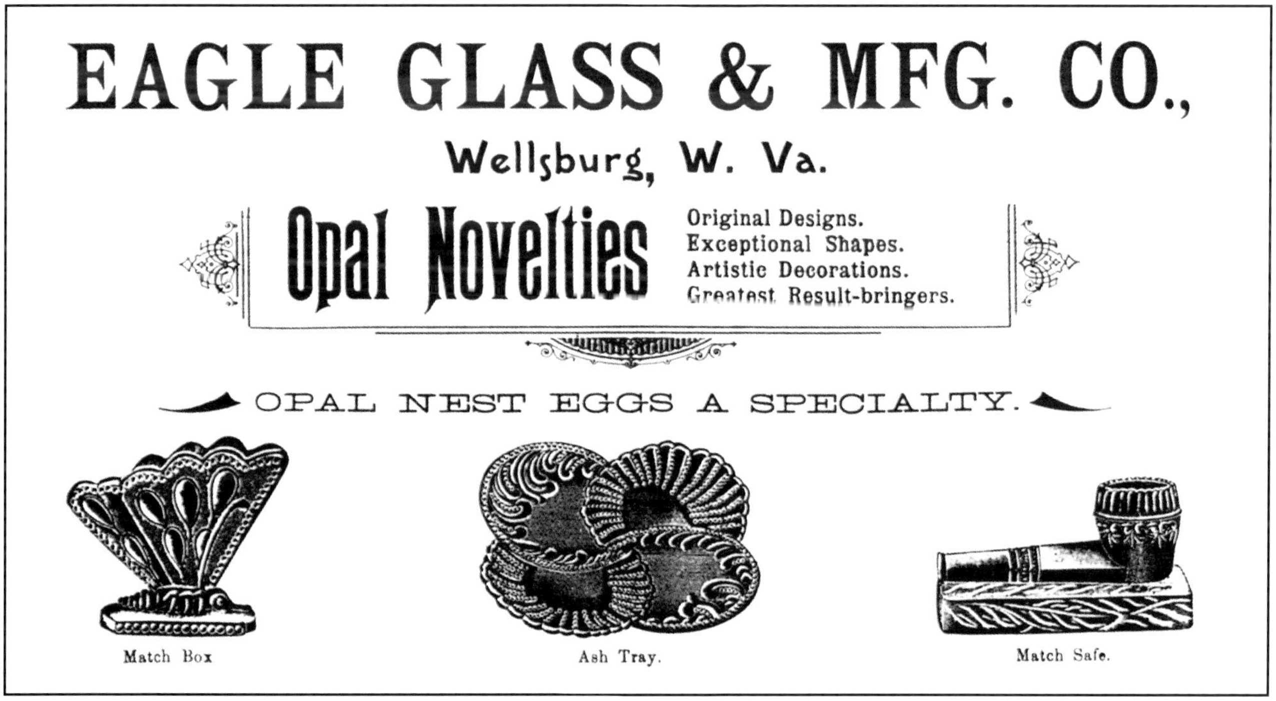

Although it is not a novelty that most collectors would be searching for, it is interesting to note an item from the *Crockery and Glass Journal* in 1882. It was written that **John Eastlake** had invented a glass bombshell, which was 4 1/2 inches in diameter, to be made of hard, tough glass an inch and a half thick. No further information was given and a search through later issues provided no additional information.

In 1906 one of the newest and most progressive industries was the **Elite Glass Works.** The owner and manager was Robert Englehardt who had been a partner in the Wheeling Decorating Company for the previous ten years. While they did not manufacture glassware, they were a decorating company. The glassware that they were decorating came from the Imperial Glass Company and it is worth mentioning because the decoration that was being applied was an *iridescent* effect that was a fast selling treatment. We now know the decoration as Carnival Glass.

In the early 1880s William K. Elson started the **Elson Glass Company** at Martins Ferry, Ohio. Although they manufactured several popular patterns, including Dewdrop, Hobnail, and Elson's Block, their moneymaking products were candy jars and druggist jars, for which Mr. Elson owned the patents. There are two novelties documented for this firm. In 1890 one of their products was a glass horn, with no description given. In 1893 the firm was manufacturing a novelty in a corded hanging rose bowl. There is little doubt that this glass works was responsible for other novelties.

When searching for a novelty manufacturer that had an enlightening product we must look at the **Enterprise Manufacturing Company** of Akron, Ohio. Their products included Luminous Match Safes among others. They advertised *the shining Auroras, luminous match safes — no bedroom should be without one, they are made of the best flint glass. The Little Keg and Baby Jumbo are very desirable for table use for salt, mustard, toothpick cups, etc.* As with any item that sold well, there were others always trying to copy them. Enterprise had this problem and included this information in their ads. They also fully warranted their products with the guarantee that the product could be returned at their expense.

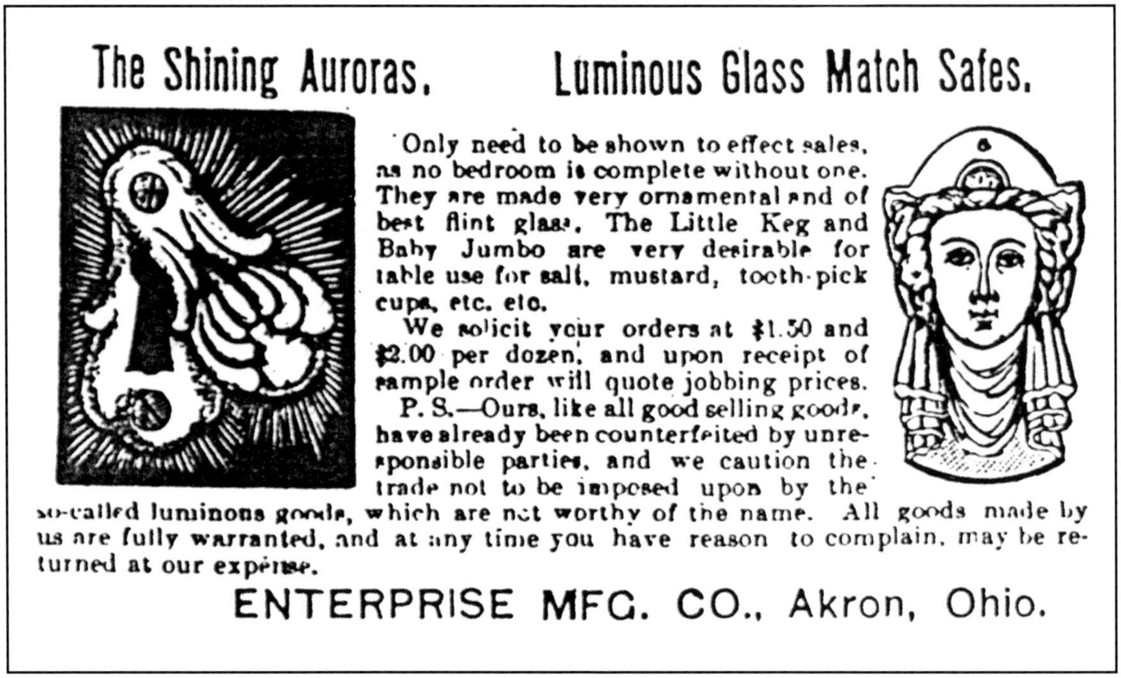

The Findlay Flint Glass Company of Findlay, Ohio, was organized in 1889 and produced glassware until the factory was destroyed by fire in 1891. It was never rebuilt. Upon opening in 1889 they produced several beautiful patterns in tableware and also a three bottle caster set resembling, and called, Squash Caster, plus a mustard in the form of an elephant's head. Next came a toothpick holder in the shape of a butterfly on a tulip and after that a toothpick holder in the form of Drawers. In their last year making glassware they produced the Pichereau's Patent Ink Stand and the Miller mustard or toothpick holder. The Miller was made in the form of a teapot and named for the designer, J. A. Miller. A debt of gratitude must be given to a gentleman named Don Smith who spent many years researching the factories at Findlay, Ohio. Don dug for shards at the factory sites and identified many patterns and novelties and placed this information in a book that is still considered the final word on the glassware made in this city. Don related to us that the Findlay Flint was his favorite factory.

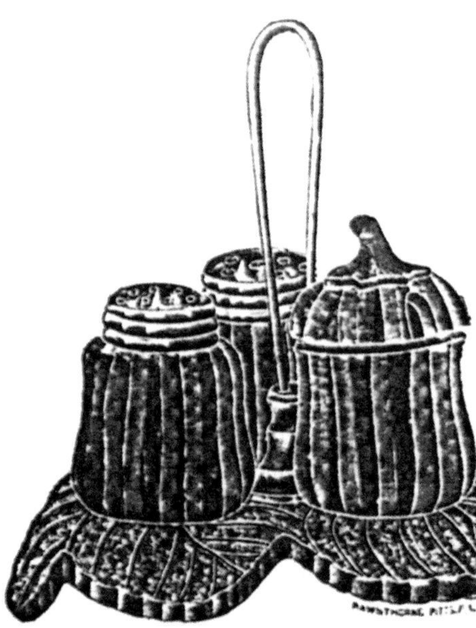

SQUASH CASTOR.

Fostoria, Ohio, was blessed with some outstanding glass companies and their products are collected today. Many novelties were made at these factories and one of the outstanding examples was made at the **Fostoria Glass Company.** The description given in *China, Glass and Lamps* was ... *lamp stands with peg socket which can be used for candlesticks — and flower holders with the same design — flower aquaria with flower holder above and a place for fish underneath — this is an elegant novelty.* There are no illustrations of this item and it is impossible to give a better description of this novelty.

The Fostoria Shade and Lamp Company, of Fostoria, Ohio, was organized in 1890. They manufactured a beautiful night lamp for the Christmas trade in 1892. It was a lamp in the form of Santa Claus. The lamp was so popular that the Consolidated Lamp and Glass Company continued its manufacture after buying out the Fostoria Shade and Lamp Company in 1894.

In 1886 **Henry Franz** of Pittsburgh, Pennsylvania, invented a *new open and shut glass-mold for forming a glass sleigh with an overhanging dashboard, having a bottom section which forms the upper side of the sleigh, the inner sides of the running gear, and the underside of the overhanging dash-board, hinged side sections provided with indented patterns for forming the external sides of the sleigh, which side sections close against one side of the bottom section, and a mold ring which rests partly on the side sections and partly on the bottom section.* The pattern on this item was called Rose Sprig. The patent was assigned to Campbell, Jones and Company for manufacturing.

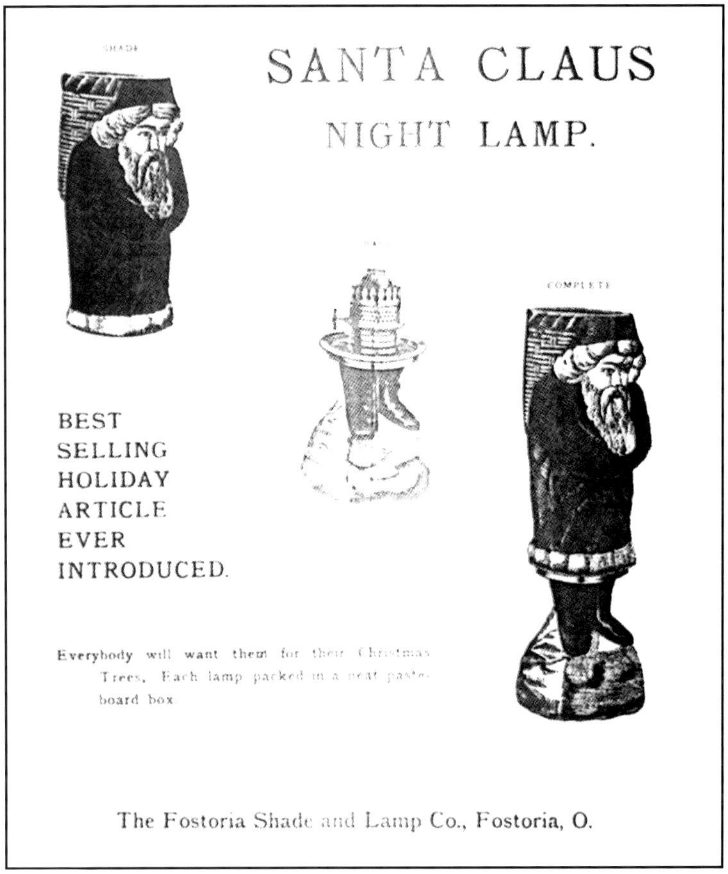

NEW GLASS-MOLD.

HENRY FRANZ, Pittsburgh, Pa., is the inventor of a new open and shut glass-mold for forming a glass sleigh with an overhanging dashboard, having a bottom section which forms the upper side of the sleigh, the inner sides of the running-gear,

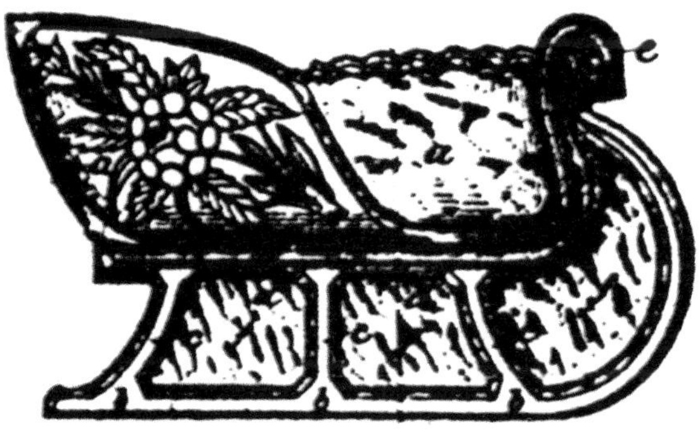

and the under side of the overhanging dash-board, hinged side sections provided with indented patterns for forming the external sides of the sleigh, which side sections close against one side of the bottom section, and a mold-ring which rests partly on the side sections and partly on the bottom section.

Gillinder & Sons was founded in 1861 at Philadelphia, Pennsylvania, and opened a second factory at Greensburg, Pennsylvania, in 1888. Most of their novelties were made at the Philadelphia works. The Greensburg plant was joined to the United States Glass Co. in 1891 as Factory G. In 1892 the Gillinder firm were making some novel night lamps, two of which were *Little Bo Peep* and *Little Jack Horner.* Their next night lamp was *Baby McKee*, which they advertised as no smell, smoke, or heat. In following advertisements there were nest eggs, ostrich eggs, duck eggs, and goose eggs. This company seemed to thrive upon the unusual as in the years following 1897 their advertisements were filled with novelties. Among the items made were *decorated hanging vases, match safes, burnt match holders, Uncle Sam's night lamp, bonbon boxes, Easter egg plates, a chick box and rabbit box, a novel egg cup with the base having the foot of a chicken, and several Easter trays.* Most of these items can be seen in the illustrations shown here.

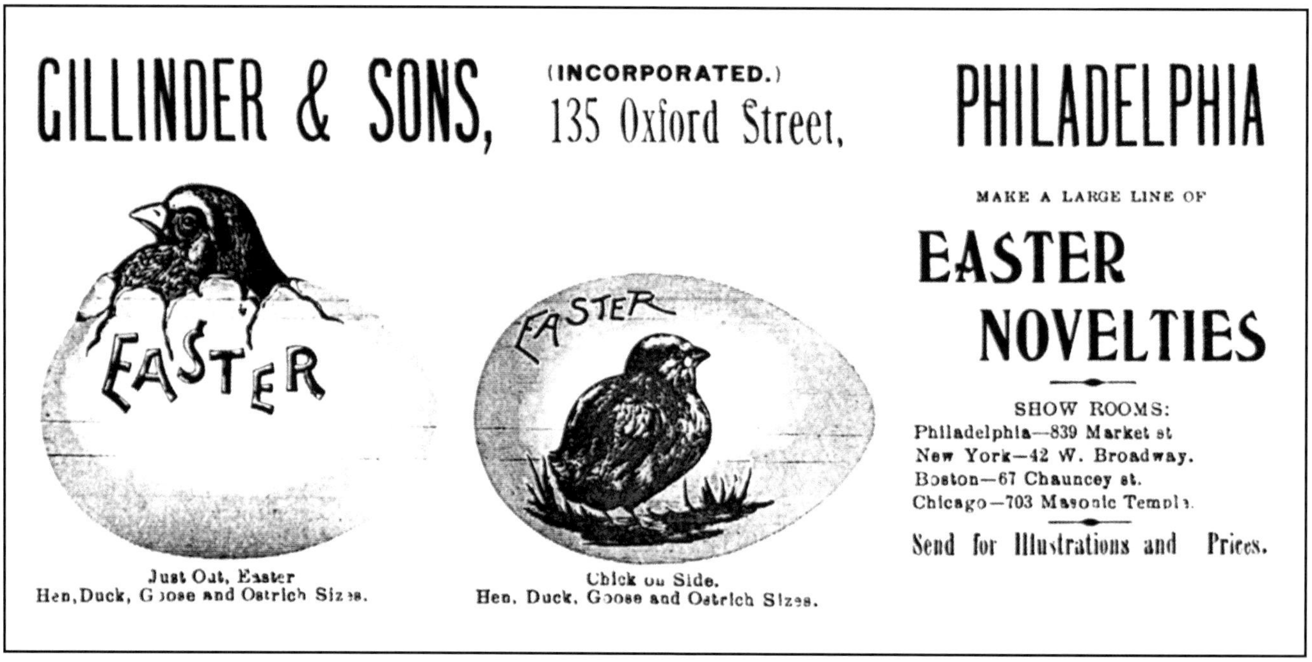

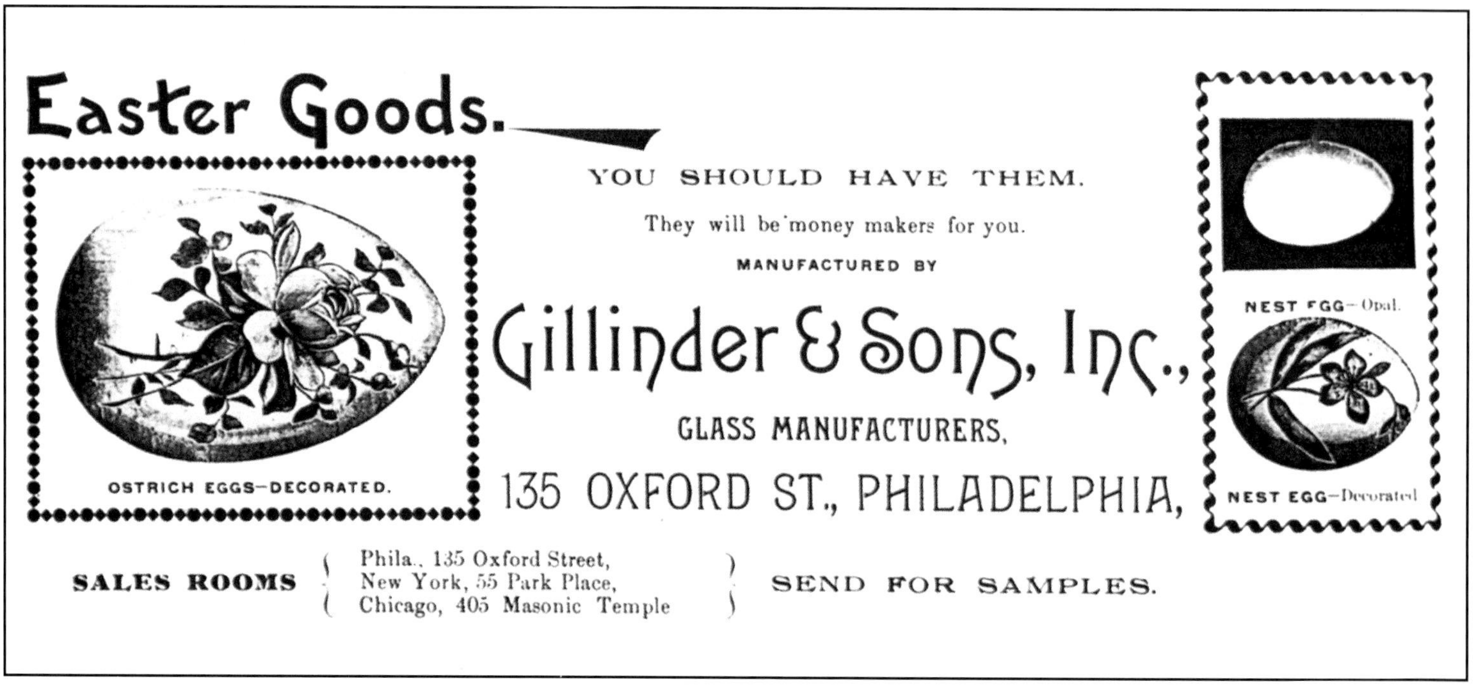

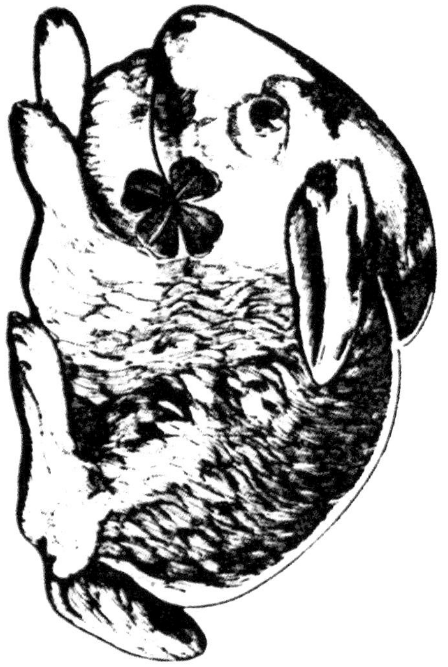

A Gillinder & Sons' Easter Tray.

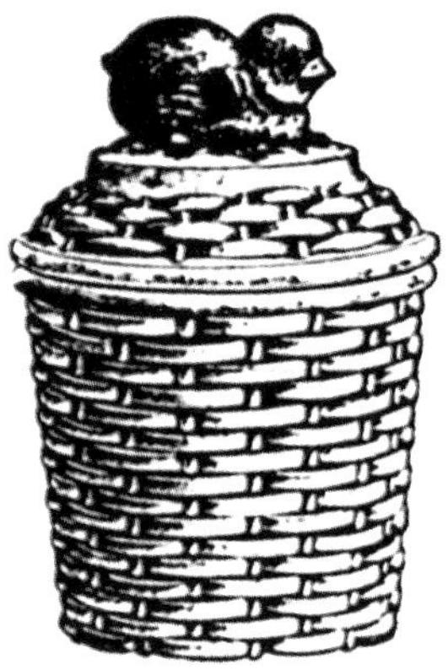

EASTER BON BON BOX.
From Gillinder & Sons, Inc.

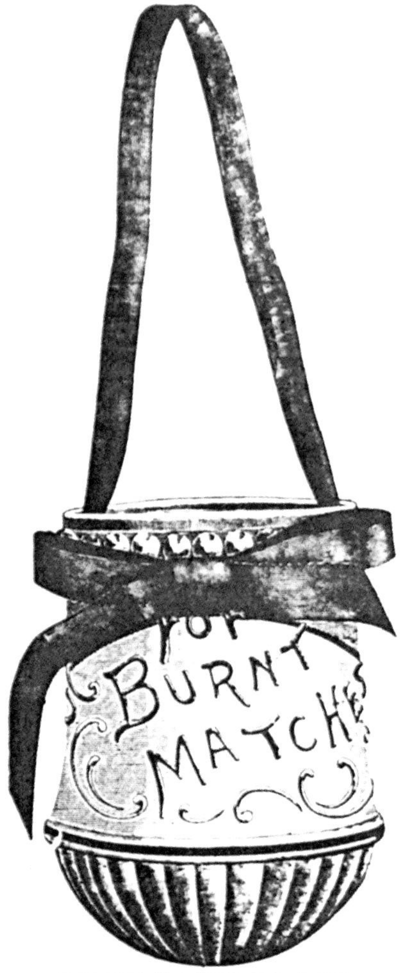

BURNT MATCH HOLDER.
Gillinder & Sons, Inc.

CHINA, GLASS AND LAMPS

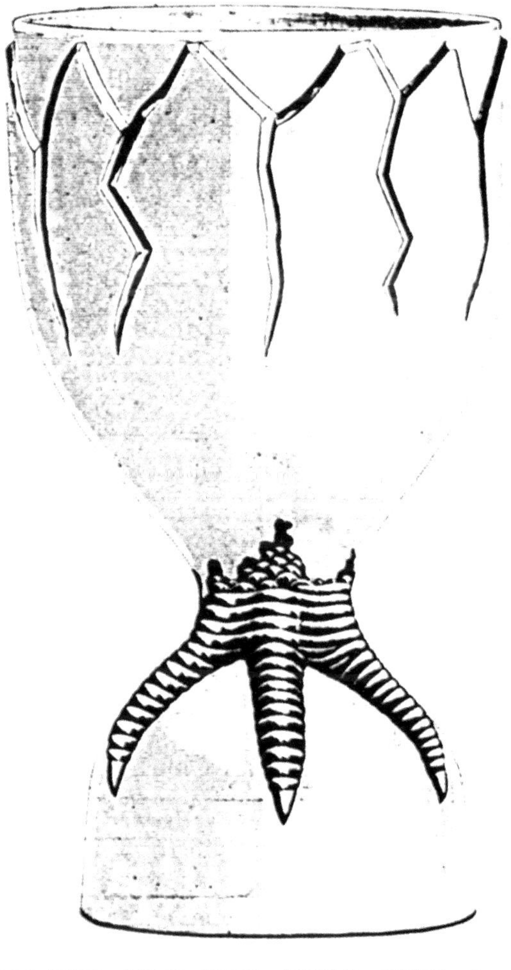

NOVEL EGG CUP, FULL SIZE, from
Gillinder & Sons, Inc.

The Greensburg Glass Company was chartered in 1890 and remained in operation as such until they became a part of the National Glass Company in 1899 as their No. 8 Glass Works. They made many tableware patterns, as they were primarily a tableware factory. Many of their patterns were ruby stained by the Oriental glass company, a decorating company. In 1891 this firm manufactured an outstanding novelty, the Stanley Caster. This was a caster set in the form of three elephant heads, the top of each holding a caster bottle. The illustration has the salt, pepper, and mustard. The advertisement caption states *also with vinegar,* but does not illustrate it.

The **Hemingray Glass Company** was organized in 1848 at Cincinnati, Ohio, and moved to Covington, Kentucky, in 1851. They manufactured glass products until 1972. Although they were best known for the manufacture of insulators, they made some outstanding novelties. They produced the K of L anvil match safe in blue, amber, and clear. They also produced a Bird dish in blue, amber, and clear. Also among the items that they manufactured were lamps in color, bottles in color, a beautiful blue basket, a leaf dish, and numerous other goods. To really appreciate this manufacturer, you should visit the website at http://www.hemingray.net

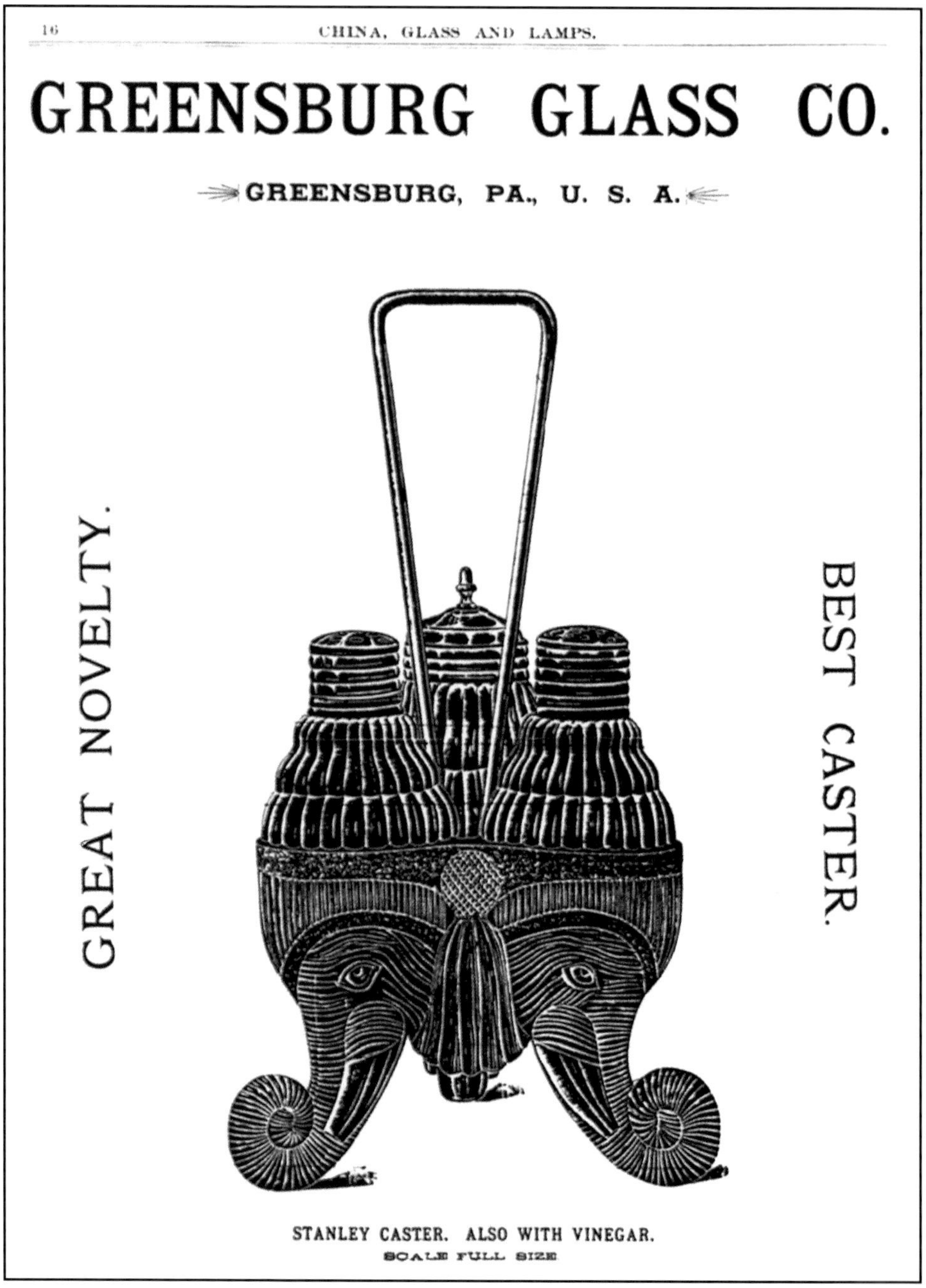

Hobbs, Brockunier and Company, which was often referred to as the **South Wheeling Glass Works** in the trade journals, made their share of novelties. Perhaps one of the first was the Turtle saltcellar. We know that they were making beautifully embossed and figural knife handles for a cutlery factory in Connecticut in 1881. They then manufactured Daisy and Button canoes that appeared in nearly every color that the firm was known to have made. They were also responsible for several items in the forms of shoes and slippers. Perhaps the most notable item that they manufactured was the one-of-a-kind vase that was a presentation piece to the President of the United States in 1887. The Wheeling Chamber of Commerce appointed a committee headed by Mr. C. W. Brockunier to decide upon a novel invitation to the President to visit the city of Wheeling. The invitation was decided to be in the form of a vase to be made at Hobbs, Brockunier and Company. The vase was of ruby, plated on white. At the mouth the color was deep ruby, and it is shaded down so that at the base it is a delicate, rich pink. The mouth of the vase is fluted, and there are spiral ribs from the rim to the base. The inscription is in old English letters, enameled. It reads: *To the President of the United States; The Chamber of Commerce has instructed the undersigned to extend to yourself and Mrs. Cleveland a cordial invitation to visit this city as guests of this Chamber, and to earnestly urge your acceptance. C. W. Brockunier, T. H. Logan, C. B. Hart, J. B. Taney, J. N. Vance, M. Riley, C. W. Seabright, Committee.*

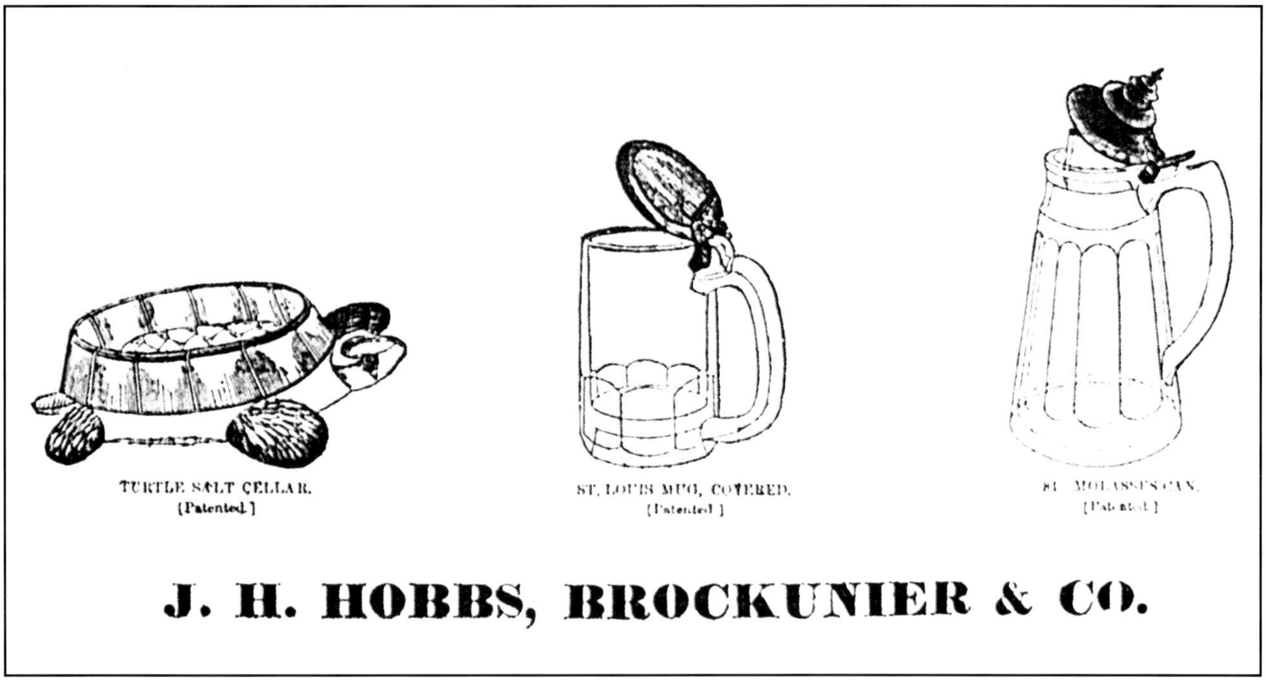

In 1907 the **Hocking Glass Company** of Lancaster, Ohio, were doing a thriving business with opal novelties. Among their wares were tomatoes, both vine ripened red and green examples, which were colored accordingly. These were used for mayonnaise dressing, bon-bons, etc. Another fruit produced was a realistically decorated pineapple. At this time they were also making pitchers, saltcellars, ten-cent vases, bureau sets, tobacco jars, and spice jars. This company had a strong start and was placing half page advertisements in *China, Glass and Lamps*.

HOCKING GLASS CO.

LANCASTER, OHIO

Will have ready and show at their various show rooms a line of

OPAL NOVELTIES, Decorated,

Consisting of staples and fancy goods, Vases, Easter Goods, etc.

CORRESPONDENCE SOLICITED.

SHOW ROOMS:

NEW YORK, BOSTON, PHILADELPHIA, 922-924 Market St. BALTIMORE, 15 Hanover St.

Although the **Indiana Tumbler & Goblet Company** of Greentown, Indiana, is best known for glassware in Golden Agate and Chocolate glass, this firm also made some outstanding novelties. They manufactured toothpick holders in the form of an old Witch and also in the form of a St. Bernard dog's head. They manufactured many covered animal dishes and a handsome Buffalo paperweight. After joining the National Glass Company as Factory No. 9, they made a toothpick holder in the form of a sheaf of wheat. Many of these items were made in chocolate glass and other colors including a beautiful Nile green. This factory was under the direction of the Jenkins family: David C., David C., Jr., Thomas, and Lewis, Jr.

In 1900 Harry Bastow, a former superintendent of the Indiana Glass Works of the National Glass Company, at Indiana, Pennsylvania, became the prime mover for the founding of the **Jefferson Glass Company** at Steubenville, Ohio. They first acquired the old Sumner Glass factory and then with Mr. Bastow as chemist or color maker they began producing some outstanding glassware that included novelties. In 1907 they moved the business across the Ohio River to Follansbee, West Virginia. They advertised novelties but many of these items were simply vases of color and opalescence.

We have found very little about some factories that manufactured a lot of glassware. We do know, however, that 1907 meant a new factory for the **D. C. Jenkins Company**. It was written in *China, Glass and Lamps* on January 12, 1907 that the D. C. Jenkins Glass Company was successor to the **Kokomo Glass Company** but in fact it was a change in name only as the ownership remained the same. Their new factory had been completed in September of 1906 and they immediately started producing glassware. The most interesting of their products would be their packer's goods as these were usually produced in novelty wares.

In 1869 David C. King and his son William King organized the **King, Son and Company** at Pittsburgh and operated it until it became a part of the United States Glass Company in 1891 as Factory K. This factory was known as the **Cascade Glass Works**. Although we found very little material about this firm in the trade journals of the time, we were fortunate that factory catalogs exist. In these catalogs we find a dog in the doghouse mustard, a sheaf of wheat match holder or toothpick holder, a hanging slipper match holder, a hanging umbrella match holder, a wall match holder in the form of an elephant's head, a snail toothpick holder, a slipper, a wall soap dish, a butter dish in the form of a stove, a butter in the shape of a helmet, and a spice barrel that resembles a barrel on wheels. They probably made many other novelties as well.

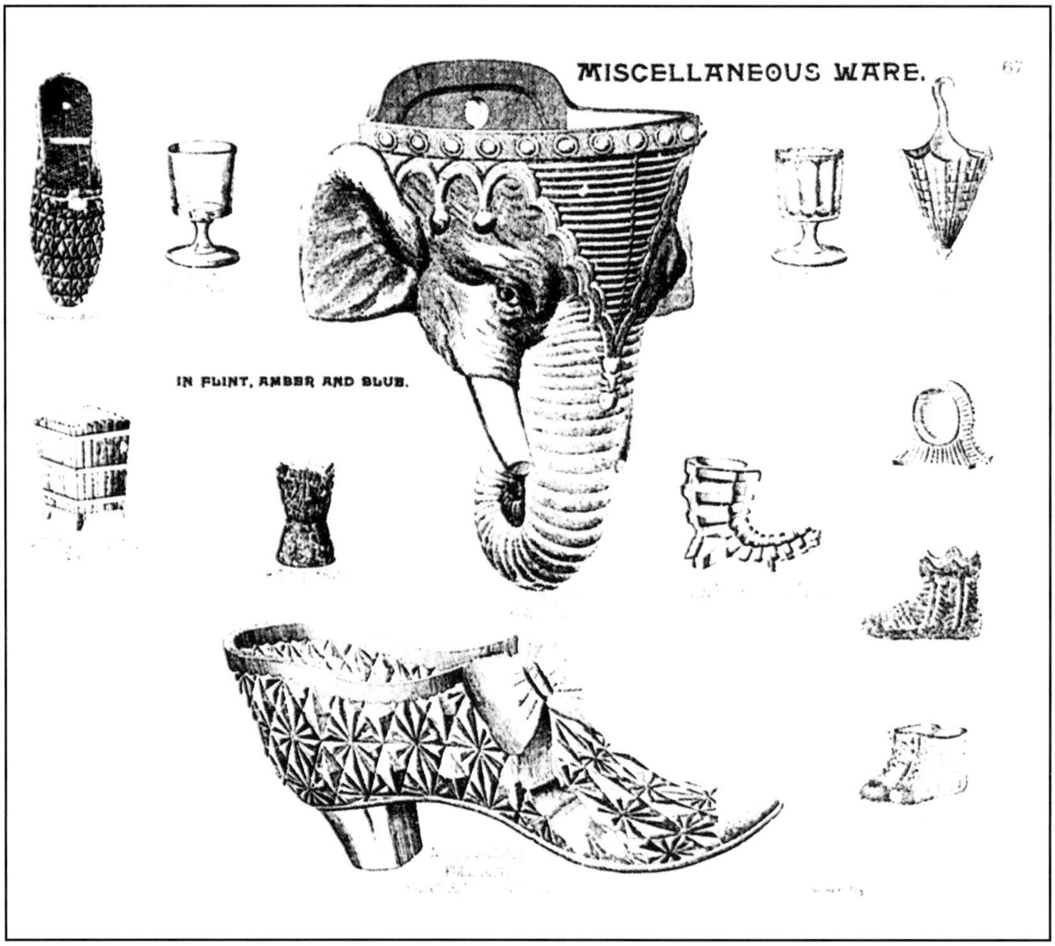

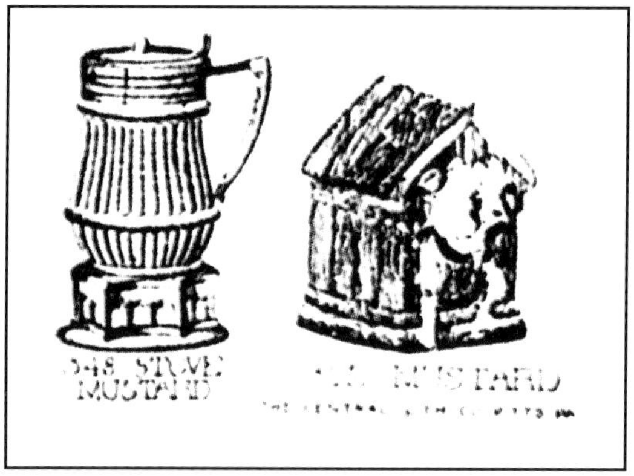

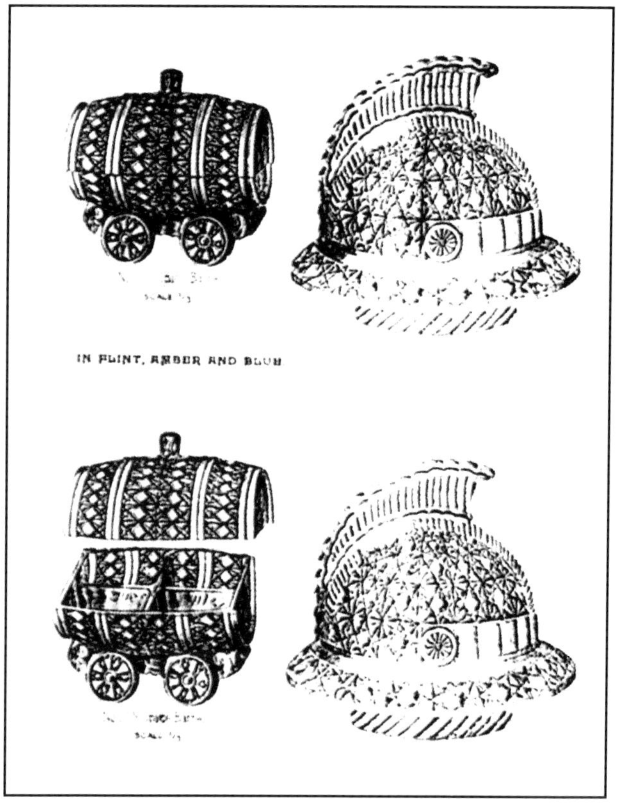

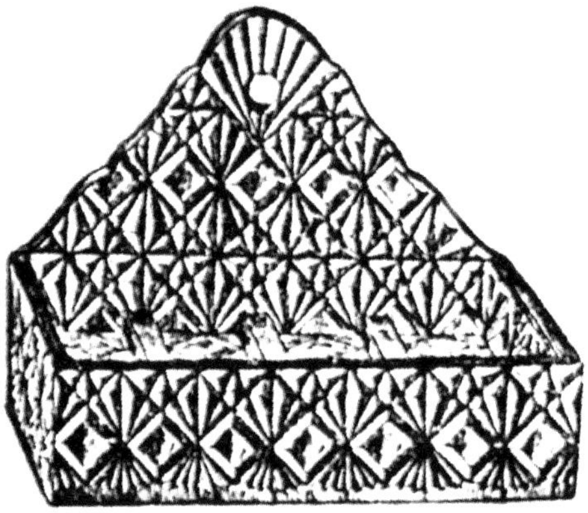

308 Bracket Soap

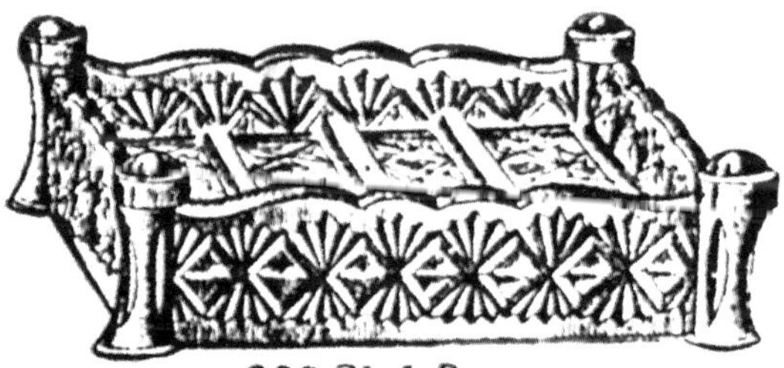

309 Slab Soap

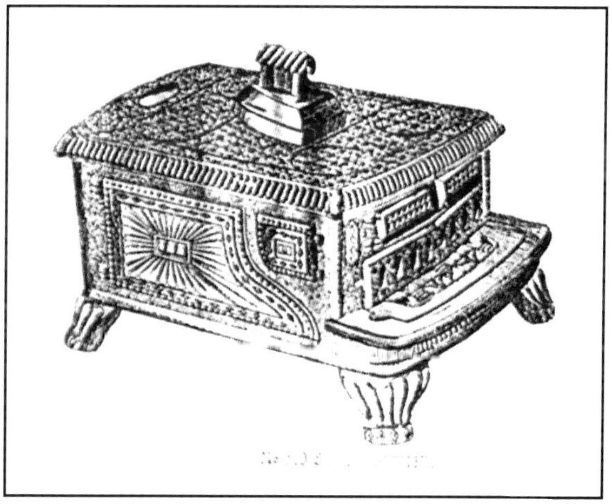

In 1872 Andrew Baggs, E. P. Rhodes, and F. C. Winship organized the **LaBelle Glass Company** at Bridgeport, Ohio. This firm manufactured tableware, lamps, bar ware, and novelties. One of their first novelties was an inkwell called the *Paragon*, and they were indeed paragons as they were described in the trade journals. They were crystal with *engraving that was beautiful and artistic.* In July of 1882 it was announced that this firm was making a pretty little bouquet holder resembling a *hammock*. Although it was not mentioned as to what colors were available in this novelty hammock, the colors that the firm was producing at the time were old gold, blue, and ruby.

The **W. L. Libby & Son Company** of Toledo, Ohio, was well known for its cut glass products; but, they also made some fine pressed glass novelties. An advertisement in the *Crockery and Glass Journal* of October 1889 illustrates three of their novelties. There was a saltshaker in the form of a dice, a salt shaped like a thimble, and a napkin ring. The patents had been applied for.

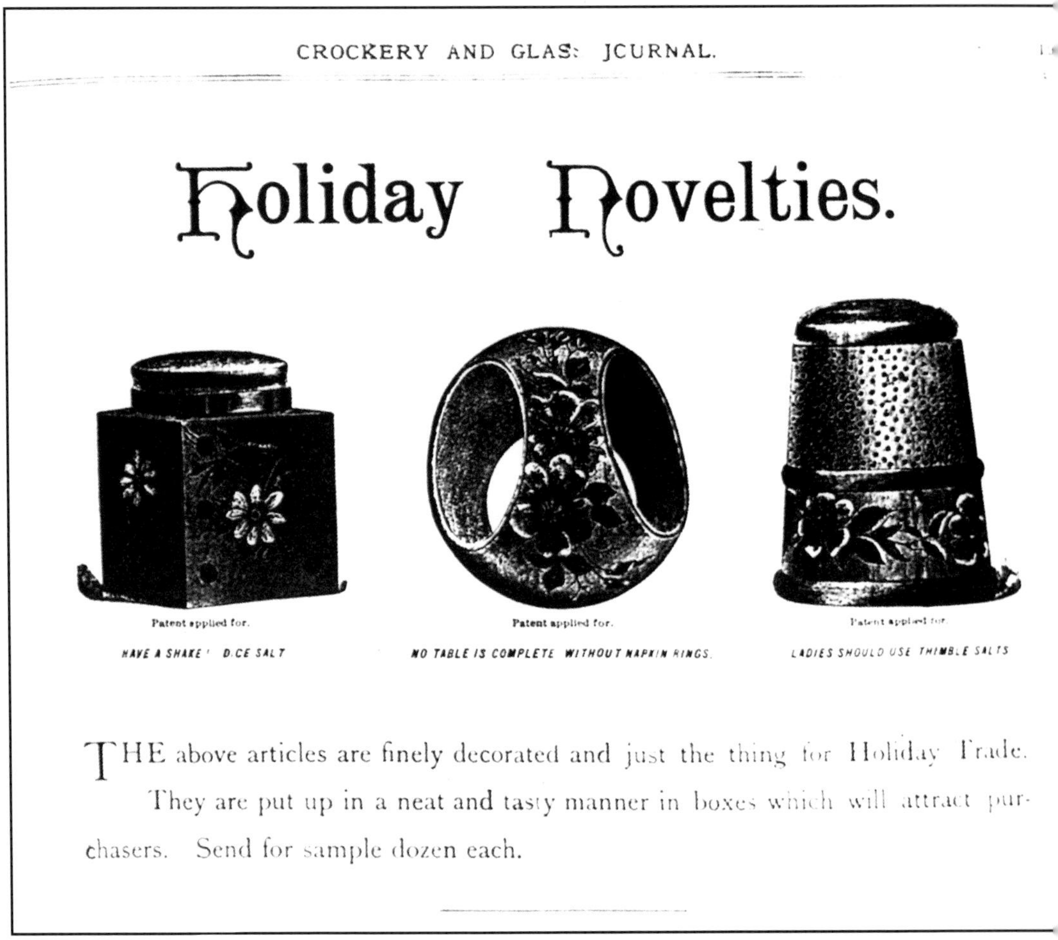

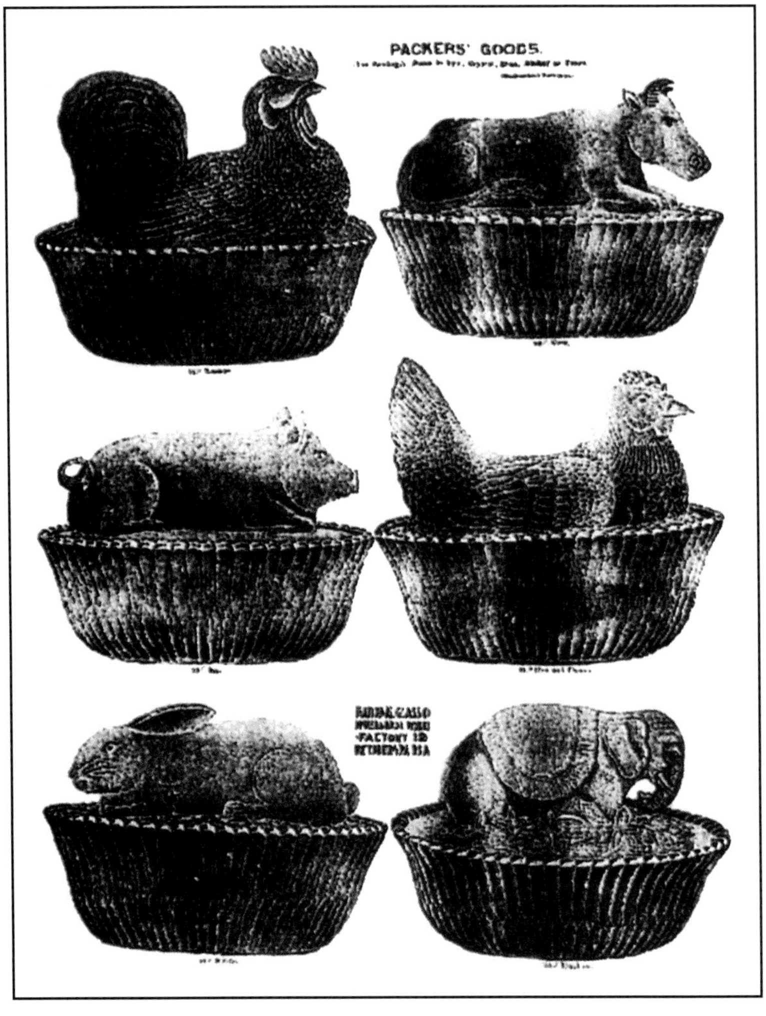

McKee and Brothers of Pittsburgh, Pennsylvania, and Jeanette, Pennsylvania, were one of the largest and longer lasting of the tableware factories. Their existence spanned the years from 1835 to 1899 without interruption. In early 1899 it was reported that *many of the novelties are very odd, but decidedly attractive and they sell like hotcakes.* Many of the items that they manufactured at the time were of opal glass. In their illustrated advertisements we find a Yachting Cap, College Straw Hat, Plug Hat match holder, Harvard card holder, puff box, Boston Bull match safe, Easter egg with chick head, Ramses 111 match safe, Heart jewel box, lock box and cover, stamp box and cover, Bijou ring stand, Parisian ring tray, Shield tray, Remember the Maine covered dish in the form of the ship, Railroad Engine, Volunteer plate, Remember the Maine plate, and a McKinley handled mug.

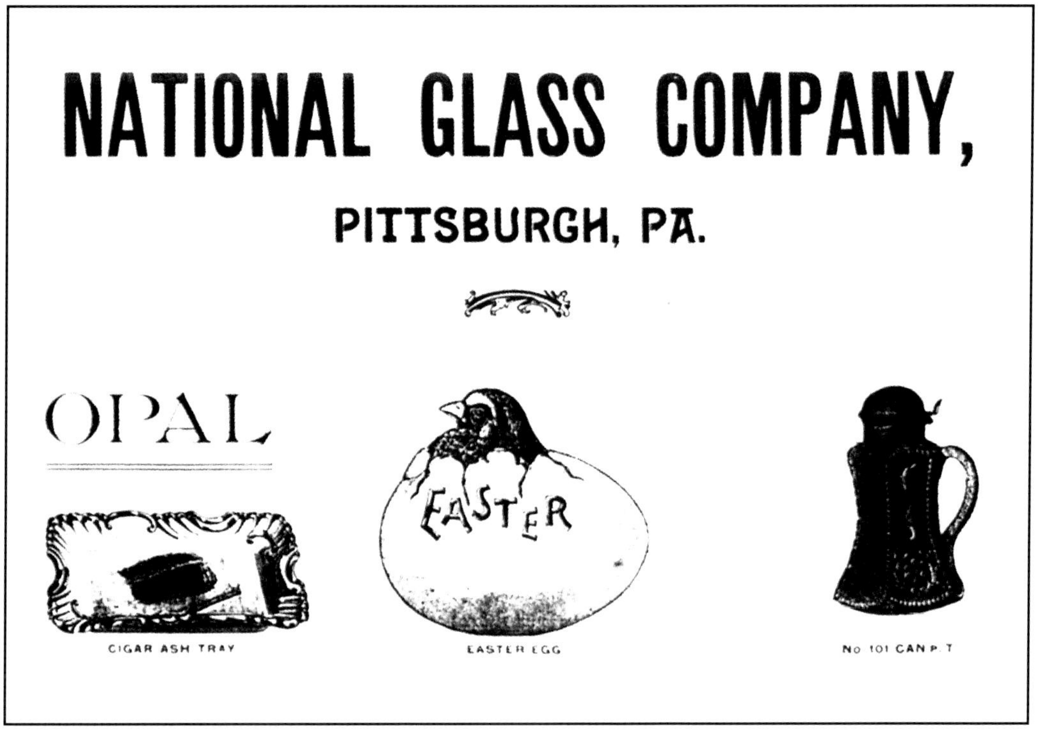
NATIONAL GLASS COMPANY,
PITTSBURGH, PA.
OPAL
EASTER
CIGAR ASH TRAY
EASTER EGG
No 101 CAN P. T

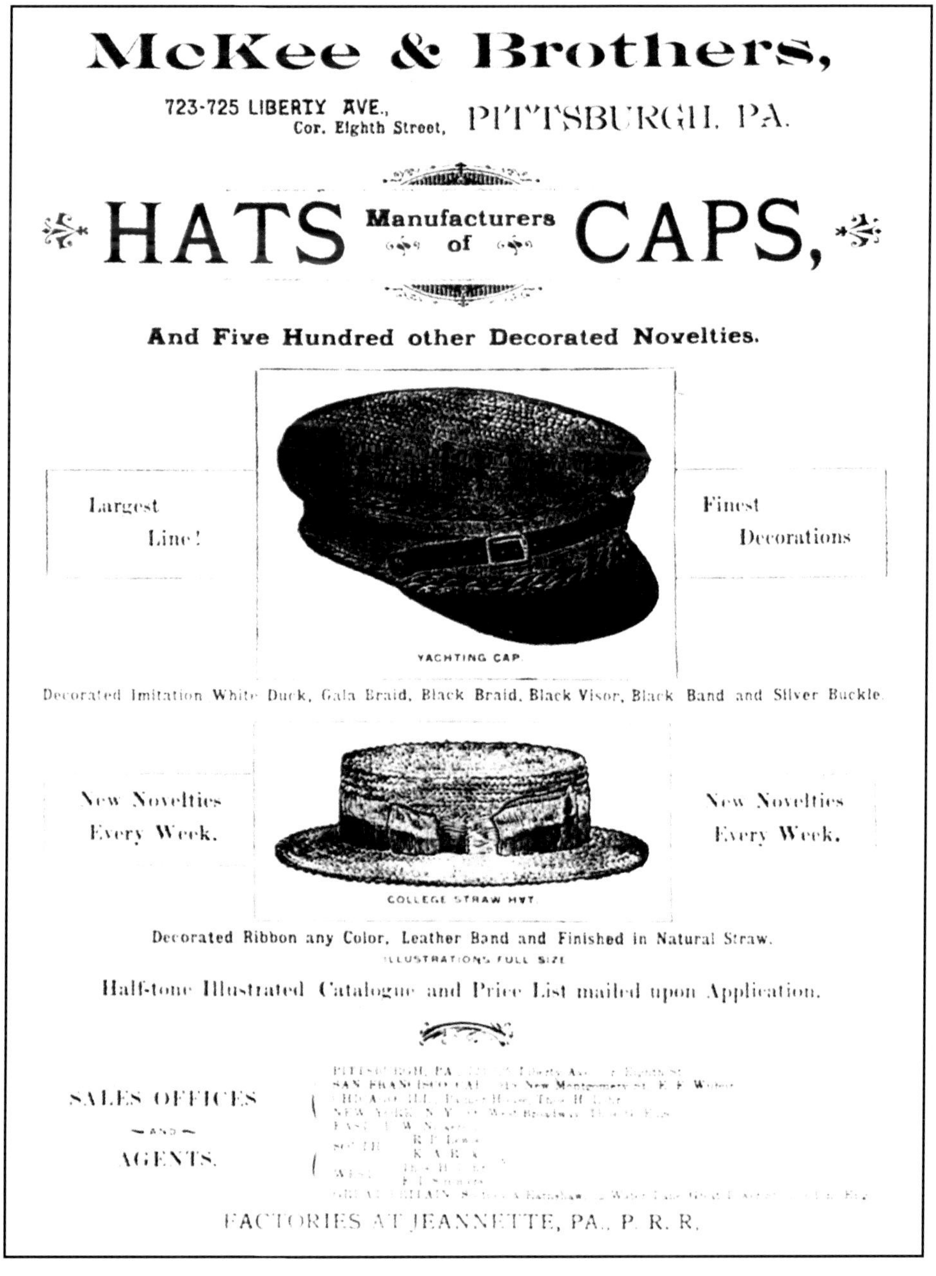
McKee & Brothers,
723-725 LIBERTY AVE.,
Cor. Eighth Street,
PITTSBURGH, PA.
HATS Manufacturers of CAPS,
And Five Hundred other Decorated Novelties.
Largest Line!
Finest Decorations
YACHTING CAP
Decorated Imitation White Duck, Gala Braid, Black Braid, Black Visor, Black Band and Silver Buckle.
New Novelties Every Week.
New Novelties Every Week.
COLLEGE STRAW HAT
Decorated Ribbon any Color, Leather Band and Finished in Natural Straw.
ILLUSTRATIONS FULL SIZE
Half-tone Illustrated Catalogue and Price List mailed upon Application.
SALES OFFICES
AND
AGENTS.
FACTORIES AT JEANNETTE, PA., P. R. R.

HE PRIZE WINN

OUR LINE EMBRACES

Comb and Brush Trays.
Pen Trays.
Pin "
Ash "
Ring "
Trinket "
Placques.
Candlesticks.
Colognes.
Caraffes.
Stamp Boxes.
Puff "
Jewel "
Fern Dishes.

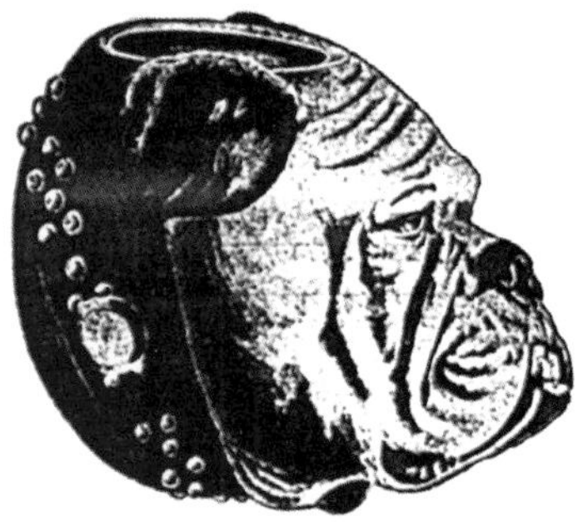

"BOSTON BULL" MATCH SAFE.

Bon Bons.
Cigar Jars.
Handkerchief Boxes.
Glove "
Collar "
Cuff "
Smoking Sets.
Manicure "
Plates.
Lock Boxes.
Card Cases.
Paste Boxes.
Card holders.
Match Safes.

Half-tone Illustrated Catalogue and Price List mailed upon Application, from our offices.

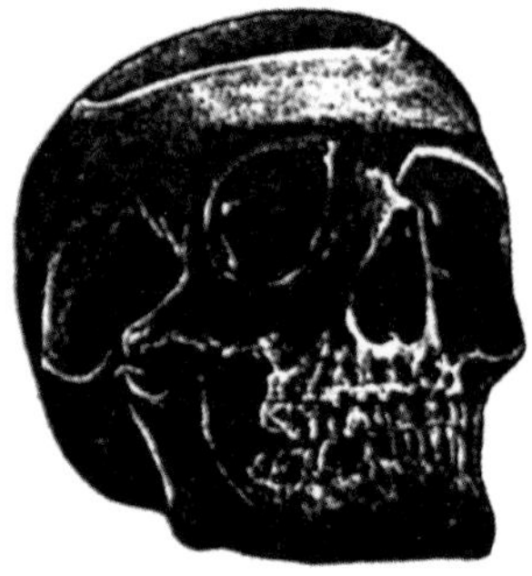

MATCH SAFE RAMESES III.

McKee & Brothers

723-725 LIBERTY AVE.,
Cor. Eighth Street, PITTSBURGH, PA.

Opal Decorated Novelties.

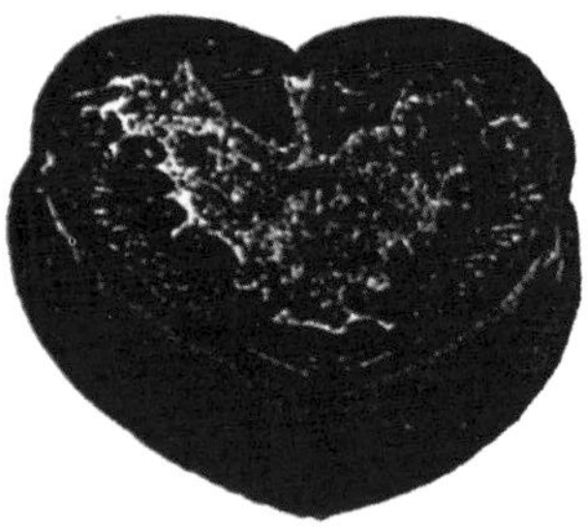

HEART JEWEL BOX.

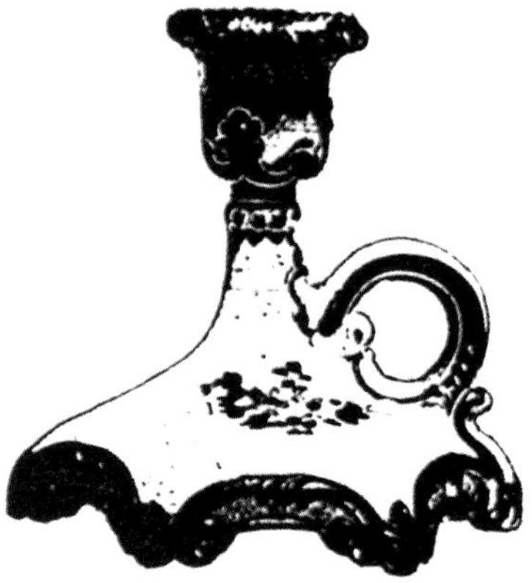

CINDERELLA CANDLESTICK.

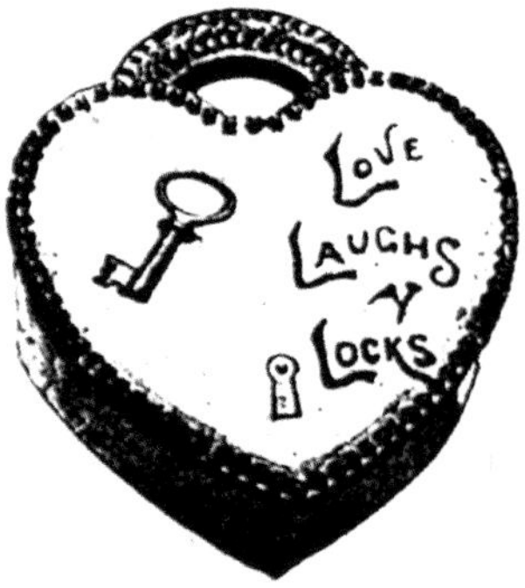

LOCK BOX AND COVER.

McKee & Brothers

PITTSBURGH, PA.

SCALE, HALF SIZE.

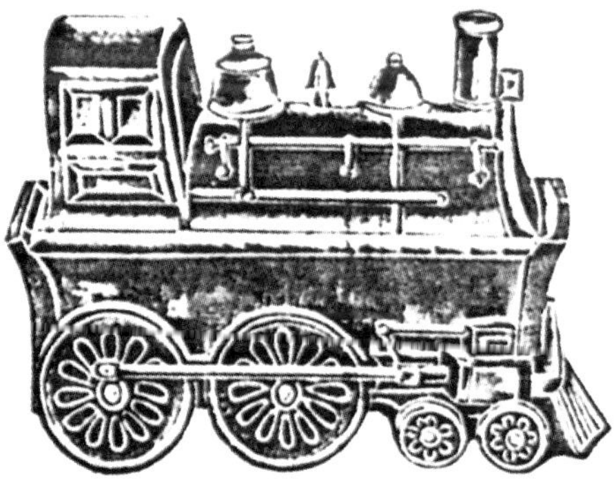

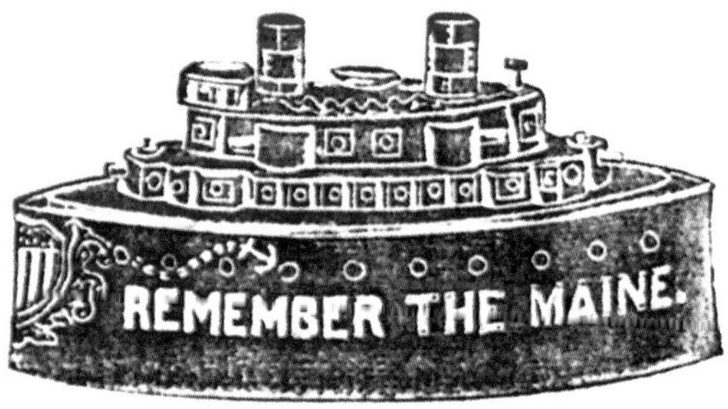

Made in CRYSTAL, GREEN, AMBER, CANARY and DEWEY BLUE.

McKee & Brothers

PITTSBURGH, PA.

SCALE, HALF SIZE.

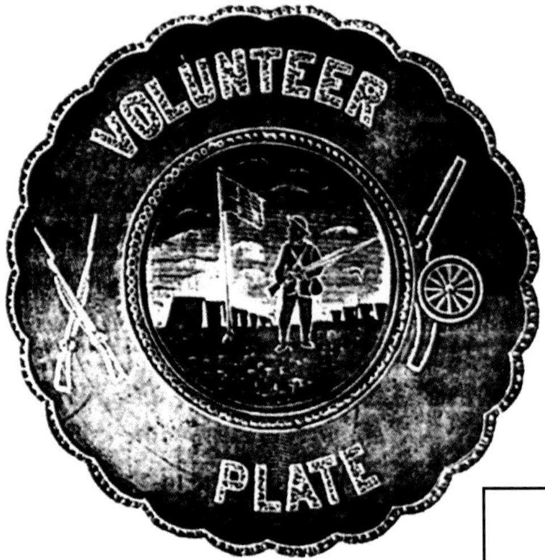

Made in CRYSTAL, GREEN,
CANARY and DEWEY B

McKee & Brothers

PITTSBURGH, PA.

SCALE, HALF SIZE.

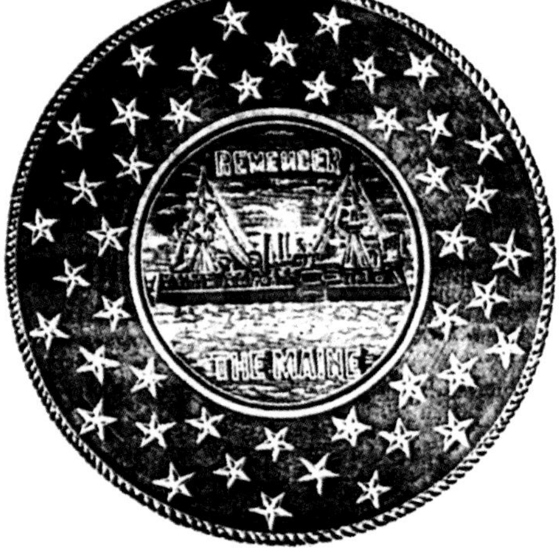

Made in CRYSTAL, GREEN, AMBER,
CANARY and DEWEY BLUE.

McKEE & BROTHERS,

PITTSBURGH, PA.

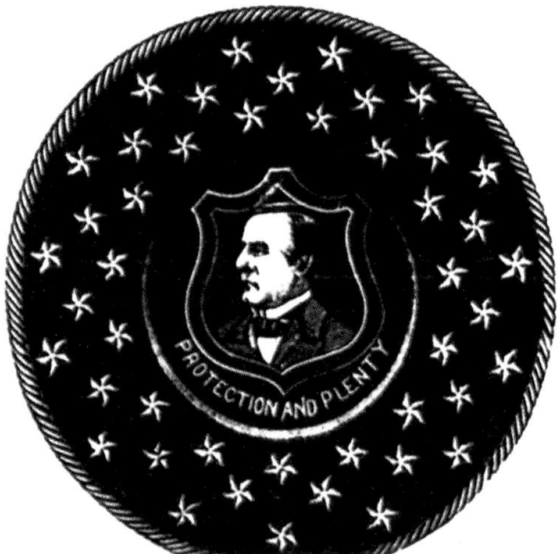

[illegible] in. McKinley Plate; also, Etched Head; also, Gold Ground.

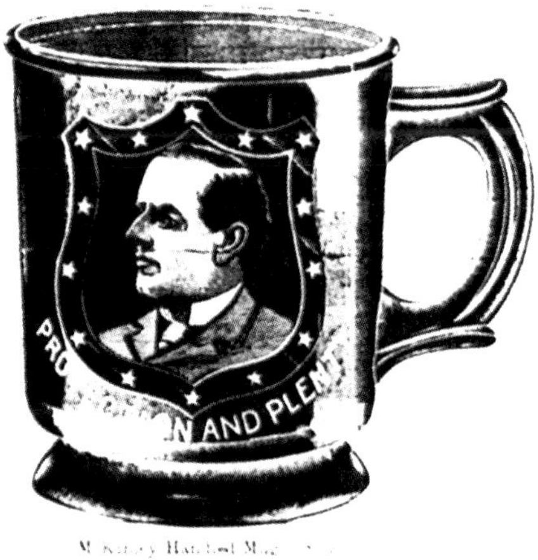

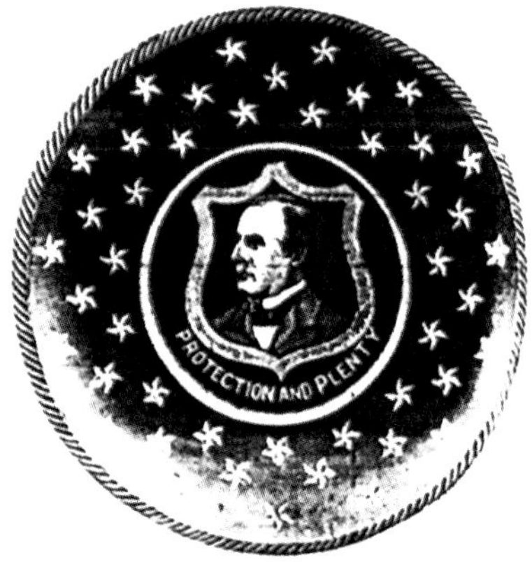

McKinley Handled Mug [illegible] [illegible] McKinley [illegible] Etched Head [illegible]

SCALE HALF SIZE

[illegible] with McKinley [illegible] with McKinley [illegible] profile [illegible]

SALESMEN.

NEW YORK: [illegible] West Broadway
SAN FRANCISCO: [illegible] Front Street
EAST— K. W. Nickerson; J. A. Harris.
WEST— Thos. H. Lohr; Frank M. Miller
SOUTH— A. J. George; H. E. Waddell

With the discovery of natural gas at Findlay, Ohio, a boom in manufacturing followed. Several glass firms were founded, one of which was the **Model Flint Glass Company.** This firm was organized in 1888 and when the gas supply diminished they moved to Albany, Indiana, in 1893. The Model Flint later became Factory 11 of the National Glass Company. Although they didn't manufacture a lot of different novelties, they did make some excellent ones. A toothpick holder in the form of a tree with a snake coiled around it was made in clear, amber, and blue. In 1892, Model Flint made *a handsome lamp called the Lion of massive shape and a large capacity for oil.* This could be the Lion lamp that has had many guessing about its origin. This lamp, which is illustrated in the photo section of this book, also has the swirl pattern of this company. Perhaps the best known and reproduced novelty made by this firm is the Lord's Supper bread plate, in an oblong shape with the representation of the Last Supper in the center and a wreath of vines surrounding it. It was said to be available in plain and etched glass.

Very little is known about the **Mosaic Glass Company** of Fostoria, Ohio. We do have an early advertisement from *China, Glass and Lamps* dated 1891 that illustrates a Swan toothpick holder, salt or cologne bottle holder. It was made in crystal and amber originally and later the color blue was available. Although this firm began operation specializing in *ornamental window glass, glass tile, and other specialties* they were also making beautiful tableware.

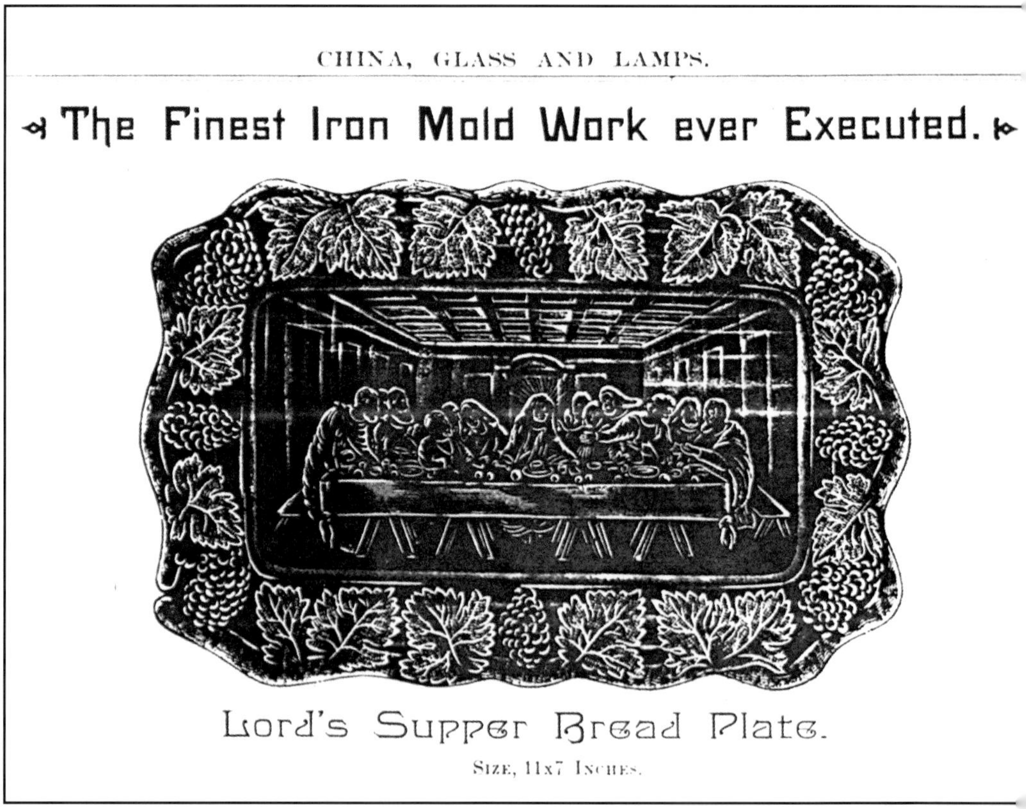

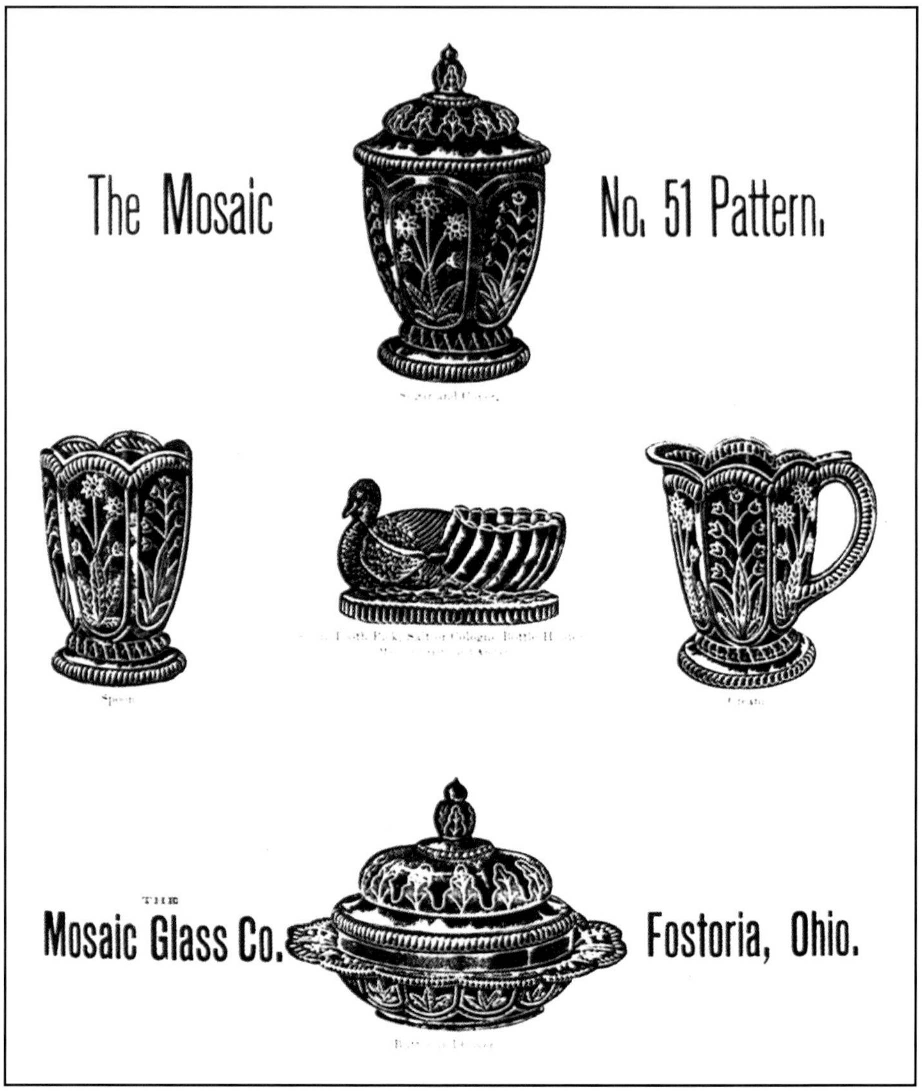

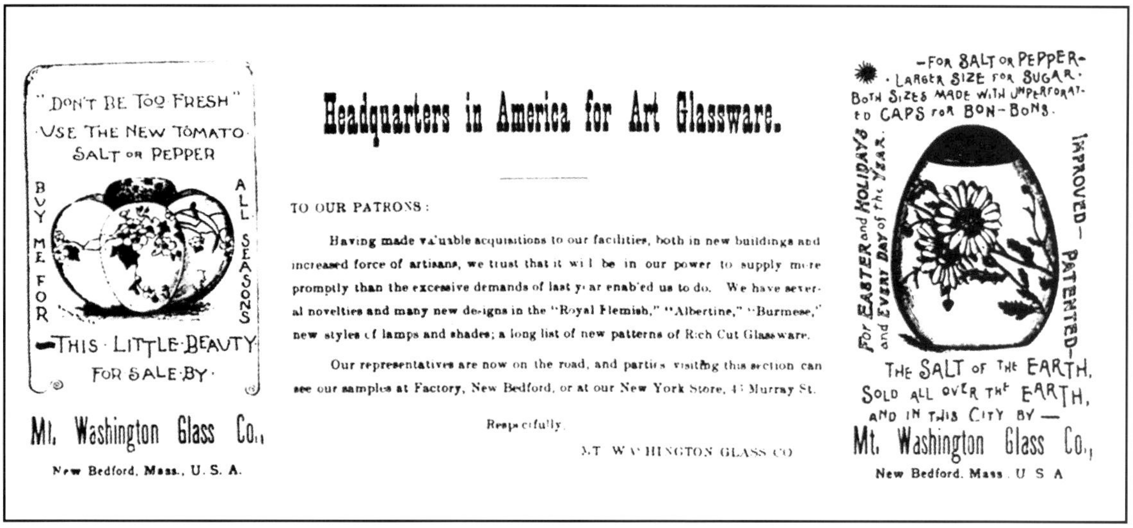

The Mt. Washington Glass Company of New Bedford, Massachusetts, was well known for their art glass, but they also made some novelties that they had to be proud of. The saltshakers that they made in 1889 in tomato or pepper shapes were outstanding as was the salt or pepper in the egg form that was also made in a larger size for sugar or with a closed lid for bon-bons. An advertisement in *Crockery and Glass Journal* dated 1891 illustrates a mushroom-shaped flower holder. The ad also states that this item makes a good toothpick holder but is manufactured for *Pansies, Violets, and Daisies.* Illustrations of Mt. Washington wares include pails, rose bowls, and flower trays. This firm was probably responsible for other novelties.

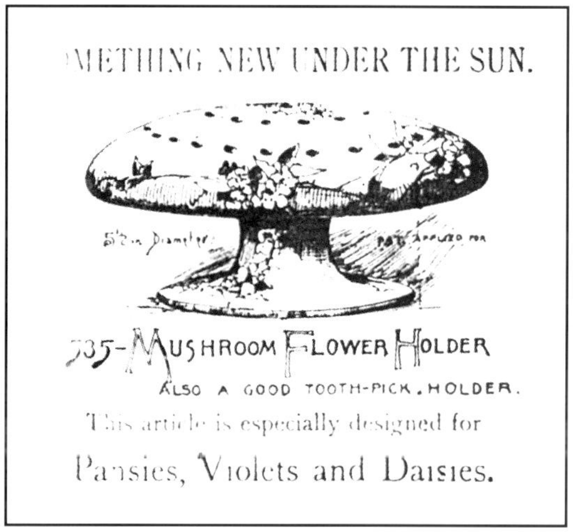

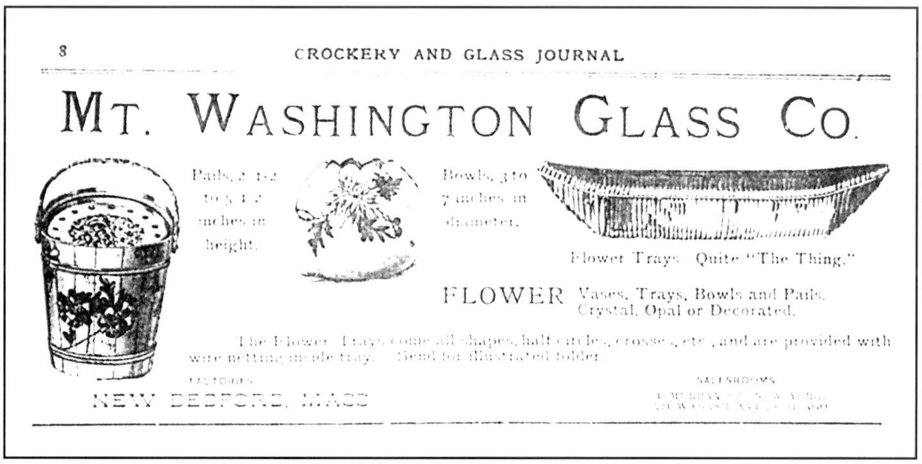

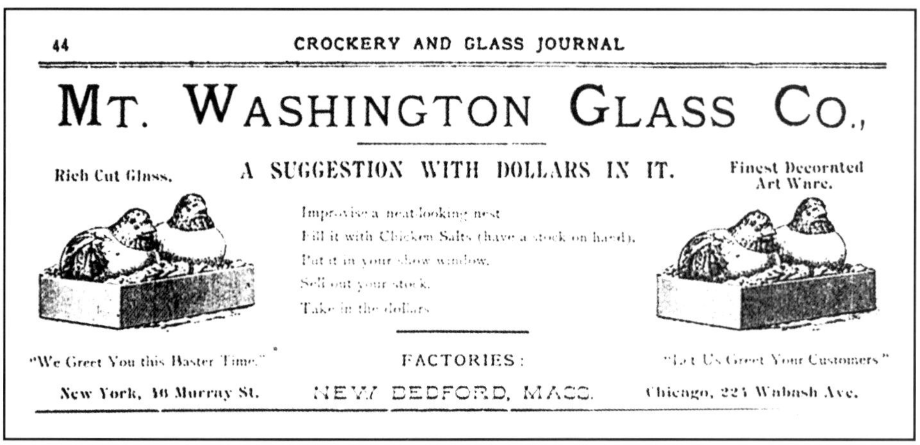

The New Brighton Glass Company were organized in 1886 and continued production of decorated goods in lamps, tableware, and novelties until 1891. It is interesting to note how fragile the glass market was because this firm refurbished their plant in late 1890 and then closed their business in the spring of 1891. Most of their products were made in clear glass. The one novelty that can be attributed to the New Brighton is the Washington Hatchet bottle. This bottle was patented and was advertised as having a screw top that was nickel-plated and cork lined.

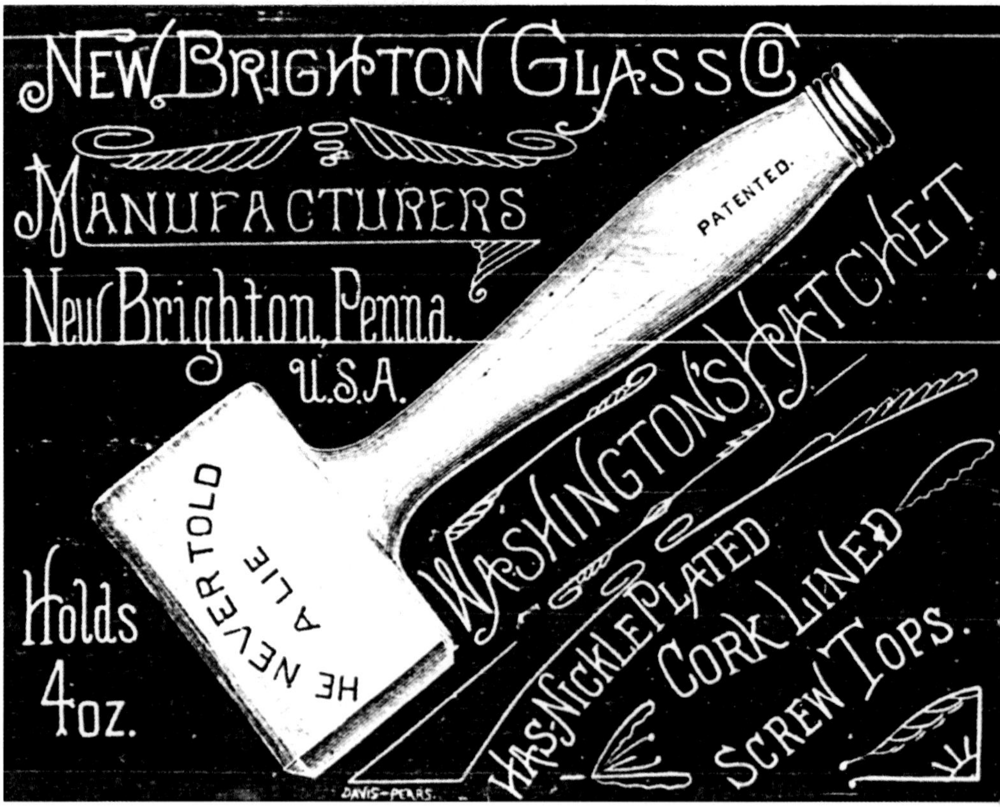

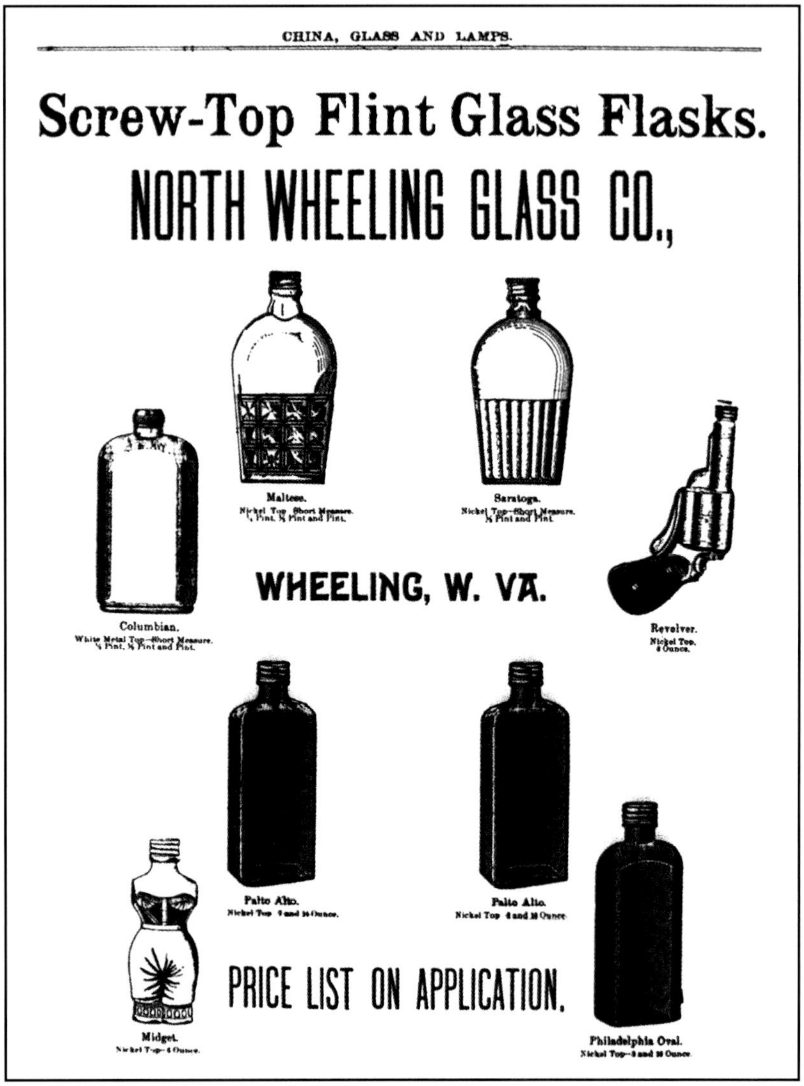

The North Wheeling Glass Company began business in 1882 and produced many varieties of bottles and flasks. In the *Crockery and Glass Journal* of October 1892 it was noted that: "The Columbian Flask, a campaign bottle with either of the candidates for President artistically etched upon one side, is one of the novelties gotten out by the North Wheeling Glass Company." This firm made many figural bottles and flasks, some examples of which are illustrated in an advertisement in 1894. This advertisement in *China, Glass and Lamps* displays illustrations of the Revolver and Midget.

The **O'Hara Glass Company, Ltd.,** of Pittsburgh, Pennsylvania, was organized in 1875 and produced quality tableware and novelties until 1891 when they became Factory L of the United States Glass Company. In 1887 they made some interesting novelties that included a *World butter dish, with the representation of the surface of the earth on it, their Toboggan pickle dish, and their Swan fruit and berry dish.*

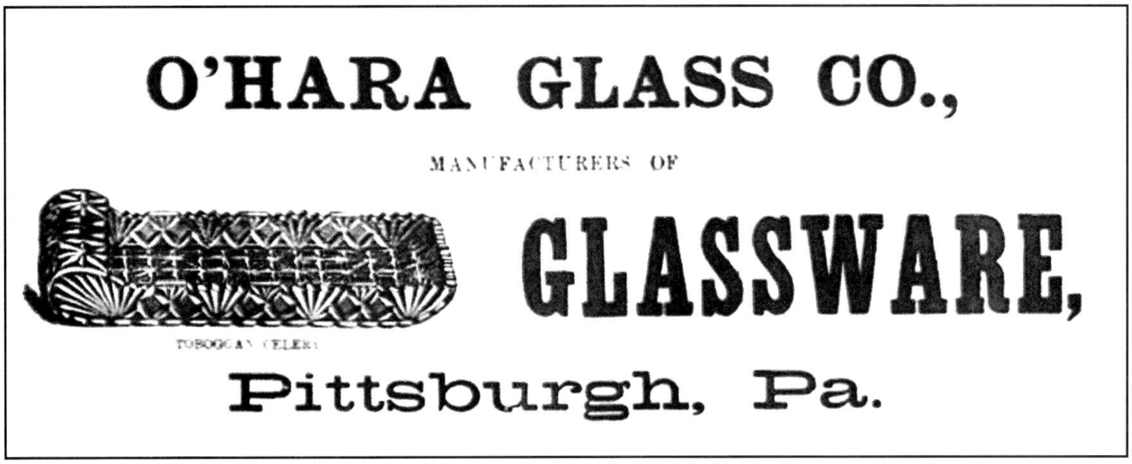

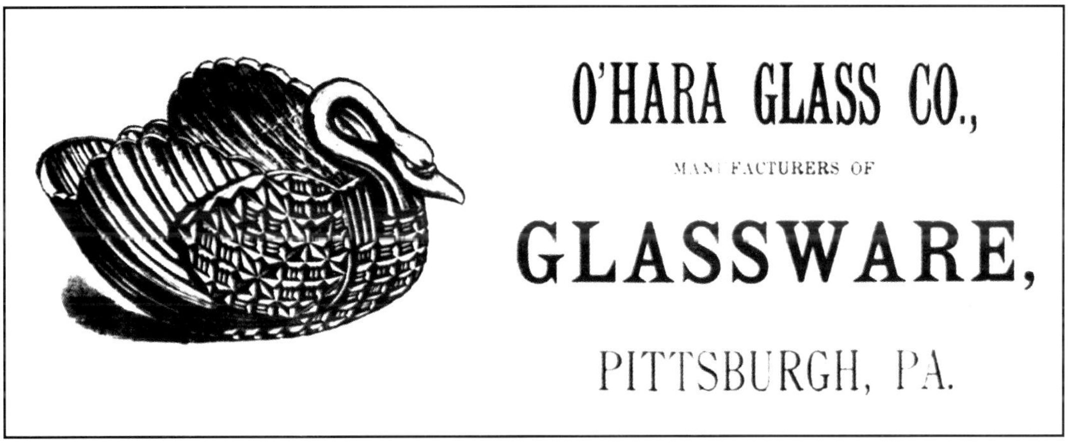

This is another of the older established firms that manufactured novelties but very little can be found in the trade journals. In July of 1890, the O'Hara placed an advertisement in the *Crockery and Glass Journal* illustrating a berry dish and an ice cream saucer in the shape of a shell.

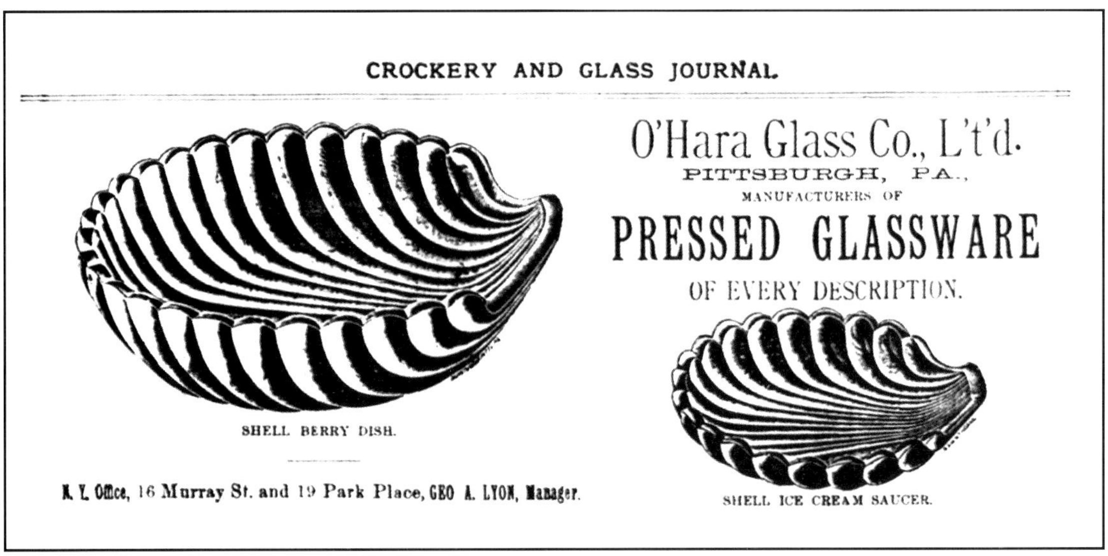

The **Richards & Hartley Glass Company** were organized at Tarentum, Pennsylvania, in 1885 after relocating from Pittsburgh, Pennsylvania, where they were originally known as Richards & Hartley Flint Glass Company. This firm was well known for the quality glassware that they produced in tableware and novelties. Among the novelties were the Kitten on a pillow toothpick holder in clear, amber, blue, and canary; Rabbit with basket toothpick holder in clear and clear with ruby stain; and a beautiful Bird salt dip.

One of the oldest and finest glass factories was started in 1865 and named **Ripley & Company.** It was located at Pittsburgh, Pennsylvania. Although their main product was tableware, they also made a few novelties. In 1891 the firm became a part of the United States Glass Company as Factory F. This is one glass company that seemed to have very few labor problems and this was probably due to Mr. Ripley. An article in the *American Glassworker* describes an incident whereby Mr. Ripley was on a business trip and on his return learned that his manager had hired a machinist to replace a mold maker. Mr. Ripley announced that his *former* manager had hired such a replacement and that *I am a mold maker, my father was a mold maker and I will not allow anyone to lower the wages of a mold maker.*

An announcement in the *Pottery and Glassware Reporter* in 1884 describes a pretty butter dish in a horseshoe shape to be known as *Maude S.* An illustrated advertisement in *China, Glass and Lamps* in 1890 shows their Climax Glass Fly Trap.

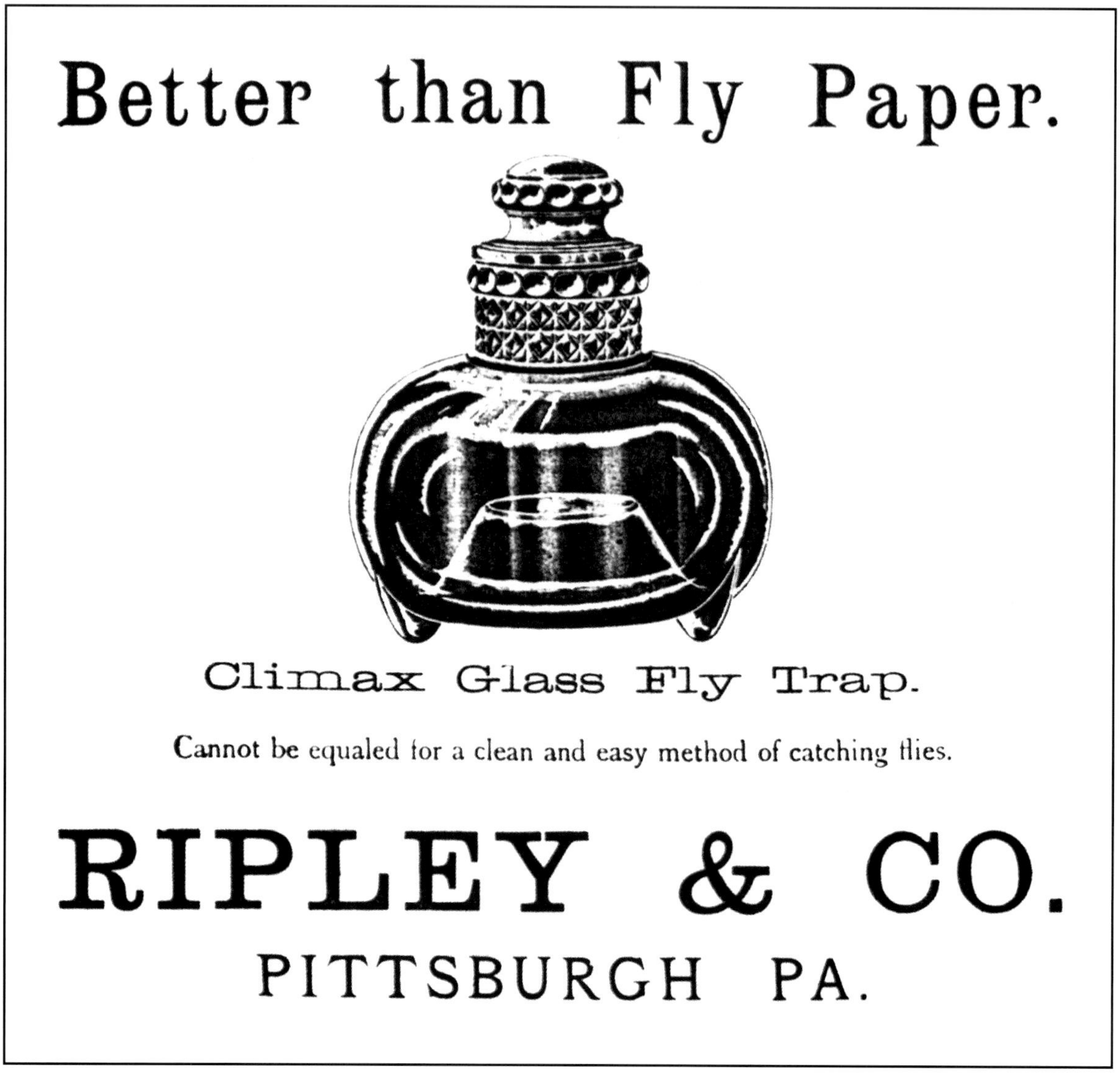

Some of the factories have had very little written about them and very little information is available about their wares. One such factory is the **Specialty Glass Company** of East Liverpool, Ohio. We do know that they issued a forty-eight page catalog in 1894 that included tableware, casters, inks, tumblers, goblets, bar goods, mustards, oils, salt and peppers, sugar shakers, fancy bottles, and lamps, among other things. It was also noted that they were manufacturing many small wares in opal and turquoise. We do have one illustration of a revolver shaped flask to be used for whisky and confections.

The **Thompson Glass Company** of Uniontown, Pennsylvania, began operations in 1889 and ended in 1896. During this period of time they had many financial problems and the factory was completely destroyed by fire in 1893. For these reasons they were not producing wares continuously. In 1894 they were manufacturing a popular Lily paperweight. It has been reported by collectors of the products of this company that they made an oblong relish dish of a bowtie pattern in a solid block for a doorstop.

One of the more specialized factories would be the **Tibby Glass Works**. As best as can be determined, the only item manufactured was a cannonball of glass. An article appearing in a *Crockery and Glass Journal* of 1882 describes that "Messrs. John Eastland and J. Bonshire, of the Tibby Glass Works have fully demonstrated that their glass shells for ordinance are a success. The shells tested were four and one half inches in diameter. The bottom of the shell is one and one-quarter inches in thickness and the sides are one and one half inches. They are about one-half the price of cast iron; they are not perishable as the old kind are, by rust, etc. and are not subject to the elements in any shape and, moreover, by actual demonstration it has been proven that the glass shell has the requisite strength and will do more execution."

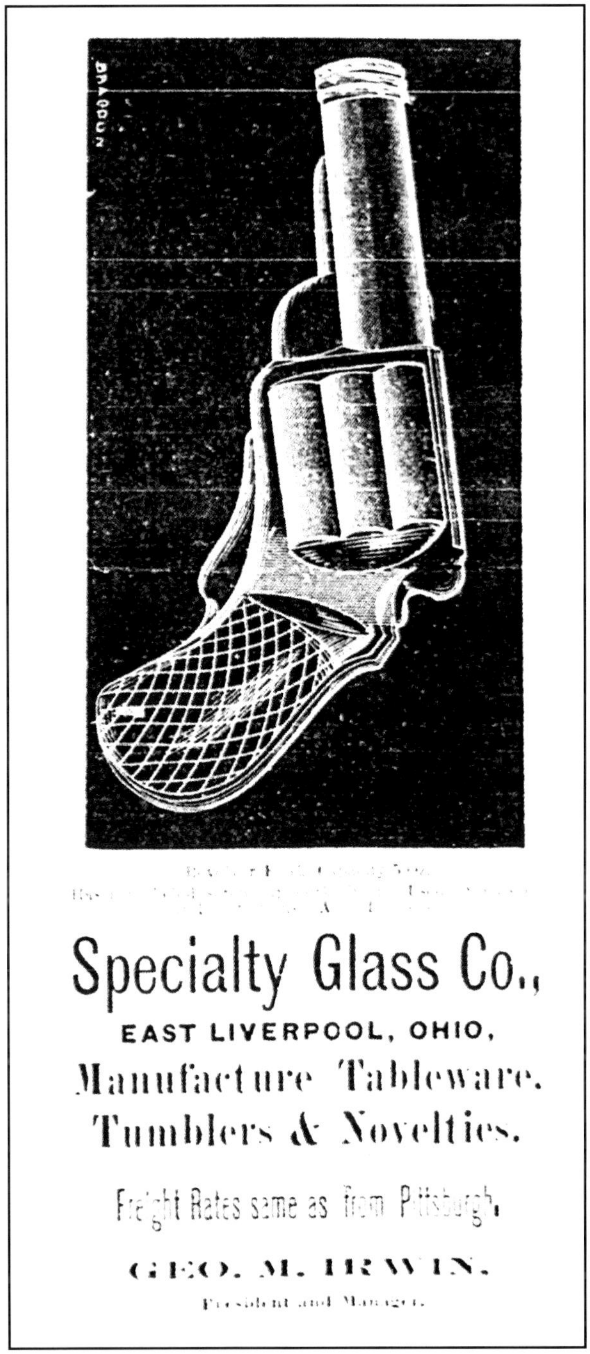

A small factory called the **Tiffin Glass Company** began in the early 1880s and changed its name in 1892 to the **Sneath Glass Company** and manufactured glassware at Tiffin, Ohio, until it burned in 1894. This was not the Tiffin Glass Company that was the successor to the United States Glass Company. This firm manufactured tumblers, tableware, and fruit jars. Toothpick holder and salt collectors seek the novelties that they made. The only documented novelties are the donkey with cart, dog with cart, and goat with cart. These items have a monkey on a slab as a cover for the cart. It is very difficult to find a cart with the cover.

The largest glass company in the United States was the **United States Glass Company**. This company was a combination of Adams and Co.; Bryce Brothers; Challinor, Taylor & Co.; George Duncan & Sons; Richards & Hartley; Ripley & Co.; Gillinder & Co.; Hobbs Glass Co.; Columbia Glass Co.; King Glass Co.; O'Hara Glass Co.; Bellaire Goblet Co.; Nickle Plate Glass Co.; Central Glass Co.; Doyle & Co.; A. J. Beatty & Sons; and the Novelty Glass Co.

Many of the products of the individual companies were continued after the giant merger in 1891. By 1892, the firm was making new and original products including tableware and novelties. An 1892 illustrated advertisement introduces their Eureka Fly Trap, which was to be used with a common tumbler.

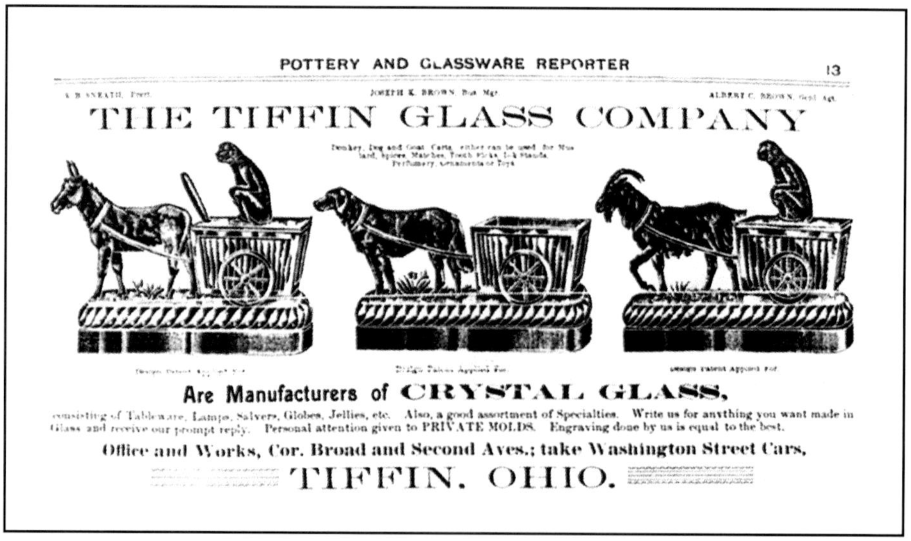

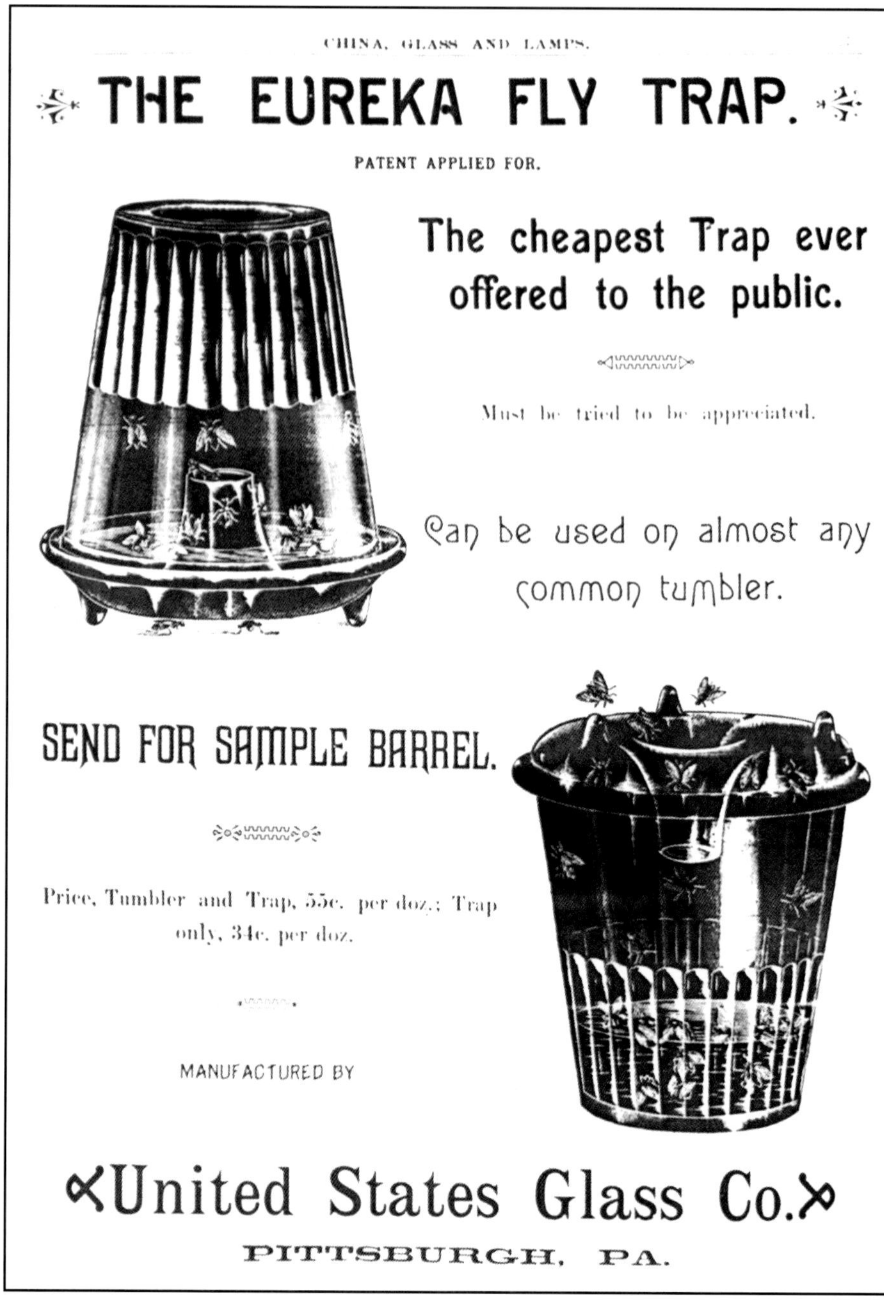

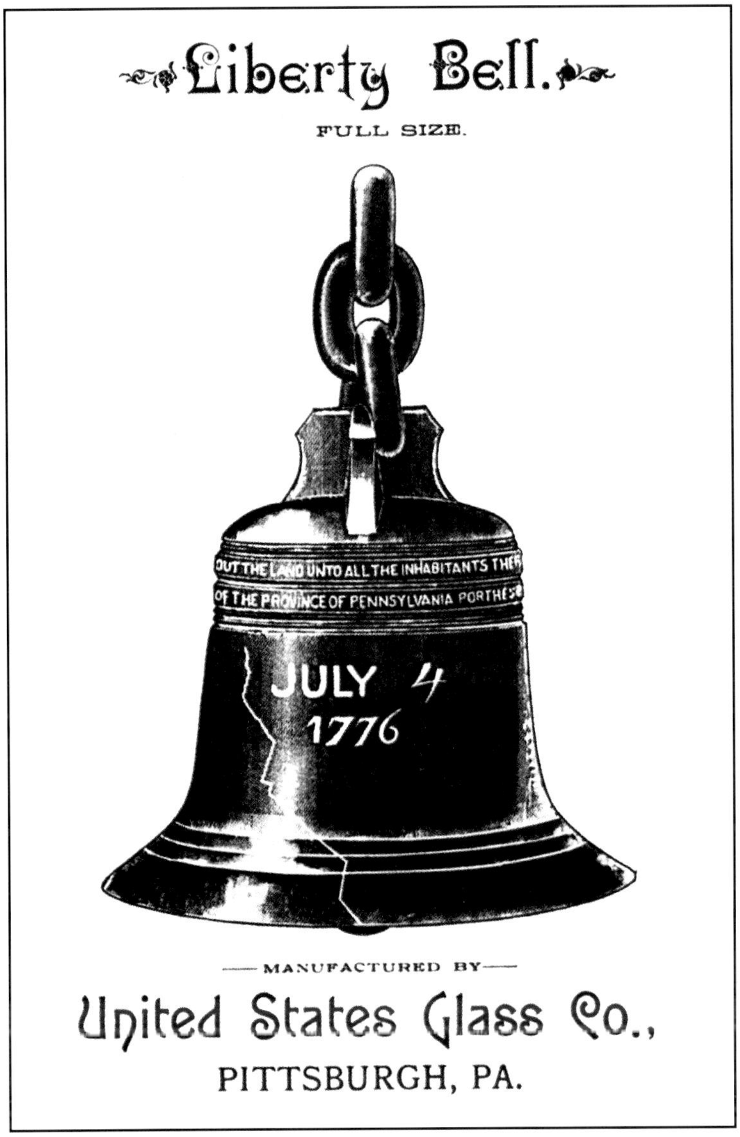

The U. S. Glass Company introduced a replica of the Liberty Bell in 1893 as shown in a trade journal ad.

An 1898 article in *China, Glass and Lamps* tells us that:

There is now an immense demand for souvenirs of all kinds bearing representations of prominent men, battle ships, Old Glory, or historic scenes connected with the past history of our country, or associated with the present struggle for freedom, in which the people of the great republic are now engaged for the purpose of adding another star to the constellation of free and sovereign states. The United States Glass Co. are offering the trade a fine line of open edge plates bearing photographic fac-similes of the Hero of Manila, the foremost and favorite Consul of the Republic; the origin of the Flag of the Free, the noble ship destroyed in the Harbor of Havana, and the Yankee Doodle, representing the immortal trio of 1776, whose ear piercing fife and soul-stirring drums aroused the minute men to immediate resistance of the invader, and instinctively recalls memories of Bunker Hill, Lexington, Concord, Saratoga and Valley Forge.

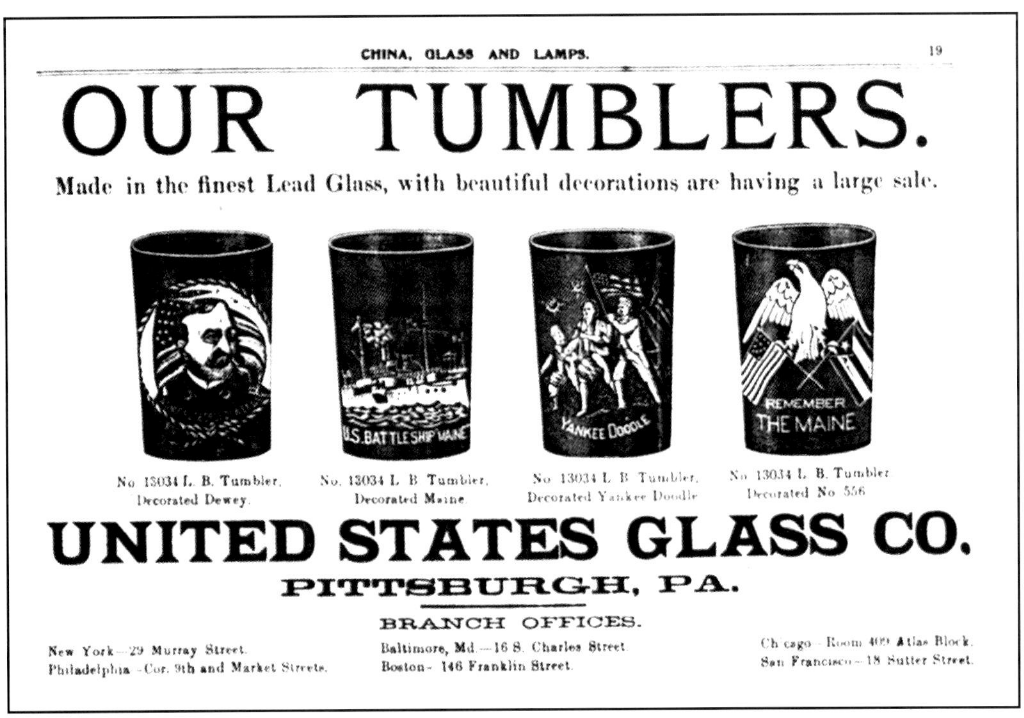

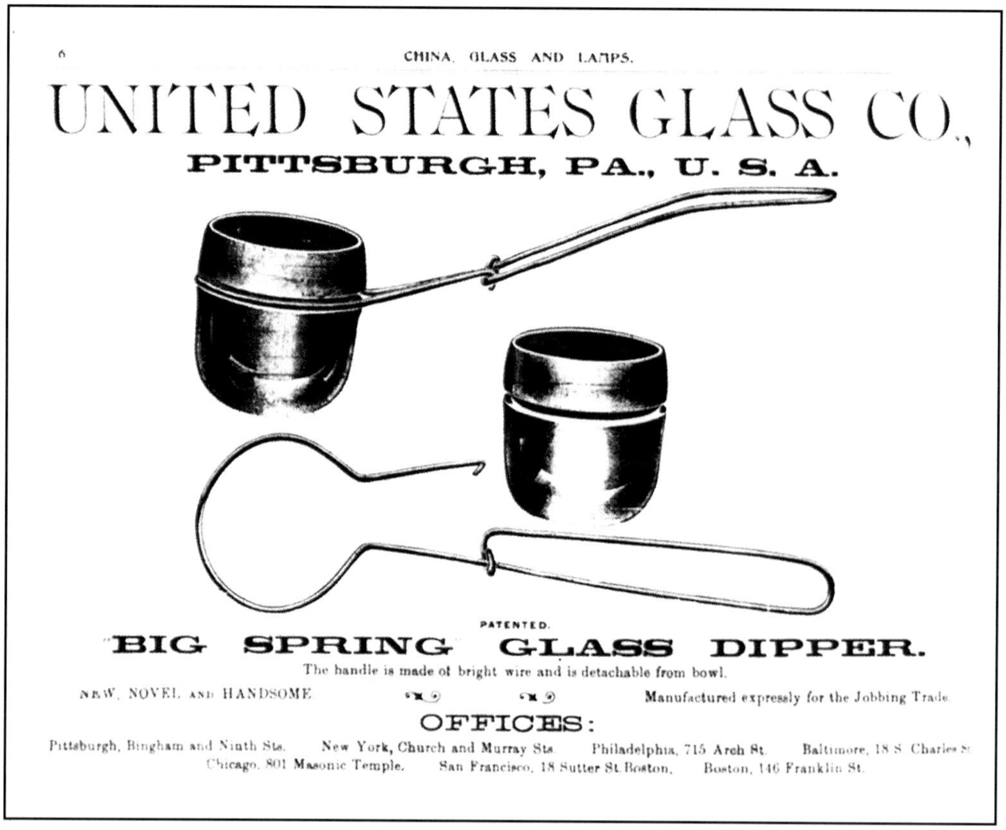

An illustrated advertisement in 1896 depicts a glass dipper with a detachable wire handle.

In 1905 one of the popular novelties of the U. S. Glass Company was their glass basket, made in six sizes, from five to twelve inches. Some were made with glass handles and some without for use with wire handles. The year 1898 saw a week set aside in Pittsburgh for the Knights Templer. Many souvenirs to mark the occasion were manufactured in glass. The U. S. Glass Co. manufactured a novelty for the Knights Templer celebration in the form of a paperweight.

In a June issue of *China, Glass and Lamps* in 1903 it was written, *Of the many progressive firms of Wheeling, W. Va., the* ***Wheeling Glass Letter & Novelty Co.*** *stands well to the front. This firm opened for business August last, and during this brief period many pleasing and attractive features have been introduced.* This was no surprise because Otto Jaeger was the man in charge. Mr. Jaeger had been the head of the etching department of Hobbs, Brockunier & Co. for many years. He then went to Fostoria, Ohio, and from there to organize the Bonita Glass Company at Cicero, Indiana. This reunited him with John Hobbs, who became a partner. When the Bonita closed in 1902, Mr. Jaeger went back to Fostoria to join the Kammerer Glass Works. His next venture was the Wheeling Glass Letter & Novelty Co. and his vast experience went with him. This firm advertised novelties and packer's goods, and specialized in private mold work. Very little can be documented about this firm.

WHEELING GLASS LETTER & NOVELTY CO.,
WHEELING, W. VA.
Manufacturers of
Glass Letters and Novelties. also Packers' Glass Ware.
Private Mold Work Our Specialty. Correspondence Solicited.

Another company making novelties was the **Westmoreland Specialty Company** of Grapeville, Pennsylvania. They manufactured many items for the Easter trade in opal glass such as eggs, rabbits, and ducks; but, one of their specialties was the souvenir items for Shrine conventions. Many of these are shown in this book. The Westmoreland Company was one of the manufacturers who managed to thrive in business for many years.

The **Windsor Glass Company** of Pittsburgh, Pennsylvania, was organized in 1886 and remained in business until 1890. This firm manufactured tableware and novelties. The only illustration of their work in novelties is a fan in the Daisy and Button pattern. An advertisement of 1886 illustrates their handiwork and verifies that they were manufacturing novelties.

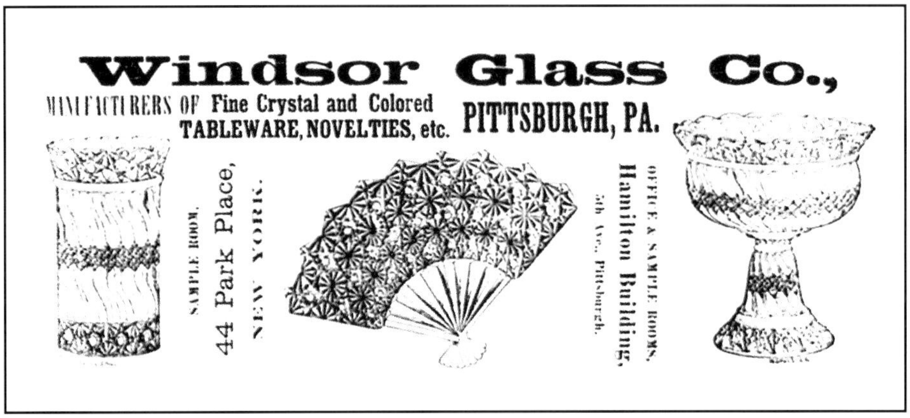

Let us turn our attention to items that appeared in the trade journals that are pertinent to novelties. In the *Crockery & Glass Journal* of 1882 it was announced that, *A patent has been granted to a Pennsylvania firm for glass shingles. They can be made in any color and will add much to architectural beauty. A roof with a colored border and opalescent body, which has been constructed of the new material, is described as very handsome.*

An article appearing in the *Crockery and Glass Journal* of 1885 relates that, *a tableware house here (Pittsburgh) has on hand an order for several thousand miniature representations of the Washington monument, to be composed of colored glass. They are exact fac-similes of the real structure, and bear besides a portrait of Washington, and suitable inscriptions. Some person in Washington has a patent on them, and they must all be finished by February 22, the day of the dedication of the real monument.*

In the *Crockery and Glass Journal* of September 1, 1887, an article appeared about a celebration at Wheeling, West Virginia and read as follows: *The past week has been a gala week in this city, and business has been wholly or partially at a standstill all the time. The occasion was the reunion of the Society of the Army of West Virginia, and Wheeling embraced the opportunity to do herself proud in making thousands feel comfortable. The manufacturers and merchants of the city were chiefs in all the movements; hence much of their time was taken up, and on Thursday of last week a great labor demonstration was the attraction, and glass canes, goblets, etc. were made in the procession as it passed along the streets.*

This then is part of the story of novelties and their manufacture. We now ask you to enjoy the photos and their values in the next section. As we have previously noted, this only scratches the surface of collecting novelties.

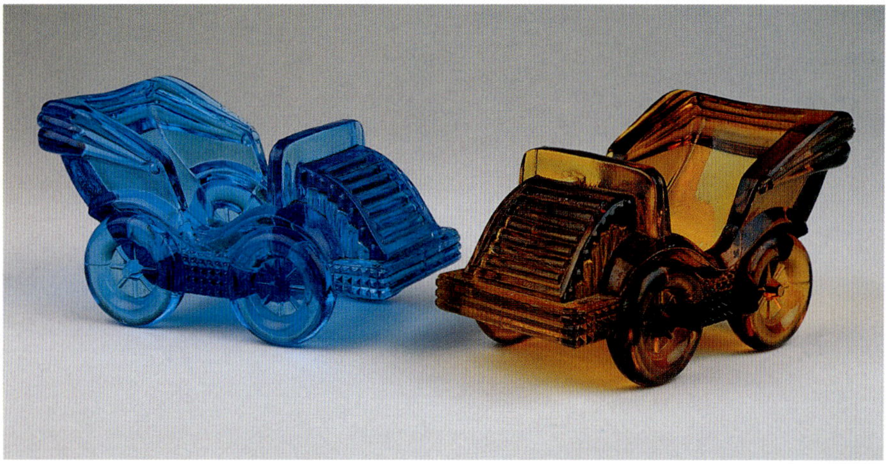

Roadsters in amber and blue are 5" in length. Maker is unknown. Circa 1890s. $85-145.

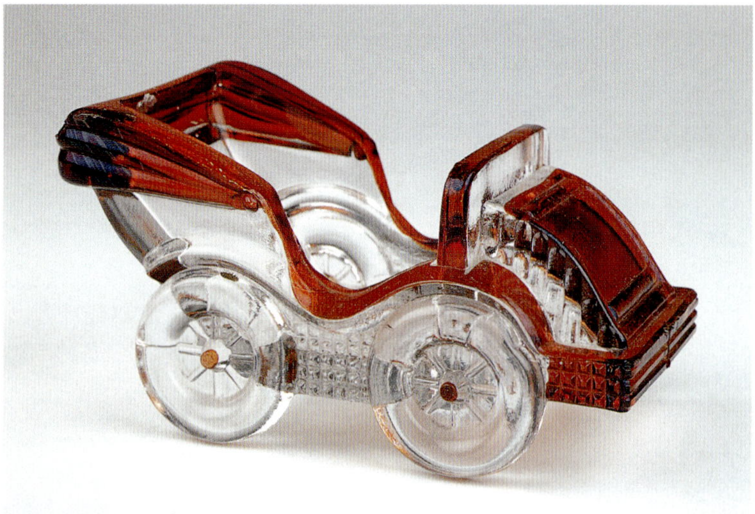

Roadster in ruby stain decoration, similar to the amber and blue except that there are no ribs on the hood. Maker is unknown. Circa 1890s. $85-150.

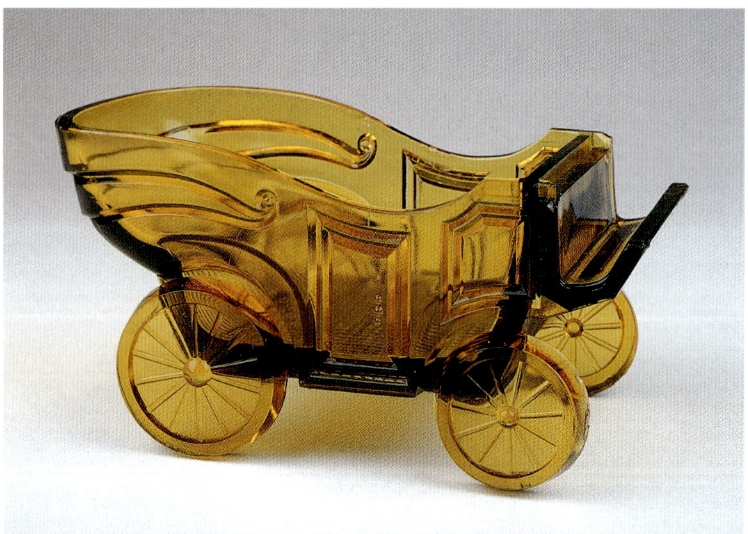

Touring Car candy dish made by the Central Glass Co., circa 1880s. It is 7" in length. $175-250.

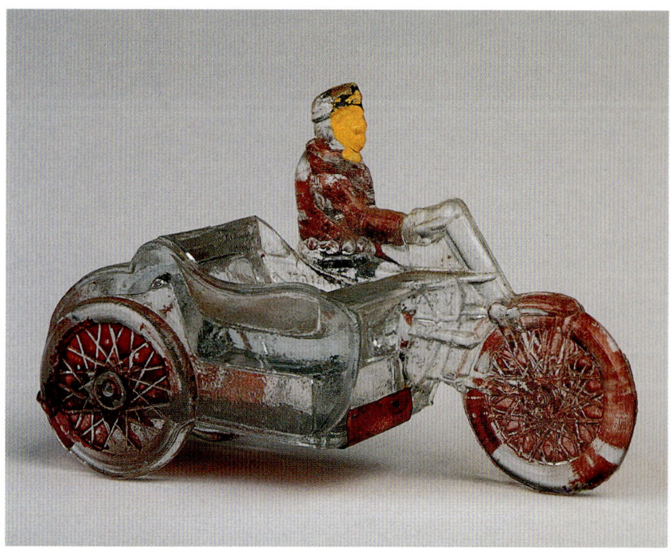

Three wheel motorcycle candy container with rider. 5" long and 3 1/4" high. $550-650.

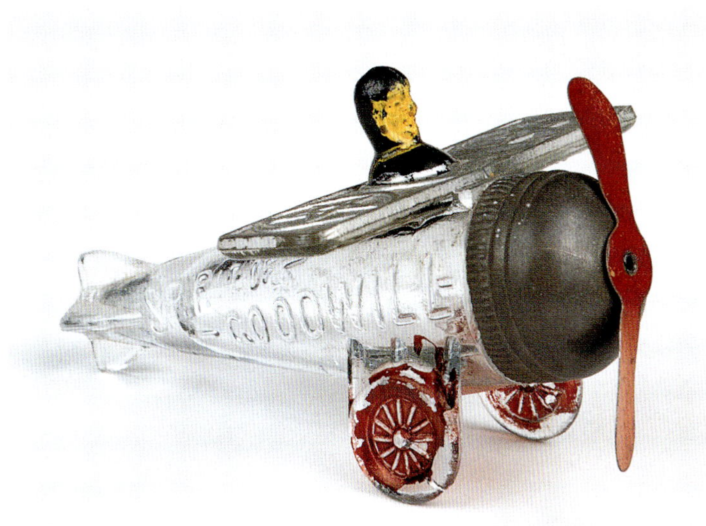

Airplane with pilot candy container, *Victory-Spirit of Goodwill*, 5" in length. $375-425.

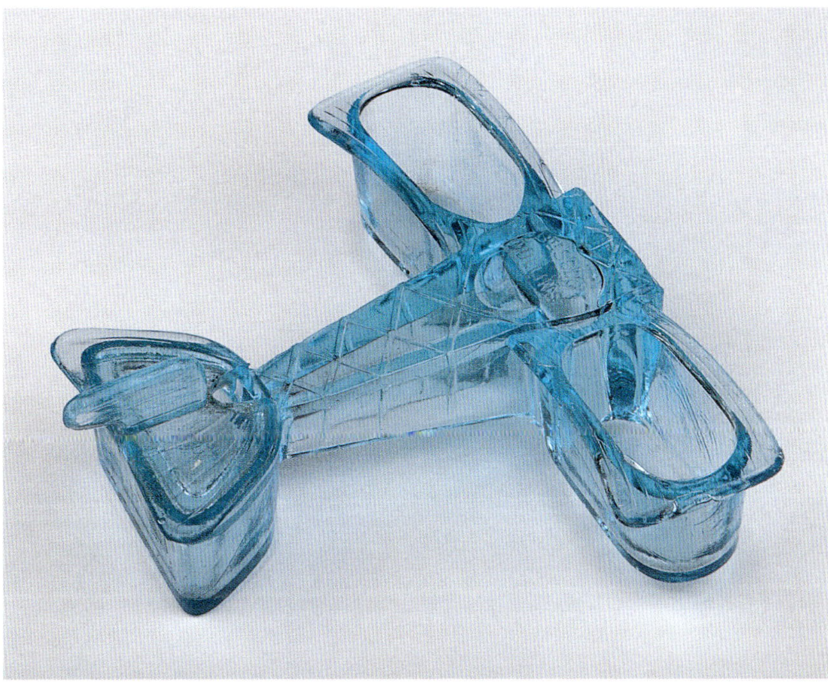

Blue Airplane condiment holder. The tail is the cover for the rear section. Marked *Depose*. 5 1/2" in length. $475-550.

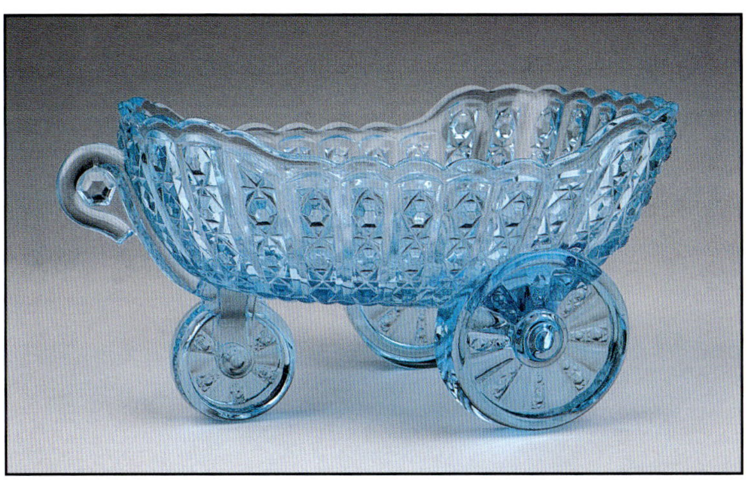

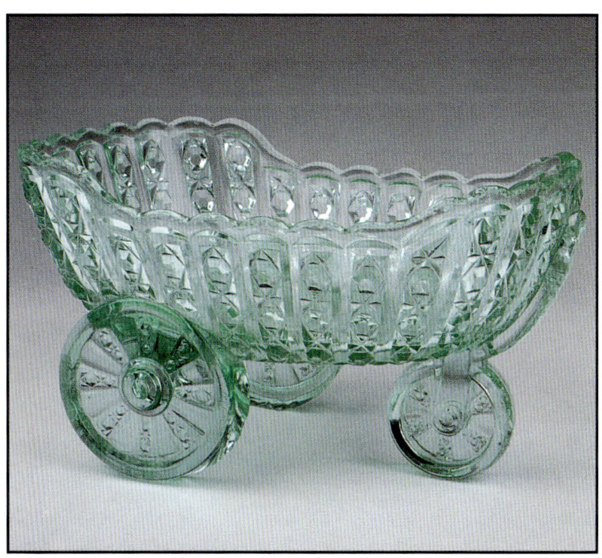

Coach bowl made by McKee and Brothers, circa 1886. Available in blue, amber, green, and clear, it is 9" in length. $95-150.

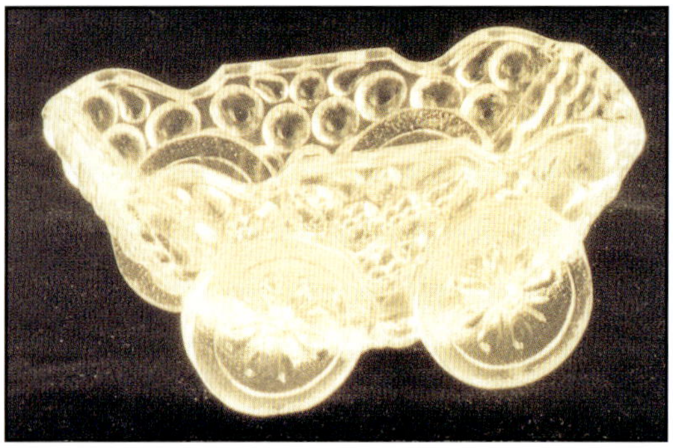

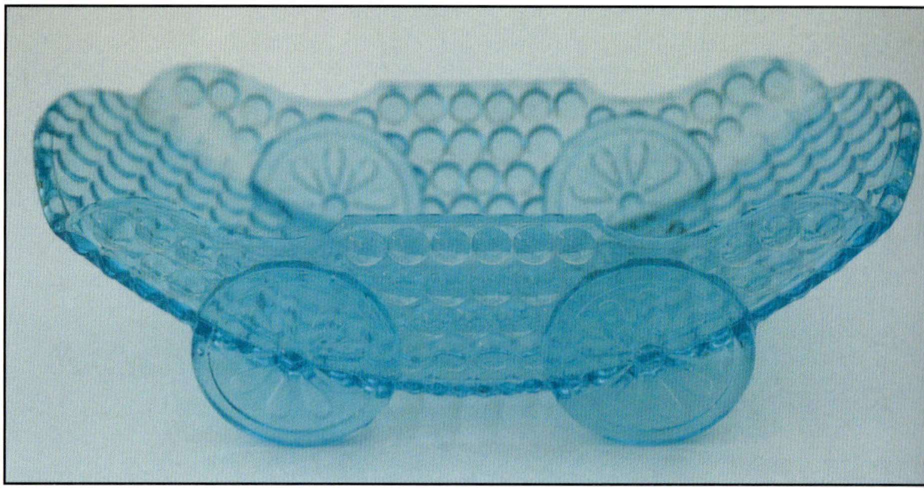

Buggy bowl in two sizes.
Small: 3 1/2" long in clear, $45-65.
Large: 8 1/2" long in blue, $200-240.

Vaseline Sleigh salt with a basket weave design, 3" long. The maker is unknown, circa 1880s. $125-195.

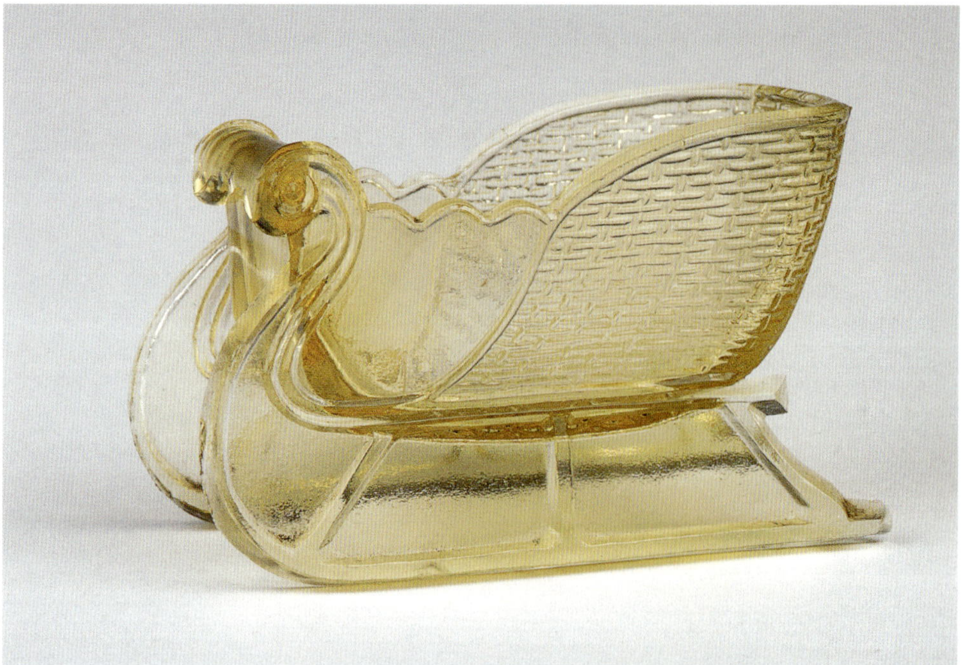

Sleigh in the Rose Sprig pattern by Campbell, Jones & Co., circa 1886. It measures 6" in length. Also available in blue, clear, and vaseline. Amber, $225-300.

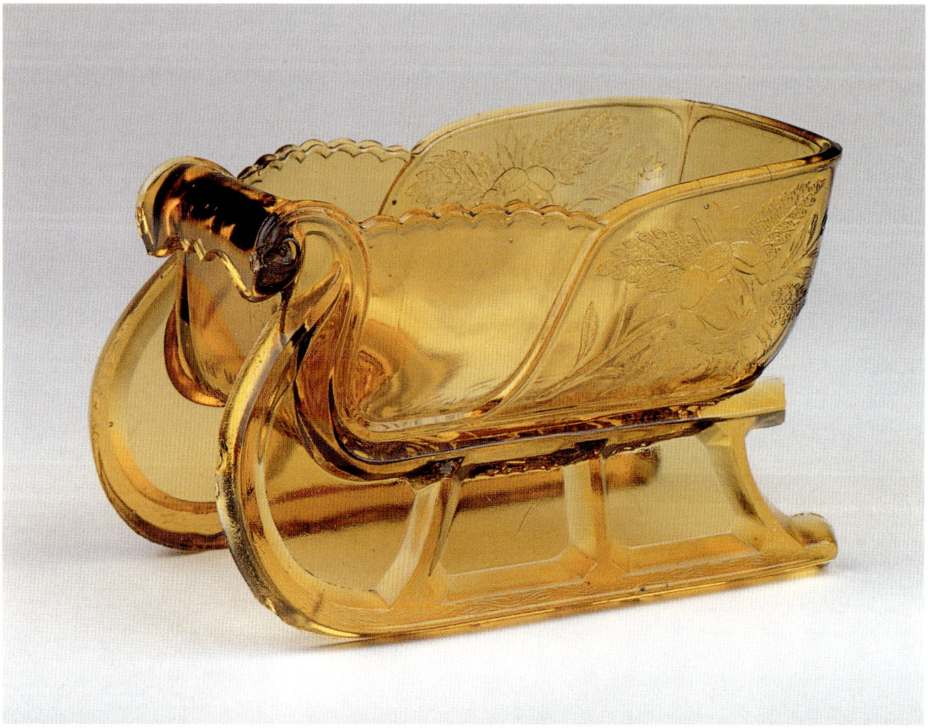

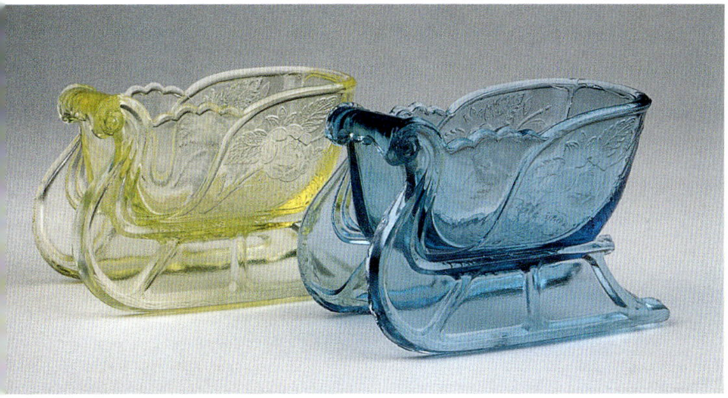

Sleigh salt dip in the Rose Sprig pattern by Campbell, Jones & Co., circa 1886. 3" in length. Also available in amber and clear. vaseline, $175-225. Blue, $175-225.

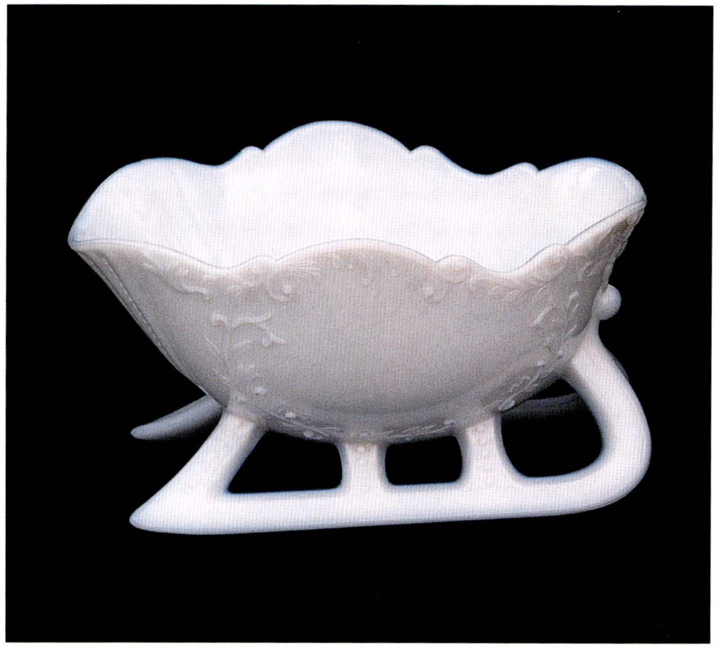

Opal Sleigh by the Westmoreland Specialty Company, circa 1900. 6 1/4" x 6 3/16" at the top rim. $75-125.

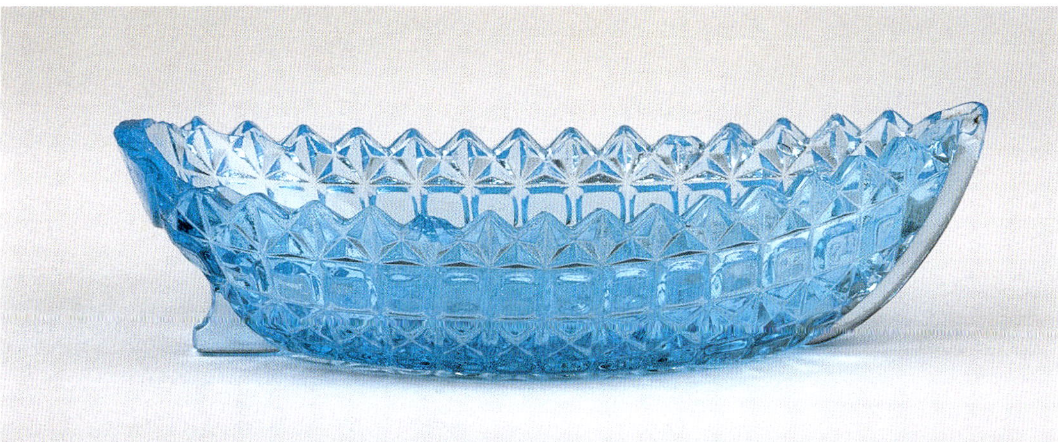

Blue *Earl* Yacht salt by Bryce Brothers, circa 1890s. Also available in amber and clear. Blue, $55-85.

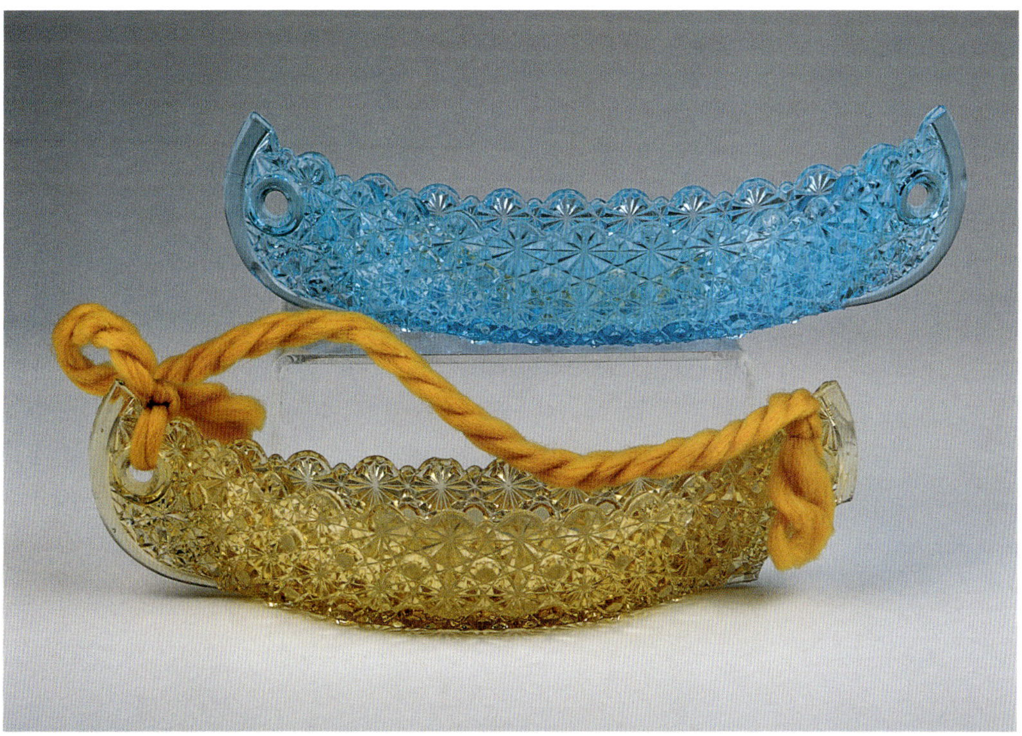

Canoe wall pocket, variations made by several companies. Daisy and button pattern. Can be found in blue, amber, clear, and clear with stained buttons or stained daisies. Circa 1880s and 1890s. $85-125.

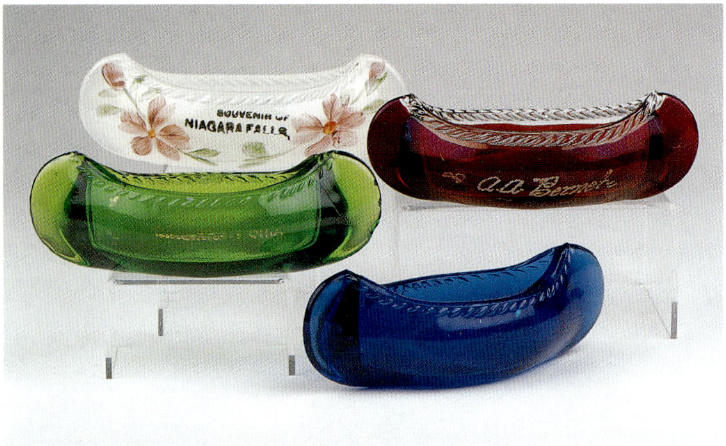

Canoes, made by the United States Glass Co., circa 1891. Can be found in clear, amber, blue, green, ruby stain, and opaque white. It is 6" in length. All colors, $65-85.

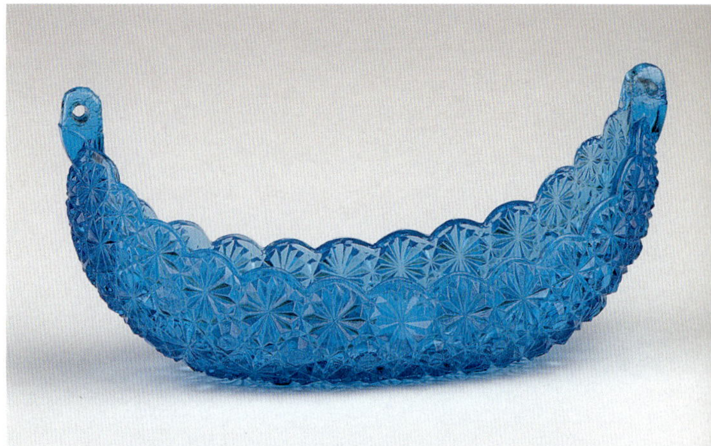

Canoe by Hobbs, Brockunier and Company, Daisy and button pattern, circa 1884. Can be found in clear, old gold, sapphire, canary, amberina, marine green, and ruby. Blue, $95-150.

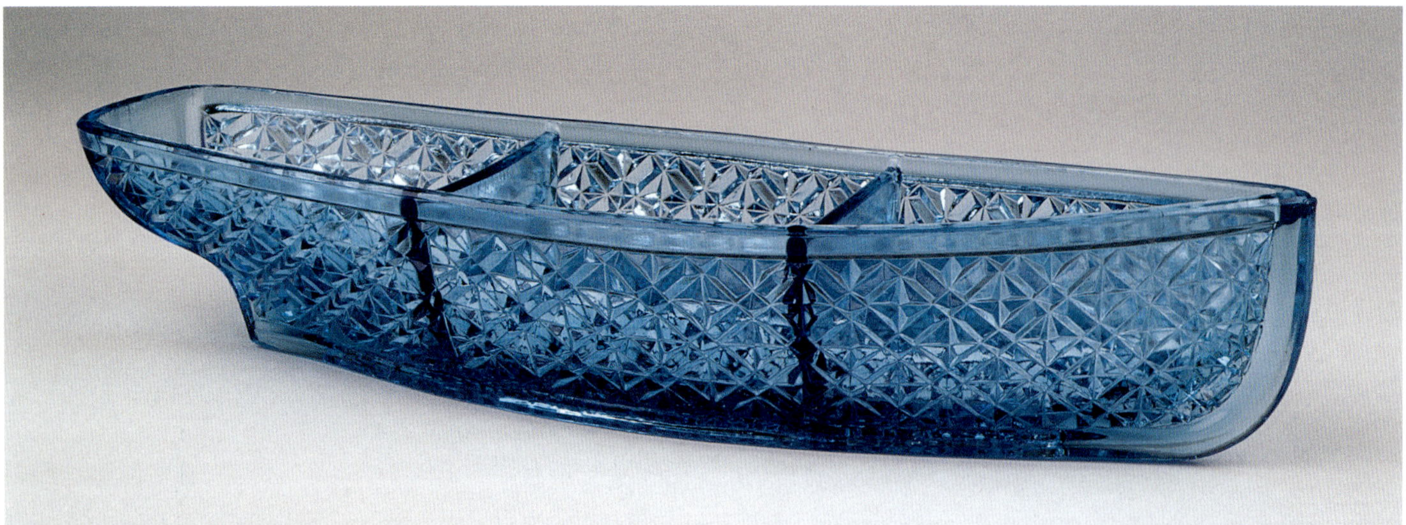

Boat shaped divided relish dish. Maker unknown. Circa 1880s. It is 11" long. Blue, $185-225.

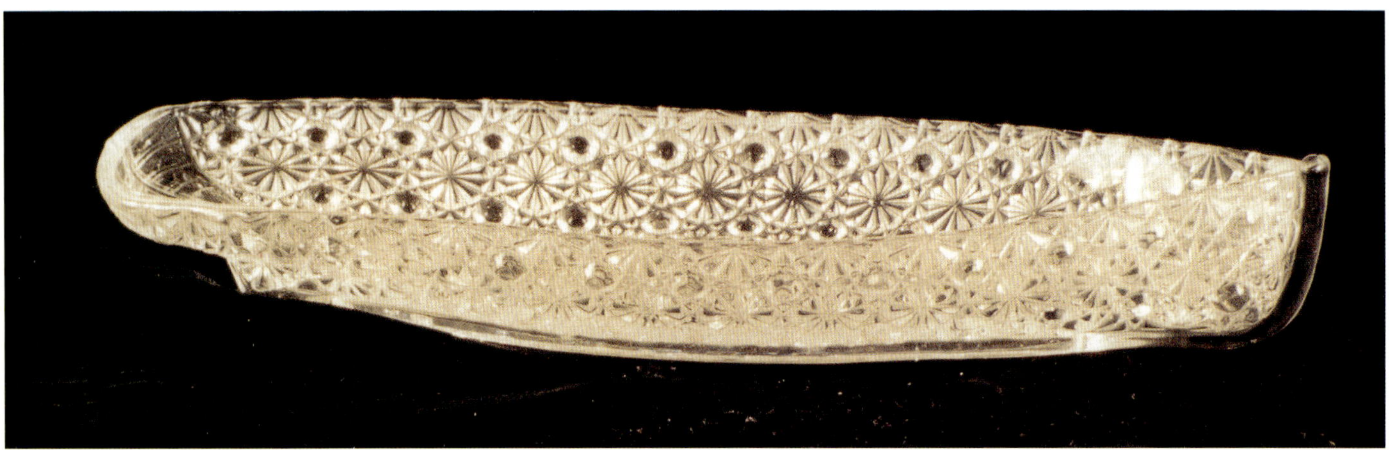

Yacht celery by Hobbs, Brockunier and Company, circa 1885. It is 14" long and 4 3/4" wide. Probably available in the many colors that this company produced. Clear, $95-150.

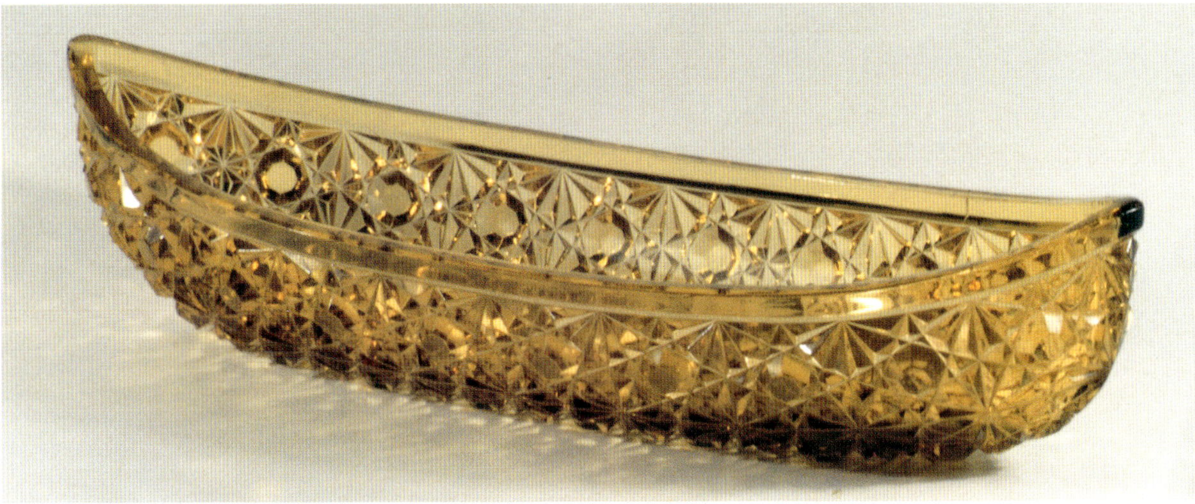

Boat by George Duncan and Sons in their Daisy and Button pattern, circa 1880s. It is 12 7/8" long and 4 3/8" wide. Amber, $95-145.

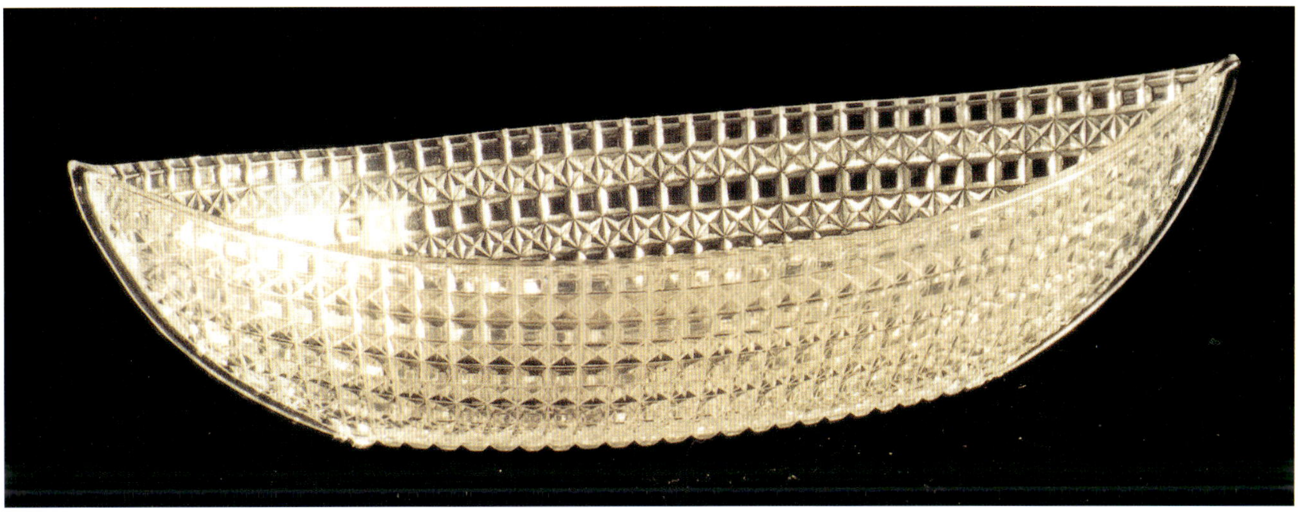

Boat by Bryce Brothers, circa 1880s. It is 12 1/2" long and 4 3/4" wide. Clear, $95-145.

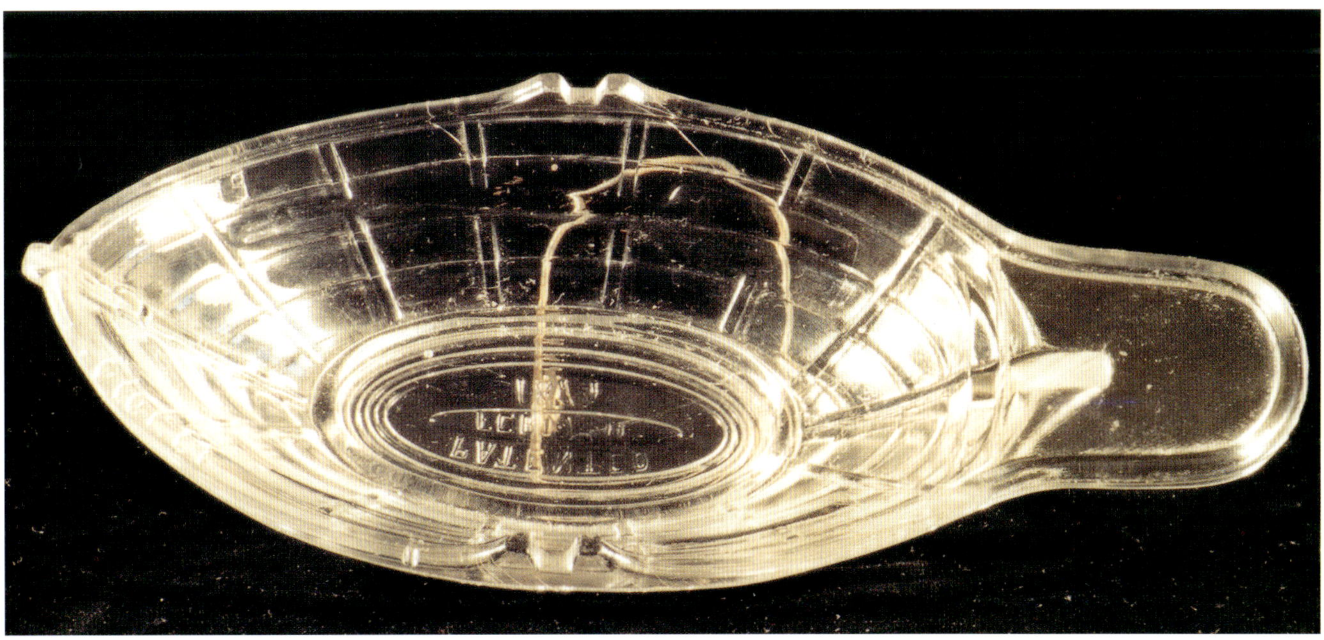

Boat shaped pickle dish. Maker unknown. Patented Feb. 17th 1874. It is 9 1/2" long and 4 1/2" wide. Clear, $175-225.

Battleship Newark made by the C. L. Flaccus Glass Co., circa 1898, in decorated Opal glass. 7 1/2" long and 4" wide. Opal, $100-150.

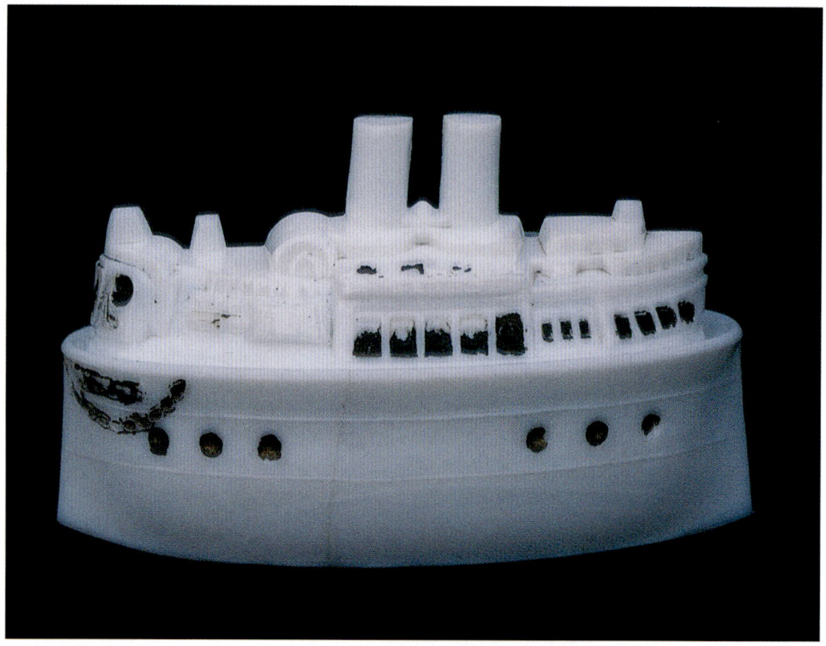

Battleship Oregon made by the C. L. Flaccus Glass Co., circa 1898, in opal. 6 1/4" long and 3 1/2" wide. Opal, $110-150.

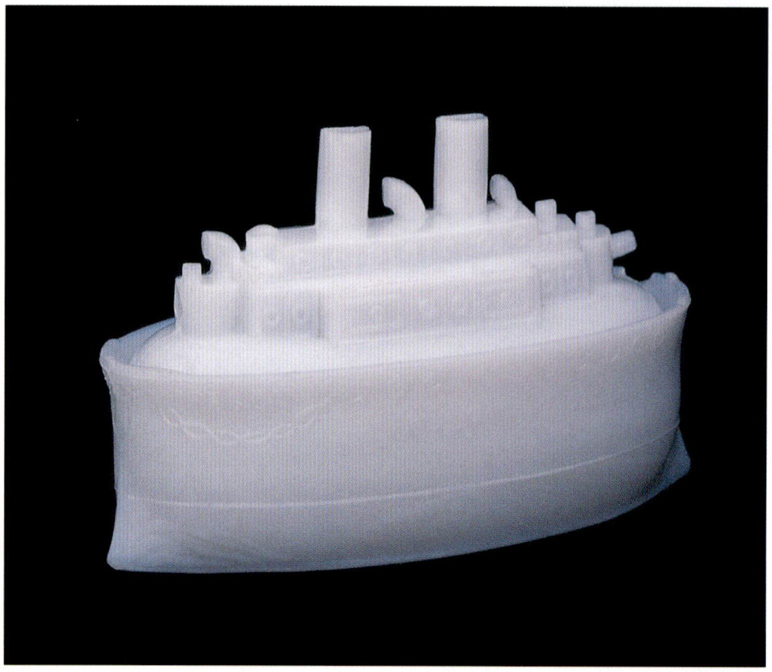

Battleship Olympia made by the C. L. Flaccus Glass Co. in clear, circa 1898. 6 1/4" long and 3 1/2" wide. Clear, $100-150.

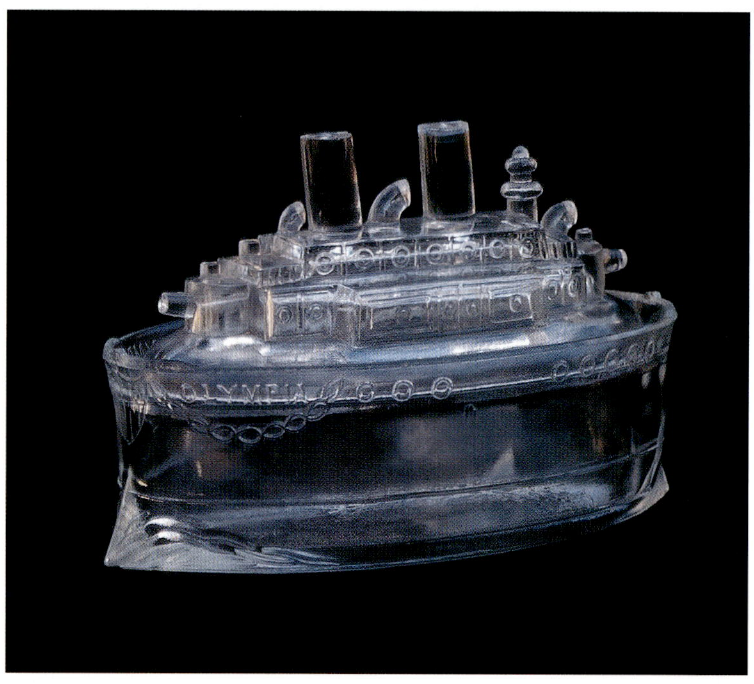

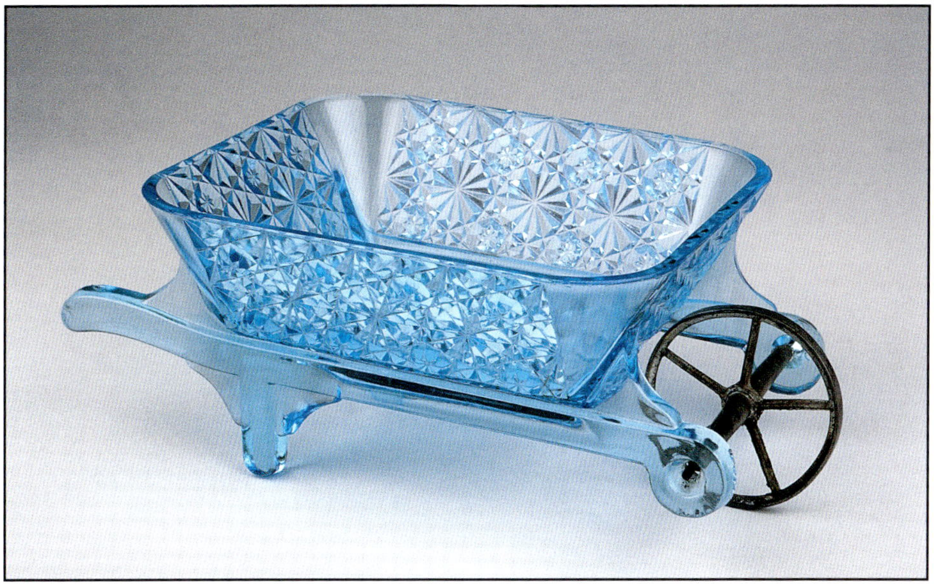

Wheelbarrow, maker unknown. Made in blue, amber, vaseline, and clear in the Daisy pattern. Circa 1880s. 8 3/4" long, 5 3/4" wide, and 3 1/2" high. Clear, $85-100. Colors, $175-210.

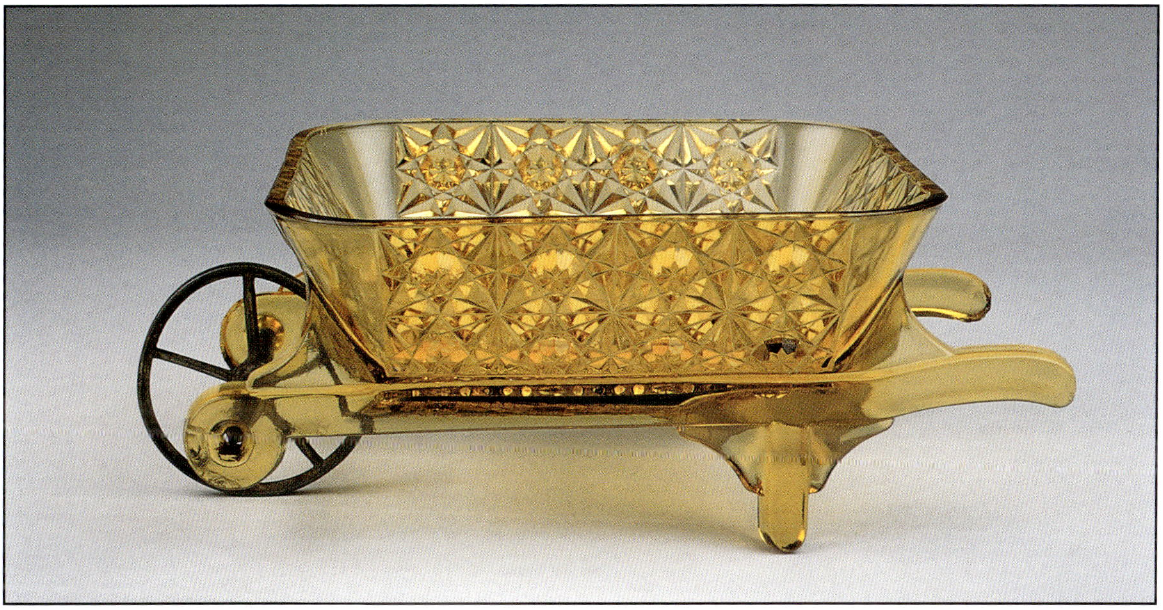

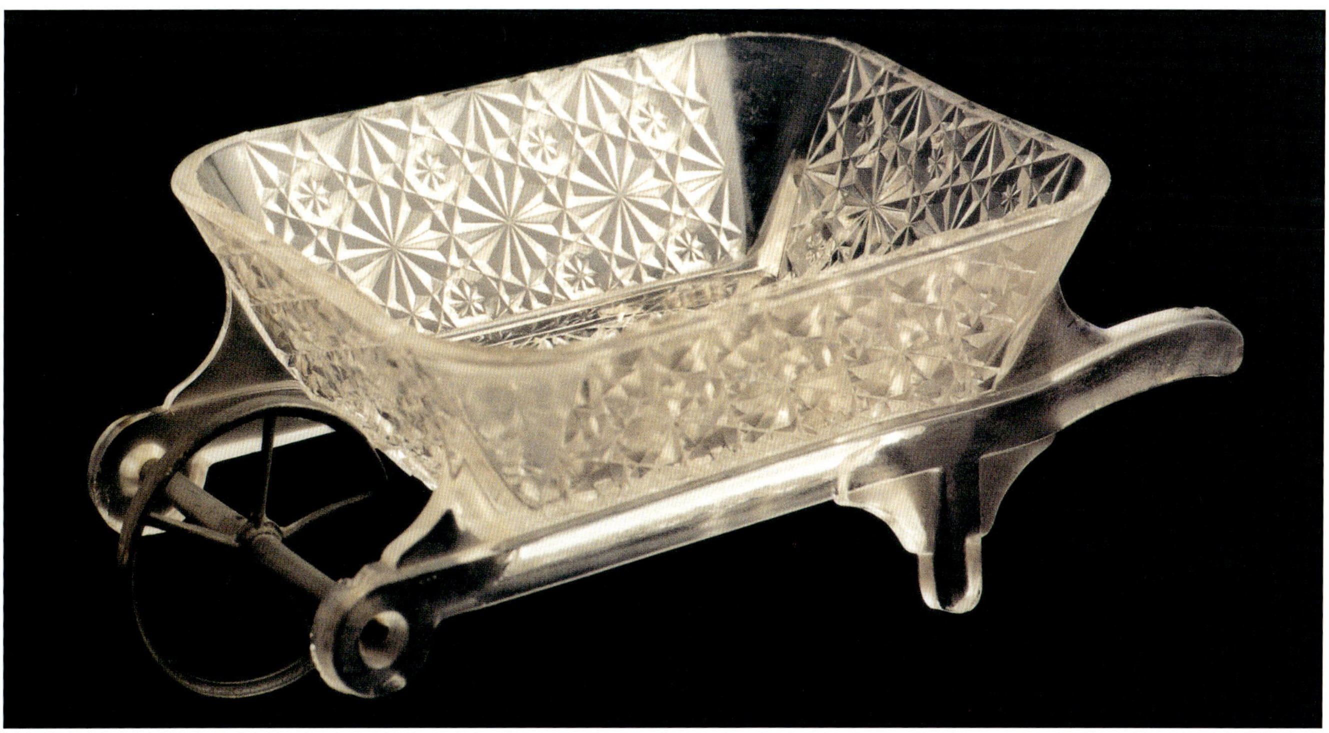

Barley pattern wheelbarrow made by Campbell, Jones and Co., circa 1882. Designed and patented by James Dalzell. Large is 8 1/4" long. Clear, $125-175. Small is 3 1/8" long. Clear, $95-145.

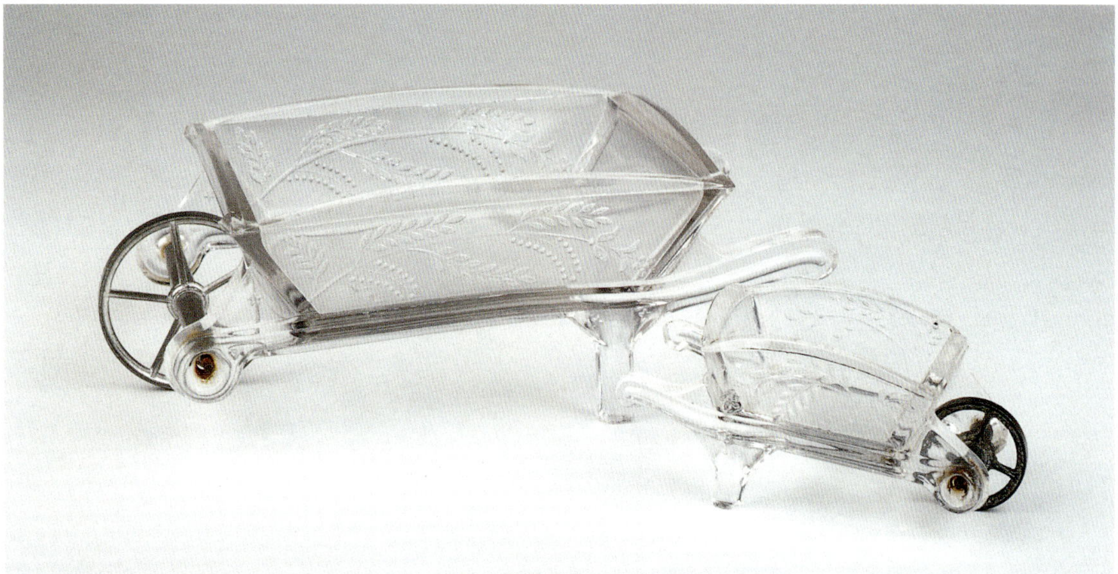

Basket weave pattern wheelbarrow, maker unknown. Circa 1800s. 9 3/4" overall length. Clear, $250-325.

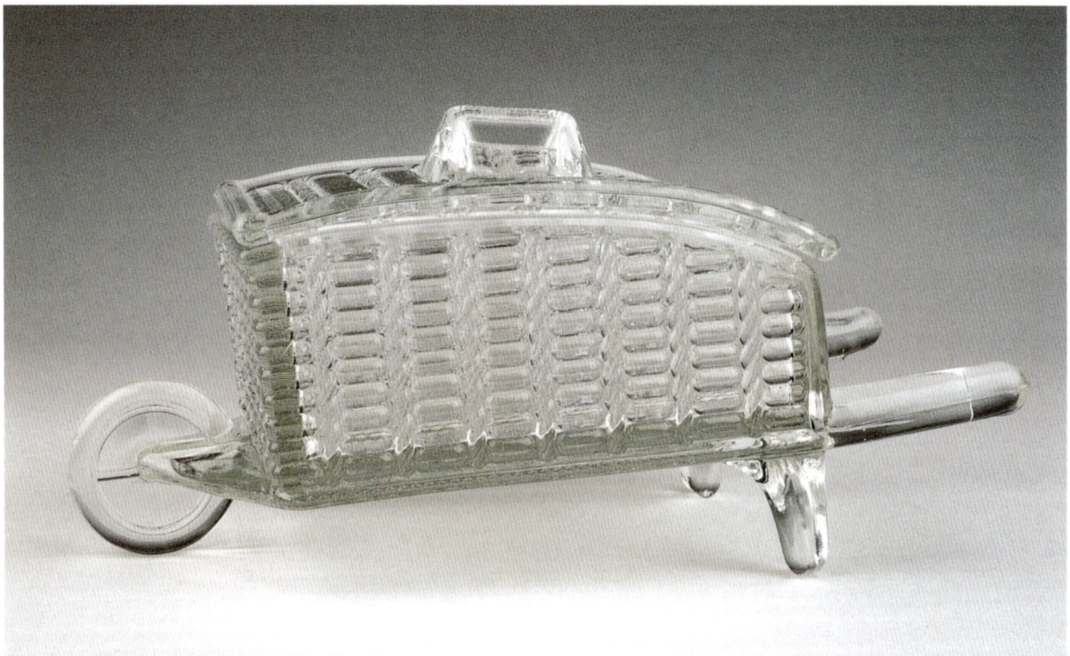

Small wheelbarrow. 3 3/8" long. Clear, $45-95.

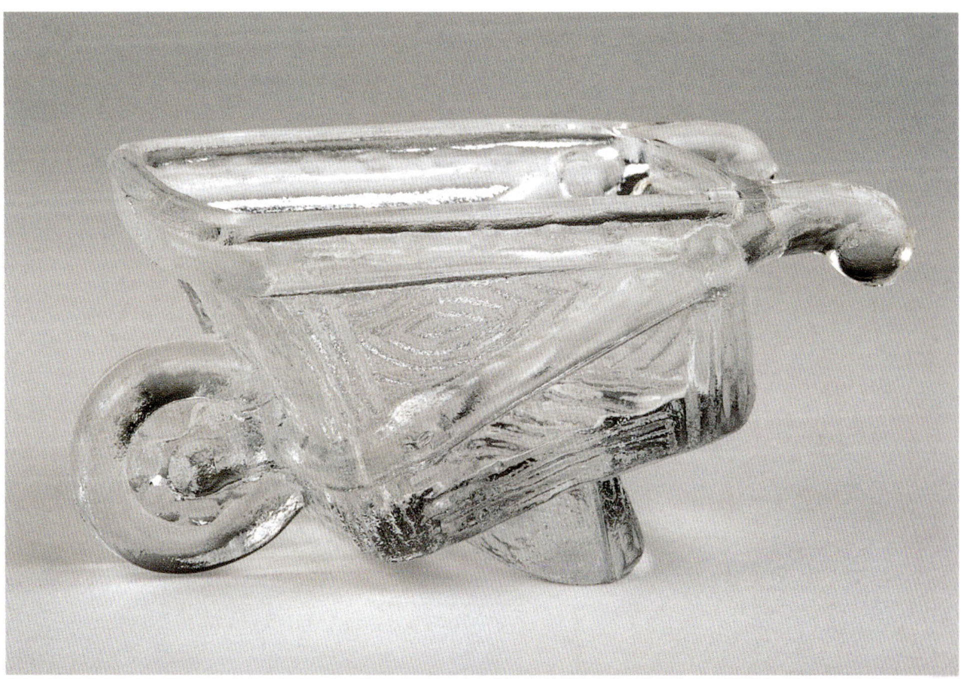

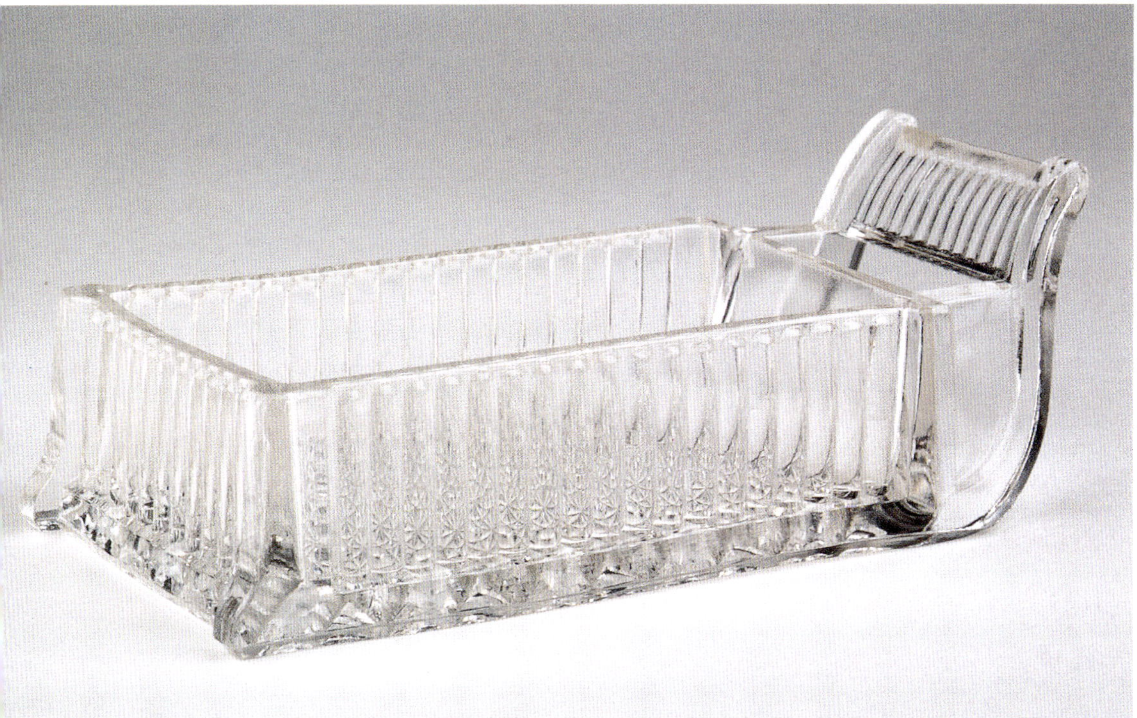

Sled made by George Duncan & Sons, circa 1883. 6" long and 3 1/8" wide. Clear, $75-135.

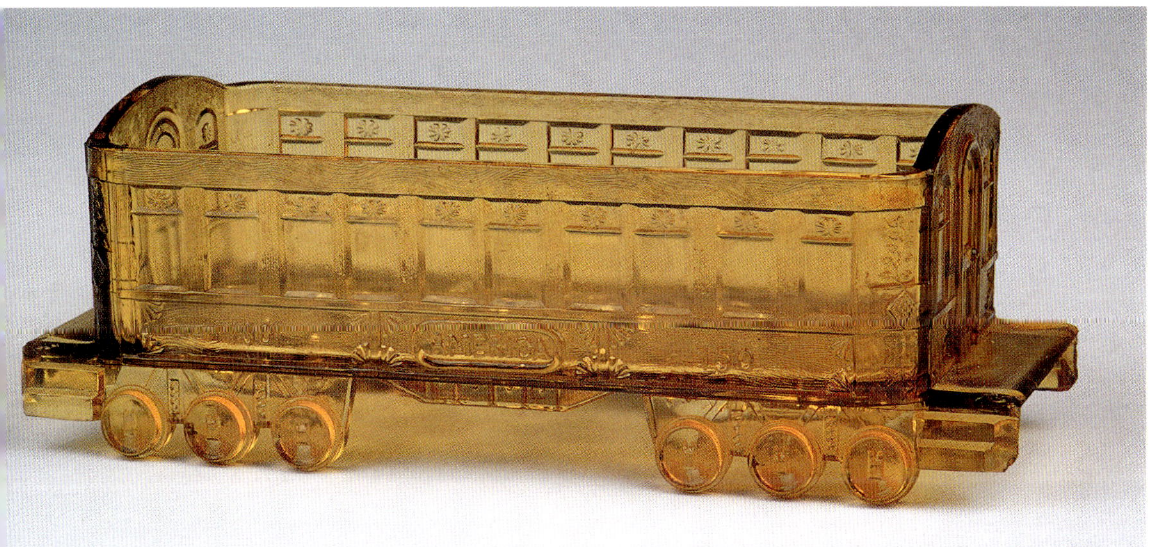

Pullman Railroad Car in amber glass. The maker is unknown, circa 1880s. 9 5/8" long. Amber, $800-950.

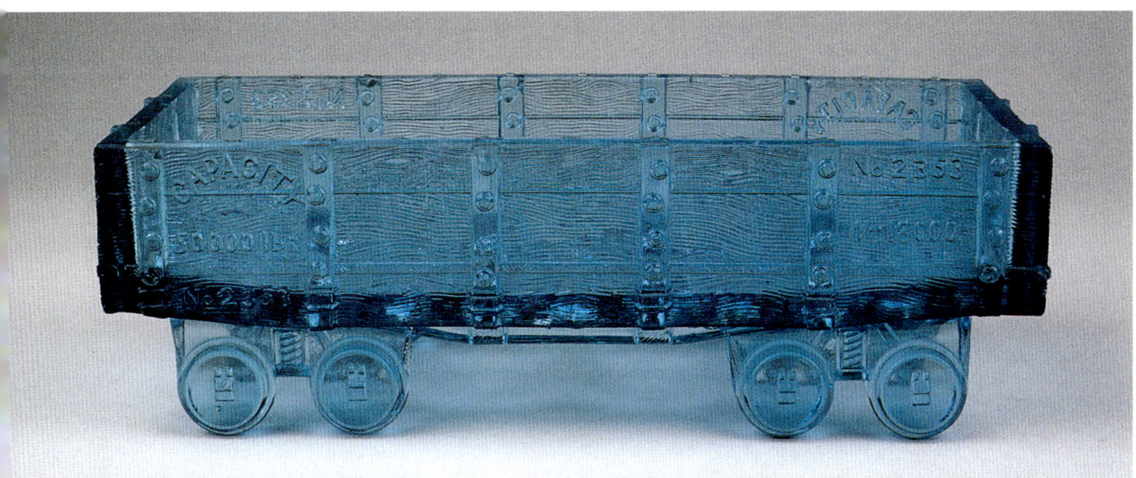

Railroad Car *America 100*. Maker unknown, circa 1890s. It is 8" in length. Blue, $ 185-225.

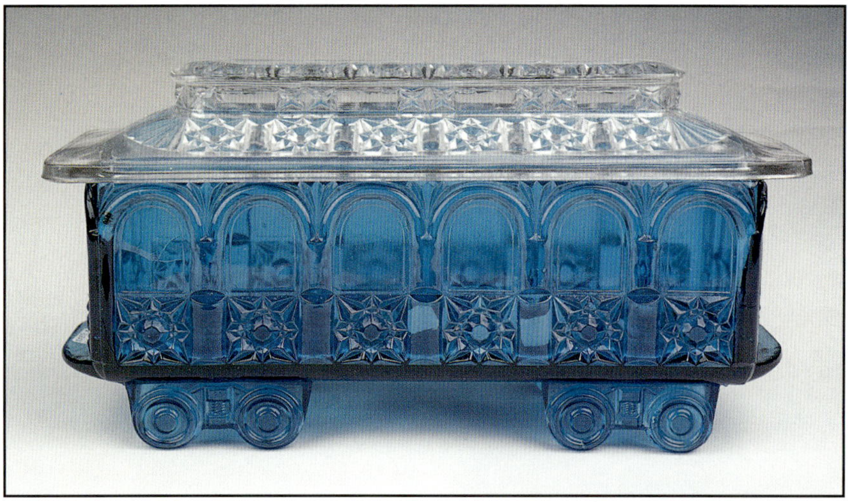

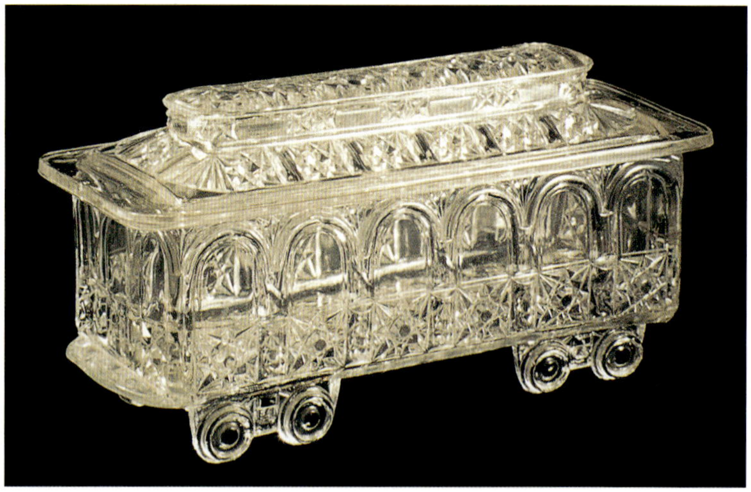

Covered Railroad Car made by the Bellaire Goblet Co., circa 1896. It was made in clear, amber, blue, and vaseline. It is 13 3/4" long and 5 5/8" wide. Clear, $600-800. Colors, $1,200-1,600.

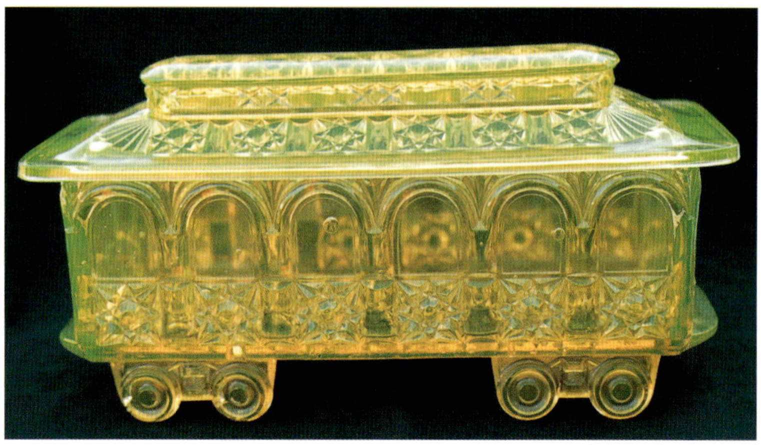

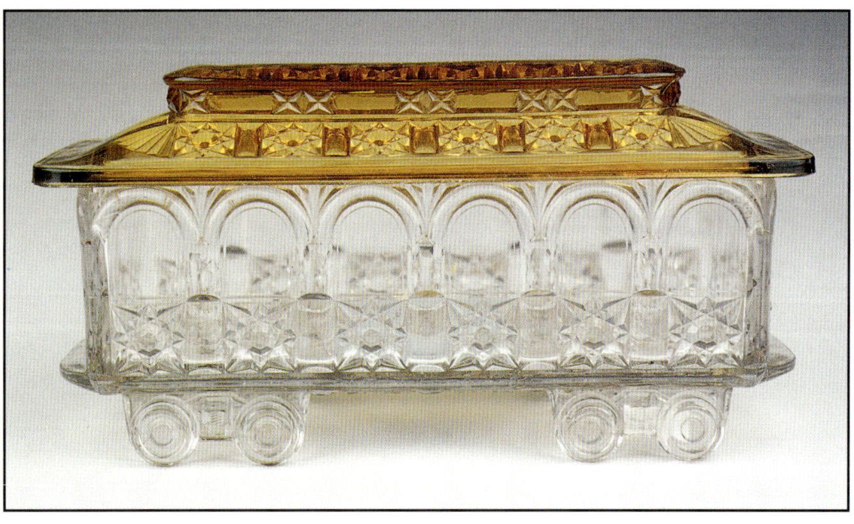

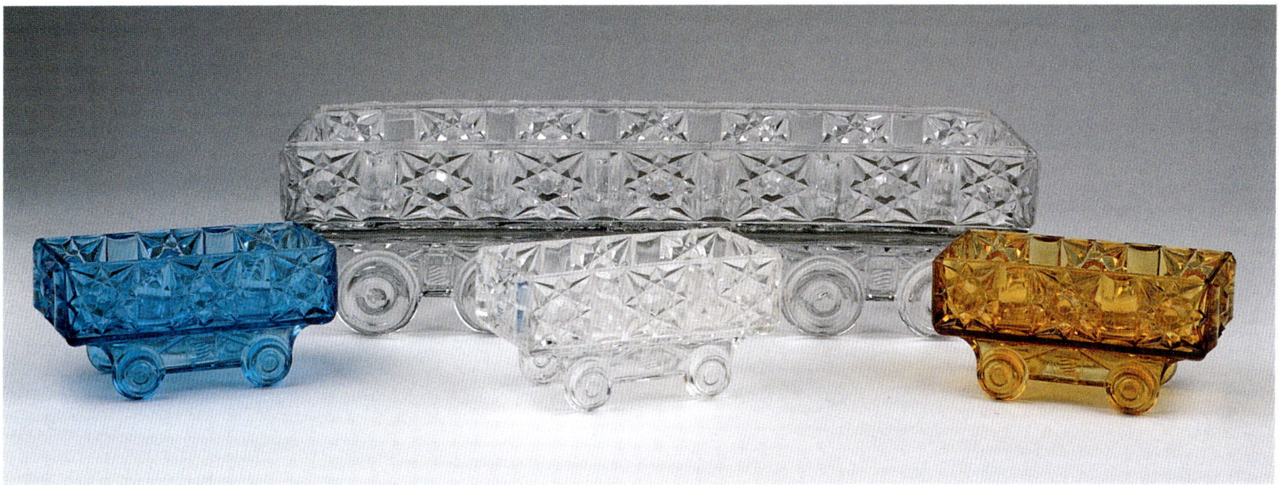

Celery and salt set in the stars and bars pattern by the Bellaire Goblet Co., circa 1886. Celery, 11" long. Clear, $125-175. Colors, $225-300. Salt, 3 3/4" long. Clear, $95-130. Colors, $125-165.

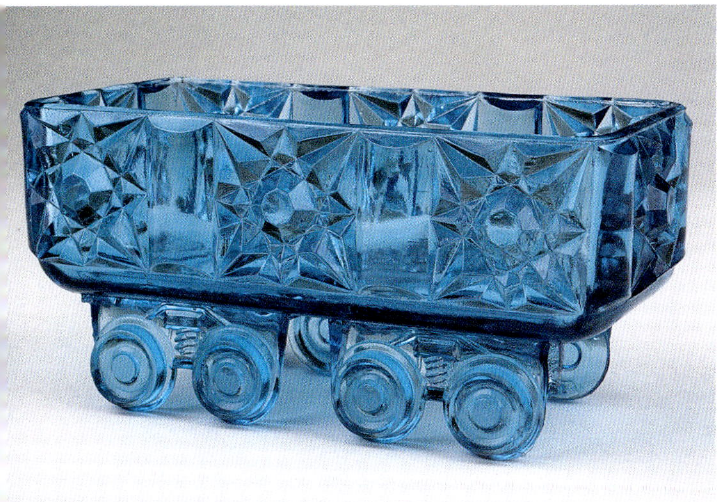

This can be used as a berry dish with the covered RR car or can be used as a master salt with the celery set. This Stars and Bars pattern car made by the Bellaire Goblet Co. is being documented for the first time. Note that this car has eight wheels, as compared to the salt, which has only four wheels. It is circa 1886 and is 4 3/4" in length. Blue, $250-300.

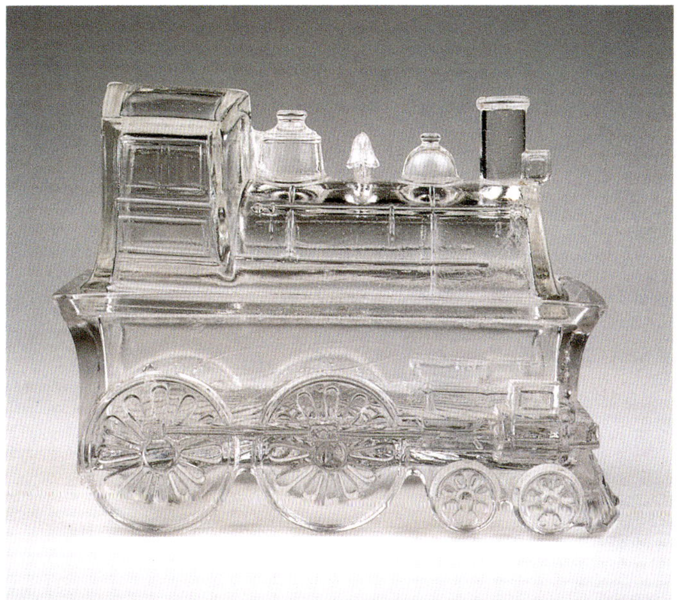

McKee and Brothers made this Railroad engine circa 1880s. It has been found in clear and green. It is 6" long. Clear, $95-140. Green, $125-165.

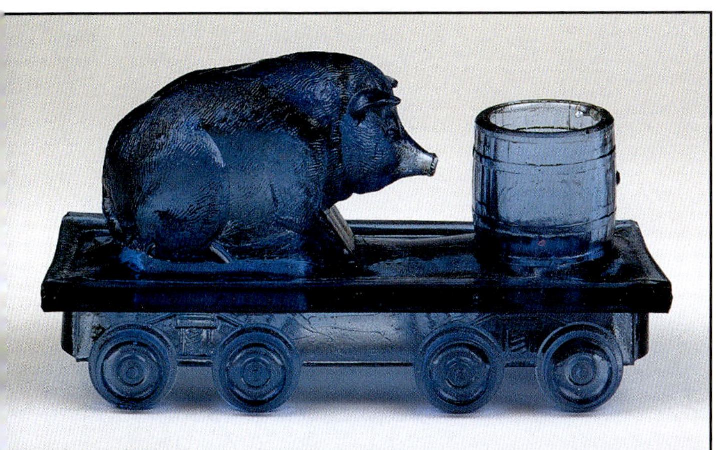

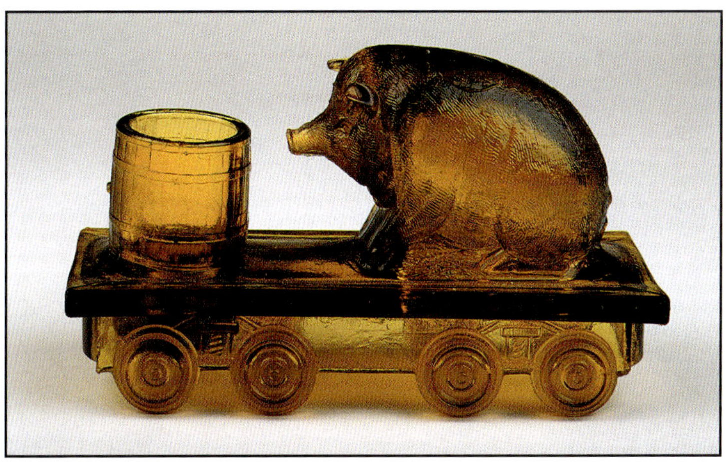

Pig on a flat car made by the Bellaire Goblet Co., circa 1880s. 3 1/8" high, 2 1/2" wide, and 5 1/2" long. Clear, $225-265. Amber, $350-385. Blue, $400-475.

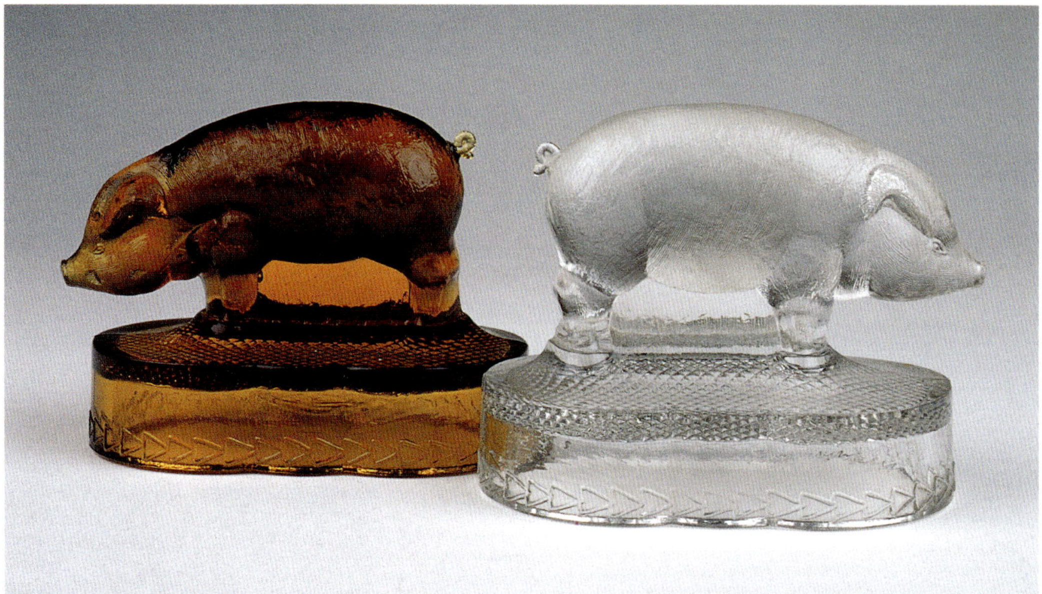

Pig paperweight made by the Bellaire Goblet Co., circa 1880s. 4 1/2" long, 2 1/2" wide, and 3 1/2" high. Clear, $70-115. Amber, $150-185. Blue, $165-225.

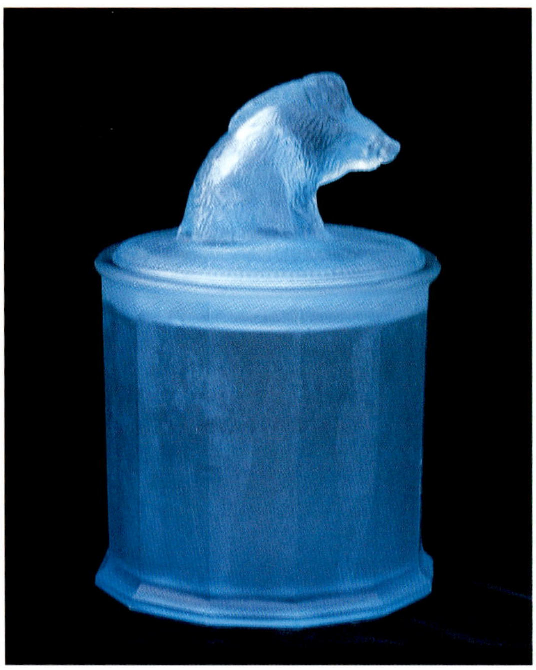

Blue Boar humidor. Maker unknown. Circa 1890. 9" high, 6" diameter. $350-400.

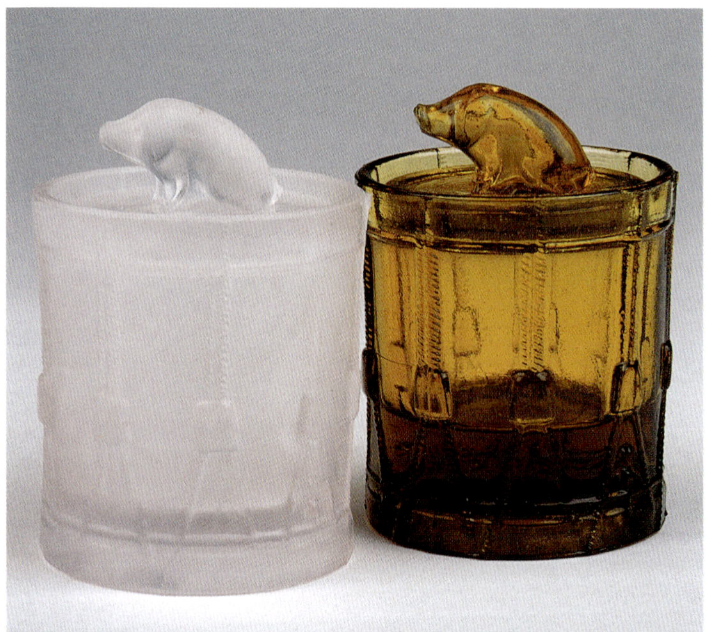

Musique by Portieux. Commonly called Pig on a drum. Circa 1933. Clear frosted, $95-110. Amber, $120-150.

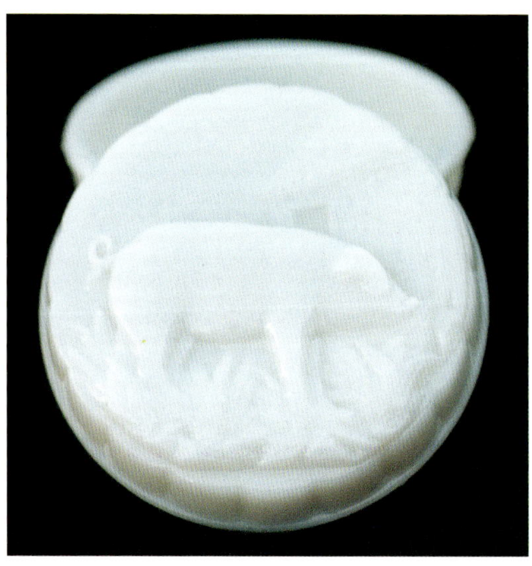

Pig covered dish. *Vallerysthal. Made in France.* 4 3/8" diameter. Date of manufactuer unknown. Opal, $900-1,100.

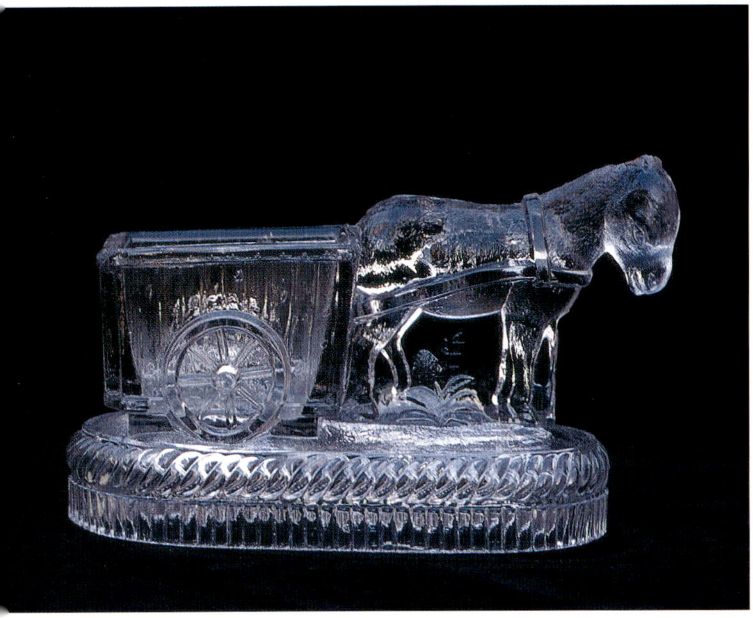

Donkey with cart made by the Tiffin Glass Co., circa 1886. 5" long and 3 1/2" wide. Lid for the cart has a monkey atop. Clear, $245-285.

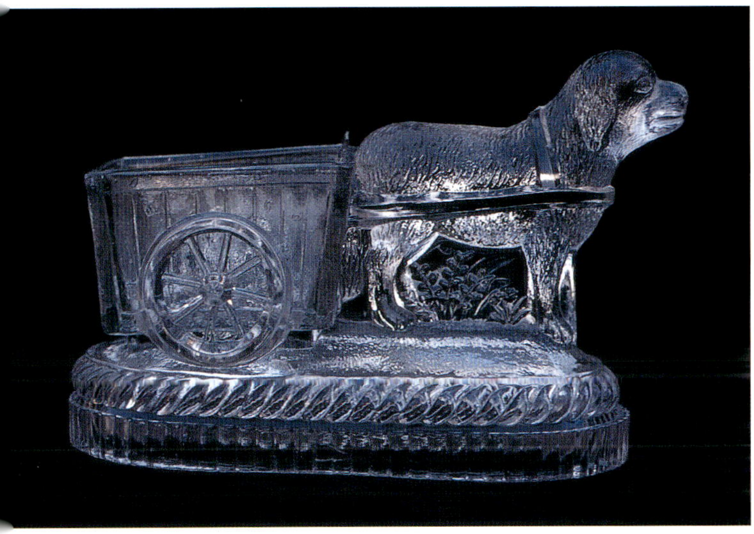

Dog with cart made by the Tiffin Glass Co., circa 1886. 5" long and 3 1/2" high. Lid for the cart has a monkey atop. Clear, $245-285.

Goat with cart made by the Tiffin Glass Co., circa 1886. 5" long and 3" high. Lid for the cart has a monkey atop. Clear, $245-285.

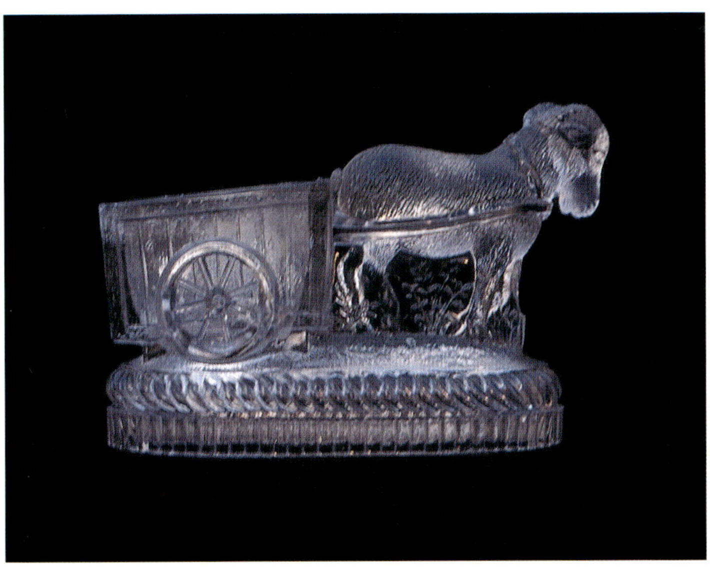

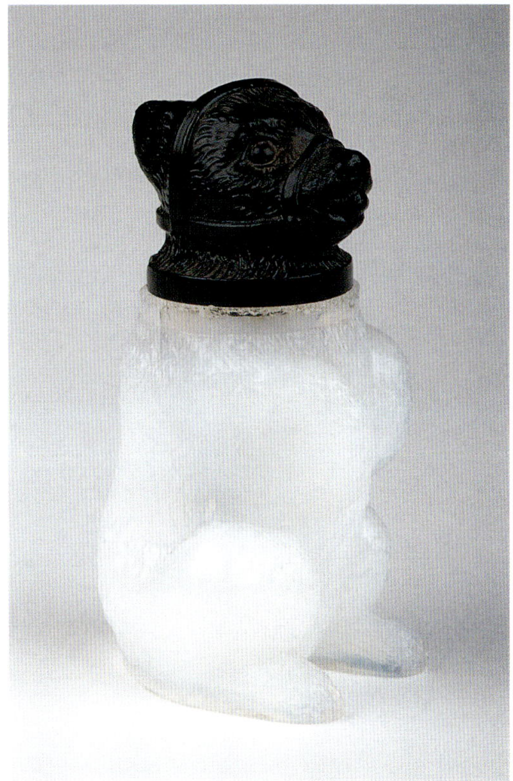

Boston & Sandwich Glass Co. bear pomade jar in opal with black opaque head, circa 1850-1887. On the bottom is an advertisement, which is not legible except for *Philadelphia*. 5" high. As pictured, $3,000+.

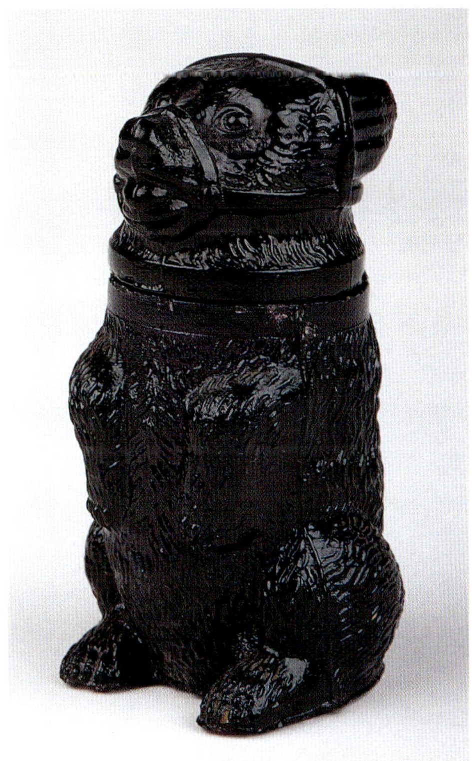

Boston & Sandwich Glass Co. black bear, circa 1850-1887, and 3 1/2" high. As pictured, $550-650.

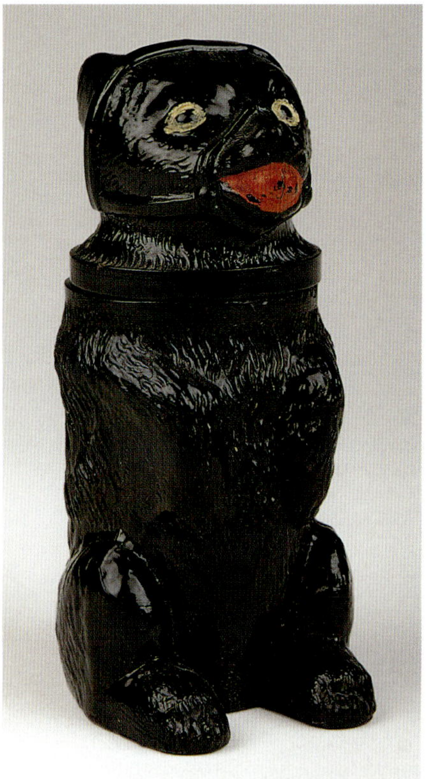

Boston & Sandwich Glass Co. black opaque bear with red mouth and white eyes, 4 1/2" high, circa 1850-1887. On the bottom is *Eugene Bize & Frigft Successors to J. Havel & Co.* $2,800+.

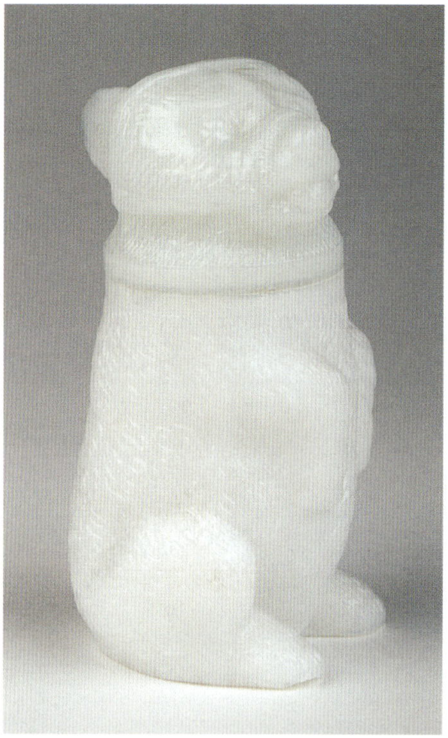

Boston & Sandwich Glass Co opal bear, circa 1850-1887. 3 7/8" high. $450-550.

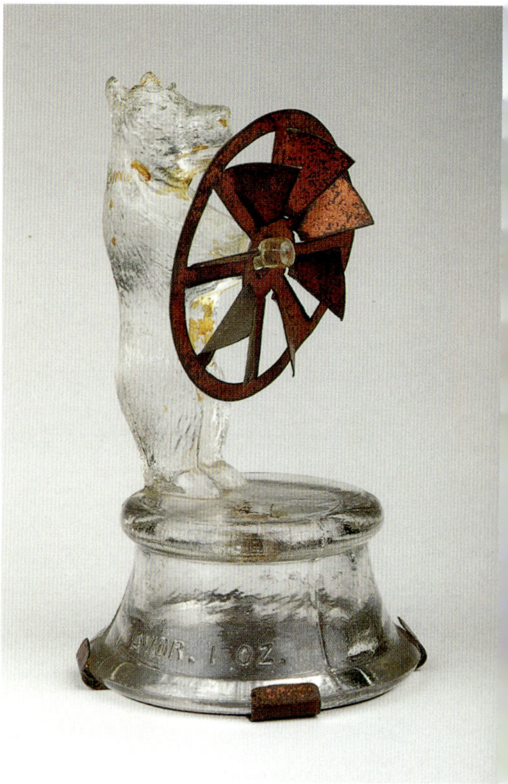

Bear candy container. Bear holding a red wind fan. Maker and date of manufactuer unknown. 4 1/2" high. $850-950.

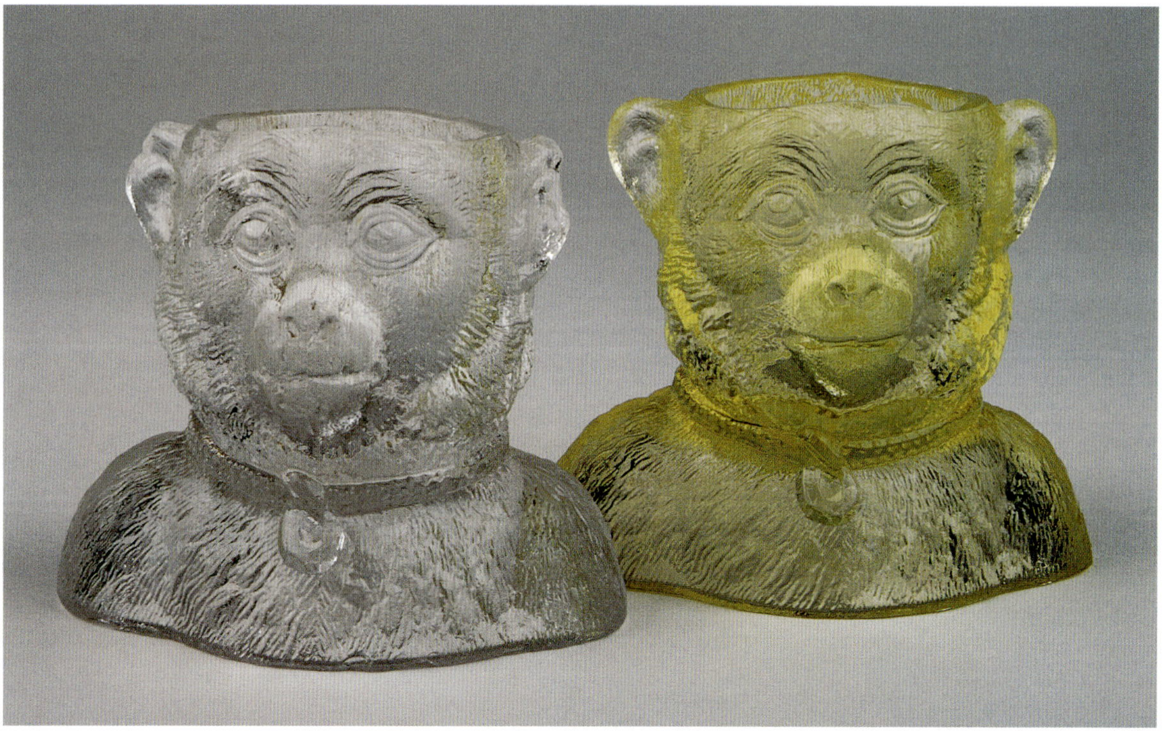

Darwin (bear) made by Richards and Hartley Glass Co., circa mid-1880s. 2 1/2" high and 2" wide. Clear, $70-80; amber, $85-95; blue, $90-100; and canary, $90-100.

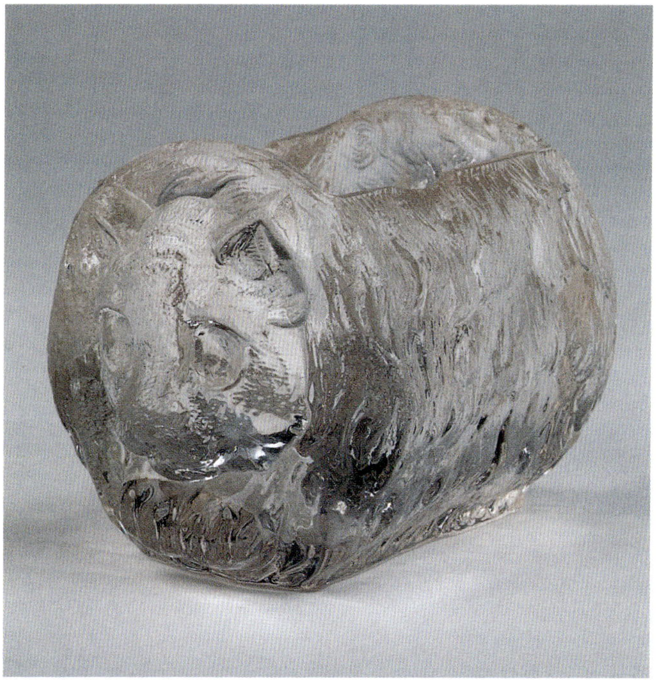

Bear in a log. Maker and date of manufactuer unknown. 2 1/2" high and 2" wide. Clear, $65-75.

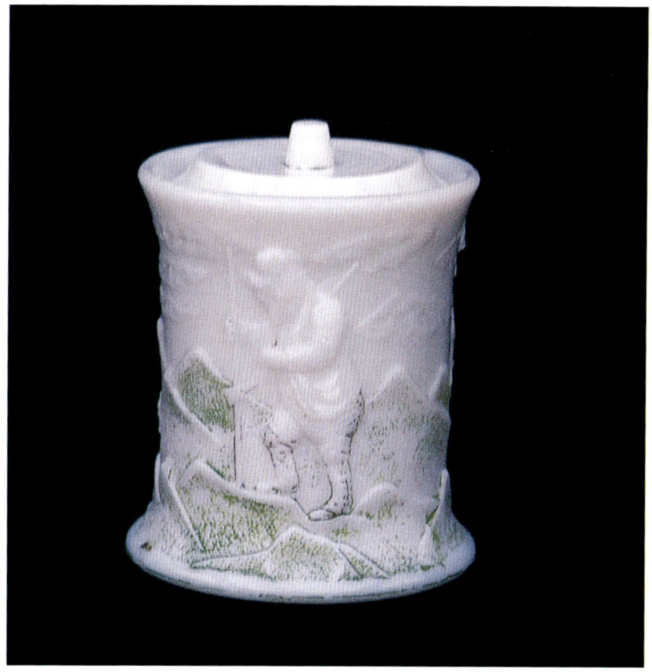

Roosevelt or Walking Bears marmalade made by Westmoreland, circa early 1900s. 4" high and 3" diameter. Opal, $130-165.

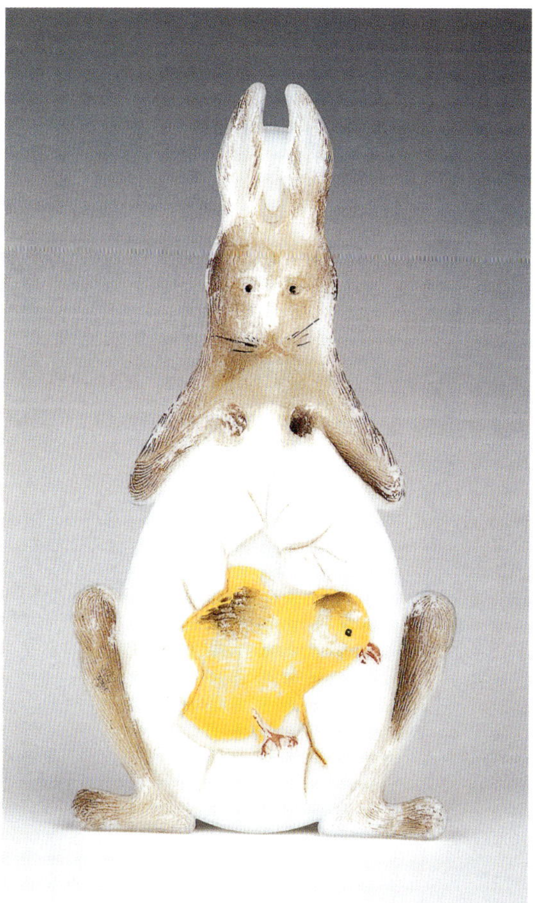

Standing Rabbit with egg and chick. Maker and date of manufactuer unknown. *Pat App For.* 7 1/4" high. Opal decorated, $2,000-2,500.

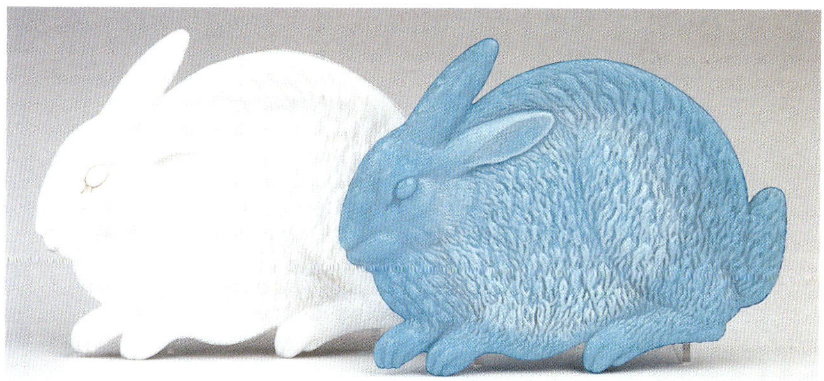

Rabbit, flat plate, maker and date of manufactuer unknown. 6" long. Opal, $325-375. Blue opaque, $425-475.

Rabbit covered dish. Opaque green with white opaque head on rib base, circa 1940. 5 1/2" long. $450-500.

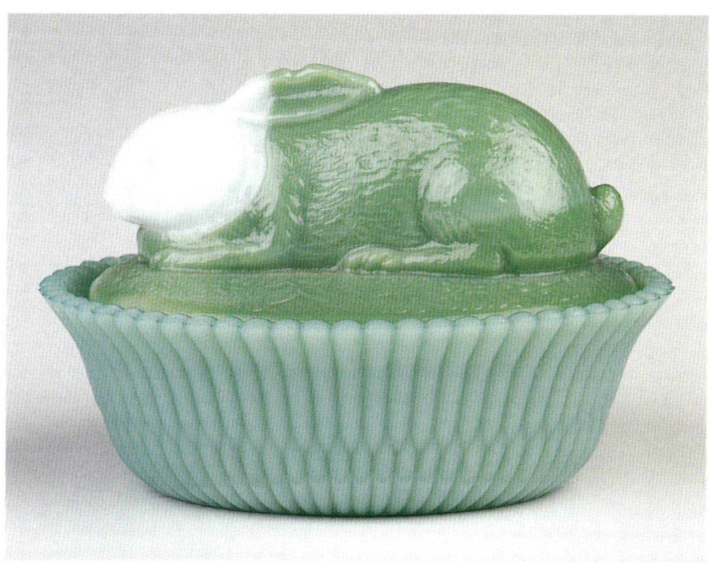

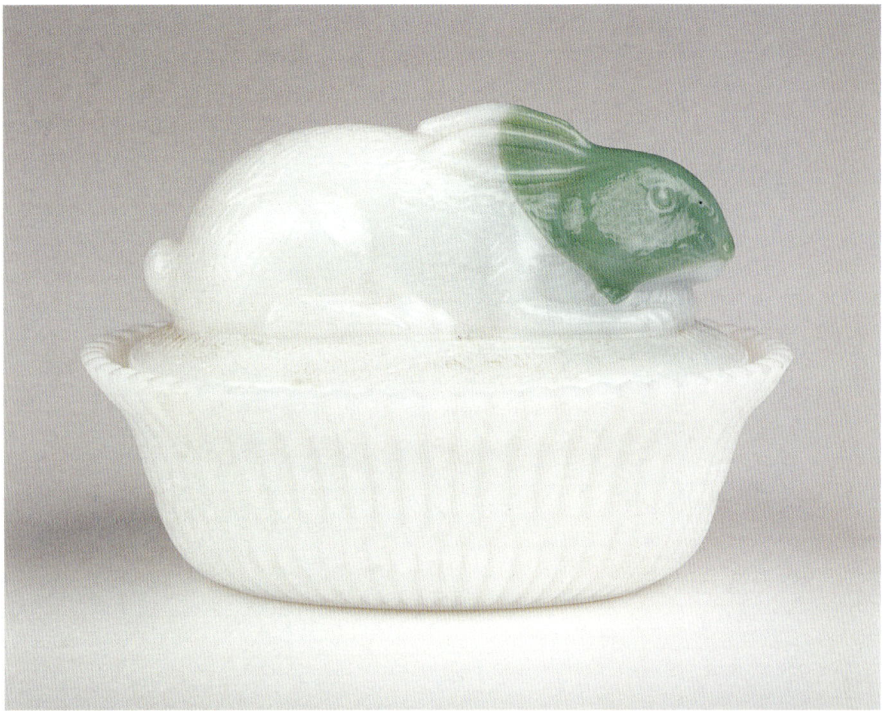

Rabbit covered dish, opal with green opaque head on rib base, circa 1940. 5 1/2" long. $450-500.

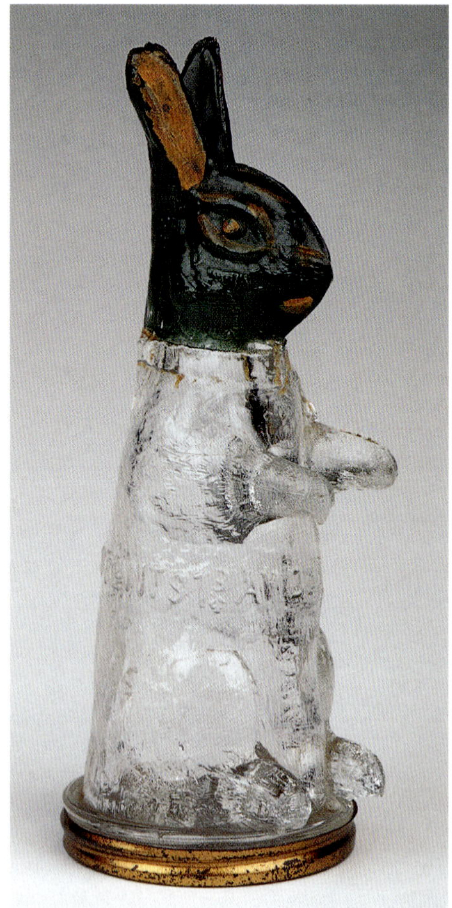

Standing Rabbit with black head candy container, maker and date of manufactuer unknown. 5 3/4" high. $450-525.

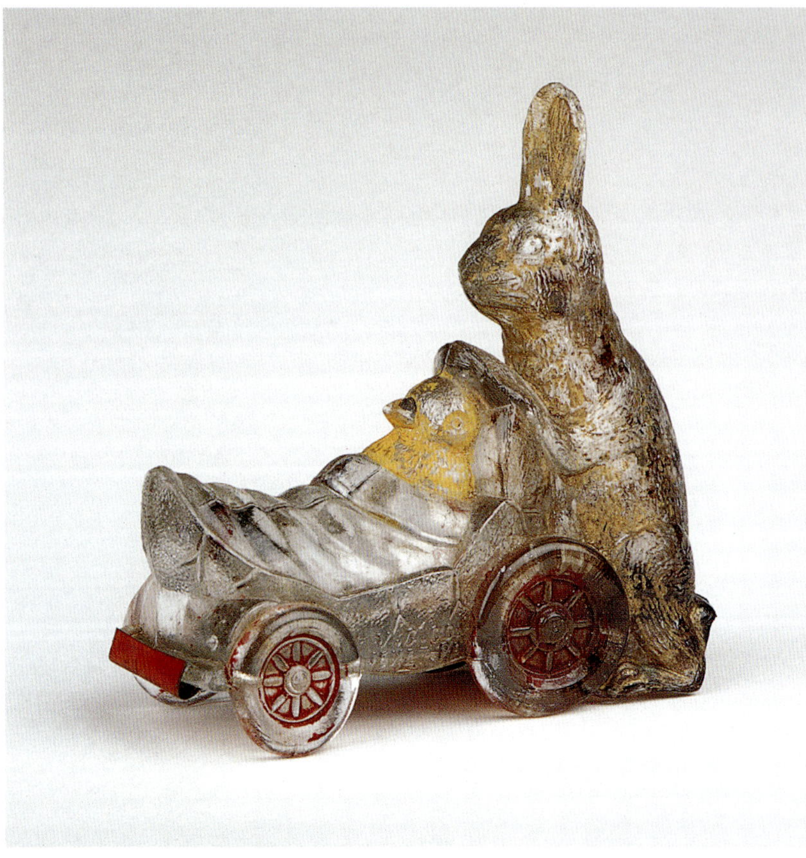

Rabbit pushing a baby buggy. *V. C. Com. Jeanette, Pa.* Date of manufactuer unknown. 4" high. $500-600.

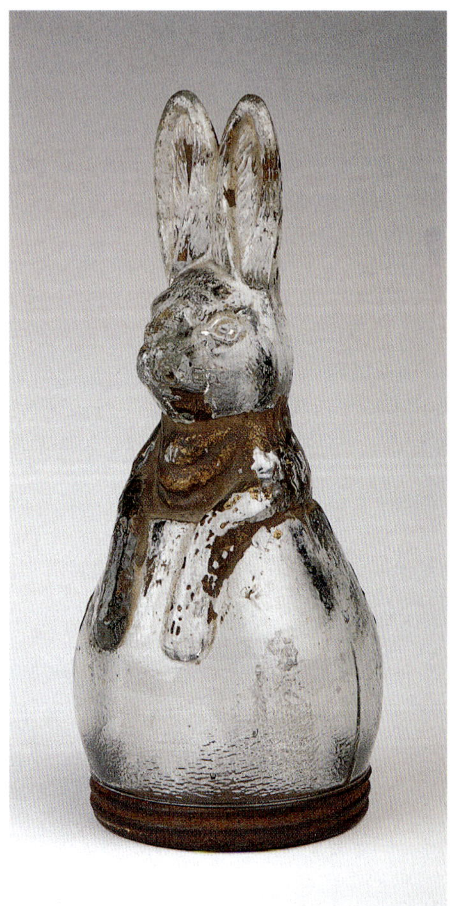

Standing Rabbit candy container, maker and date of manufactuer unknown. Marked *USA*. 5 1/4" high. $200-250.

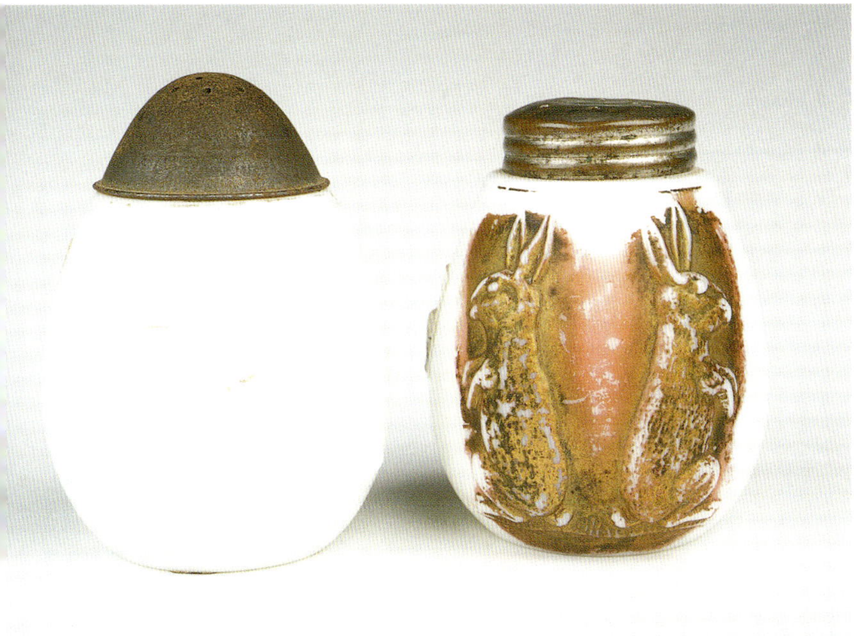

Salt and Pepper shakers. Opal with rabbits and chickens made by the Eagle Glass & Mfg. Co., circa 1900. 2 1/2" high. $145-175.

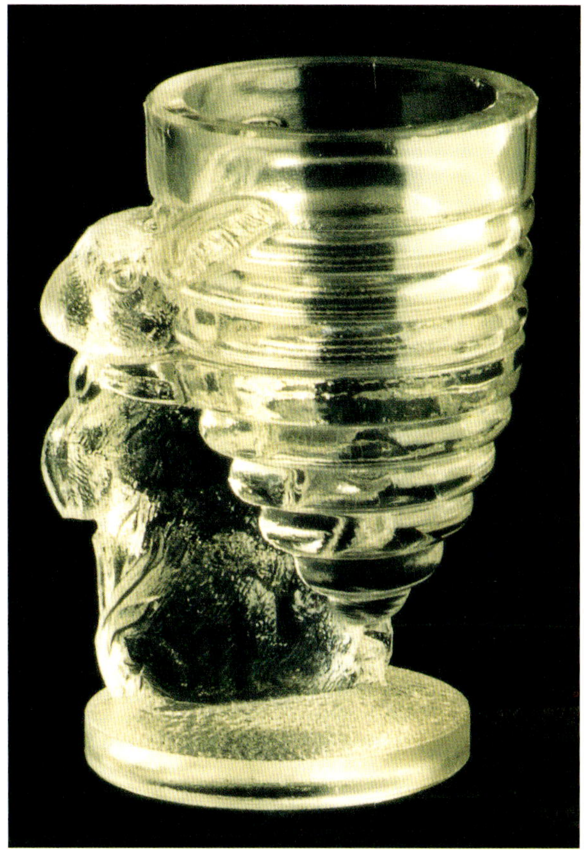

Rabbit with basket made by the Richards and Hartley Glass Co., circa 1880s. 3 3/8" high. Clear, $80-90.

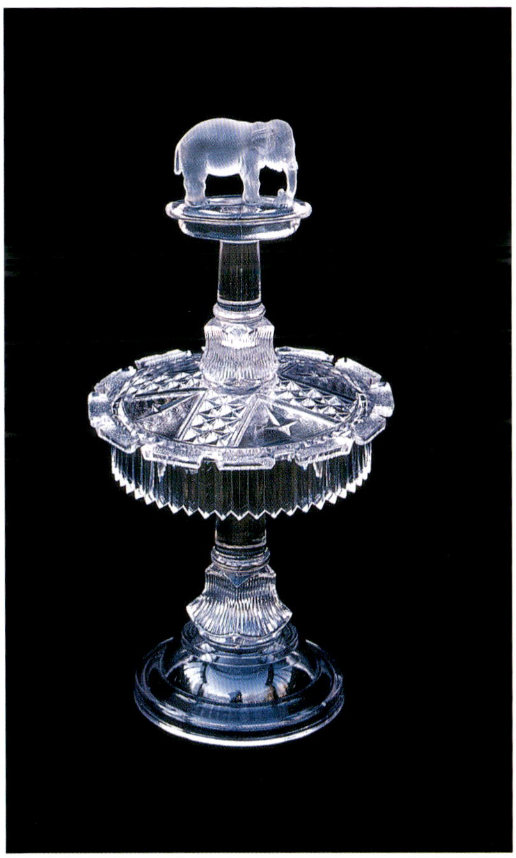

Jumbo spoon rack made by the Canton Glass Co. and designed by David Barker, circa early 1880s. 11" high. $700-1,100.

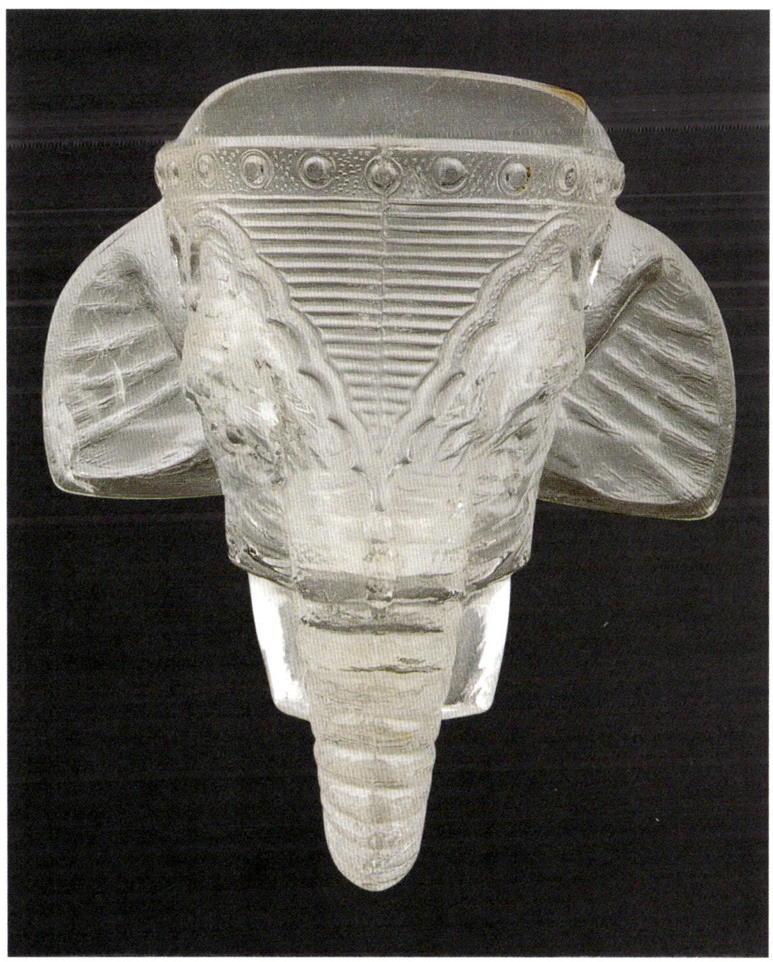

Elephant wall match made by King and Company, circa 1891. Clear, $85-125.

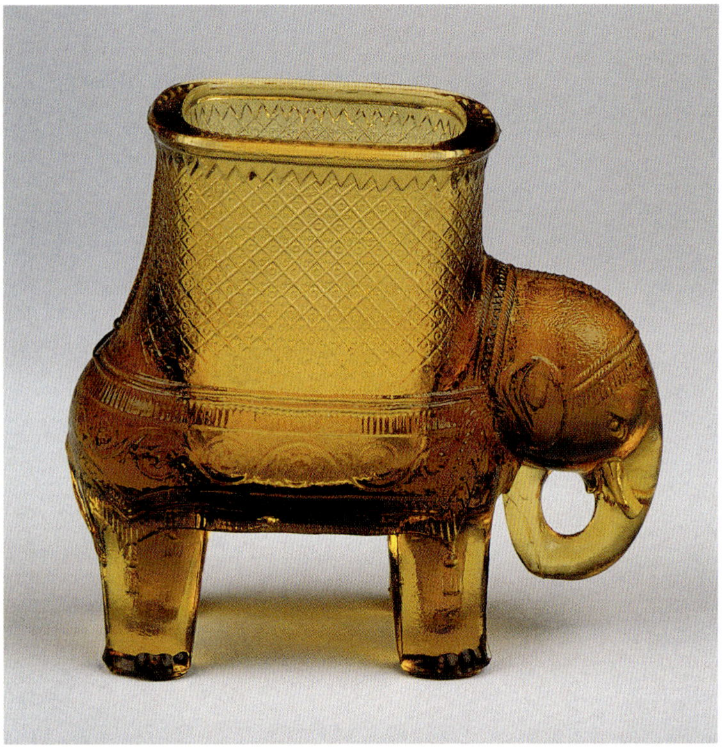

Baby Mine made by the Enterprise Manufacturing Co., circa 1883. Clear, $45-85. Colors, $65-145.

Standing elephant with trunk down, satin finish. Maker and date of manufactuer unknown. 6" long and 4 3/8" high. Clear, $375-425.

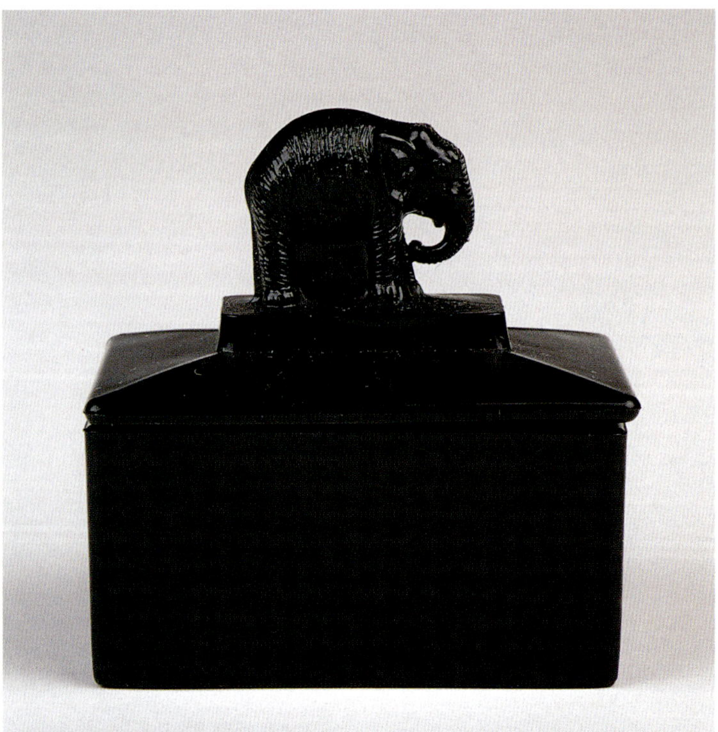

Black opaque box with a black opaque elephant finial, maker unknown, circa 1920s. 3 5/8" wide and 3 5/8" high. $225-275.

Boy on an elephant in opaque blue made by Vallerysthal, circa 1901. 7 1/2" long. $1,500-1,800.

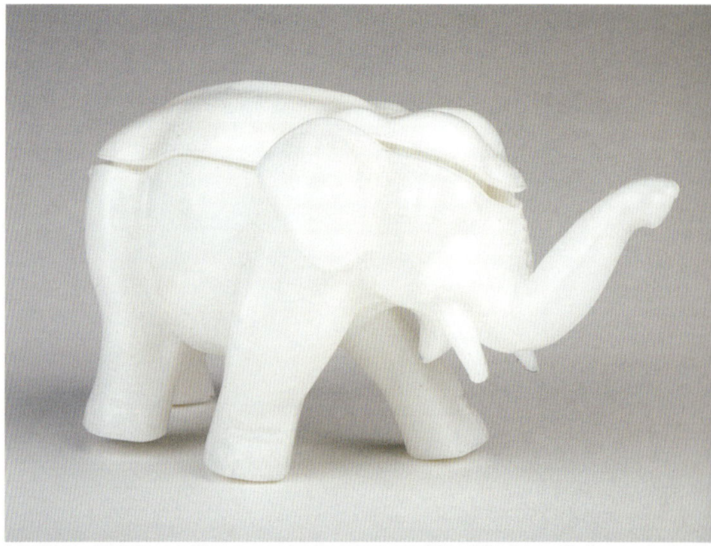

Opal elephant with cover, trunk up. Maker and date of manufactuer unknown. 6" long. $300-350.

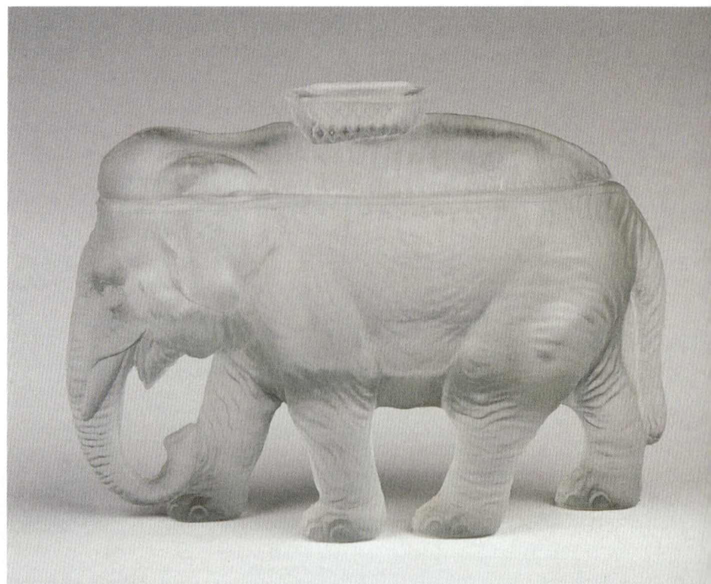

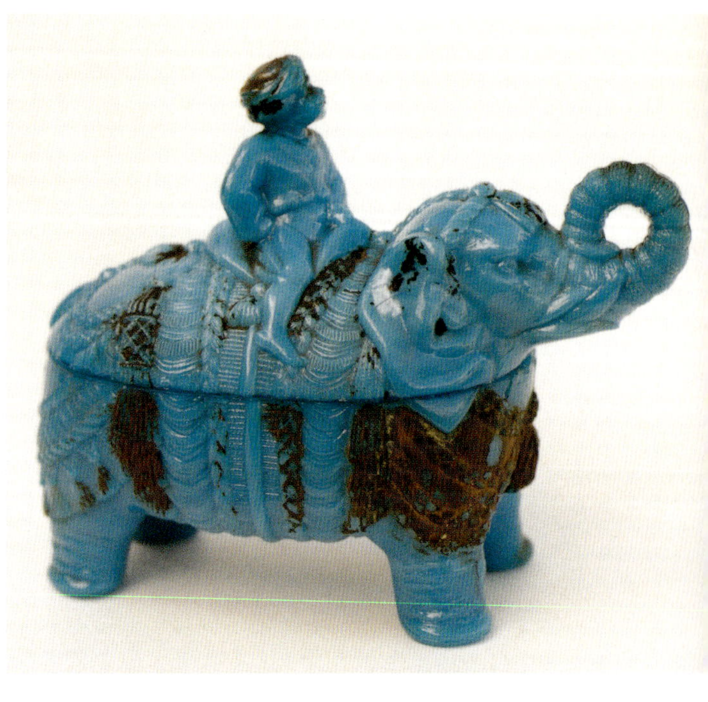

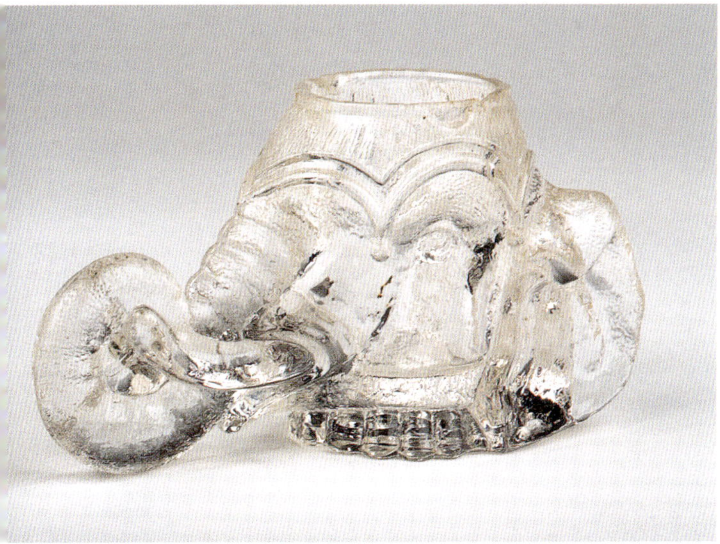

Elephant head mustard or toothpick holder made by the Findlay Flint Glass Co., circa 1889-1891, 2 3/8" high and 4 3/8" long. Clear, $75-125. Blue or amber, $250-350.

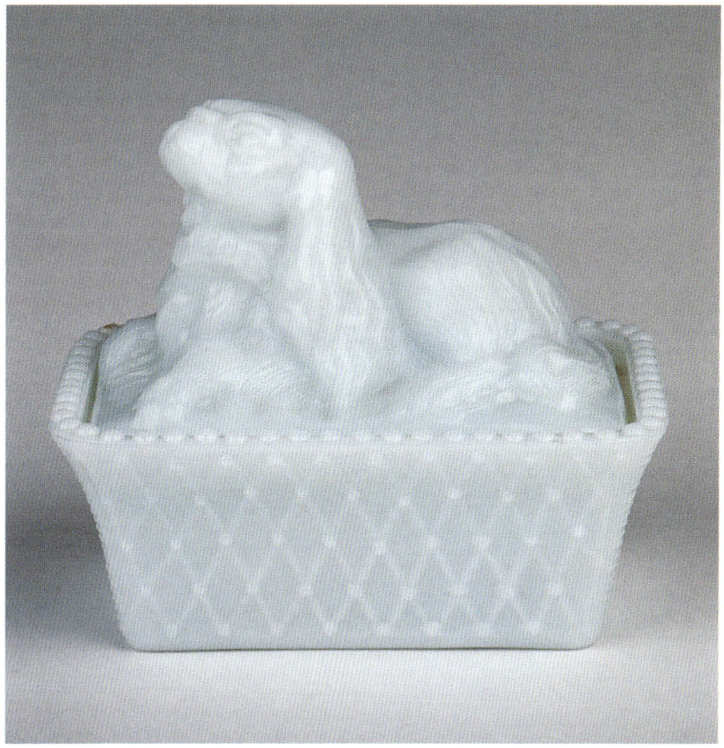

Spaniel dog on a square cross-thatched base in opal made by the Boston and Sandwich Glass Co., date of manufactuer unknown, 5" wide. Opal, $950-1,000.

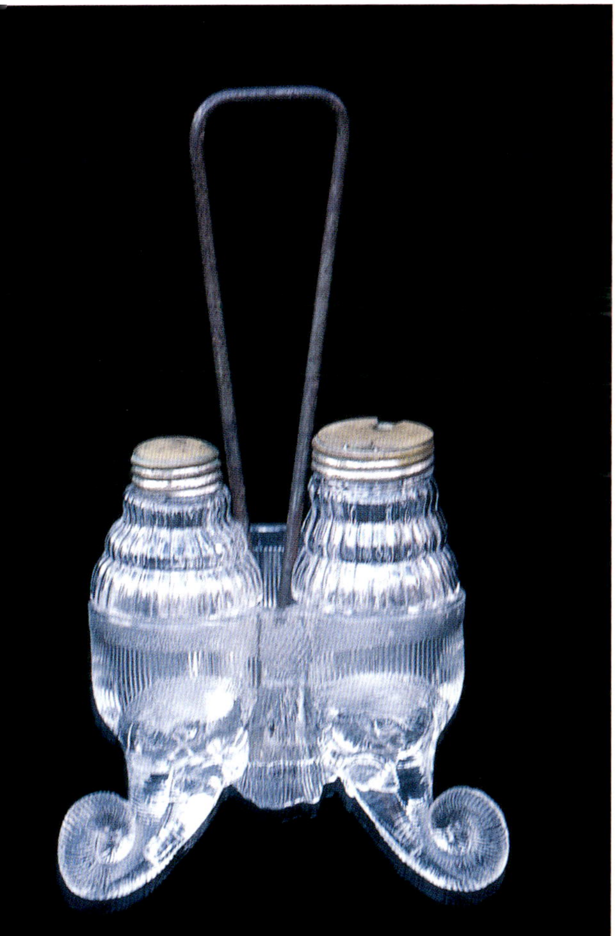

Stanley castor set made by the Greensburg Glass Co., circa 1891, 6" high and 5" wide. Clear, $450-550. Colors, $2,000-2,500.

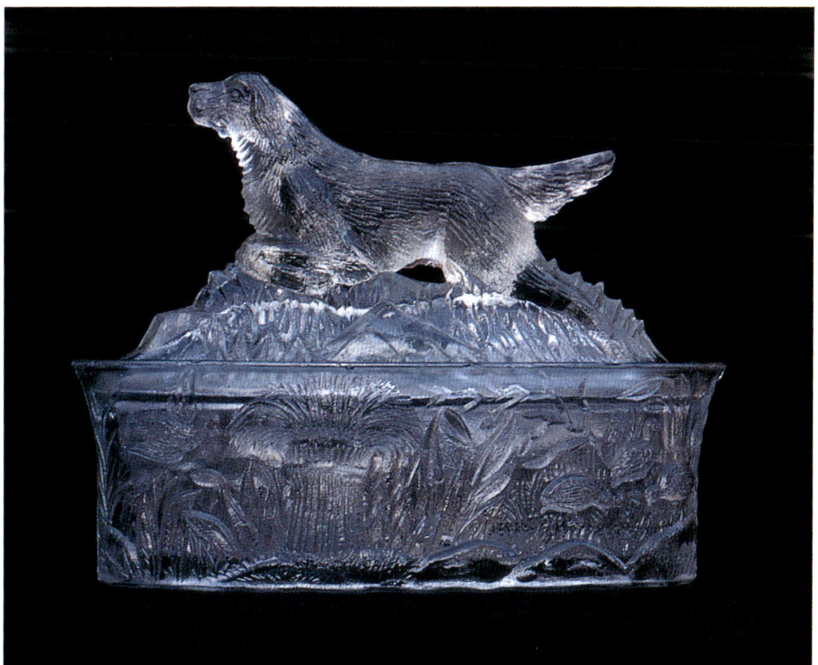

Dog lid on a Quail in wheat base covered dish made by the C. L. Flaccus Glass Co., circa 1890s, 6 1/2" long and 3 1/8" wide. $175-250

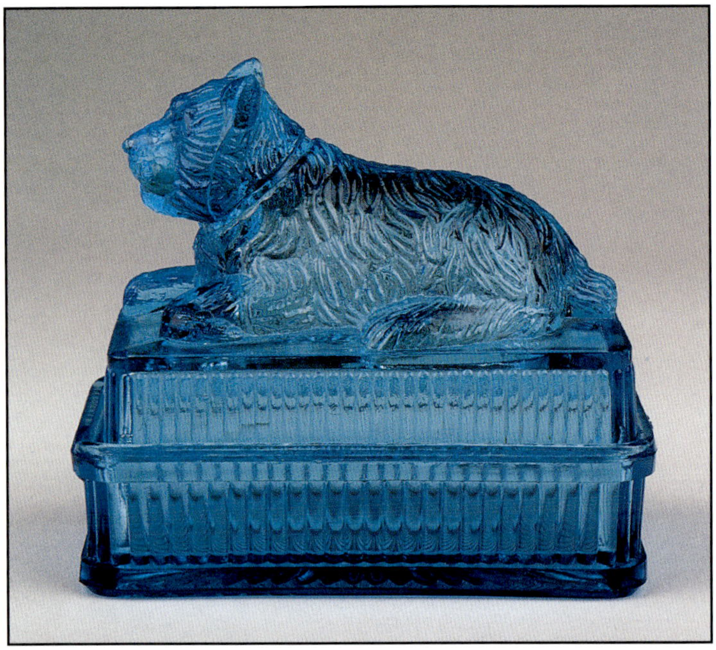
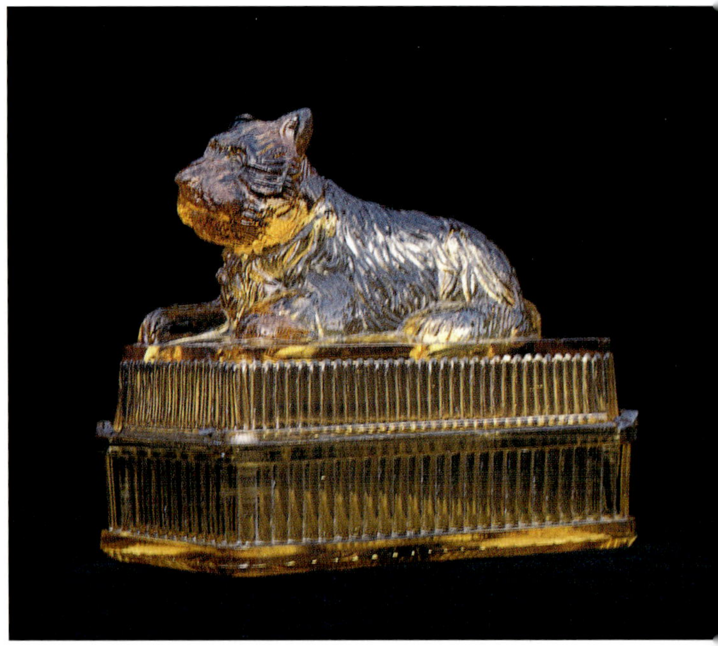

Terrier covered dish in amber and blue. Maker unknown, circa 1880s. 5" long and 3" wide. Amber, $150-200. Blue, $185-225.

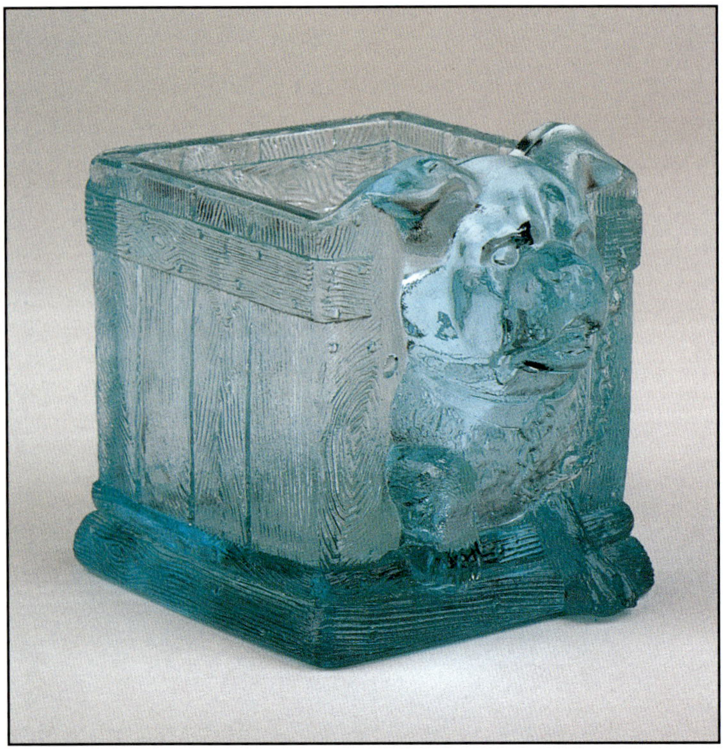
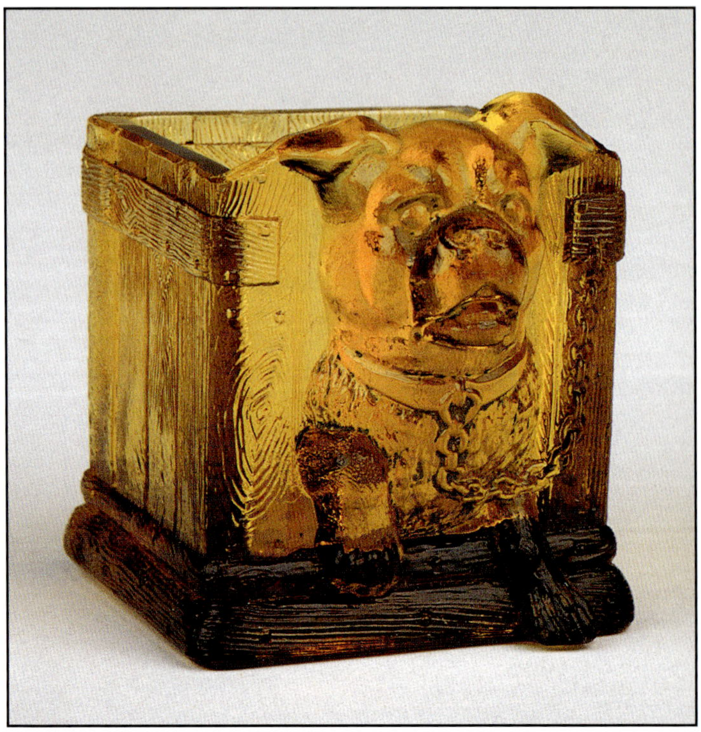

Dog House toothpick holder. This originally had a cover and was a condiment container made by King, Son and Co. Circa late 1880s. 2" high and 2" wide. Colors, $75-100.

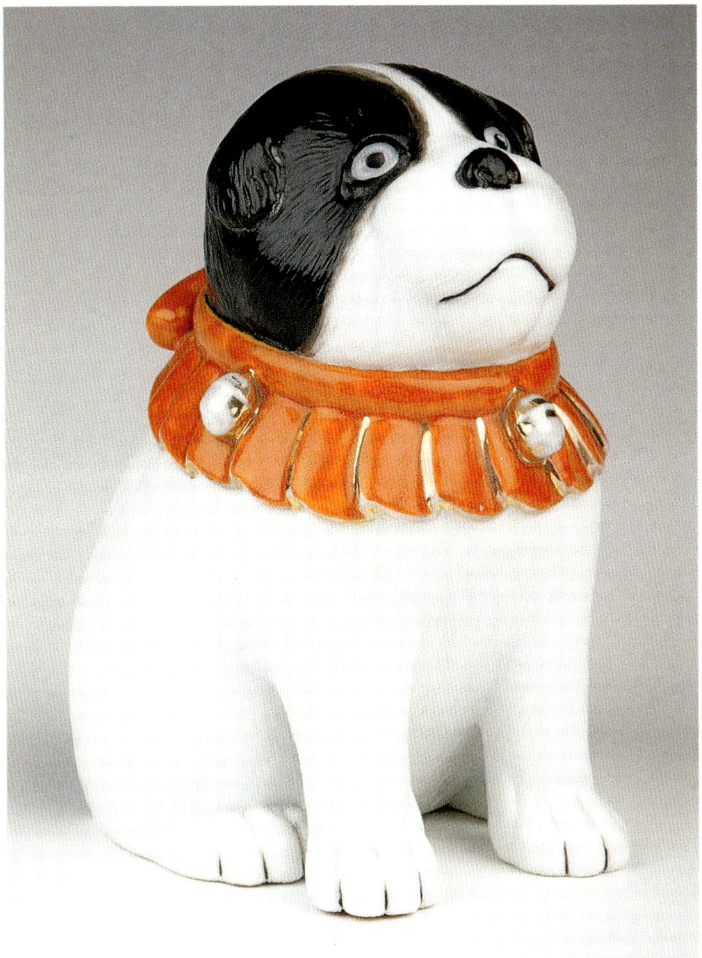

Dog in opal with black with a red collar painted decor, maker and circa are unknown. It is 5 1/4" high and very lightweight due to the very thin glass. The paws are well pressed on the underneath side and are decorated red. It is probably foreign made. $1,800-2,000.

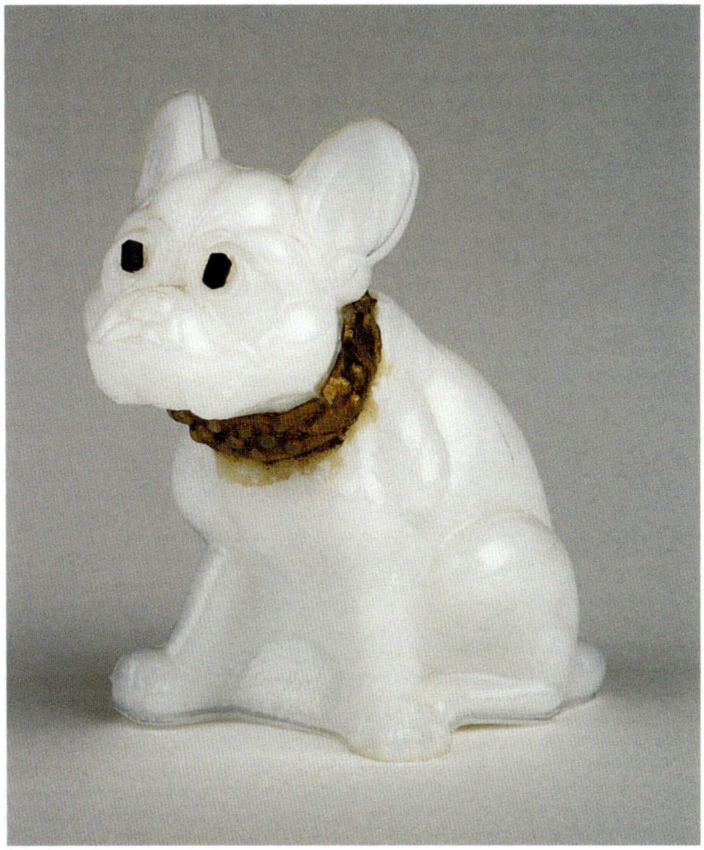

Dog in opal with attached black eyes and a gold collar, maker and date of manufactuer unknown, 2 3/4" high. $115-150.

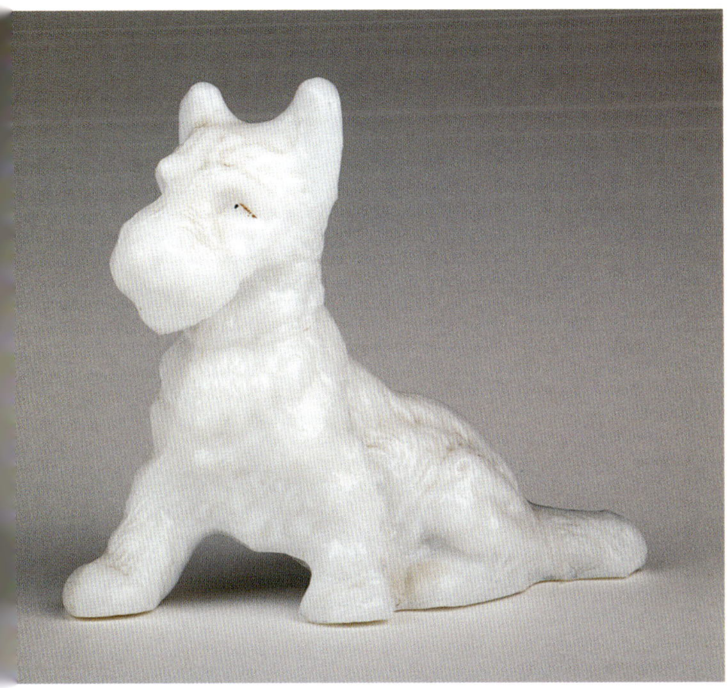

Opal dog paperweight, maker unknown, circa 1920s, 5" high. $175-200.

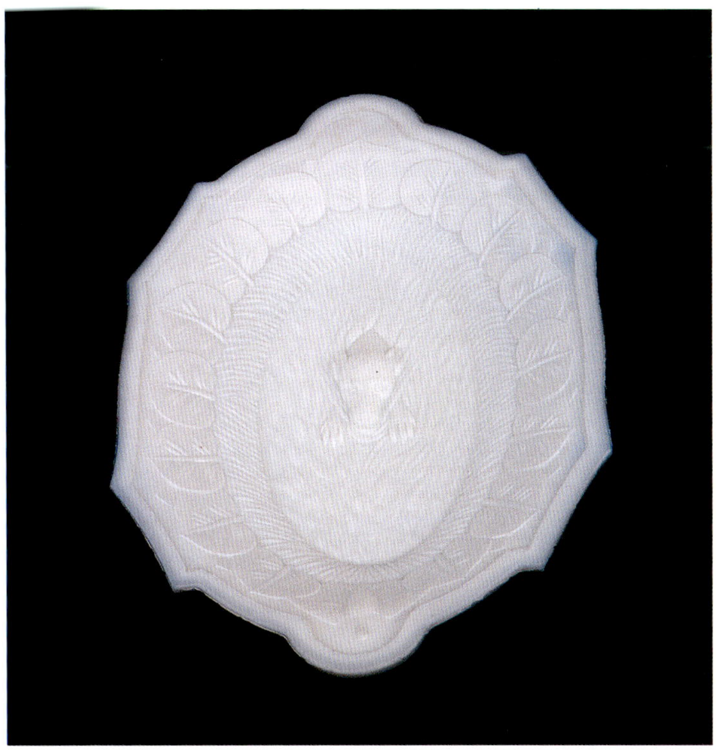

Retriever Platter, maker uncertain, circa 1890, 13" long. Opal, $110-150.

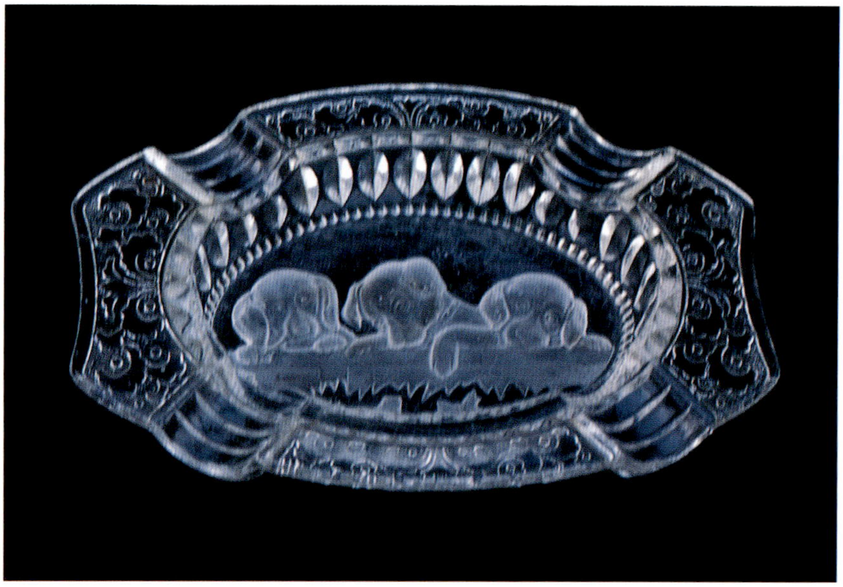

Three puppies cigar tray. Maker and date of manufactuer unknown, 6 1/2" x 4 3/4". Clear, $150-185.

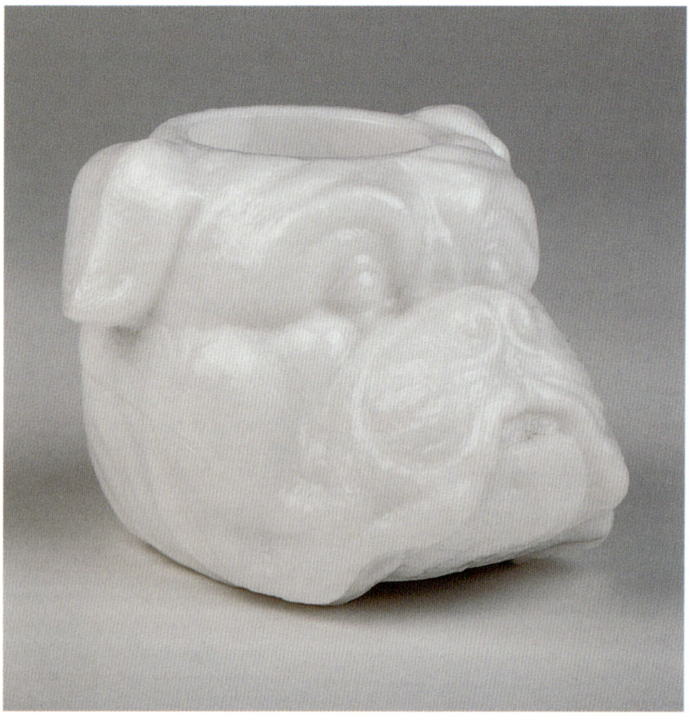

Boston Bull match safe in opal made by McKee and Brothers, circa 1899, 2 1/2" high and 3 1/2" wide. Clear, $100-135; opal, $150-185.

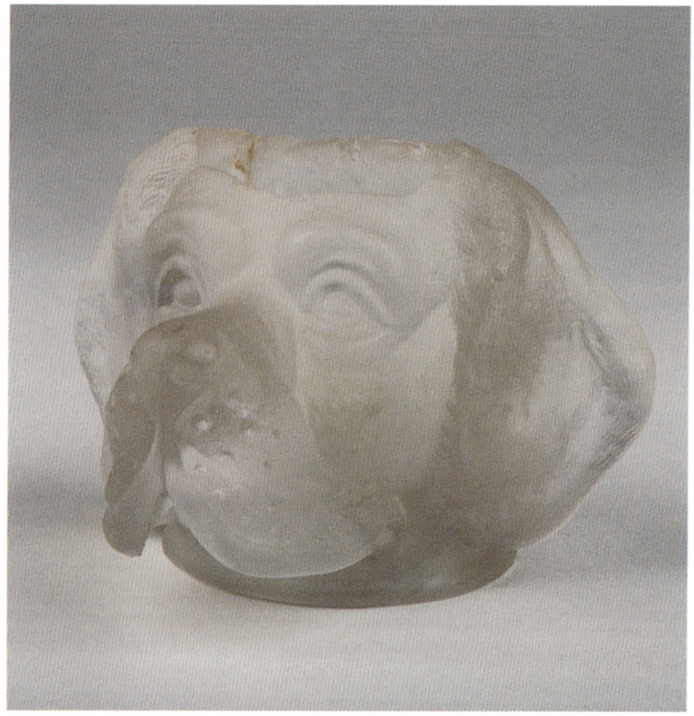

St. Bernard match safe made by the Indiana Tumbler and Goblet Co., date of manufactuer unknown, 2 3/8" high and 3 1/2" wide. Clear, $135-150. Clear with satin finish, $150-195. Nile green, $245-285.

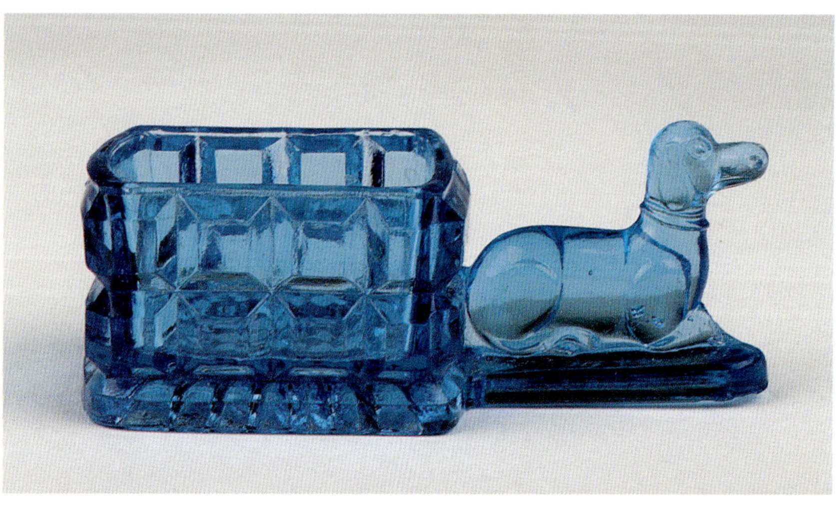

Dog salt dip made by the Central Glass Co., circa 1889. Colors, $95-145.

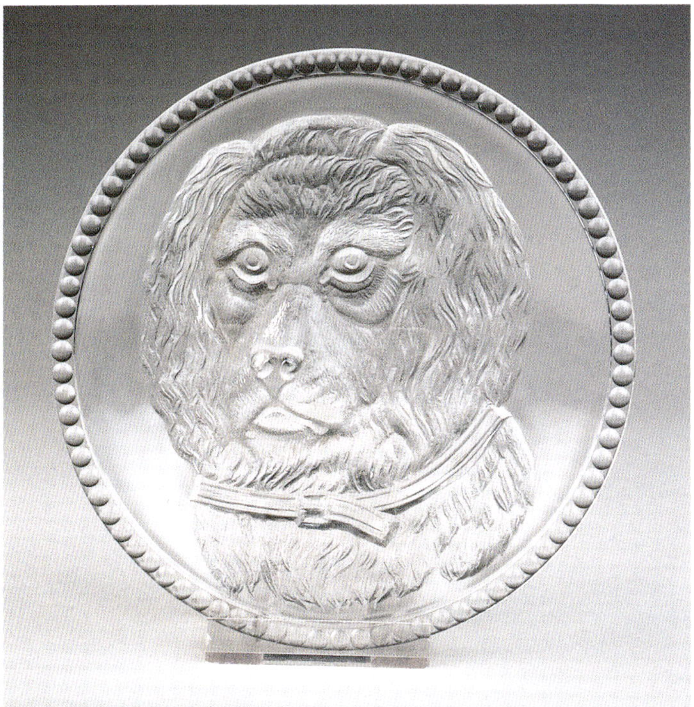

Pet dish. Dog made by the Columbia Glass Co., circa 1888. Clear, $85-125.

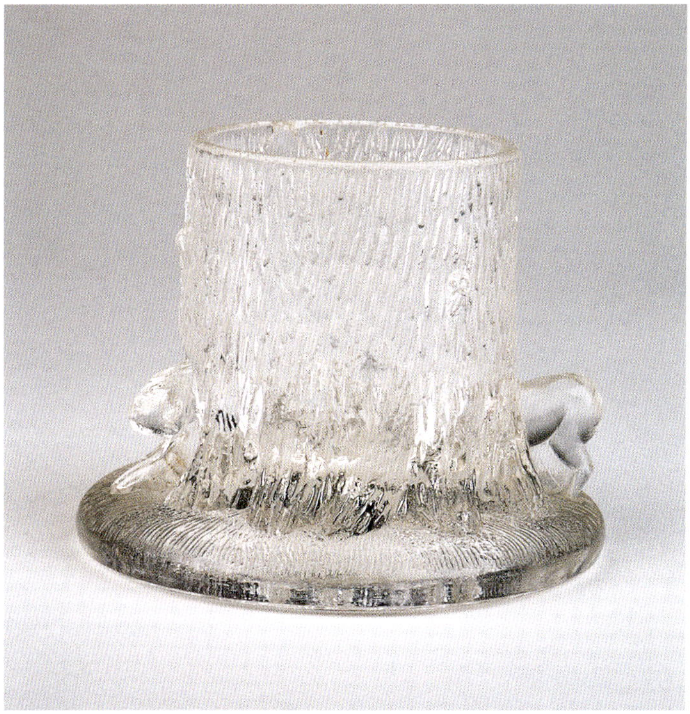

Dog chasing rabbit through tree stump toothpick holder, 2 3/8" high and 2" wide. Clear, $60-75.

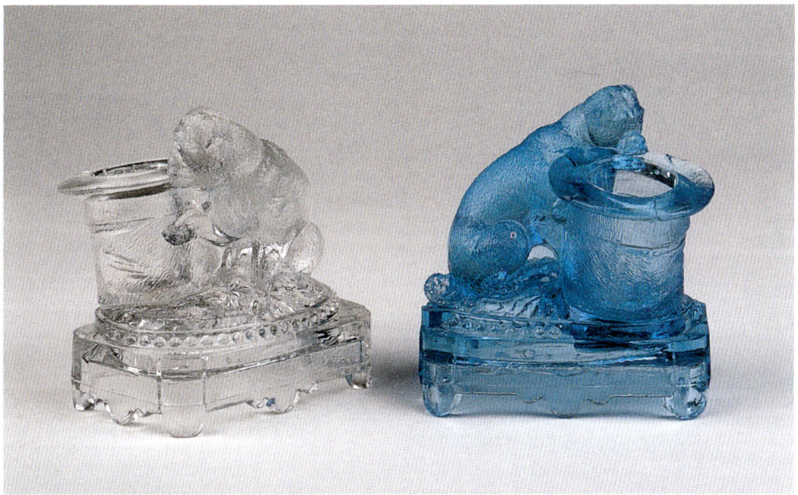

Dog and hat was made by the Belmont Glass Co., circa 1885, 2 3/4" high and 1 1/4" wide. Clear, $50-60. Blue, $80-95.

Dog with baskets double saltcellar made by Vallerysthal, circa 1890, 2" high and 3" wide. Clear, $75-125.

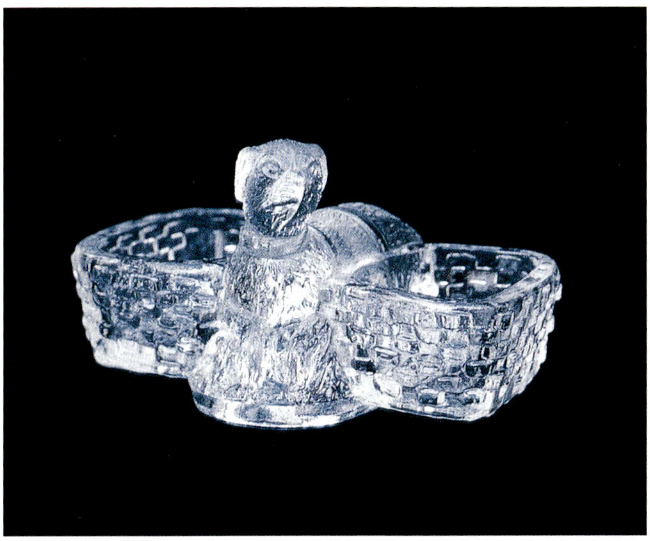

Setter dog covered dish made by Vallerysthal, circa 1908, 6" x 4". $275-295.

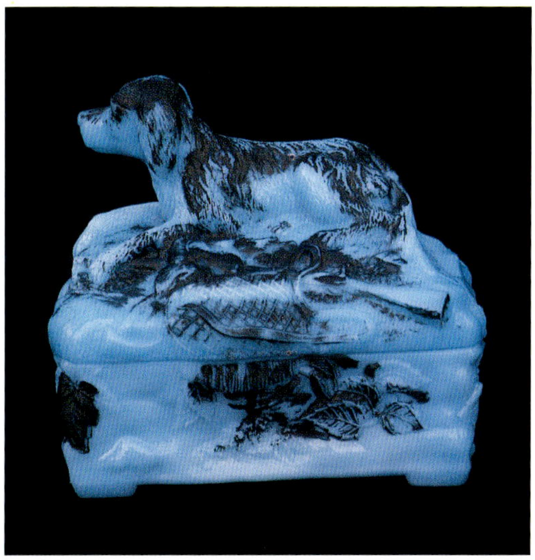

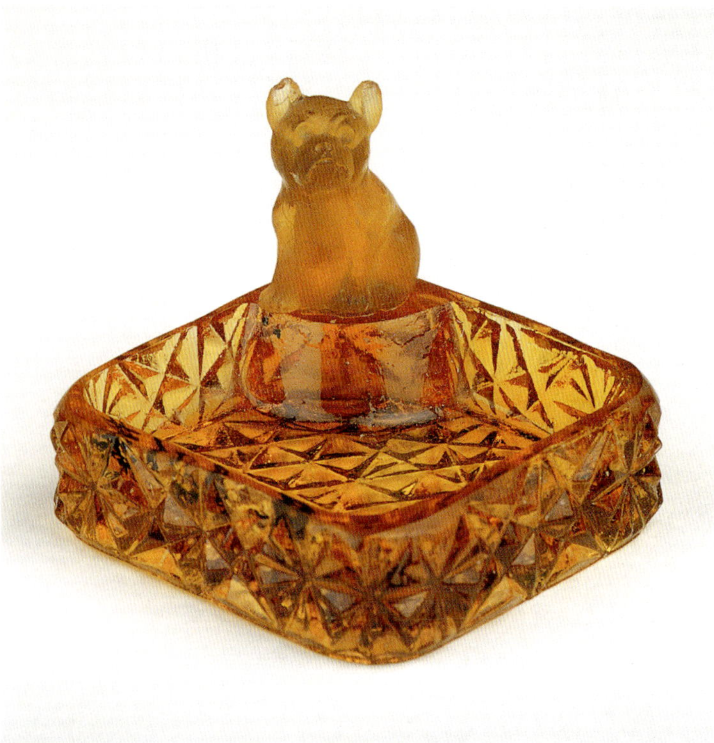

Square Daisy and Button pattern base with a dog in the center, maker and date of manufactuer unknown, 2 1/2" square base. Amber, $175-225.

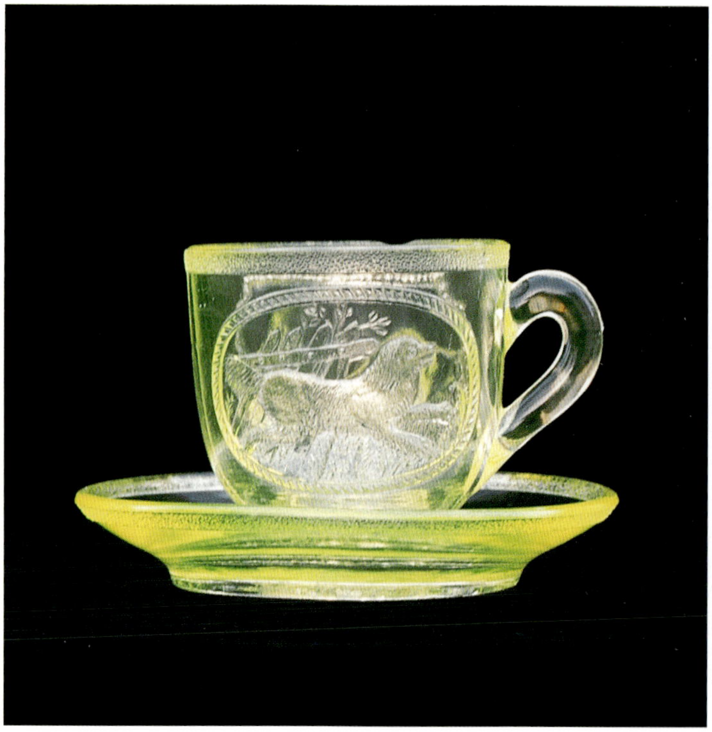

Cat on a cushion toy cup and saucer, made by the U. S. Glass Co. at their factory F, circa 1891, 2 1/4" diameter. $140-185.

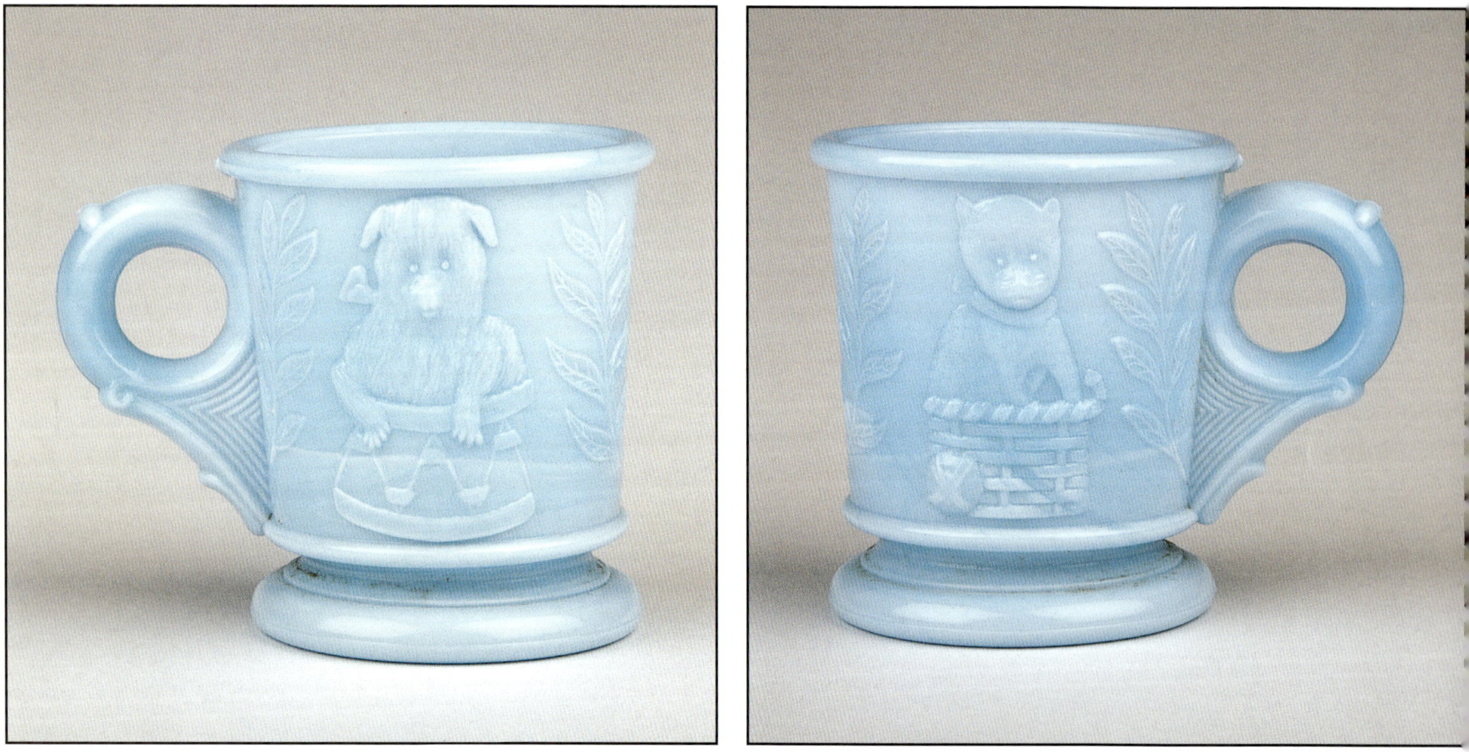

Opaque blue cup with puppy on one side and kitten on the reverse, maker and date of manufactuer unknown, 2 1/2" high. $120-140.

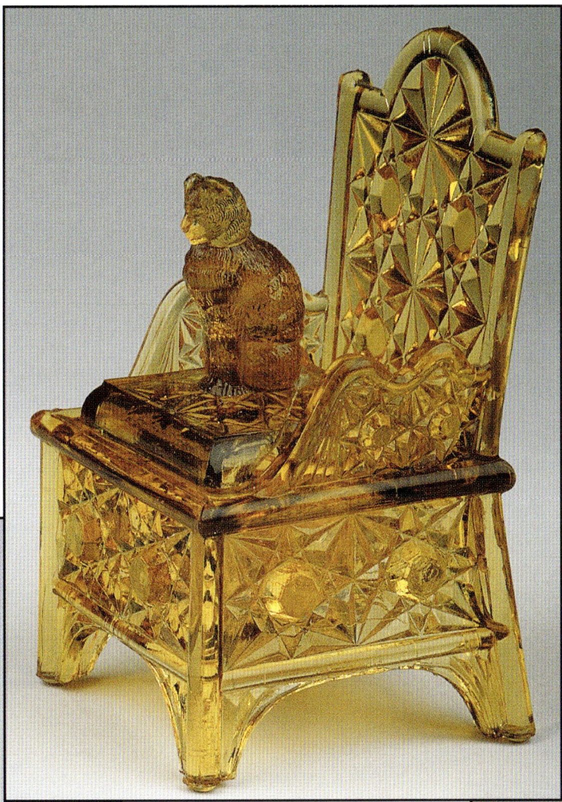

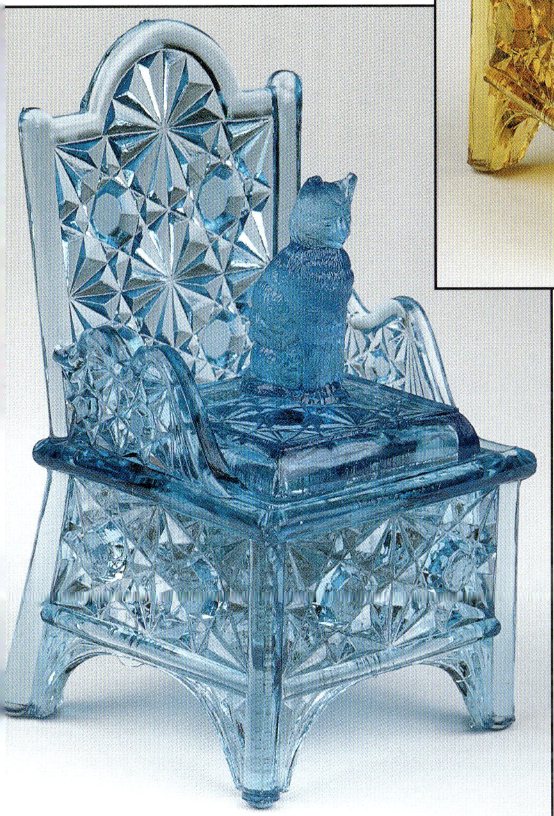

Chair inkwell with kitten lid made by the Canton Glass Co., circa 1880s, 4 1/2" high and 2" wide. Clear, $185-250. Colors, $295-375.

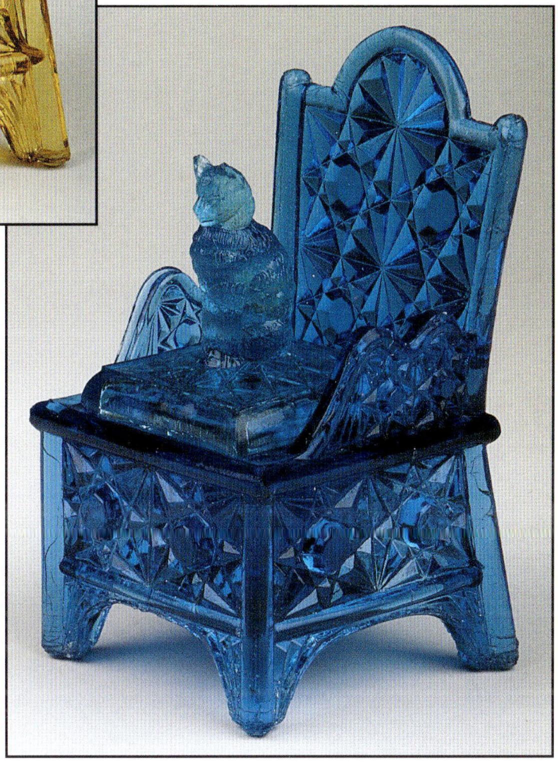

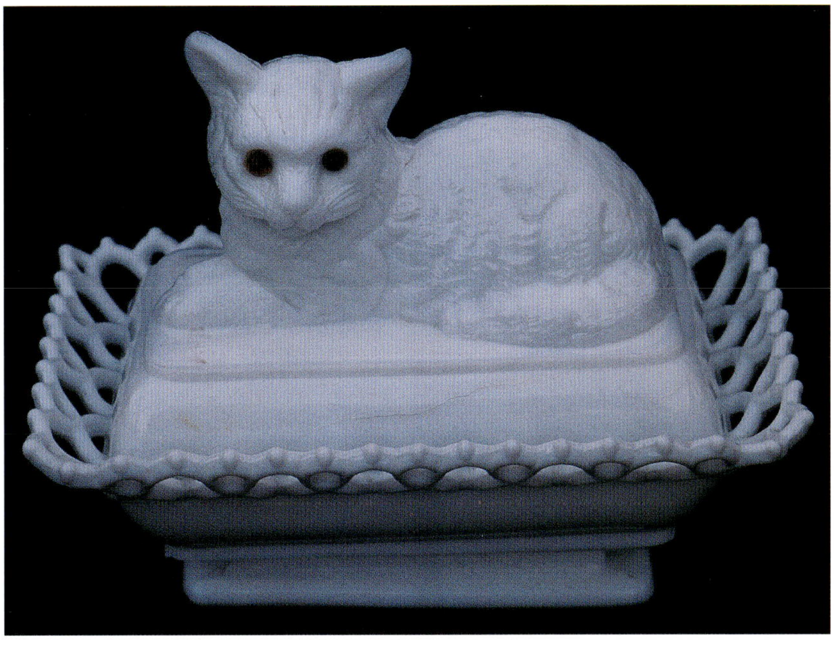

Cat covered dish made by Atterbury and Co., circa 1889, 6 3/8" long. Opal, $150-175.

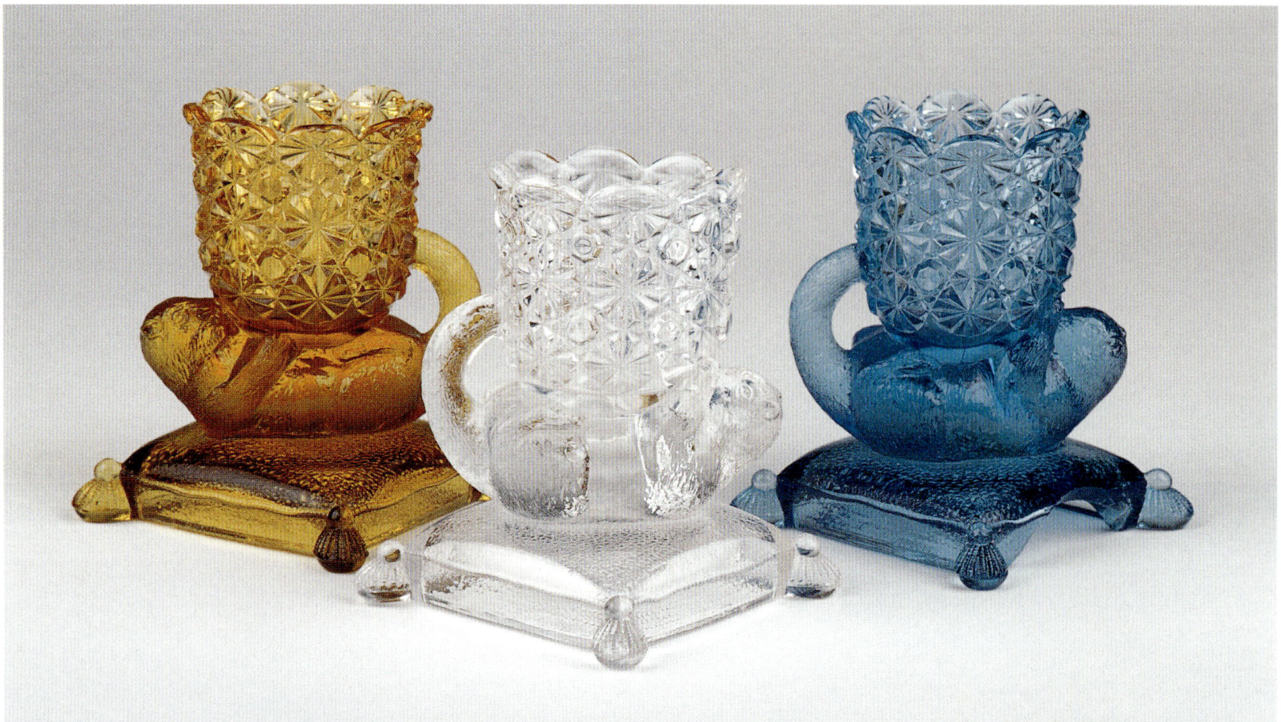

Kitten on a pillow toothpick holder made by Richards and Hartley Glass Co., circa 1889, 3 1/2" high and 3" wide at the base. Clear, $85-125. Colors, $125-165.

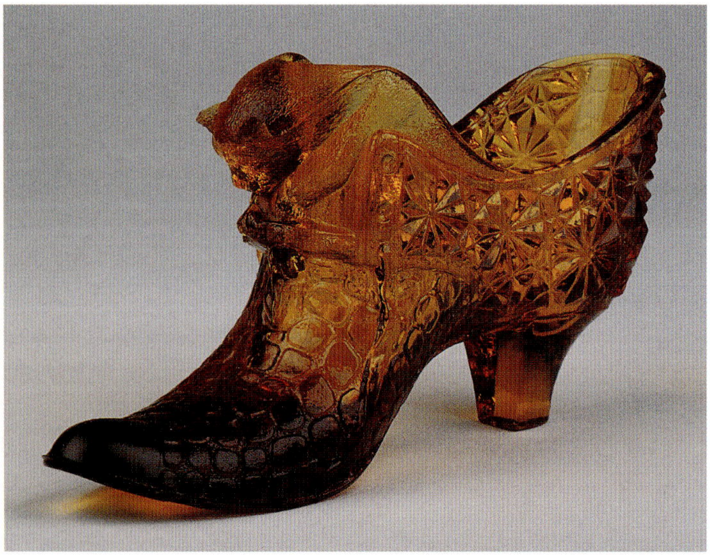

Kitten in shoe perfume bottle packing container, as noted in original advertisement, made by the Columbia Glass Co., circa late 1880s. Clear, $35-50; colors, $45-65. Beware of many reproductions.

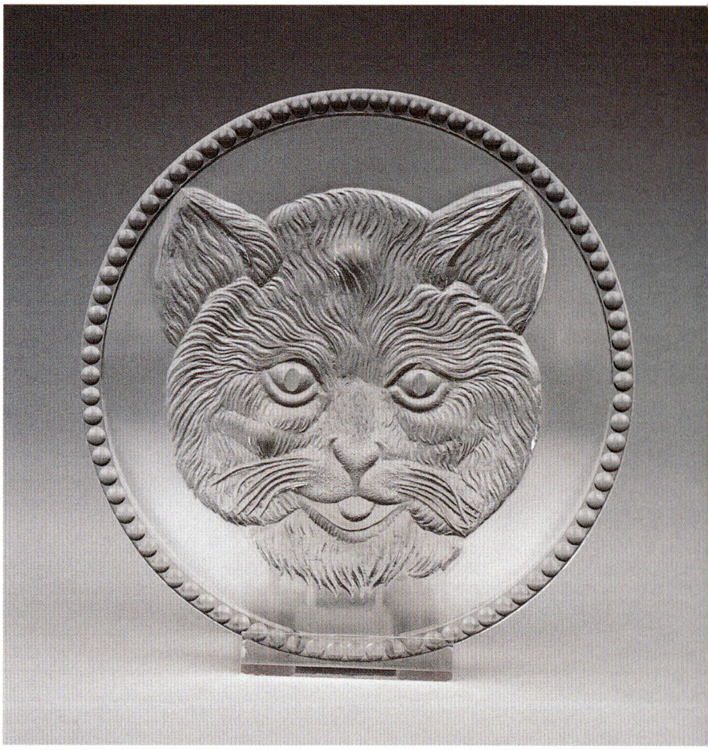

Pet dish kitten made by the Columbia Glass Co., circa 1888. Clear, $85-125.

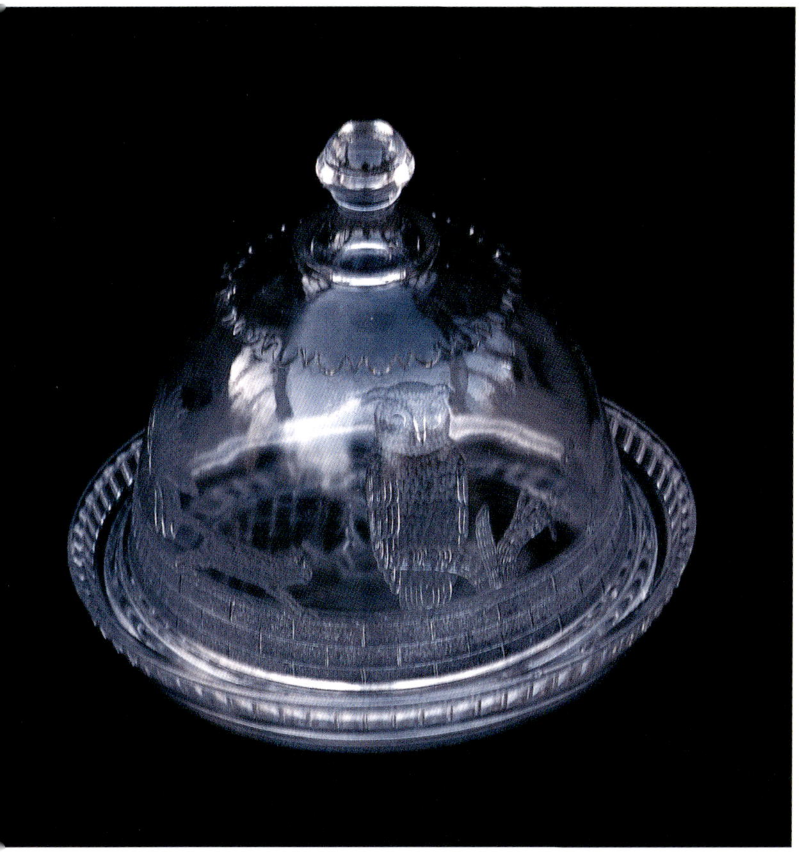

Owl and pussycat cheese dish which the owner attributes to Adams and Co., circa 1880, base diameter is 8". Clear, $500-600.

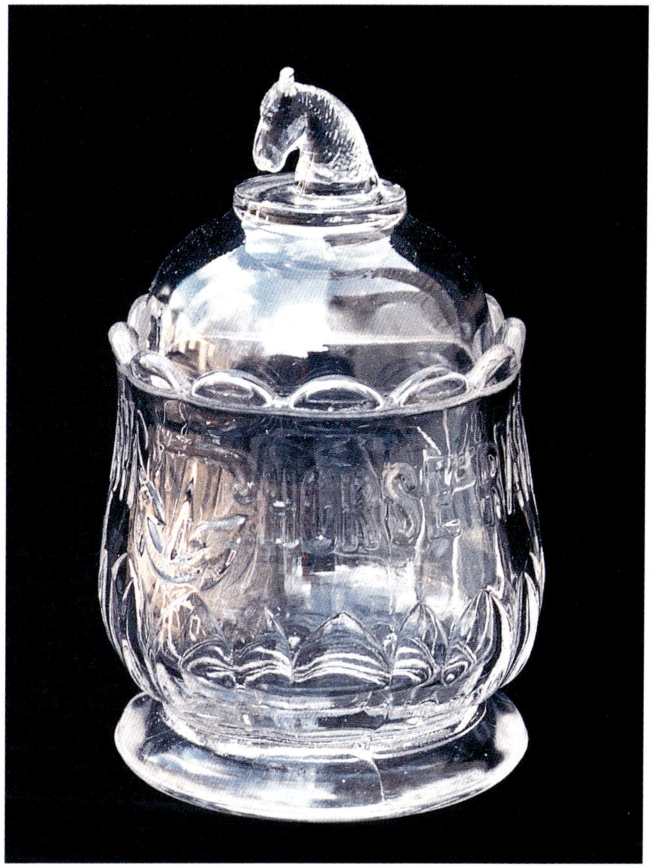

Horse head finial horseradish container, maker and date of manufactuer unknown, 5" high and 3" diameter. Clear, $120-135.

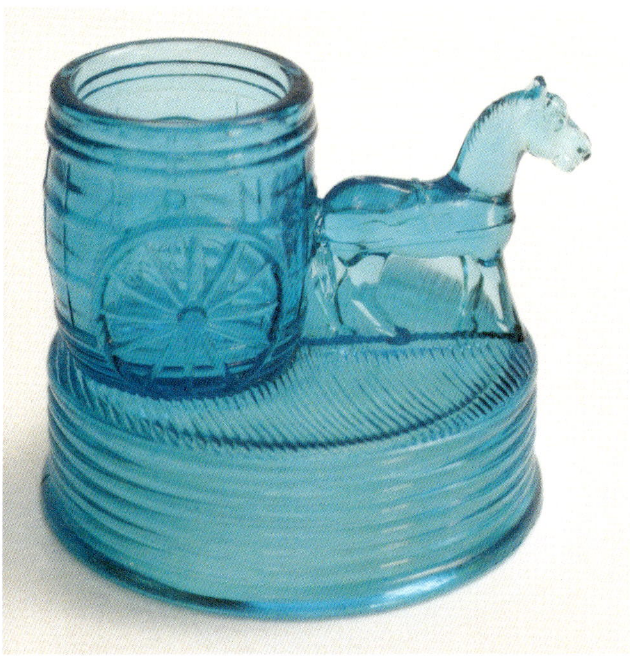

Horse with cart toothpick holder made by the Central Glass Co., circa mid-1880s. Amber, $150-175. Blue, $210-240.

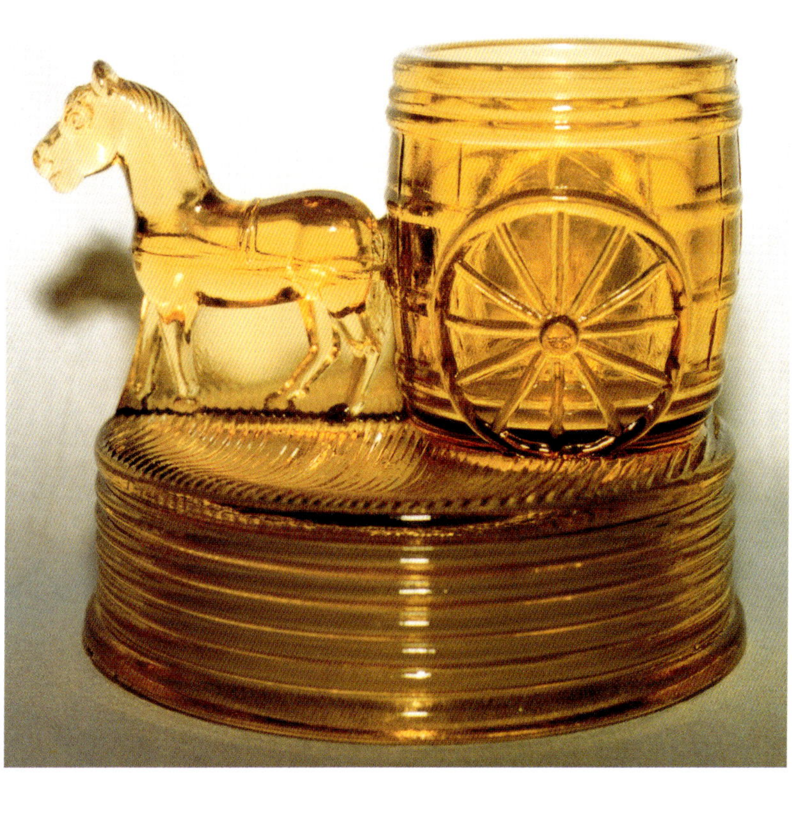

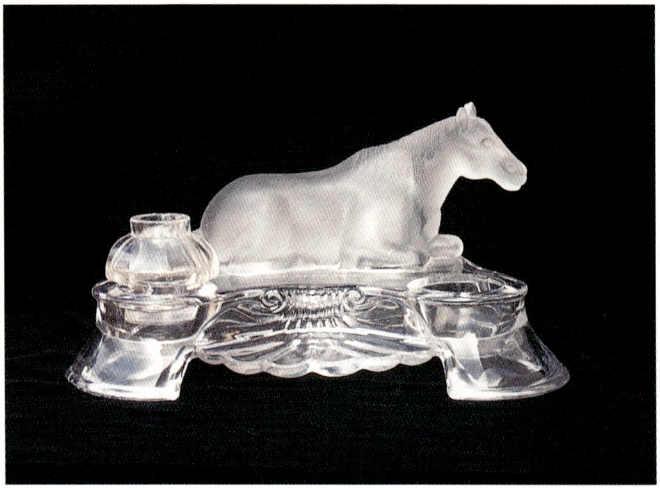

Recumbent Horse inkwell made by the Central Glass Co., circa 1880s, 4 1/4" high and 9" long. Clear, $240-285.

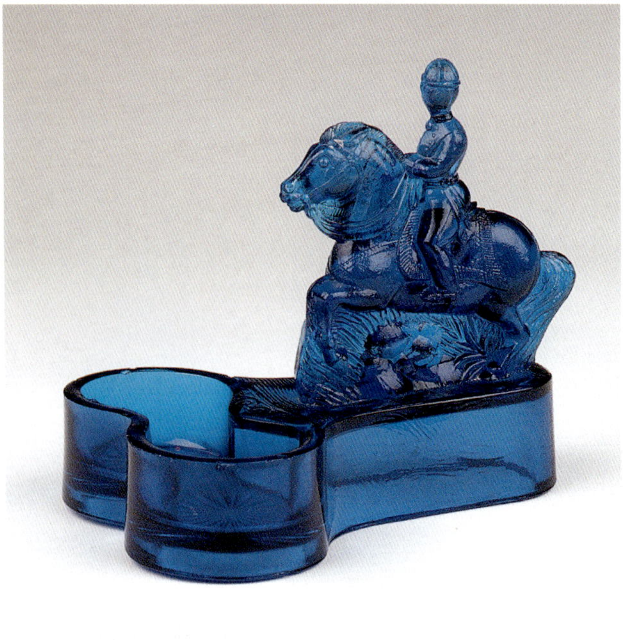

Blue Jockey holder for salt and pepper shakers, maker and date of manufactuer unknown. 6" long. $225-300 without shakers.

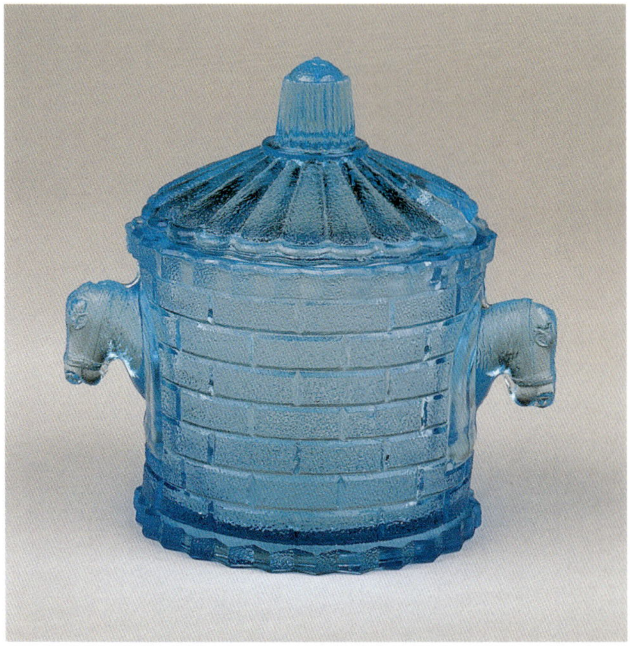

Mustard with Horse head handles made by Adams and Company and continued by the United States Glass Company in 1891. 4" x 4 1/4". Blue, $185-225.

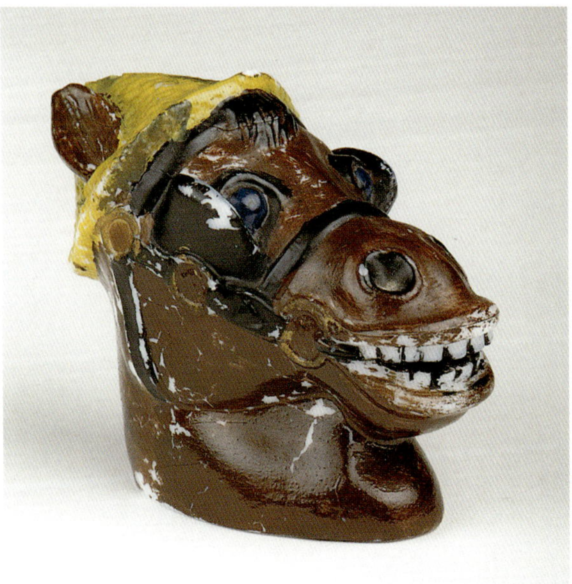

Opal glass Donkey head with brown paint and yellow cap, maker and date of manufactuer unknown, 5" x 4". $550-650.

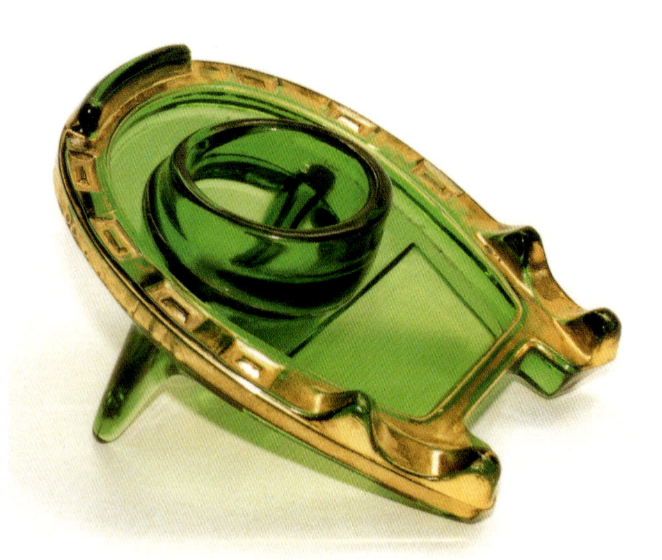

Horseshoe inkwell, maker and date of manufactuer unknown, 4 1/4" long and 3 1/2" wide. Green with gold decoration, $135-160.

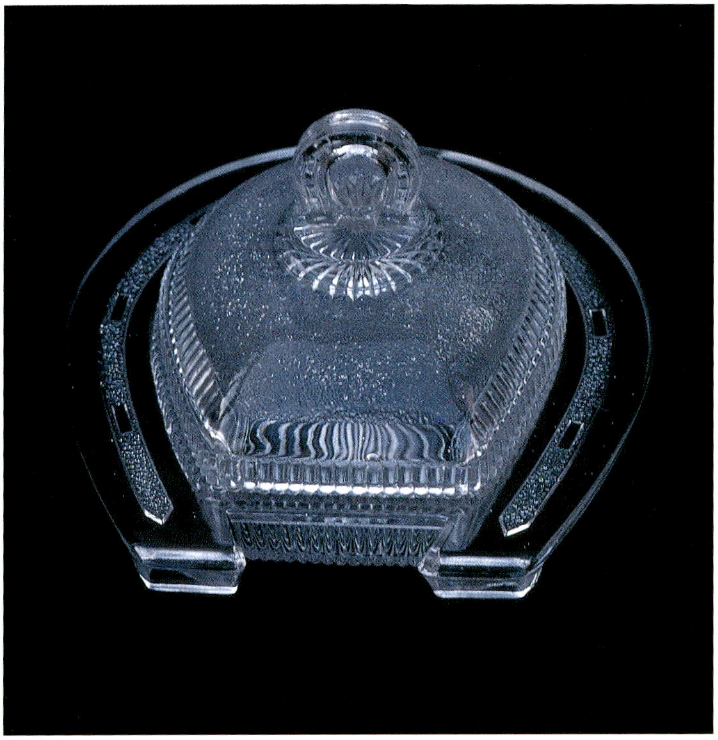

Maude S butter dish made by Ripley and Co., circa 1884. The base rim is 6 7/8" by 6 5/8". Clear, $175-225.

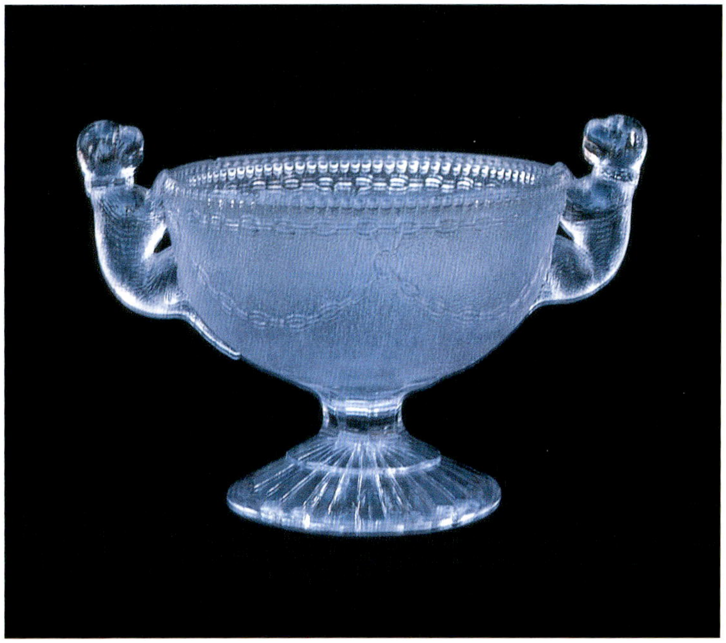

Dog and Cat open sugar made by Davidson, circa 1895, 4 1/2" diameter. The dogs are boxers. Open, $170-190; with lid, $350-380.

Opal decorated Monkey water pitcher, maker and date of manufactuer unknown, 9" high. $950-1,250.

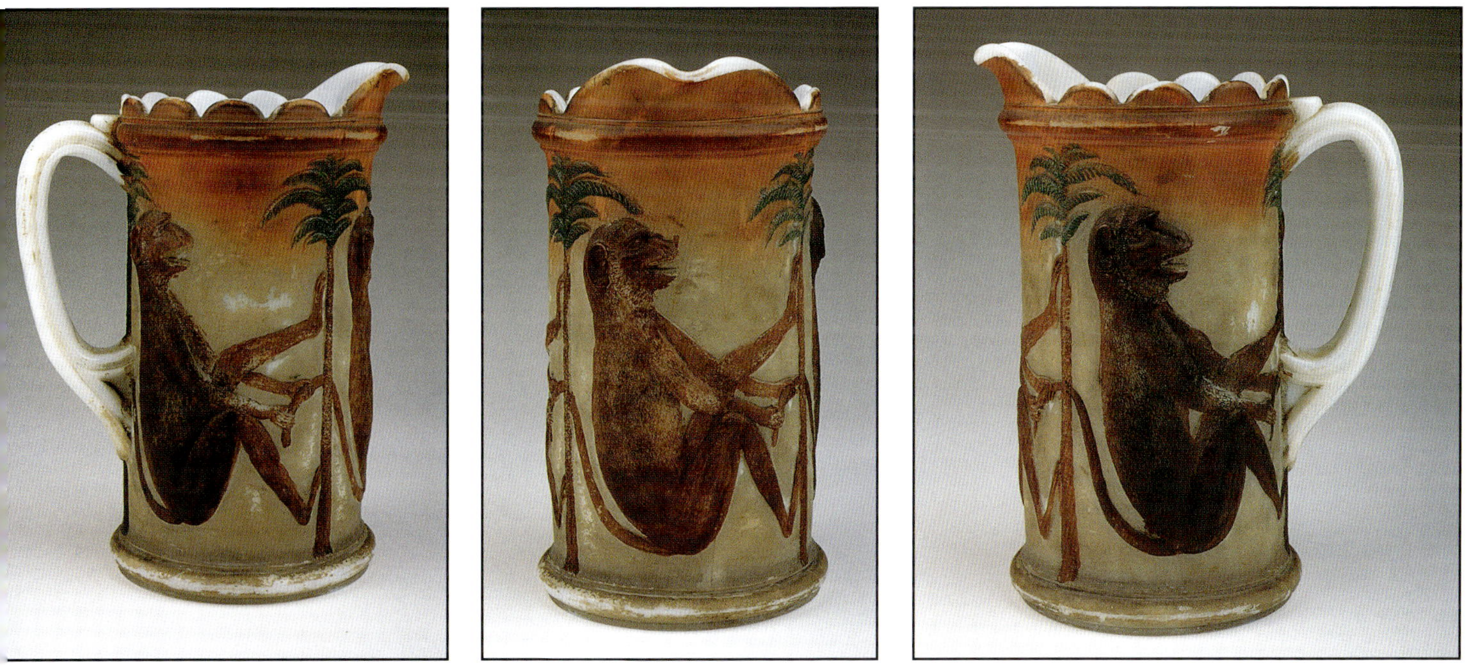

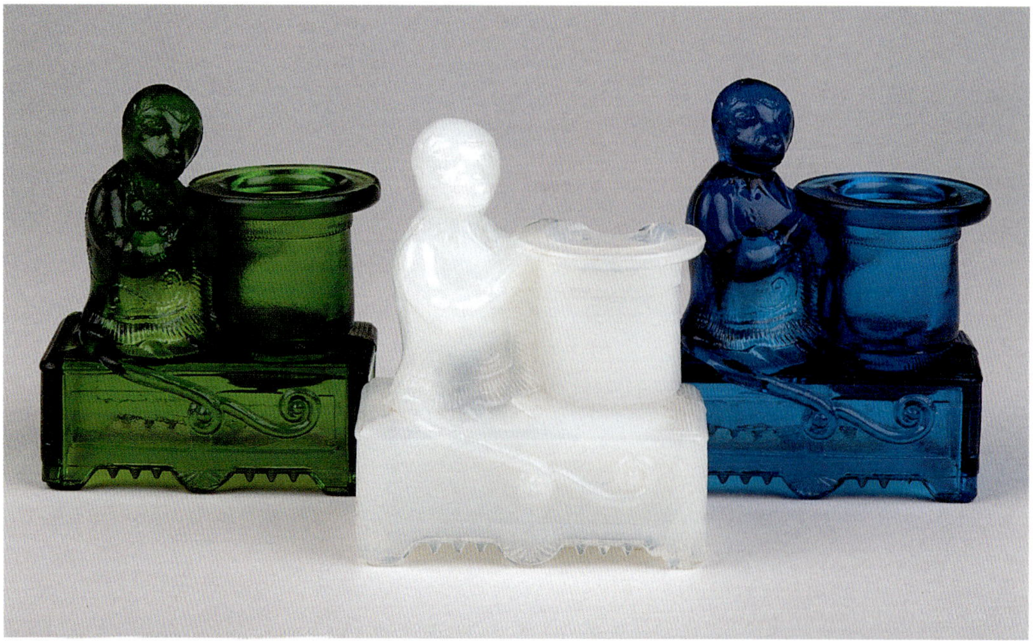

Monkey with Hat toothpick holder, maker and date of manufactuer unknown. 2 1/2" high and 3" long. Clear, $50-70. Colors, $90-135.

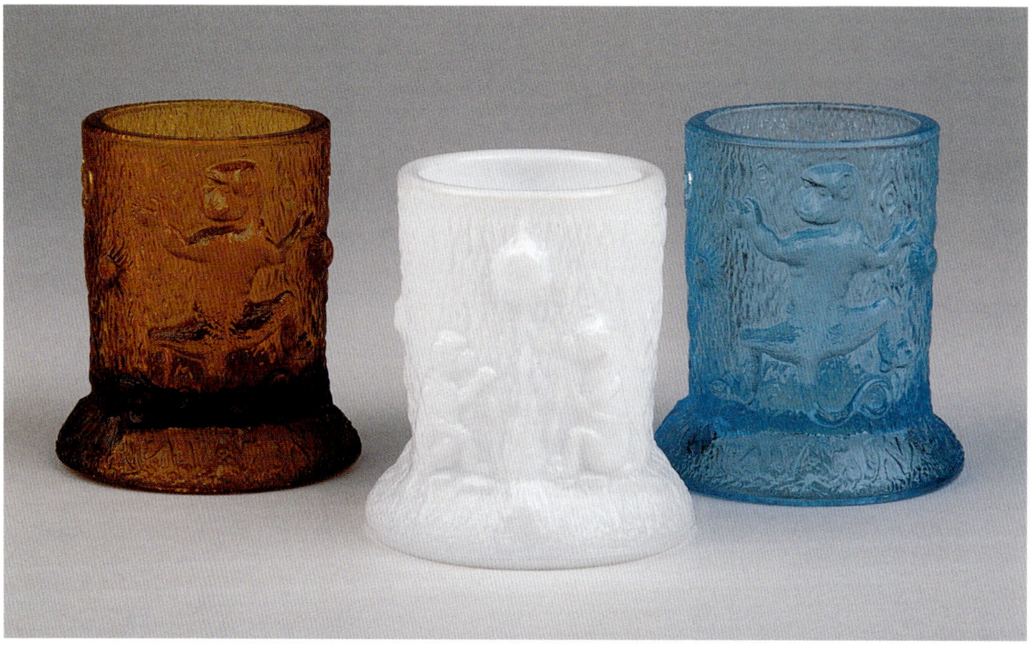

Monkey on a Stump toothpick holder made by the United States Glass Co., circa 1904. 2 1/2" high and 2" wide. Clear, $45-60. Colors, $50-75.

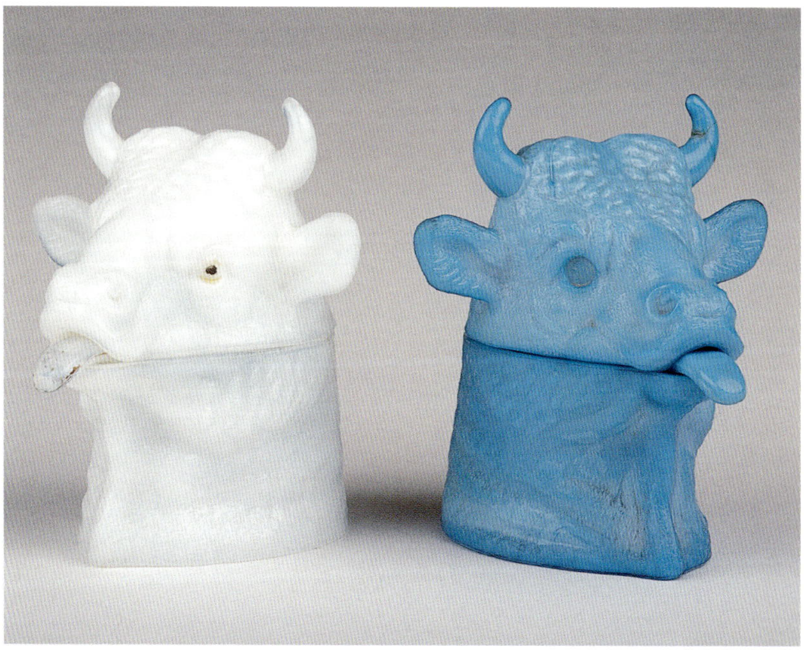

Bull's Head mustard made by Atterbury and Co., circa 1888, 4 1/2" high. Opal, $190-225. Blue opaque, $490-525.

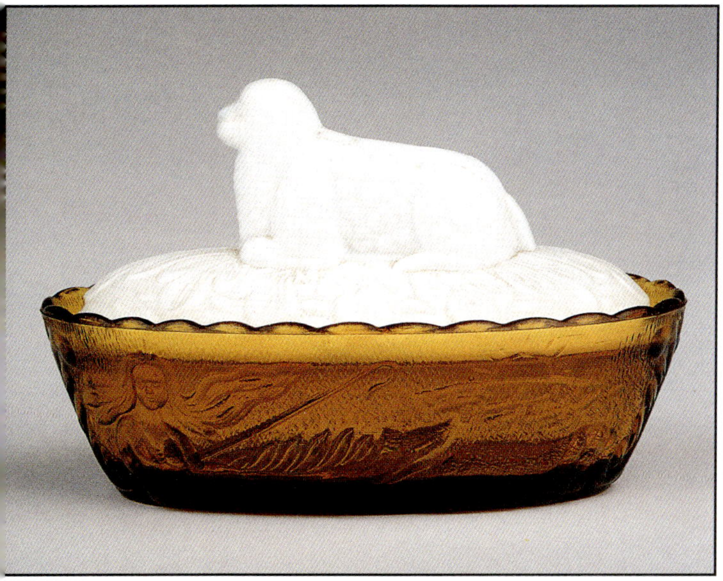

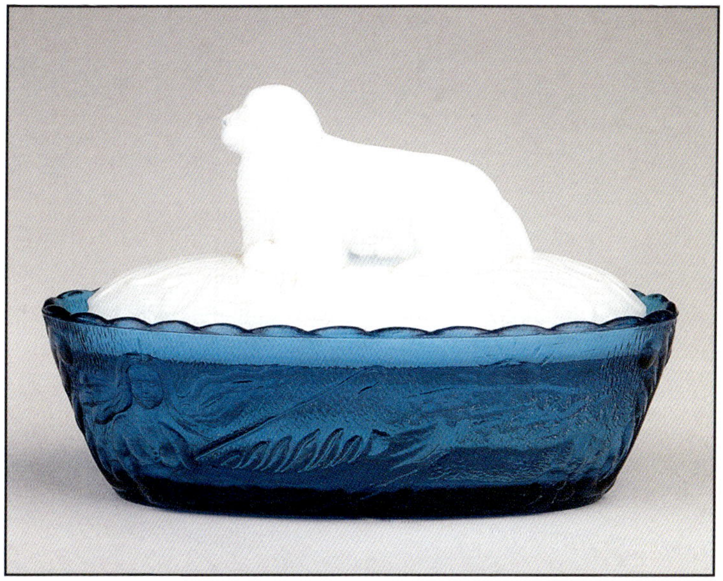

Sheep covered dish known by some collectors as *Little Bo Peep*, made by C. L. Flaccus Co., circa late 1880s, base 6" long. All colors, $875-950.

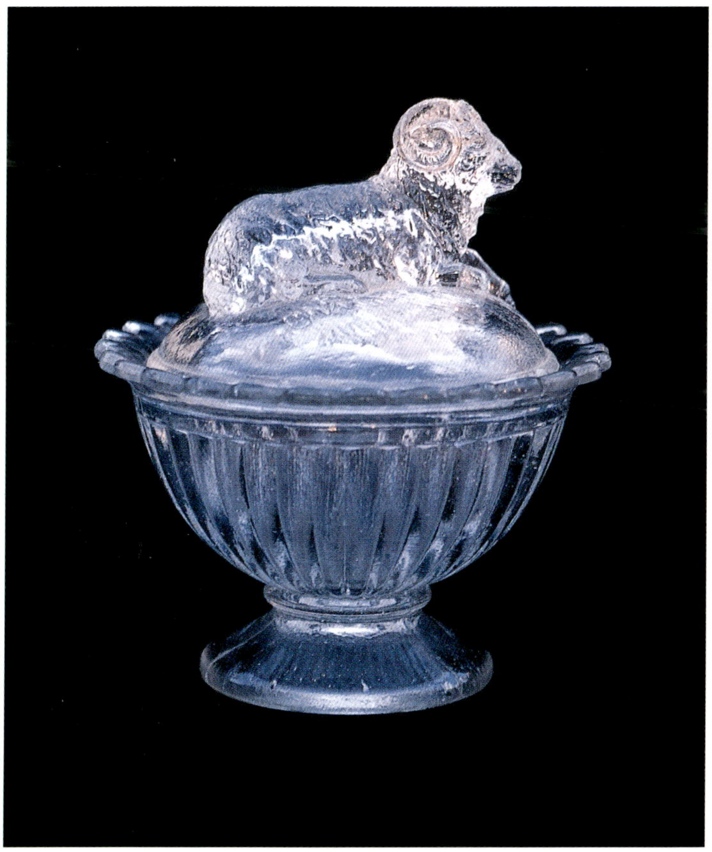

Ram salt, date of manufactuer unknown, 3 3/4" high and 3 1/4" diameter. Clear, $125-140.

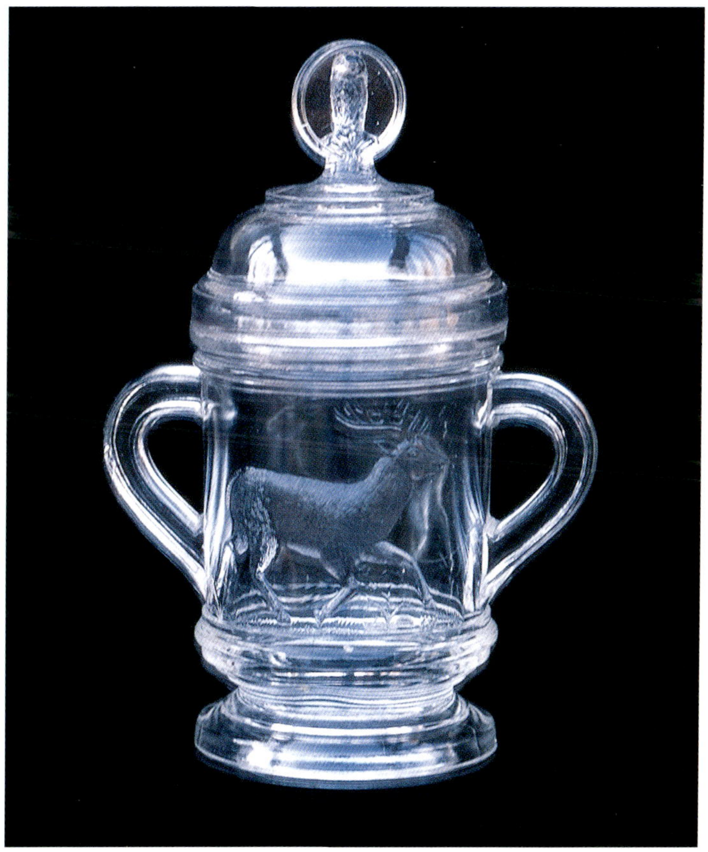

Lone Elk marmalade jar, maker unknown, circa 1870s, 7" high and 3" diameter. $275-300 with the original Parrot and Fan lid.

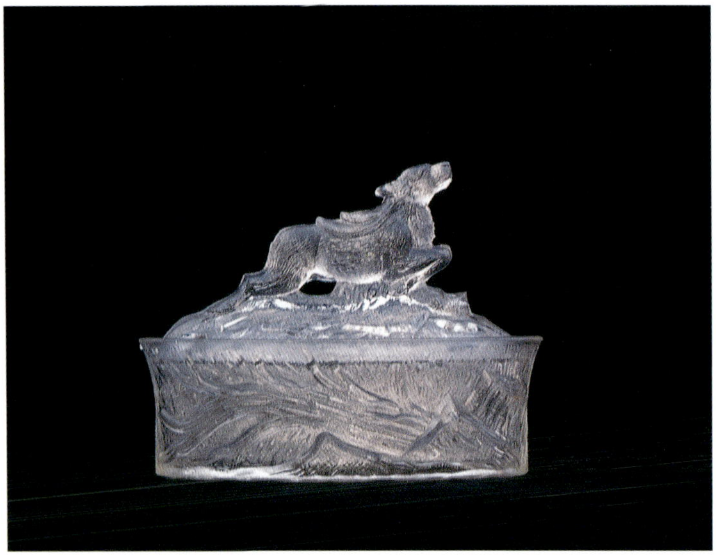

Deer on Fallon Tree made by the C. L. Flaccus Glass Co., circa 1890s, 6 1/4" long and 3 1/2" wide. Clear, $200-235.

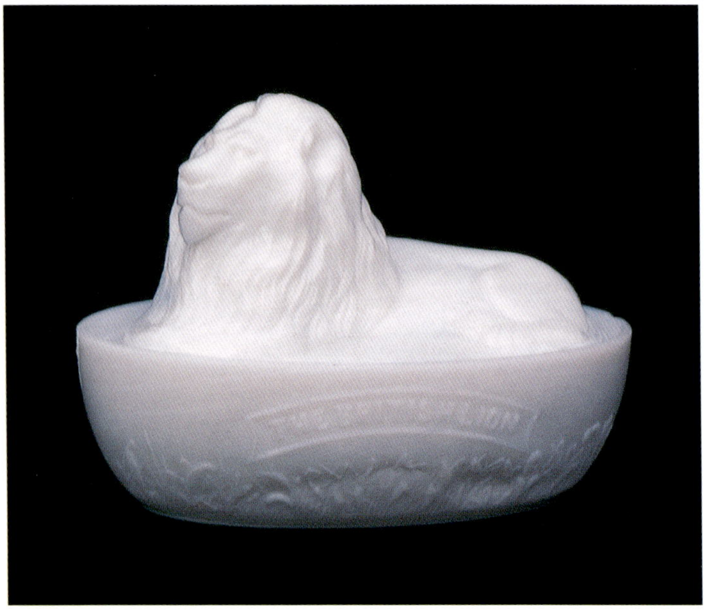

The British Lion, maker unknown, circa 1870s, 6 1/4" x 3 1/2". Opal, $145-175.

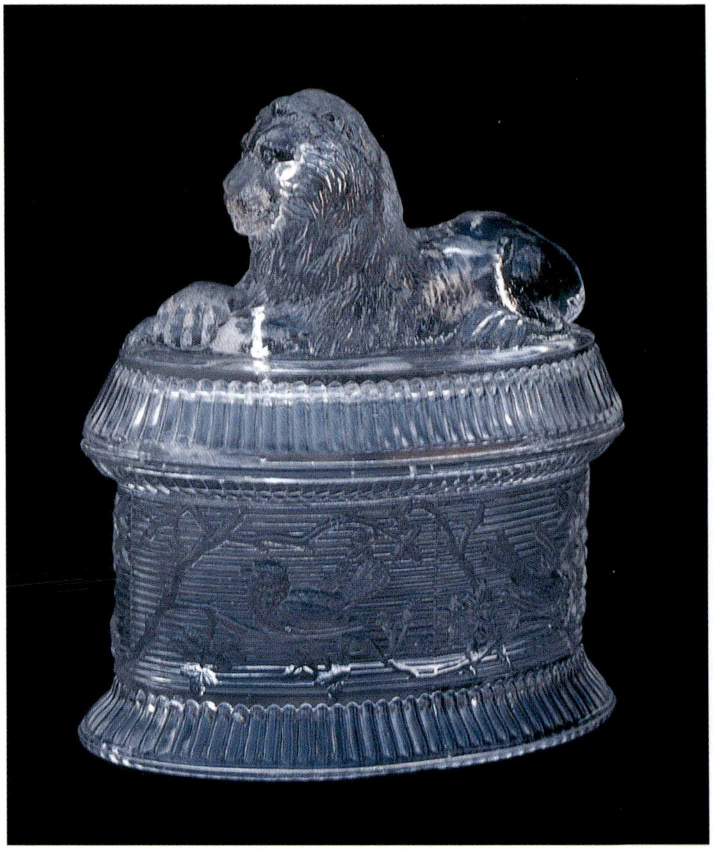

Majestic Lion covered dish, maker unknown, circa late 1870s. Clear, $350-375.

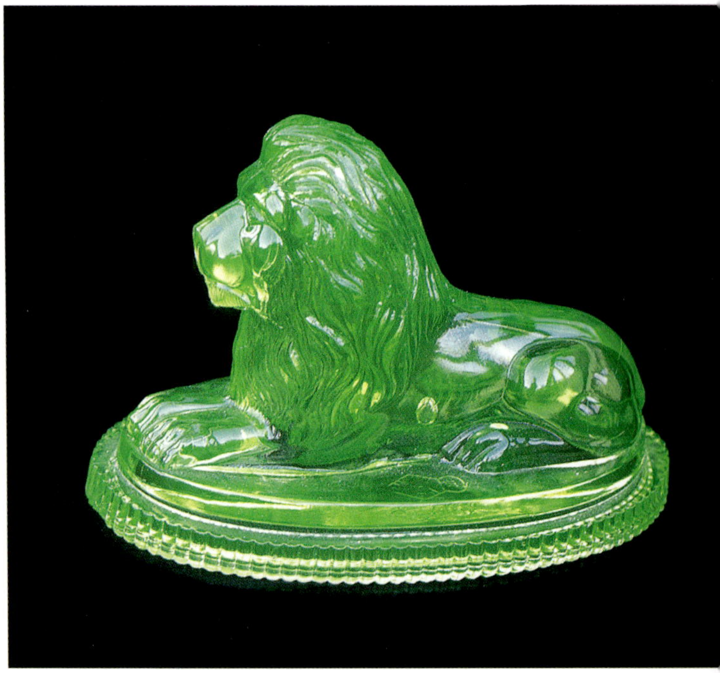

John Derbyshire's Green Lion, circa 1874, 7 1/4" x 4 1/4". $265-295.

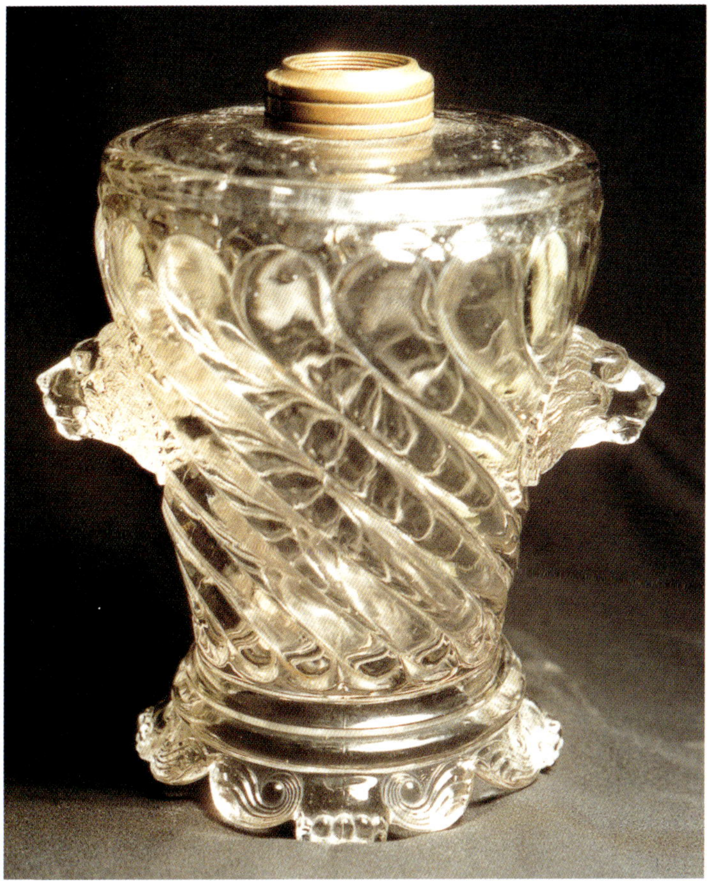

Lion Lamp made by the Model Flint Glass Company, circa 1892. This attribution is made by the description in the text and by the Twist pattern attributed to the Model Company. Clear, $275-300.

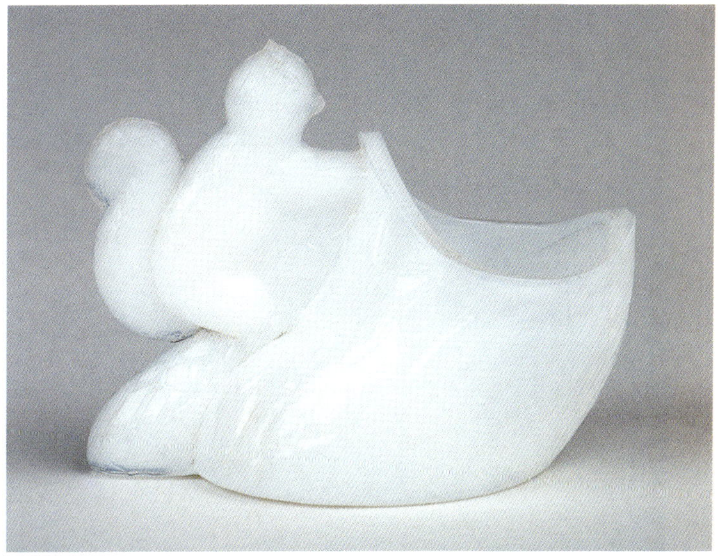

Opal squirrel saltcellar, maker and date of manufactuer unknown. $100-135.

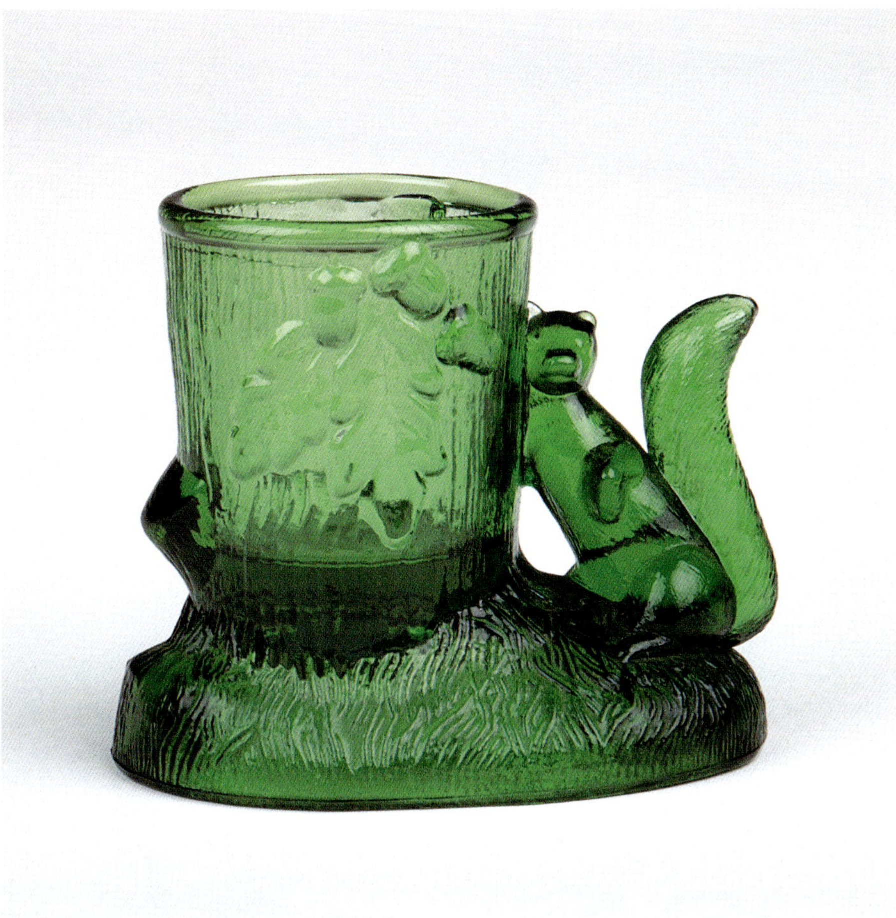

Green squirrel with tree trunk toothpick holder, maker and date of manufactuer unknown, 3" high. $130-150.

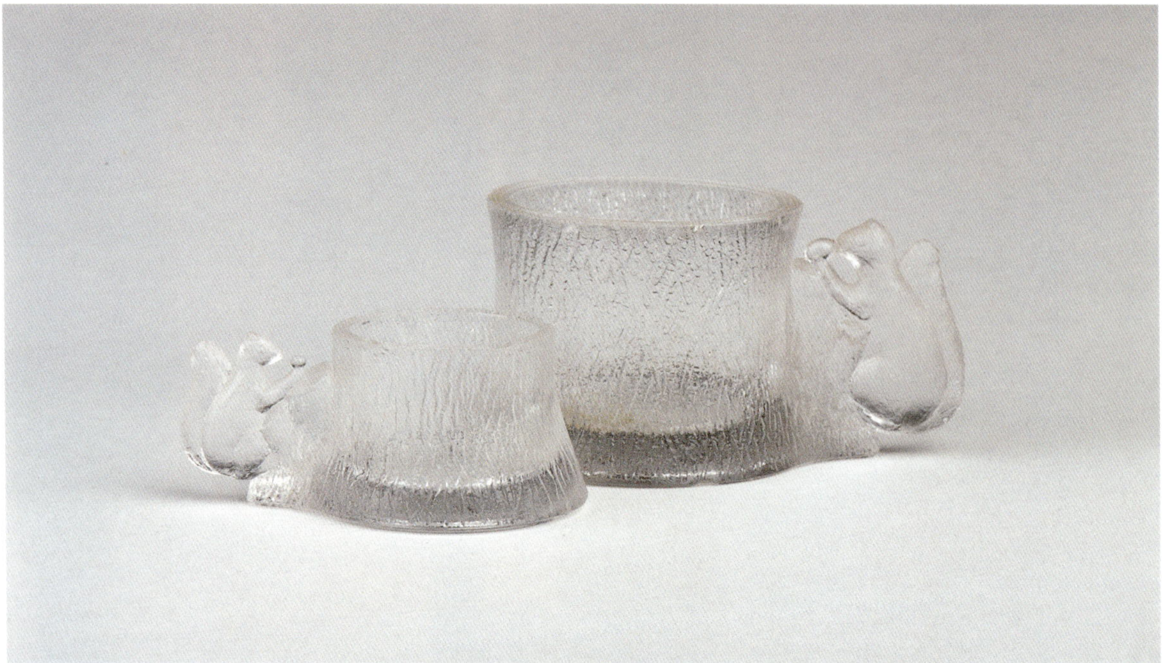

Squirrel saltcellars.
$75-95.

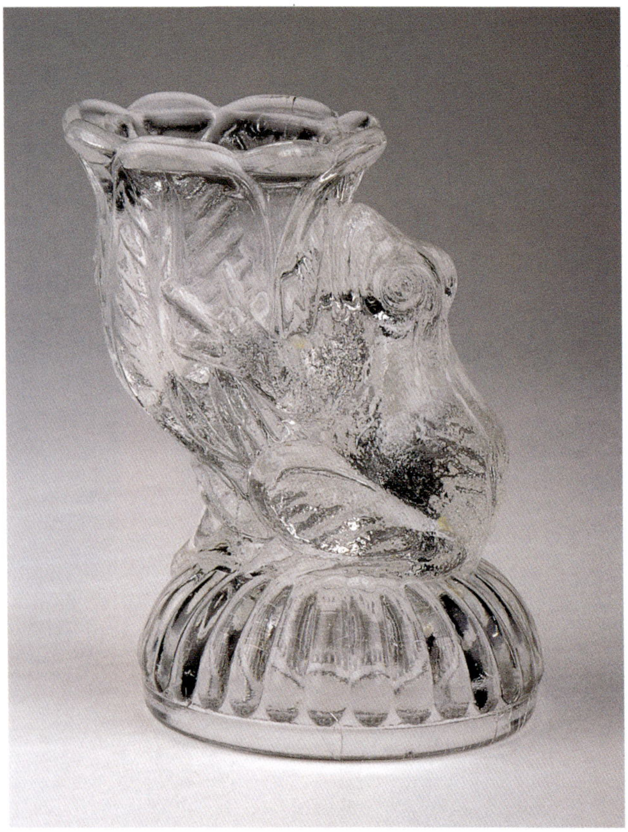

Frog, also known as Frog on Lily Pad, made by the Co-operative Flint Glass Co., circa 1880s, 3 1/2" high and 2" wide. Clear, $35-45. Colors, $45-65.

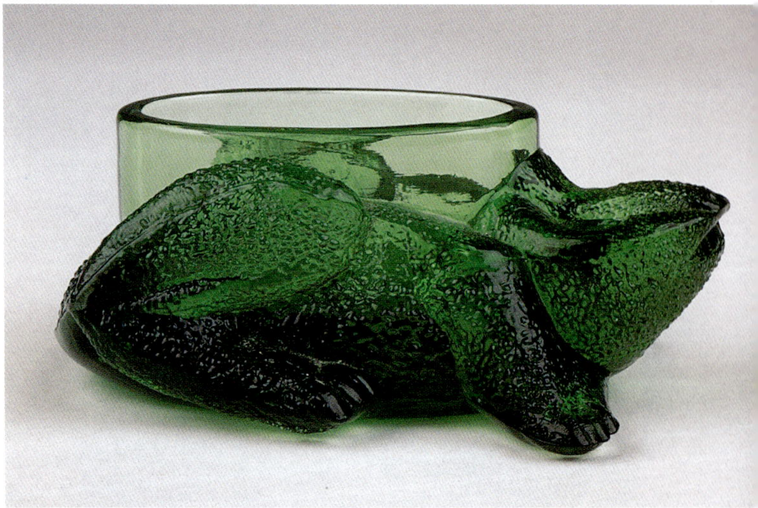

Green Frog saltcellar, maker and date of manufactuer unknown.
$85-125.

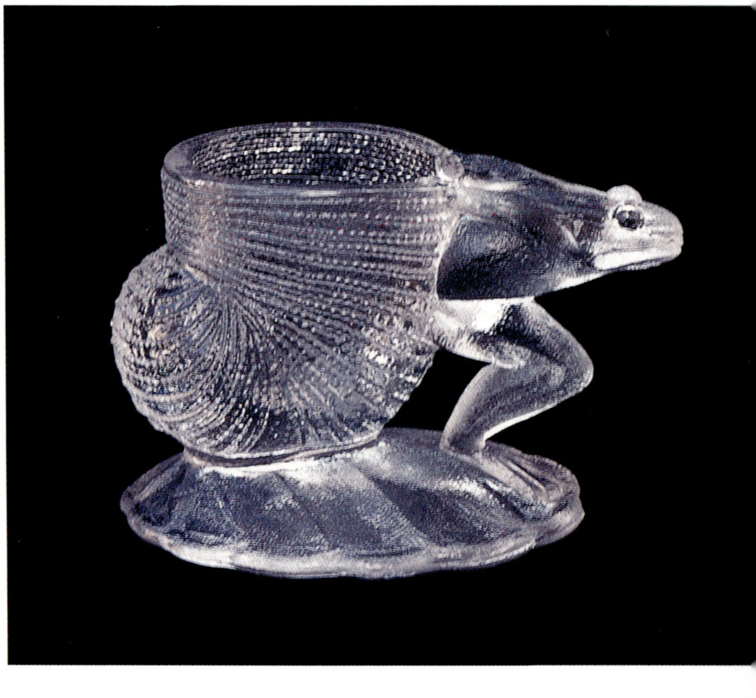

Frog and Shell made by the Ohio Flint Glass Co., circa 1897, 3 3/4" x 1 1/2" at the top. Clear, $125-135.

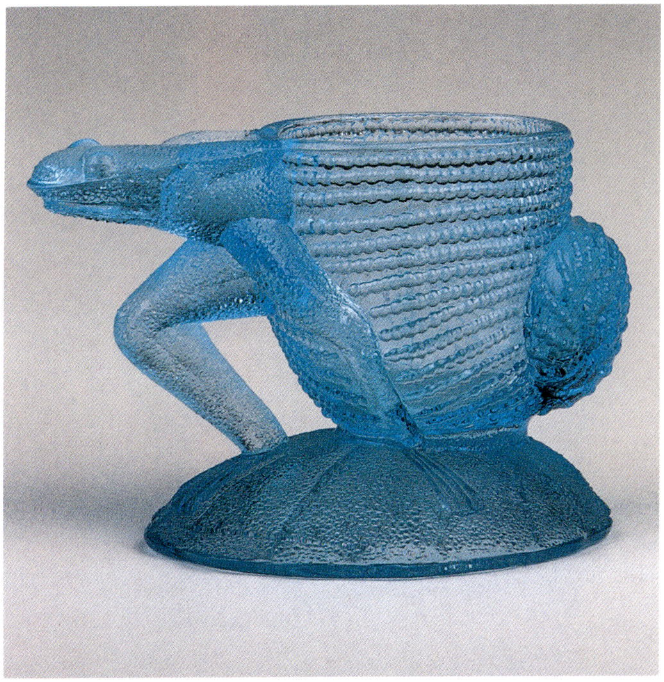

Reproduction of Frog and Shell by L. G. Wright.

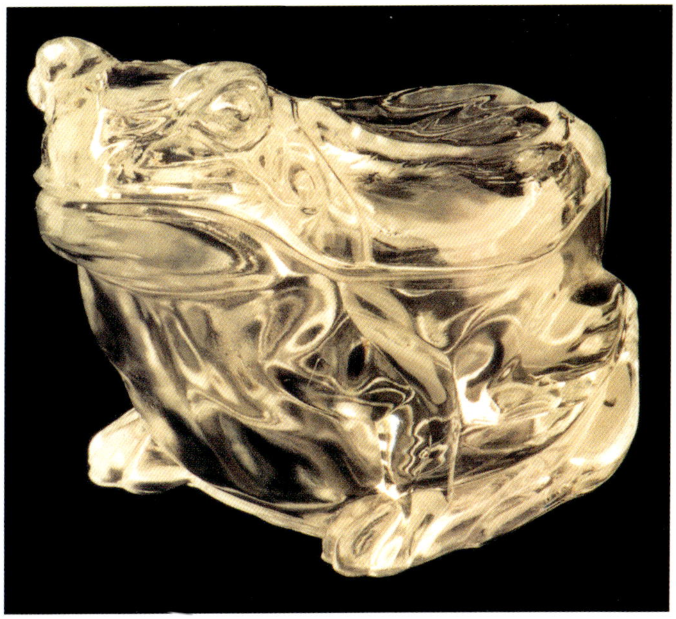

Frog covered dish made by the Co-operative Flint Glass Co., 5 1/2" long and 3 3/4" high. Clear, $75-125.

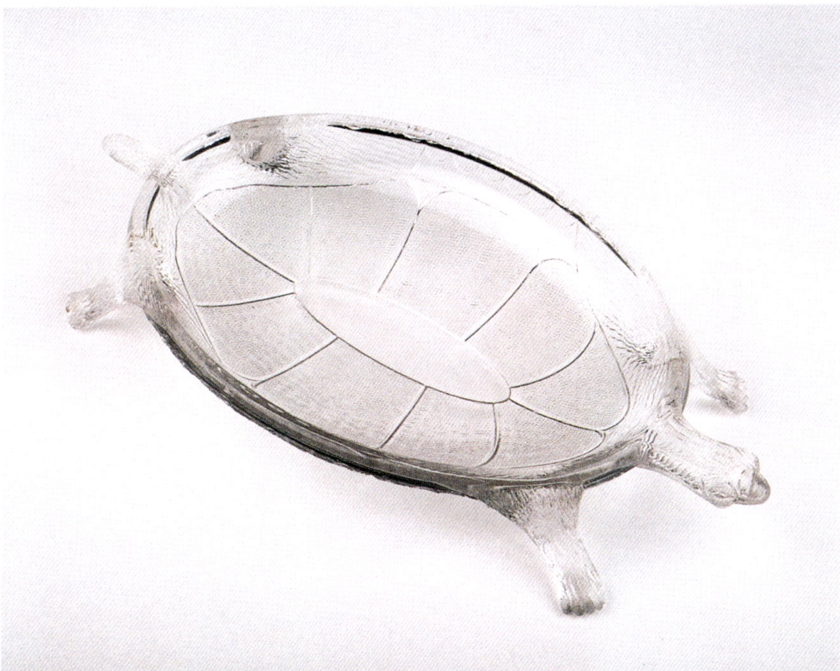

Turtle relish dish, maker and date of manufactuer unknown, 10" long. Clear, $85-125.

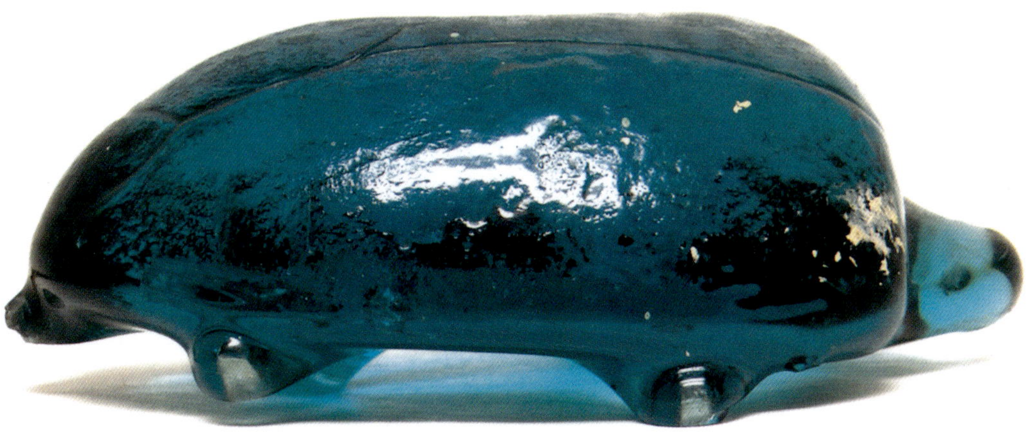

Turtle whimsy made by the workers *after hours* at the Hemingray Glass Co. Clear, amber, and blue, $100-300.

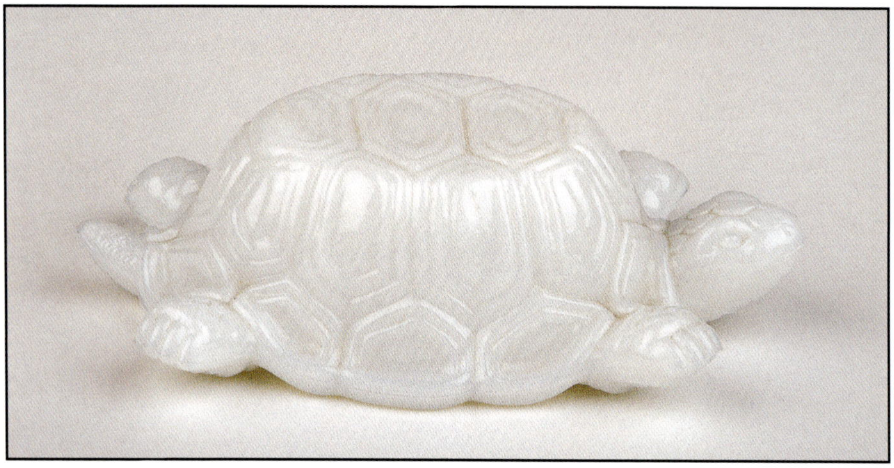 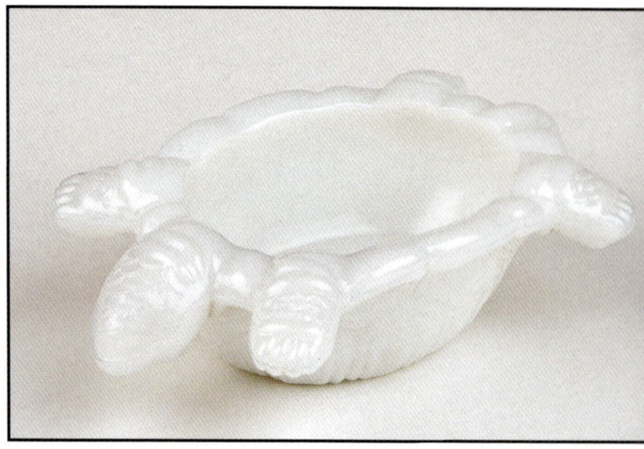

Opal Turtle made by Hobbs, Brockunier & Co., circa 1875, 4 3/8" long. Opal, $185-225.

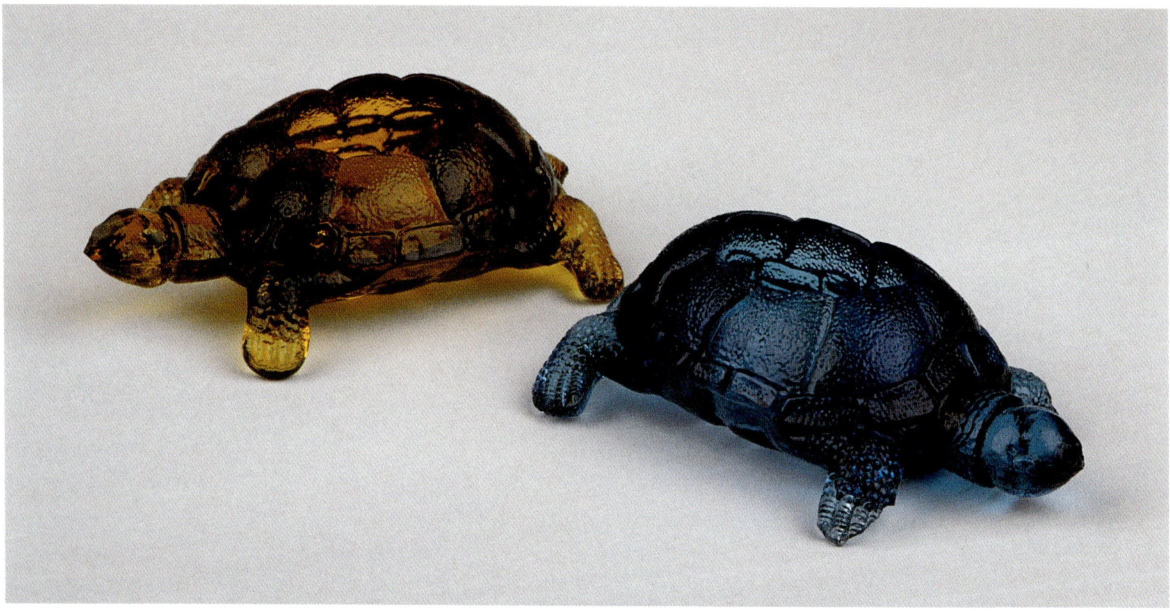

Turtle saltcellar made by the Bellaire Goblet Co., circa 1886-1890, 3 3/8" long. Clear, $75-95. Amber, $125-145. Blue, $135-165.

Turtle saltcellar made by Hobbs, Brockunier & Co., circa 1875, 3 1/8" long. Clear, $75-95. Opal, $145-185.

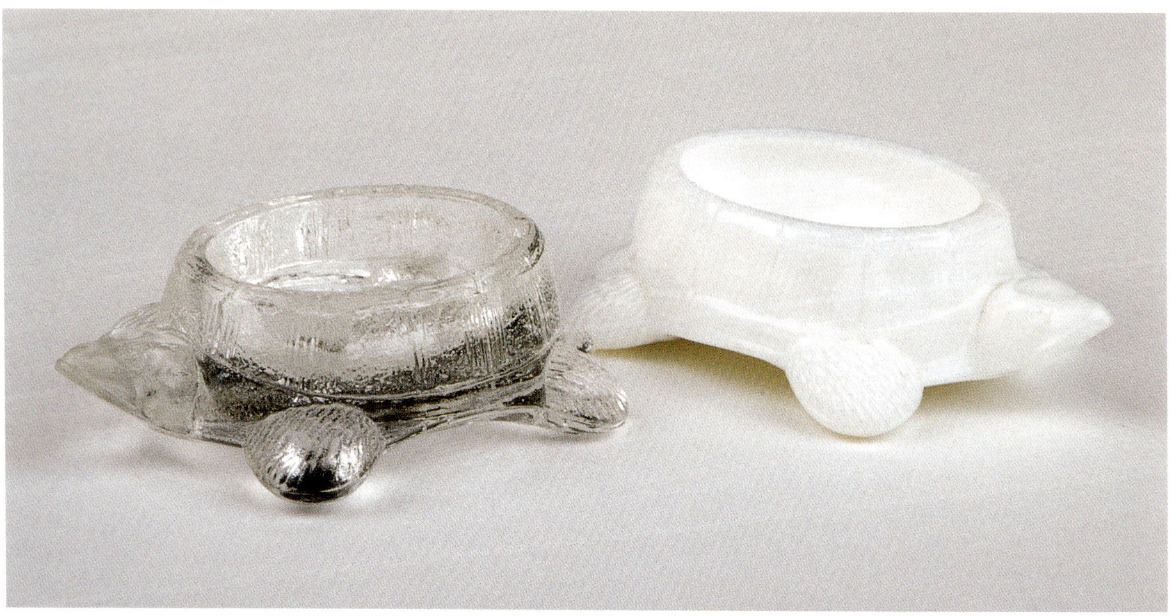

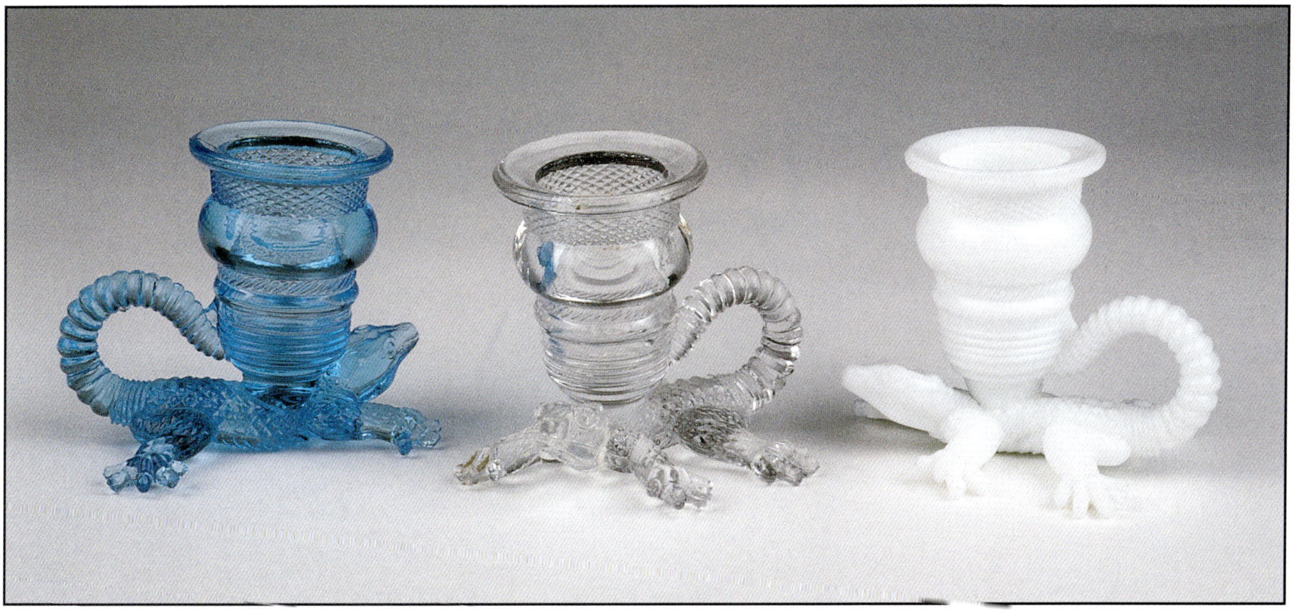

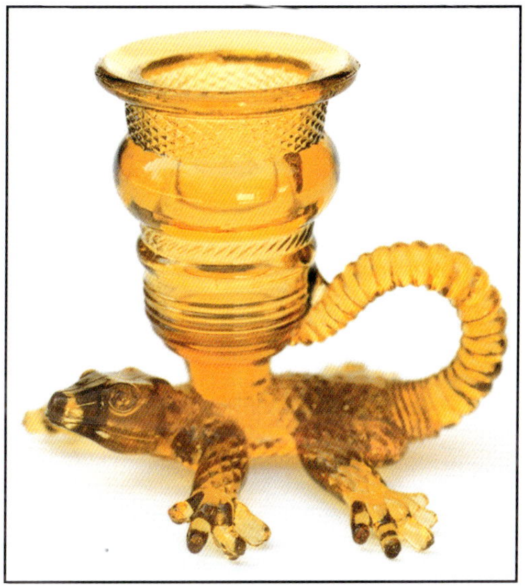

Alligator, maker unknown, circa 1890, 3" high and 3 5/8" wide. Clear, $180-195. Amber, $240-260. Blue, $280-325. Opal, $240-260.

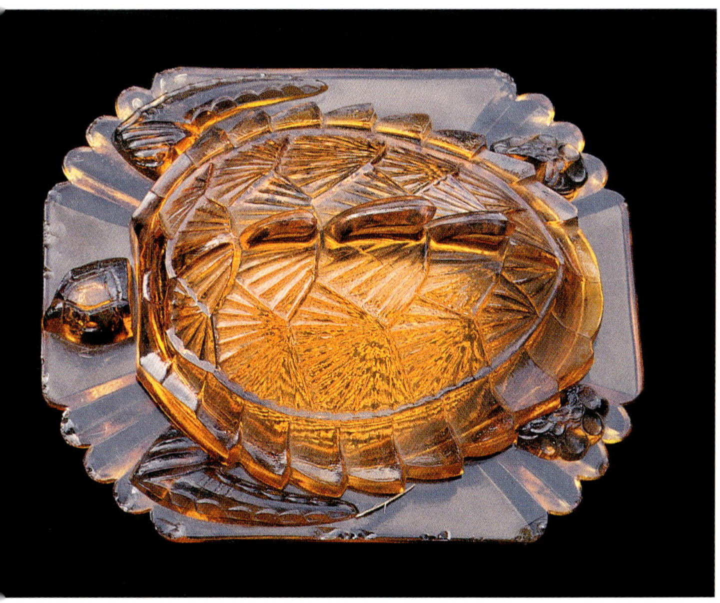

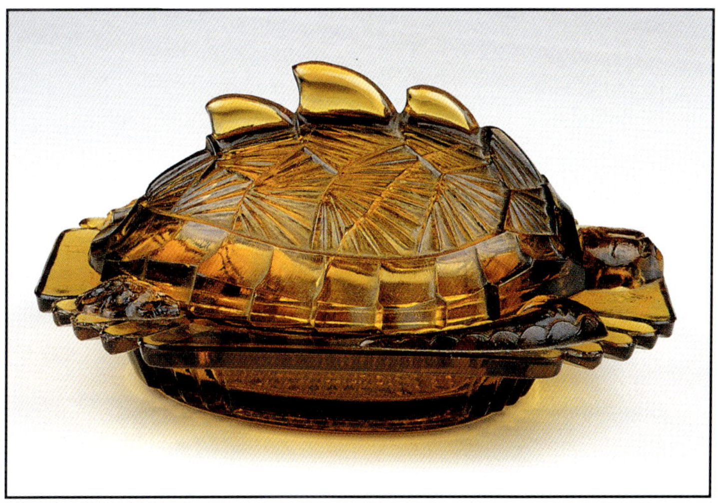

Sea Turtle butter dish, maker and date of manufactuer unknown, 7" long. $250-350.

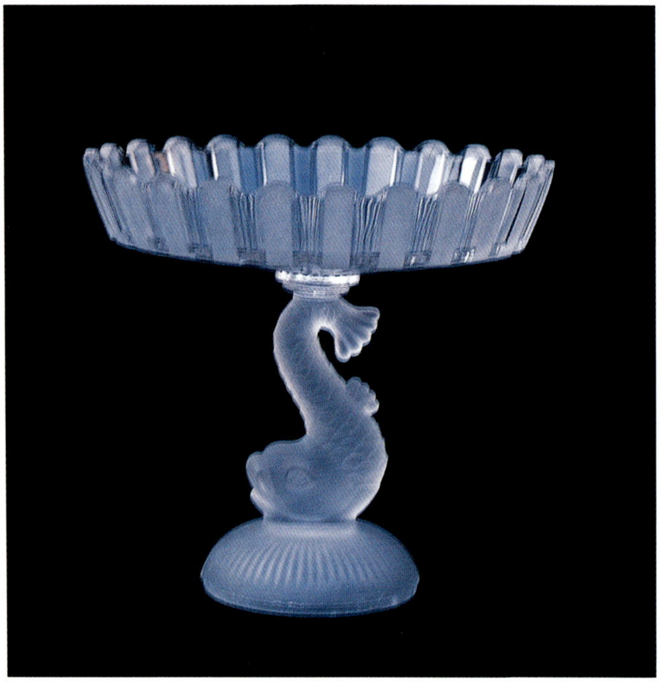

Ribbon Dolphin compote made by Bakewell, Pears & Co., circa 1870, 10 1/2" diameter. $245-265.

(*Below*) Dolphin covered dish made by the Indiana Tumbler and Goblet Co. All illustrated here are minus lids. From the left are saw tooth mouth in red agate, $300-350; smooth mouth in chocolate, $400-450; smooth mouth in golden agate, $600-650; and serrated mouth in chocolate, $125-150. Values are for complete items with covers.

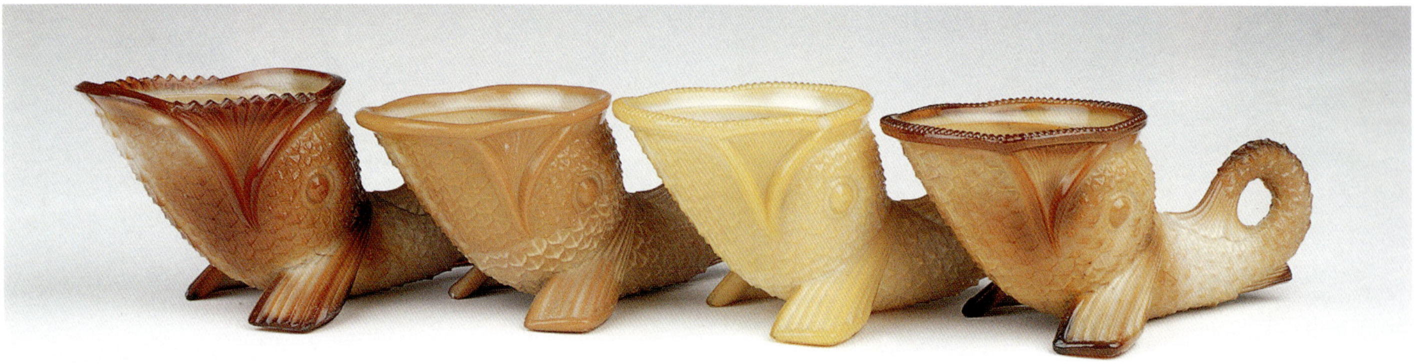

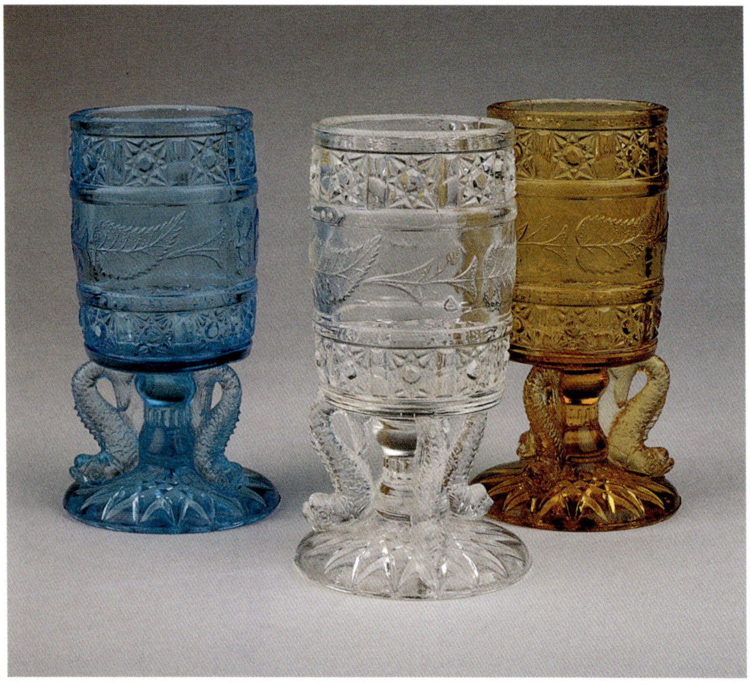

Dolphin match holder, maker and date of manufactuer unknown, 4 1/2" high and 2" wide. Clear, $40-50. Colors, $70-85.

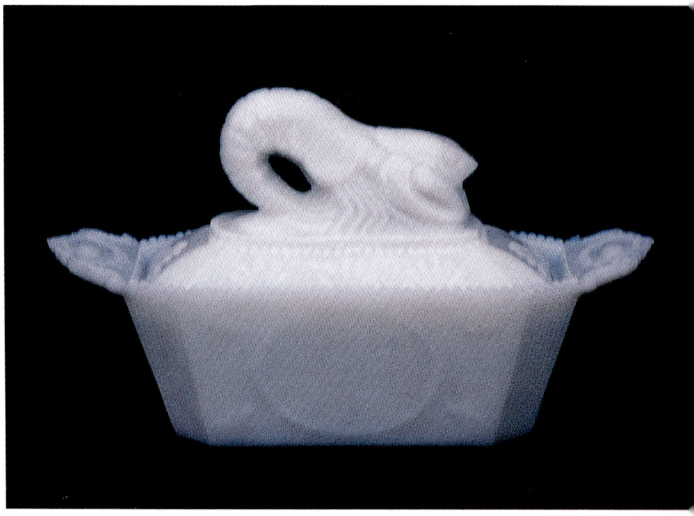

Crawfish covered dish made by the Westmoreland Specialty Co., circa 1890, 7 3/4" x 3 3/8". Opal, $220-240.

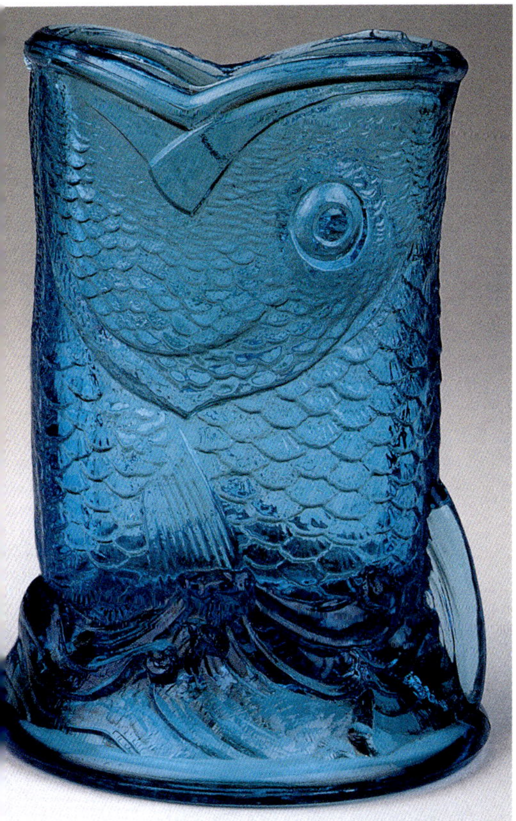

Menagerie spoon holder for children's table set made by Bryce, Higbee and Co., circa 1886. 3 1/2" high and 2 1/4" wide. Clear, $85-95. Amber, $100-115. Blue, $125-145.

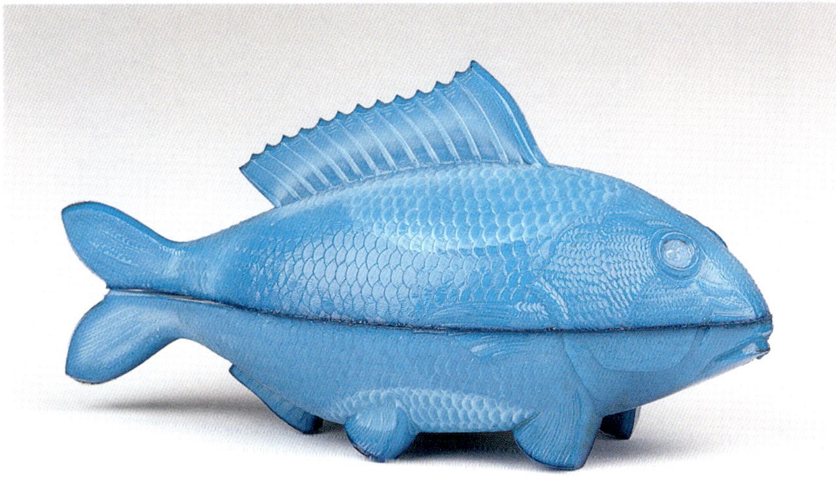

Fish covered dish made by Atterbury and Co., 8 1/2" long. Blue opaque, $2,000-2,250.

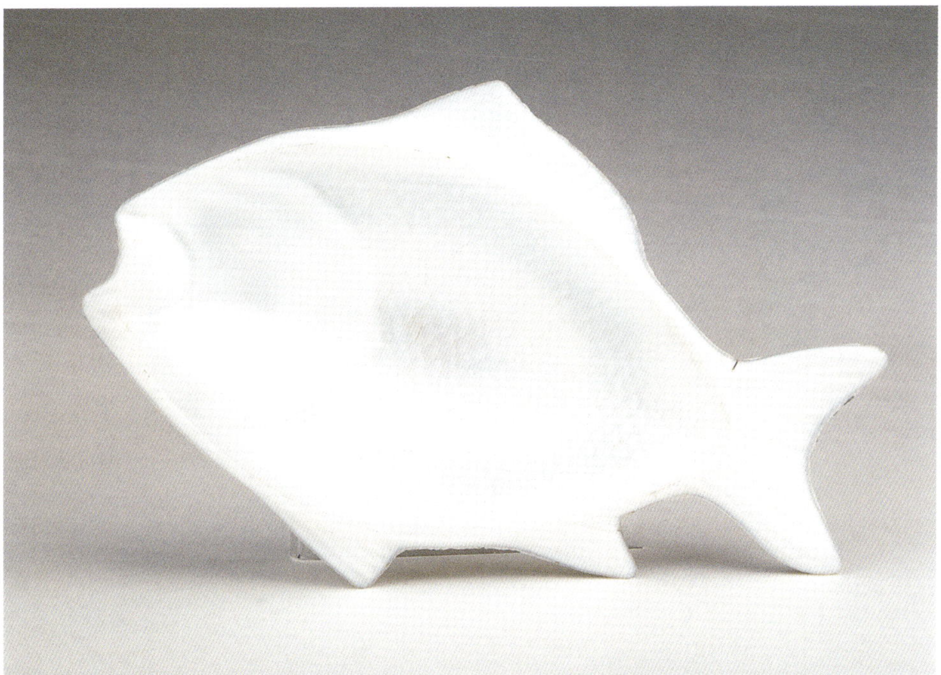

Fish made by Atterbury and Co. *Patented June 4 1872*. 9 5/8" long. Opal, $50-70.

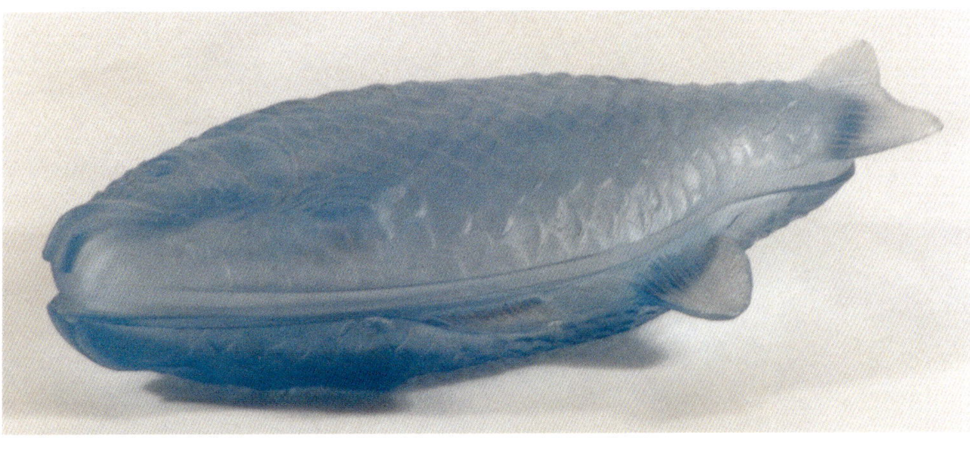

Fish covered dish, maker and date of manufactuer unknown, 8 1/4" long and 4 3/4" wide. Blue, $200-250.

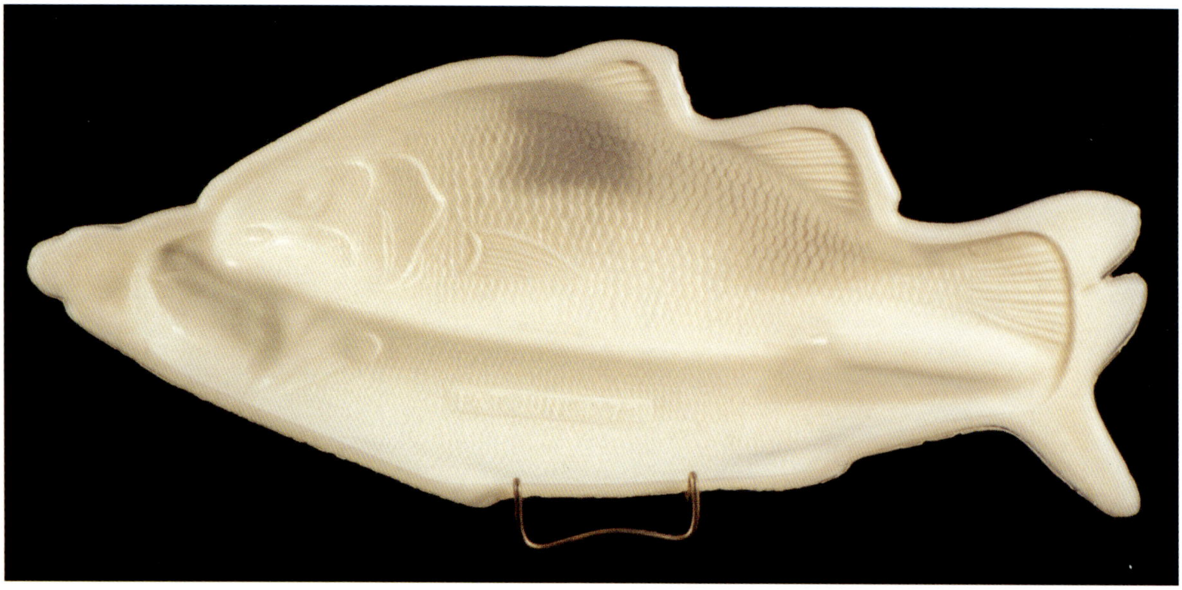

Fish pickle dish made by Atterbury and Co. *Pat. June 4 '72*. 11" long and 4 1/2" wide. Opal, $150-200.

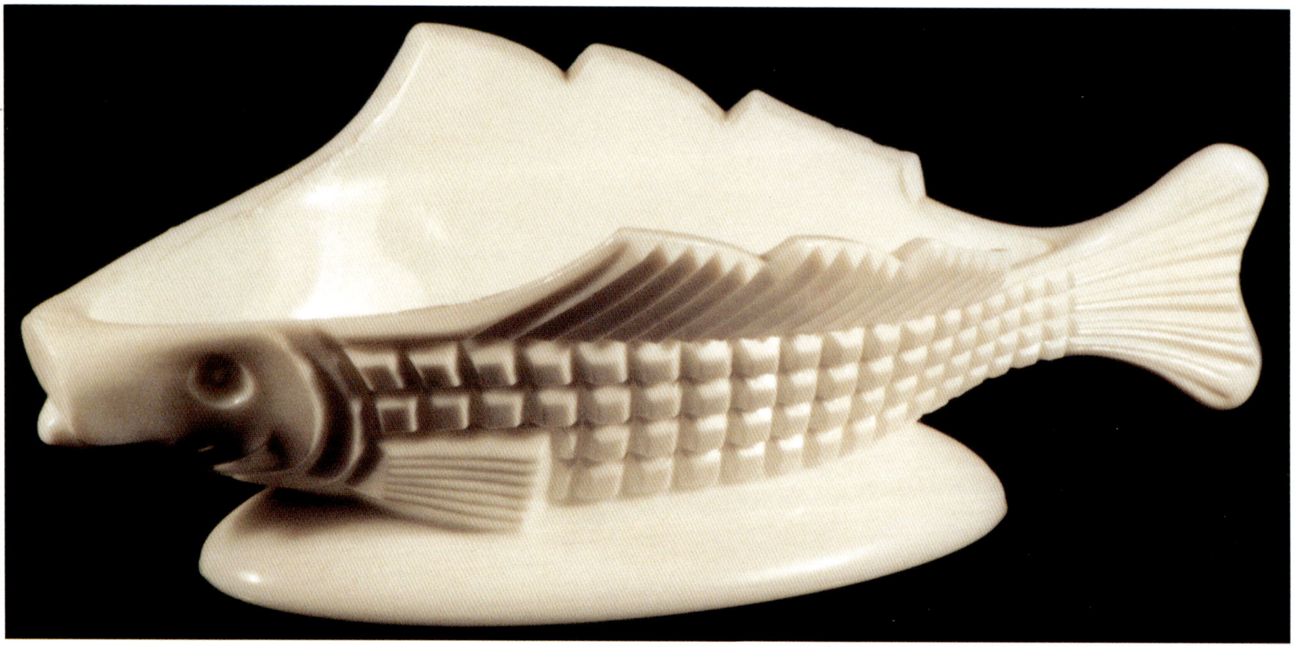

Fish pickle dish made by Challinor, Taylor and Co., circa 1891, 9" long and 4 3/8" wide. Opal, $200-250.

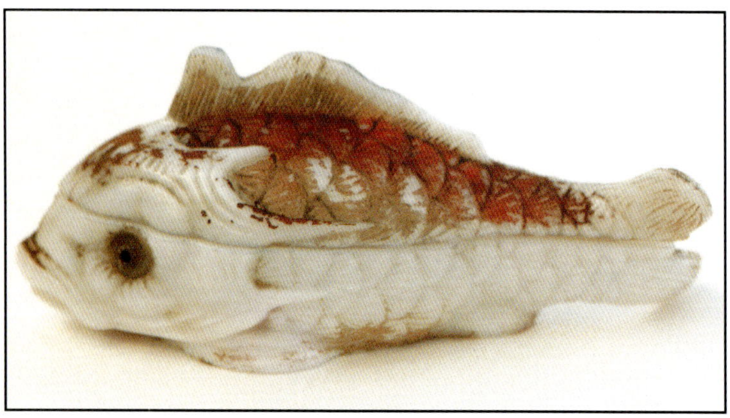

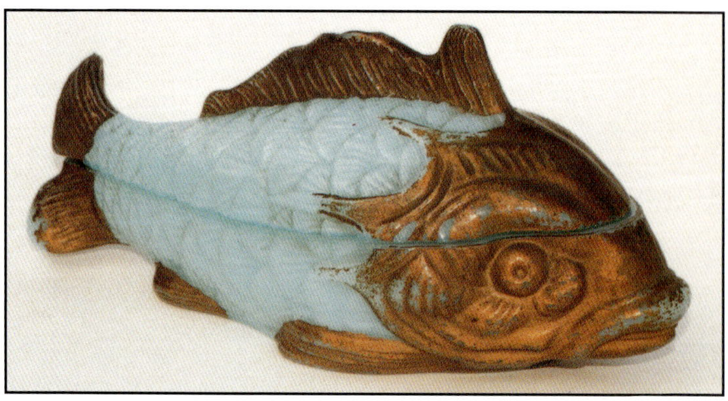

Fish covered dish made by Vallerysthal, circa 1901, 7 1/2" long. Opal, $250-300. Blue opaque, $500-700.

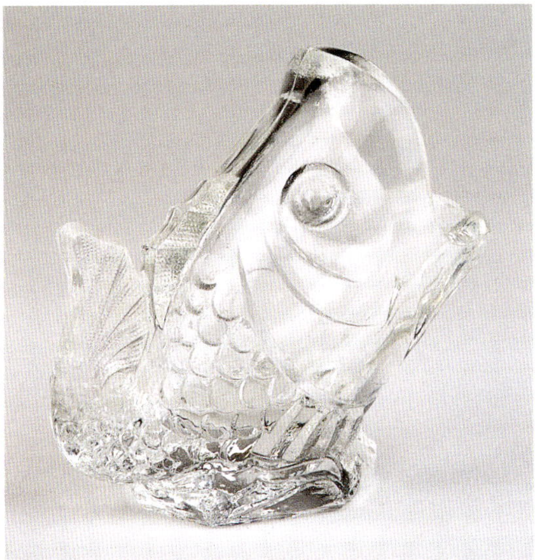

Fish toothpick holder, maker and date of manufactuer unknown, 3" high and 1 3/4" wide. Clear, $45-55. Blue, $55-65.

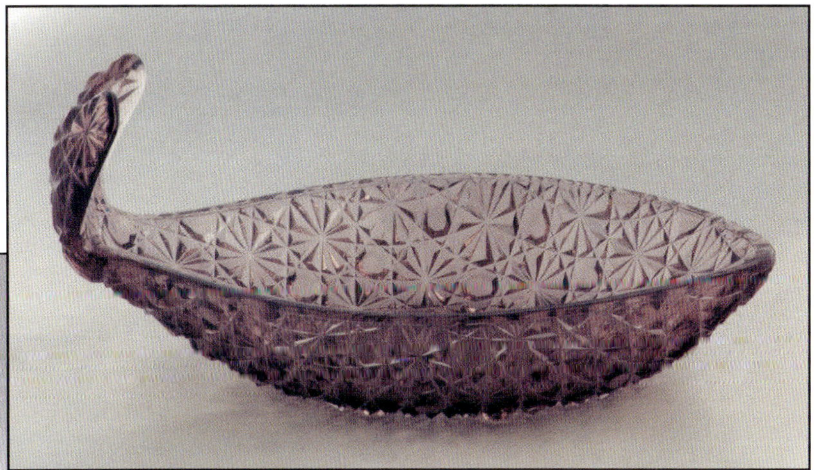

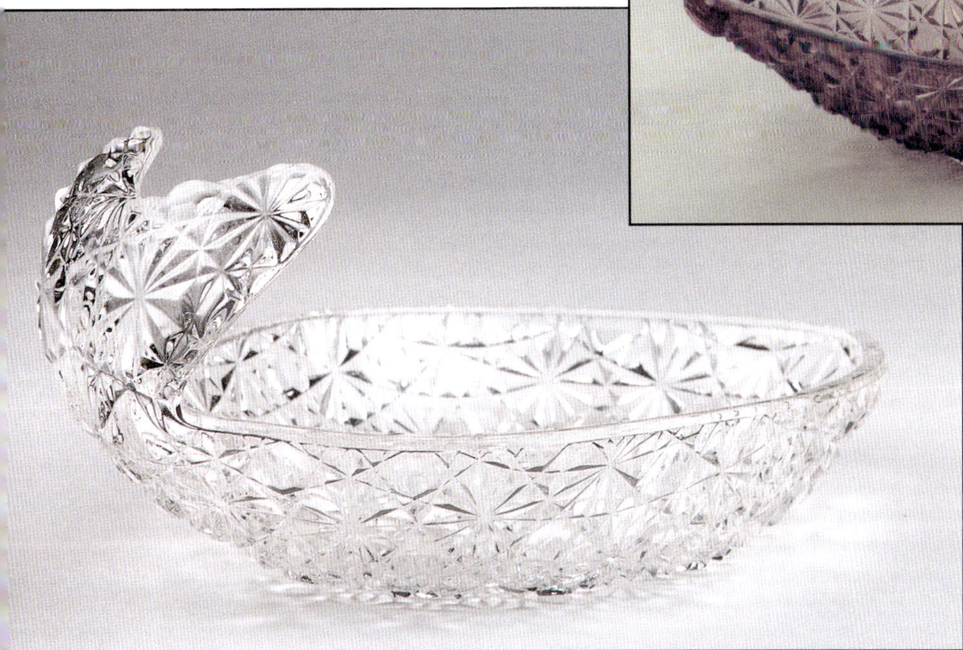

Fish relish dish in the Fashion pattern made by Bryce Brothers, circa late 1880s, 5 3/4" long and 4" wide. Clear, $55-70. Amethyst, $90-125.

Entwined Fish covered dish made by Atterbury and Co., circa 1889, 7 1/2" diameter. Opal, $200-235.

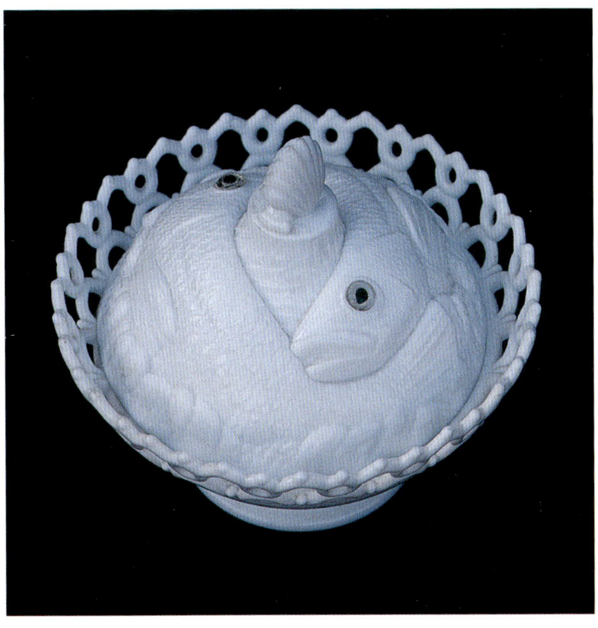

Fish covered dish made by the Central Glass Co., circa 1890, 10" x 3 1/4". Clear frosted, $225-265.

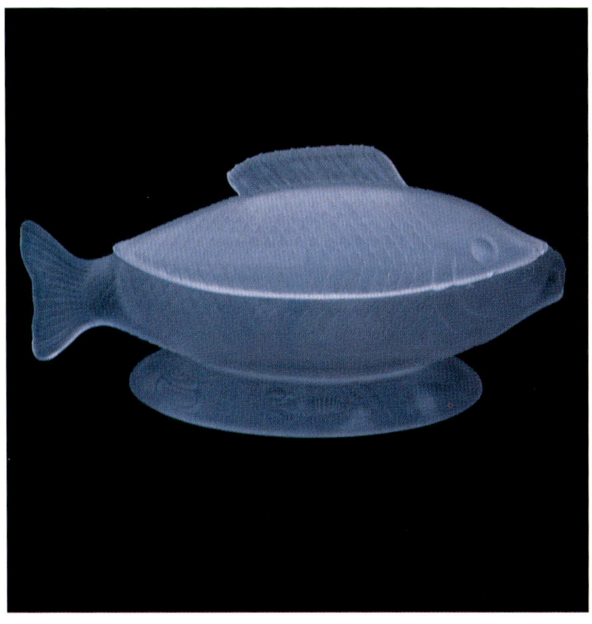

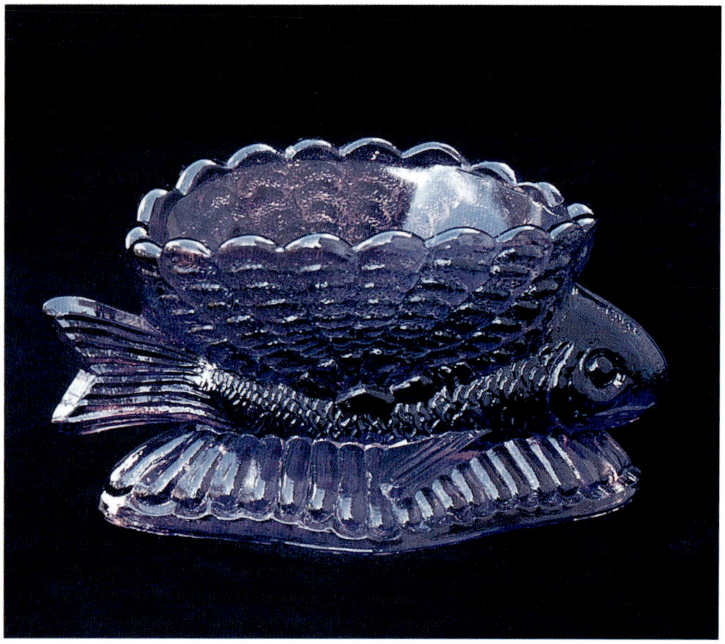

Flying Fish salt, maker unknown, circa 1890-1900, 2 3/8" high and 4" long. $120-140.

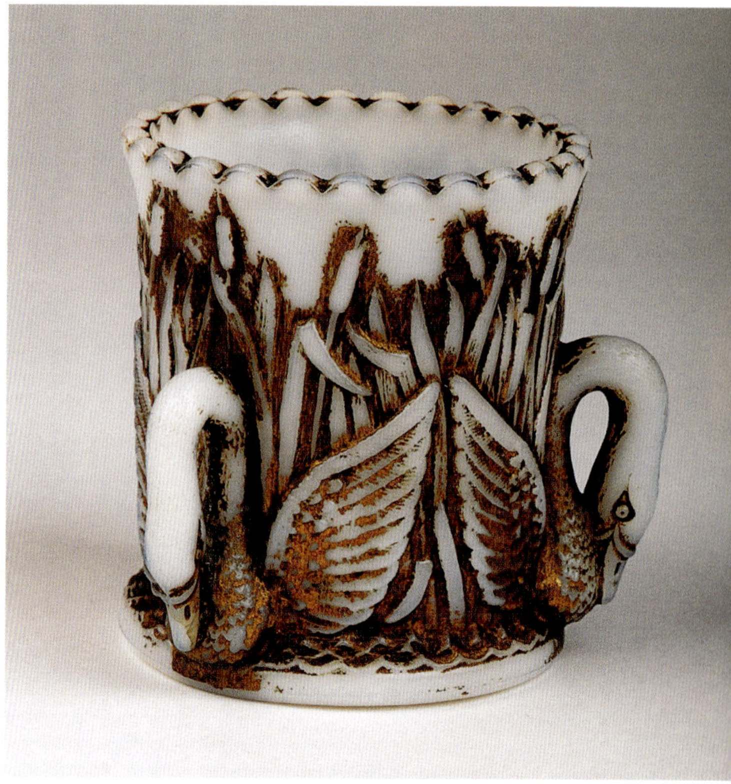

Swans in Rushes toothpick holder made by the Westmoreland Specialty Co., date of manufactuer unknown, 2 1/4" high and 2" wide. Opal, $50-70.

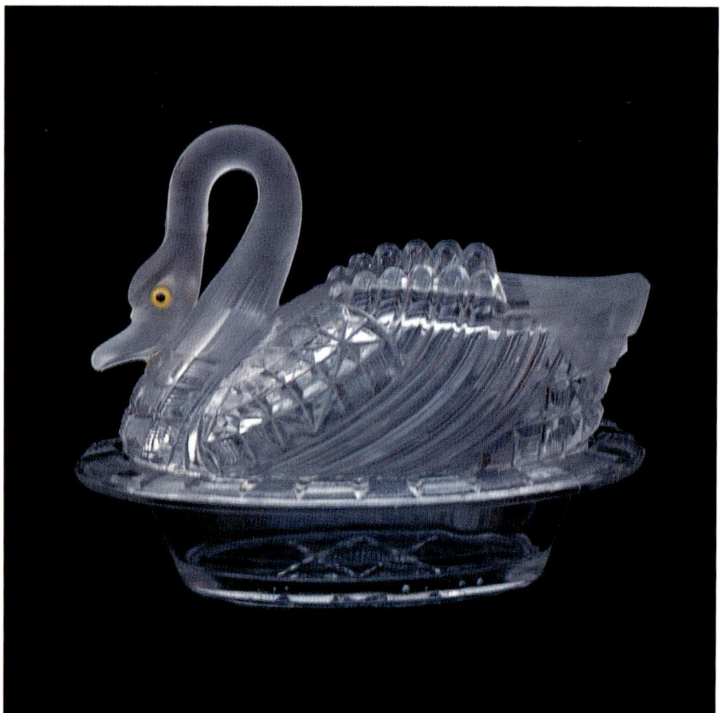

Swan, of the Challinor, Taylor Glass Co. Farm Yard Collection, circa 1891, 8" x 6 3/4" at the rim. $150-185.

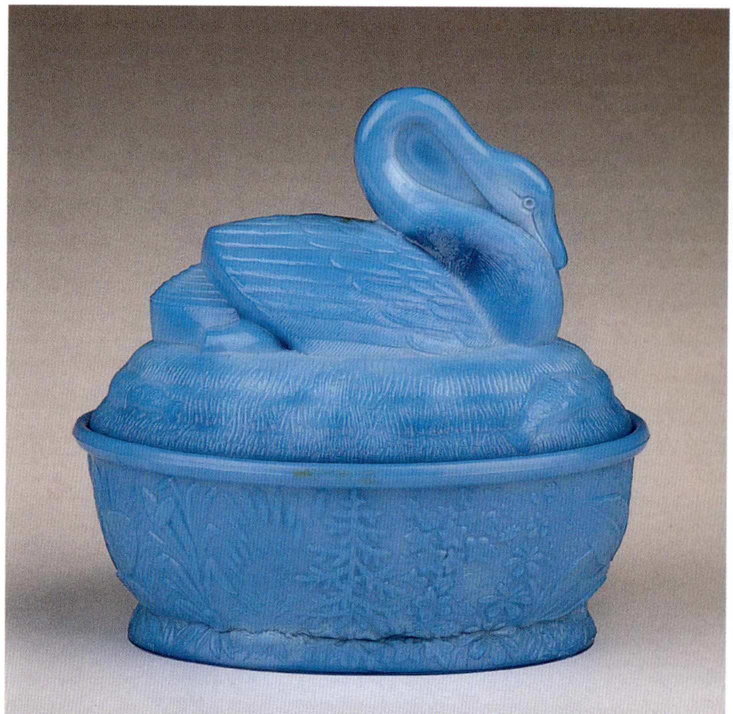

Swan covered dish made by Challinor, Taylor and Company, 7" long. Opal, $600-675. Blue Opaque, $2,500-2,750.

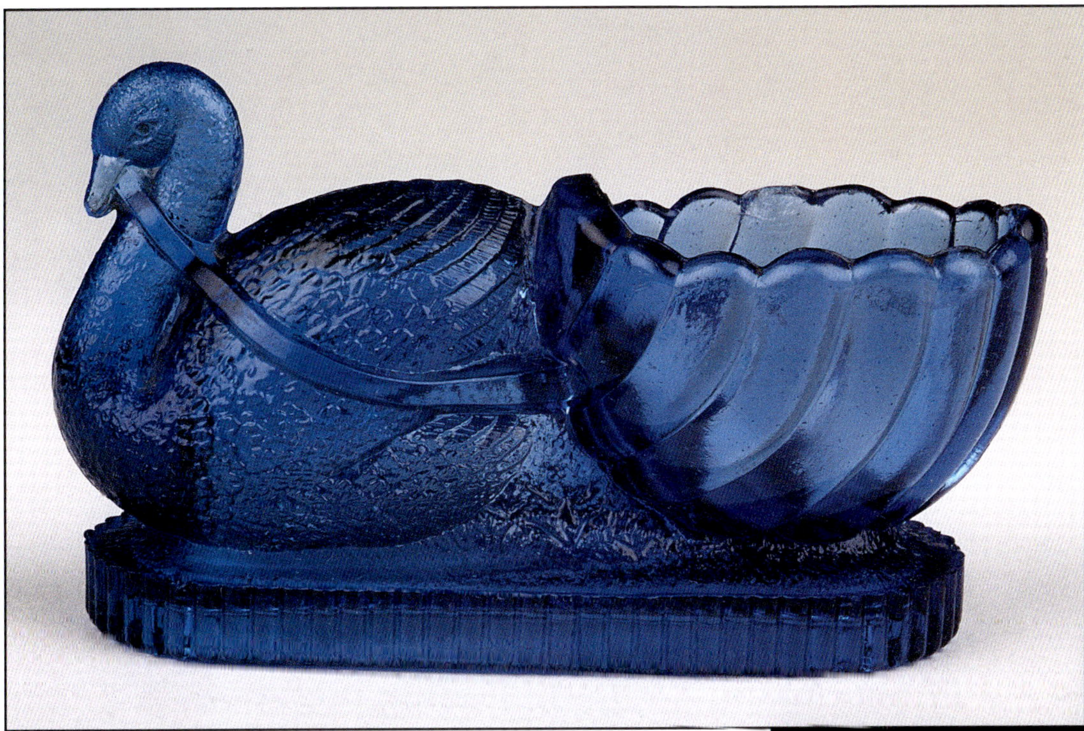

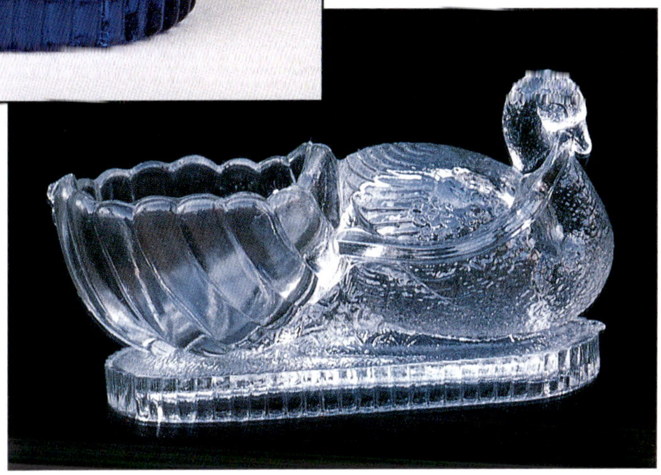

Swan toothpick holder made by the Mosiac Glass Co., circa 1891. Clear, $85-100. Amber, $150-160. Blue, $165-180.

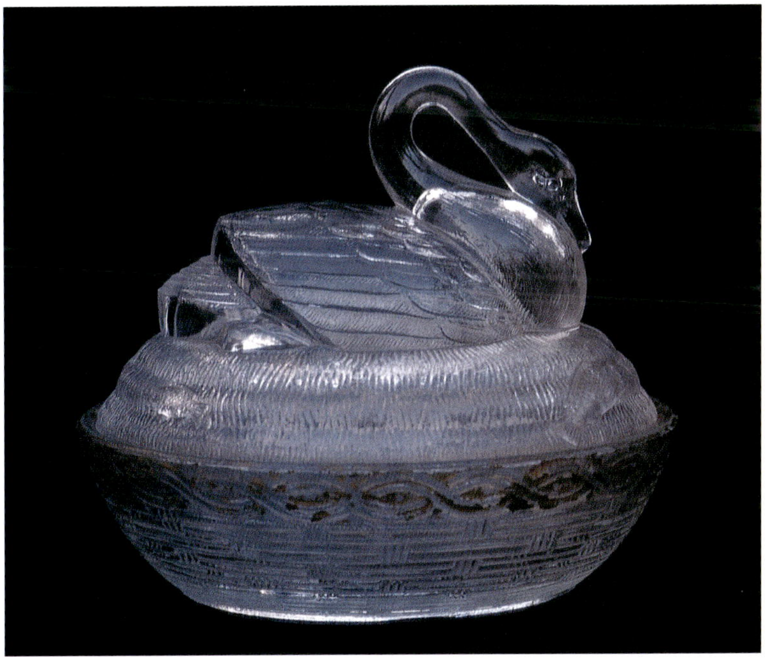

Swan covered dish made by Challinor, Taylor and Co., circa 1891, 7" x 5 1/2". Clear, $280-310.

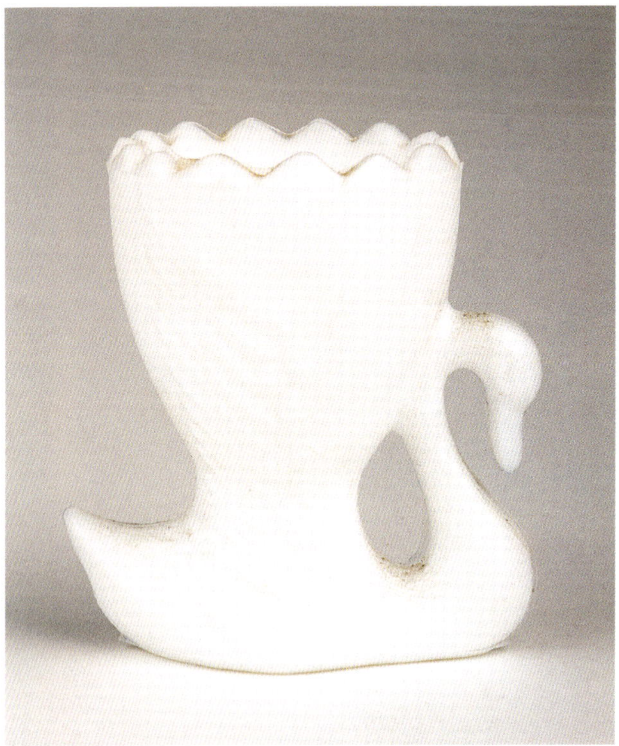

Swan opal toothpick holder, maker and date of manufactuer unknown, 2 1/2" long. $95-110.

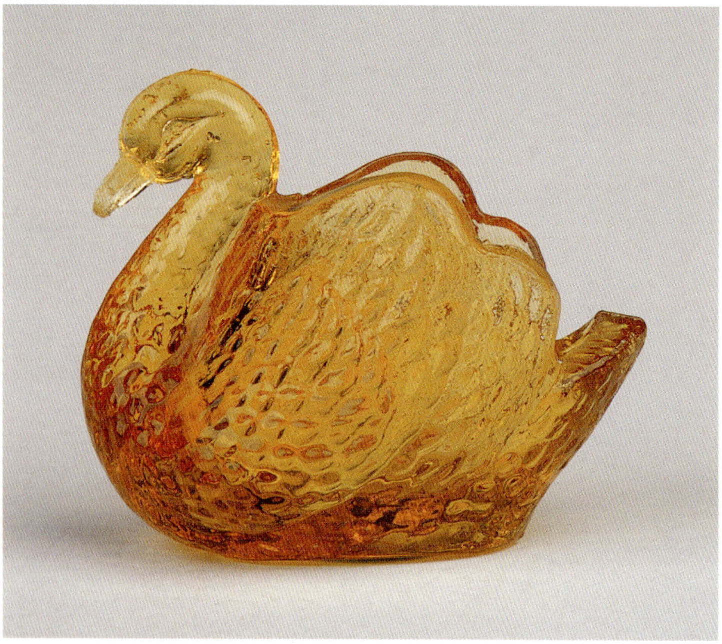

Swan toothpick holder, maker and date of manufactuer unknown, 2 1/2" long. Amber, $40-60.

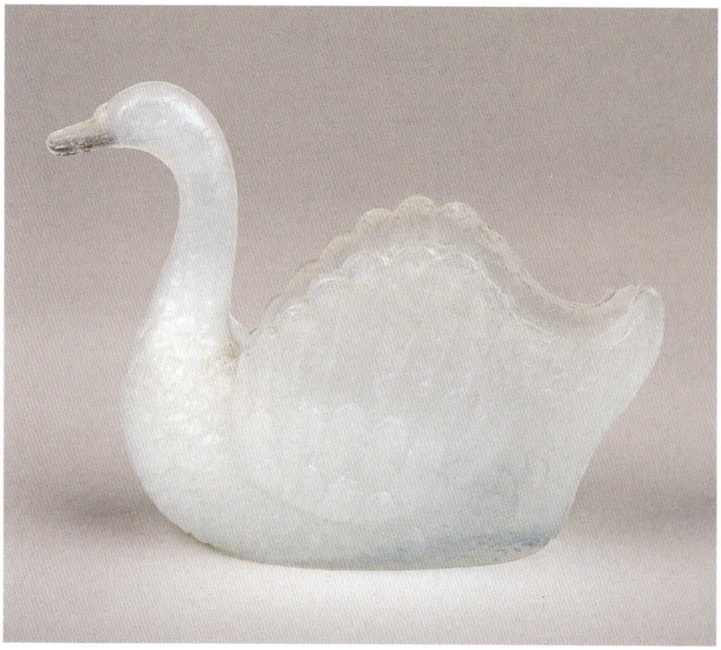

Swan saltcellar, maker and date of manufactuer unknown, 2 1/4" long. Opal, $45-55.

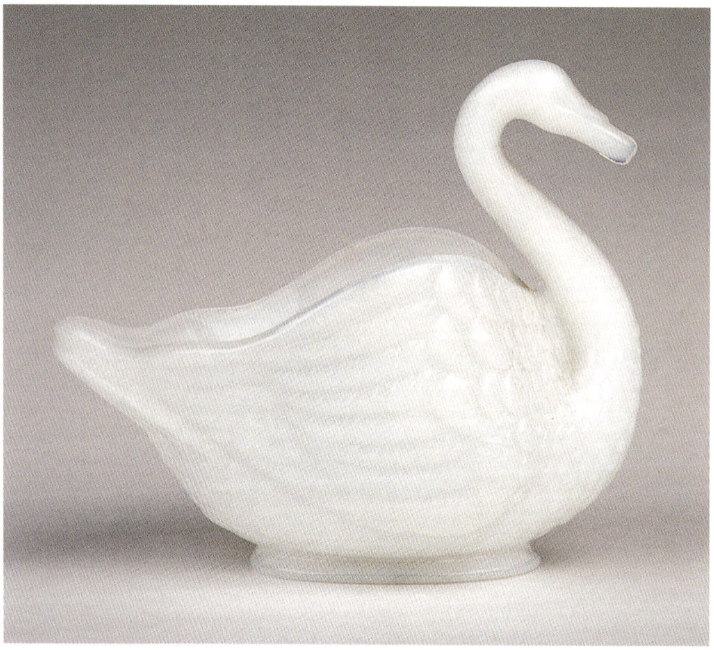

Swan, opal, maker and date of manufactuer unknown, 5" long. Opal, $90-100.

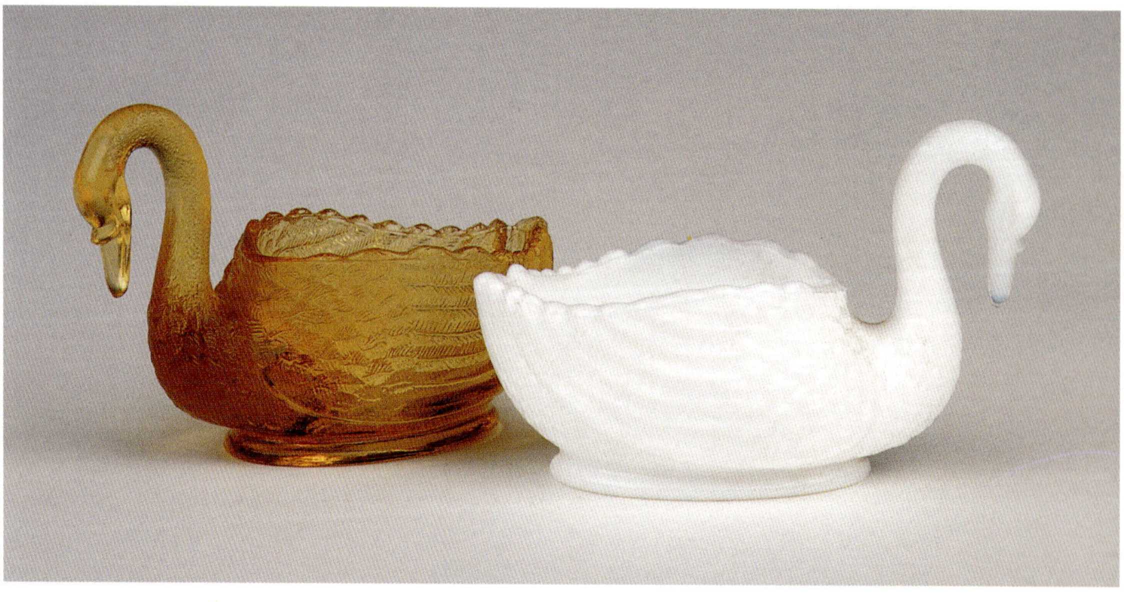

Swan saltcellar, maker and date of manufactuer unknown, 3 3/4" long. Amber, $40-60. White opaque, $45-65.

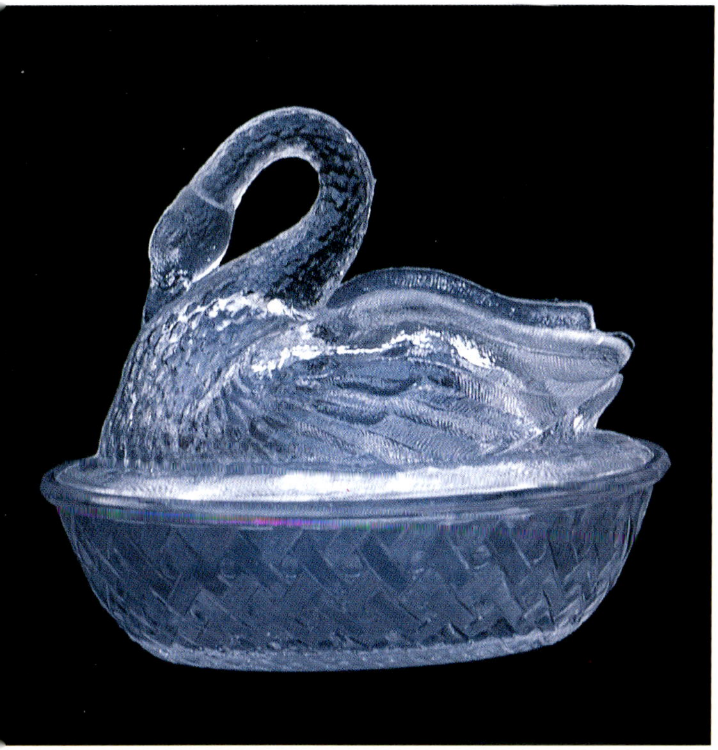

Swan made by the Belmont Glass Co., circa 1884, 6 1/4" high and 7" long. $200-225.

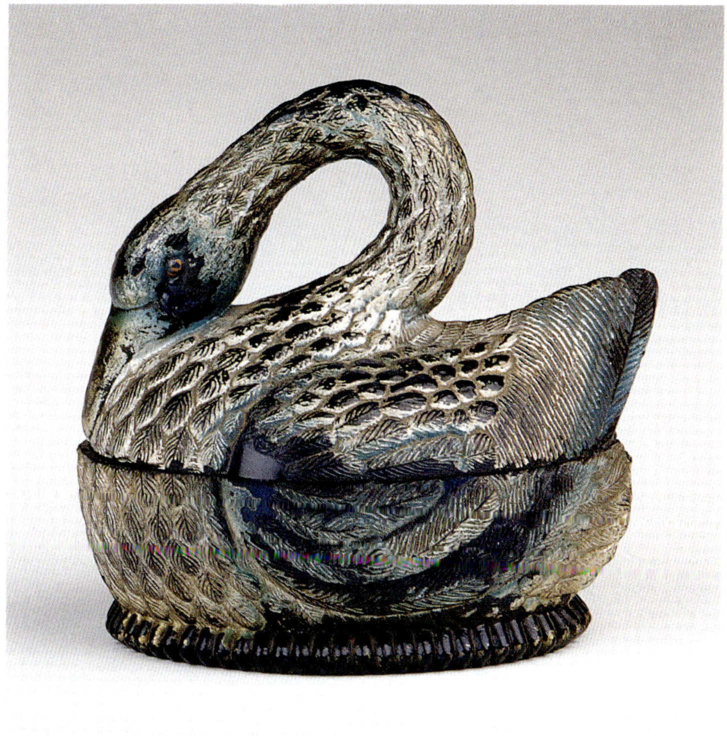

Swan covered dish made by Vallerysthal, date of manufactuer unknown, 5 1/2" long. Cobalt blue with gold, $500-550.

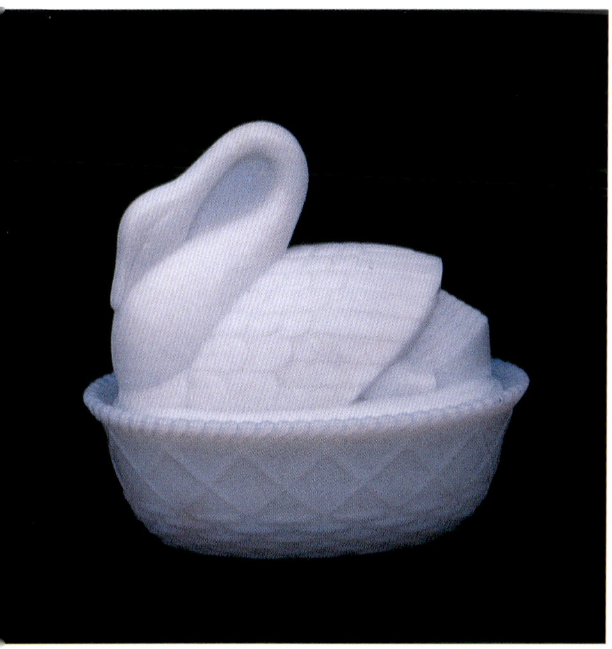

Swan made by the Westmoreland Specialty Co., circa 1890s, 5 1/2" x 4 1/2". Opal, $85-110.

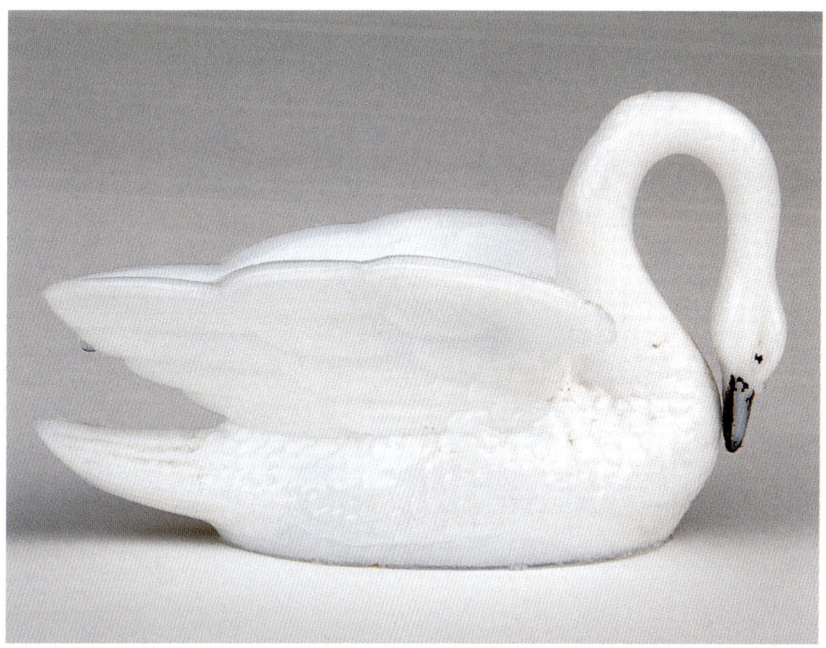

Opal Swan, head down with a black bill, made by Gillinder and Sons, date of manufactuer unknown, 5 1/2" long. $125-150.

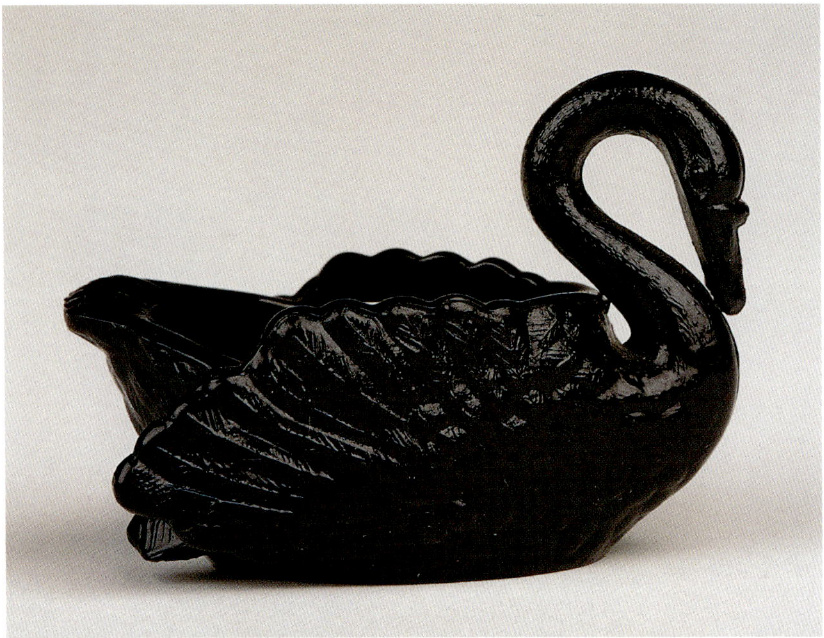

A black opaque Swan made by the Cambridge Glass Co., 3 1/4" long. $75-100.

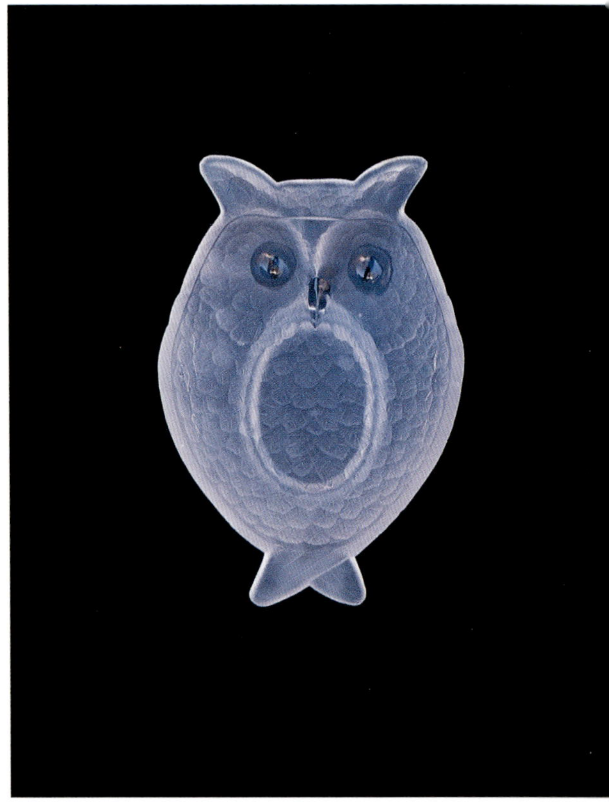

An Owl pickle dish made by the Central Glass Co., circa 1880s. 8" long. Clear, $80-90.

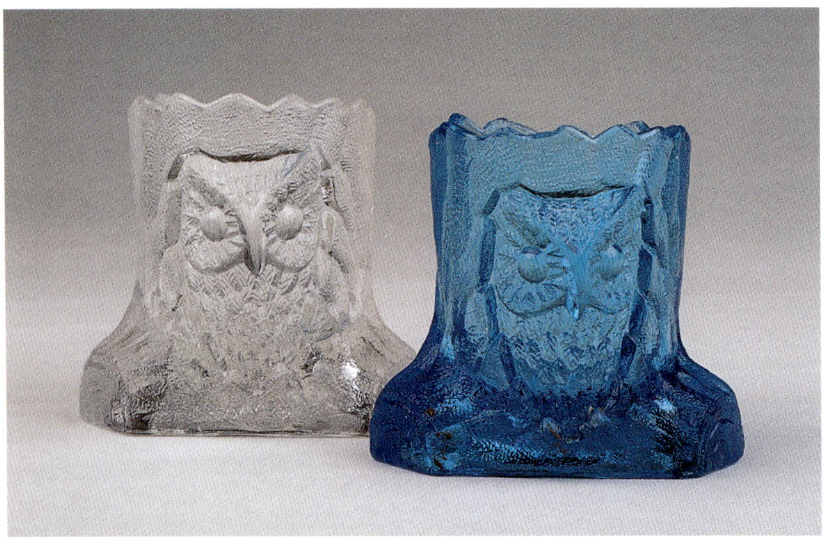

Owl in a Stump toothpick holder made by the Central Glass Co., circa 1880s, 2 1/2" high and 2 3/4" wide. Clear, $50-60. Blue, $70-95.

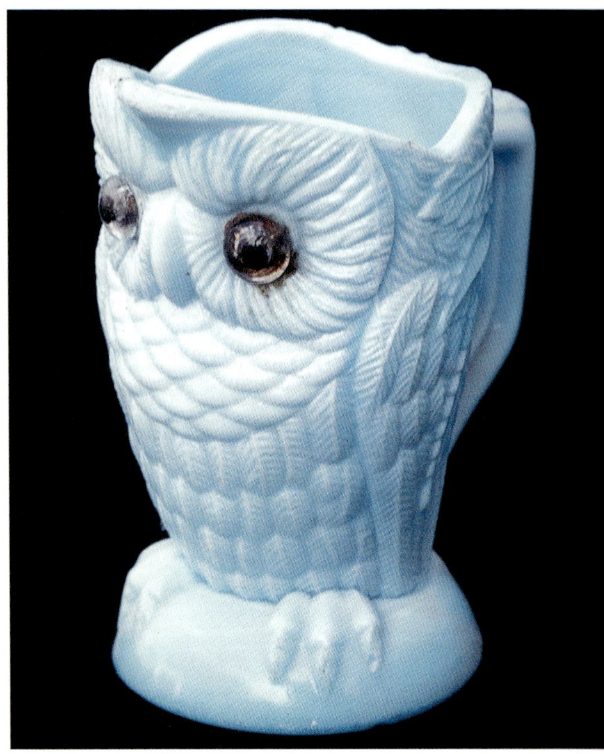

A blue opaque Owl cream pitcher made by Challinor, Taylor & Co., circa 1885. 3 5/8" high. Blue opaque, $60-85.

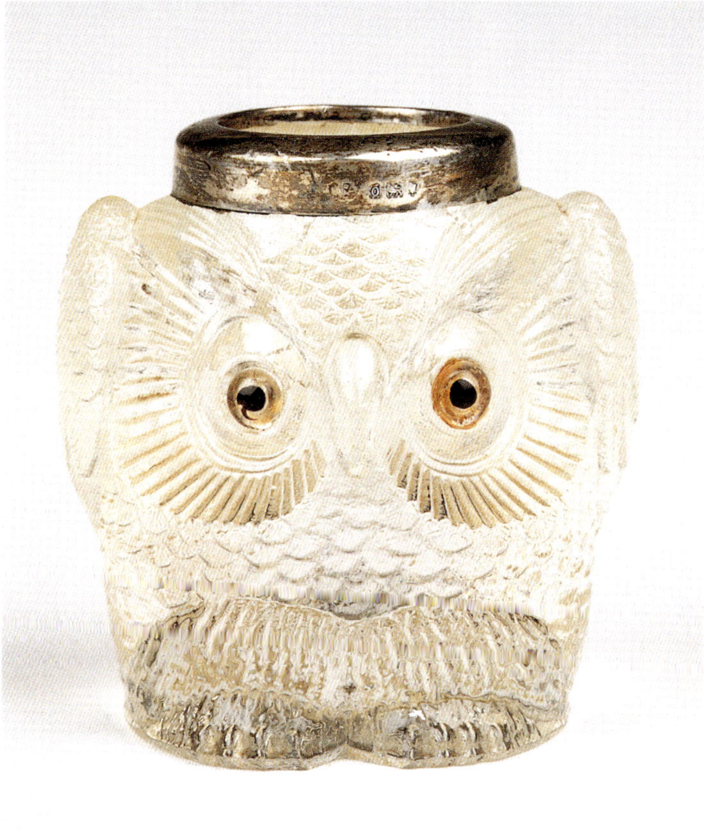

Owl head match holder, foreign made, 3" high. Clear, $190-200.

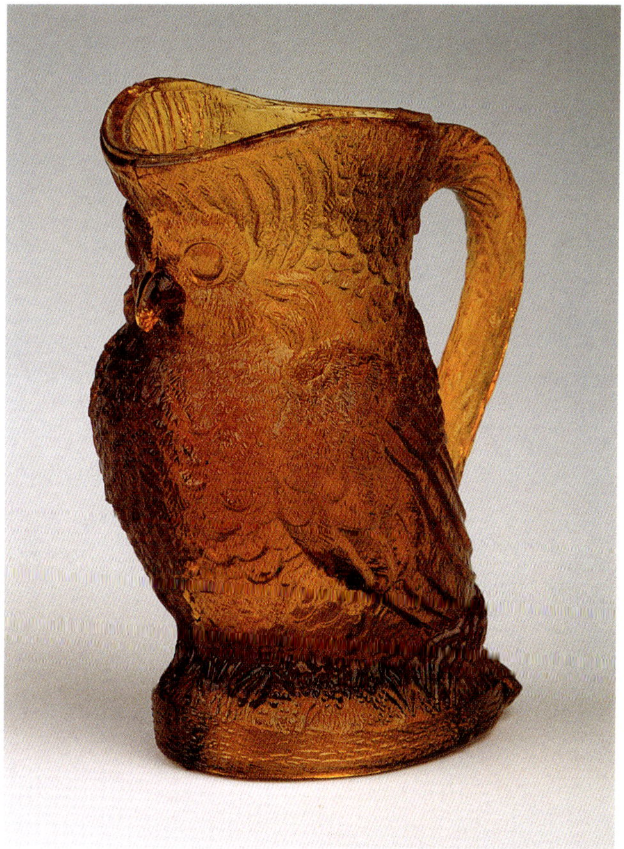

Owl cream pitcher, 3 3/4" high. Amber, $275-295.

Owl with black eyes standing on a pedestal of two books. 3 1/2" high. Probably used as a paperweight. Opal, $125-150.

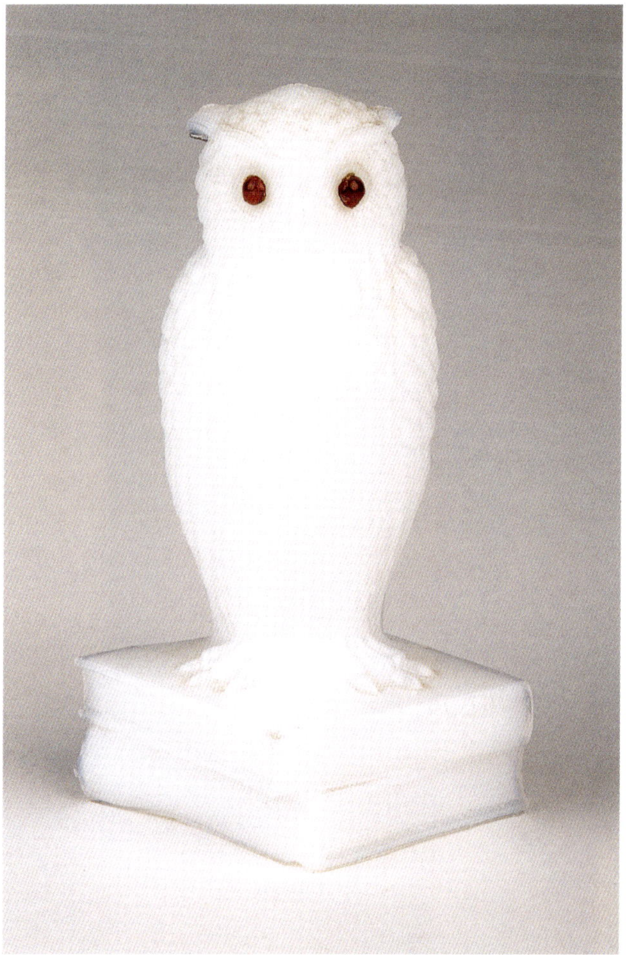

Opal Baby Owl toothpick holder, maker and date of manufactuer unknown. 2 1/2" high and 2" wide. Opal, $50-60. Opaque blue, $60-75.

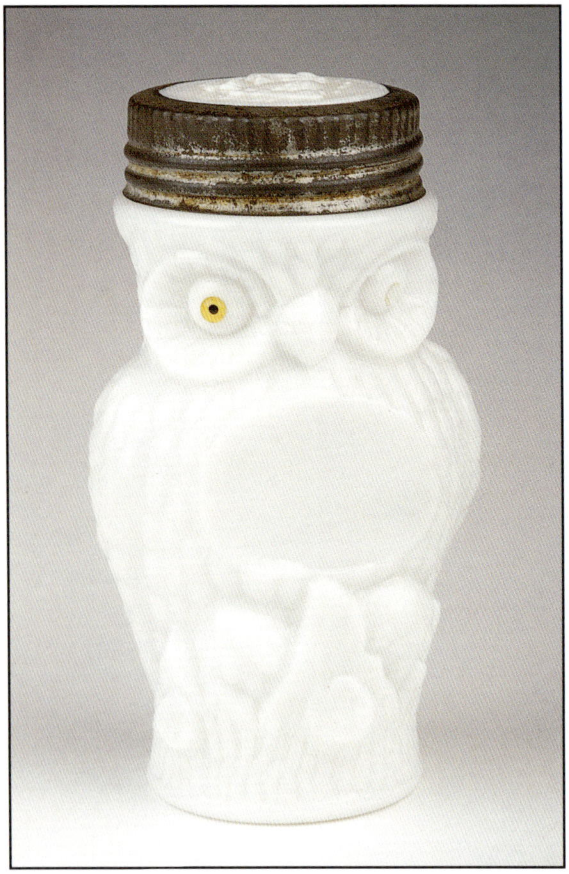

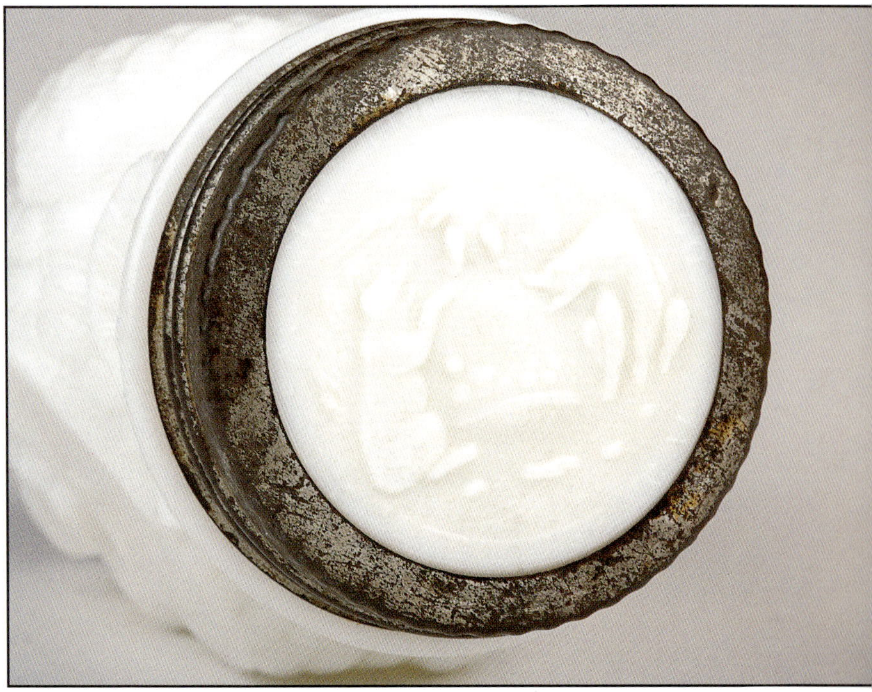

Opal full figure Owl canning jar with extremely rare Eagle and Bear lid. Jar and lid measure 6 3/4" high. Opal, $450-500.

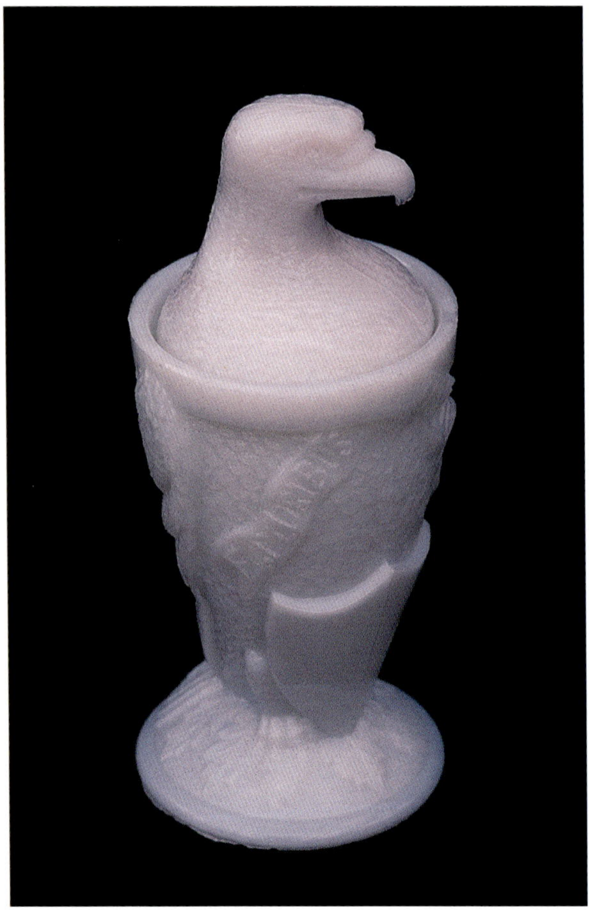

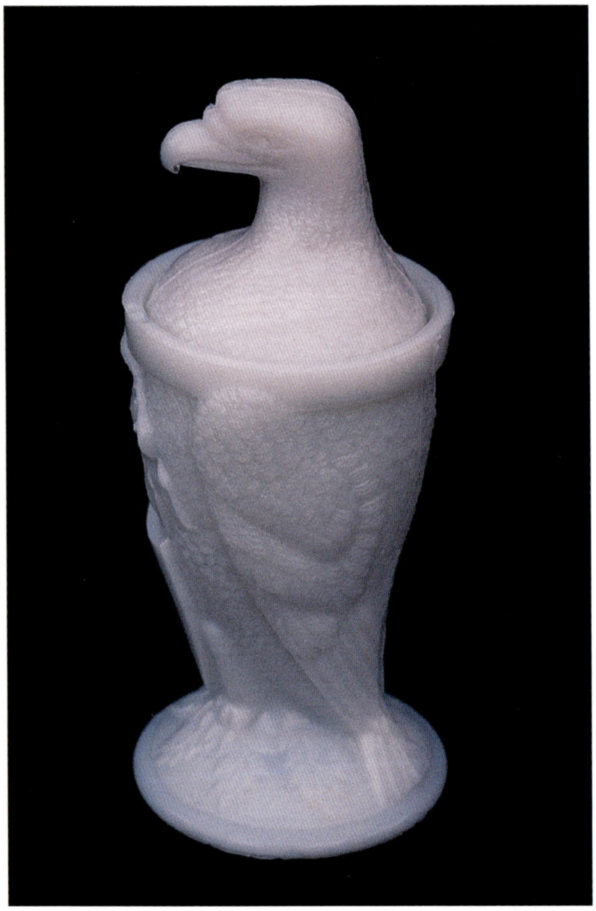

Old Abe covered jar made by the Crystal Glass Co., date of manufactuer unknown, 6" high and 2 3/4" diameter. Opal, $170-200.

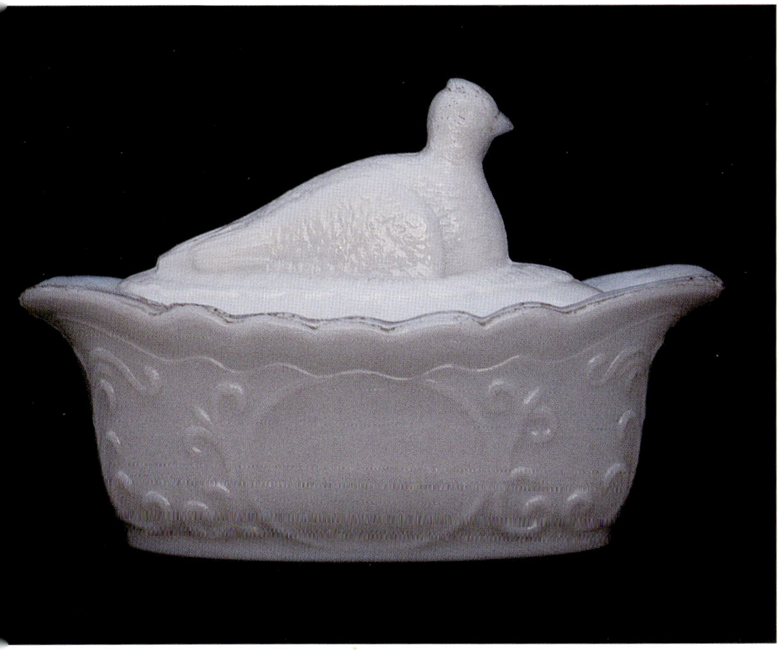

A Dove mustard container, circa 1890s. 6 1/2" x 3". Opal, $125-150.

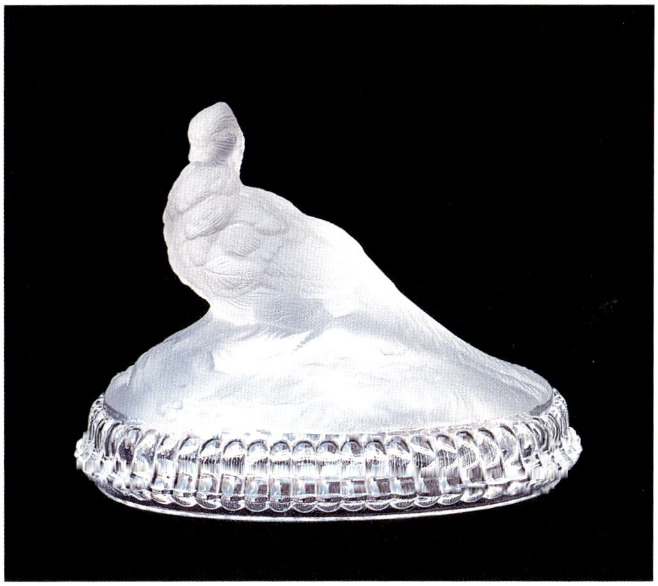

Partridge paperweight, circa 1870, 6" long. Clear frosted, $150-175.

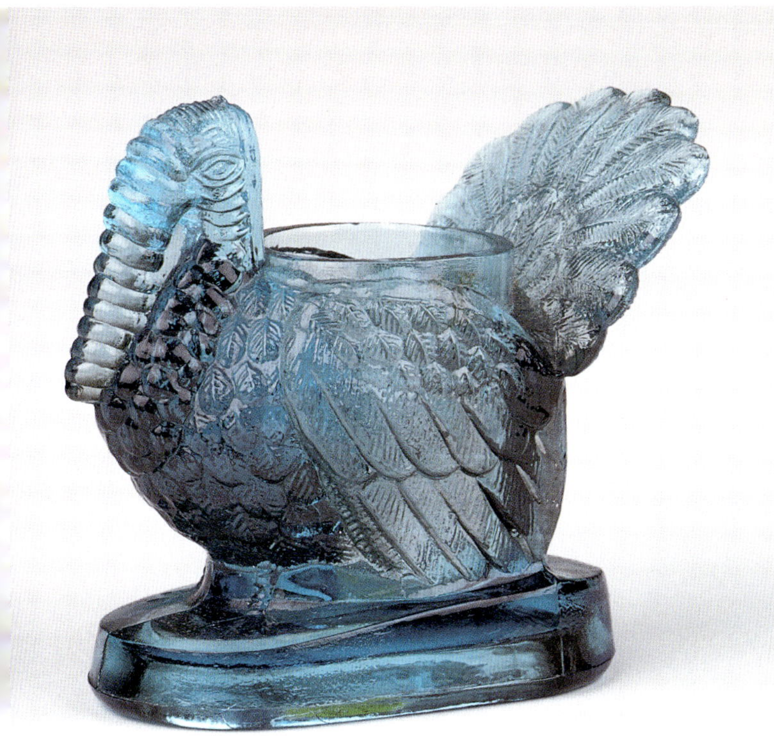

A Turkey toothpick holder, no information available. Blue, $85-135.

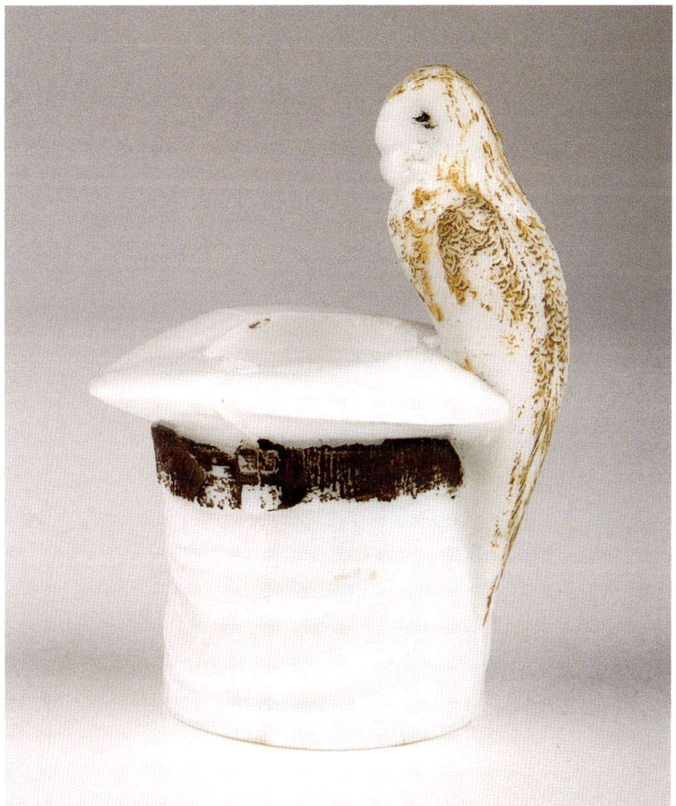

Parrot with Top Hat toothpick holder, date of manufactuer unknown, 2 1/8" high and 2 1/4" wide. Opal, $60-75.

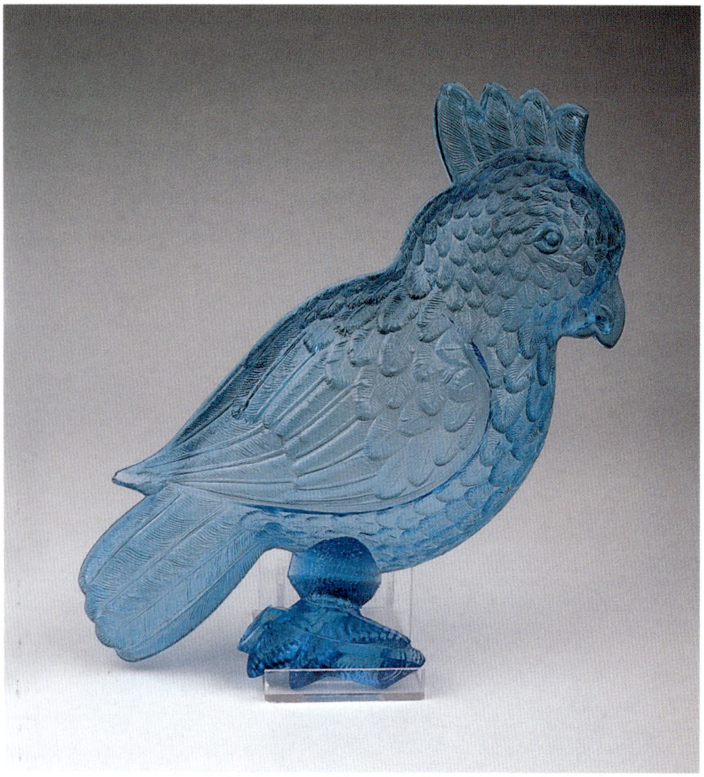

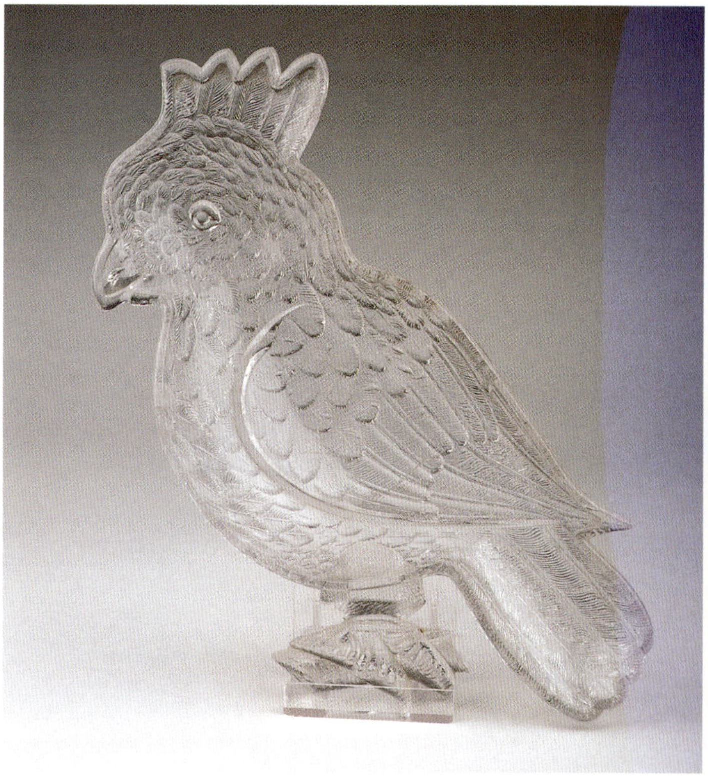

Parrot relish or pickle dish, maker unknown, 9 1/2" high. Clear, $85-125. Blue, $145-170.

A Blue opaque Duck covered dish by Vallerysthal. 5 1/2" long. Blue opaque, $290-315.

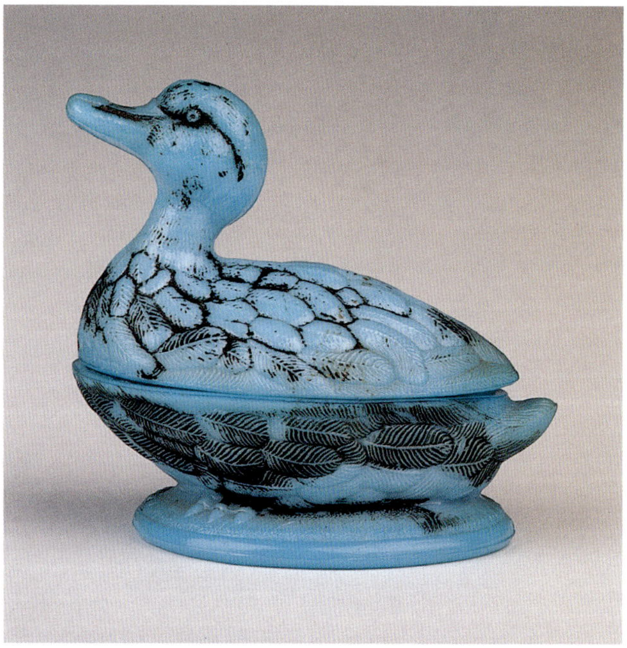

A Duck open salt made by Portieux, date of manufactuer unknown, 5" long. Blue opaque, $100-150.

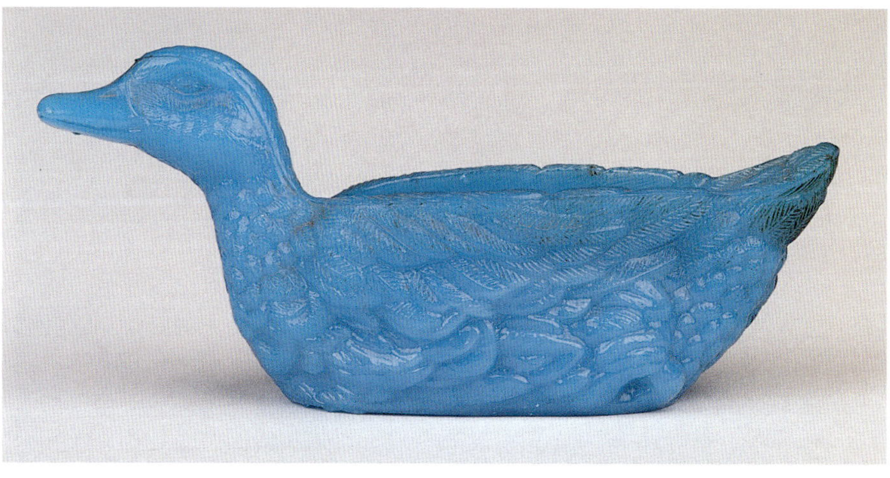

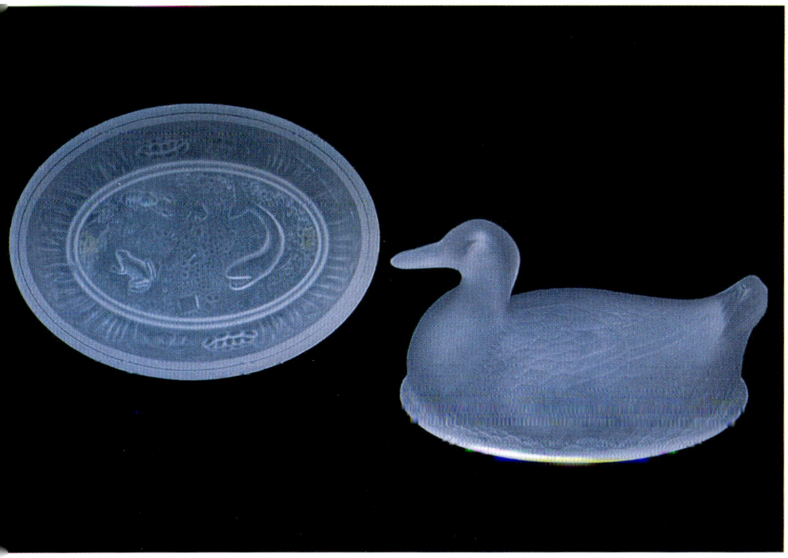

A Duck on a Duck Pond base made by the Central Glass Co., circa 1890. 7" x 5 1/4". $200-235.

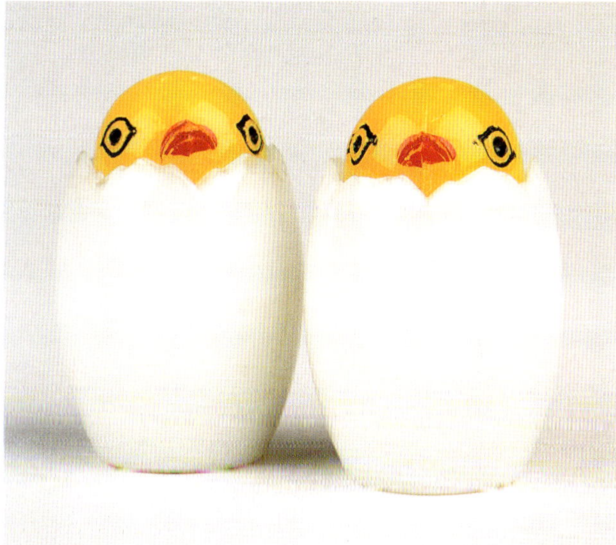

Bird salt and pepper shakers, opal with opaque yellow tops, 2" high. $545-575 pair.

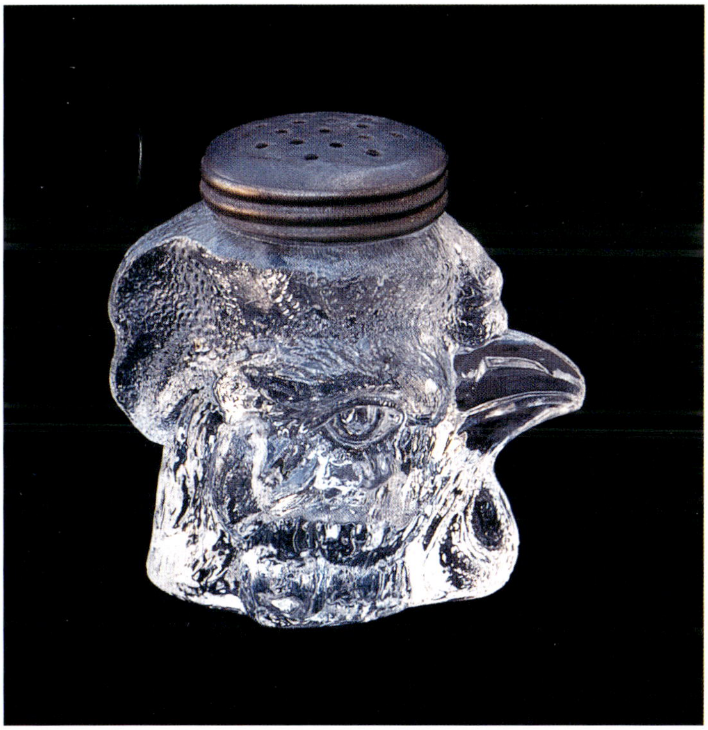

A Rooster Head saltshaker, circa 1800s, maker unknown, 3" high. $110-125.

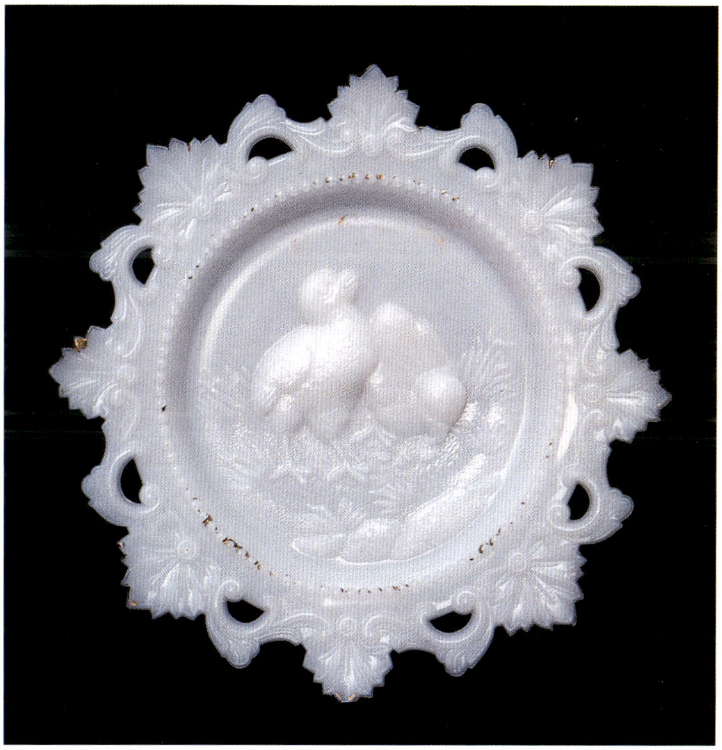

An Easter Chicks plate made by the Westmoreland Specialty Co., circa 1900, 7" diameter. Opal, $45-55.

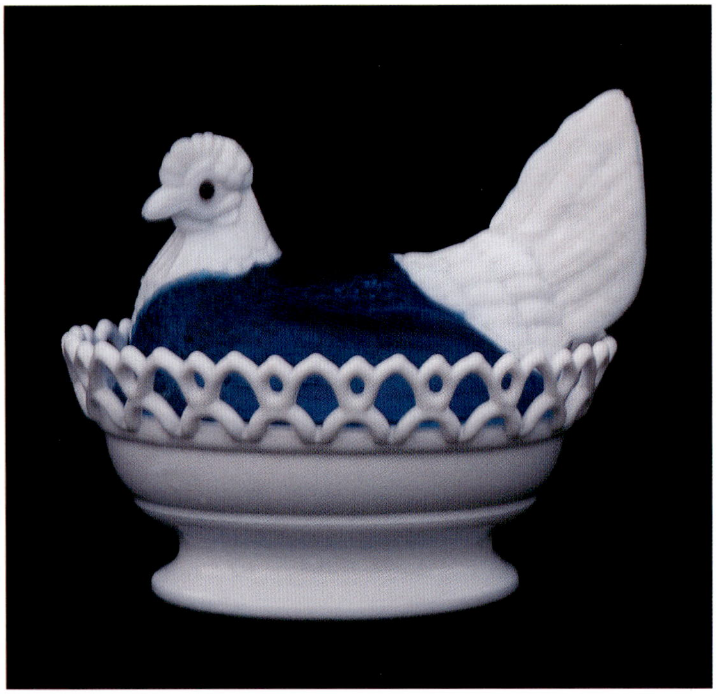

An opal Hen with blue opaque body covered dish made by Atterbury & Co., circa 1891, 8" x 6". As pictured, $400-450.

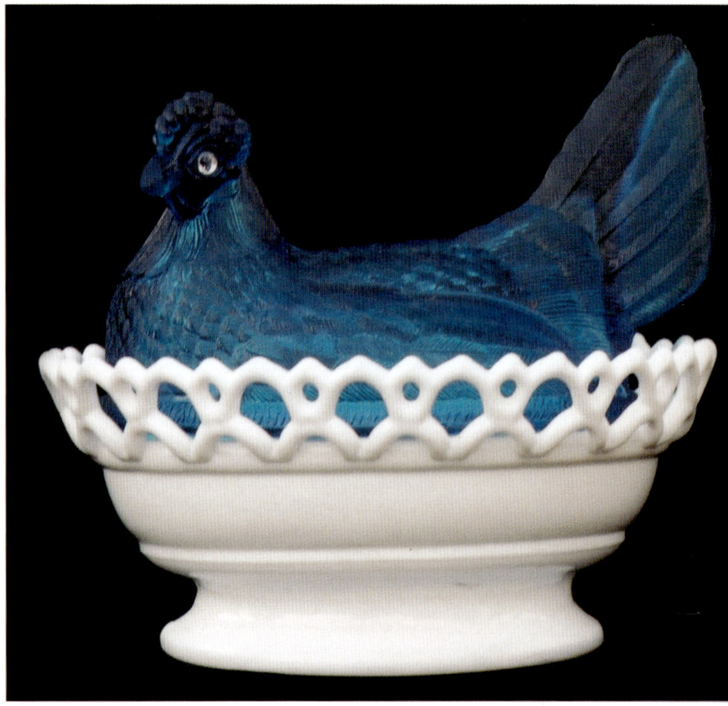

A blue opaque Hen on an opal base covered dish made by the Atterbury & Co., circa 1890, 6" x 8". As pictured, $220-240.

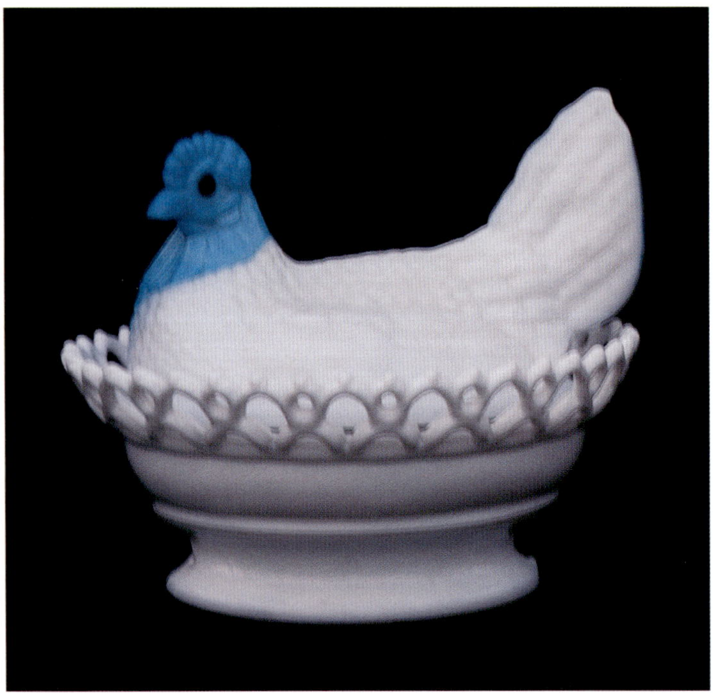

An opal Hen covered dish with a blue opaque head made by Atterbury & Co., circa 1890, 8" x 6". As pictured, $215-245.

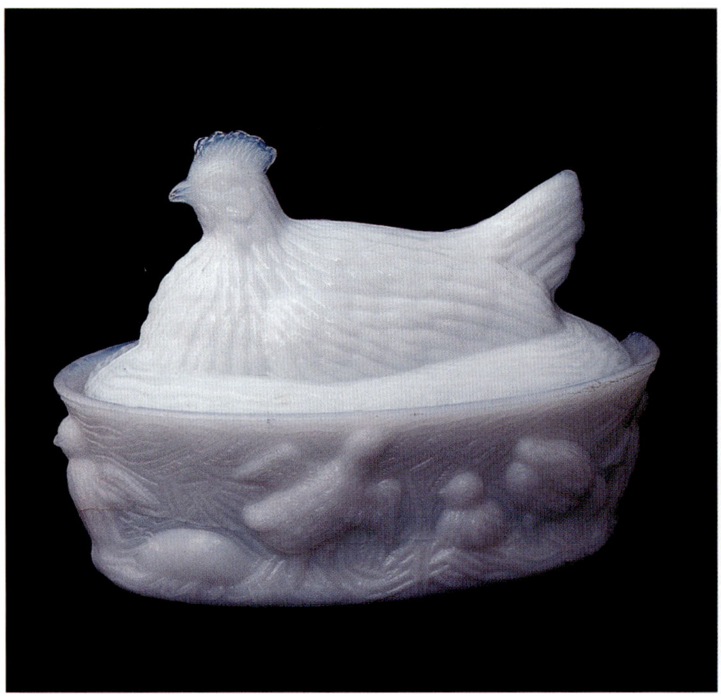

An opal Hen on an opal base with Chicks made by the C. L. Flaccus Glass Co., circa 1890s, 6 1/4" x 3 3/4". As pictured, $200-225.

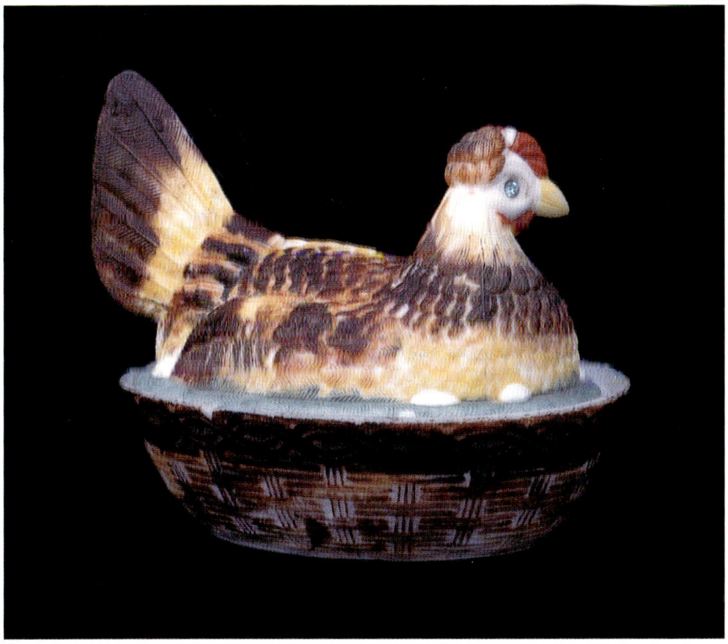

An opal Hen, decorated, from the Farm Yard Collection made by the Challinor, Taylor and Co., circa 1891, 7" x 5 1/2". As pictured, $245-265.

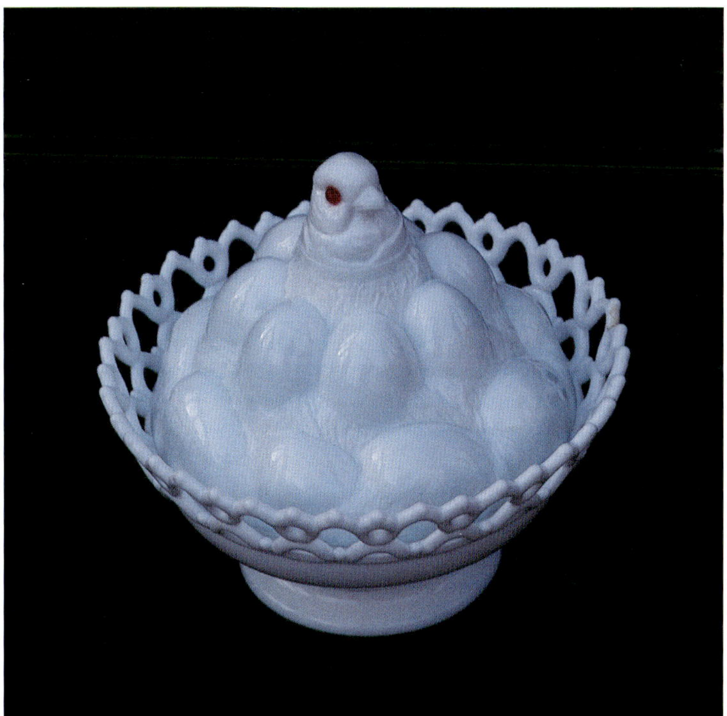

An opal Chick and Eggs covered dish made by the Atterbury & Co., patented August 6, 1889, 7 1/2" diameter. $145-165.

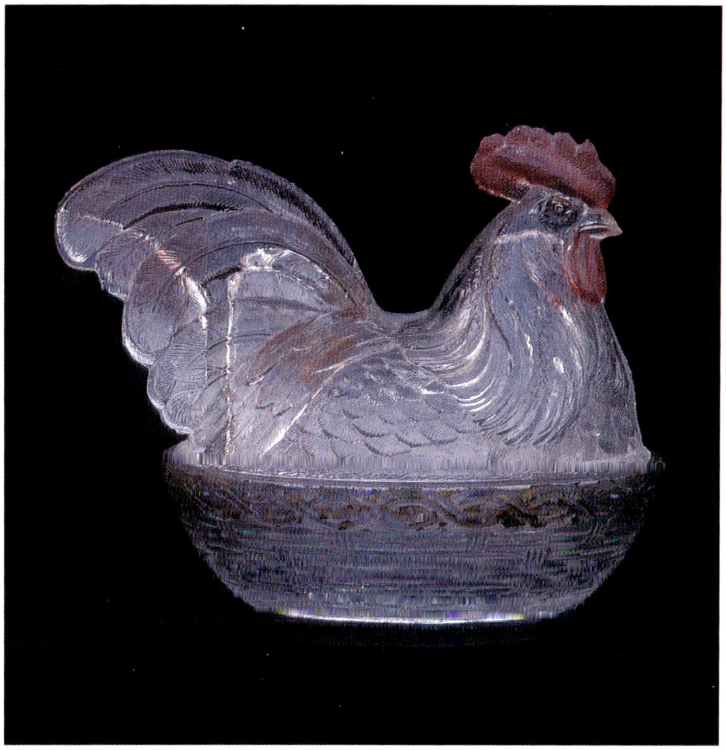

A clear decorated Rooster covered dish from the Farm Yard Collection made by the Challinor, Taylor and Co., circa 1891, 7" long and 5 3/4" wide. $290-325.

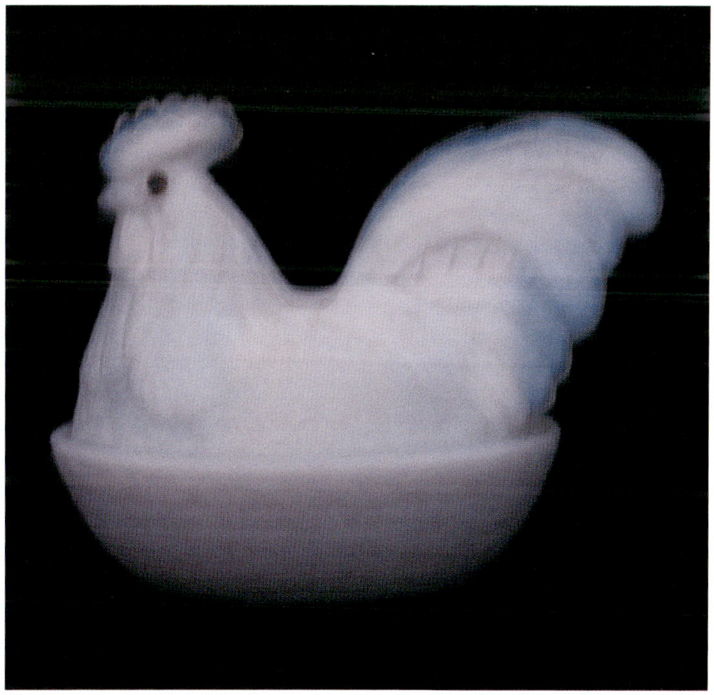

An opal Rooster from the Farm Yard Collection made by the Challinor, Taylor and Co., circa 1891, 7" x 5 1/2". $145-165.

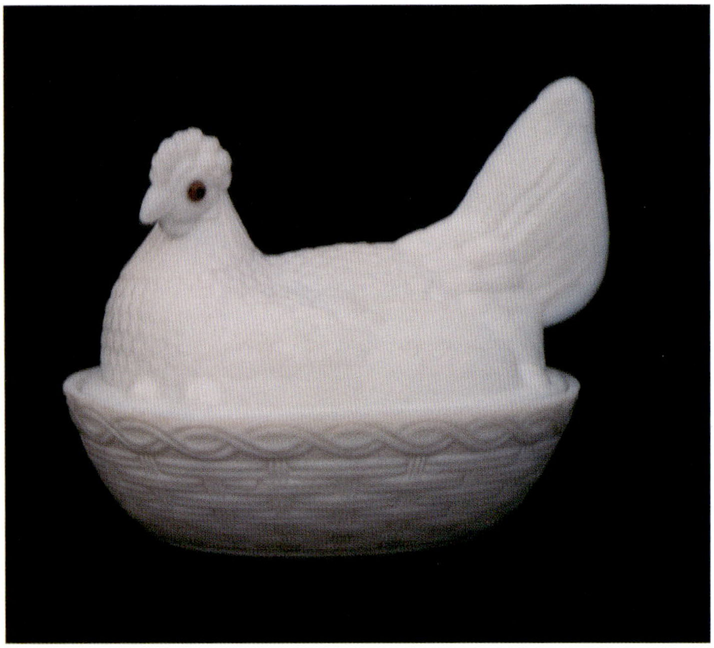

An opal Hen covered dish of the Farm Yard Collection made by Challinor, Taylor & Co., circa 1891, 7" x 5 1/2". $100-125.

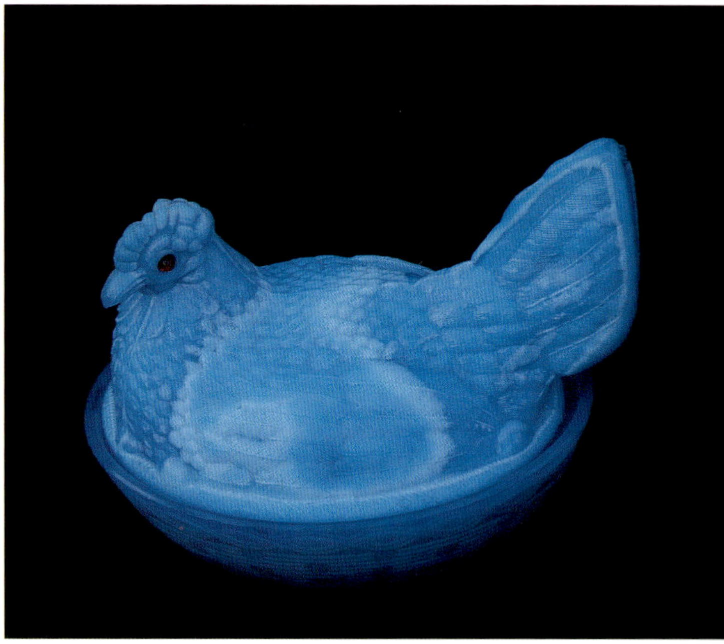

A mosaic *deuce* Hen on a blue opalescent base made by Atterbury & Co., circa 1890, 7" x 5 1/2". $1,500-1,700.

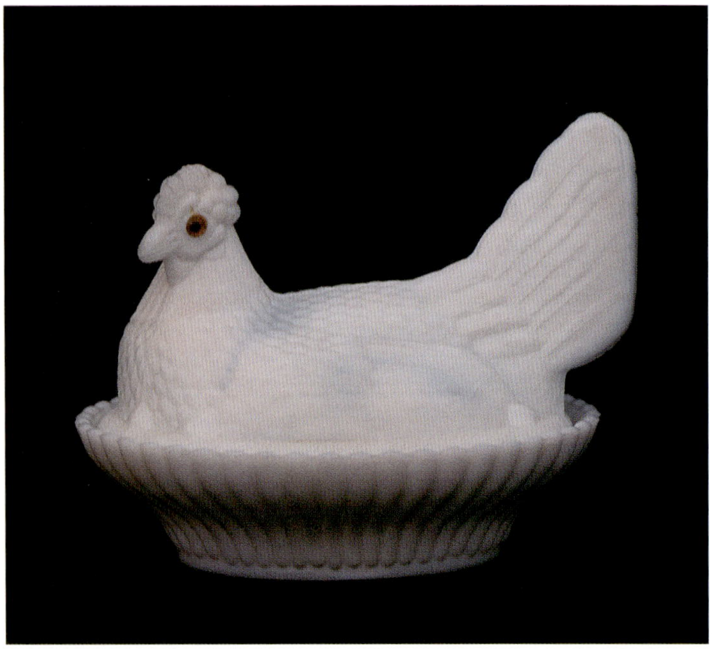

An opal Hen covered dish made by Atterbury & Co., circa 1890, 7" x 5 1/2". $150-180.

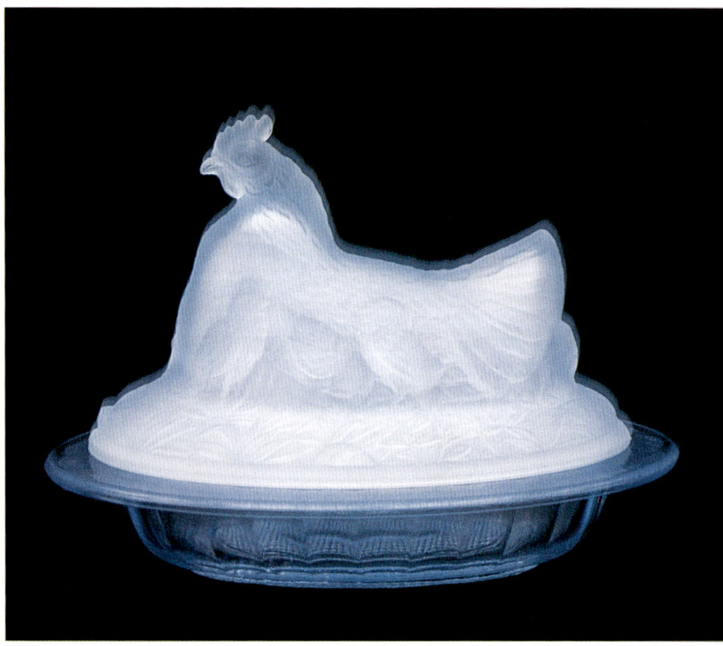

A light blue Hen covered dish by Sowerby, circa 1920, 7" x 4 1/2". $100-120.

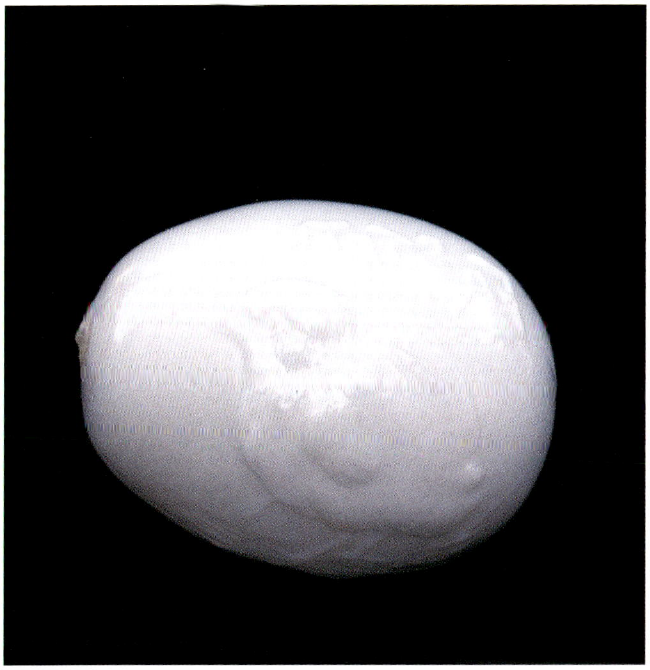

An opal Easter Egg with an embossed Chick, circa 1899, the maker was probably one of the lesser-known factories such as Bonita, 3" long. $55-65.

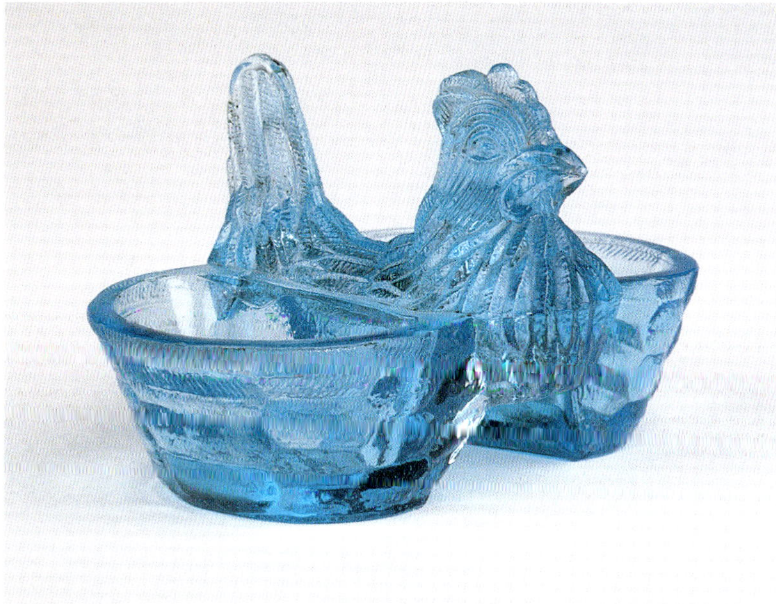

Bird double salt, date of manufactuer unknown, 4 1/2" long. Blue, $170-185.

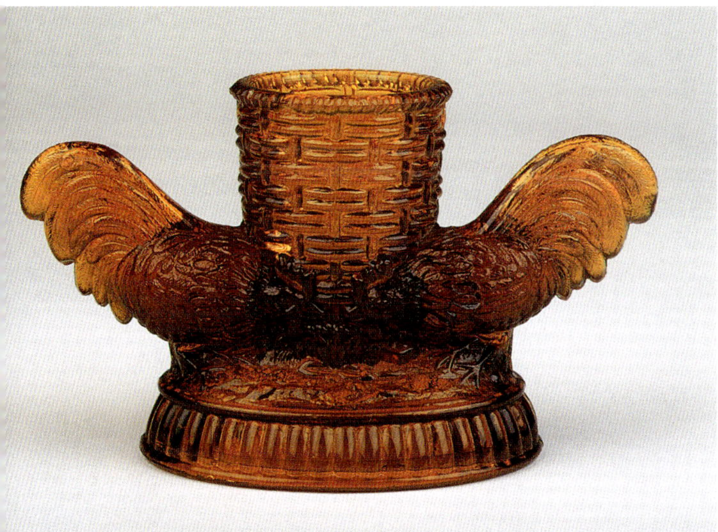

A Two Roosters toothpick holder, maker and date of manufactuer unknown, 3" high and 1 5/8" wide. Clear, $60-70. Amber, $80-95.

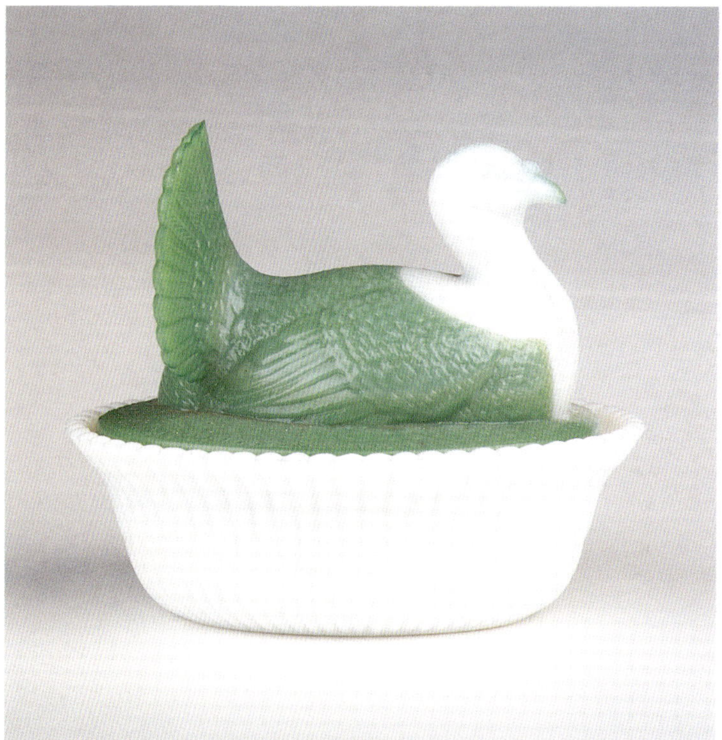

Green opaque Turkey with an opal head and rib base covered dish, 5 1/2" long. $450-475.

Bird driving a car candy container, *Jeanette*, date of manufactuer unknown, 4 1/4" long. $350-450.

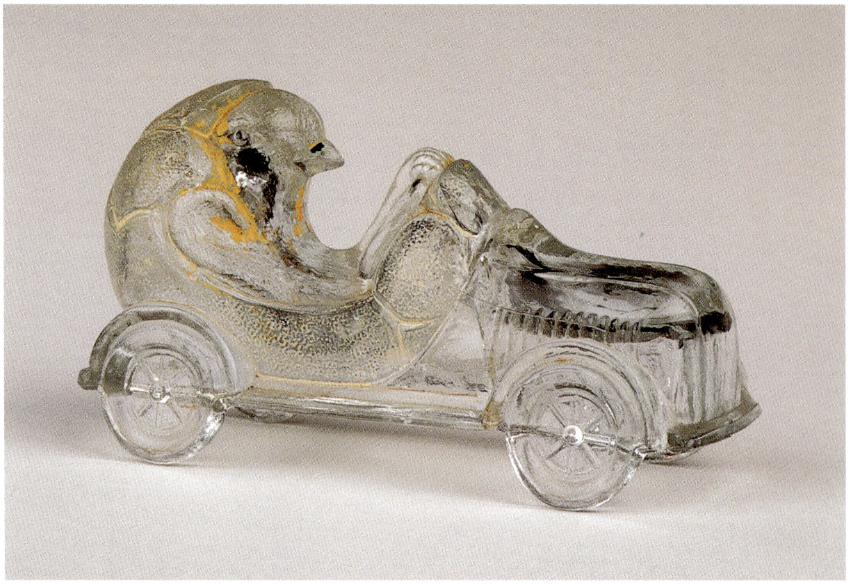

Opal Basket with Four Chicks, maker unknown, 4 3/8" long. $800-850.

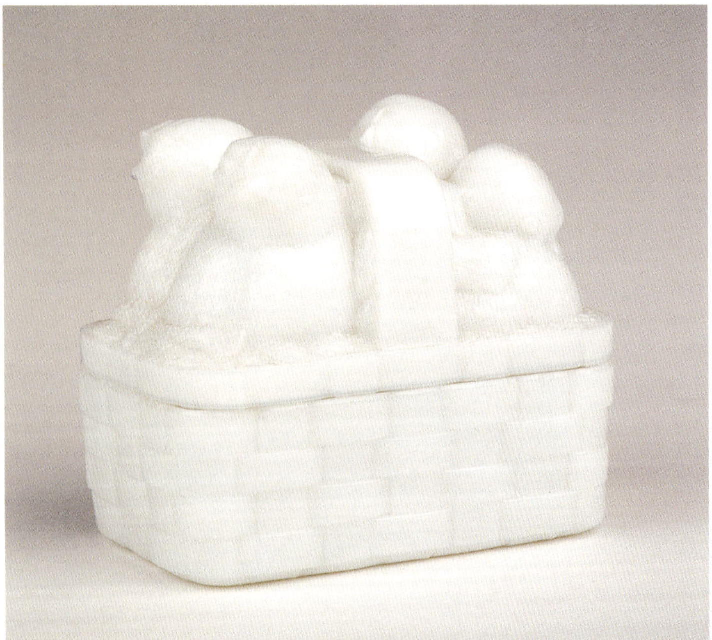

Just Out toothpick holder made by Gillinder & Sons, circa 1876. Clear with satin finish, $125-135.

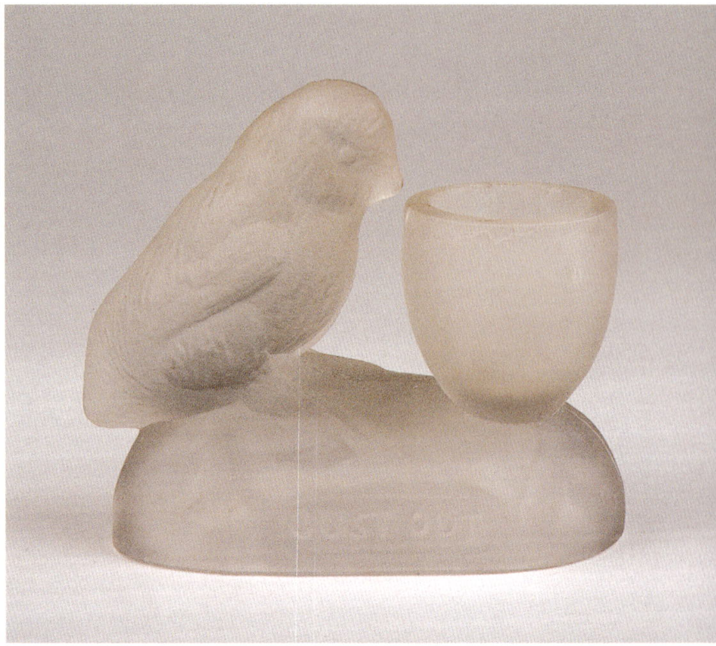

A variety of Bird saltcellars, makers and date of manufactuer unknown. Amber, $90-95. vaseline, $95-100. Blue, $70-80.

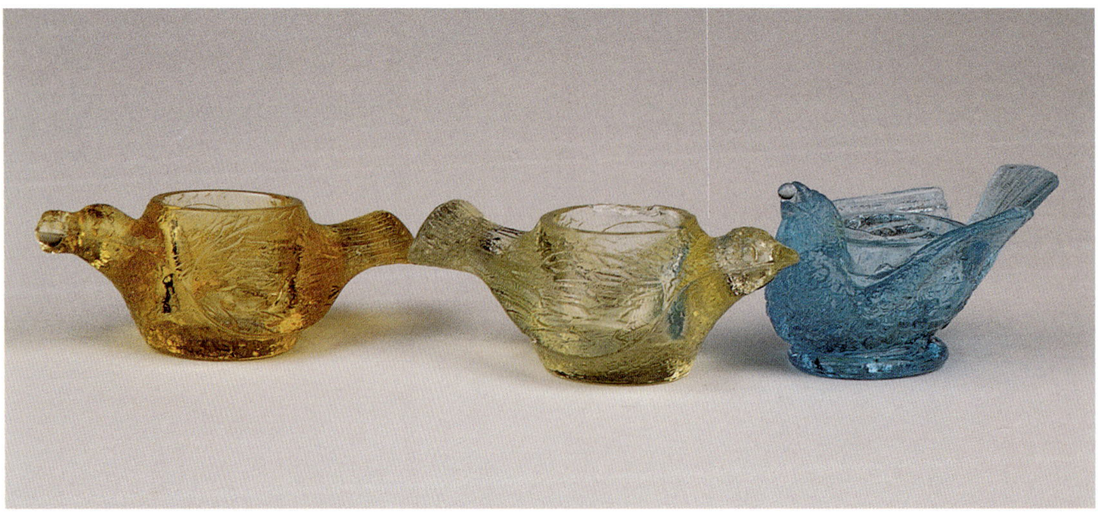

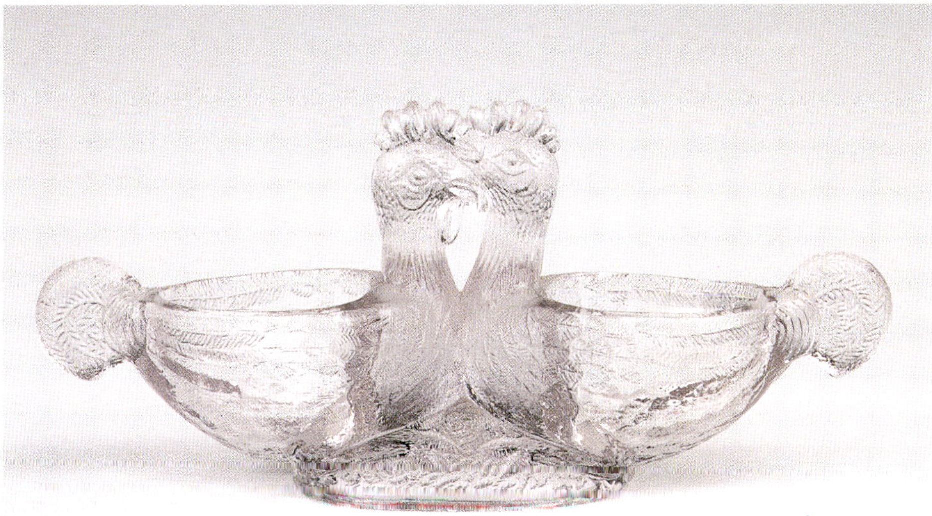

A Two Bird double saltcellar made by Vallerysthal, 6" long. Clear, $170-185.

Bird with Cherry toothpick holder, it also was made with a cover to be used as a mustard container, maker and date of manufactuer unknown, 2 1/2" high. Amber, $140-175. Amber with cover, $300-325.

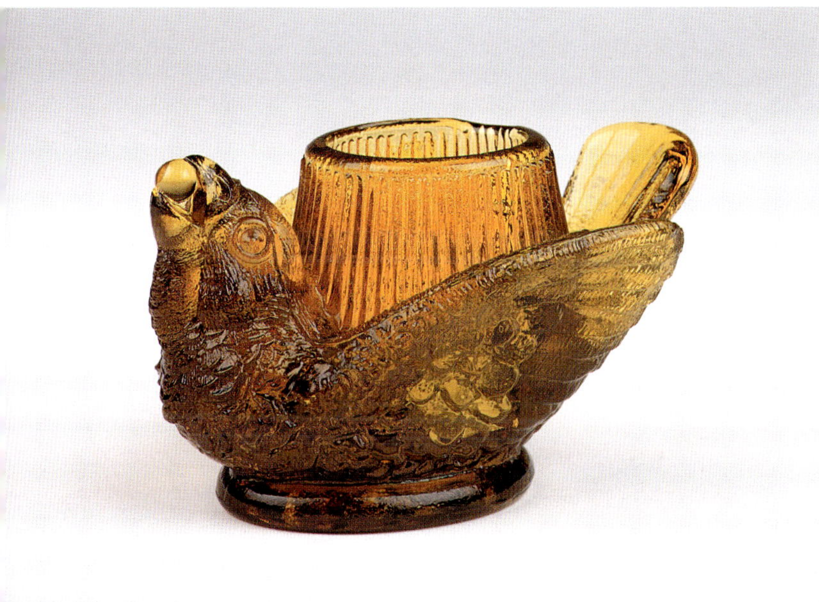

Bird with head stretching upward, saltcellar, 2 1/2" long. Blue, $185-235.

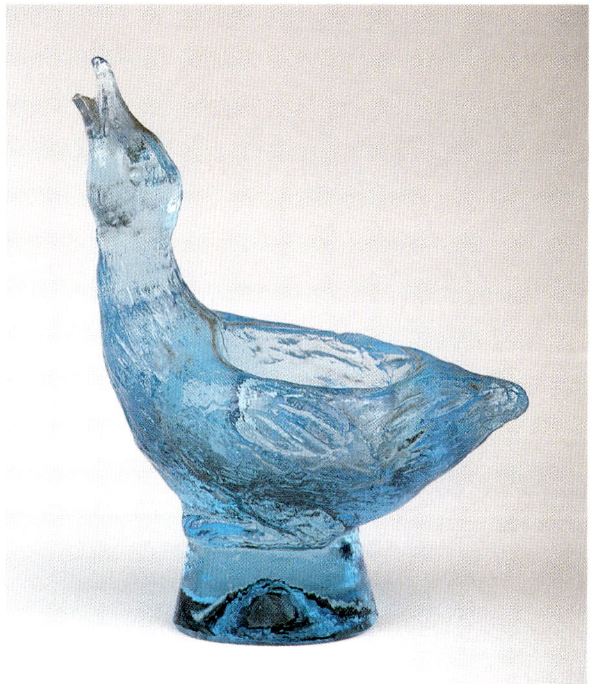

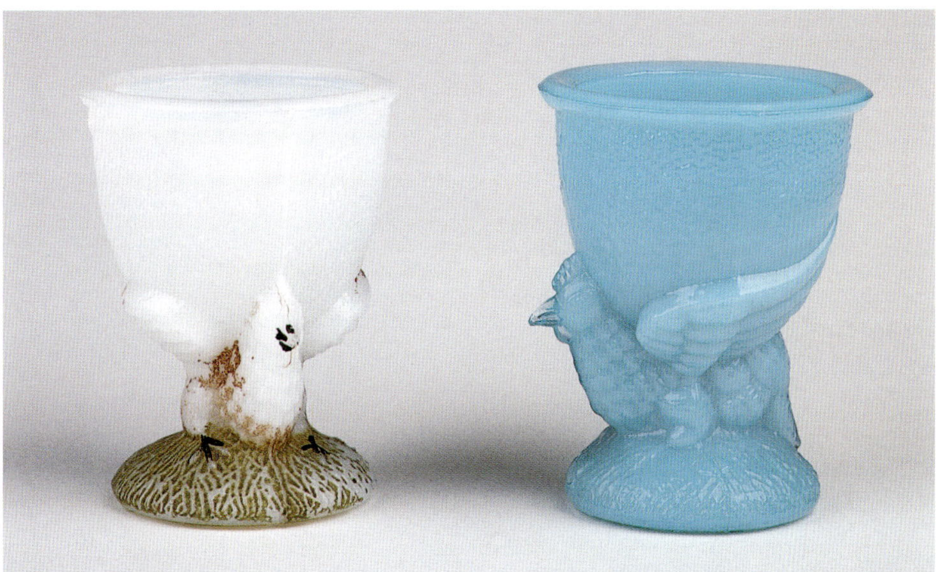

Chicken eggcup made by Vallerysthal, 2 1/2" high. Opal, 35-50. Opaque blue, $60-75.

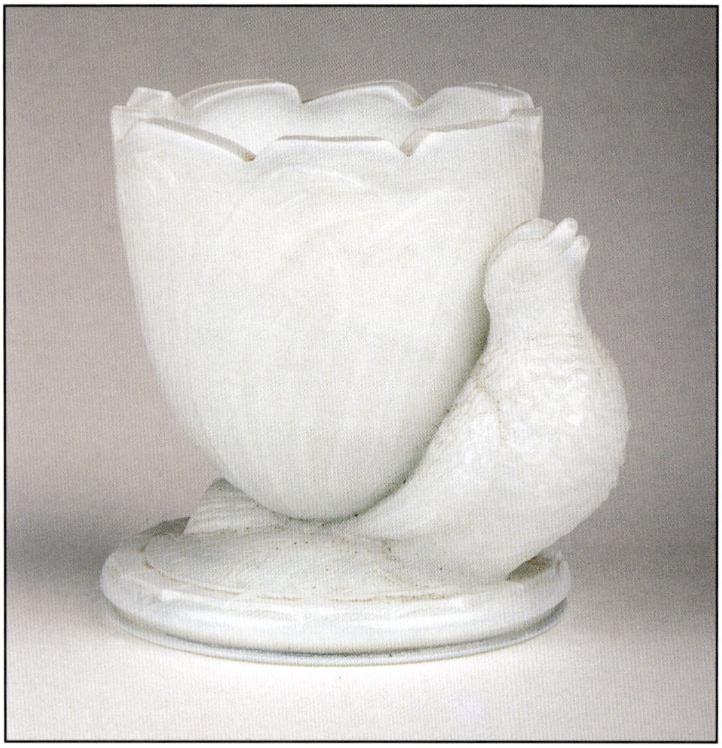

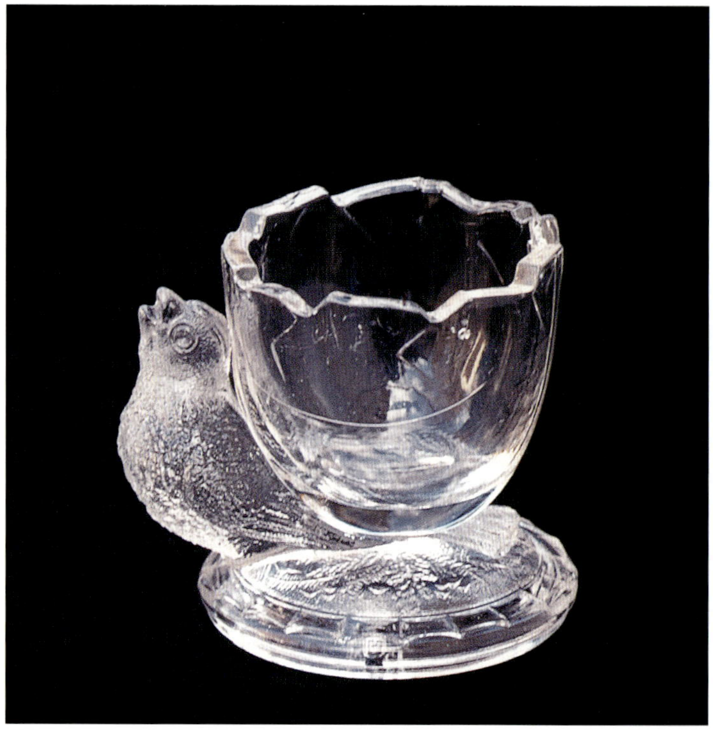

Bird in Egg Shell toothpick holder, circa 1890, maker unknown. 2 1/2" high and 2 3/8" diameter at the base. Clear, $70-80. Opal, $80-90.

Bird and Nest saltcellar, maker and date of manufactuer unknown, 3 1/2" long. Clear, $50-60.

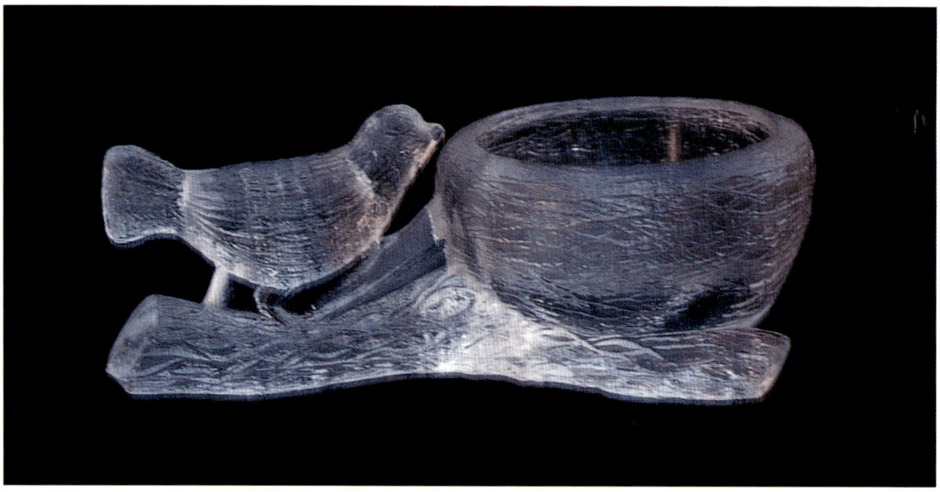

Chick in Egg saltcellar, circa 1890, 2 5/8" high. Clear, $25-35. Blue, $90-145.

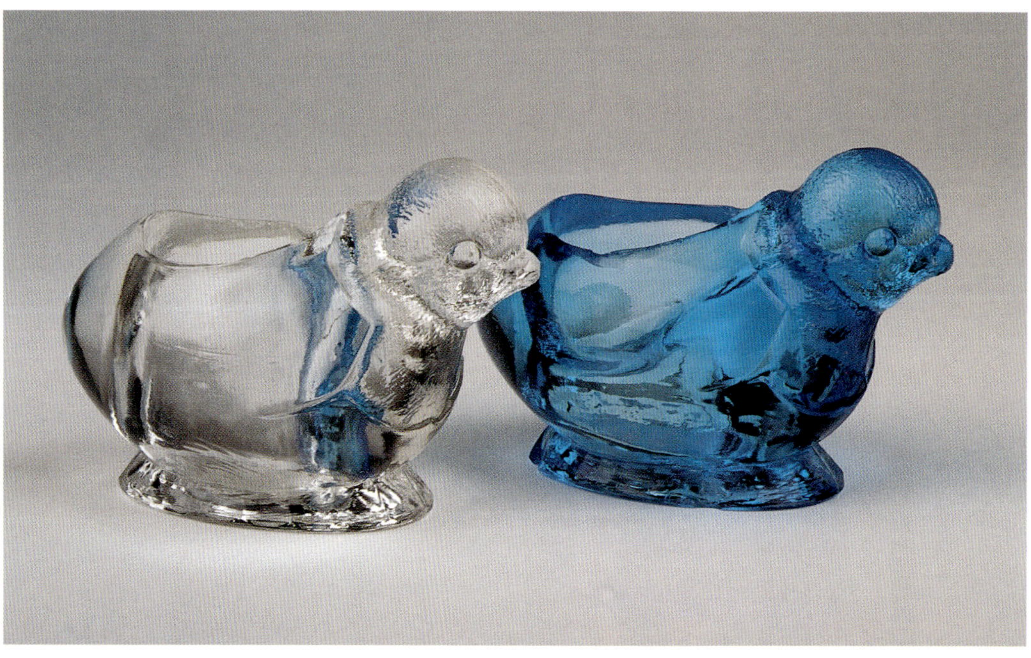

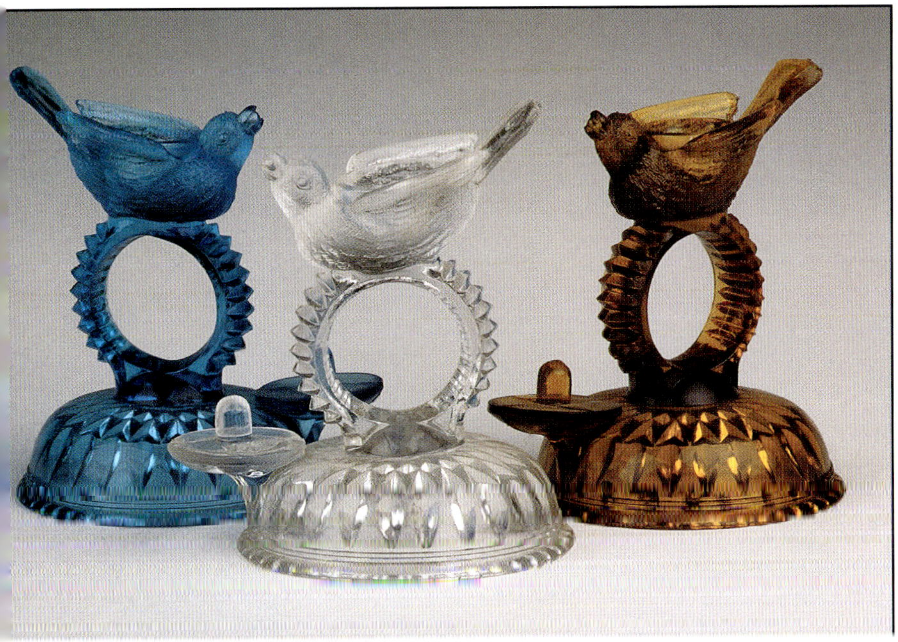

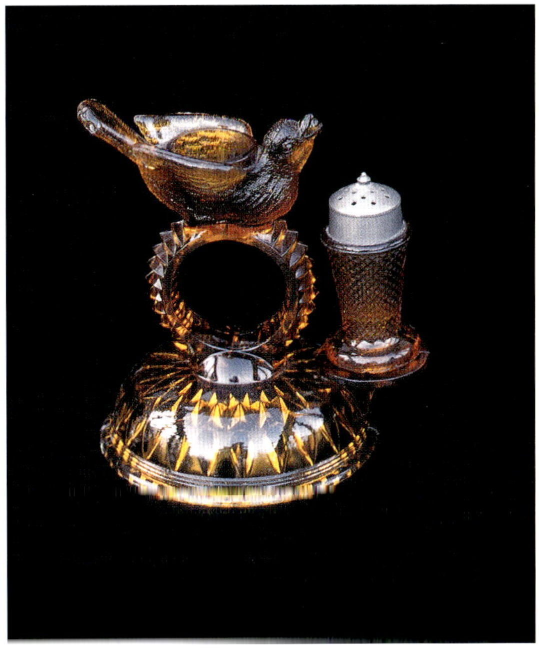

Bird combination napkin holder and saltcellar, circa 1875, 5" high and 4" diameter at the base. Clear, $170-190. Color, $350-425. Values are for complete pieces.

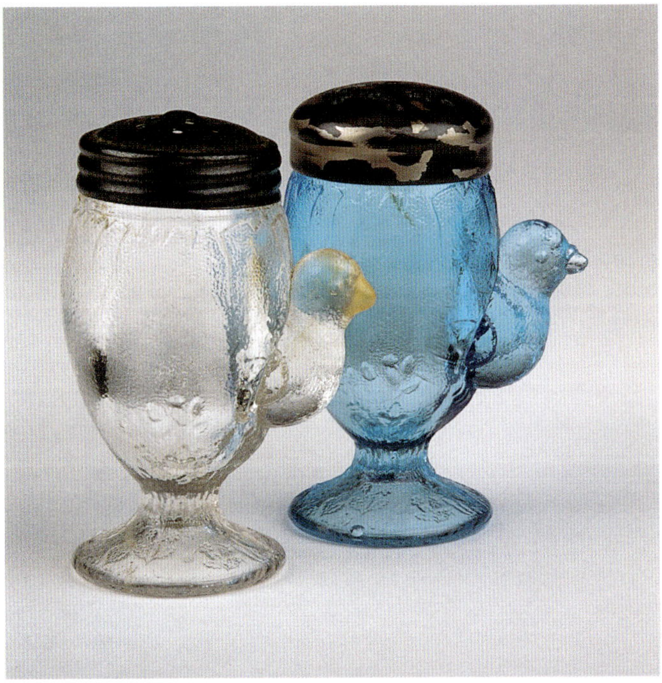

Early Bird shaker made by the Columbia Glass Co., circa late 1880s, attribution made by shards found at the factory site, 2 7/8" high and 1 5/8" wide. Clear, $110-125. Amber, $165-180. Blue, $180-195.

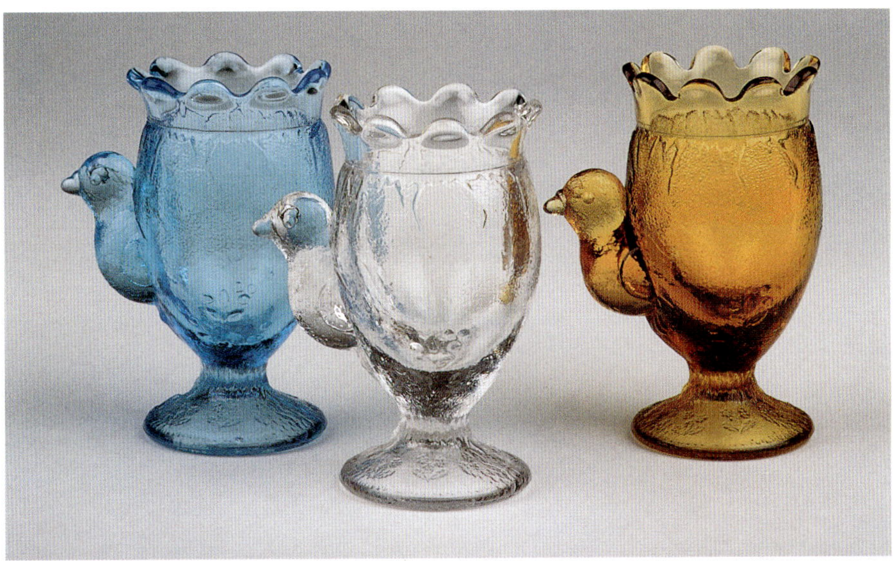

Early Bird toothpick holder made by the Columbia Glass Co., circa late 1880s, attribution made by shards found at the factory site, 2 7/8" high and 1 5/8" wide. Clear, $110-125. Amber, $165-180. Blue, $180-195.

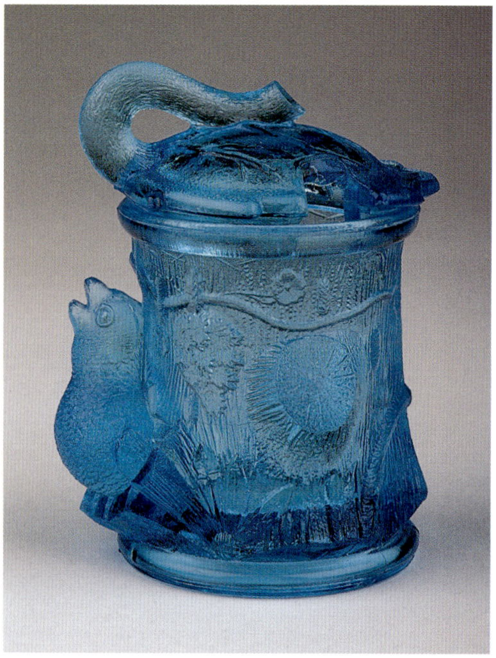

Stump or Bird and Tree made by McKee and Brothers, circa 1886, 2 3/4" high and 2" wide. This is illustrated in an old factory catalog as a mustard and, without the lid, as a toothpick holder. Clear, $45-50. Amber, $65-75. Blue, $80-85.

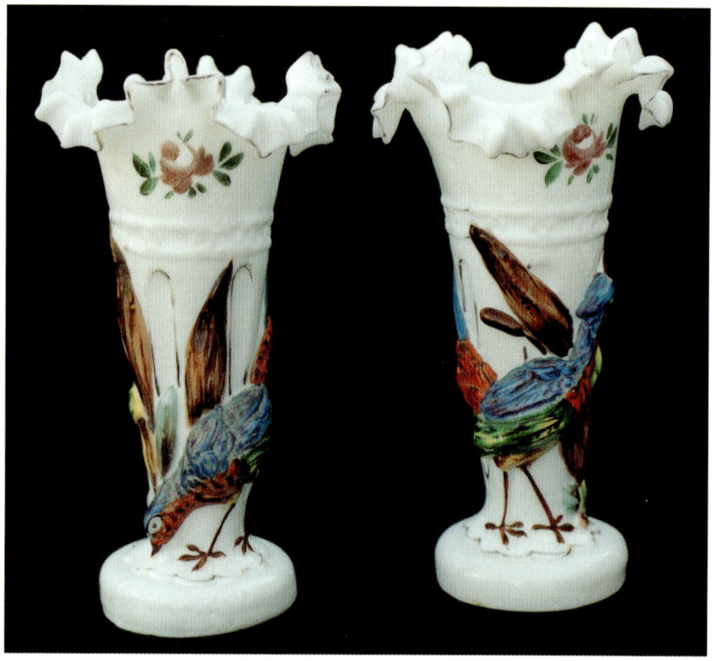

Vase with decorated birds in high relief. Maker and date of manufactuer unknown, 9" high. Opal decorated, $225-275 pair.

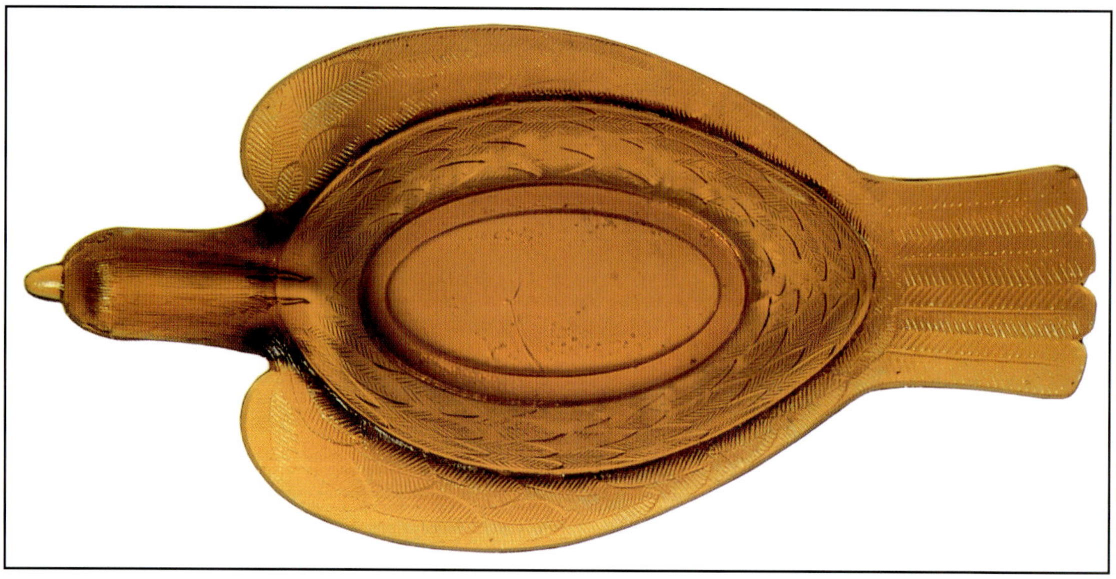

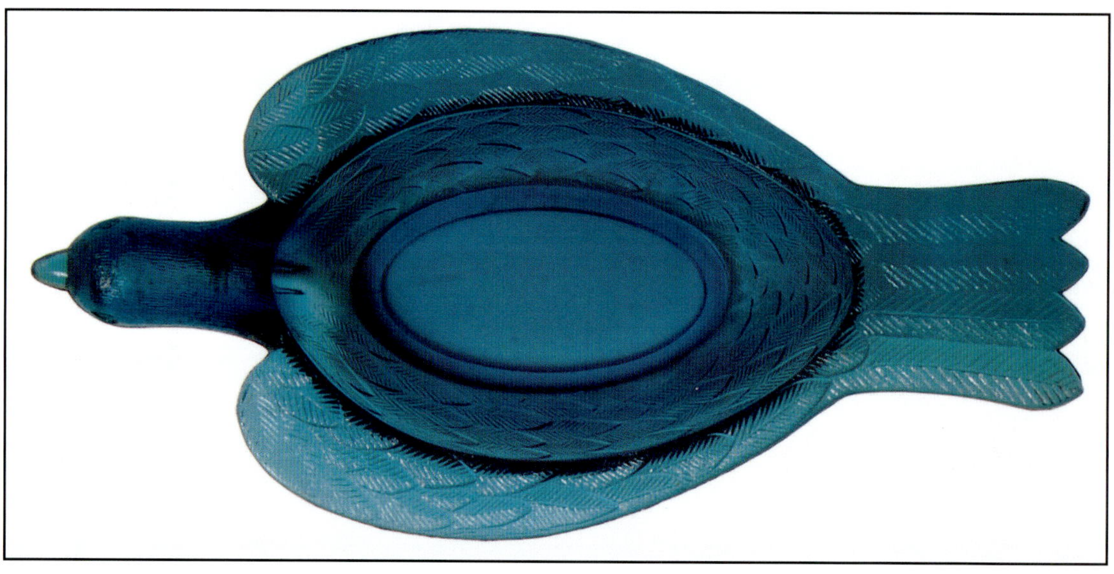

Bird dish made by the Hemingray Glass Co., patented Feb. 1, 1876, design patent 8,942. Made in amber, yellow amber, clear, light blue, peacock blue, peacock opaque white, clambroth, purple pink opaque, dark pink opaque, and other colors. Clear, $75-95. Color, $125-150.

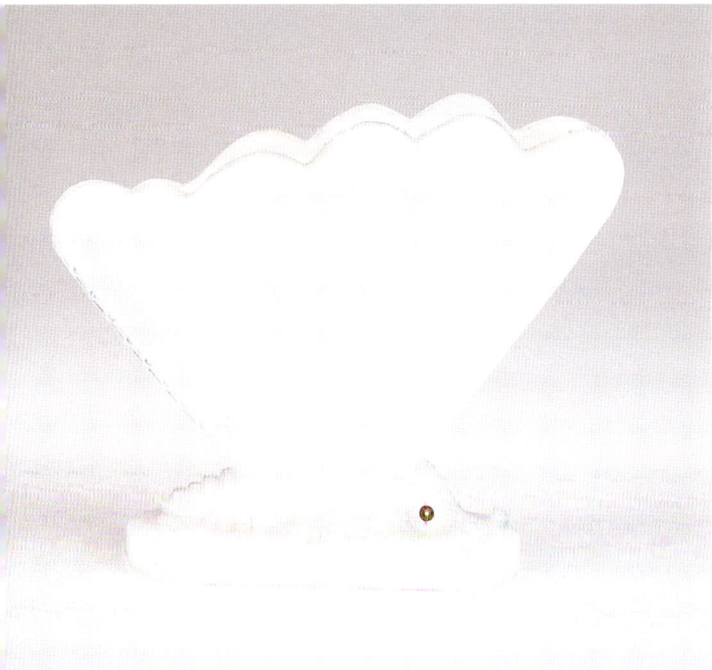

Butterfly toothpick holder made by the Eagle Glass and Manufacturing Co., circa 1899. 2 3/4" high and 1 1/4" wide. Opal, $45-55.

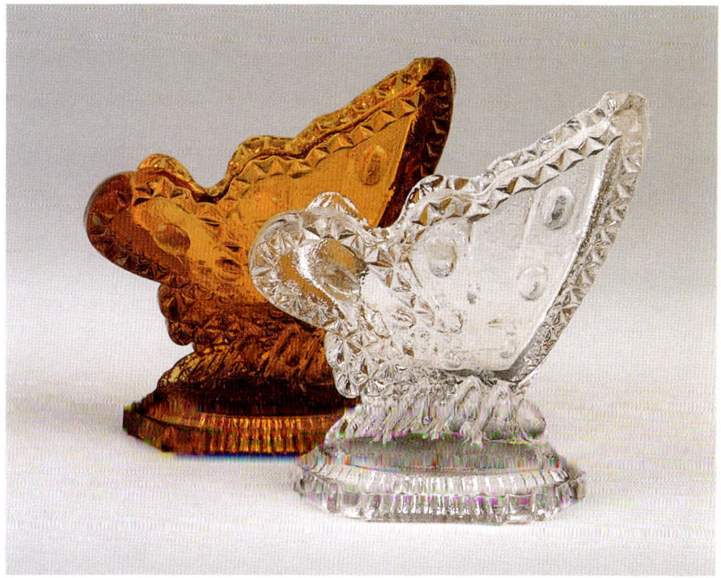

Butterfly toothpick holder made by the Buckeye Glass Co., circa 1887. 2 3/8" high. Clear, $40-55. Amber, $65-80.

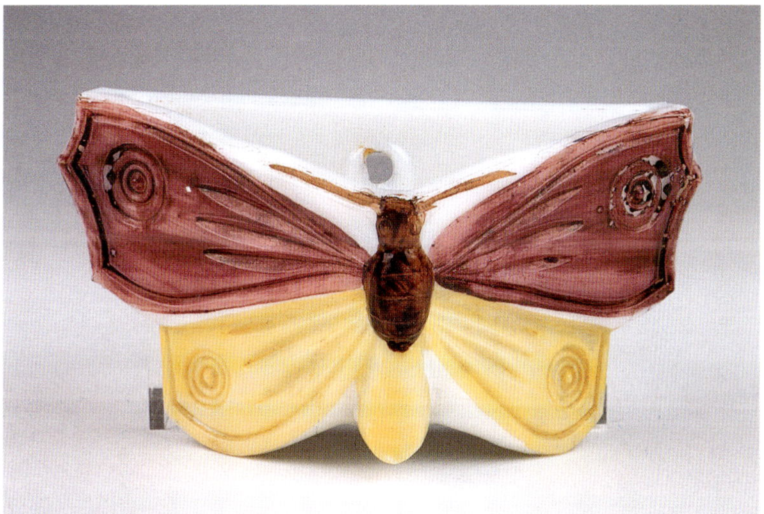

Butterfly match holder made by Challinor, Taylor and Co., circa 1890s. 2 1/4" high and 4 1/2" wide. Decorated opal, $95-145.

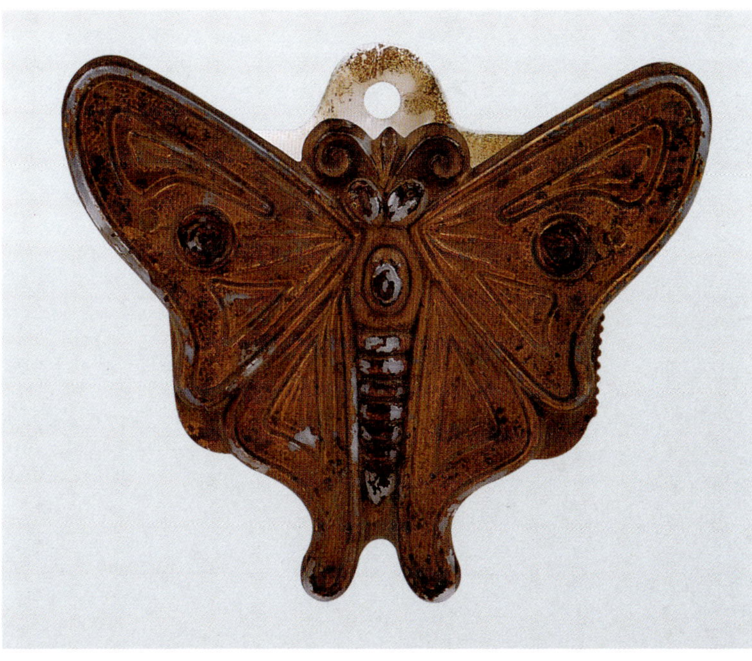

Butterfly match holder, maker unknown, circa 1889, 1 3/4" high and 4 1/4" wide. Decorated opal, $95-145.

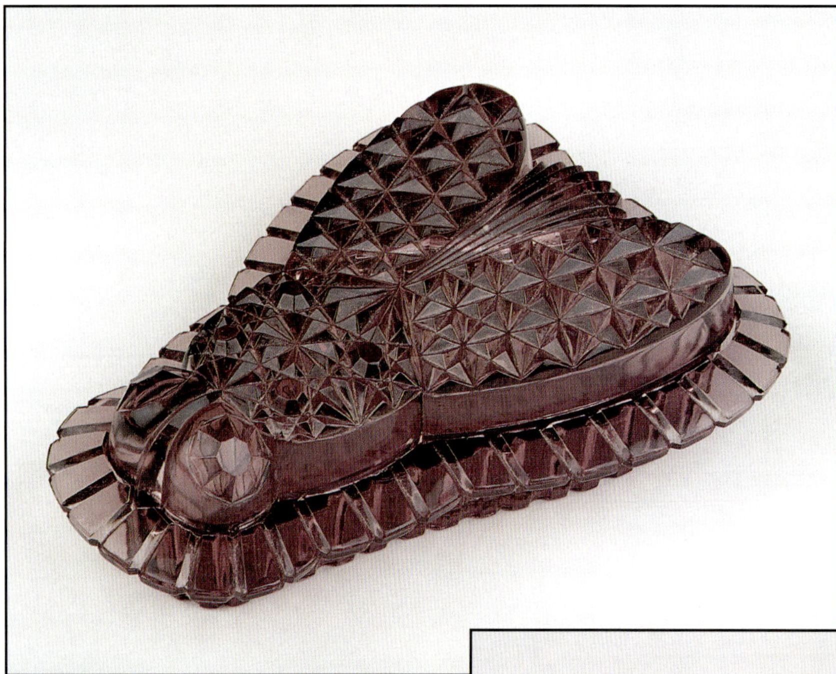

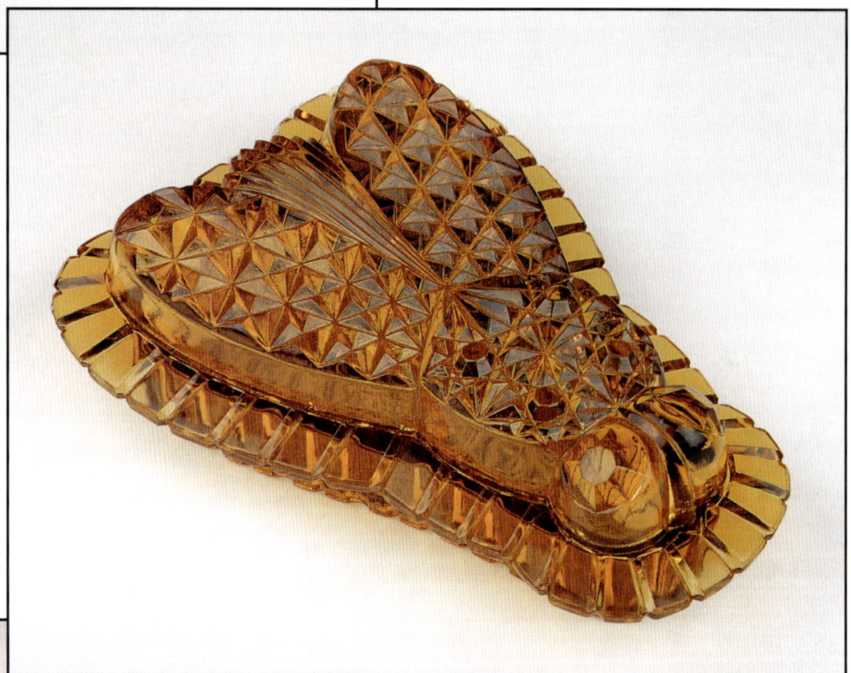

Fly covered dish, maker unknown, circa late 1880s. 8 1/2" long. Amethyst, $325-400. Amber, $290-350. vaseline, $325-400. The amethyst dish shown here is repaired in the old method; it has a staple over a crack in the lid.

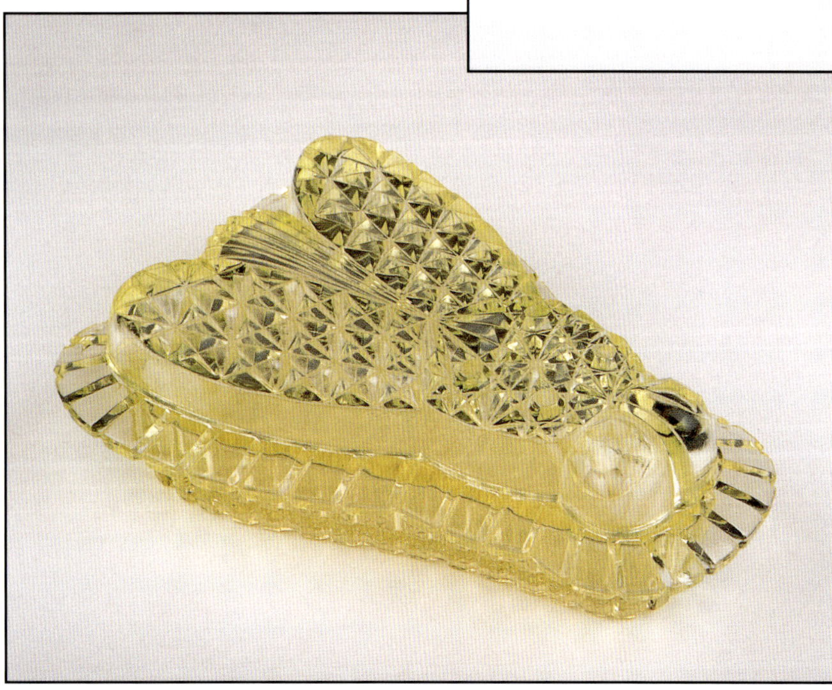

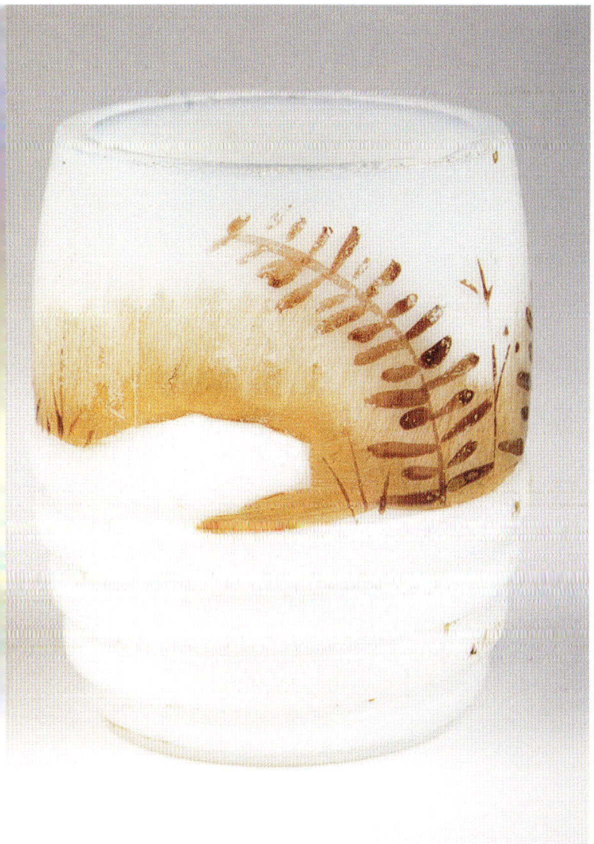

Coiling snake toothpick holder, maker unknown, circa late 1890s. 2 1/4" high and 2" wide. Decorated opal, $45-60.

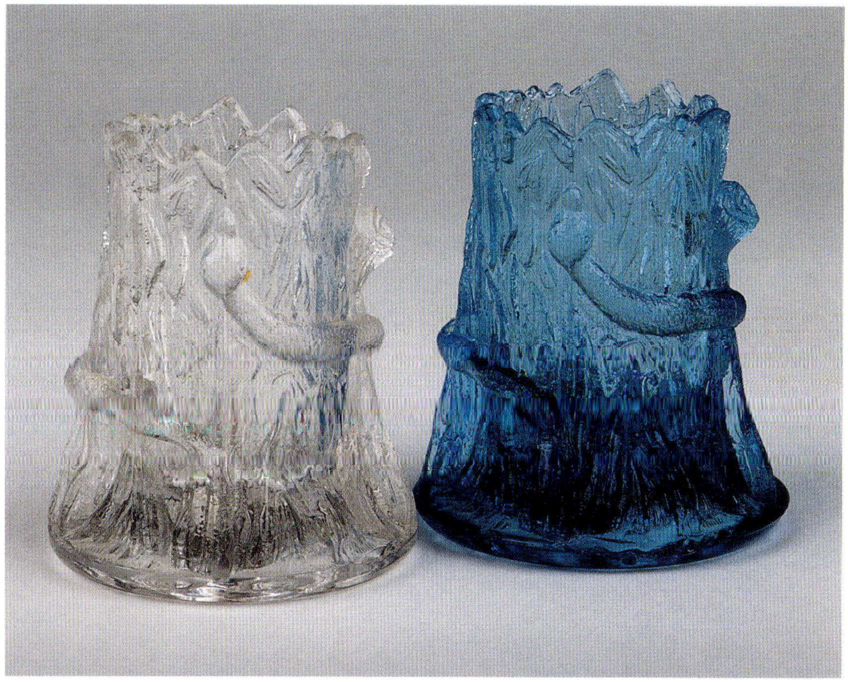

Snake on a Stump toothpick holder made by the Model Flint Glass Co., circa 1892. 2 5/8" high and 2 3/8" wide. Clear, $40-60. Amber, $65-80. Blue, $80-100. This was reproduced by L. G. Wright.

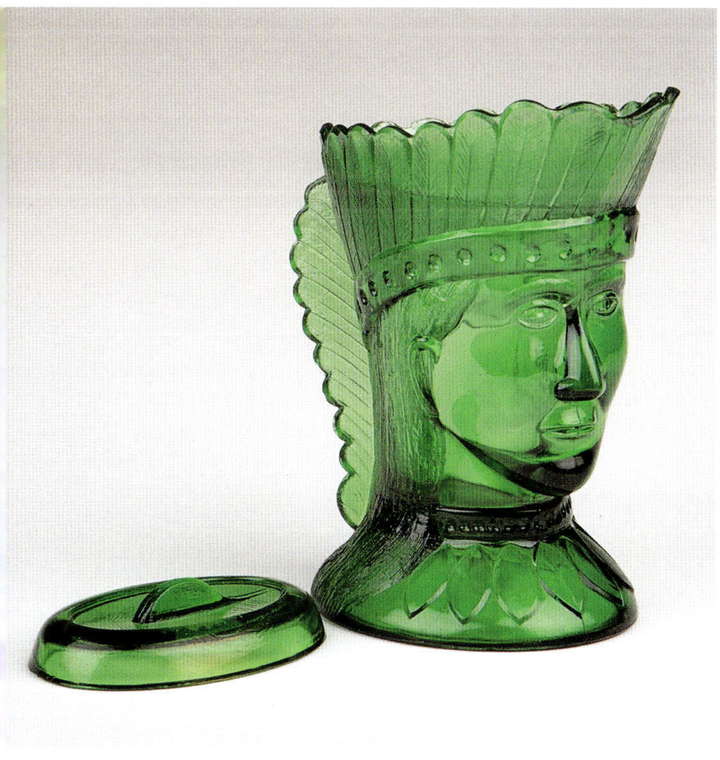

Indian Head pitcher in emerald green made by the Indiana Tumbler and Goblet Co., circa 1900. It is 9" high. Most of these are missing the lid because the lid easily falls inside the pitcher and breaks. This lid was photographed off so as not to accidentally cause breakage. Emerald green, $2,500-2,750.

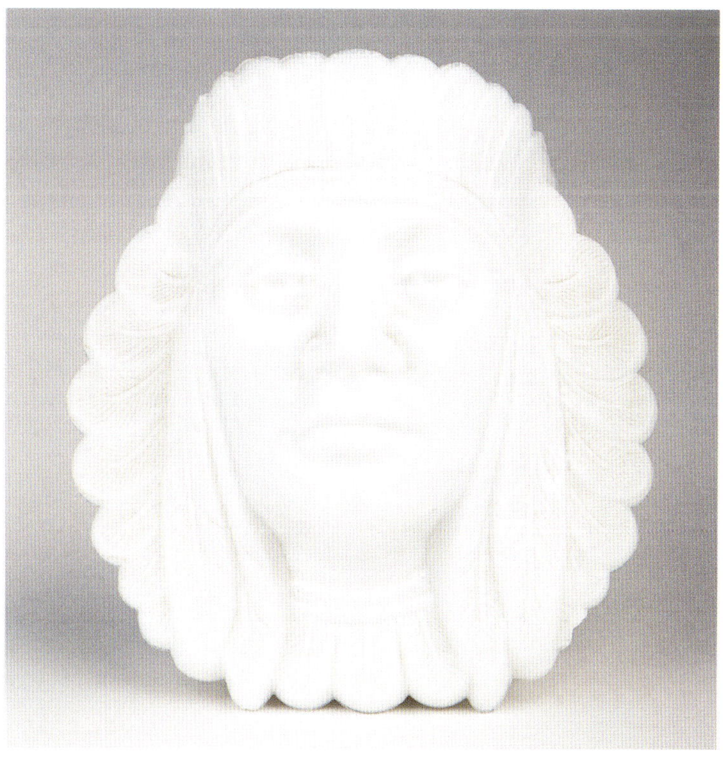

Opal Indian in full headdress match holder made by the Challinor, Taylor and Co., circa 1891. 5" high. $200-250.

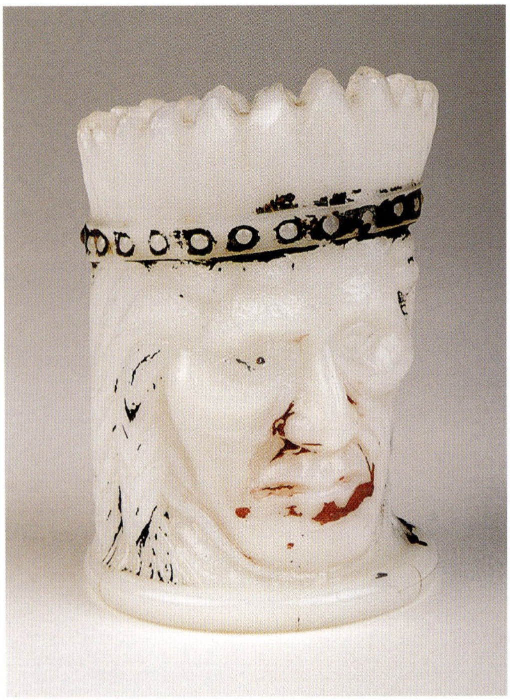

Indian head match holder in decorated opal. $85-110.

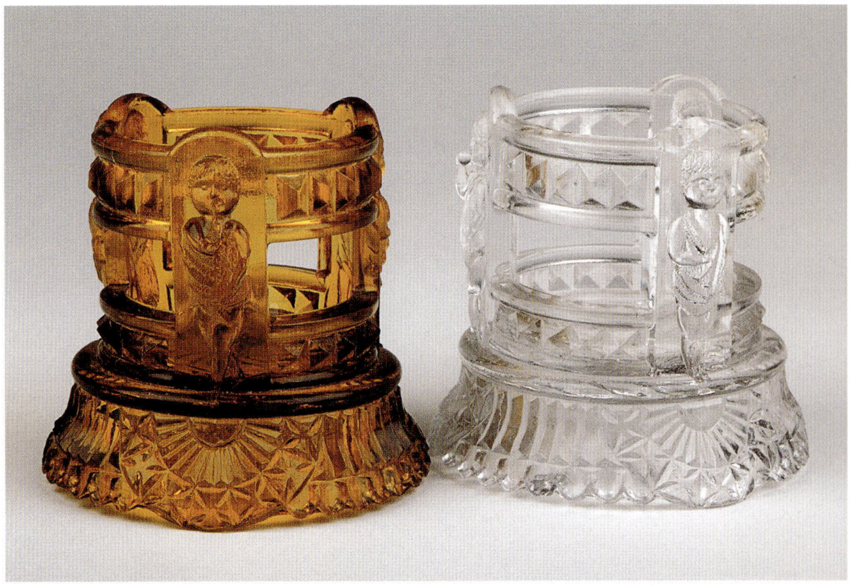

Egyptian toothpick holder made by the Aetna Glass and Manufacturing Co. in 1887. 2 3/4" high and 2 1/4" wide. Clear, $90-110. Amber, $140-160. Blue, $165-185.

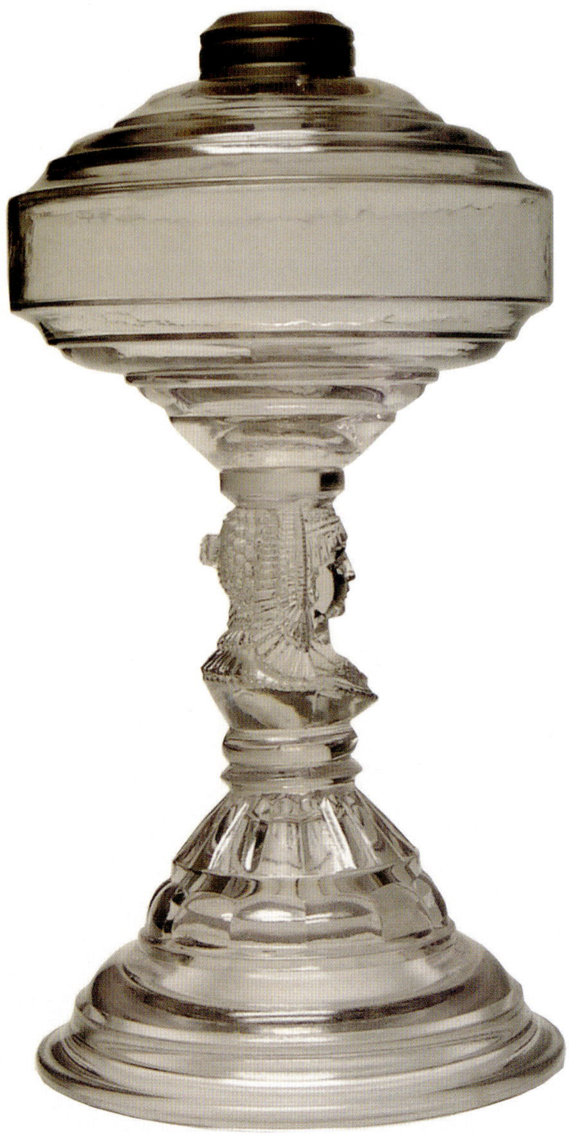

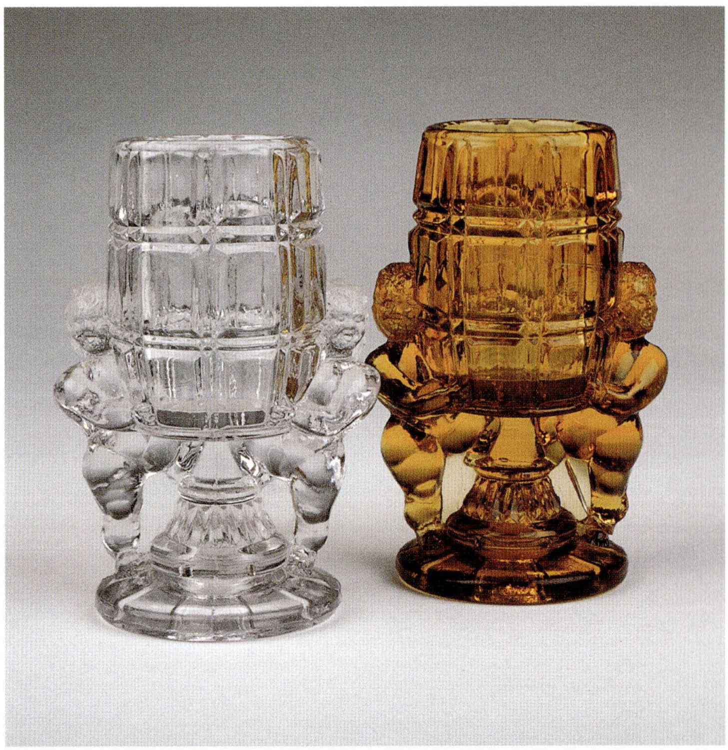

Peek-a-boo toothpick holder made by the McKee Glass Co., circa 1904. 3 3/4" high and 1 7/8" wide. Clear, $60-70. Amber, $70-85. Blue, $70-85.

Egyptian Lamp made by the Hemingray Glass Company. Clear, $1,200.

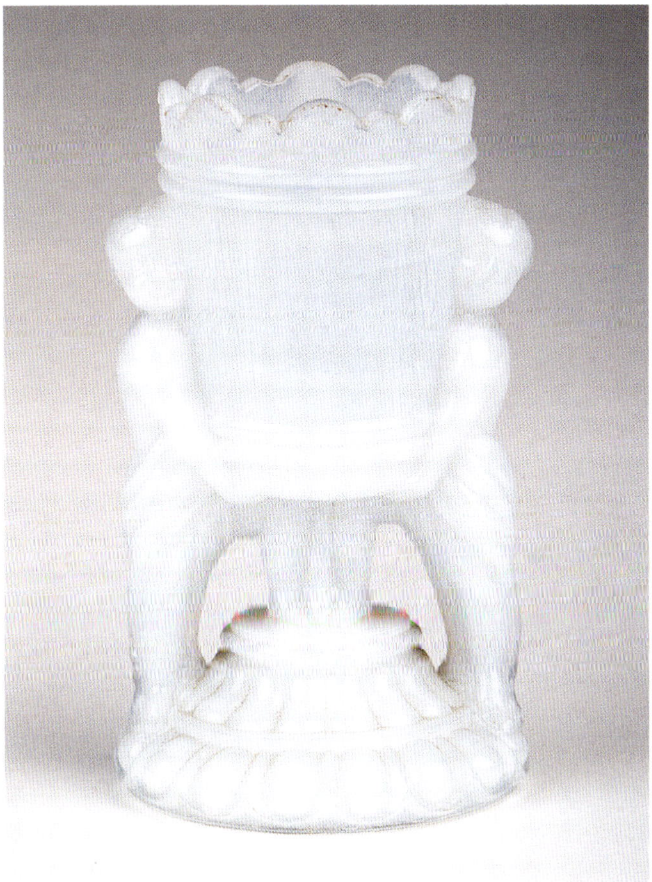

Two Cherubs match or toothpick holder by Vallerysthal, circa early 1900s. 4 1/2" high. Opal, $275-325.

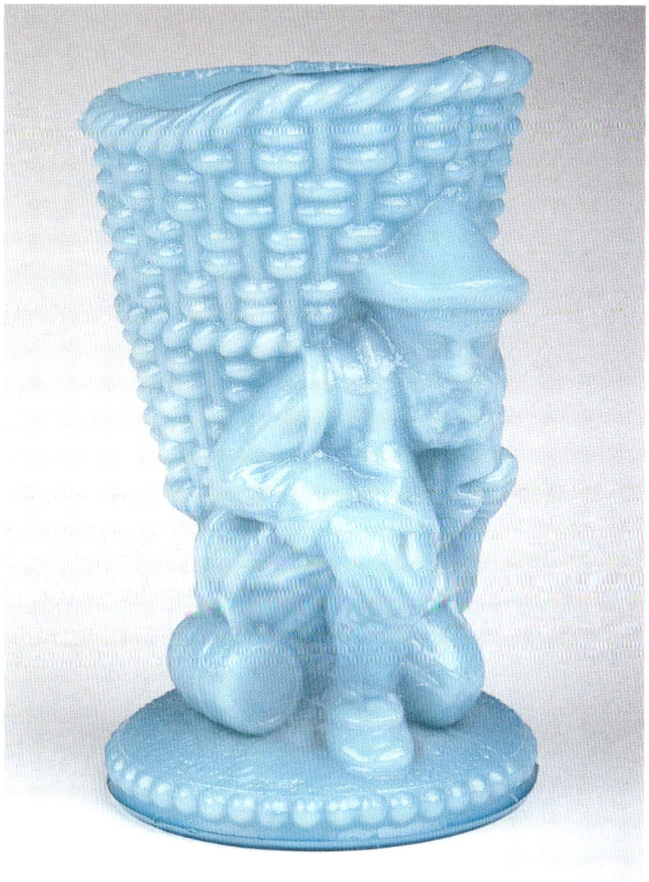

Man with Pack made by Portieux, circa early 1900s. 3 1/2" high. Blue opaque, $150-185.

Old Man with Pack and a match striker on the front. $210-240.

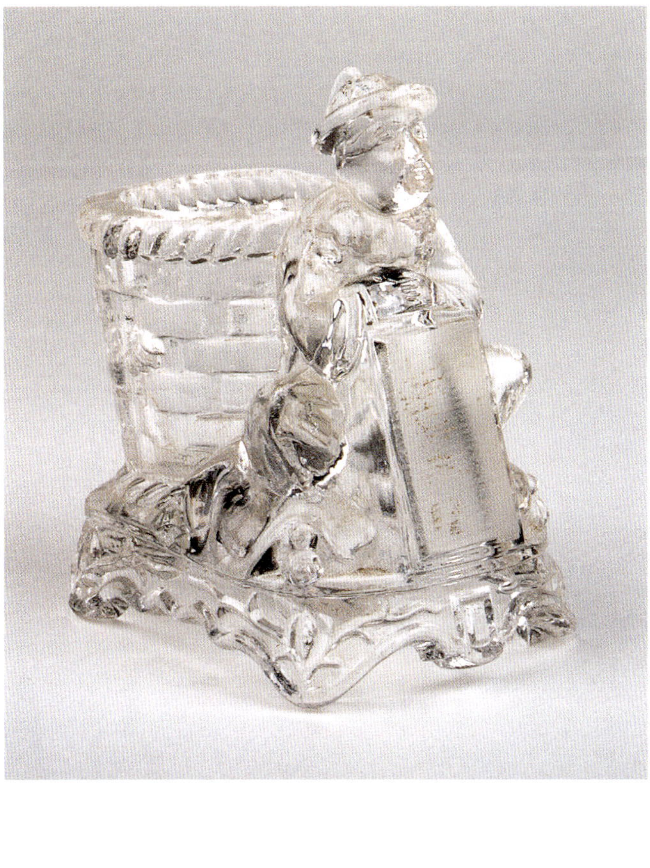

Old Man with Pack and a match striker on the front. $210-240.

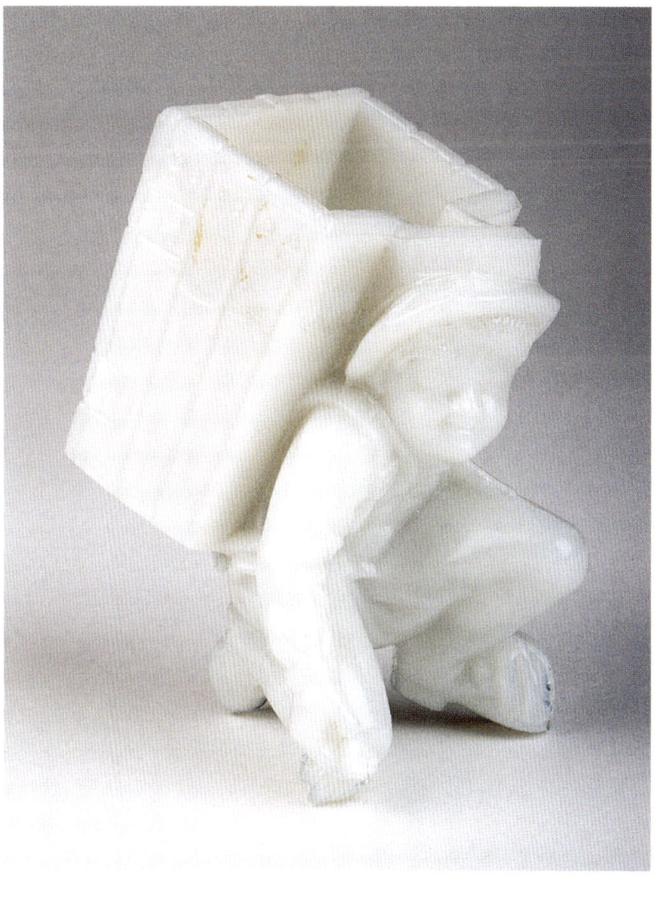

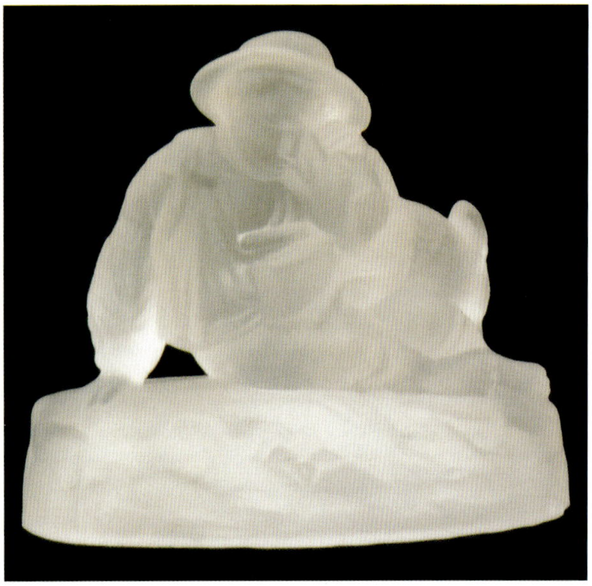

(Left) *The only love you can buy*, made by Gillinder and Sons in 1876. 4 3/4" high and 5 1/2" wide. $235-265.

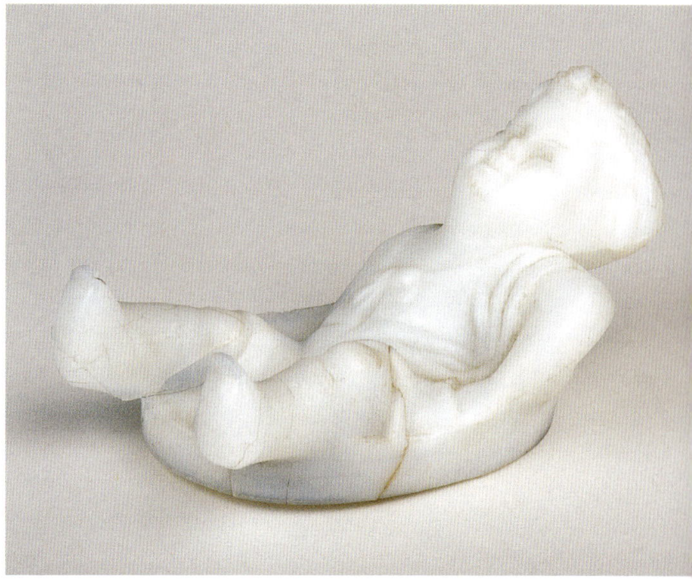

Opal Baby matchbox, a cover for an opaque black hat base. The lid is 4 3/4" long. Opal lid on a black base, a complete item, $950-1,000.

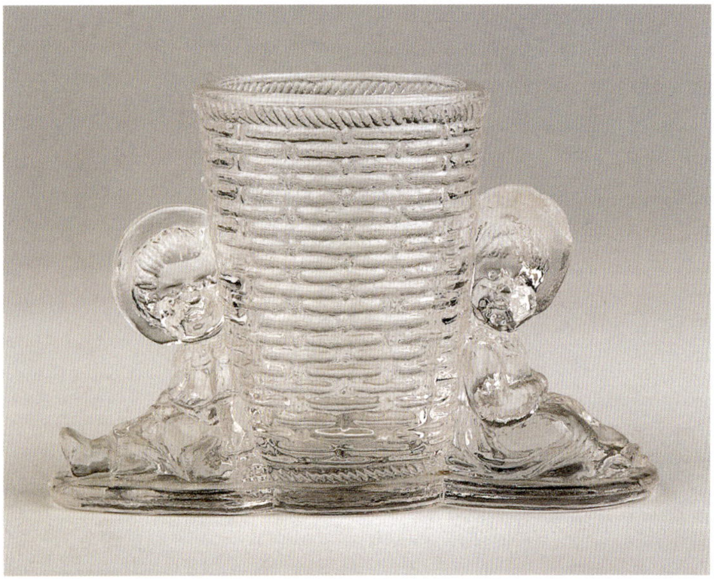

Peek-a-boo made by the Ohio Flint Glass Co., circa 1897. 2 1/2" high and 1 5/8" wide. Clear, $55-75.

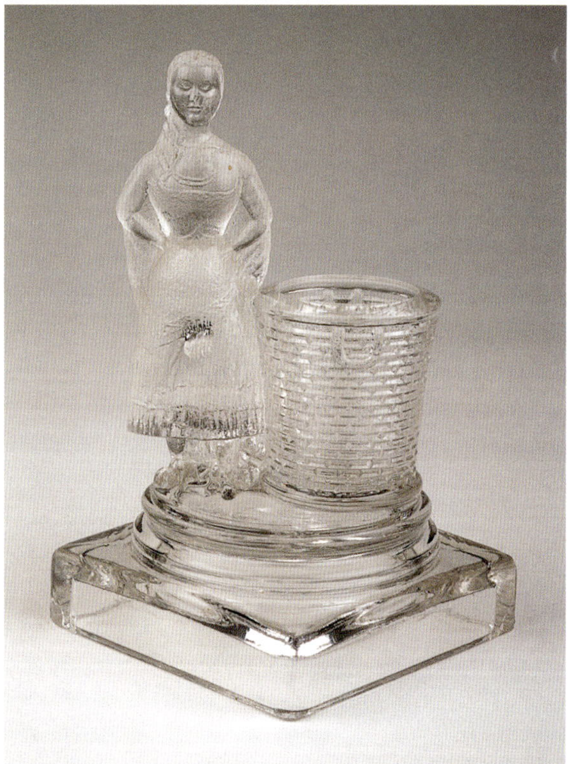

Pretty Maiden toothpick holder. 5 1/4" high and 3 1/8" wide on the base. $75-90.

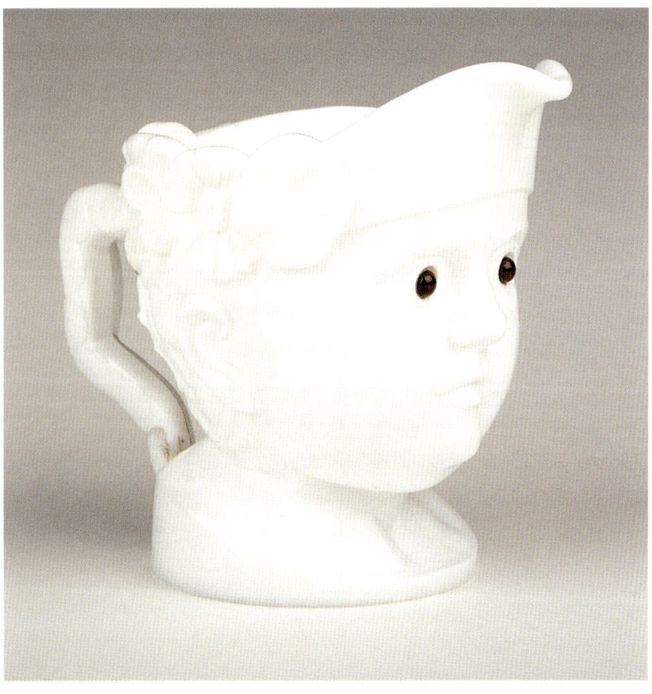

A cream pitcher in the figure of a child's head. Maker and date of manufactuer unknown. Opal, $185-225.

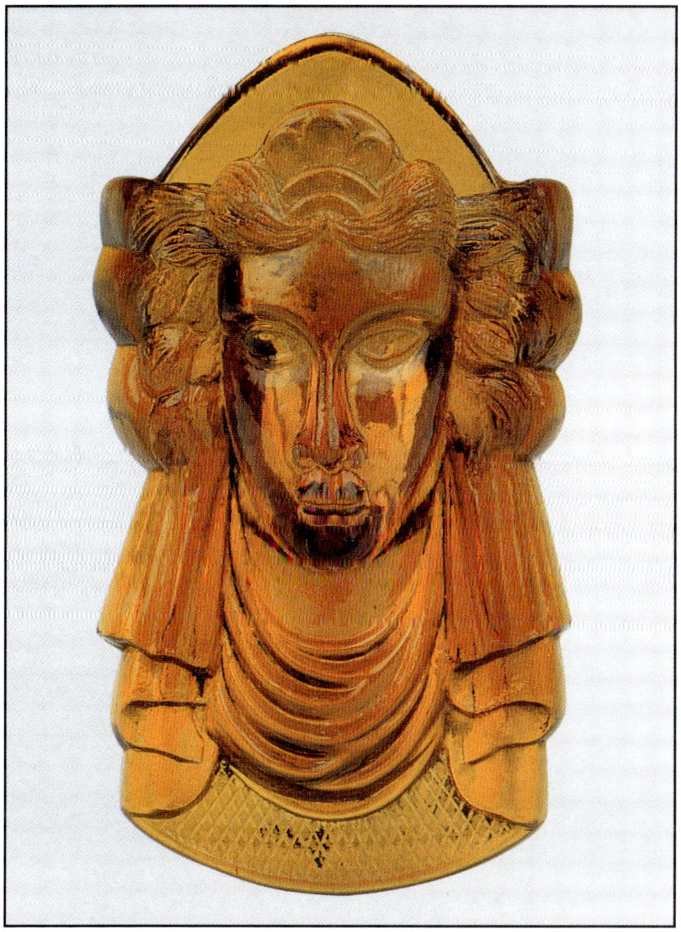

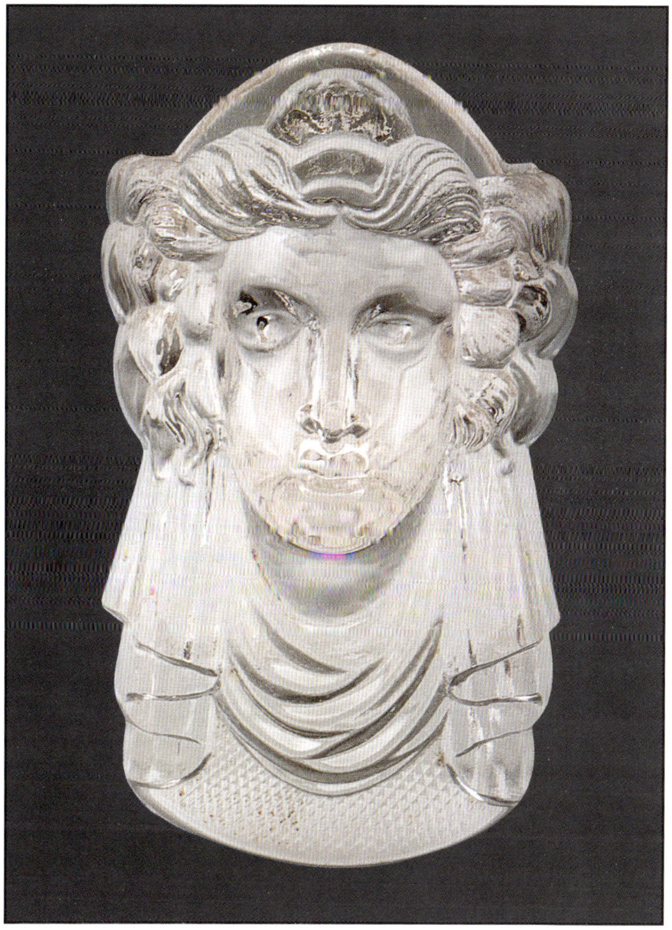

Wall match holder, sometimes called Jenny Lind, made by the Enterprise Glass Co. 4 1/2" high. Clear, $65-85. Amber, $120-150.

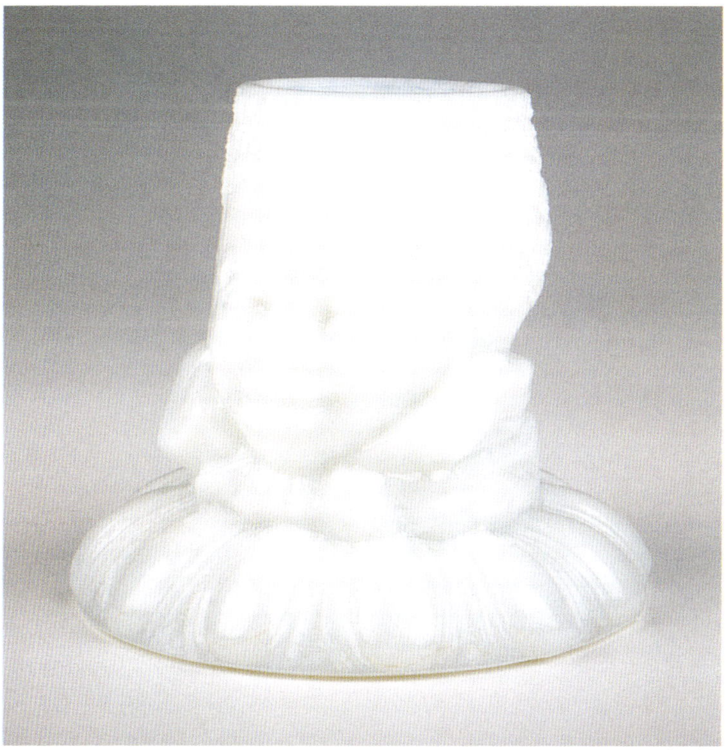

Negro Boy match or toothpick holder, maker unknown, circa 1900. Opal, $85-125.

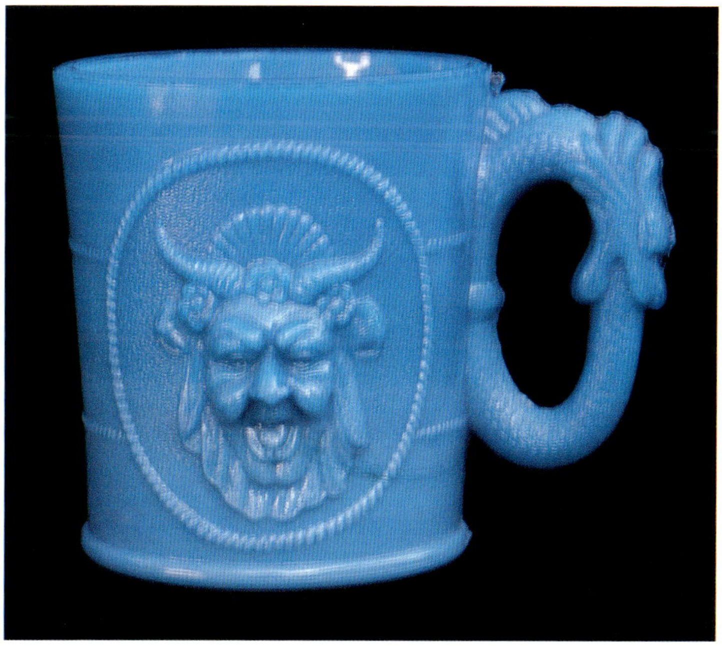

Mephistopheles Dragon handled mug, circa 1885. 3 3/8" high and 3" diameter. $145-165.

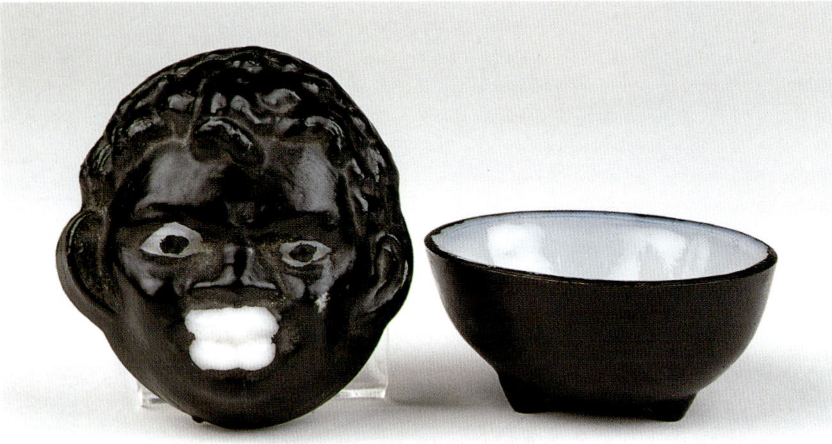

Negro Boy covered box, opal inside and black decorated outside. 2 3/8" diameter. $850-950

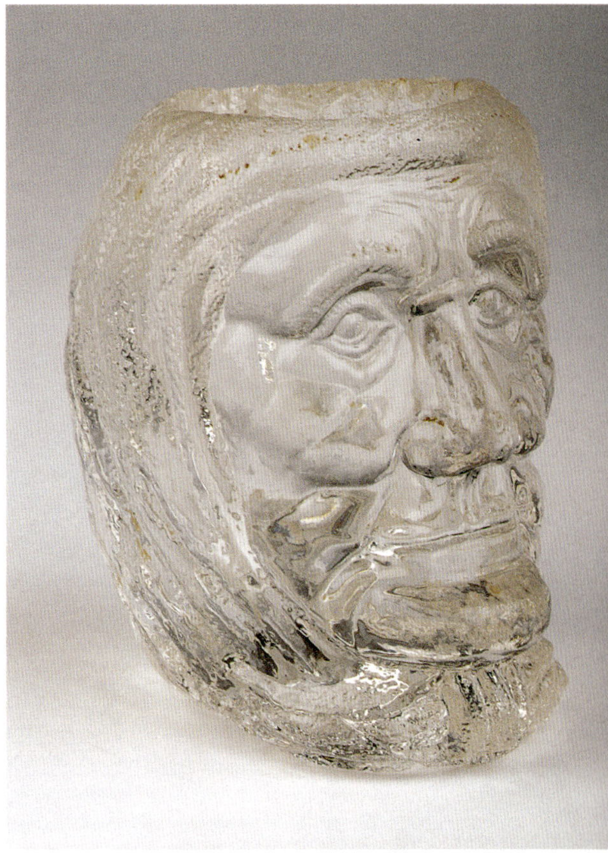

Old Witch toothpick holder made by the Indiana Tumbler & Goblet Company. 2 5/8" high and 2 3/4" wide. Clear, $80-90. Has been reproduced.

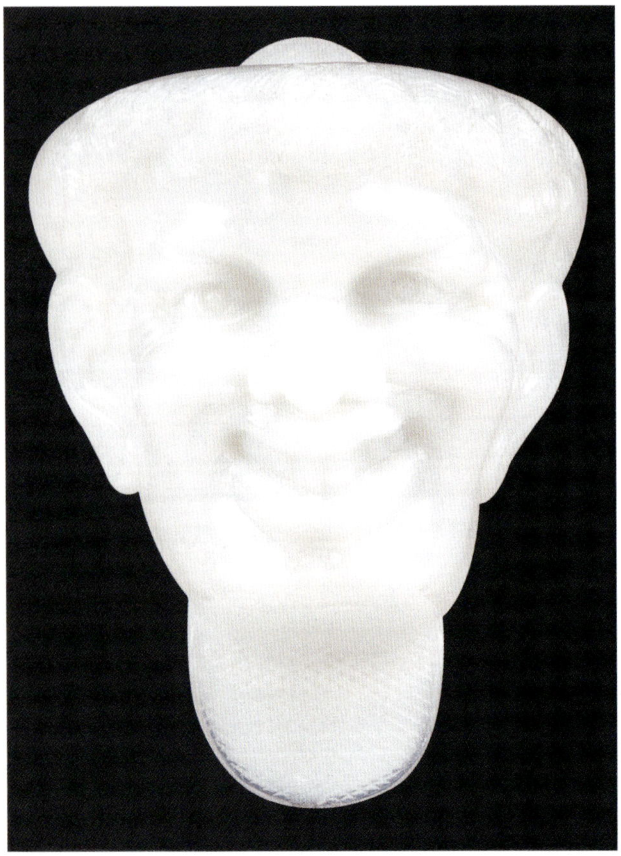

Jester match holder. *Patent June 13, 1876*. Opal, $100-125.

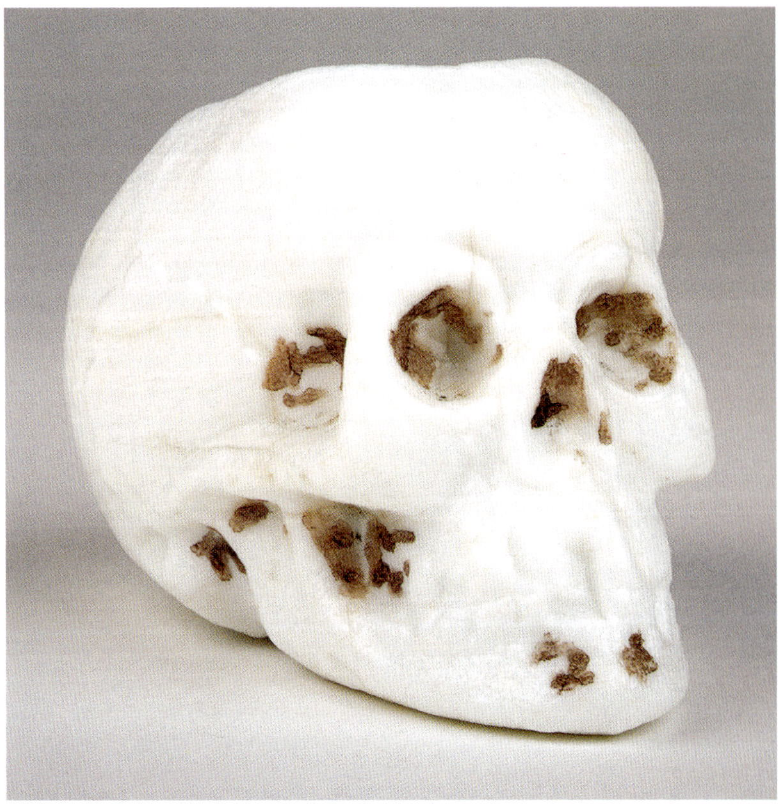

Ramses 111 toothpick holder made by McKee and Bros., circa 1899. 2 1/2" high. Opal $225-265.

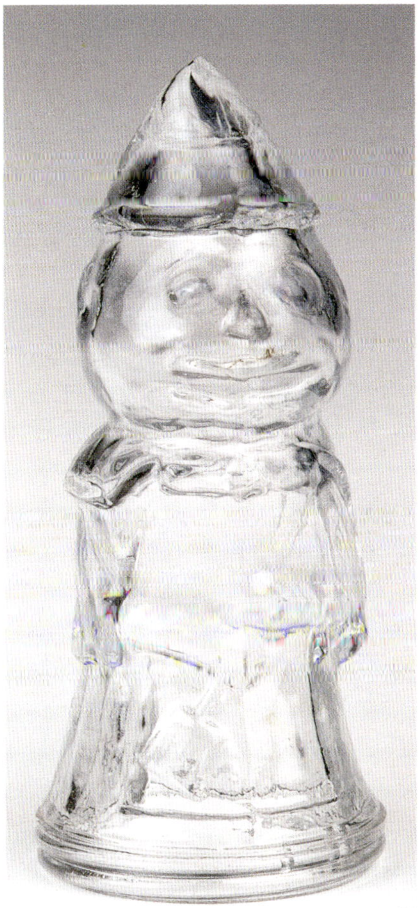

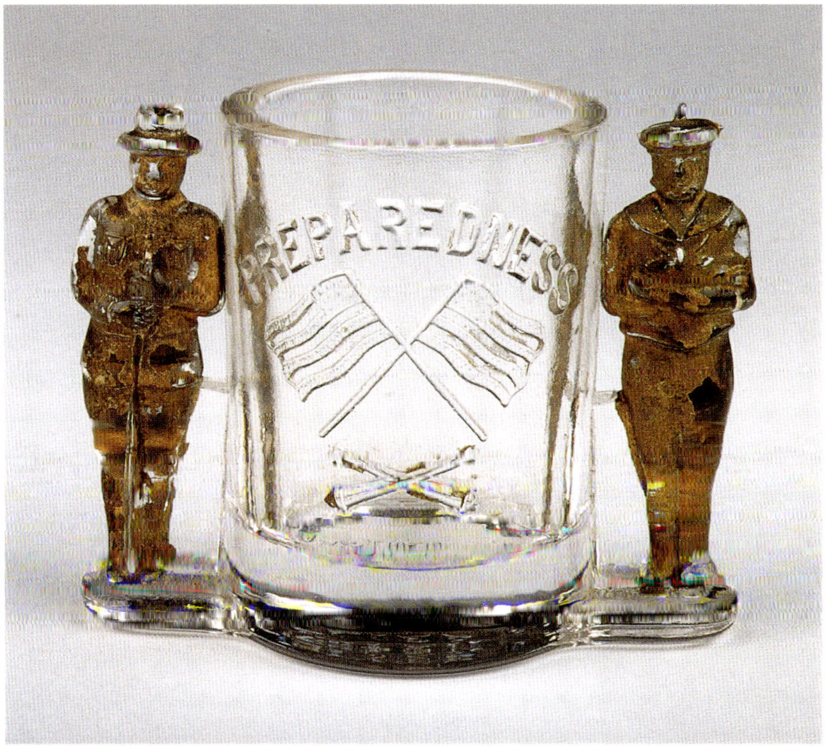

Preparedness toothpick holder, circa 1917. Clear with gold, $190-225.

Punkin Head candy container. 4 5/8" high. Clear, $450-550.

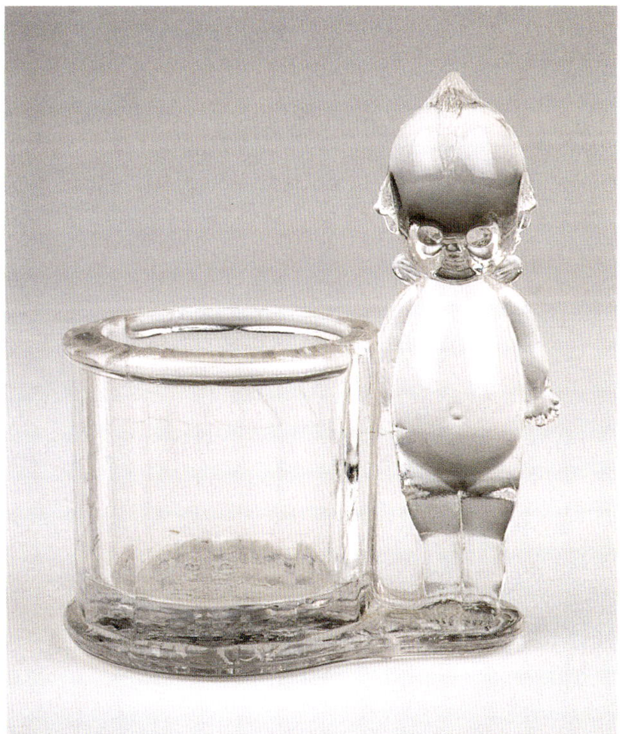

Kewpie candy container made by Geo. Borgfeld. The containers are marked with their name and *Reg. U S Pat. Off. Des. Pat. 3650.* 1 3/4" high and 1 3/4" wide. Clear, $45-65. Has been reproduced and marked Taiwan.

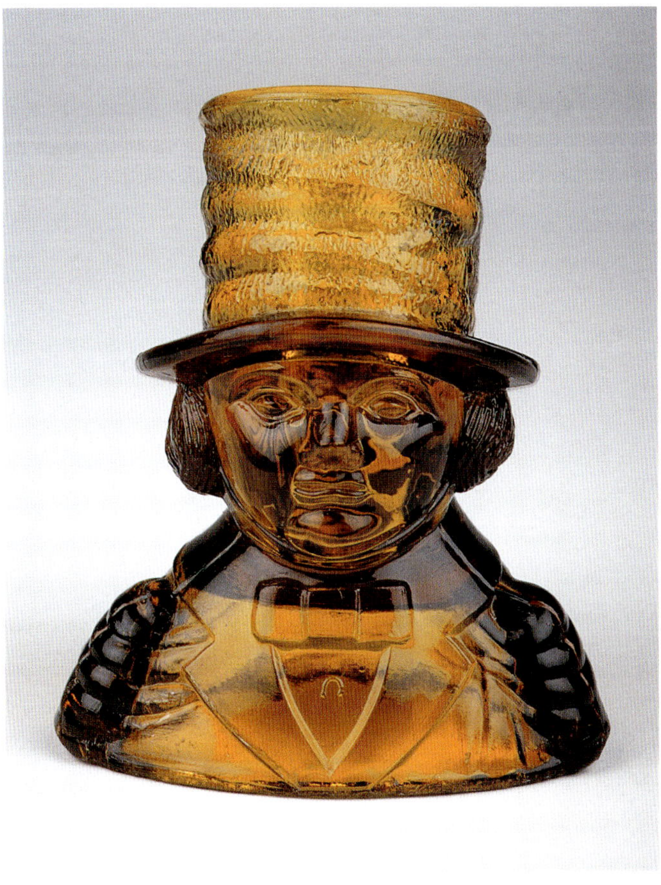

Man in top hat toothpick holder. Amber, $185-225.

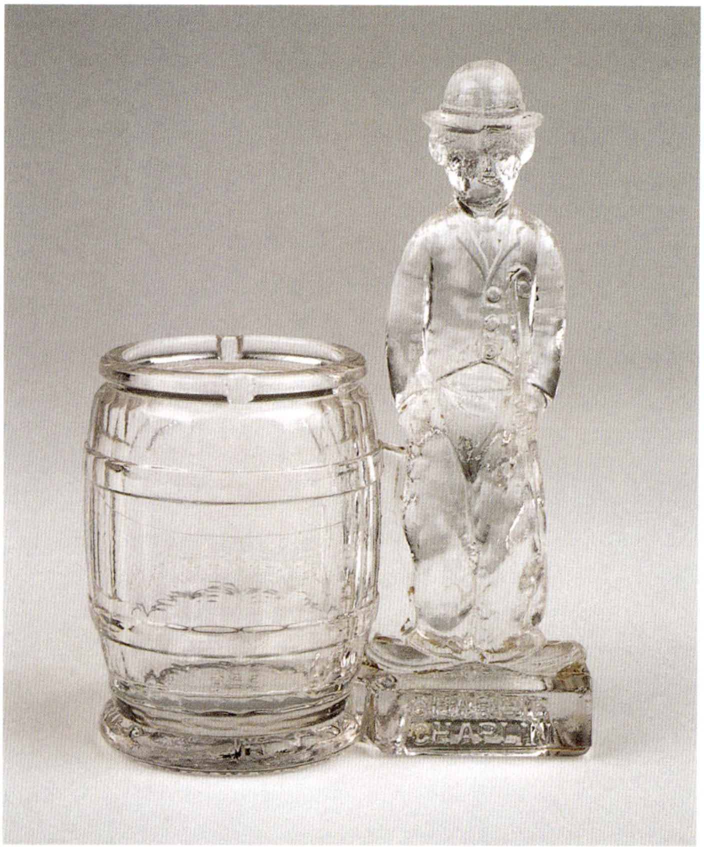

Charlie Chaplin candy container. 2 1/8" high and 1 5/8" wide. Clear, $60-70.

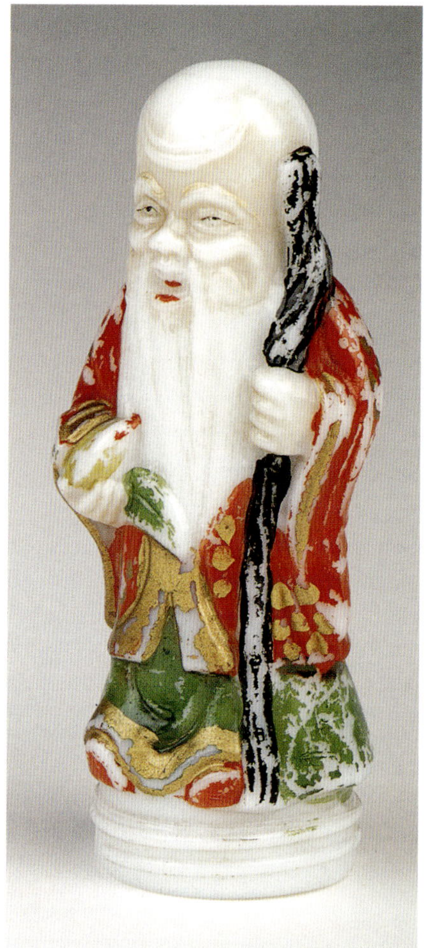

Santa candy container decorated opal. 5" tall. $2,100-2,300.

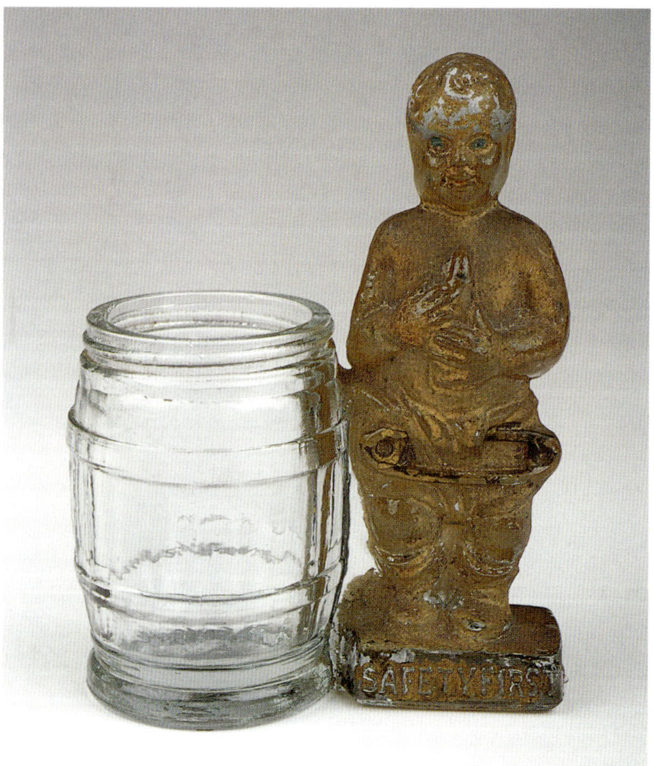

Safety candy container getting its name from the safety pin on the diaper and the word safety on the base, 3 3/8" high. Clear with gold decoration, $125-155.

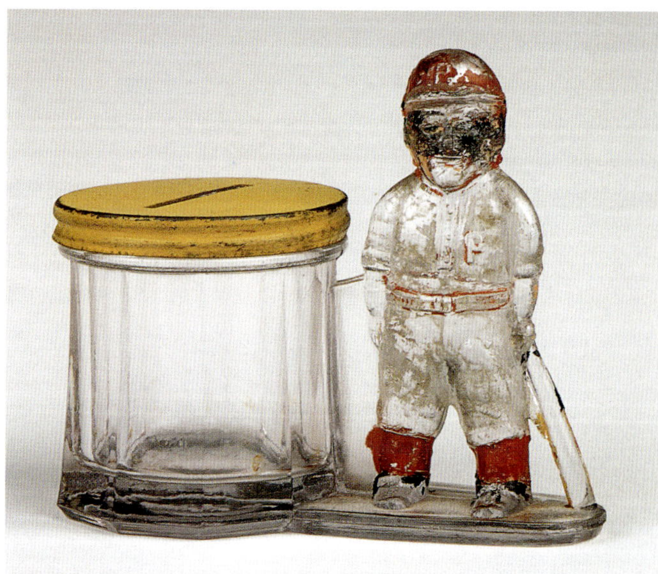

Baseball player candy container-bank: the player has the letter P on his cap and jersey. 4" high. Clear decorated, $1,500-1,800.

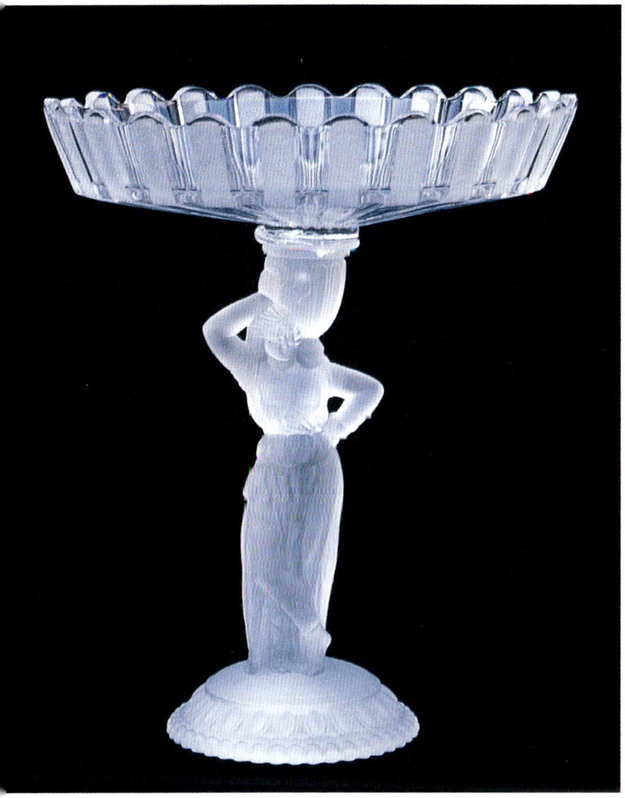

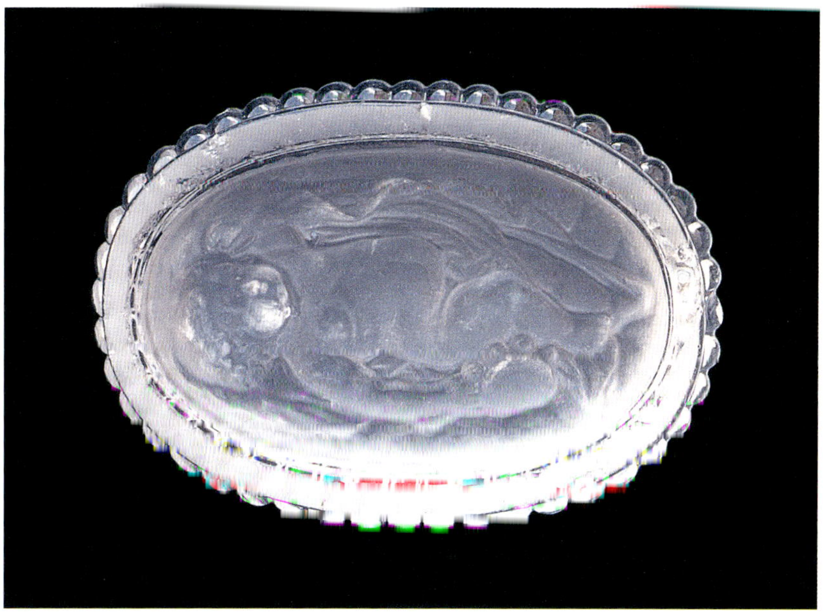

Infant Moses paperweight, circa 1880s, 4 1/4" long. $85-125.

Rebecca at the Well compote made by Bakewell, Pears and Co., the bowl being the Ribbon pattern, circa 1870. 12 1/2" high and 10 1/2" diameter. $350-600.

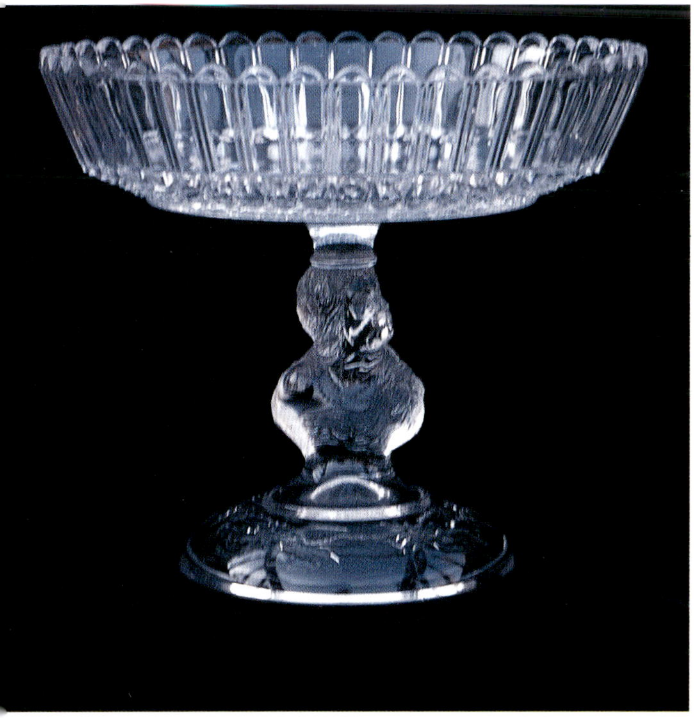

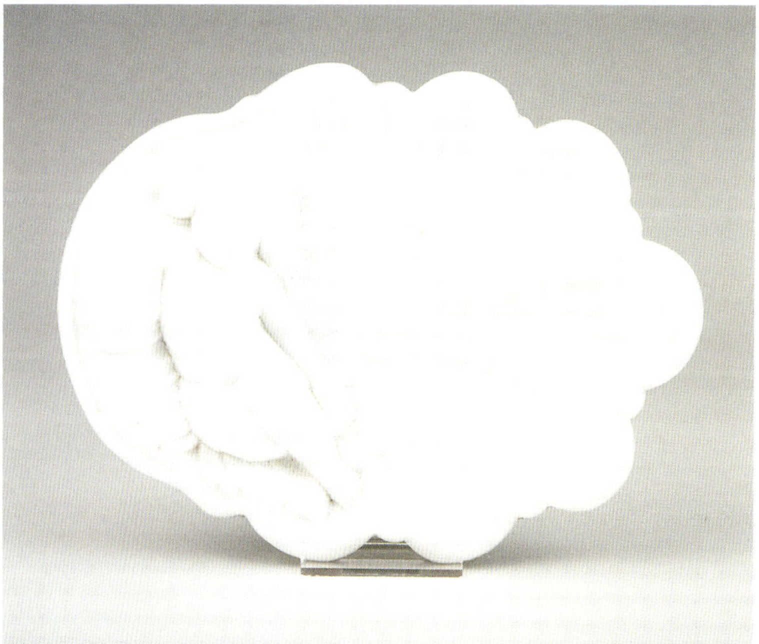

Baby on a Shell. Opal. $135-145.

Jenny Lind Majestic Crown compote made by Challinor, Taylor and Co., circa 1877. 7 1/2" high. $100-125.

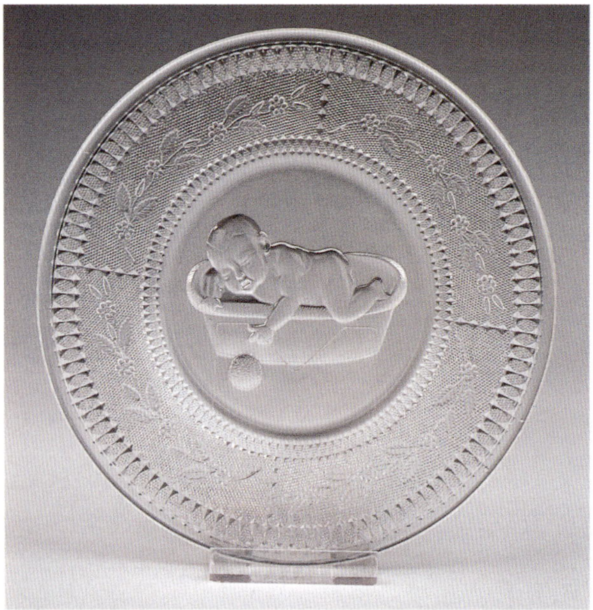

Dot pattern plate with Baby center made by the Findlay Flint Glass Co., circa 1890. 7" diameter. Collectors know this pattern as Stippled Forget Me Not. Clear, $60-85.

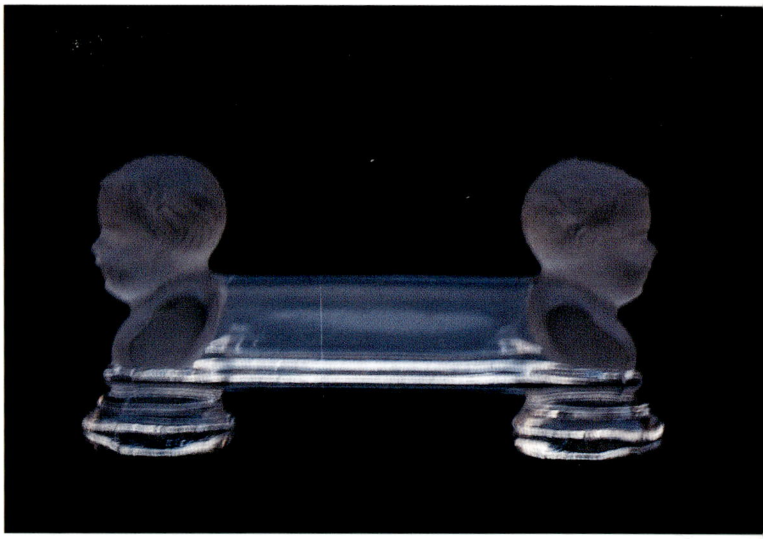

Baby Head knife rest, circa 1875. 4 1/4" long. Clear frosted, $85-100.

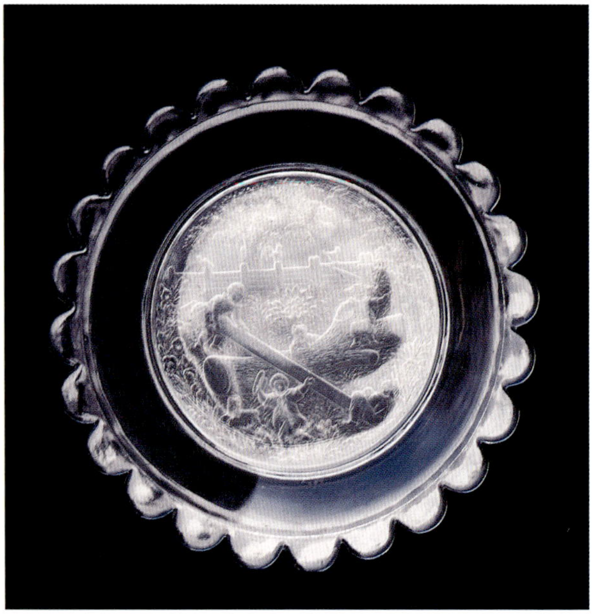

Seesaw plate, circa 1875. 10" diameter. Clear, $155-180.

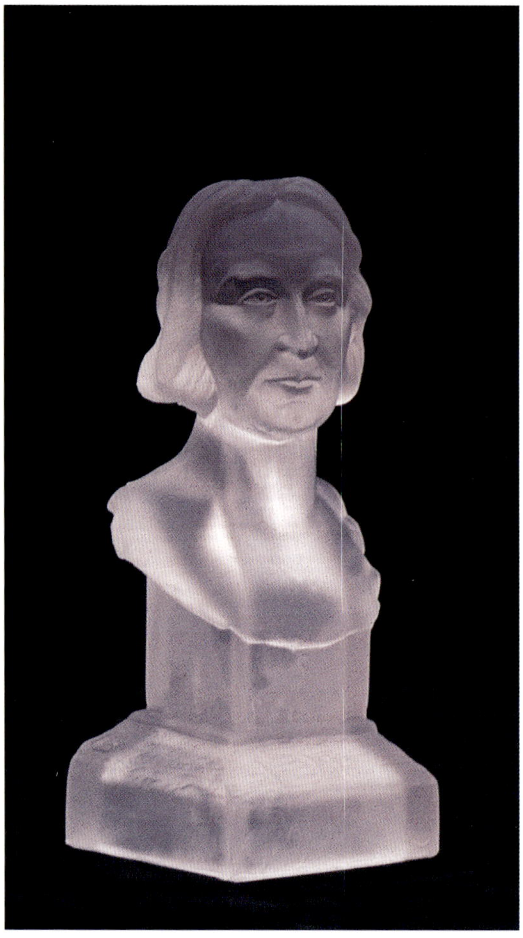

Bust of Columbus Statuette, circa 1880. 5 1/2" high. Clear frosted, $100-125.

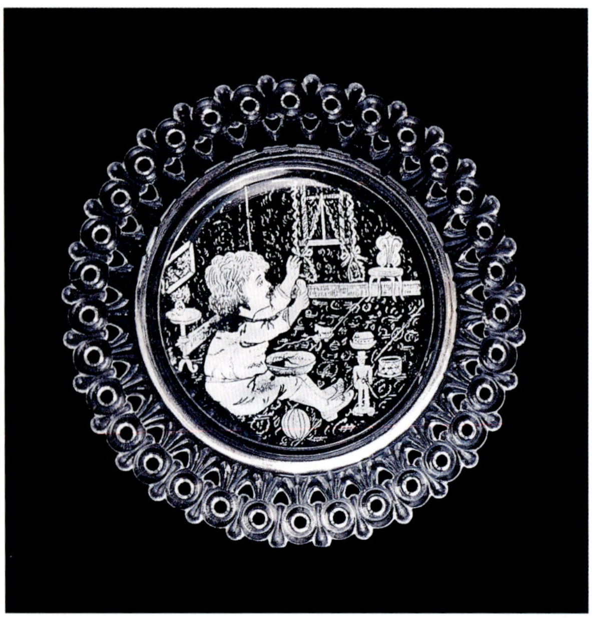

Little Jack Horner egg and dart plate, circa 1889. 5 1/2" diameter. Clear, $70-90.

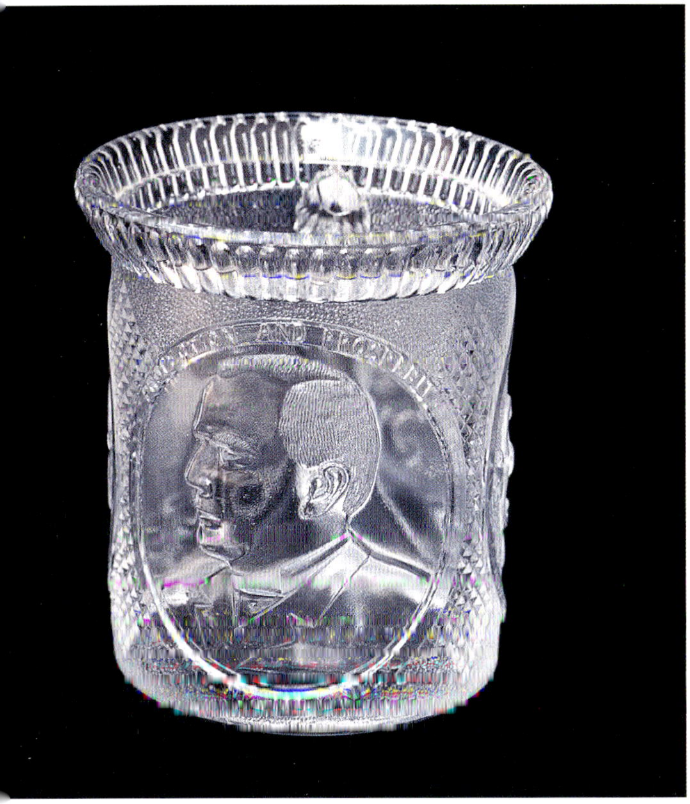

McKinley Protection and Plenty mug made by McKee and Brothers, circa 1896. 3 1/2" high. $75-100.

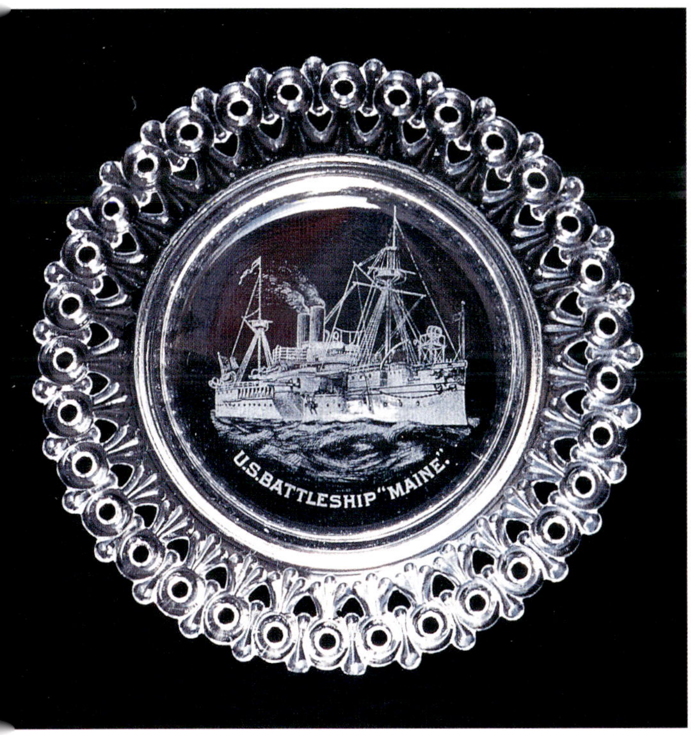

U S Battleship Maine egg and dart plate, circa 1900. 5 1/2" diameter. $20-40.

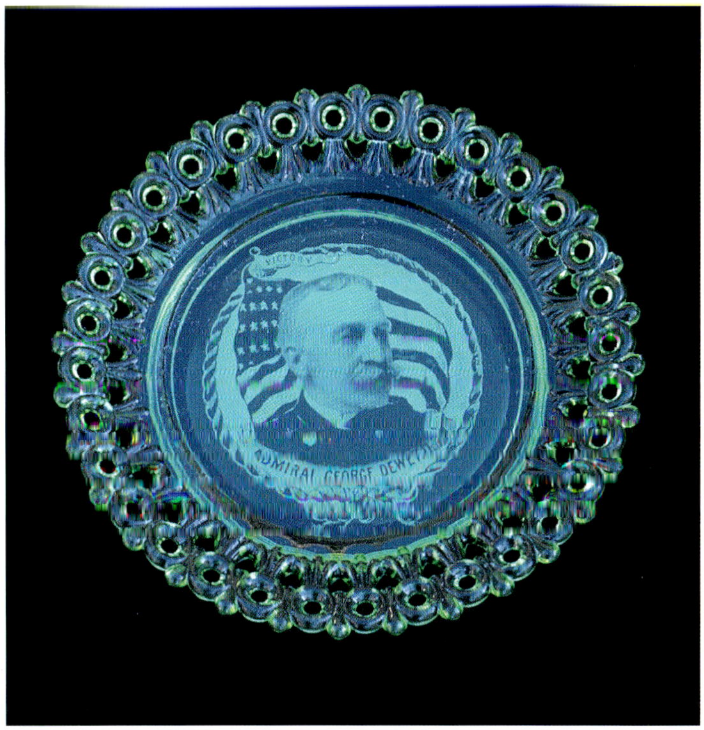

George Dewey plate, circa 1900. 5 1/2" diameter. Green, $75-100.

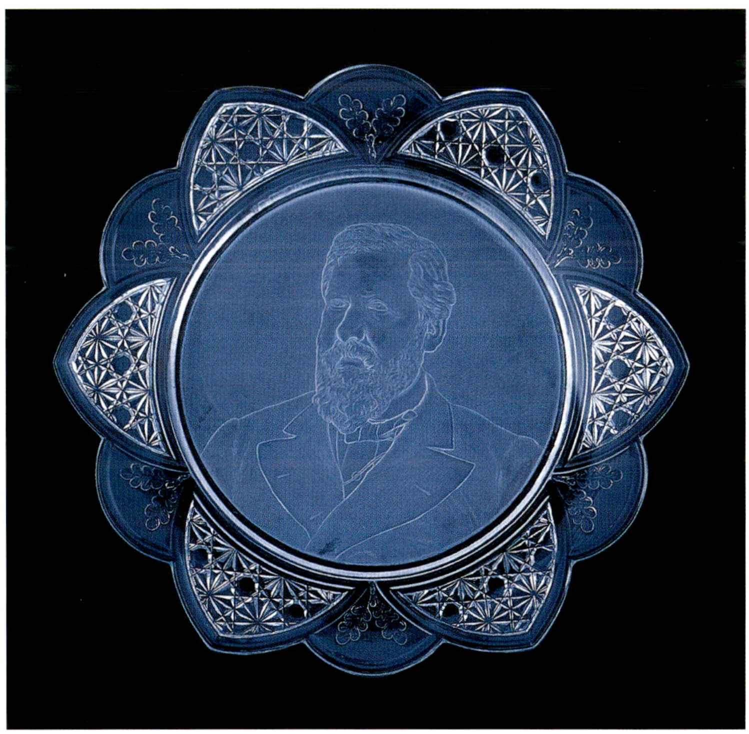

James G. Blaine portrait plate for the election of 1884, made by Gillinder and Sons. 11 1/2" diameter. $300-350.

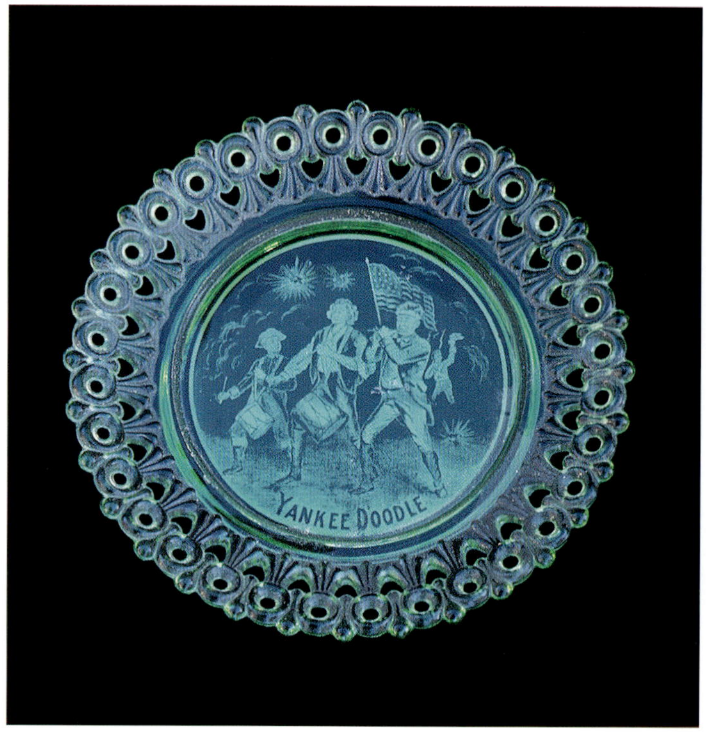

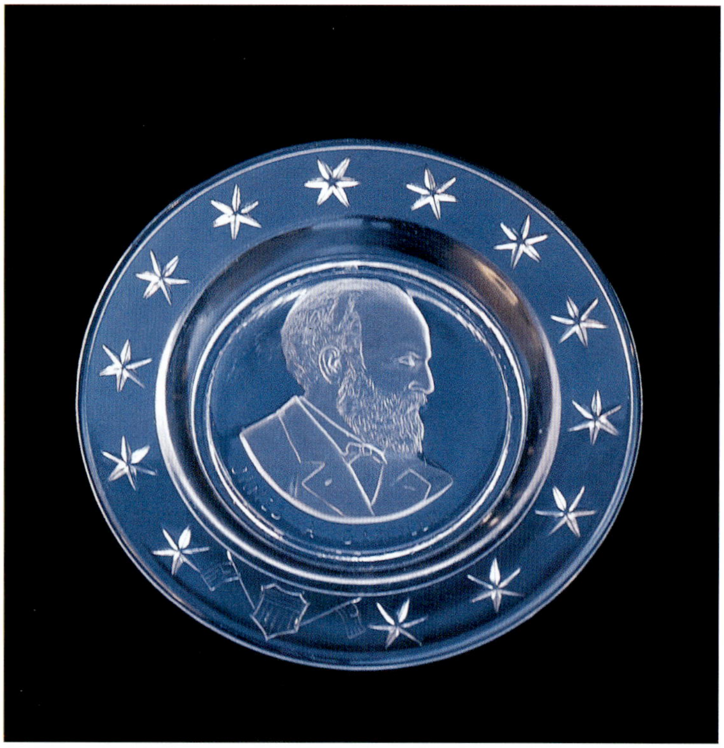

Garfield plate. 6" diameter. $85-100.

Yankee Doodle plate patterned after the *Spirit of '76* painting by Archibald Willard. Circa 1900. Green, $75-100.

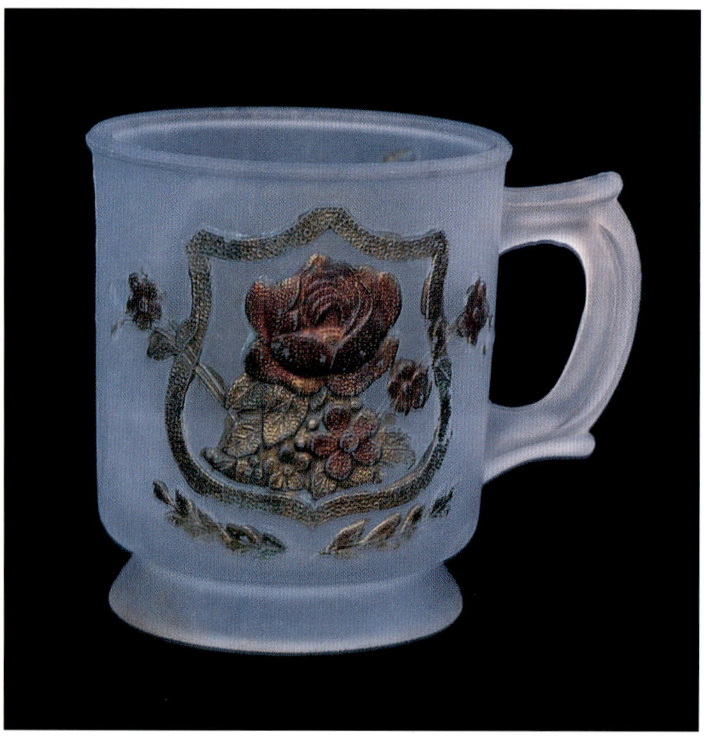

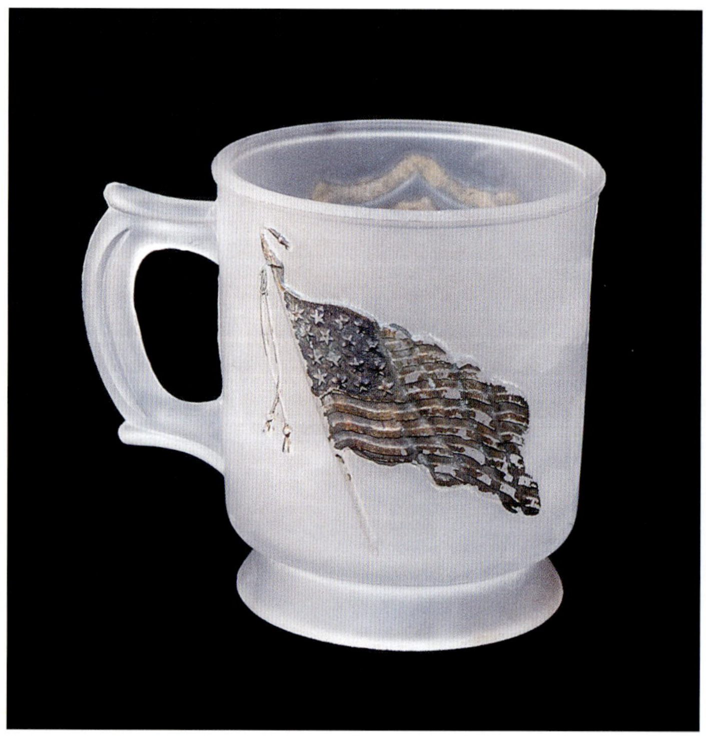

Tennessee Statehood mug with Cherokee Rose on one side and the Flag on the other. 3 1/2" high and 3" diameter. $125-150.

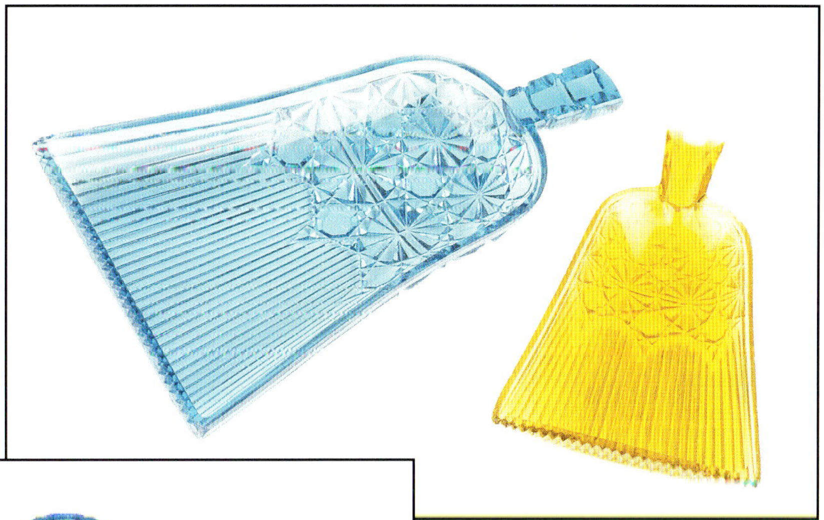

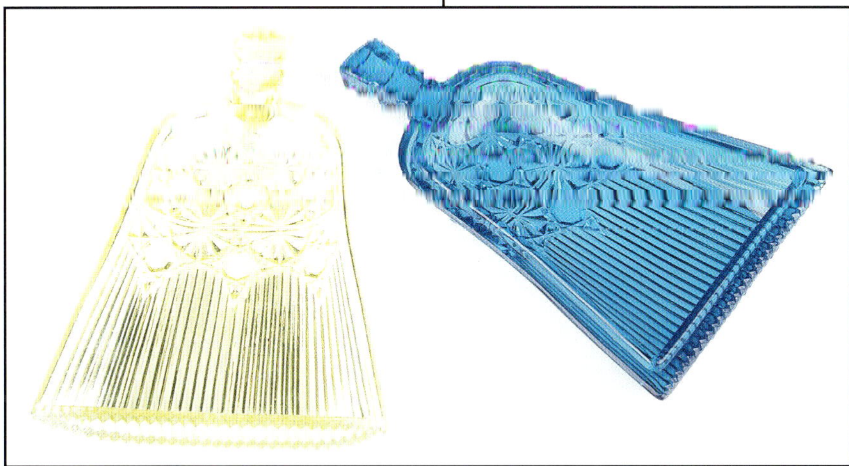

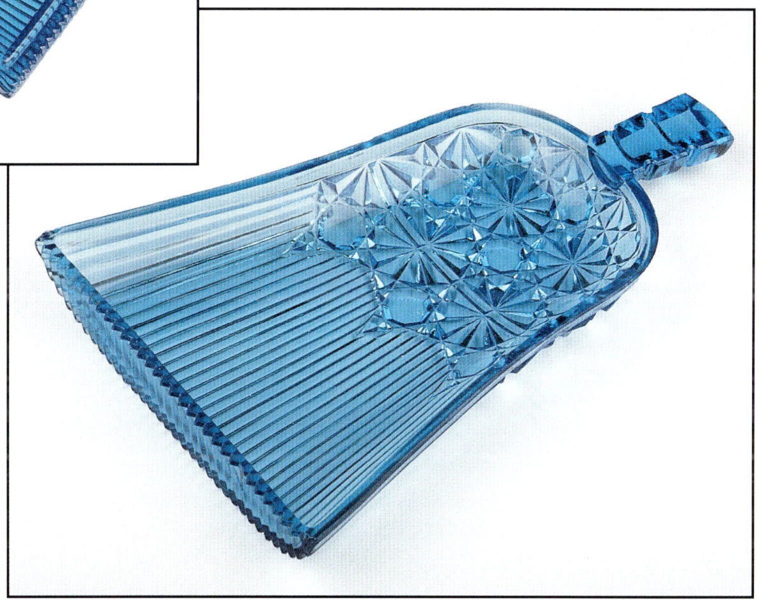

Whisk Brooms of various sizes made by several factories in the late 1880s. Blue, 8 1/2", $65-85. Blue and vaseline, 7 1/2", $65-85. Amber, 6 1/4", $40-55.

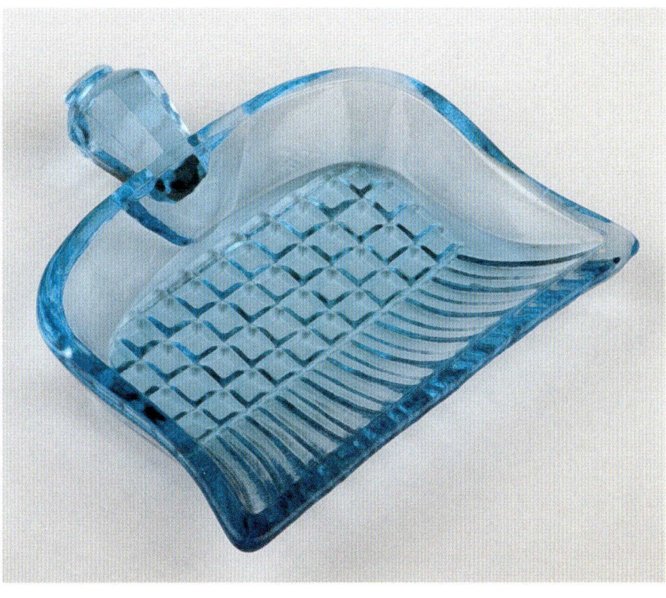

Dust pan made by the Indiana Tumbler and Goblet Co. $85-110.

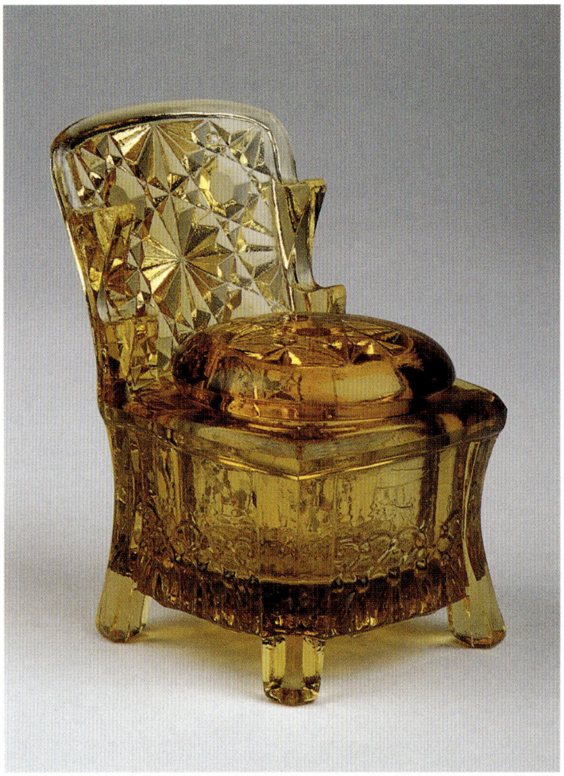

Chair inkwell made by the Canton Glass Co., 3" high. $300-350.

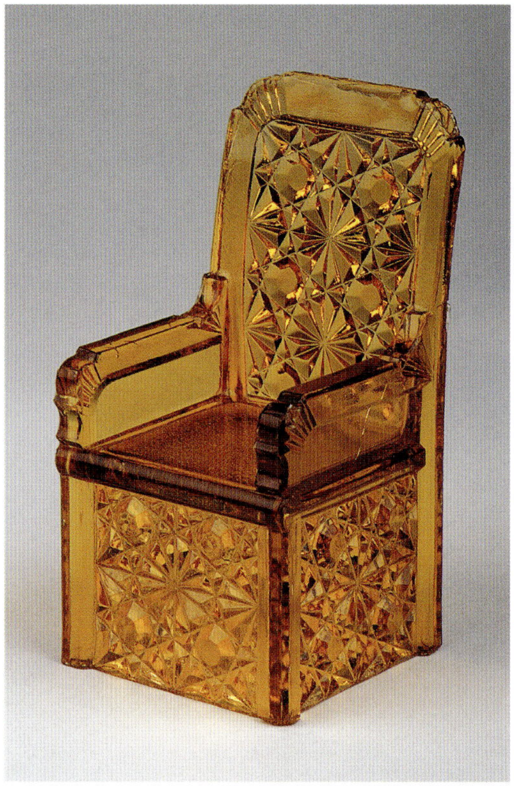

Chair made by Geo. Duncan and Sons, circa late 1880s. 4" high and 2 1/8" wide. Amber, $90-125.

Anvil, fine cut pattern made by the Windsor Glass Co., circa 1886. 2 1/8" high and 1 1/4" wide. Blue, $65-85.

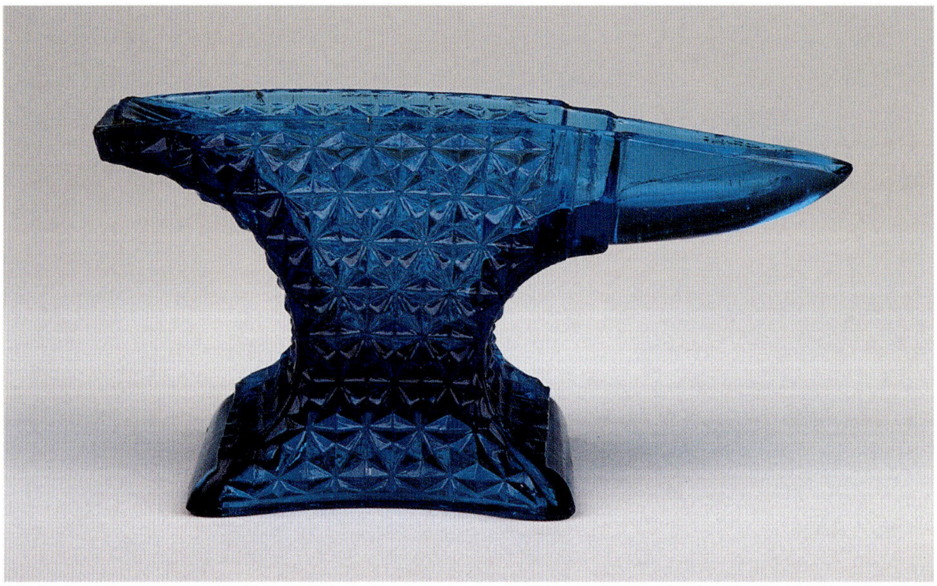

Anvil, daisy and button pattern, made by the United States Glass Co., circa late 1890s. 2" high and 1 5/8" wide. Amber, $65-75. Blue, $70-90.

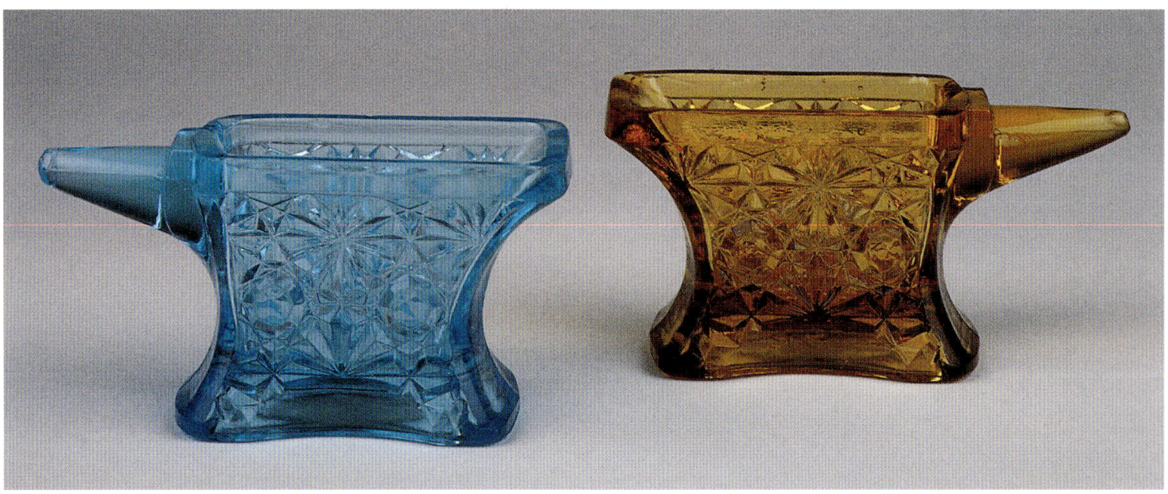

Ice Box sugar bowl, 5 1/4" high and 3 1/2" wide. Opal, $290-325.

Anvil, daisy and button pattern, made by the Co-operative Flint Glass Co., circa mid-1880s, 2" high and 2 1/8" wide. Amber, $40-50. Opal, $55-65.

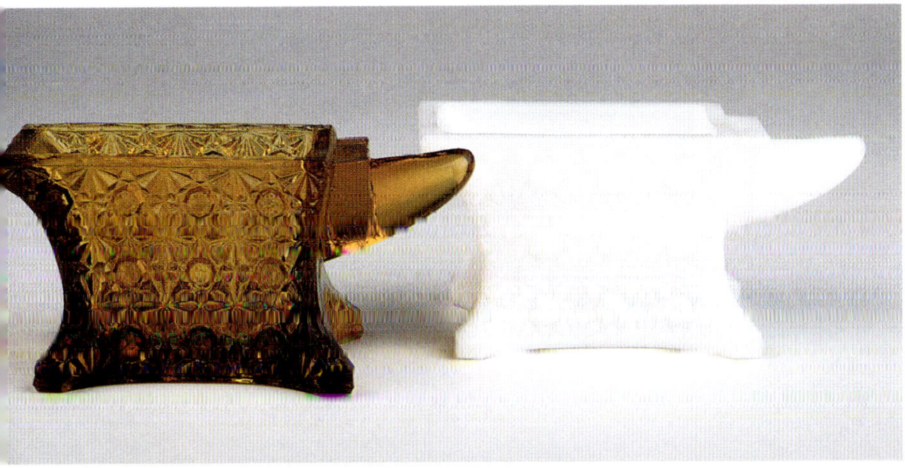

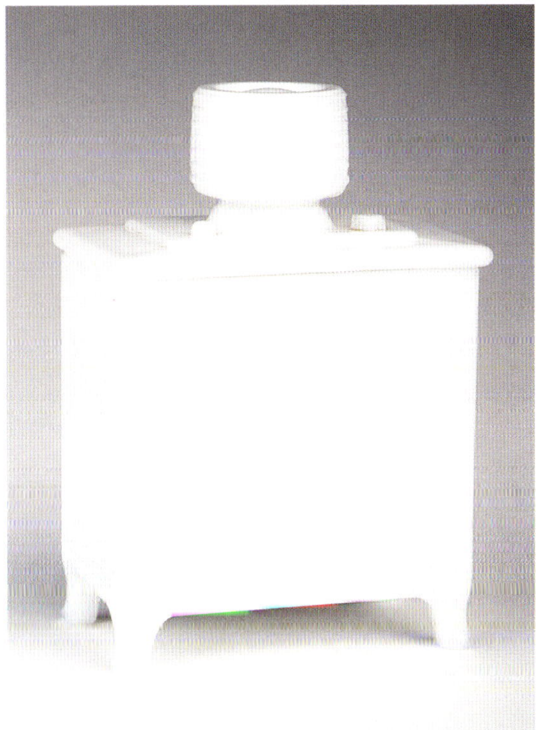

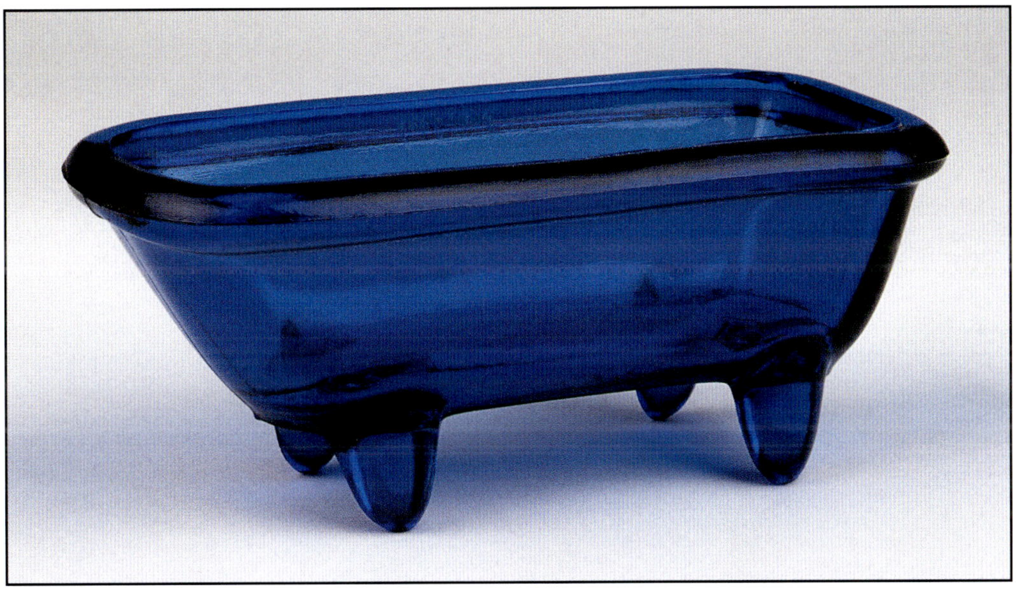

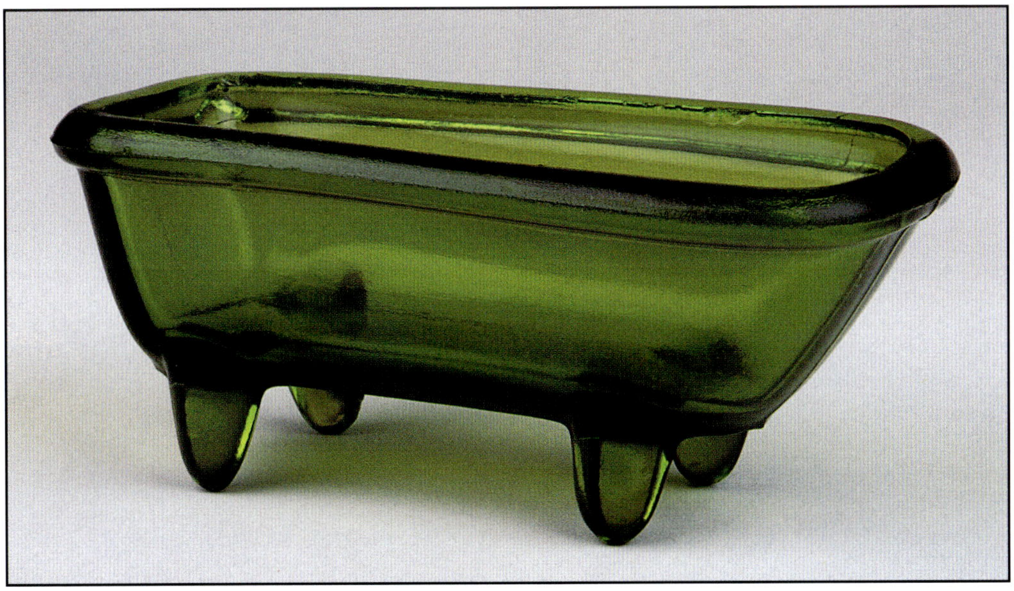

Bathtub made by the United States Glass Co., circa 1892. 5 7/8" long. Green, $45-65. Blue, $50-70.

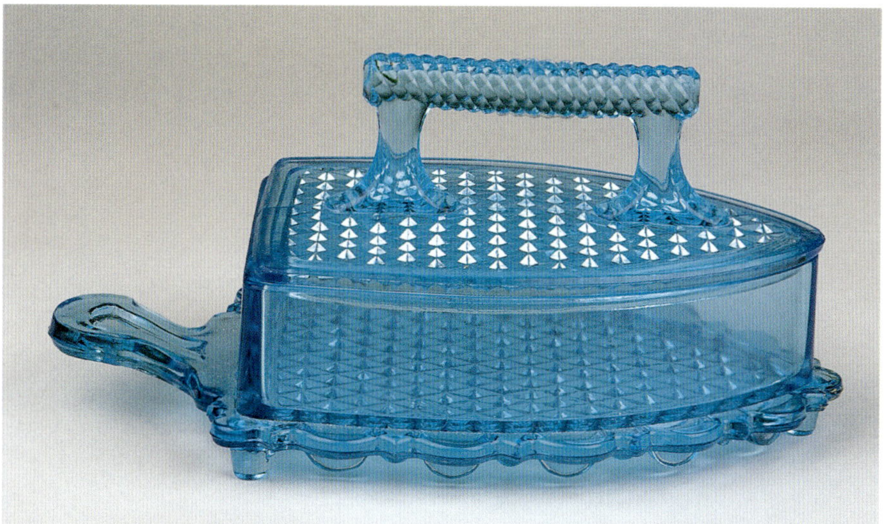

Flat Iron butter dish, circa 1890s. Blue, $80-90. Beware of reproductions.

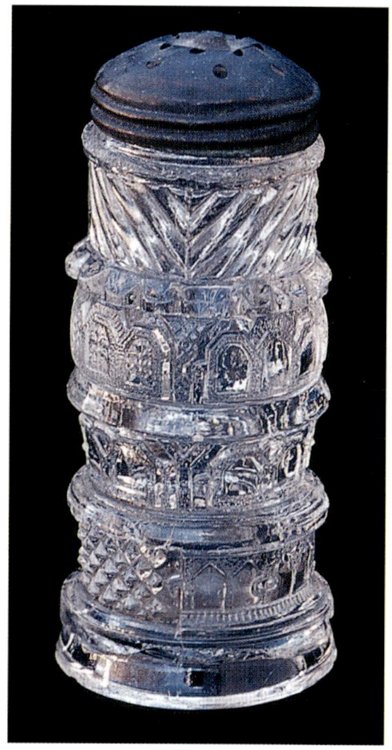

Stove saltshaker, circa early 1880s. 4 1/2" high. $80-100.

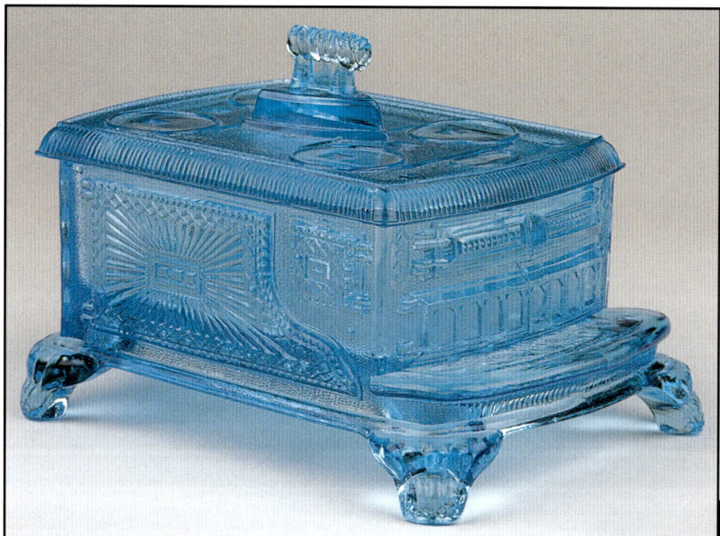

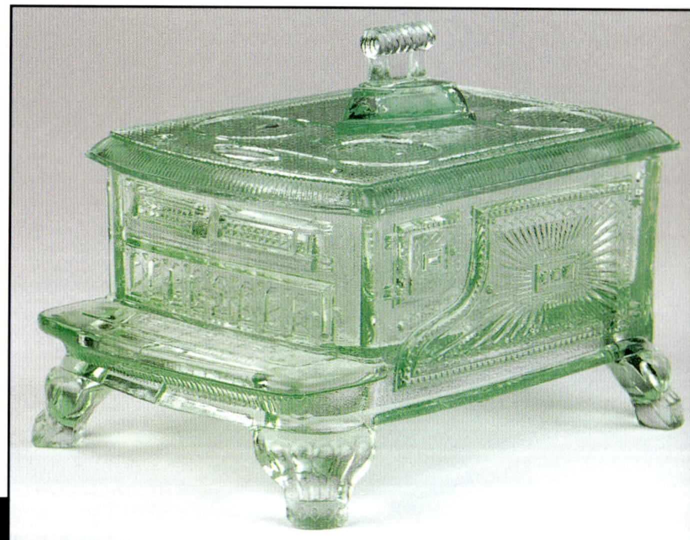

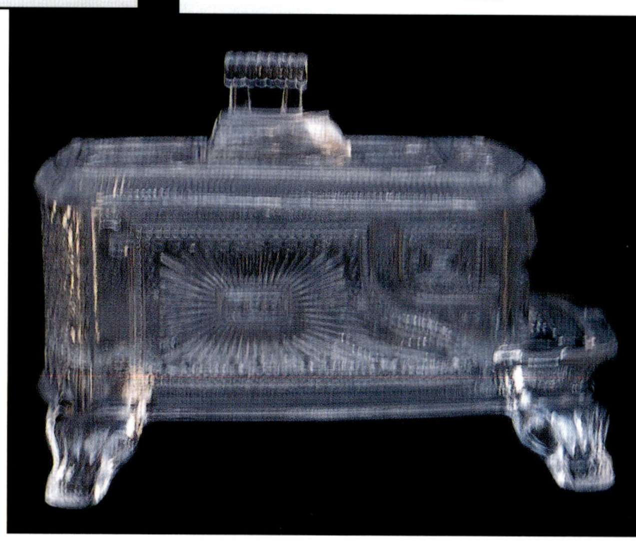

Stove figural butter dish made by King, Son and Co in the late 1880s. Base: 7" x 4 1/2". Lid: 6 1/2" x 4 1/2". Clear, $110-130. Blue, $130-150. Green, $130-150.

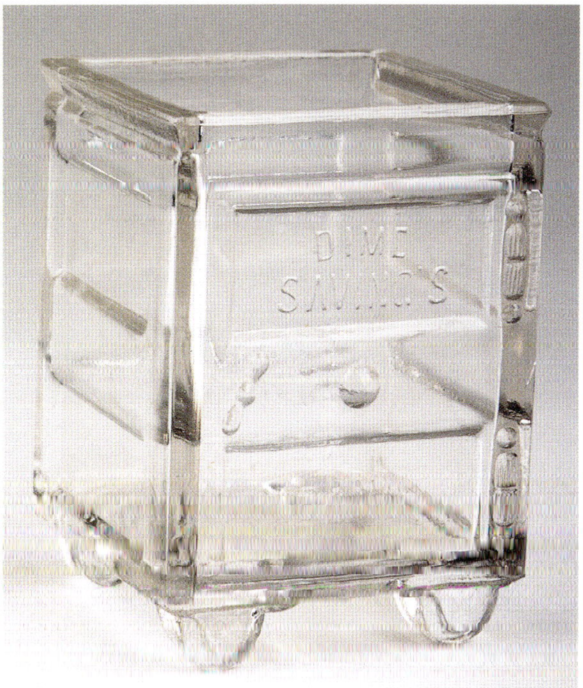

Safe candy container, *Dime Savings Bank-C D Kenny Co.-Teas and Coffee*. 2 3/4" high and 2 1/8" square. $85-120.

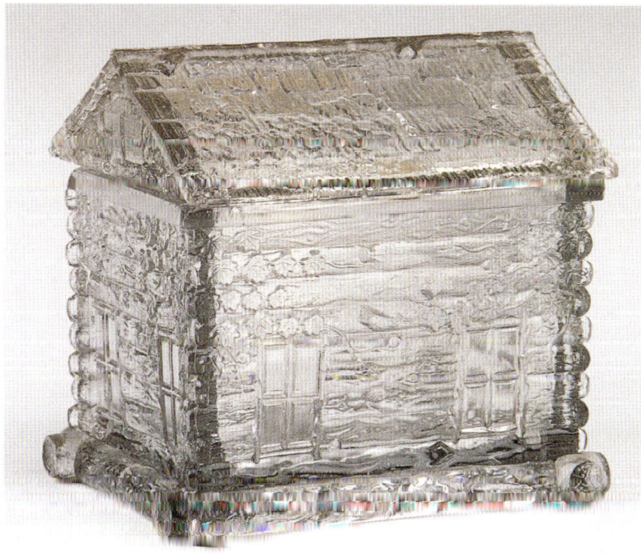

Log Cabin with vines on all sides. Although there are two windows on each side and an attic window at each end, this log cabin has no doors. 3 1/2" high, 3 1/2" long, and 2 5/8" wide. $385-425.

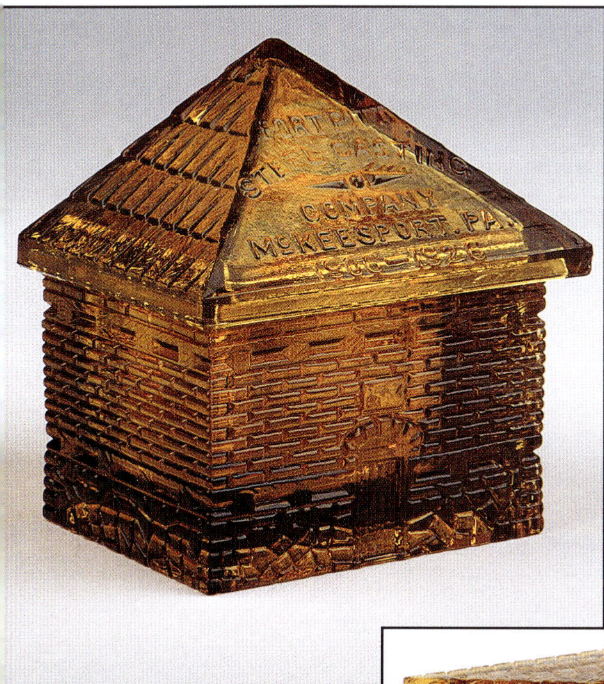

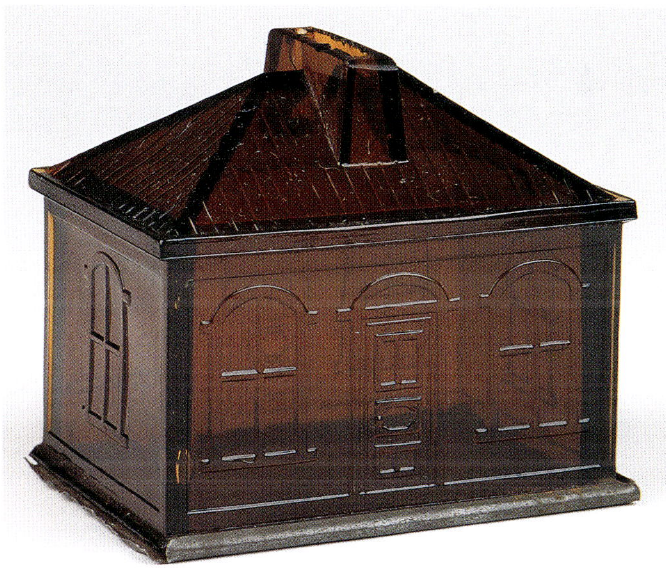

Bank made by McKee and Brothers, circa 1880. An 1880 catalog illustrates it as a *Cabinet Bank*. Dark amber, $285-325.

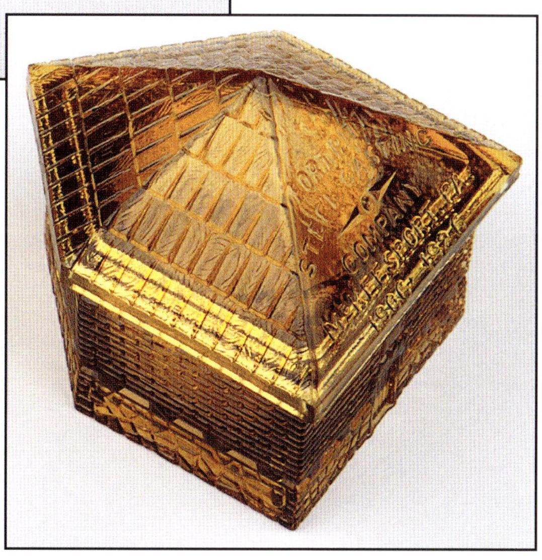

Inkwell with *Ft Pitt Steel Casting Company, McKeesport, Pa 1908-1926* on the lid. *Block House 1764 A D – Coll-Bouquet, Pittsburg, Pa* on the base. 2 5/8" wide. Dark amber, $250-300.

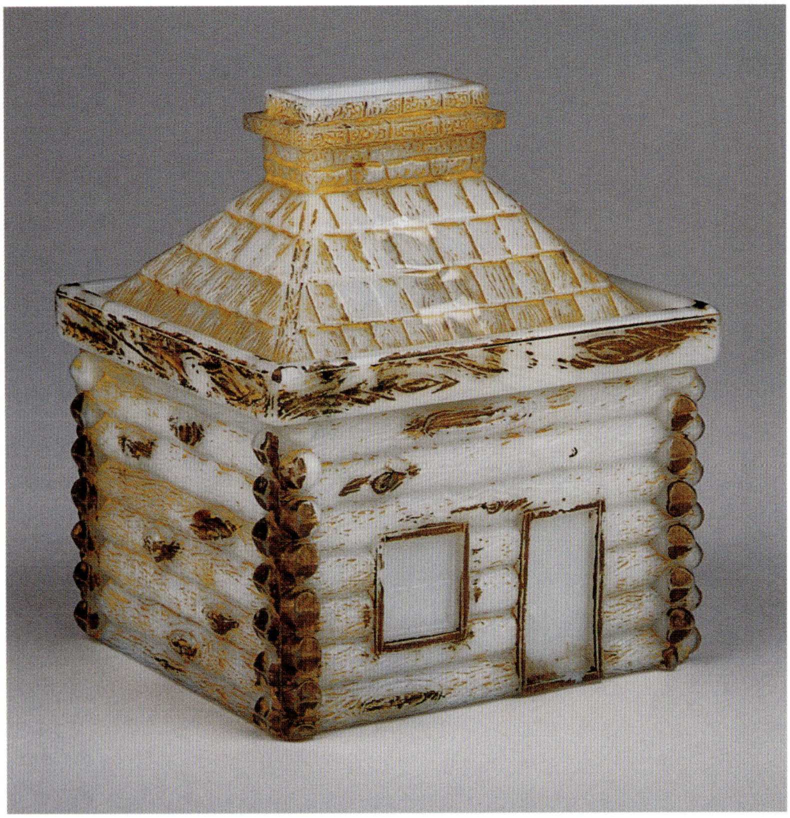

Log Cabin mustard container-bank made by the Westmoreland Specialty Company. 3 3/8" x 3 1/8" at the base. Opal, $175-225.

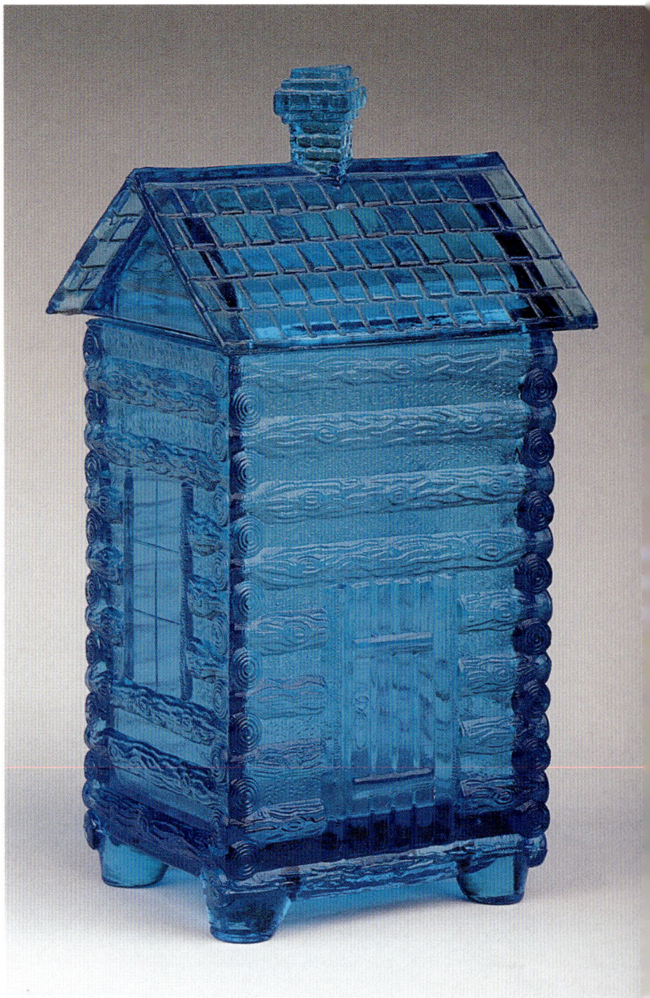

Log Cabin pattern pickle dish made by the Central Glass Company, circa 1880s. 7" high. Blue, $950-1,250.

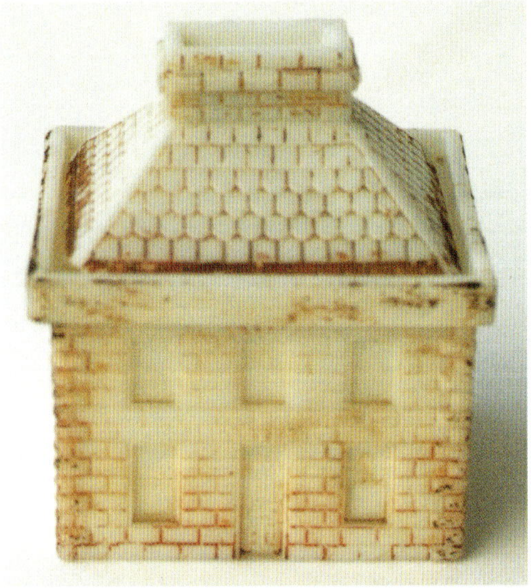

Brick Schoolhouse mustard container-bank made by the Westmoreland Specialty Company. As was the Log Cabin, this item was packed and sold containing prepared mustard. 3 1/4" x 3 3/4" x 4". Opal, $175-225.

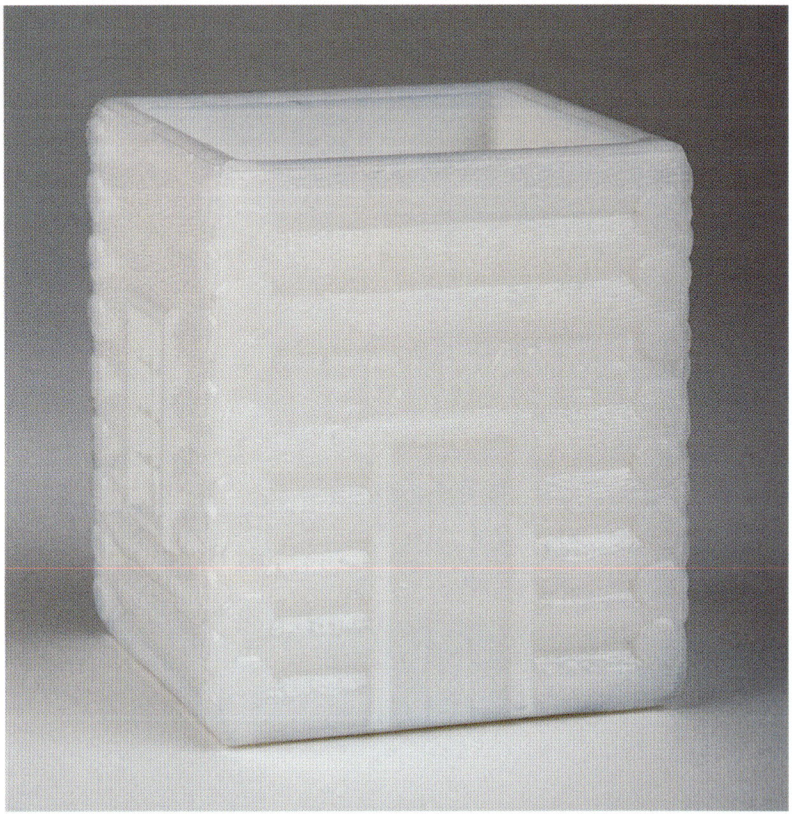

Log Cabin container *Tecumseh*, 2 1/2" high. Should have a lid. Complete Opal, $95-125.

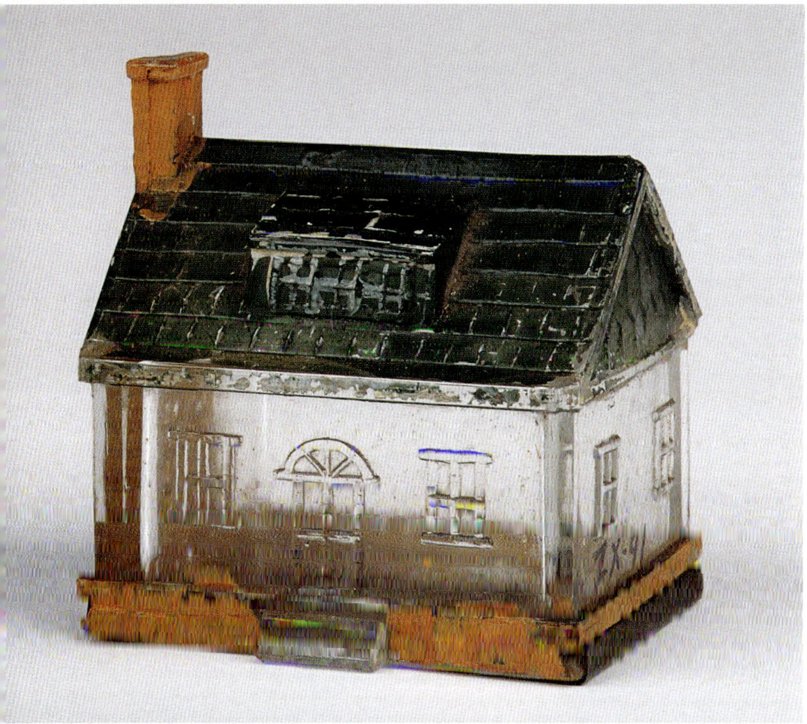

House candy container, 2 3/4" long and 2 1/8" wide. Clear decorated, $400-500.

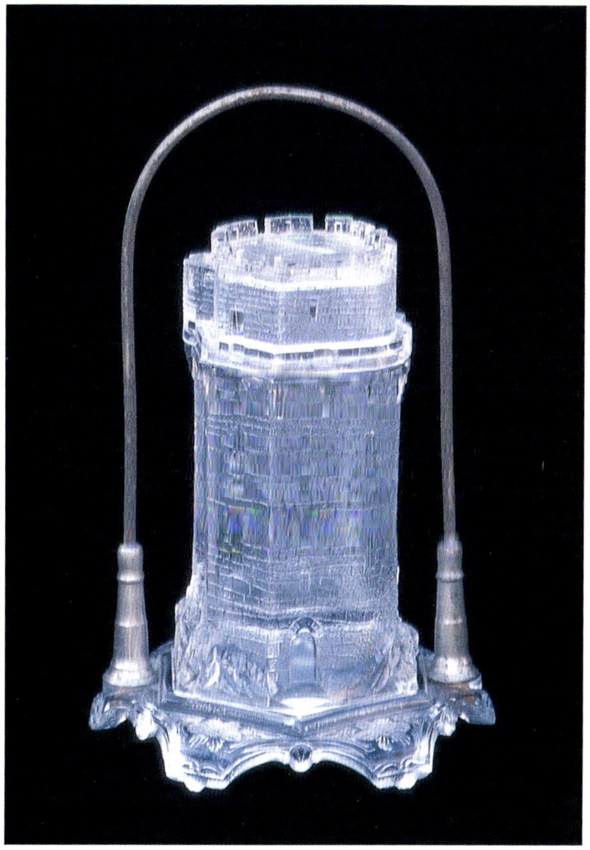

Knobby Castle pickle caster made by the Aetna Glass and Manufacturing Company, first advertised in 1886. 8" high and 4" wide. Clear, $450-600.

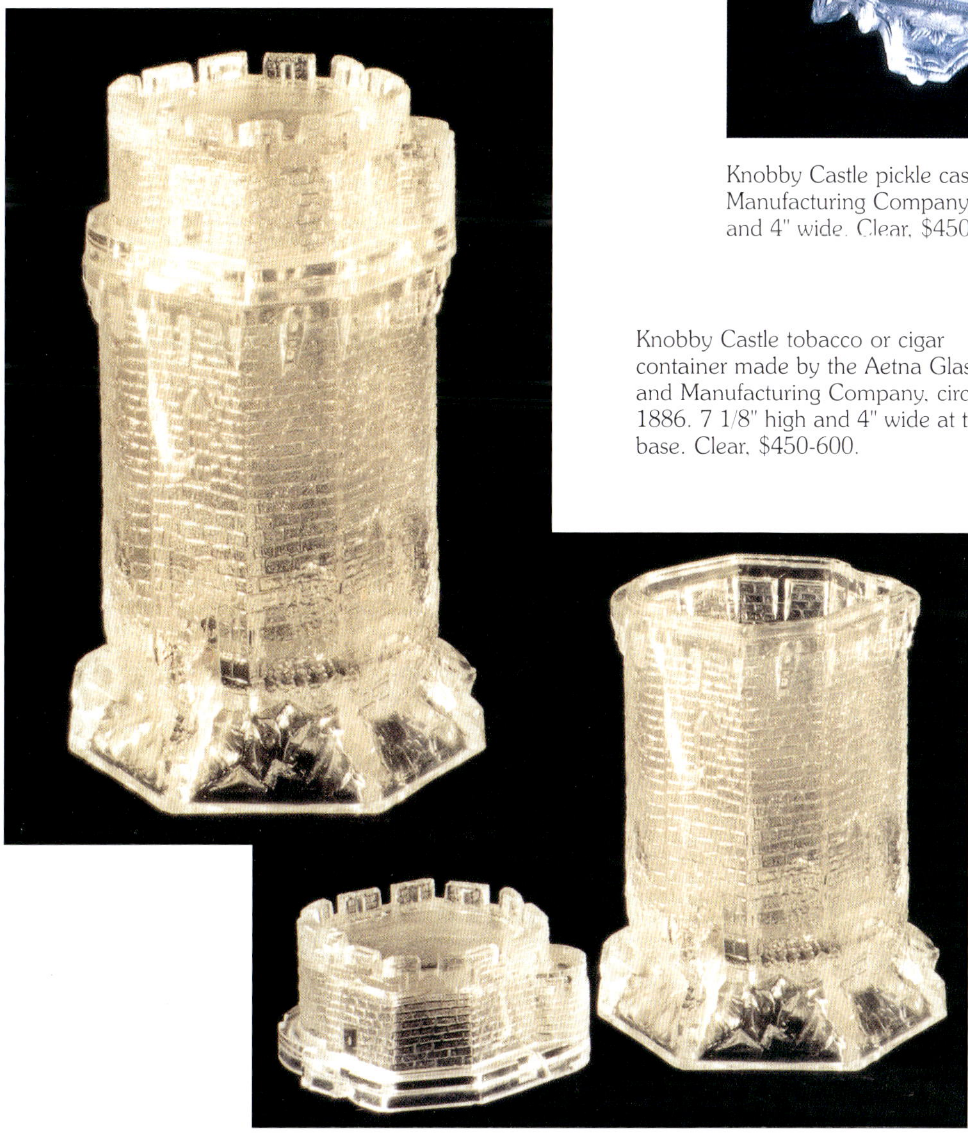

Knobby Castle tobacco or cigar container made by the Aetna Glass and Manufacturing Company, circa 1886. 7 1/8" high and 4" wide at the base. Clear, $450-600.

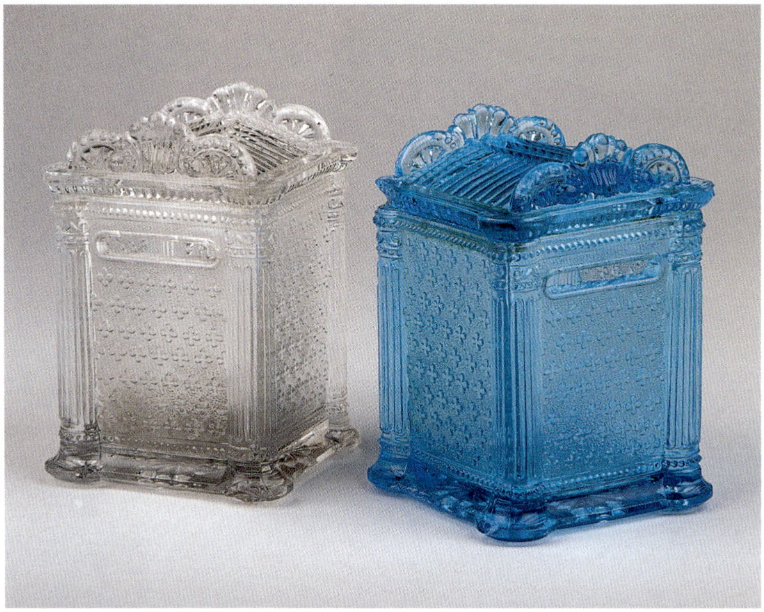

Savings Bank bank, 4" high. Clear, $85-125. Blue, $125-165

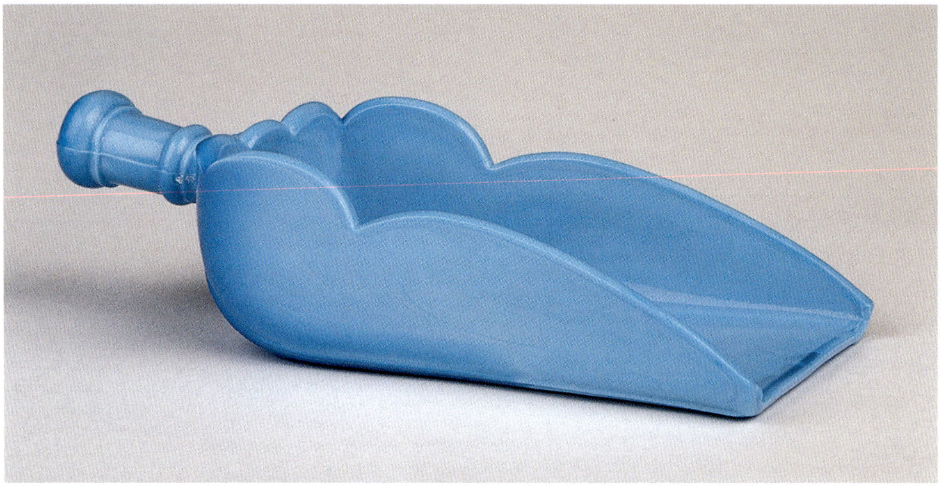

Blue opaque candy scoop, maker and date of manufactuer unknown. 7" long. $170-185.

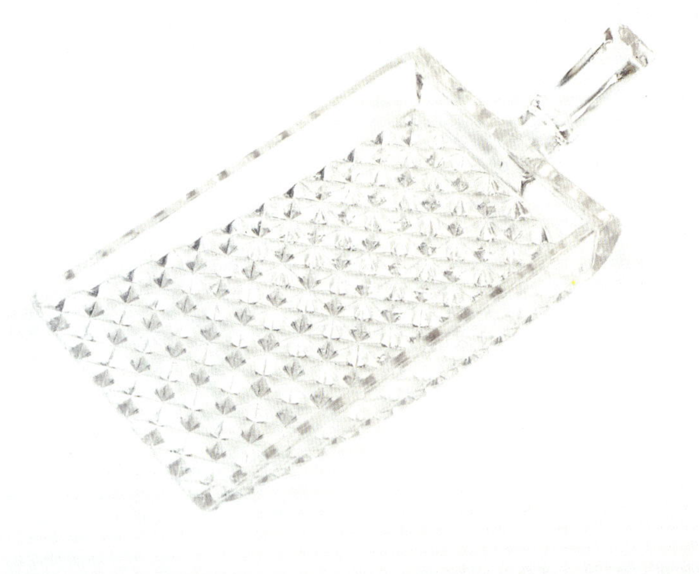

Candy Scoop in the fine cut pattern, 8 1/2" long. Clear, $85-125.

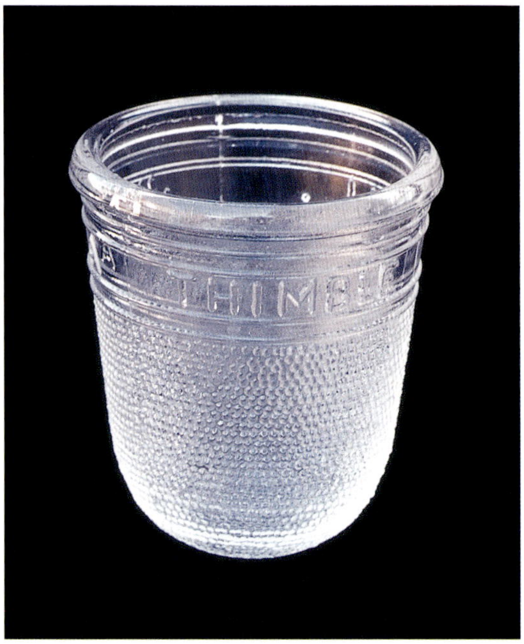

Thimble shot glass, *Just A Thimble Full*, by George Davidson, circa 1885. 2 1/2" high. Clear, $75-120.

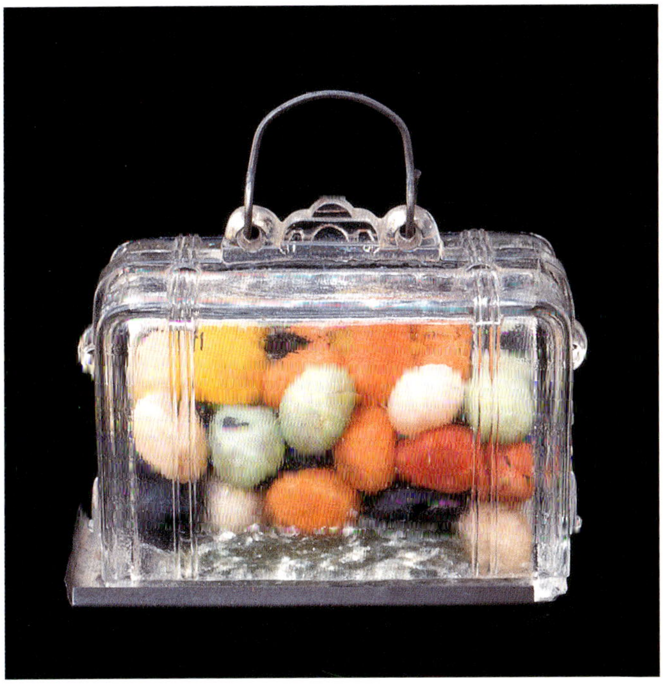

Suitcase candy container made by the Westmoreland Specialty Company, circa 1906. 3 3/4" long. As shown, $150-200.

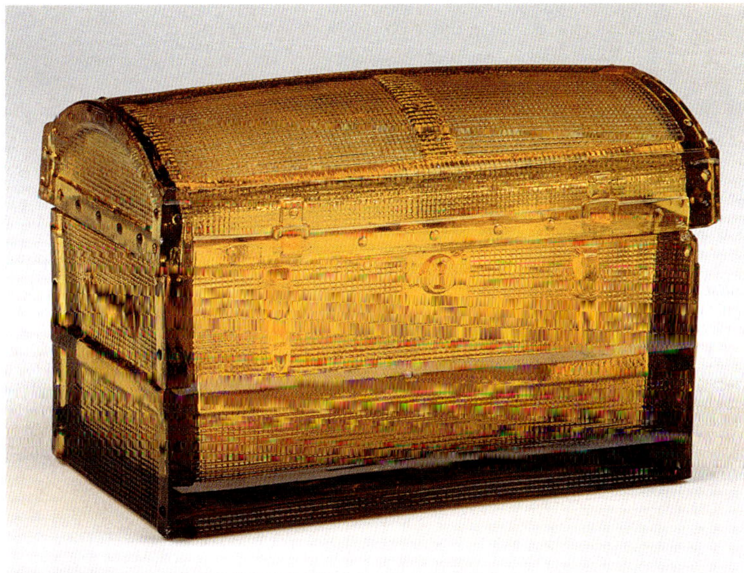

Amber Trunk with a hinged lid, maker and date of manufactuer unknown, 4" long. Amber, $195-245.

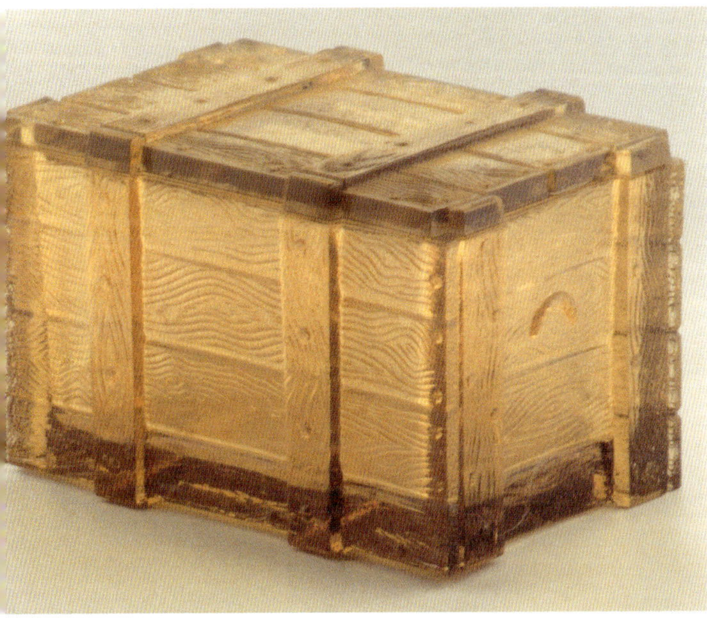

Trunk or Box by Vallerysthal, some are marked with the Vallerysthal name in the bottom. 3 7/8" long and 2 5/8" wide. Amber, $85-125.

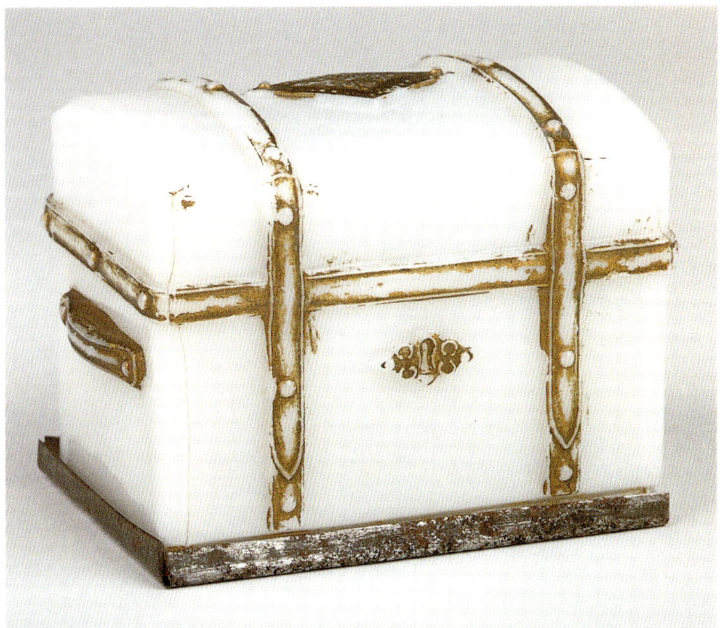

Trunk candy container in opal decorated in gold. 2" high, 2 7/8" long, and 2" wide. As shown, $165-210.

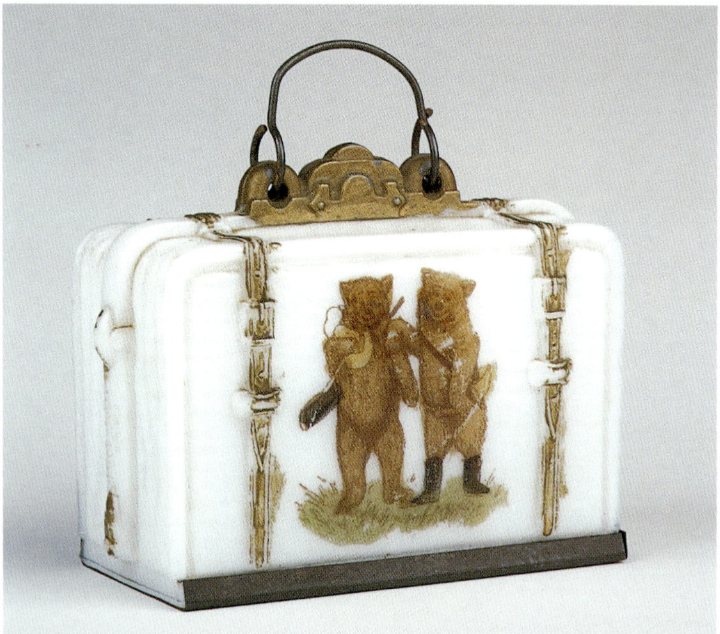

Suitcase candy container in opal decorated with Roosevelt bears and made by the Westmoreland Specialty Company. 4" long and 2" wide. As shown, $325-375.

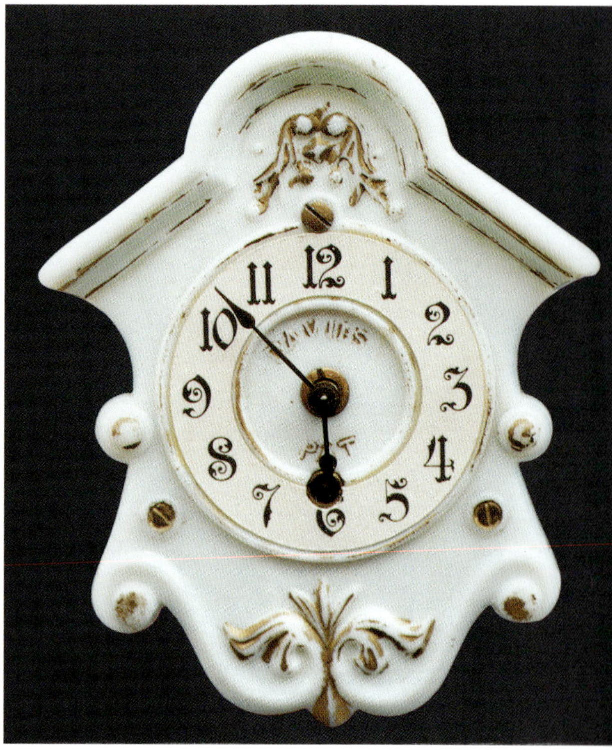

Clock, *Davies Patented* printed on the face, 7" high and 5 1/2" wide. Opal with original works and pendulum, $1,200-1,500.

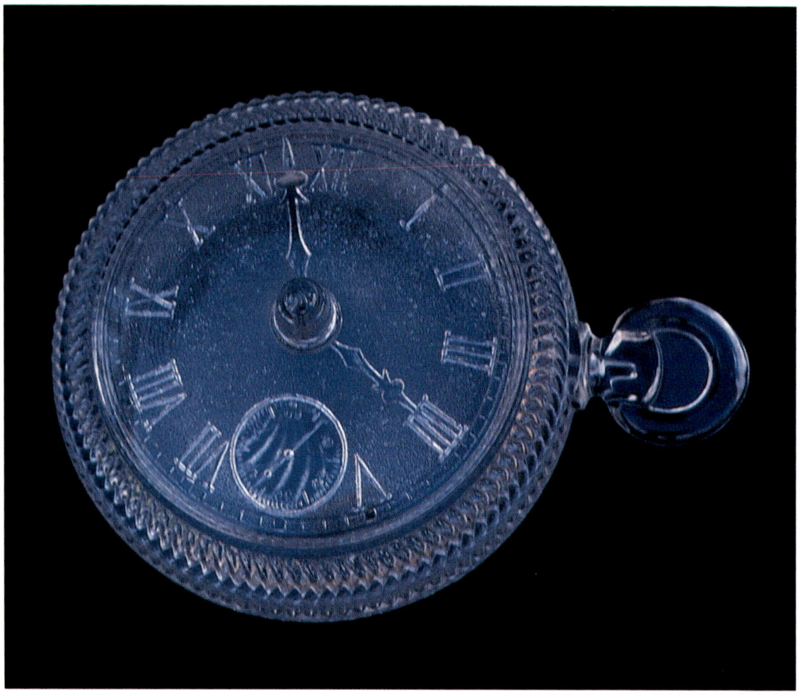

Pocket Watch butter dish made by Adams and Company, circa 1891. 6 1/4" diameter. Clear, $200-240. This is the original; the Imperial Glass Company made reproductions.

Tambour Art Glass Mantle Clock made in the daisy and button pattern by the McKee Glass Company, circa 1920-1925. It was made in clear, amber, amethyst, canary, blue, and green. Blue, $245-285.

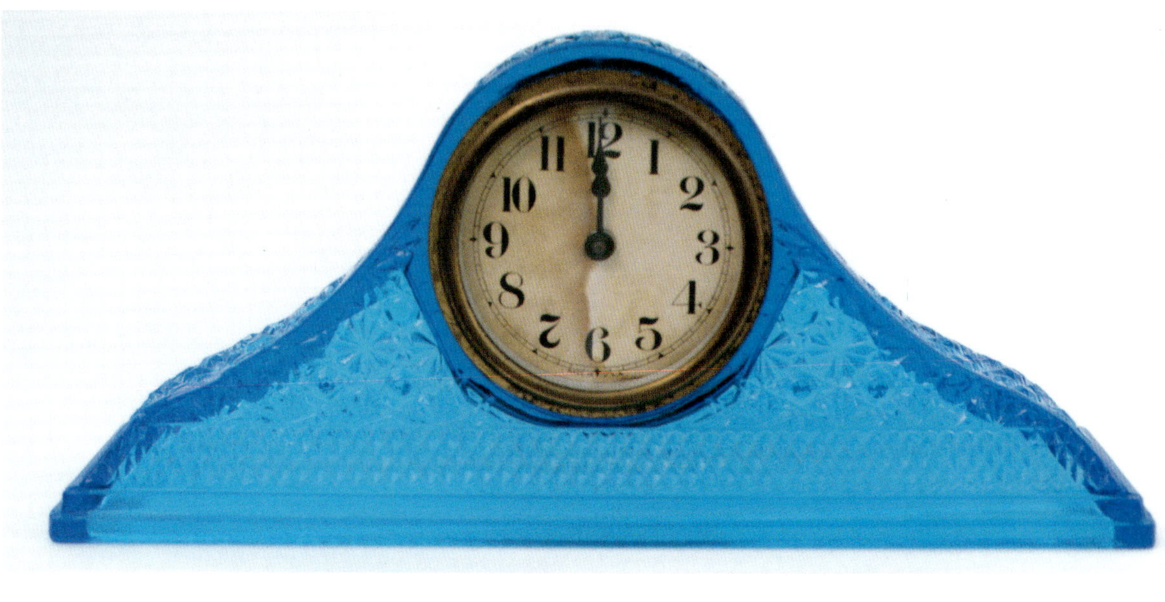

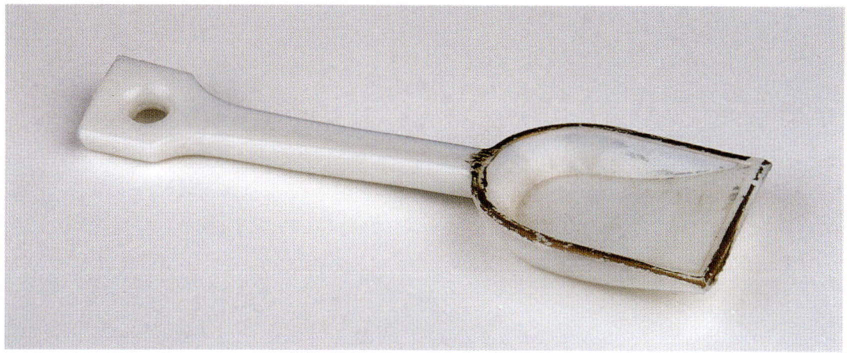

Spade in opal. A reissue by the United States Glass Company in 1891. 8 1/2" long. Opal, $90-125.

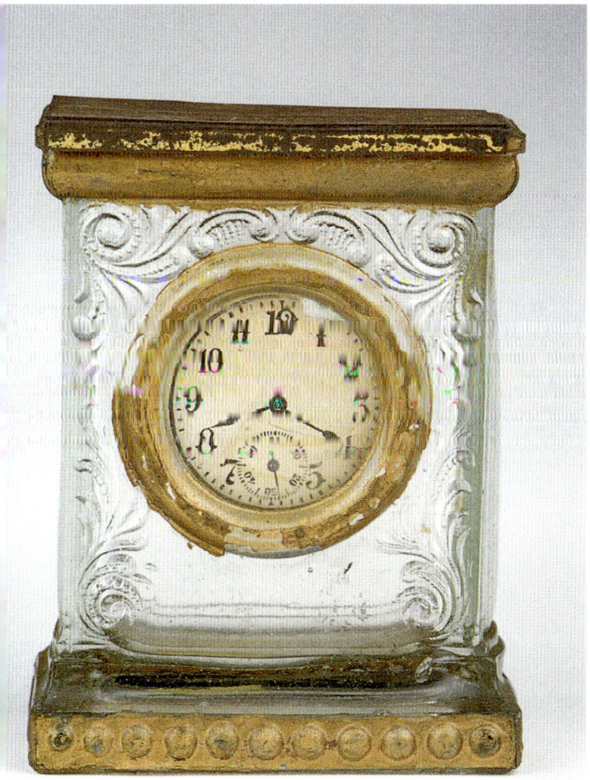

Clock candy container. 3 3/4" high and 3" wide. Clear, $90-110.

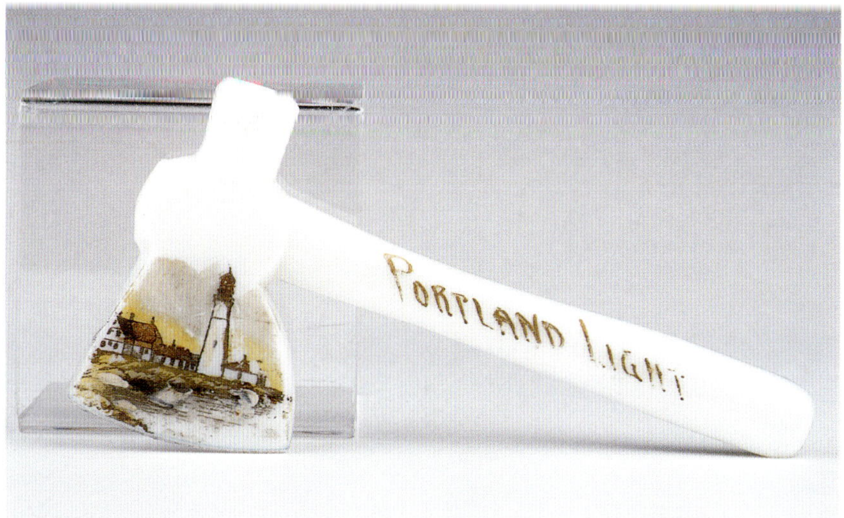

Hatchet, *Portland Light*, picturing a Light House. Made by the United States Glass Company, circa late 1890s. 6 1/4" long. Opal, $100-150.

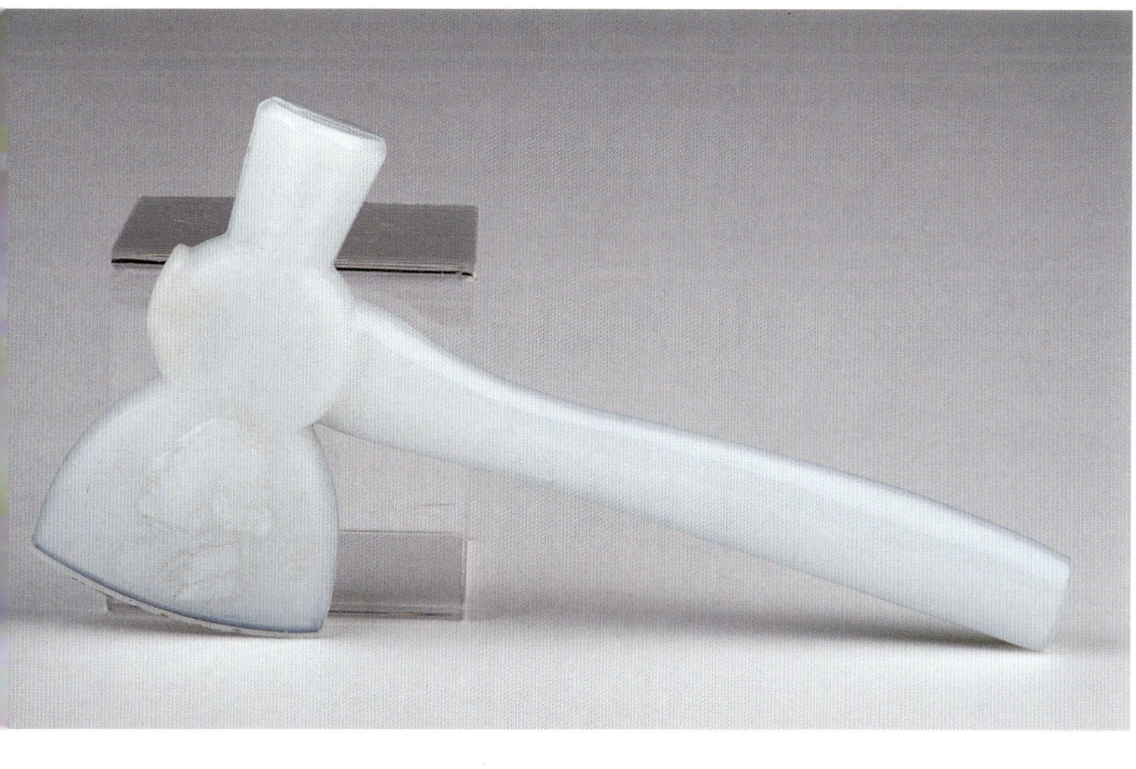

Washington Hatchet, *Worlds Fair 1893*, made by the Libby Glass Company, Toledo. 8" long. Opal, $175-225. Clear, $110-125.

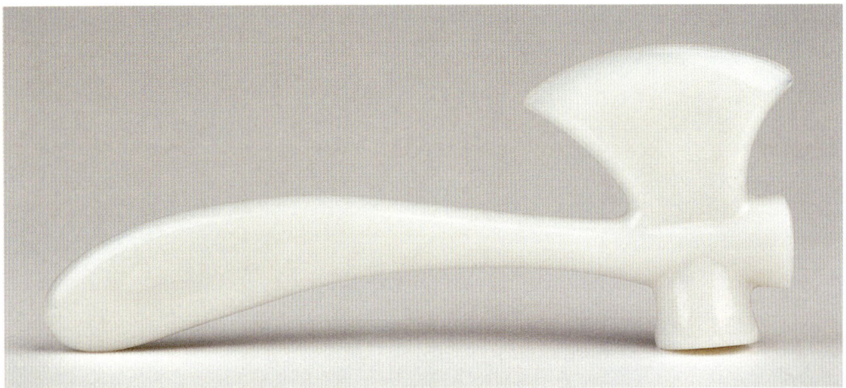

Hatchet, opal and no design. 6" long. $60-70.

Hatchet with floral design and metallic handle end, 7 1/8" long. Opal, $115-135.

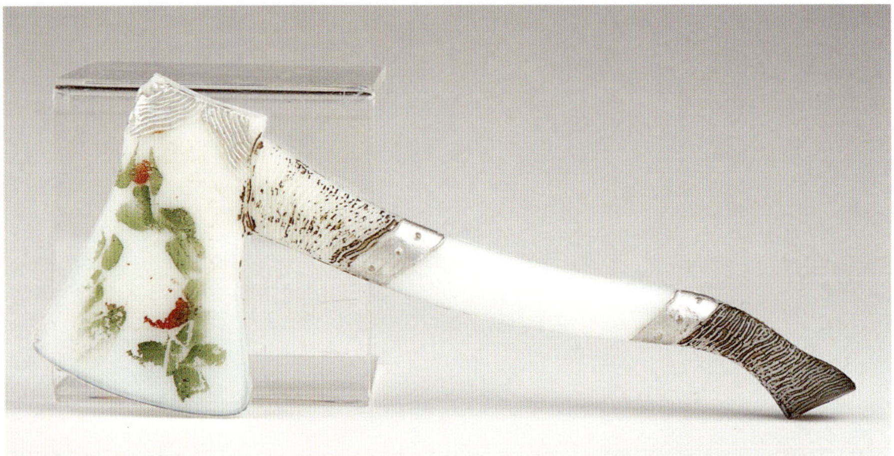

Hatchet with Indian in full color and *Pan American Buffalo 1901* made by the Cambridge Glass Company in 1903, a reissue of the National Glass Company product. 7 1/4" long. Opal decorated, $215-245.

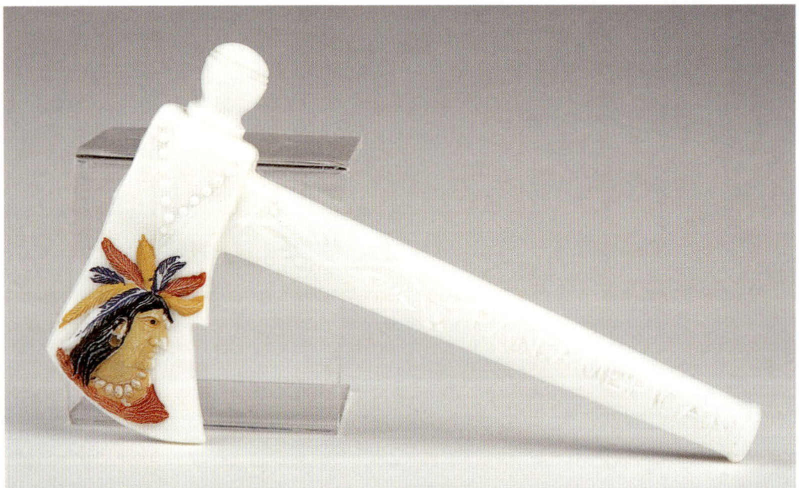

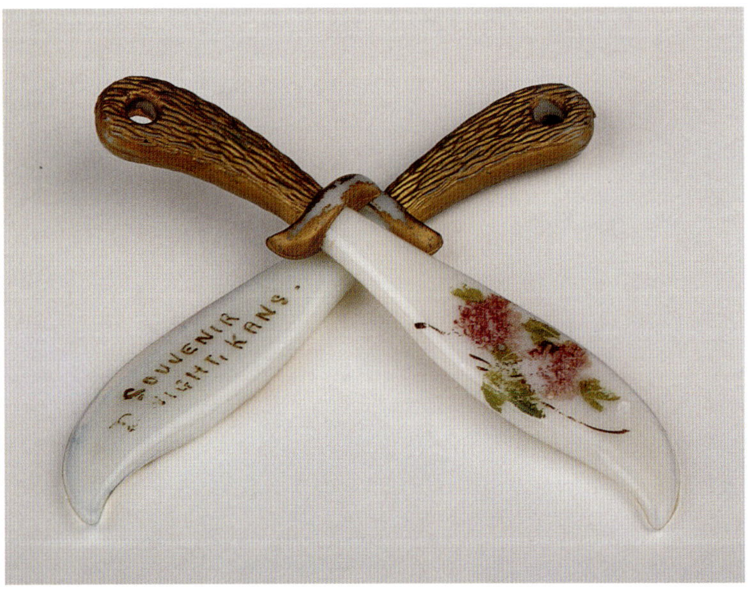

Opal knifes, decorated and souvenir. Opal, $85-100.

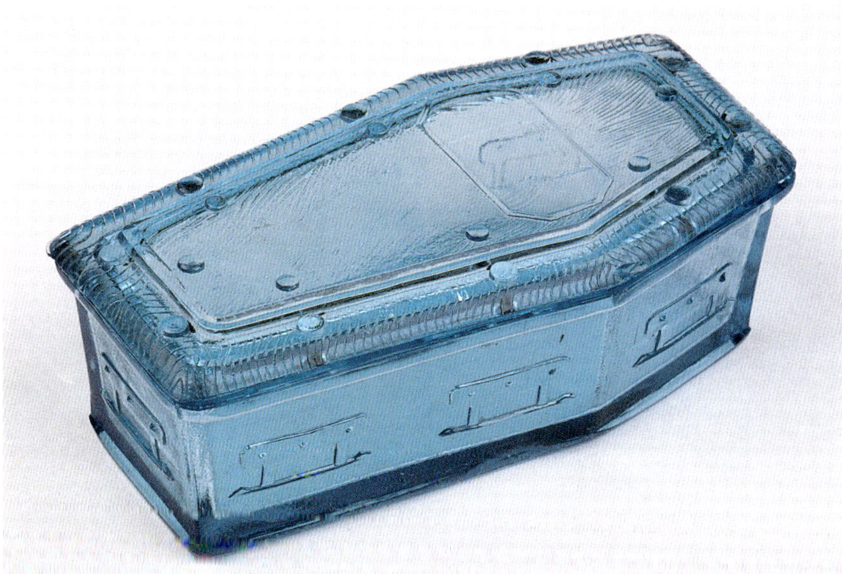

Coffin trinket box, date of manufactuer unknown. 4 3/4" long. Blue, $375-400.

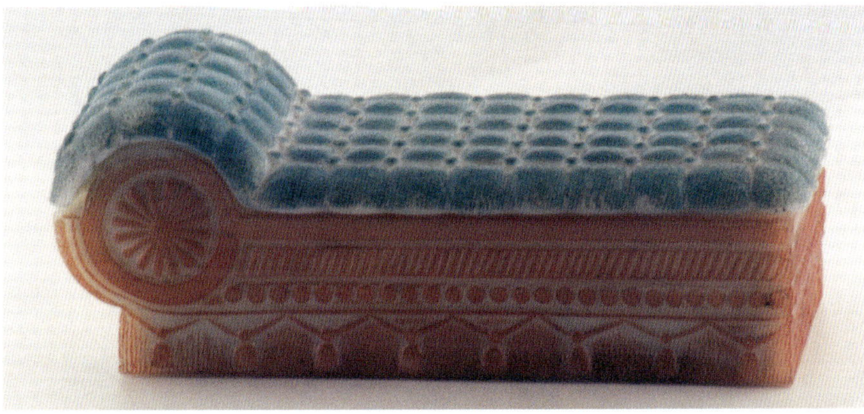

Fainting Couch, decorated opal. 5" long and 2 1/8" wide. Opal decorated, $350-425. Opal, no decoration, $175-250.

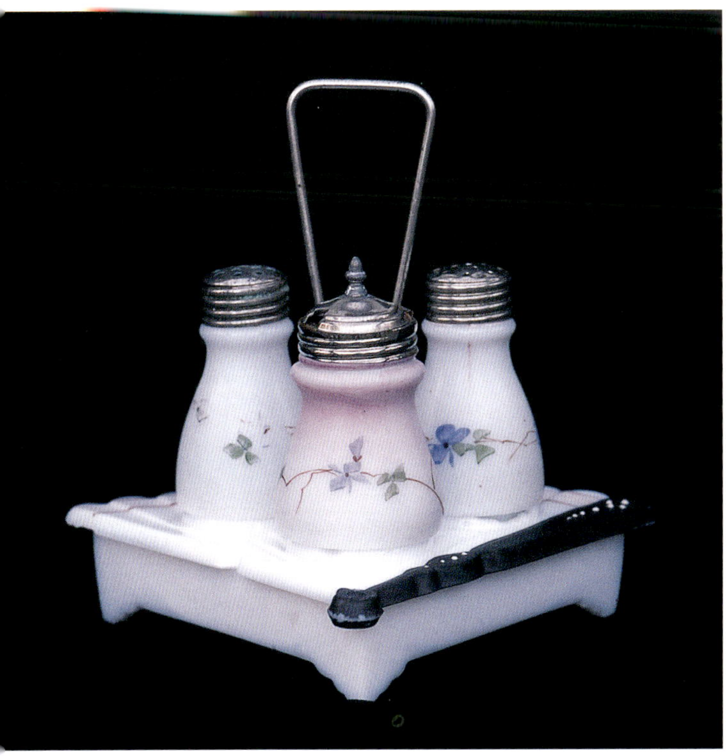

Fan condiment set made by Dithridge and Company, circa 1894. 7" wide. Opal, $110-145.

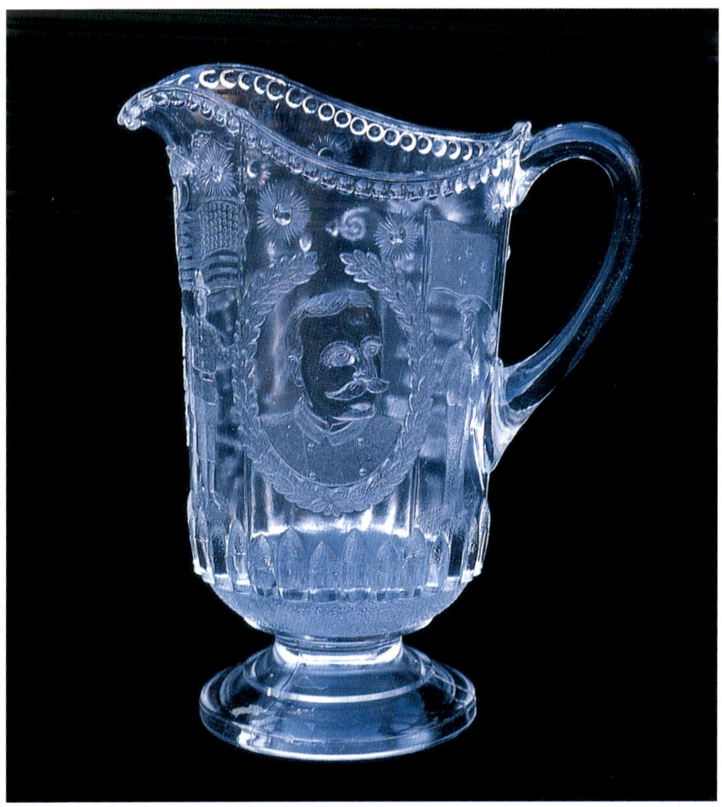

Gridley pitcher made by the Beatty-Brady Glass Company, circa 1898, 9" high. A Spanish American War item. $140-160.

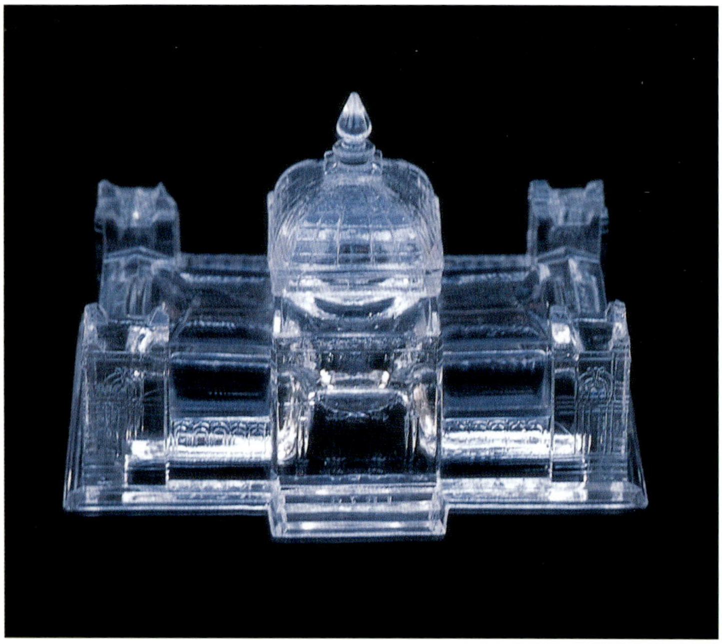

Centennial Memorial Hall inkwell by Charles Yockel, circa 1876, 4 1/2" high and 6 1/2" wide. $650-750.

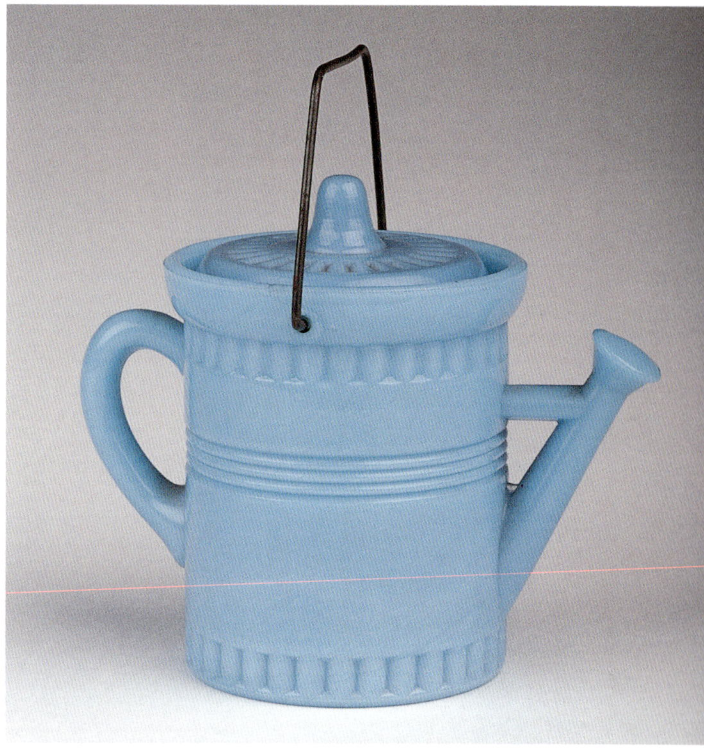

Blue opaque Water Can, circa 1910s. 4" high and 5" wide. $165-185.

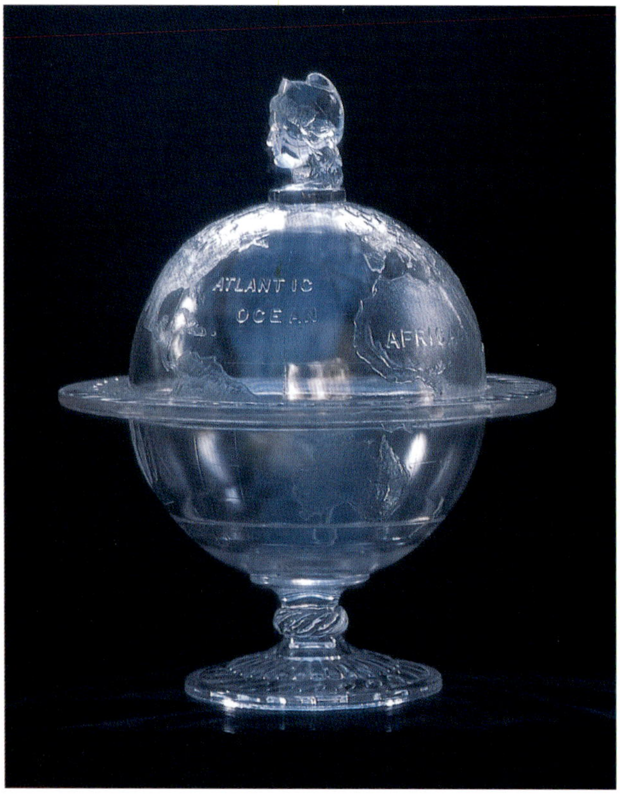

Terrestrial Globe butter dish made by the O'Hara Glass Company, circa 1876. 9" high and 8" diameter. $2,000-4,000.

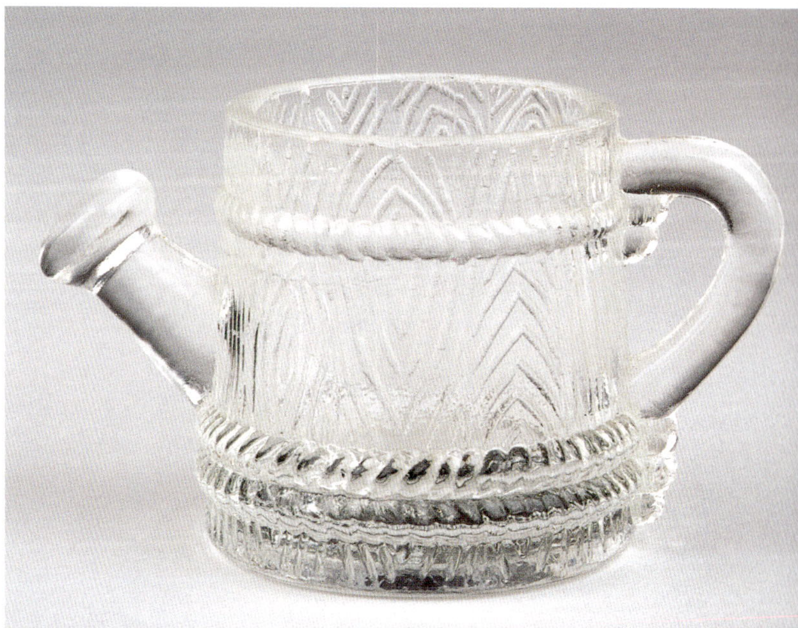

Water can, maker and date of manufactuer unknown. Clear, $45-65.

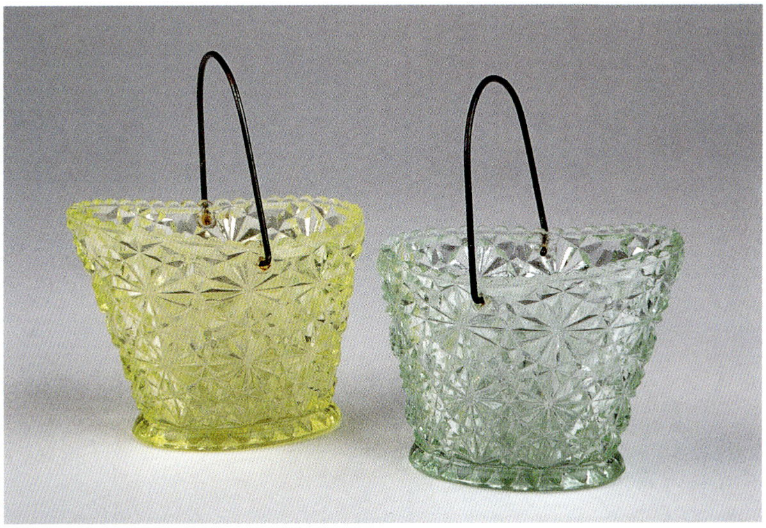

Coal Hod in the daisy pattern. 1 7/8" high. Apple green, $75-90. Yellow, $75-90.

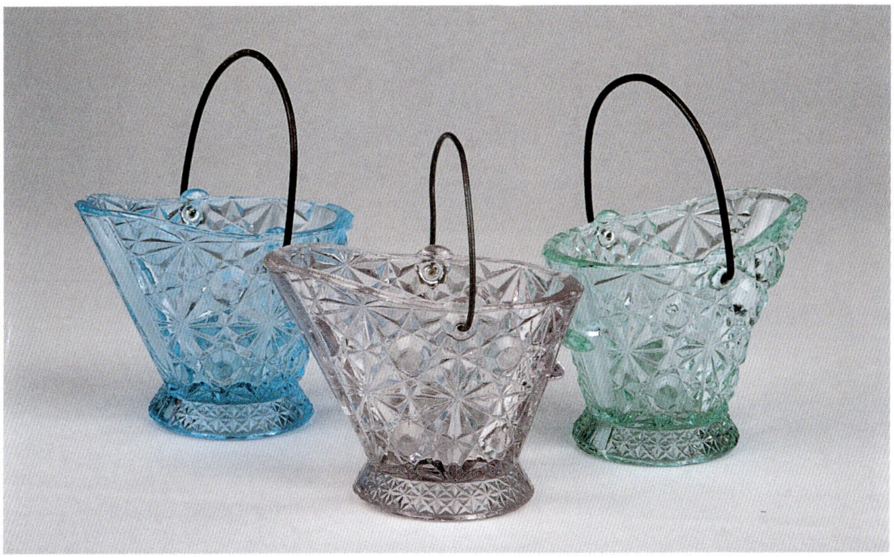

Coal Hod in the daisy and button pattern made by the Adams and Company and reissued by the United States Glass Company in 1891. 2" high. Clear, $35-45. Apple green, $75-95. Blue, $75-95.

Coal Hod toothpick or match holder made by Bryce Brothers, circa late 1880s. 2 3/8" high and 2" wide. Amber, $75-90. Blue, $80-100.

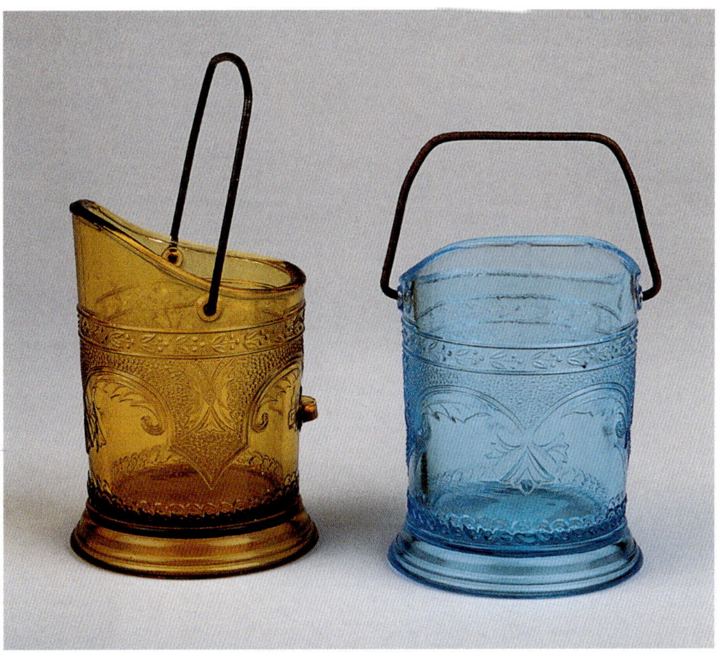

Coal Hod toothpick or match holder in the diamond point pattern. 2 1/2" high and 2" wide. Blue, $145-160.

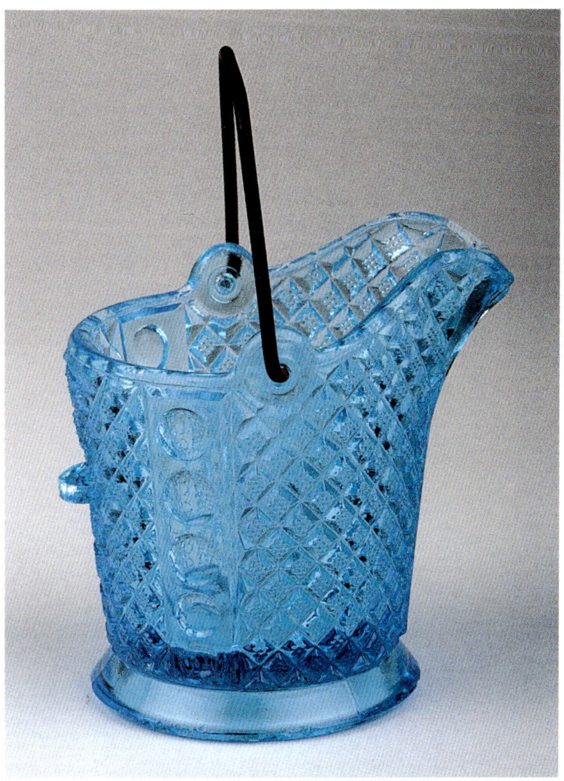

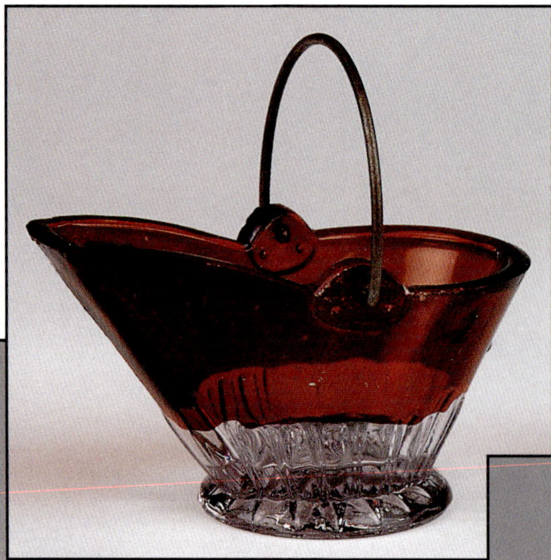

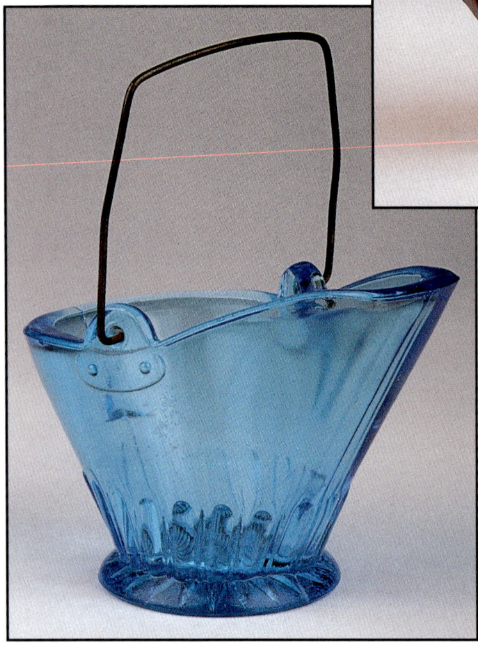

Toy Coal Bucket made by the United States Glass Company, circa early 1890s. 2" high, 2" wide, and 4" long. Ruby Stain, $50-65. Blue, $85-100. Opal, $85-110.

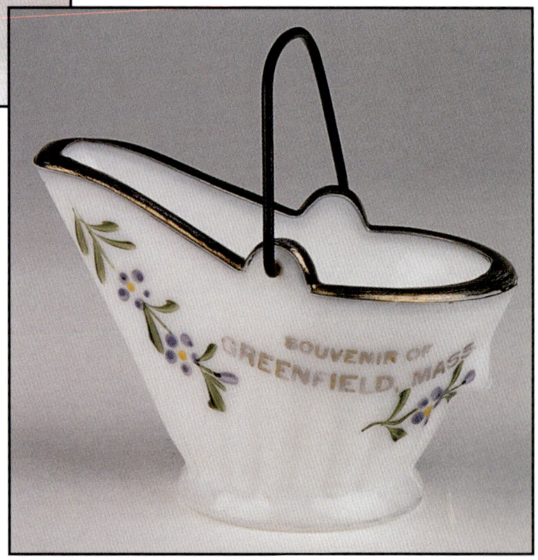

Carpet Bag wall match. The base is 2 3/4" x 1 5/8". Opal decorated, $160-195.

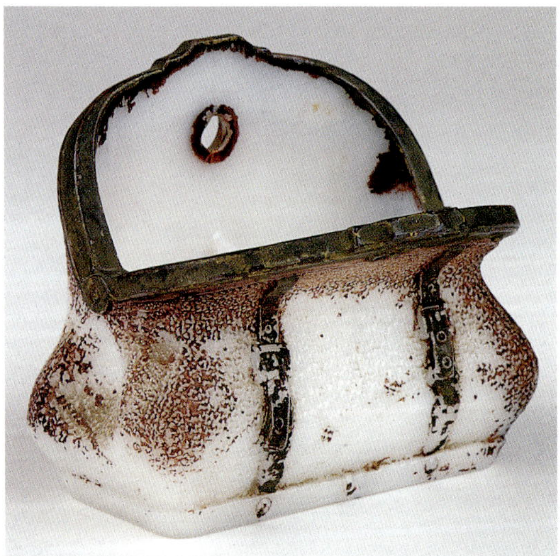

(Below) Purse toothpick or match holder in the fine cut pattern. 2" high and 1 3/4" wide. Blue, $95-110. Canary, $95-110. Amber, $95-110.

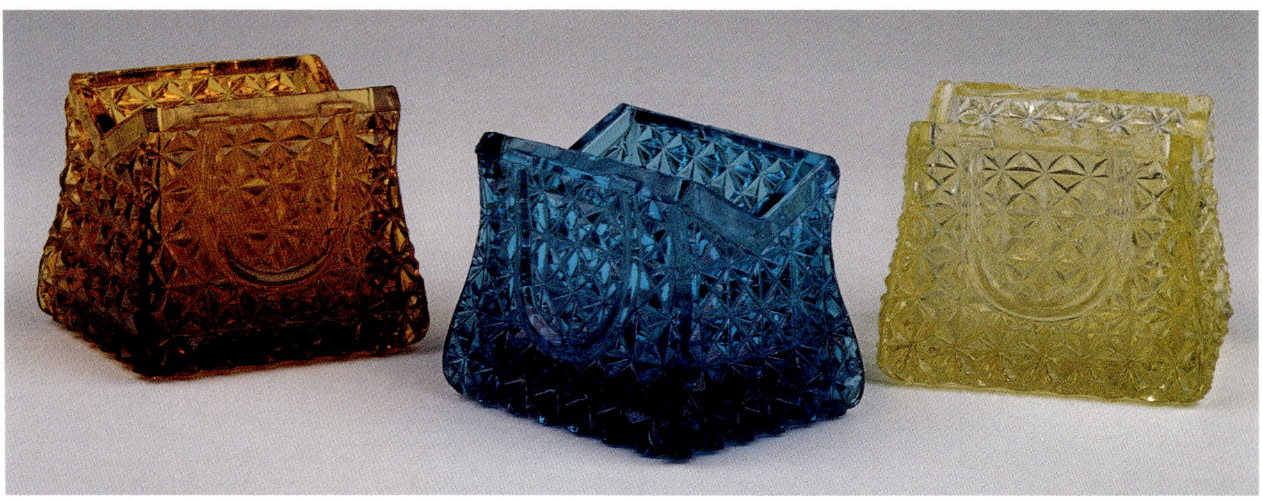

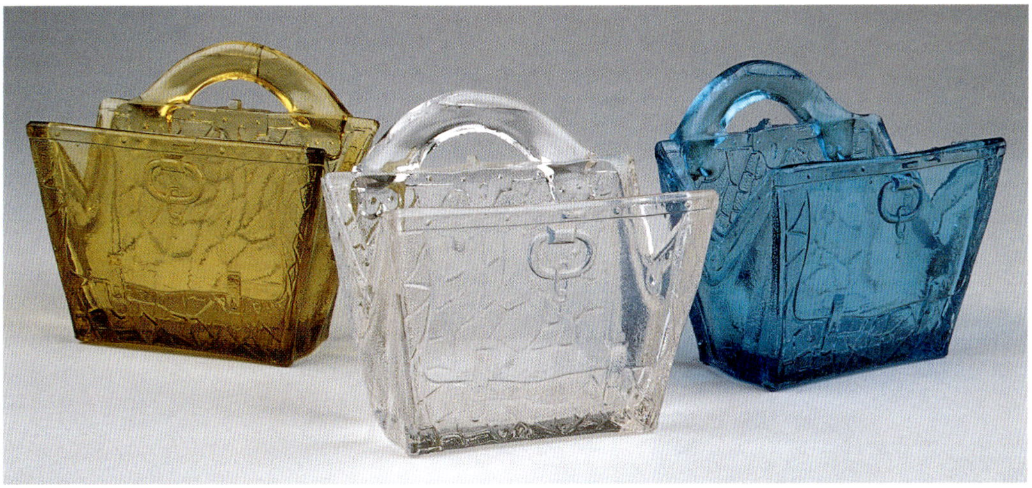

Valise toothpick or match holder. 2 1/8" high and 2 7/8" wide. Blue, $110-125. Clear, $85-110. Amber, $110-125.

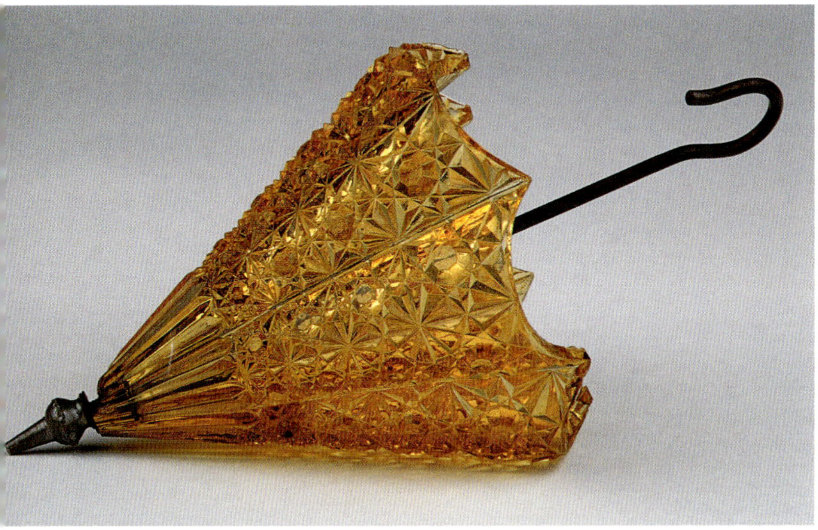

Umbrella designed by A. Heisey and made by Geo. Duncan and Sons in the late 1880s. 3 3/8" diameter and 7 1/2" long. Amber, $275-325.

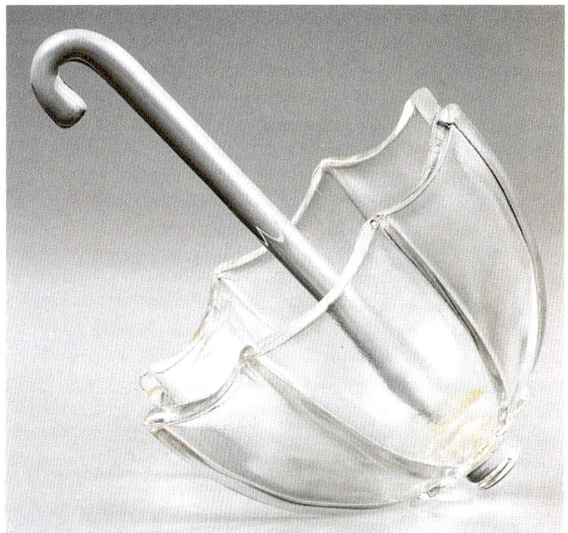

Umbrella, maker and date uncertain. 3 1/2" diameter. Clear, $45-65.

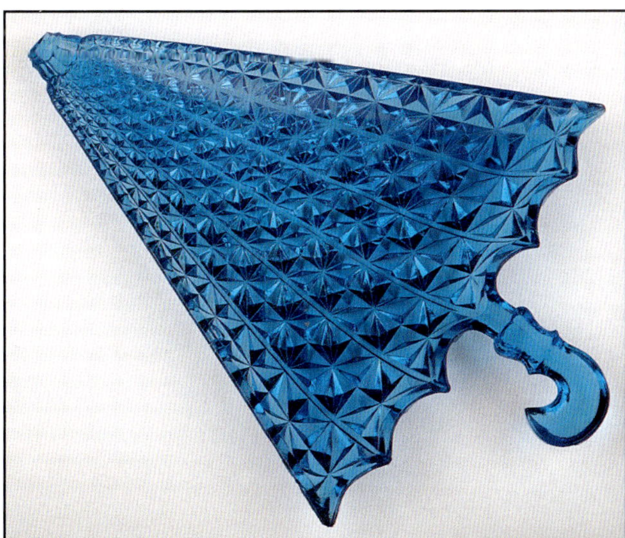

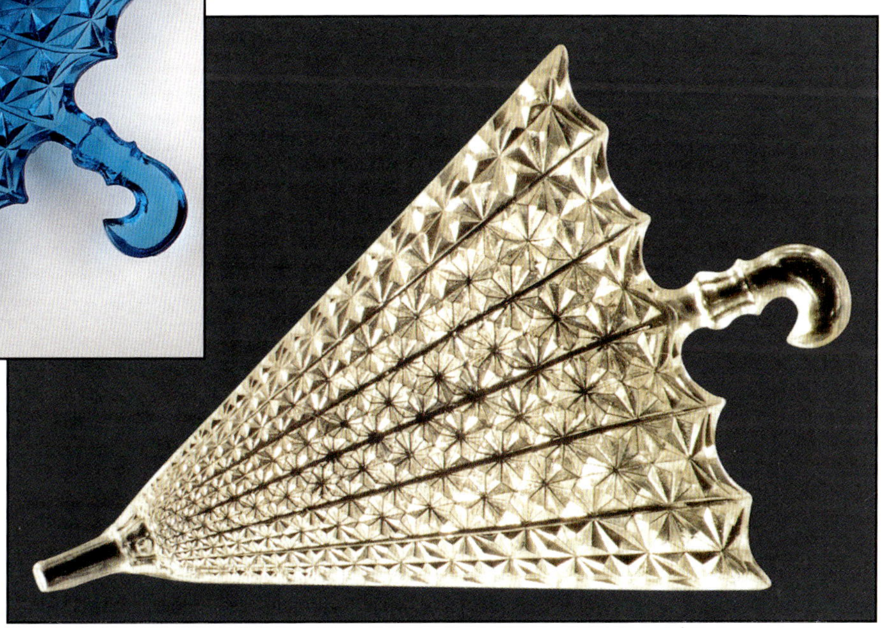

Umbrella relish or pickle dish. 9 1/2" long and 6 3/8" wide. Clear, $65-75. Blue, $85-110.

Umbrella. 4 1/2" diameter and 6" long. Opal decorated, $385-450.

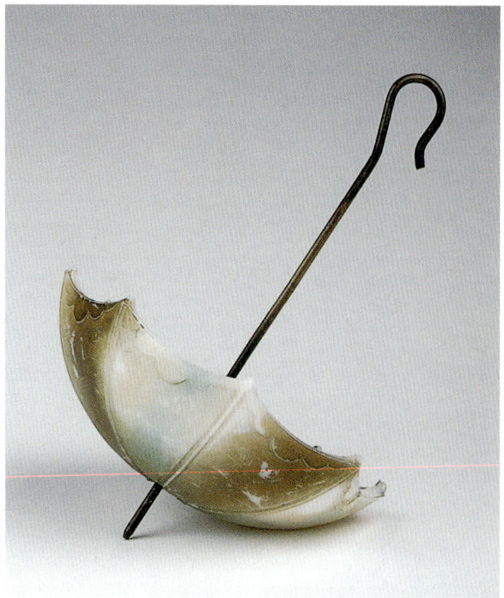

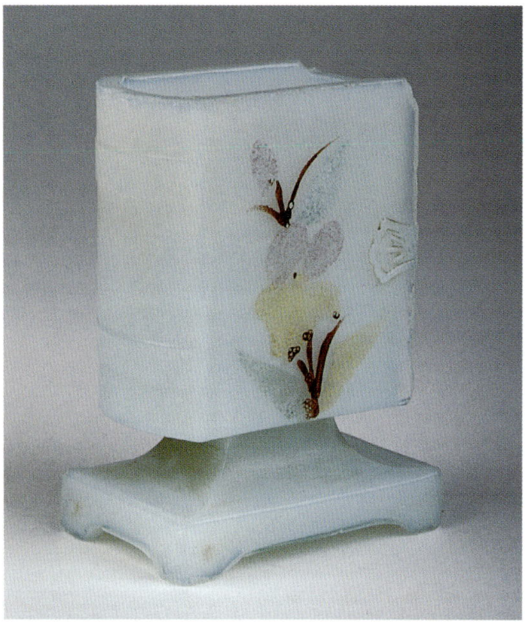

Parlor Album match or toothpick holder. 3" high, 1 1/4" wide, and 6" long. Opal, $120-140. Opal decorated, $135-160.

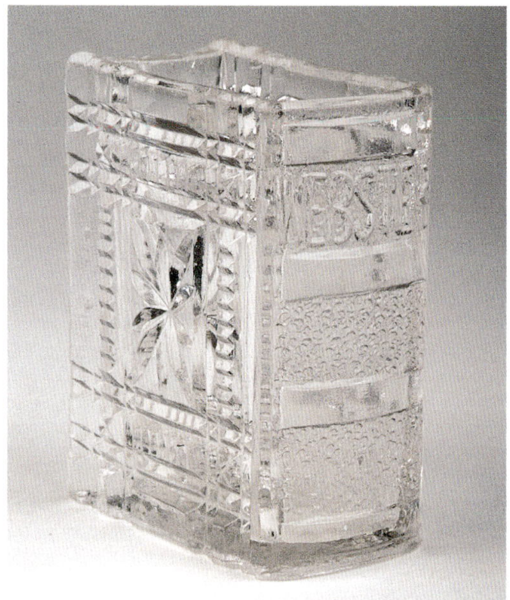

Webster Dictionary. 2 1/2" high, 1 1/4" wide, 2 1/4" long. Webster is printed on the spine of the book. Clear, $160-180.

Book match or toothpick holder made by the Adams and Company, circa late 1880s. 3" high, 1 3/8" wide, and 2 1/4" long. Clear, $65-80. Amber, $90-110. Blue, $100-125. Opal, $110-140.

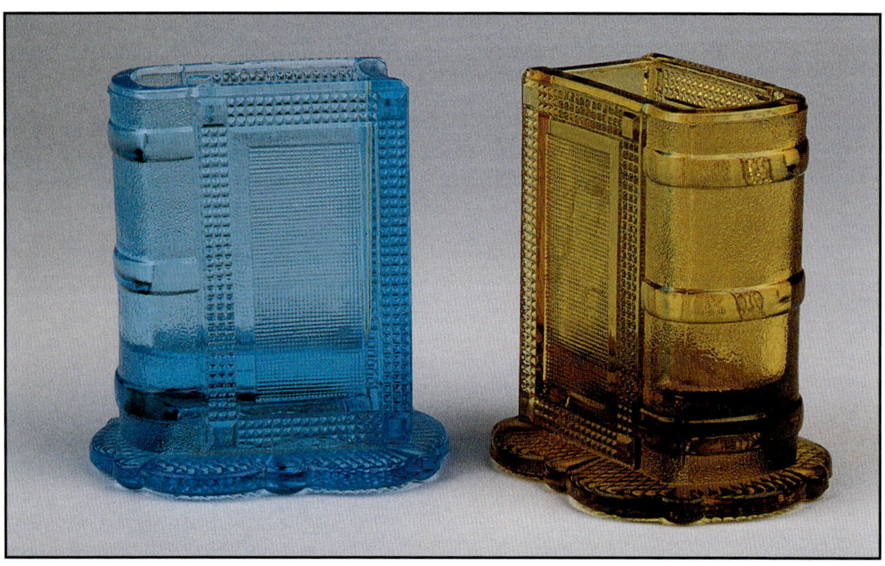

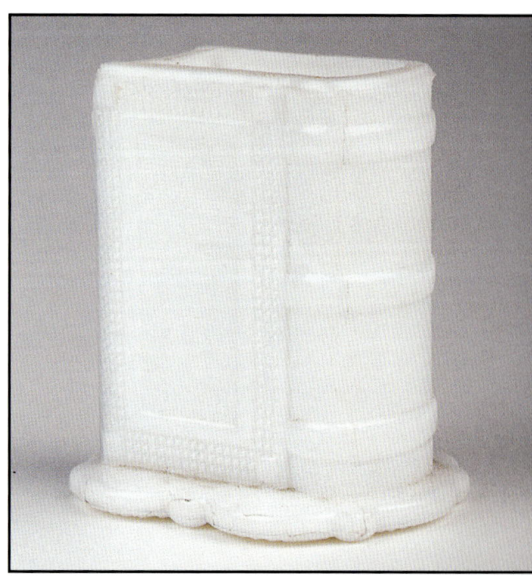

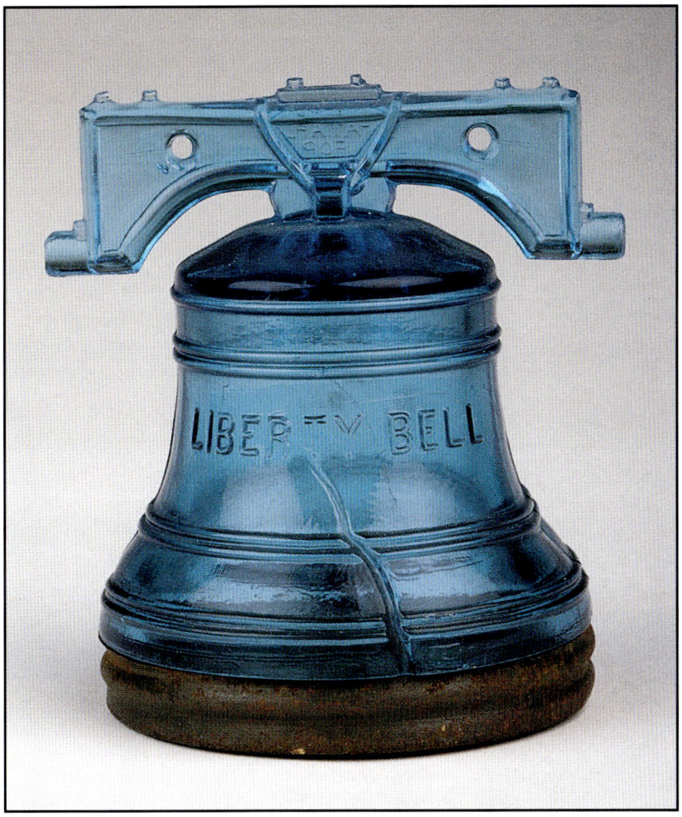

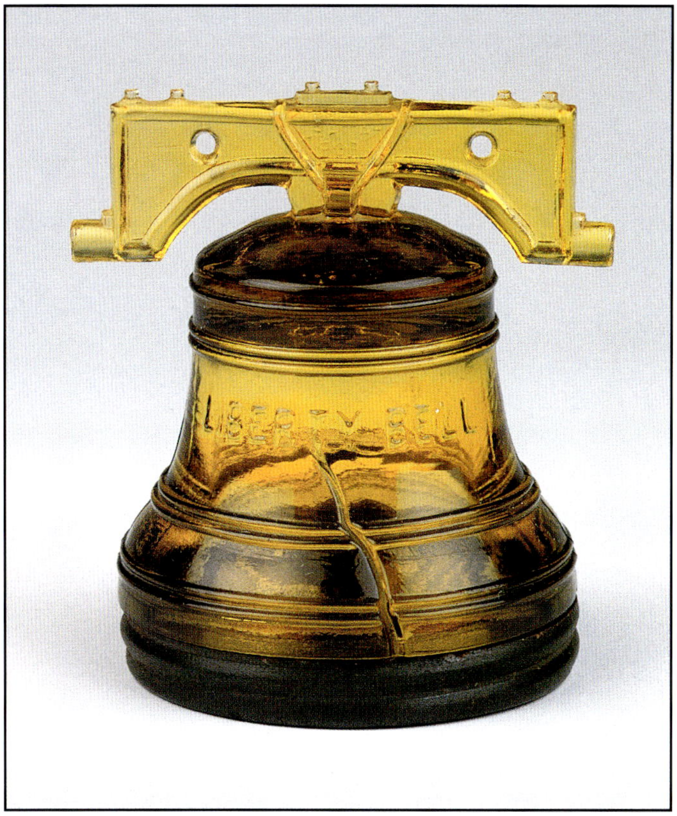

Liberty Bell candy container marked *Patent Applied For.* 3 1/2" high and 2 3/4" diameter. Amber, $135-150. Blue, $145-165.

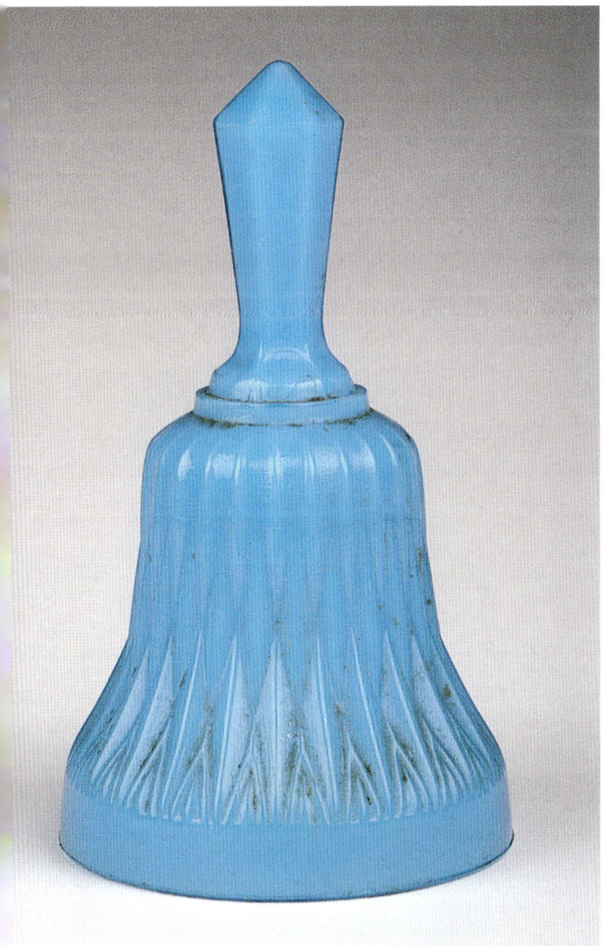

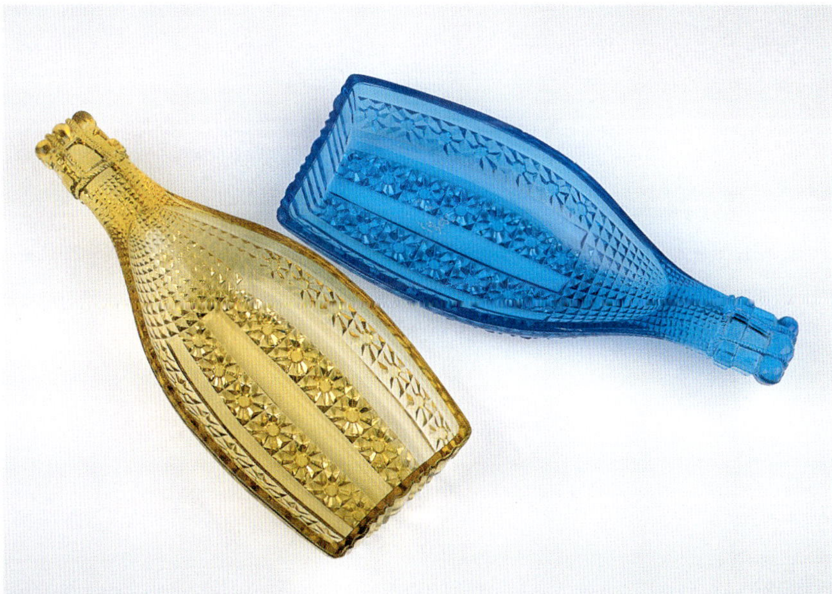

Bottle shaped pickle dish made by the Central Glass Company as illustrated in an 1889 catalog. 8 1/4" long. Blue, $145-160. Canary, $145-160.

Bell, circa 1920s. 5 1/2" high and 3 3/8" wide. Blue opaque, $120-135.

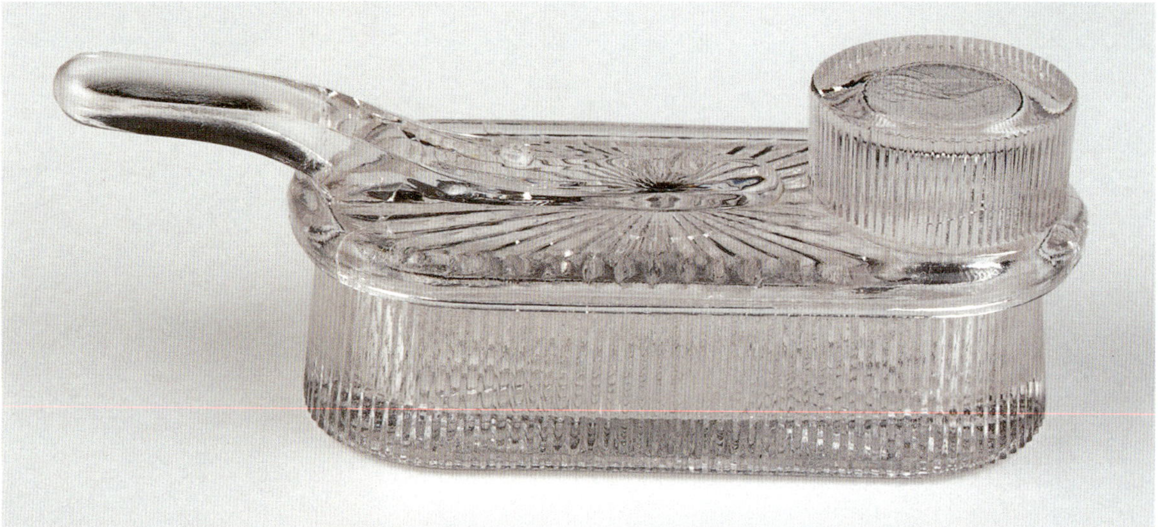

Shoe Brush match holder made by Adams and Company, circa 1890. 5" long. $150-165.

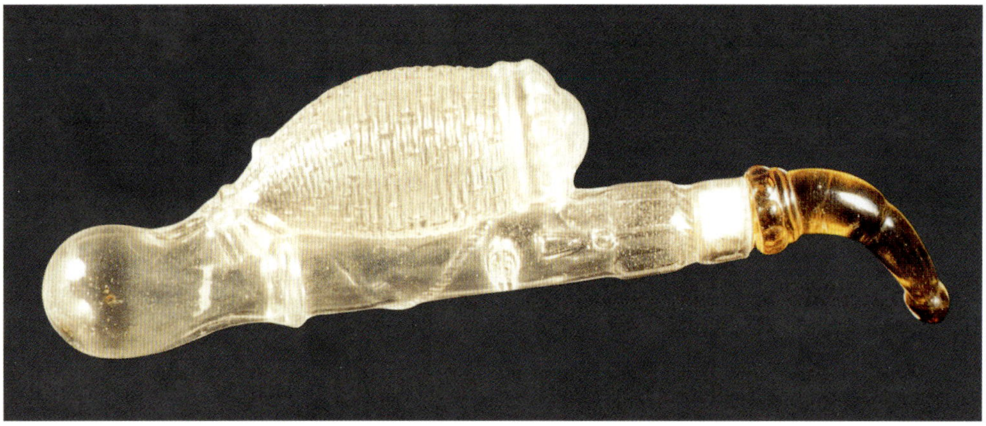

Old German Pipe flask made by the Dalzell, Gilmore, and Leighton Company, circa 1890. 10 1/2" long. Clear with amber as shown, $165-200.

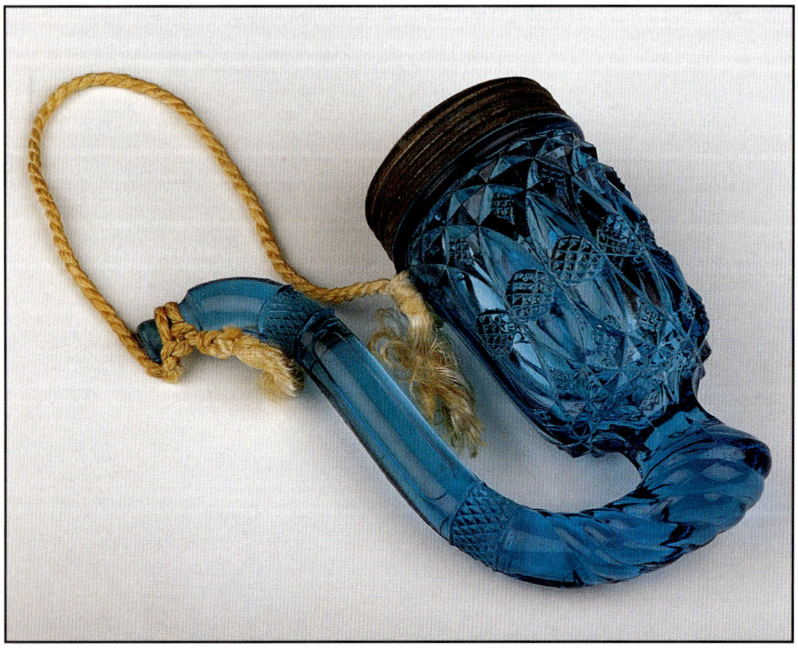

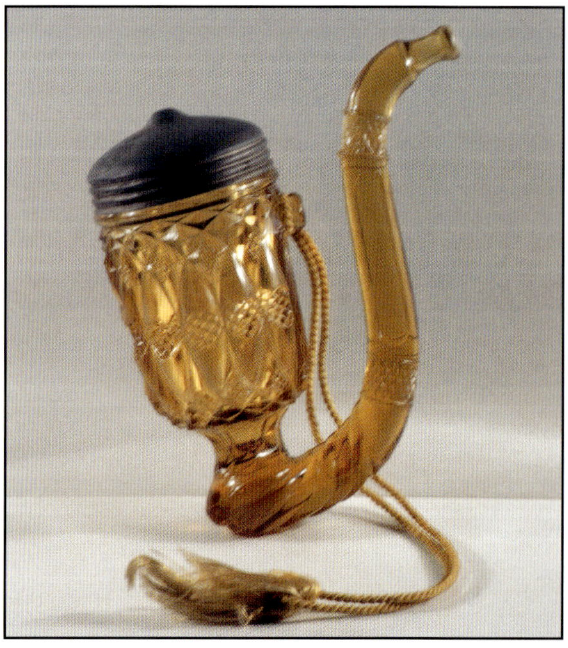

Pipe flask with cord designed by Julius Proeger, circa 1890. 5" high. Amber, $165-185. Blue, $175-200.

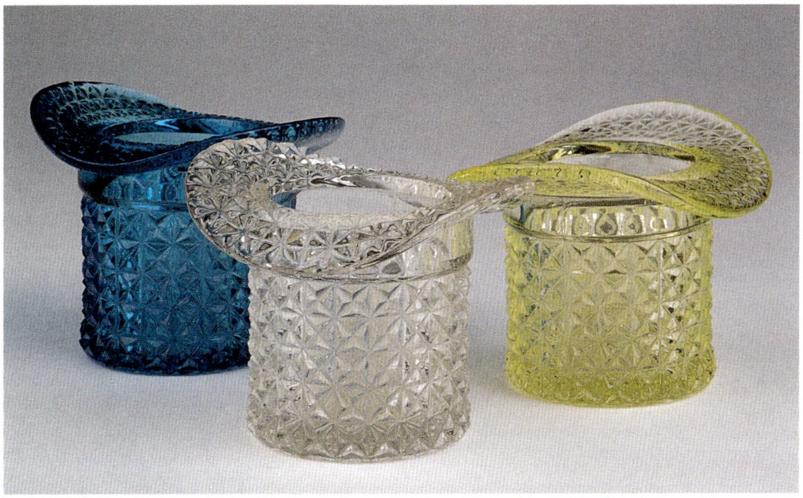

Hat match or toothpick holder in the fine cut pattern, circa 1886. 2 3/8" high. Clear, $32-42. Amber, $38-48. Blue, $50-60. Canary, $50-60.

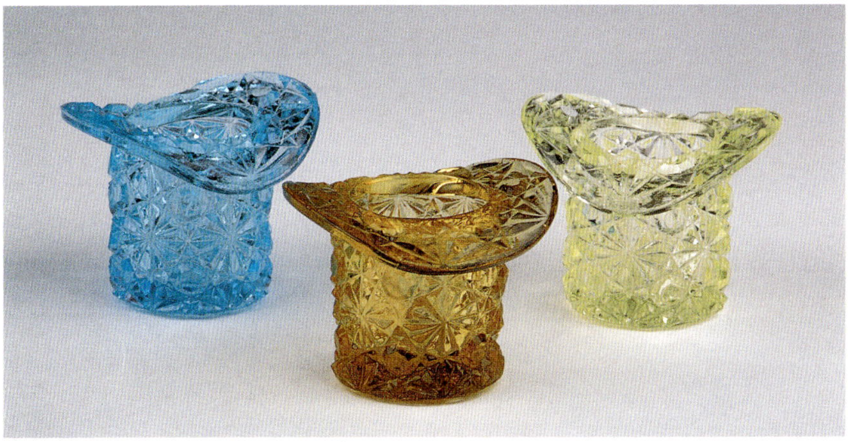

Hat match or toothpick holder in the Daisy and Button pattern made by the Geo. Duncan and Sons, circa 1885. 2 5/8" high. Blue, $40-60. Amber, $25-40. Canary, $30-40.

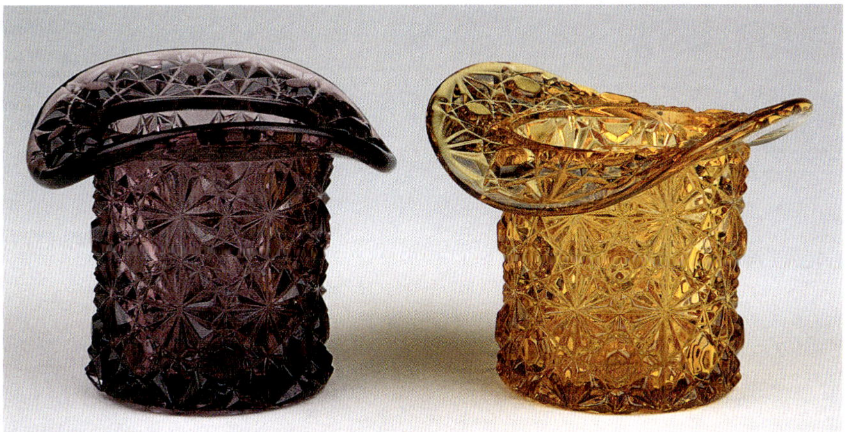

Hat toothpick or match holder in the daisy and button pattern, circa 1900. Amber, $35-45. Amethyst, $50-60.

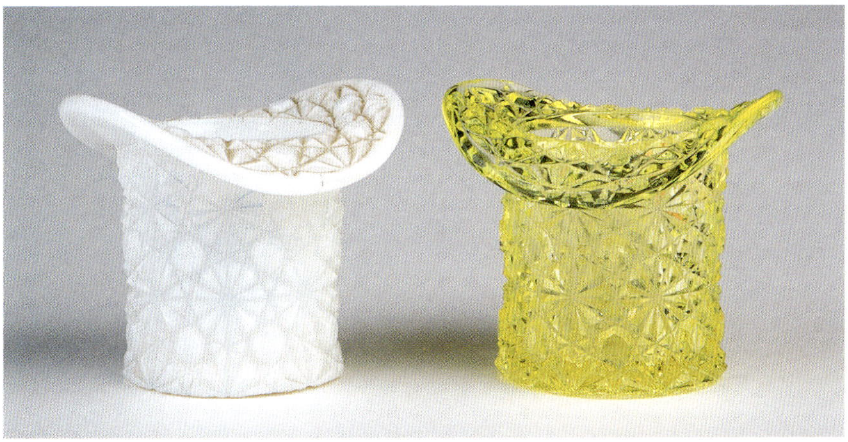

Hat toothpick or match holder in the daisy and button pattern, circa 1900. Canary, $55-65. Opal, $ 70-85.

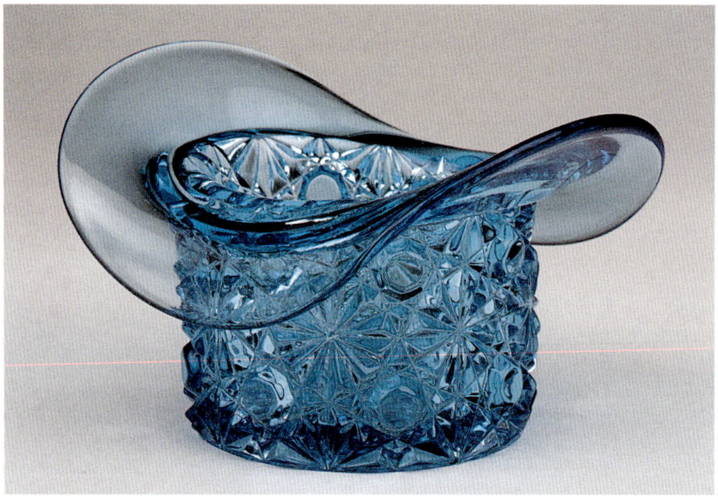

Hat match holder in the daisy and button pattern. This was pressed in a tumbler mold and the sides were turned down to form a brim for the hat. Blue, $65-85.

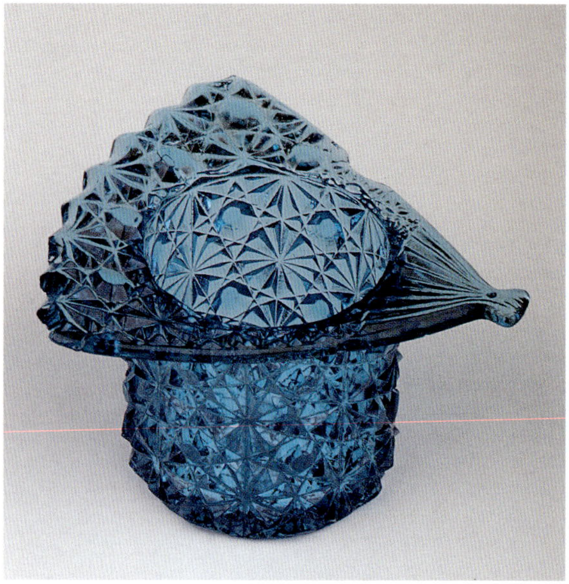

Hat match holder in the daisy and button pattern, the brim in the shape of a fan. Blue, $70-95.

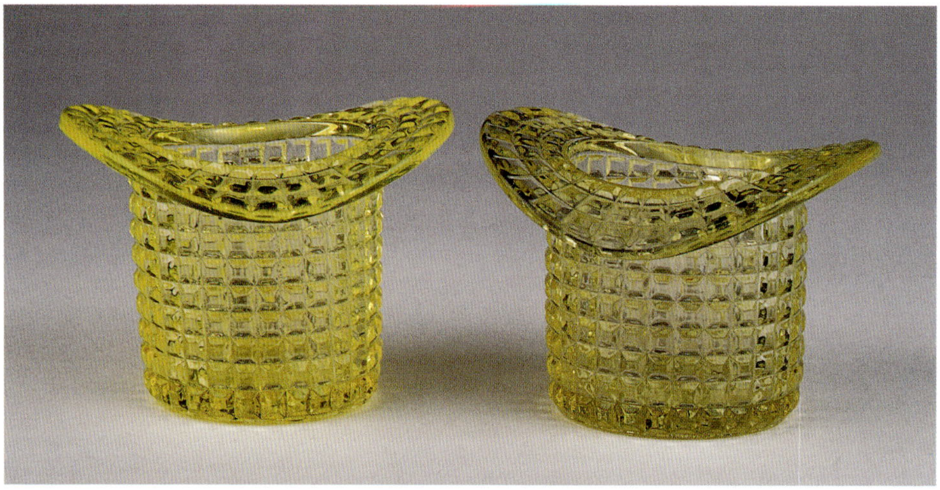

Hat match holder in a tapered block pattern made at the Rochester Glass Works by the National Glass Company, circa 1902. 2 1/4" high and 2" in diameter. Canary, $60-75.

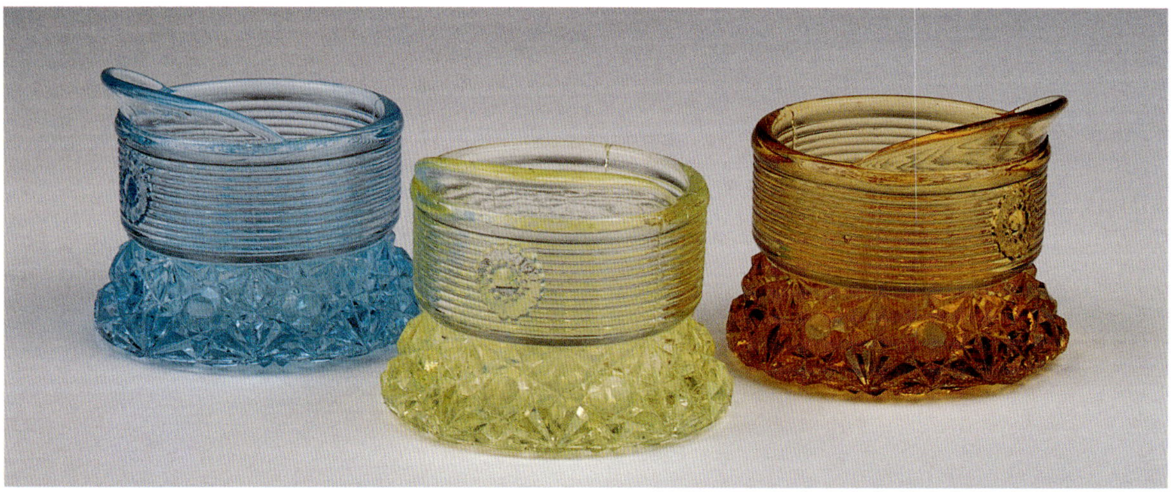

Little German Band Cap salts made by Geo. Duncan and Sons, circa 1886. 1 7/8" high and 2 1/2" diameter. Clear, $55-65. Amber, $65-80. Blue, $125-140. Canary, $125-140.

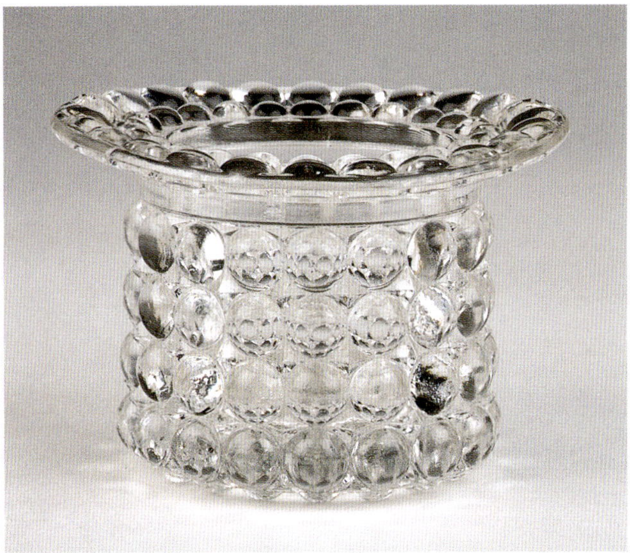

Hat match holder in the thousand eye pattern made by the Richards and Hartley Glass Company, circa 1888. 2" high and 2" in diameter. Clear, $60-75. Amber, $65-80. Apple Green, $70-85. Blue, $75-95. Canary, $70-85.

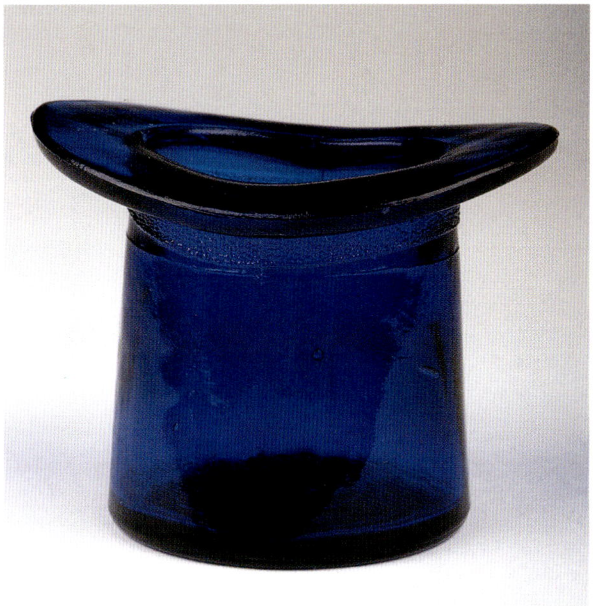

Hat match holder, maker unknown. Blue, $55-70.

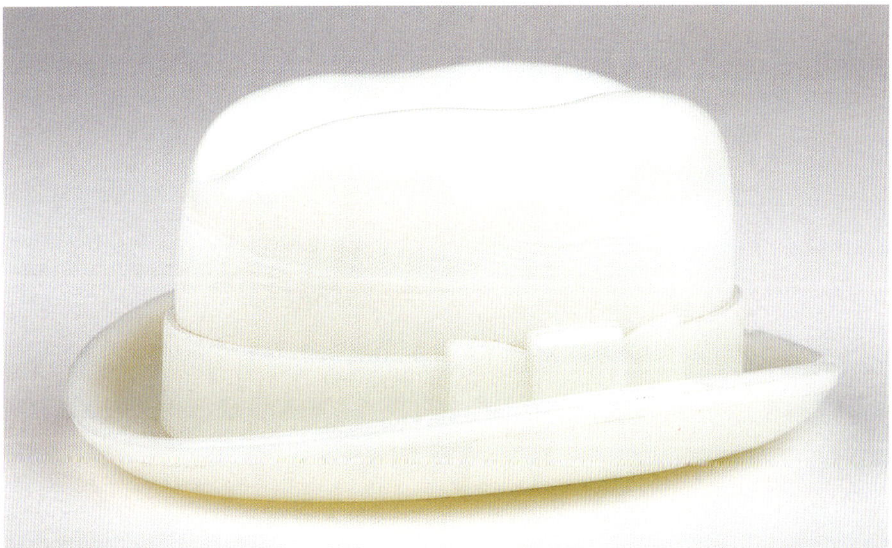

Derby hat made by McKee and Brothers, circa 1889. 2 7/8" high. Opal, $135-150.

Straw Hat made by McKee and Brothers, circa 1889. This hat was made for the McKinley-Bryan presidential campaign. 1" high and 4" long. Clear, $75-85. Straw color, $135-150.

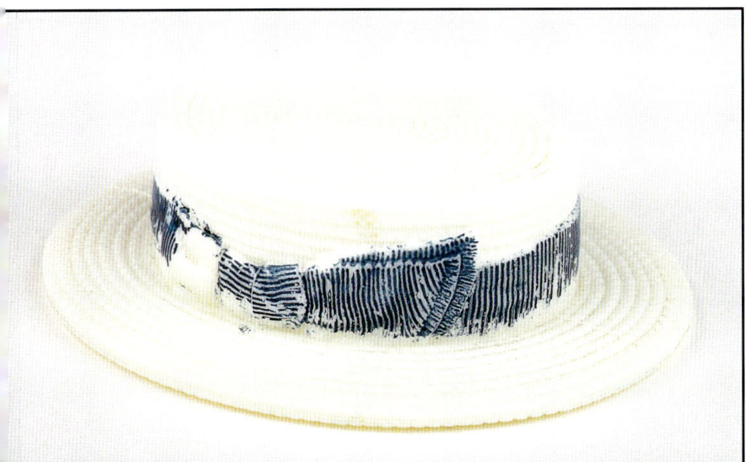

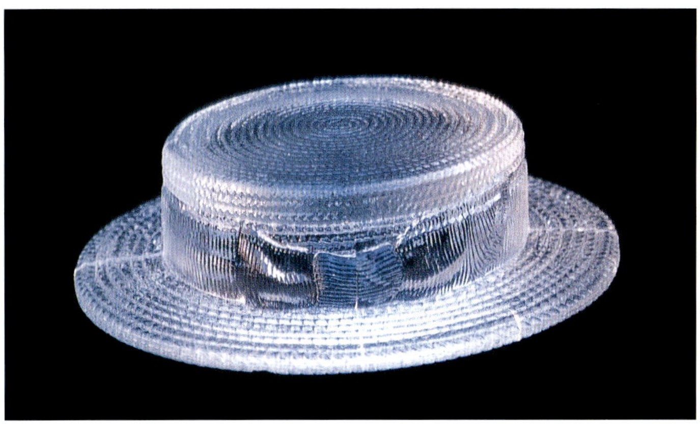

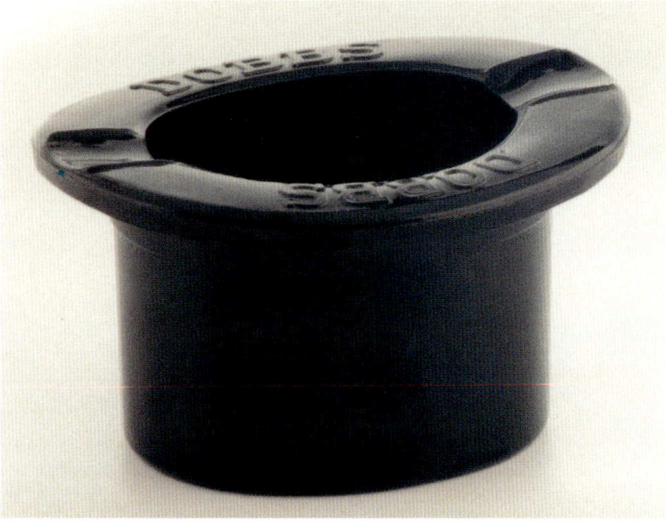

Hat match holder or ashtray, *Dobbs.* This could be an advertising piece for Thomas Dobbs, who was a representative in New York for several glass companies. 4" long and 3 1/4" wide. $200-250.

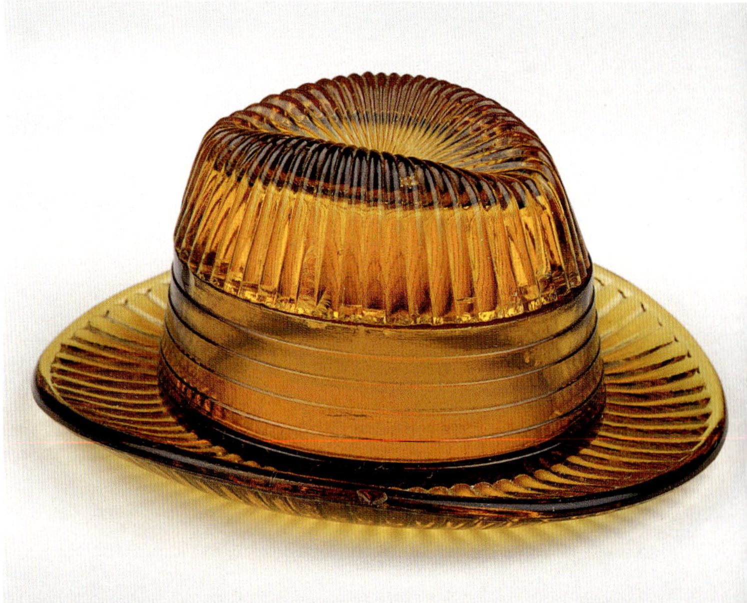

Hat container with the crown of the hat forming a lid. 3" high. Amber, $175-195.

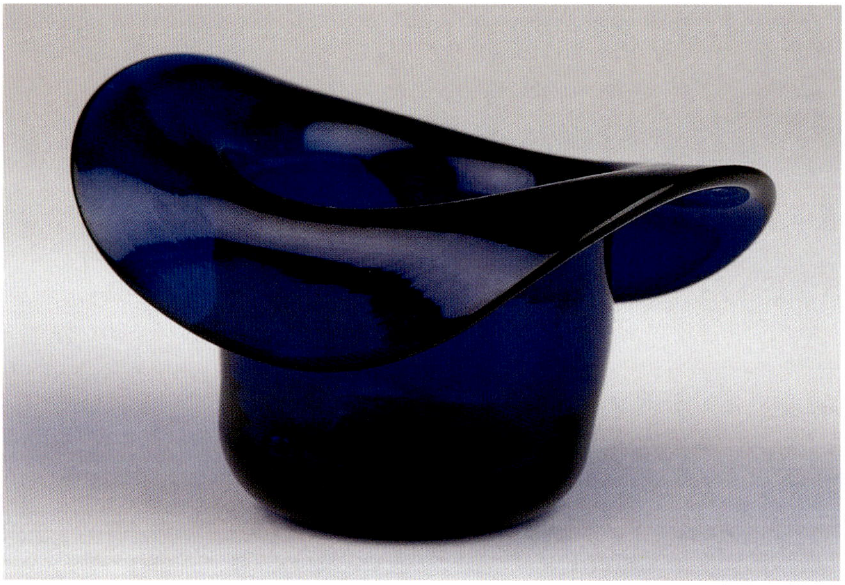

Hat match or toothpick holder in blown glass. Blue, $45-65.

Harrison Hat pattern number 16014, made by the United States Glass Company as illustrated in an 1892 catalog. *He's All Right* and *The Same Old Hat*. 2 1/4" high and 3 3/8" wide. Blue opaque, $250-300.

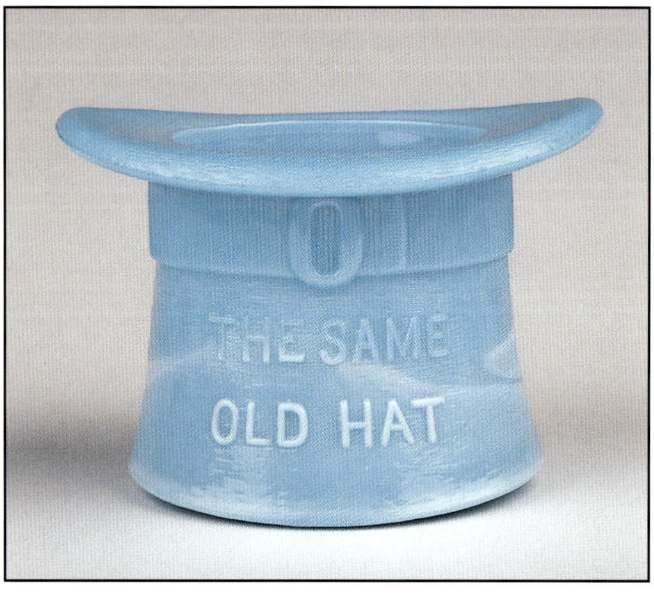

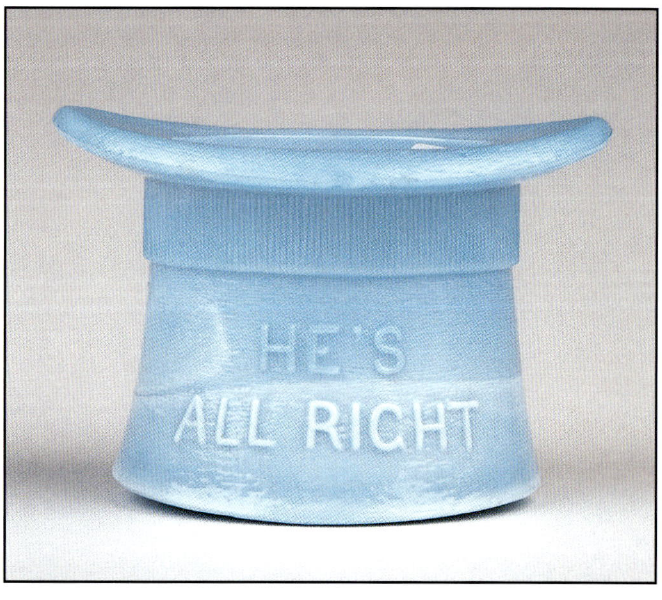

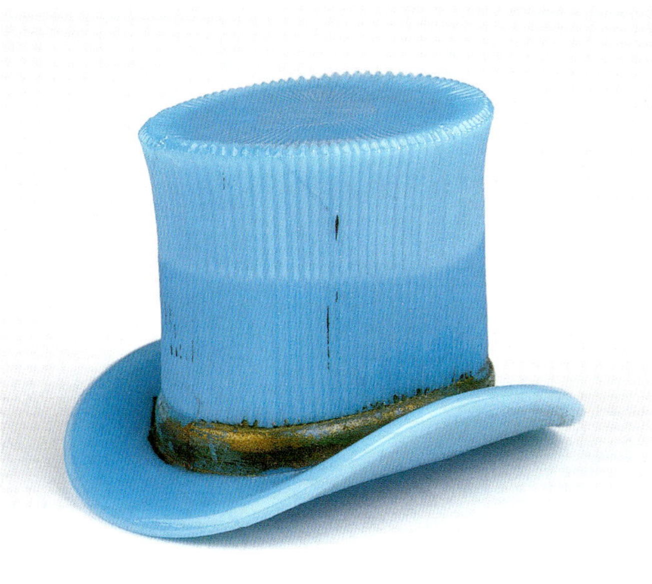

Top Hat match holder, 2 1/4" high and 3 1/4" wide. Blue opaque, $100-125.

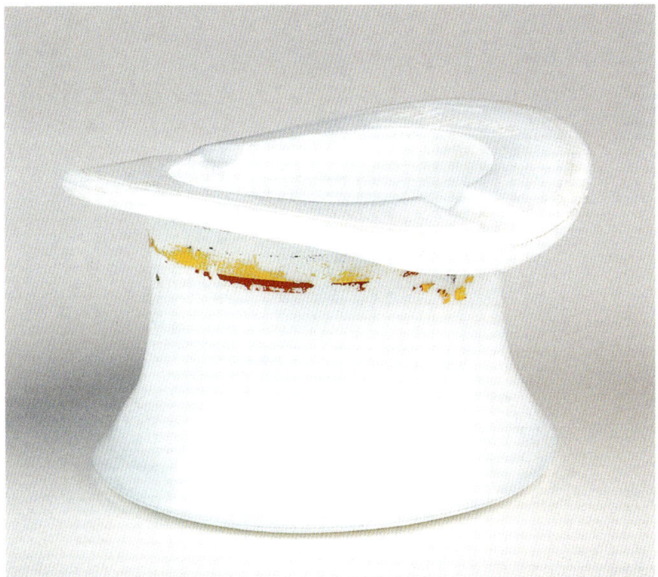

Hat ashtray or match holder. *Magnus* and *Depose* marks. 2 1/2" high and 4 1/2" wide. Opal, $130-150.

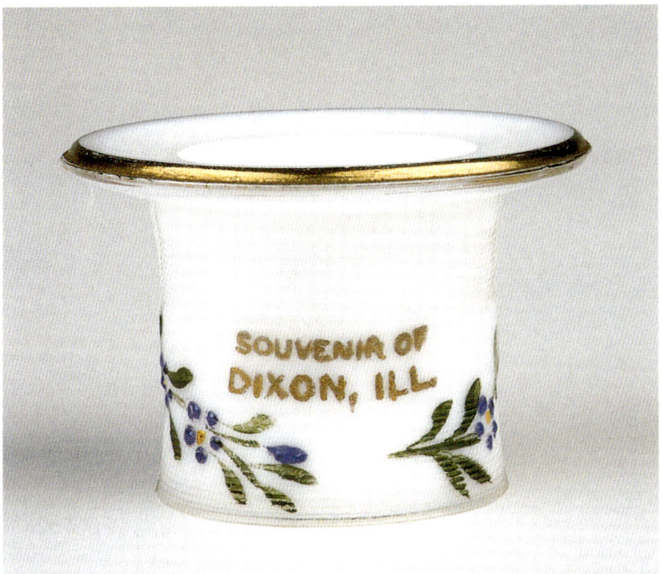

Hat match holder, *Souvenir of Dixon, Ill.*, 3 1/4" wide and 2 1/4" high. Opal, $75-95.

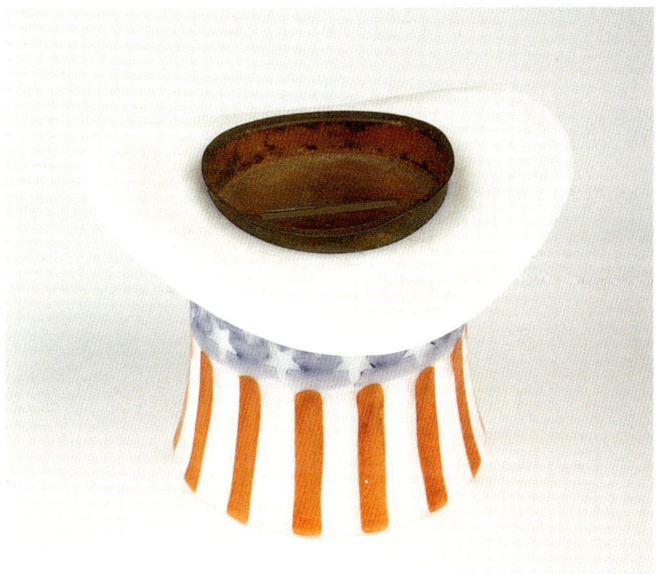

U S Hat, bank and packer's container made by the Westmoreland Specialty Company, circa 1900. 3 3/4" wide and 2 3/4" high. As shown, $65-100. With lid, $85-125.

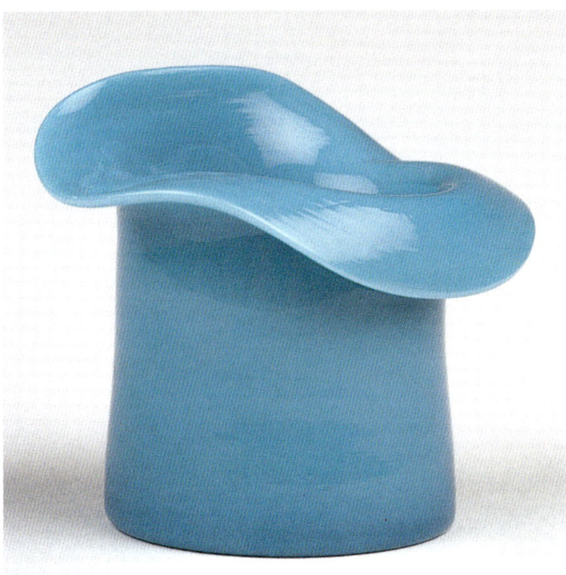

Hat match holder in blown glass. One side of the brim is turned up and the other side down. 2 1/4" high and 3" wide. Blue opaque, $85-110.

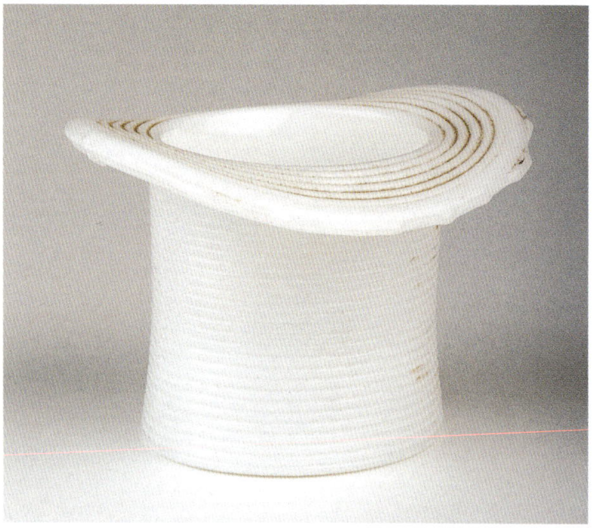

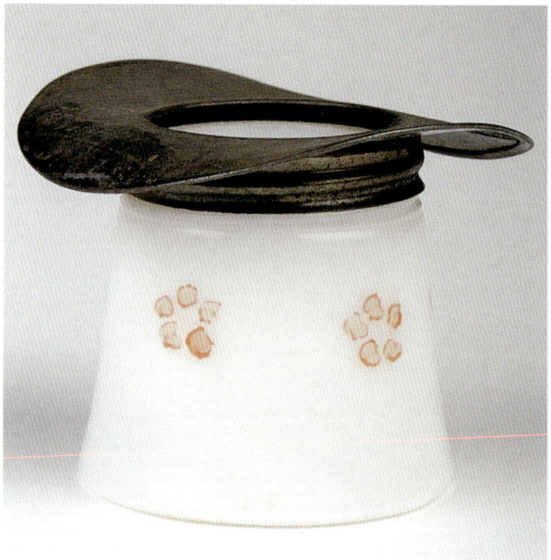

Saratoga Hat, match or toothpick holder illustrated in a 1903 Cambridge Glass Company catalog, made earlier by a factory of the National Glass Company. 2 1/4" high and 3 1/4" wide. Opal, $60-80. Clear, $30-35. Blue, $45-55. Amber, 35-40.

Hat match or toothpick holder, originally a political item. Note that it has a metal brim. 3" wide and 2" high. As shown, $190-200.

Hat match or toothpick holder, maker unknown. 2 1/2" high and 3 1/4" wide. Green, $45-55.

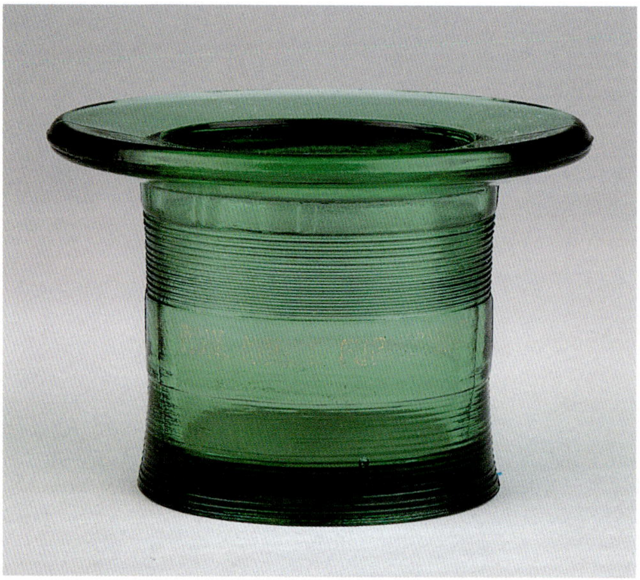

Helmet Butter Dish in the daisy and button pattern made by King, Son, and Company, circa late 1880s. Lid diameter: 5 3/8". Clear, $385-435.

Jockey Cap butter dish. The front panel of the cap is identical to that of the Helmet butter. Circa late 1880s. Inner brim of the cap is 5 1/2" in diameter. Clear, $325-400.

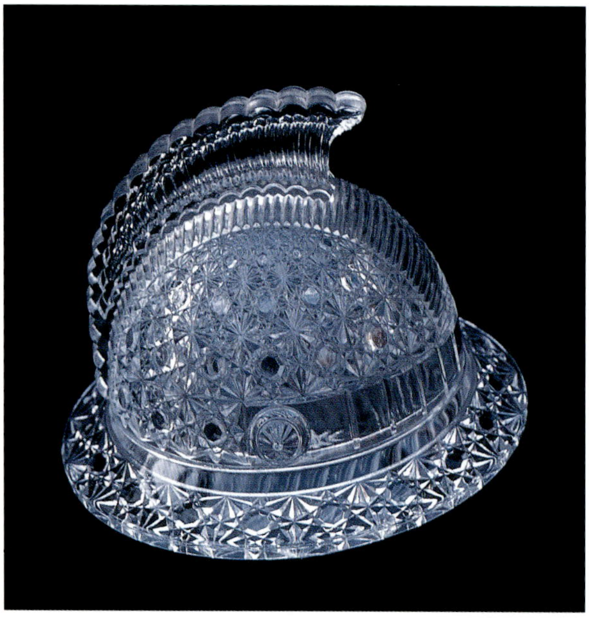

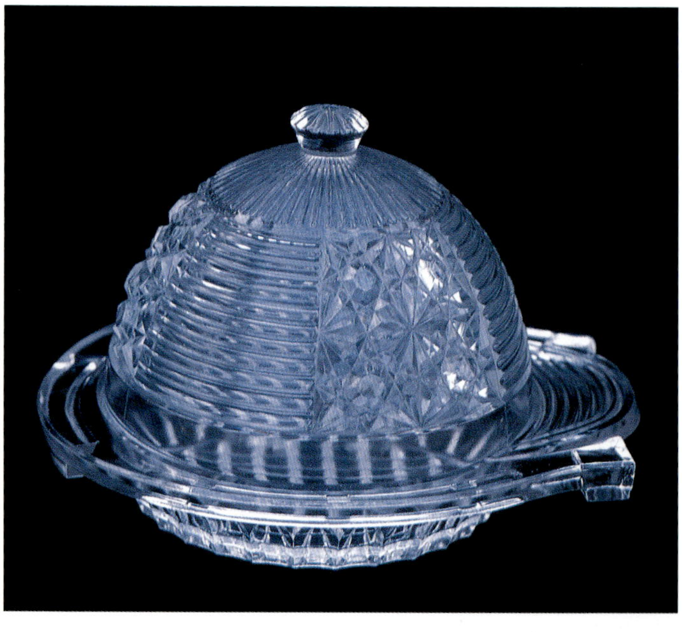

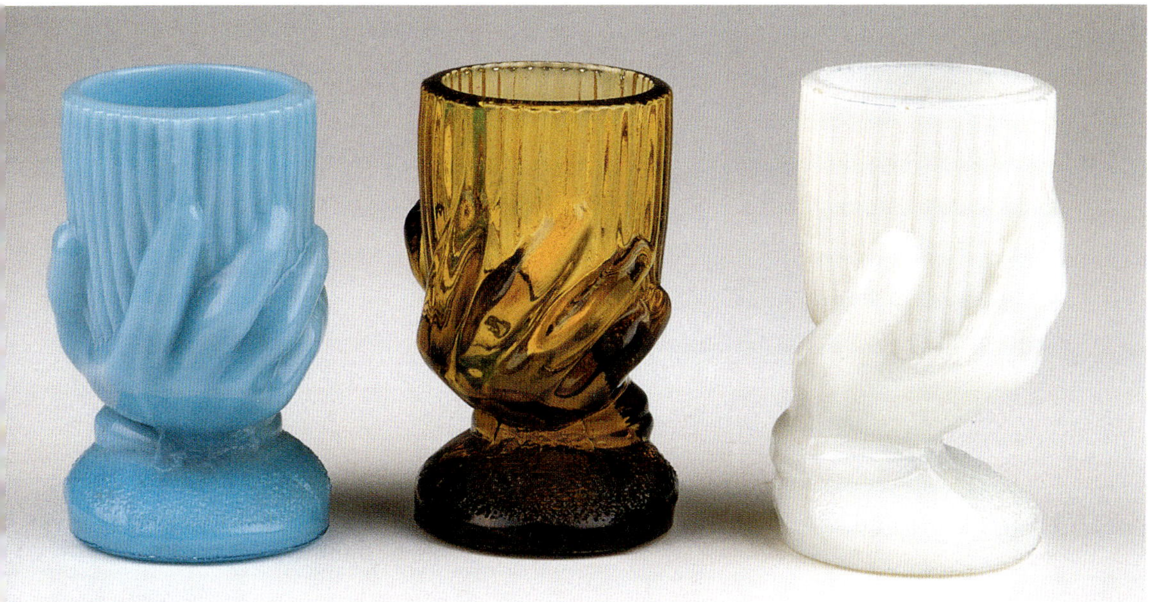

Beggar's Hand toothpick or match holder by Portieux. 3 1/2" high and 2" wide. Blue, $90-100. Amber, $80-90. Opal, $75-95.

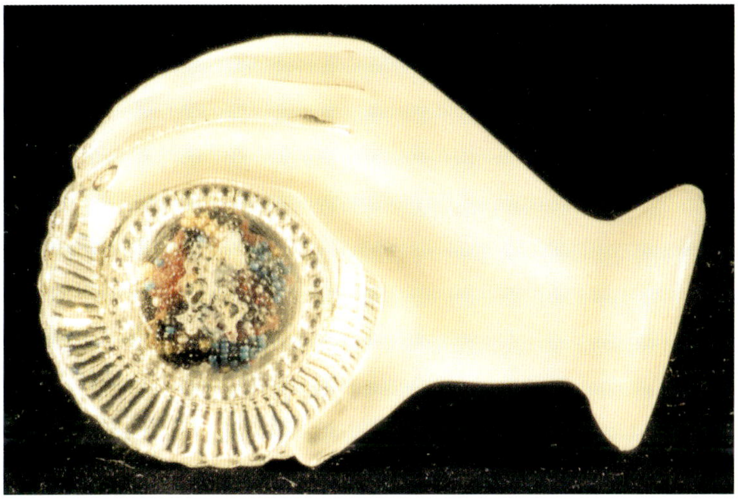

Hand Paperweight. 4" long. Maker unknown. As shown, $150-200.

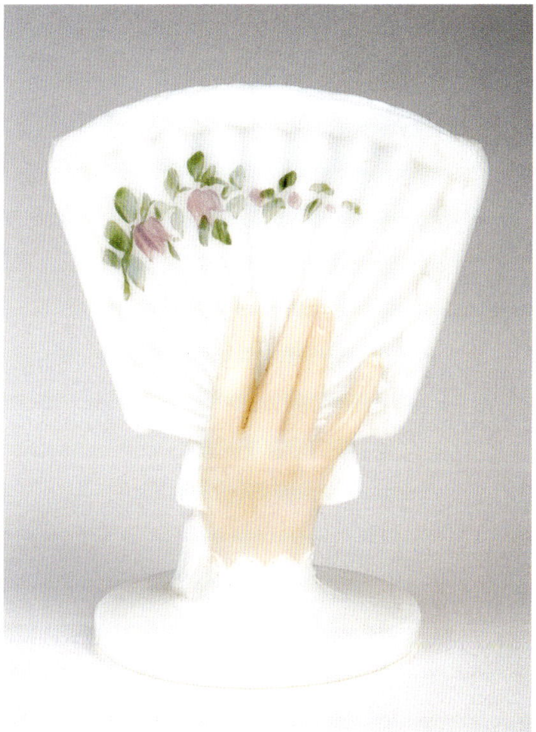

Hand with Fan match holder. 4 3/8" high. Opal, $65-75

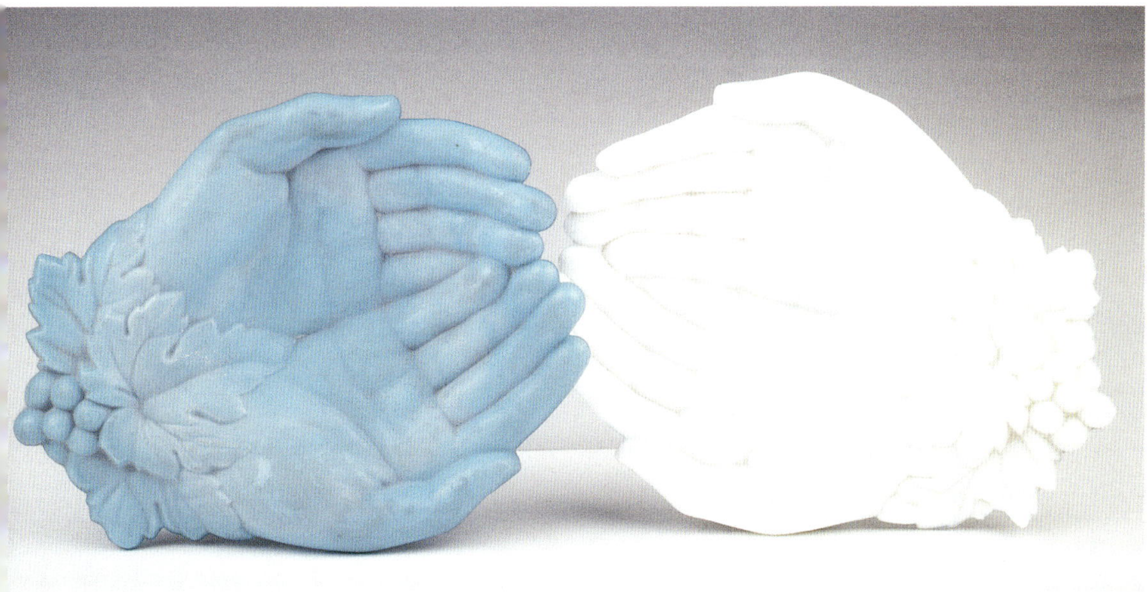

Hands, unknown use. 7 1/2" long and 6" wide. Opal, $70-80. Blue opaque, $145-165.

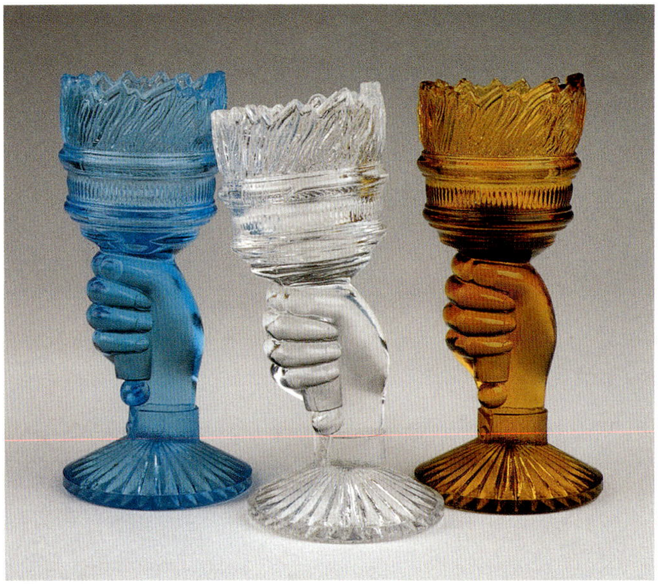

Hand with Torch toothpick holder, circa 1876. 3 3/4" high and 1 5/8" wide. Clear, $60-75. Amber, $70-85. Blue, $90-110.

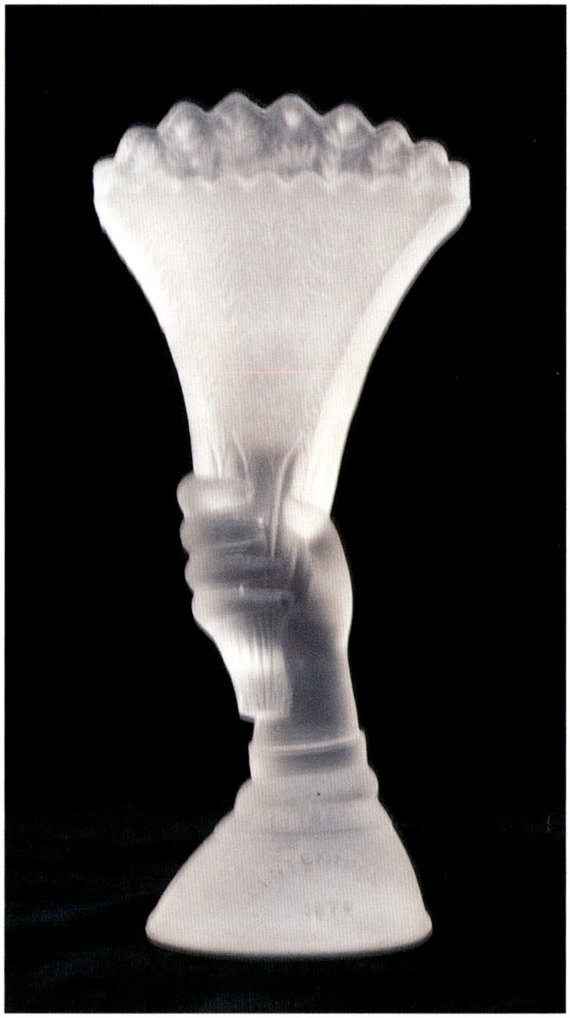

Centennial Hand Vase made by Gillinder and Company, circa 1876. 7 1/8" high. $75-110.

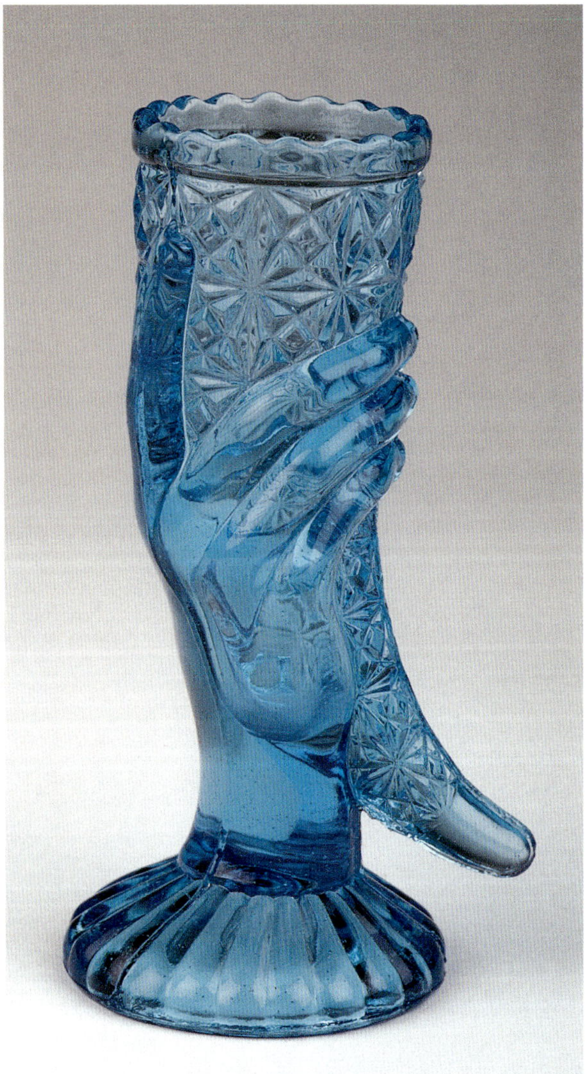

Cornucopia Vase made by the Geo. Duncan and Sons Company, circa late 1880s. 5" high and 2 1/4" diameter on the base. Blue, $60-85.

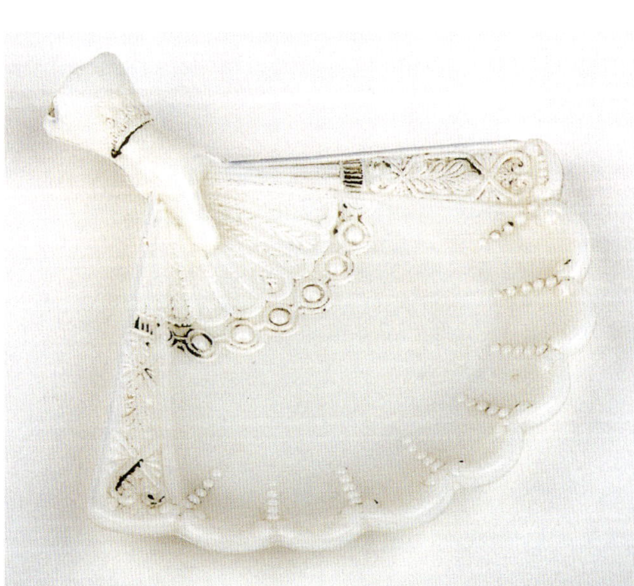

Hand with Fan, unknown use, circa late 1890s. 5 5/8" wide. Opal, $65-80.

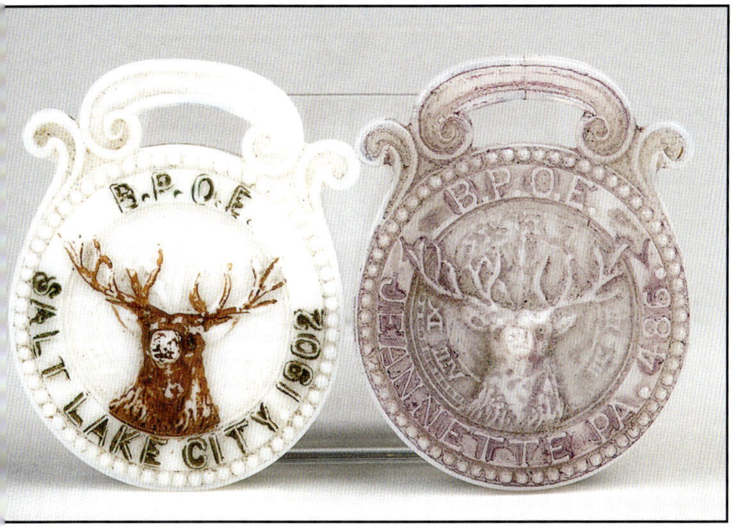

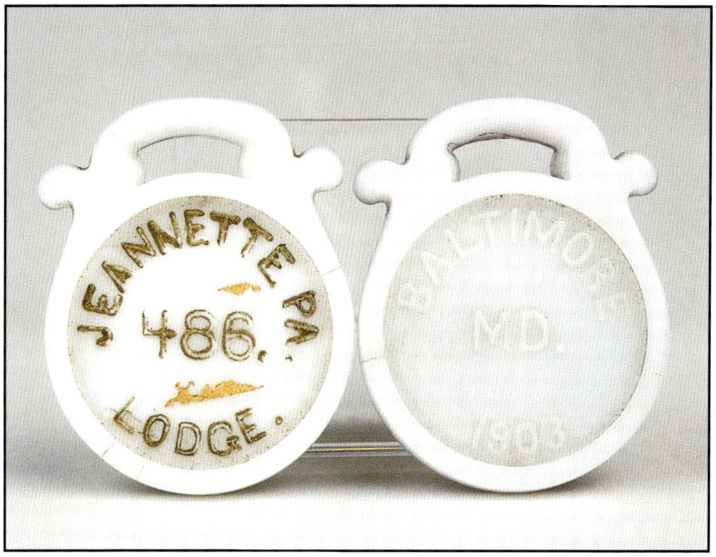

Watch Fobs, No. 1 – obverse: *BPOE Salt Lake City 1902*; reverse: *Jeanette Pa Lodge 486*. No. 2 – obverse: *BPOE 486 Jeanette Pa*; reverse: *Baltimore Md 1903*. 2" high and 1 1/2" wide. Opal, $350-385.

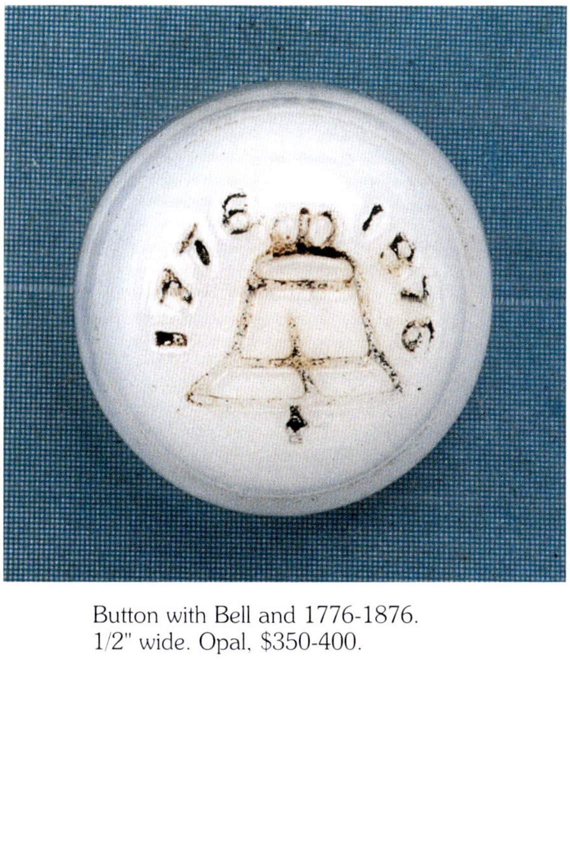

Button with Bell and 1776-1876.
1/2" wide. Opal, $350-400.

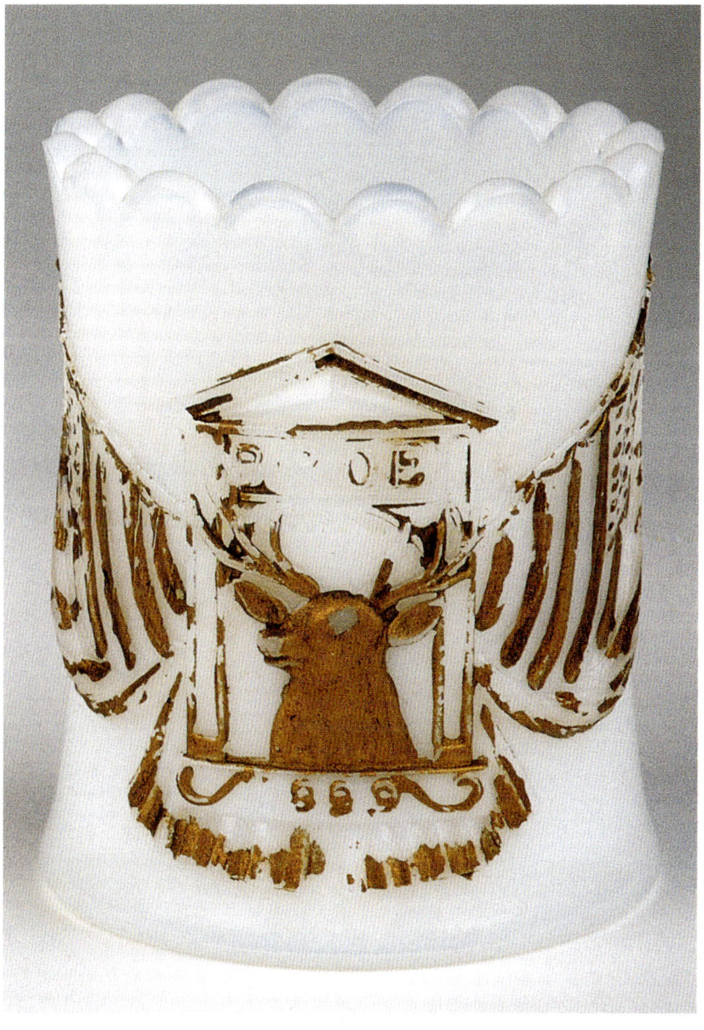

BPOE toothpick holder, date and maker unknown. 2 3/8" high and 2" wide. Clear, $65-75. Opal, $130-145.

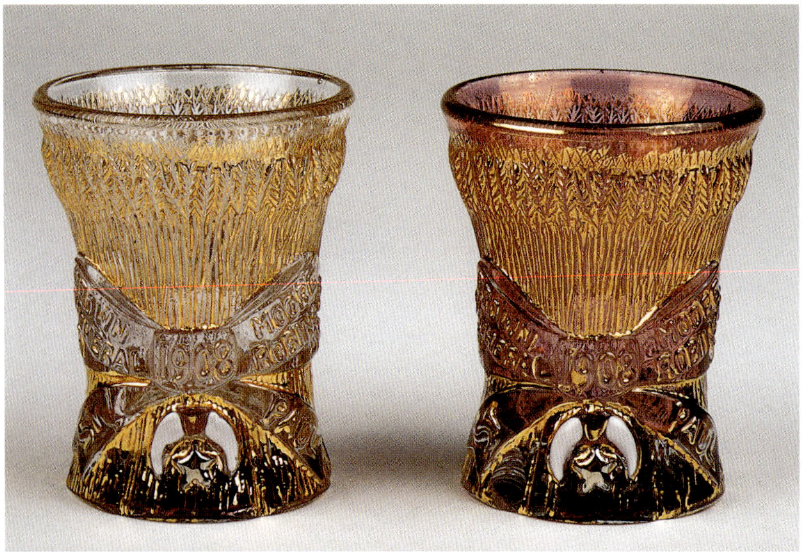

Sheaf of Wheat toothpick holder made by the Westmoreland Specialty Company for the Shrine convention of 1908. 2 1/8" high and 1 5/8" wide. Clear with staining, $190-235.

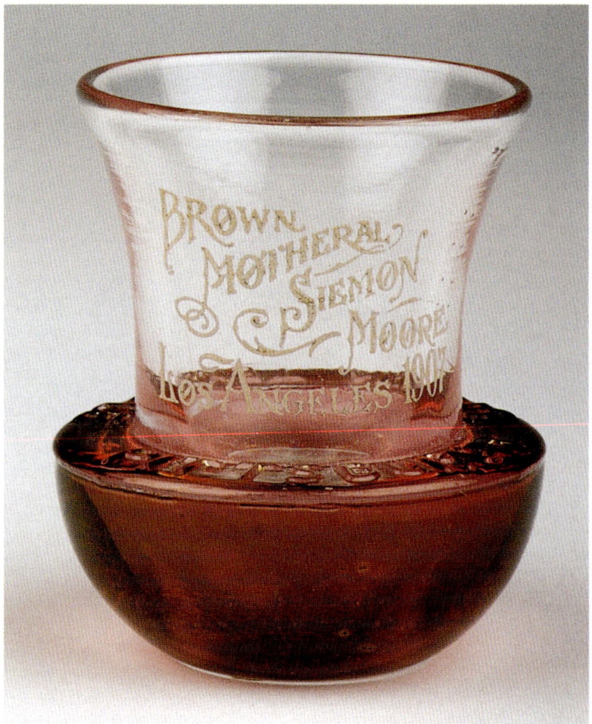

Shrine souvenir toothpick holder made by the Westmoreland Specialty Company for the Los Angeles Shrine convention of 1907. 2 1/2" high and 1 1/4" wide. $190-235.

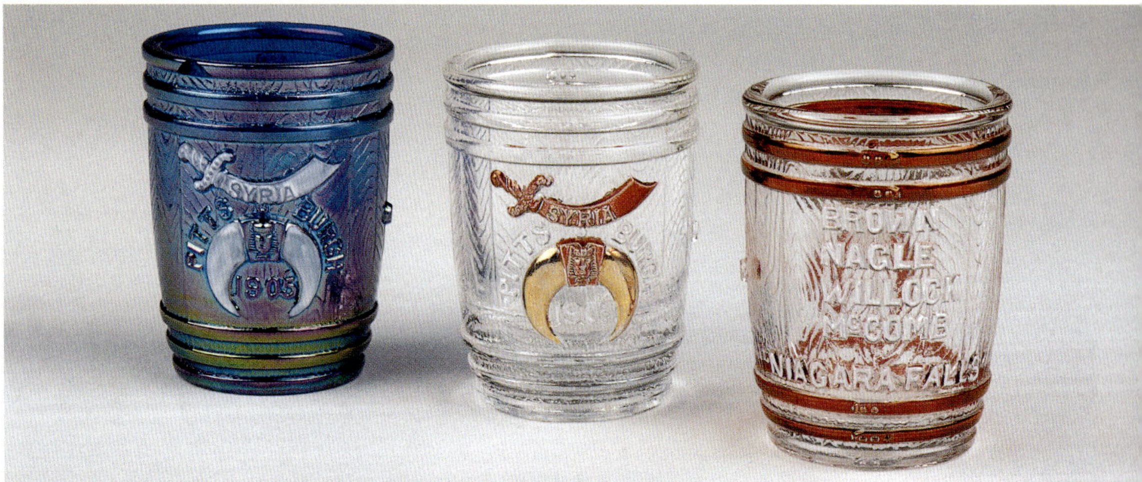

Barrel toothpick holder made by the Westmoreland Specialty Company for the Shrine convention of 1905 at Niagara Falls, New York. 2 1/2" high and 1 1/2" wide. Clear with staining, $190-235. Cobalt iridescent, $190-235.

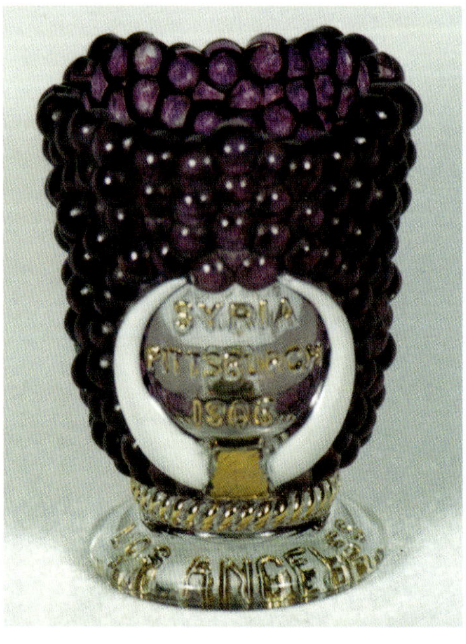

Grapes toothpick holder made by the Westmoreland Specialty Company for the 1903 Shrine convention. 2 1/2" high and 1 7/8" wide. As shown, $190-235.

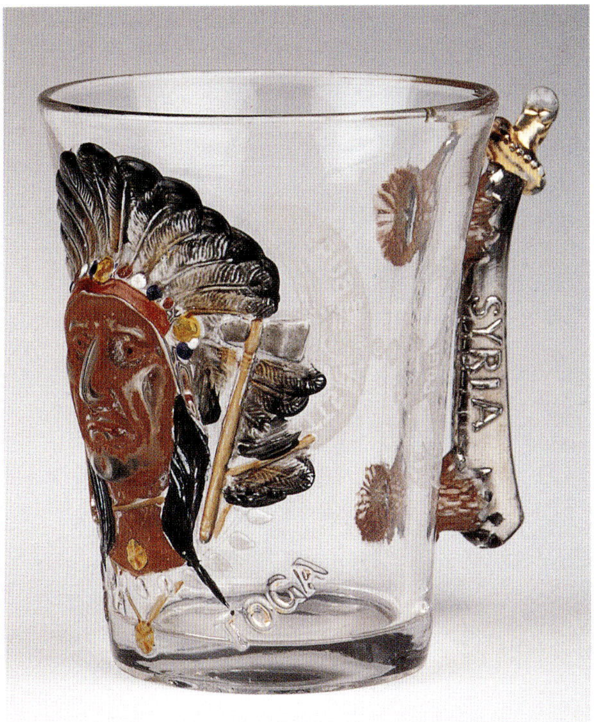

Saratoga mug made by the Westmoreland Specialty Company for the Shrine convention of 1903. 3 1/2" high. Clear with stain, $125-150.

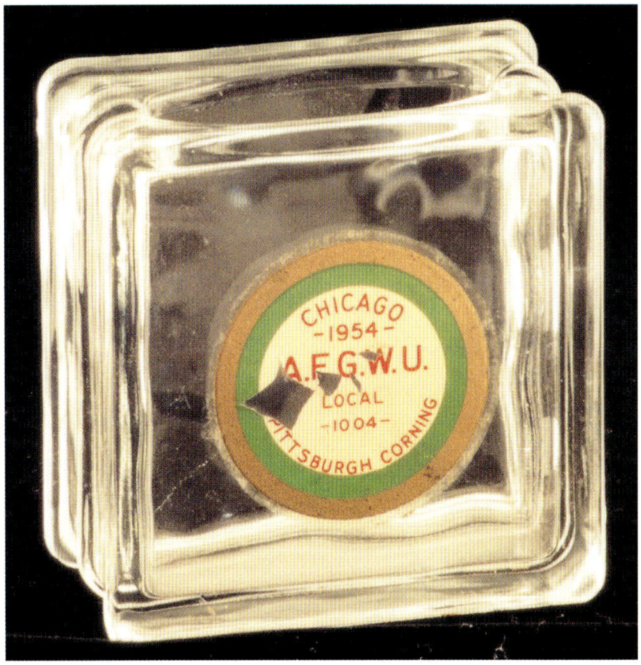

Bank, souvenir of Local 1004 of the American Federation of Glass Workers Union, circa 1954. 3 1/2" square. $25-45.

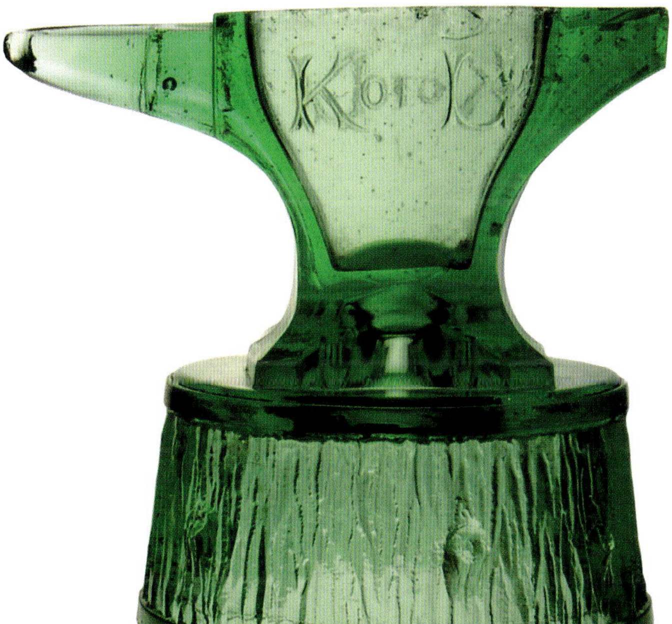

K of L match safe made by the Hemingray Glass Company, patented March 1, 1887. Design patent number 17,148. Known colors are amber, peacock blue, and depression glass green. Depression glass green, $750-850.

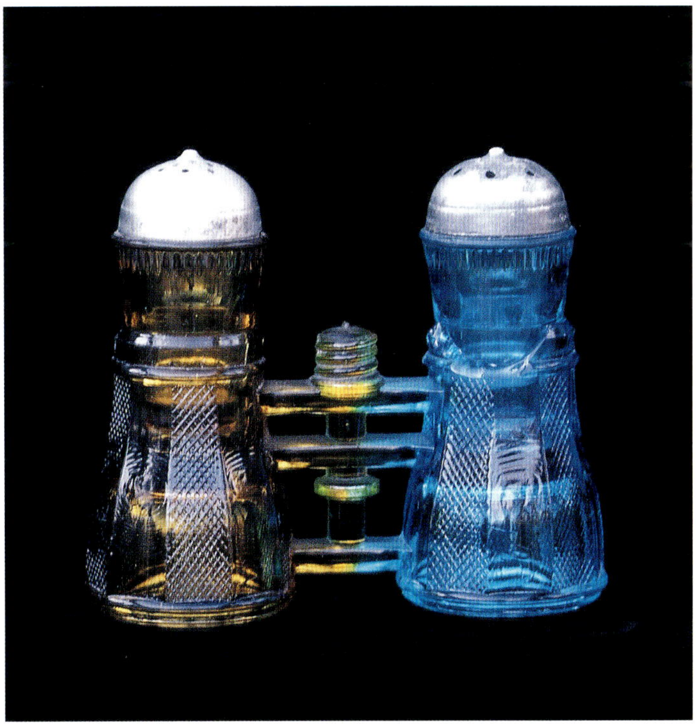

Binoculars salt and pepper shakers, maker uncertain, circa 1890. 4 1/2" high and 5 1/2" wide. As shown in sapphire and amber combination, $300-350.

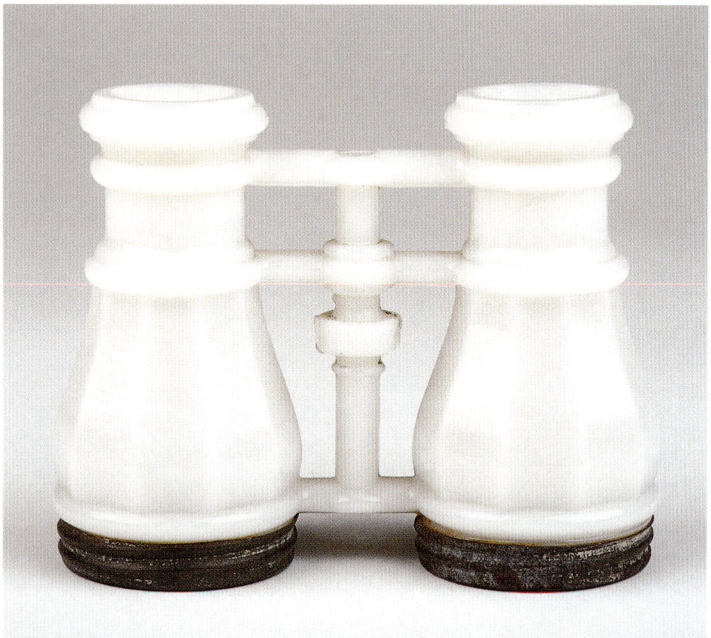

Binoculars candy container, circa late 1890s. 3" high. Opal, $165-195.

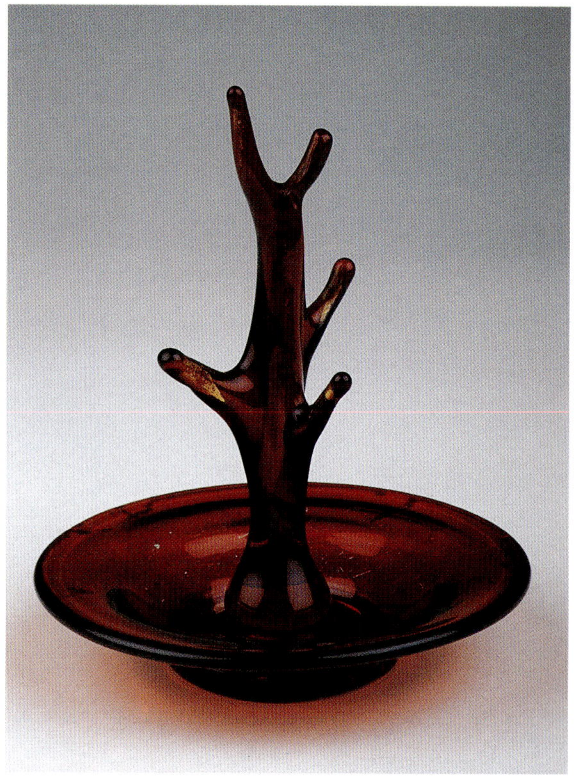

Ring Tree. 4" high and 3 1/2" base diameter. Ruby Stain, $125-150.

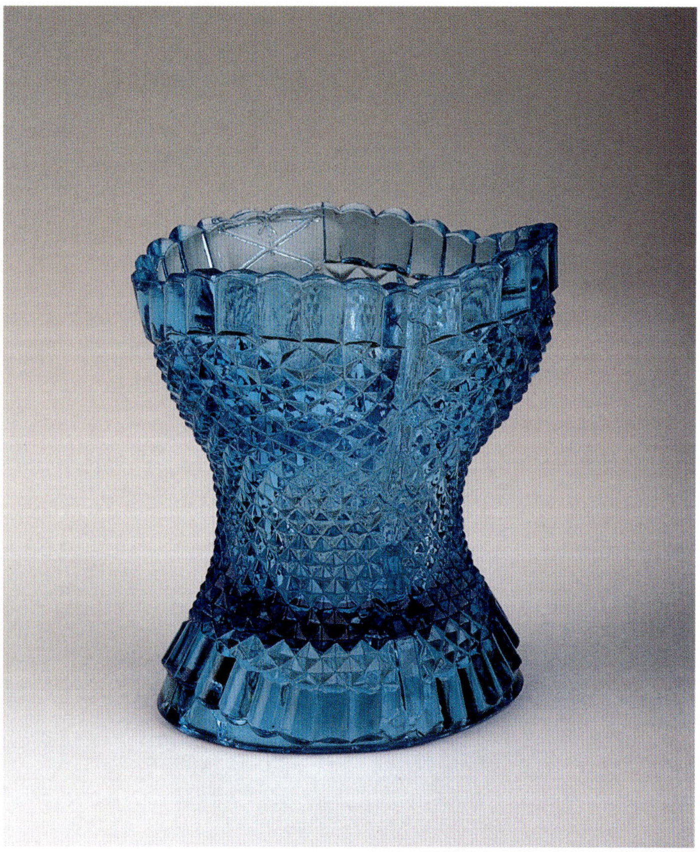

Corset toothpick holder made by the Bellaire Goblet Company, circa 1899. 2 7/8" high and 2 1/2" wide. *Patent Appl'd For* on the base. Clear, $125-140. Amber, $190-225. Blue, $215-245.

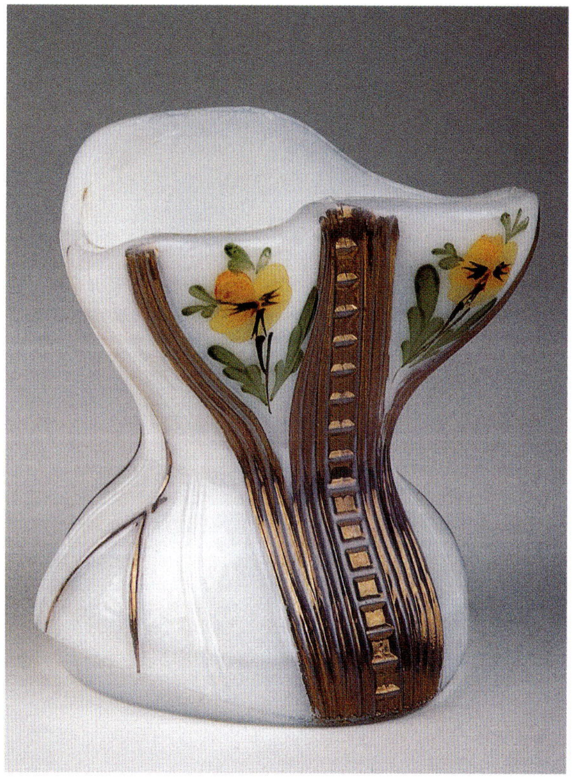

Tight Corset toothpick holder. 3" high and 2 1/2" wide. Opal, $100-125. Opal decorated, $120-145.

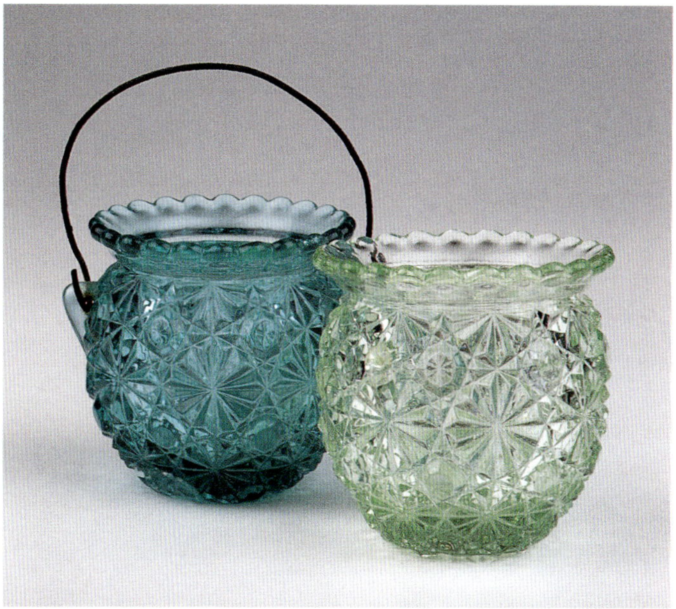

Kettle in the daisy and button pattern, in many ways matches the Mikado pattern toothpick holder of Richards and Hartley and could have been made from the same mold, circa 1885. Note the stars on the buttons. 2 1/4" high and 2 3/8" wide. Blue, $65-85. Apple Green, $65-85.

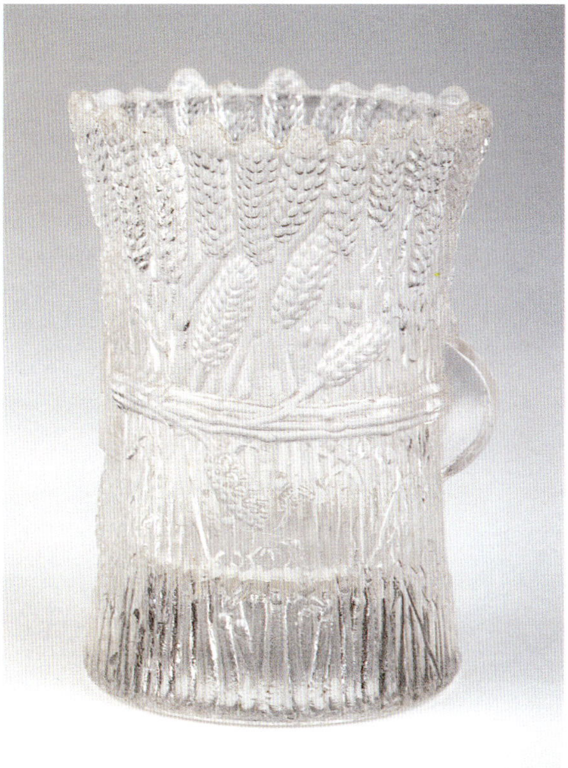

Sheaf toothpick made by the Dalzell, Gilmore & Leighton Company, circa 1898. This is documented by a Dalzell, Gilmore & Leighton catalog of the late 1890s. 3" high and 1 1/3" wide. Reproduced by the National Glass Company at their #9 glass works from the original mold. Dalzell Clear, $85-100. Amber, $140-180. National Chocolate, $500+. Nile Green, $180-250.

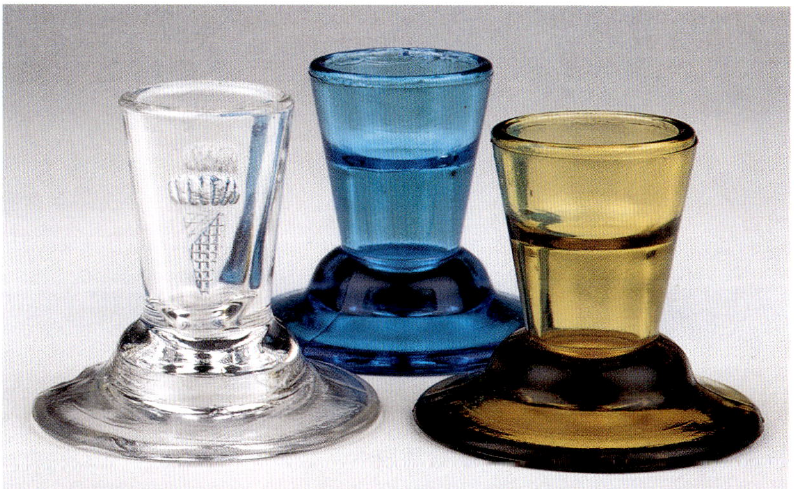

Ice Cream Cone Holder. 2 1/2" high. The clear one has an ice cream cone on it. Clear, $35-45. Amber, $35-45. Blue, $35-45.

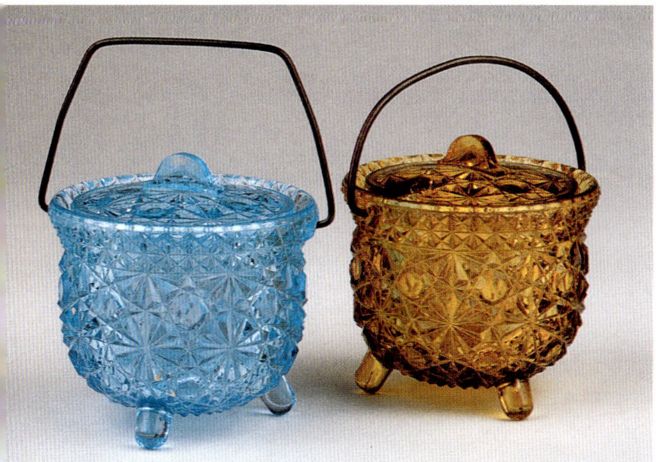

Kettle mustard or horseradish in the daisy and button pattern made by Adams and Company, circa late 1880s. 2 1/2" high and 3" wide. Amber, $60-75. Blue, $60-75.

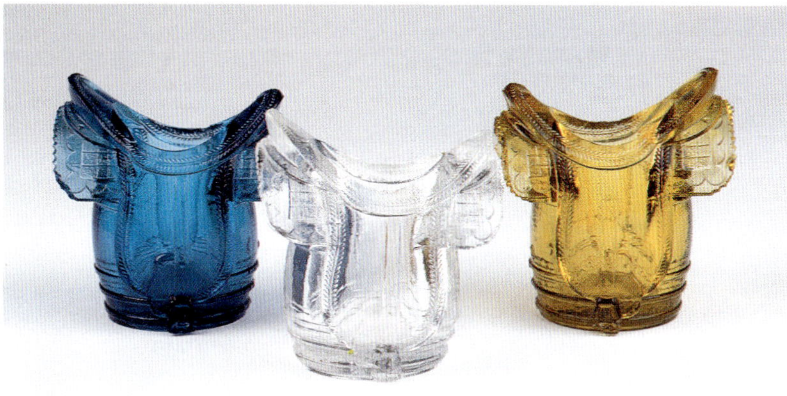

Saddle toothpick holder. 3" high and 3" wide. Reproductions are slightly smaller. Clear, $35-45. Amber, $45-55. Blue, $45-55.

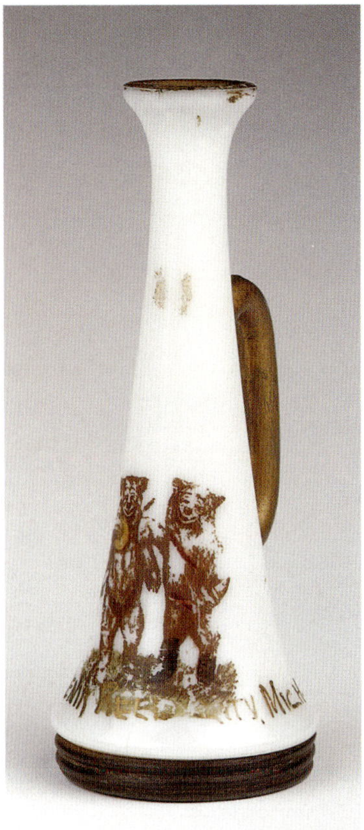

Horn, container with Roosevelt bears decoration. 5 1/2" high. Opal with bears, $290-325.

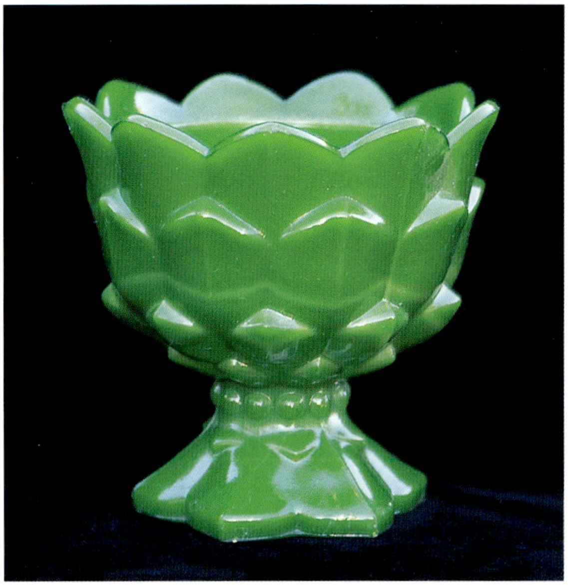

Artichoke open sugar by Vallerysthal, circa 1908. 4" high and 4" wide. Emerald Green opaque open sugar, $120-150. Emerald Green opaque covered sugar, $240-260.

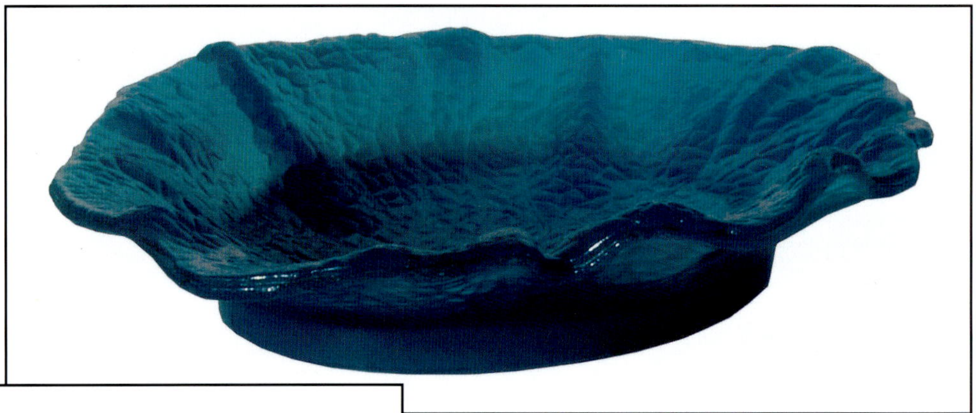

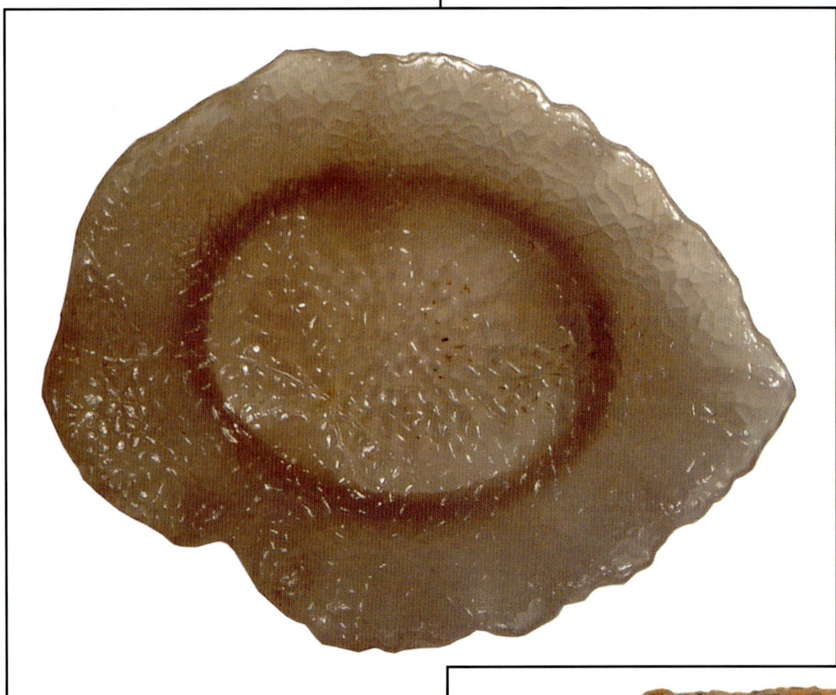

Leaf dish made by the Hemingray Glass Company, made in all the many colors of the bird dishes. All colors, $75-150.

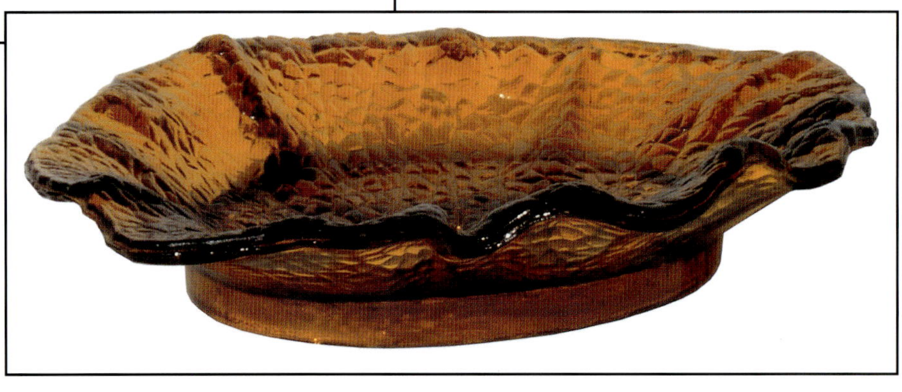

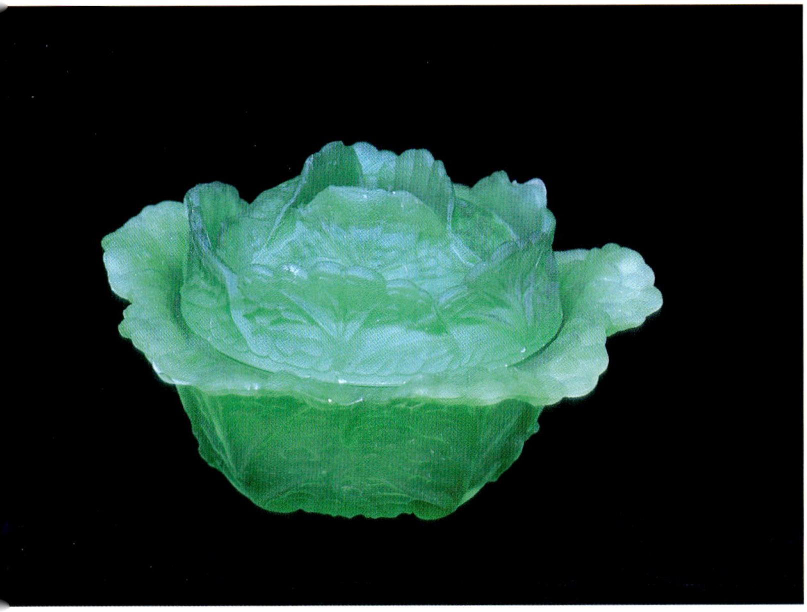

Cabbage butter dish by Vallerysthal, circa 1890. 6 1/2" diameter. Emerald green, $95-125.

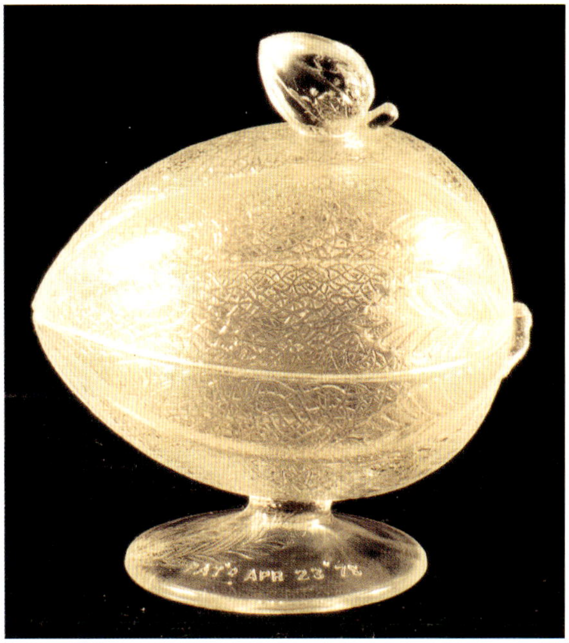

Melon butter dish, *Pat'd Apr. 23 '76*. 5 1/2" high and 5 1/4" long. $80-135.

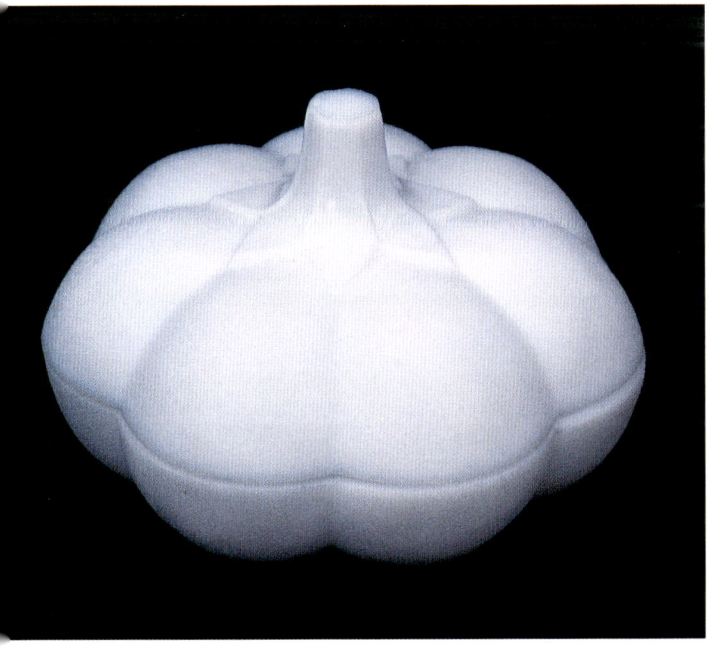

Tomato butter dish made by the Challinor, Taylor & Company, circa 1883. 6" in diameter. $100-125.

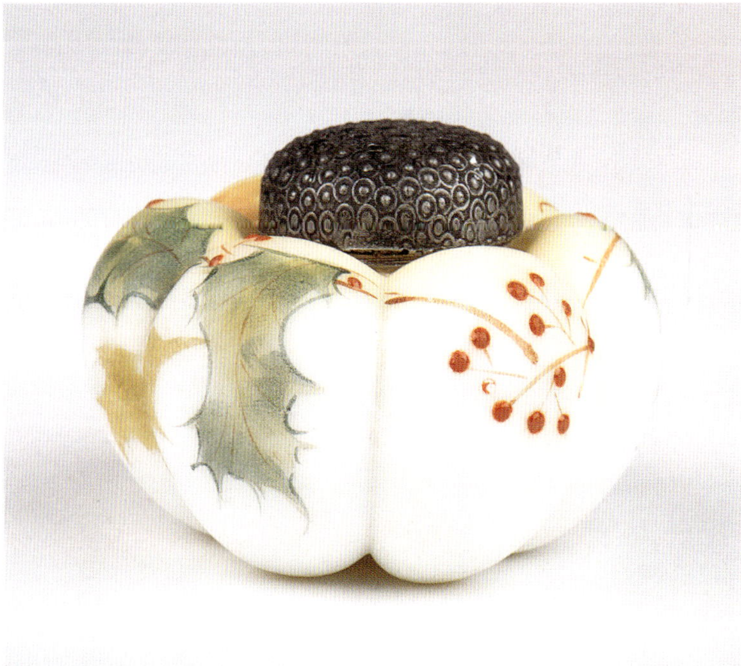

Tomato saltshaker made by the Mt. Washington Glass Company. As decorated with holly, $175-225.

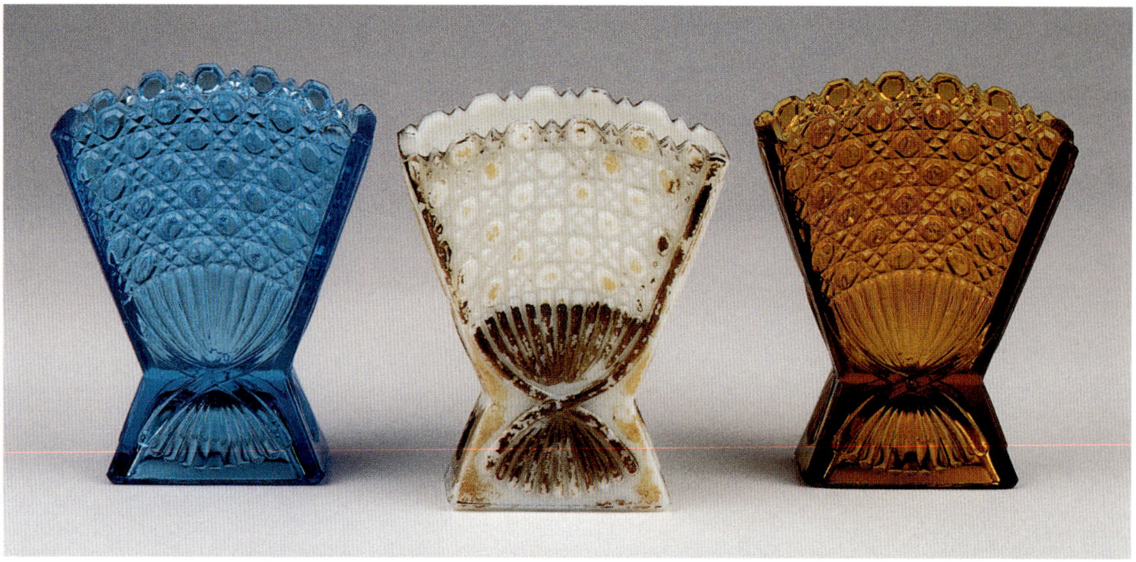

Fan toothpick or match holder in the cane pattern made by the United States Glass Company, circa 1898. 3 7/8" high and 3 1/4" wide. Clear, $50-60. Amber, $70-80. Blue, $85-95. Opal with gold decoration, $65-75.

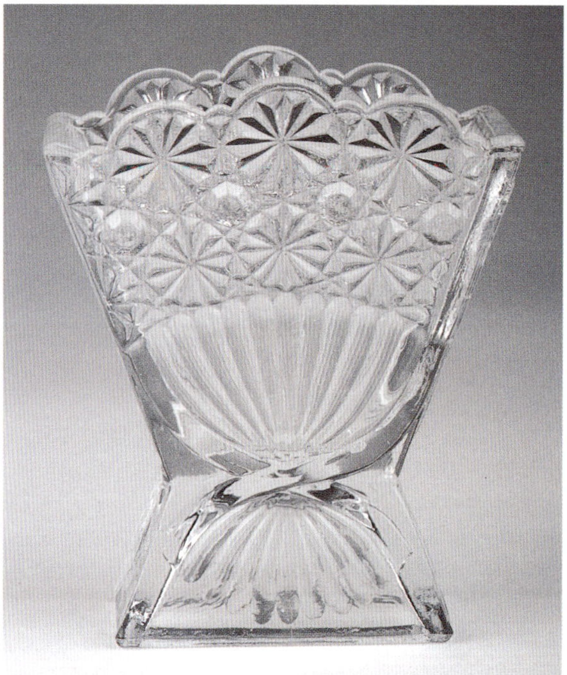

Fan toothpick or match holder in the daisy and button pattern. 3 7/8" high and 3 1/4" wide. Clear, $45-60.

Fan dish in the jersey swirl pattern made by the Windsor Glass Company, circa late 1880s. 8 7/8" long and 7 1/2" wide. Clear, $55-65. Blue, $85-95.

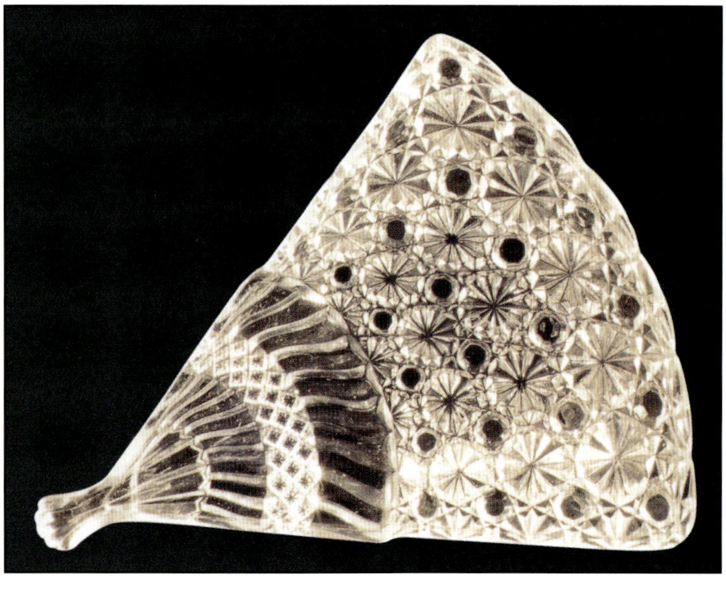

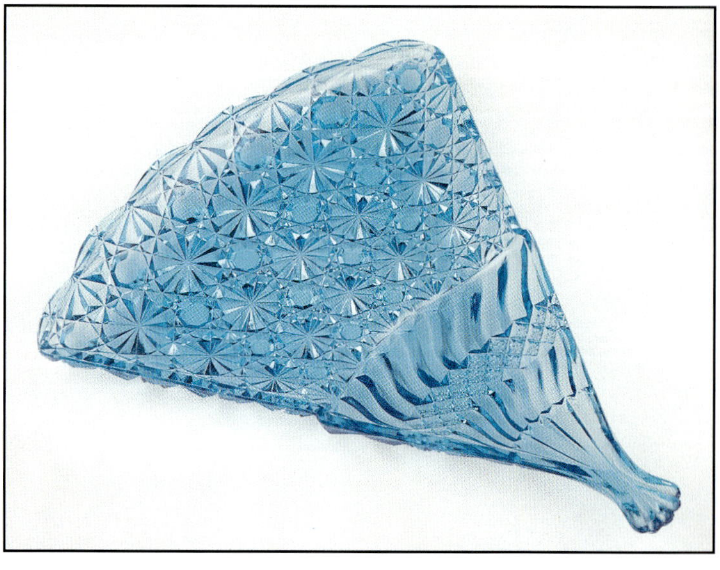

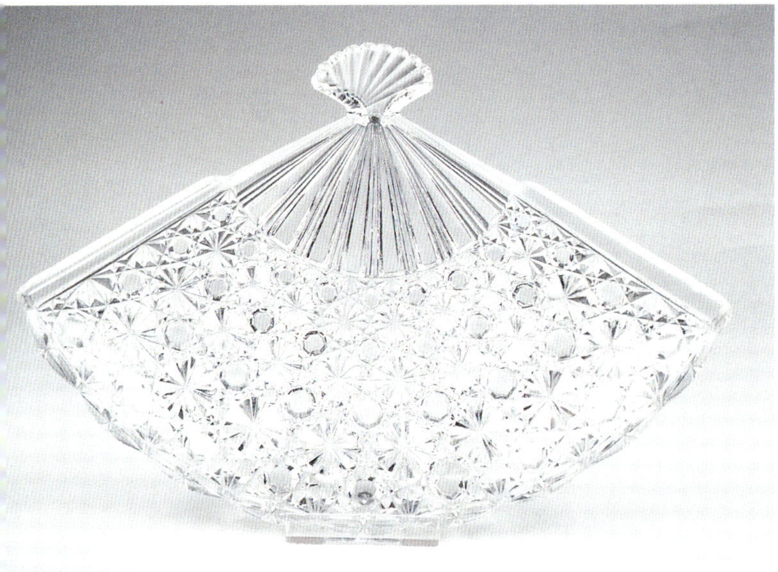

Fan dish, possibly a relish tray, in the daisy and button pattern. 7 1/4" x 10 3/4". Clear, $55-65.

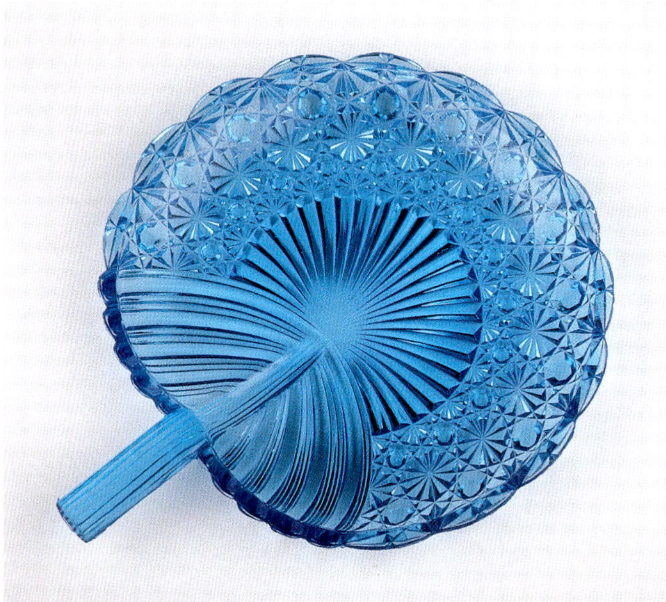

Fan relish dish has a daisy and button pattern, maker and date of manufactuer unknown. 7" diameter. Blue, $70-90.

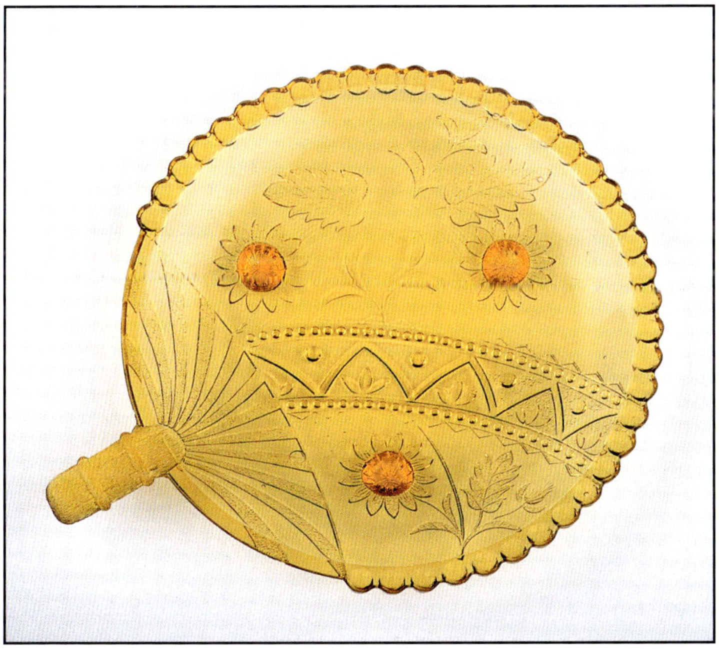

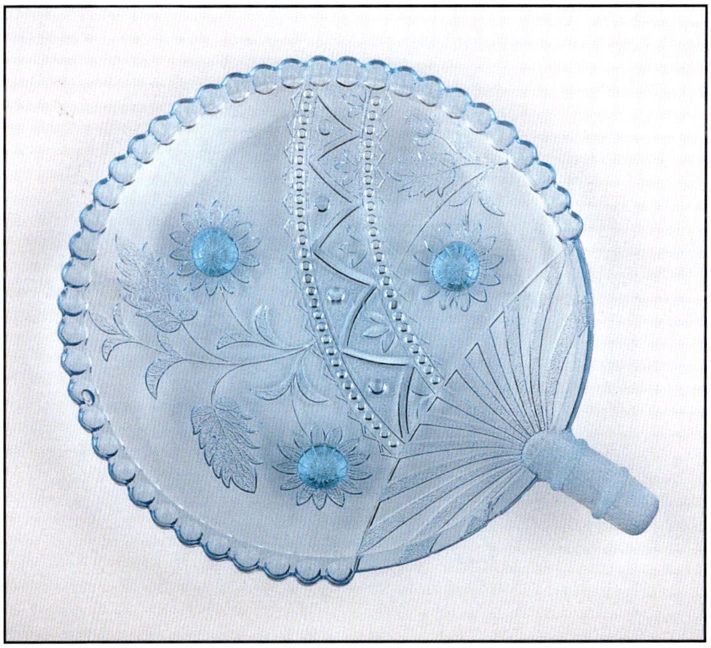

Fan relish dish, maker uncertain. 7" in diameter. Amber, $75-95. Blue, $75-95.

Basket toothpick holder made by the Westmoreland Specialty Company. 1 7/8" high and 1 7/8" wide. Opal with gold decoration, $35-45.

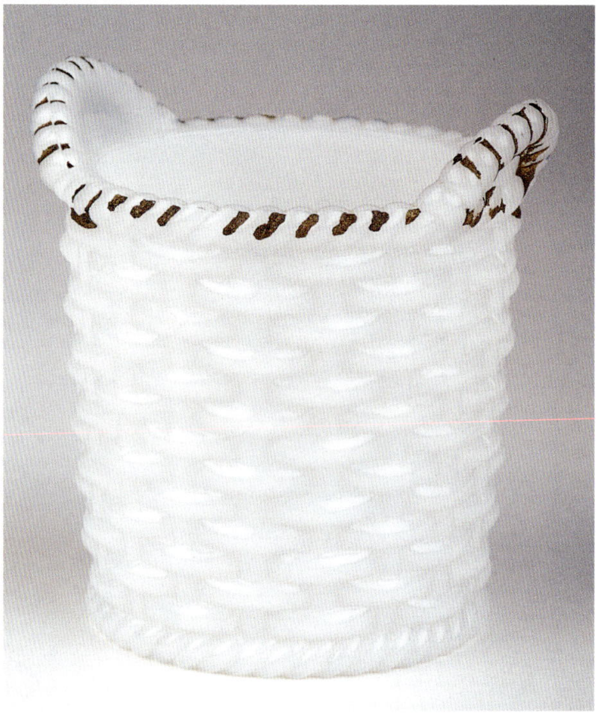

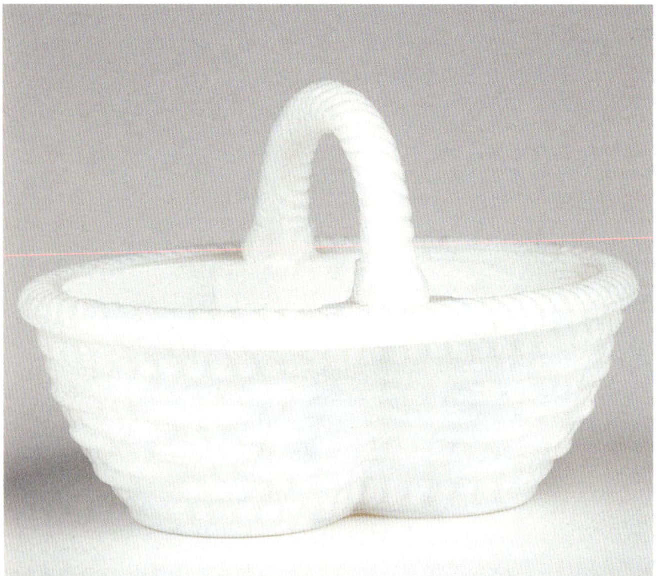

Handled Basket made by Atterbury and Company, *July 21, 1874* on the base. 3 3/4" long. Opal, $45-65.

Basket match or toothpick holder by Vallerysthal. 4 3/4" long. Opal, $70-85.

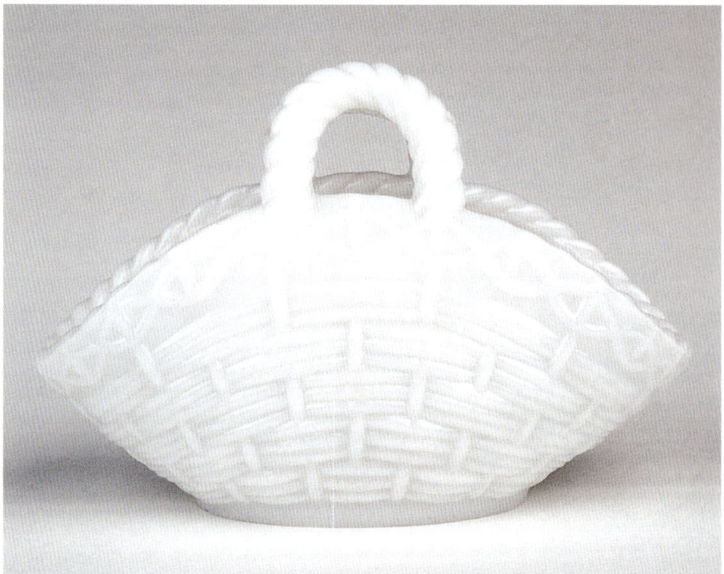

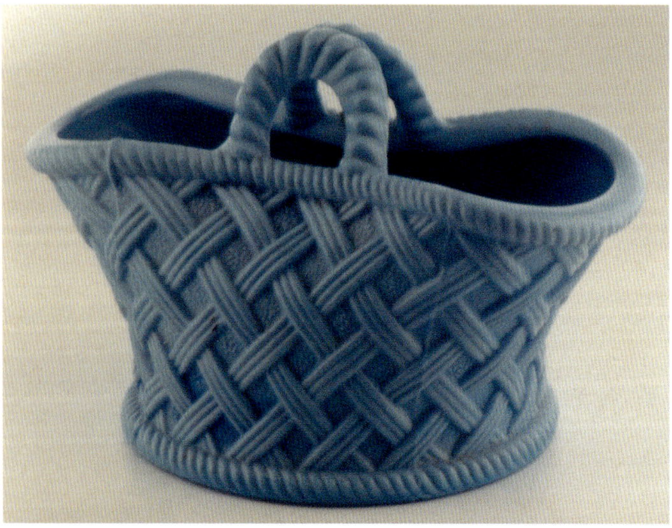

Basket match or toothpick holder by Sowerby. 4 3/8" long and 3" wide at the base. Blue opaque, $75-125.

Basket with a wire handle match holder, chicken on one side and a rabbit on the reverse. 4 1/4" long. Opal decorated, $245-265.

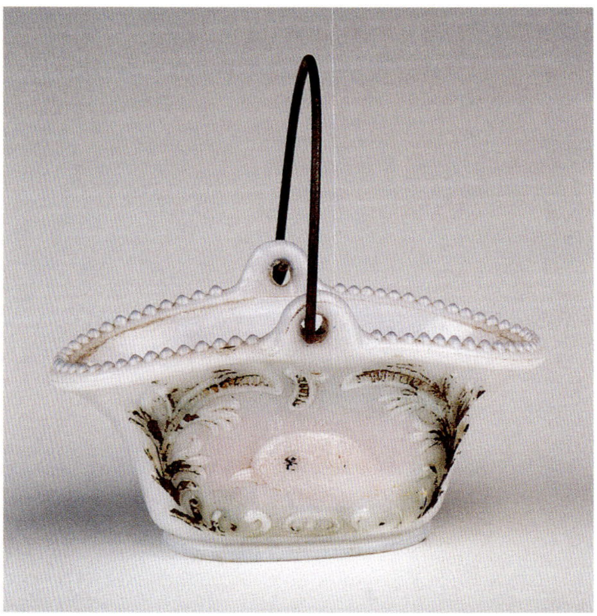

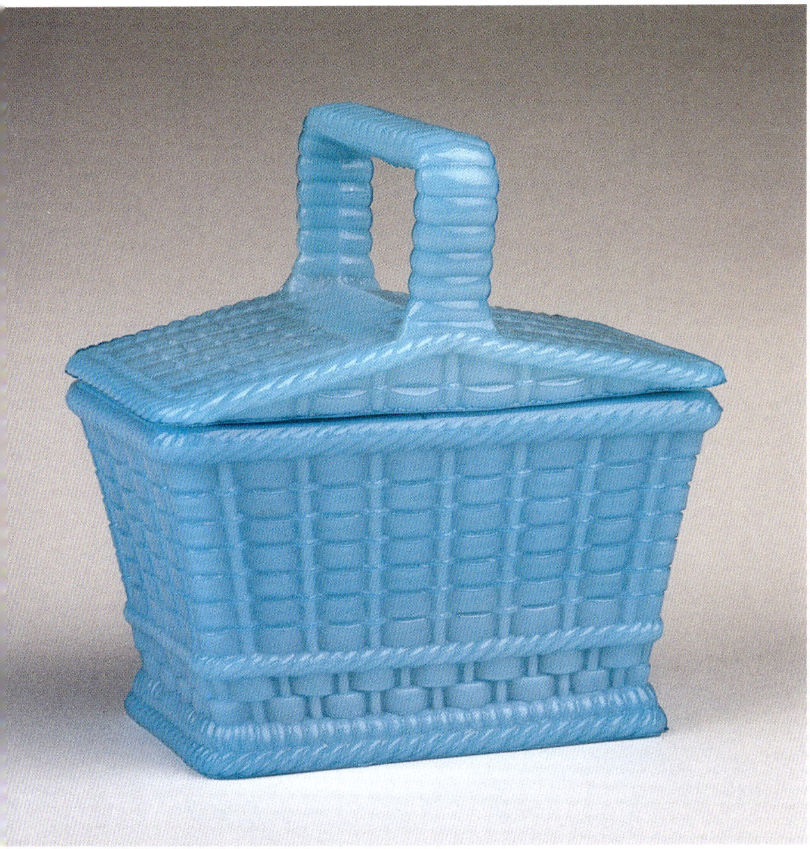

Covered Basket by Portieux. 5 1/4" high and 5" wide. Blue opaque, $170-190.

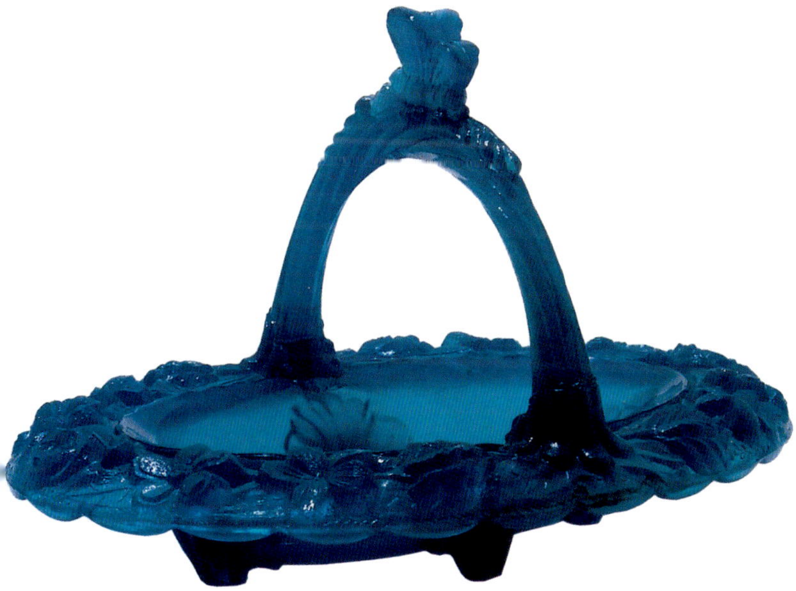

Basket made by the Hemingray Glass Company, two patent dates on the bottom: *July 21st 1874* and *April 5 1881*. Made in all the Hemingray colors, as was the Bird dish. As shown, $200-250.

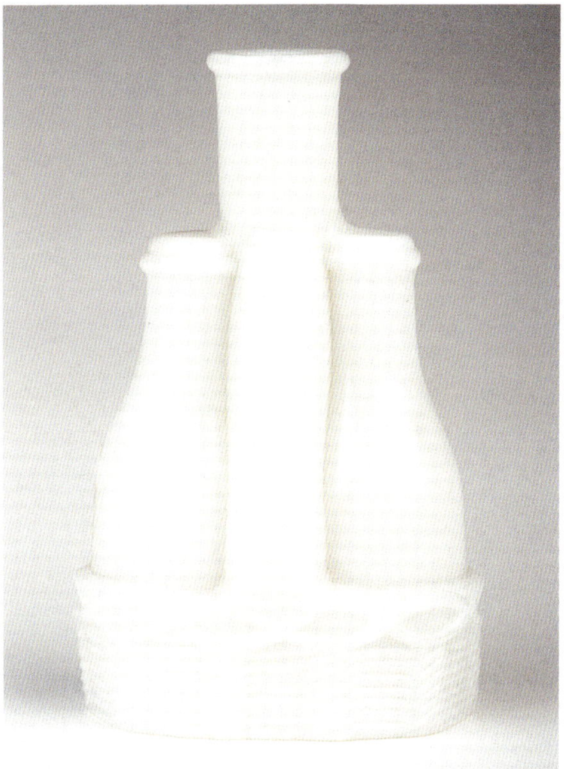

Milk Bottles in a Carrier, candy container. 4" high. Opal, $290-320.

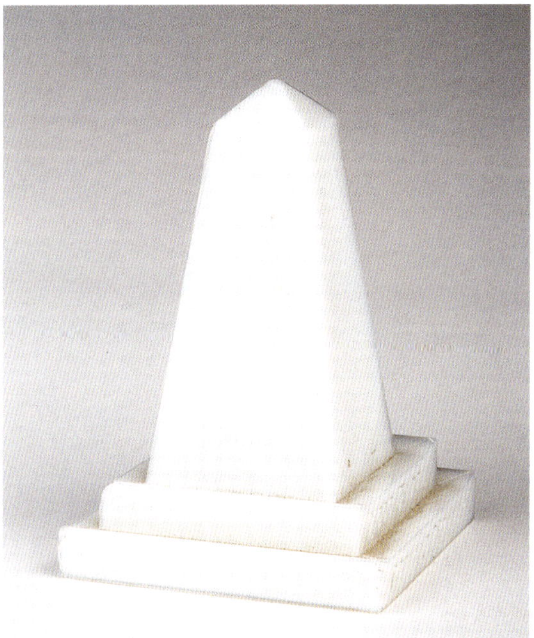

Monument advertising piece reading: *Compliments of W D Simmons advertising*. Opal, $385-425.

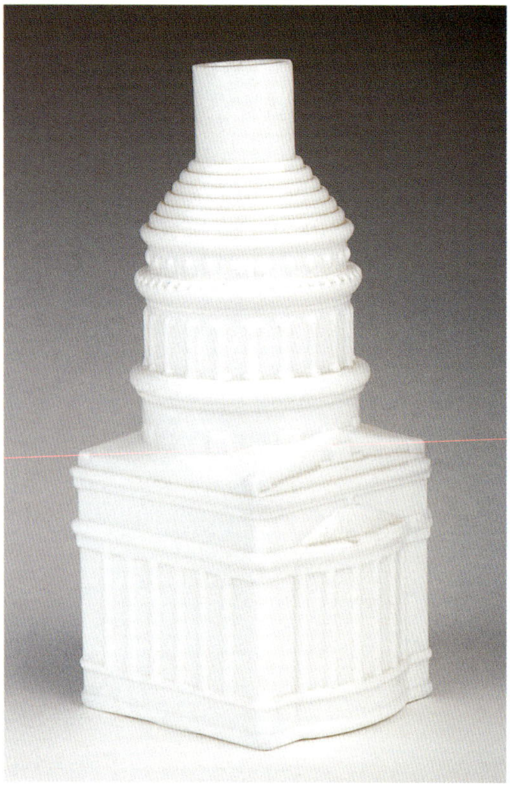

Grants Tomb bottle. The stopper is a bust of Grant. Circa 1893. 8" high. Without stopper in opal, $325-365. With stopper, $950-1,050.

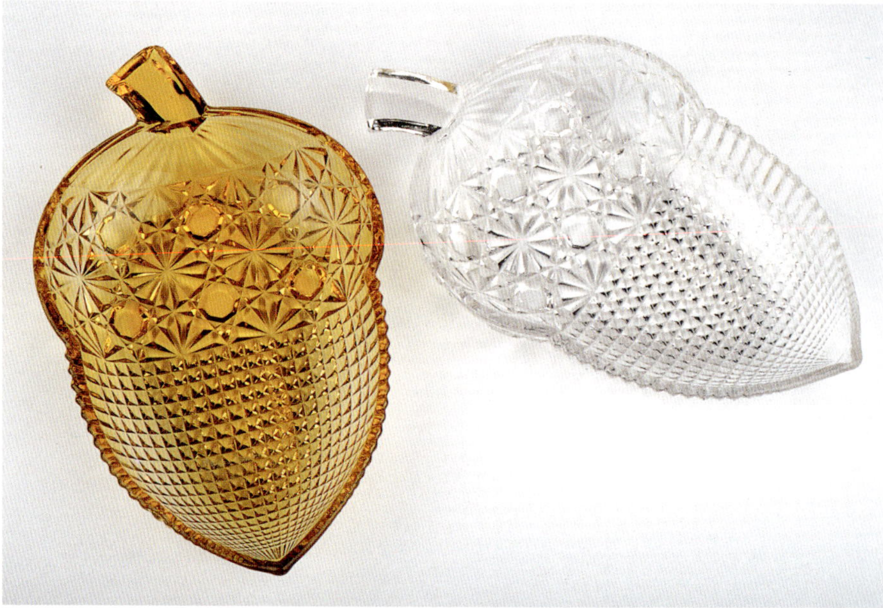

Acorn pickle dish made by Doyle & Company, circa late 1880s. 8 1/4" long. Clear, $70-95. Amber, $85-110.

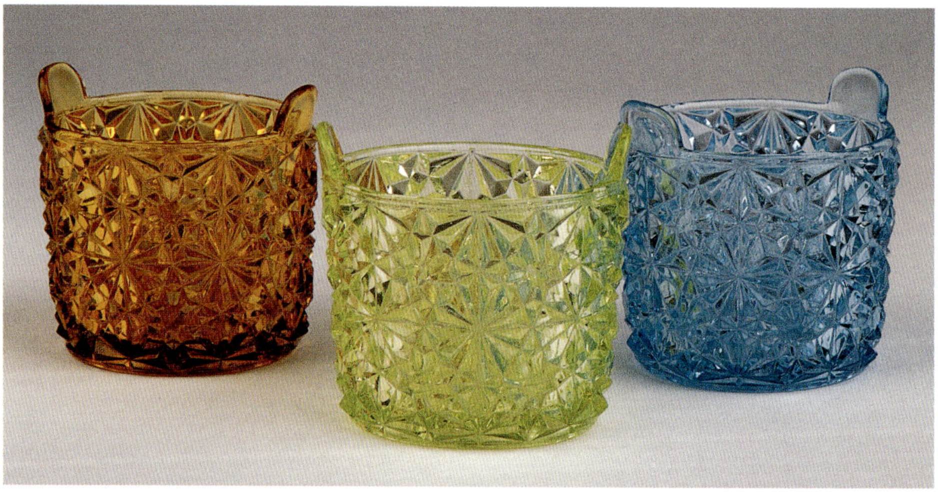

Ice Bucket toothpick holder No. 300 pattern made by the Aetna Glass and Manufacturing Company, circa 1886. Amber, $50-65. Blue, $60-85. vaseline, $60-85.

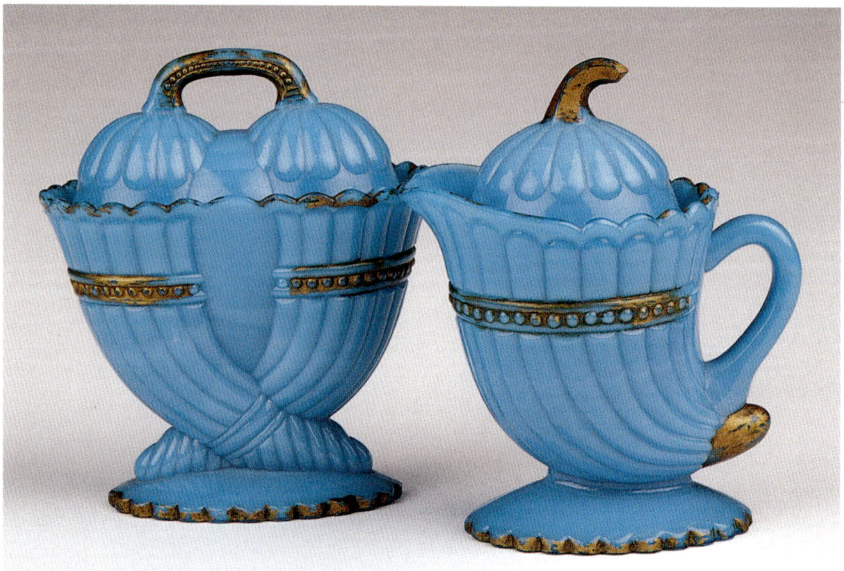

Cornucopia pattern sugar and cream pitcher made by the Westmoreland Specialty Company, circa 1905. Sugar and cream are each 5 1/4" high. Blue opaque sugar, $65-80. Blue opaque cream pitcher, $75-100.

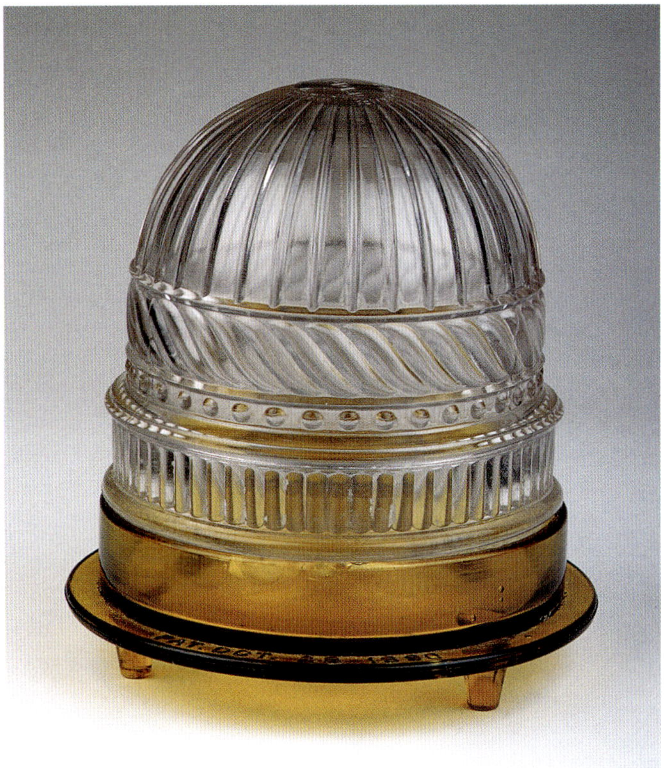

Fly Trap, *Pat Oct 28 1890*, 7 3/8" high. $225-250.

Eagle 1776-1876 medallion, *America Celebration. Her Works Praise Her. Woman's Pavilion.* 2 1/4" diameter. Opal, $190-225.

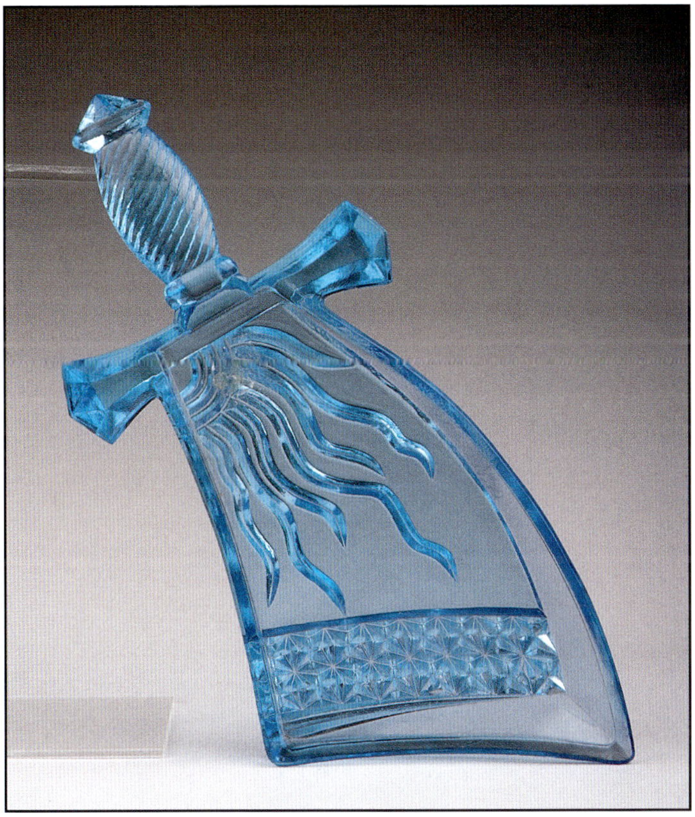

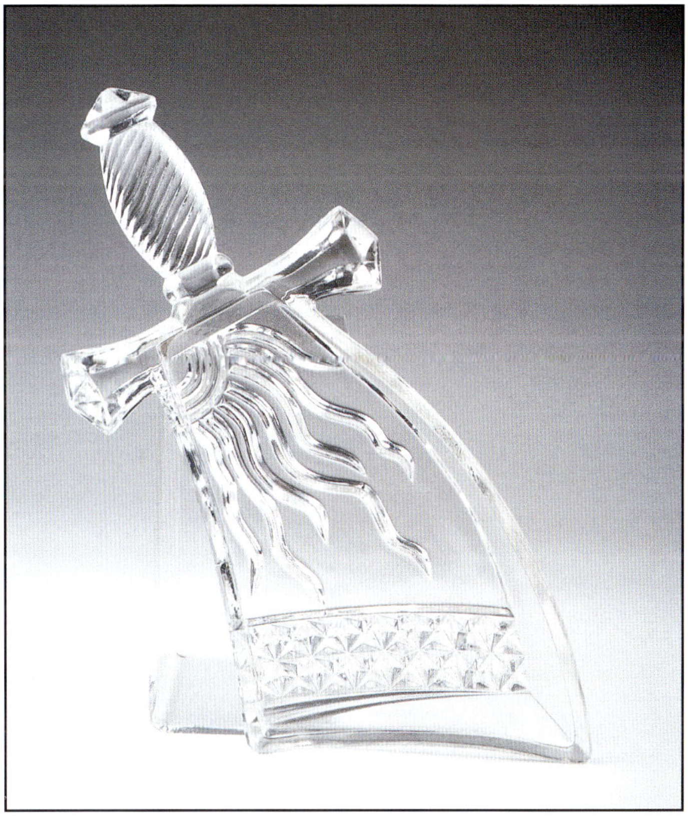

Flaming Sword pickle dish. 10 1/4" long. Clear, $65-85. Blue, $80-110.

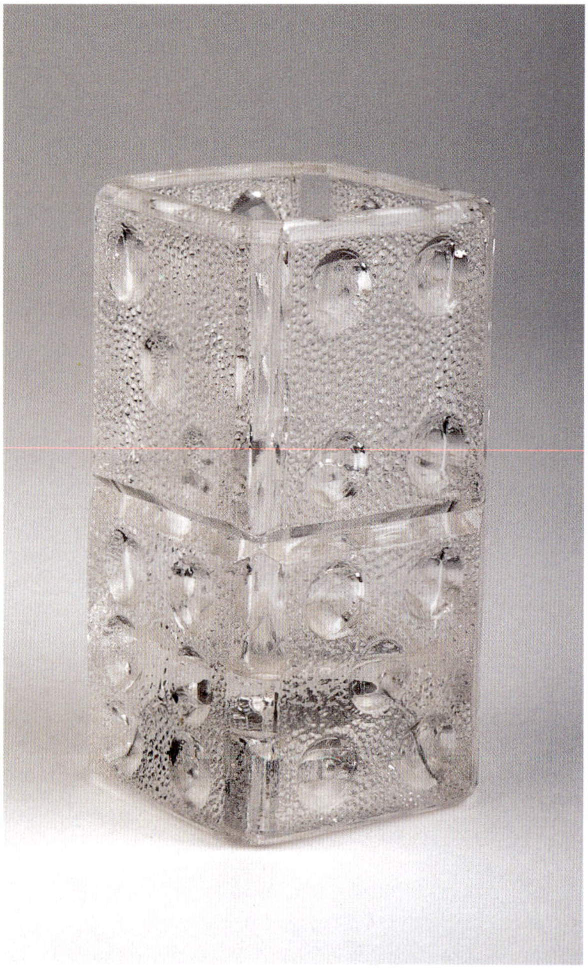

Domino toothpick holder. 2 5/8" high and 1 1/2" wide. Clear, $65-85.

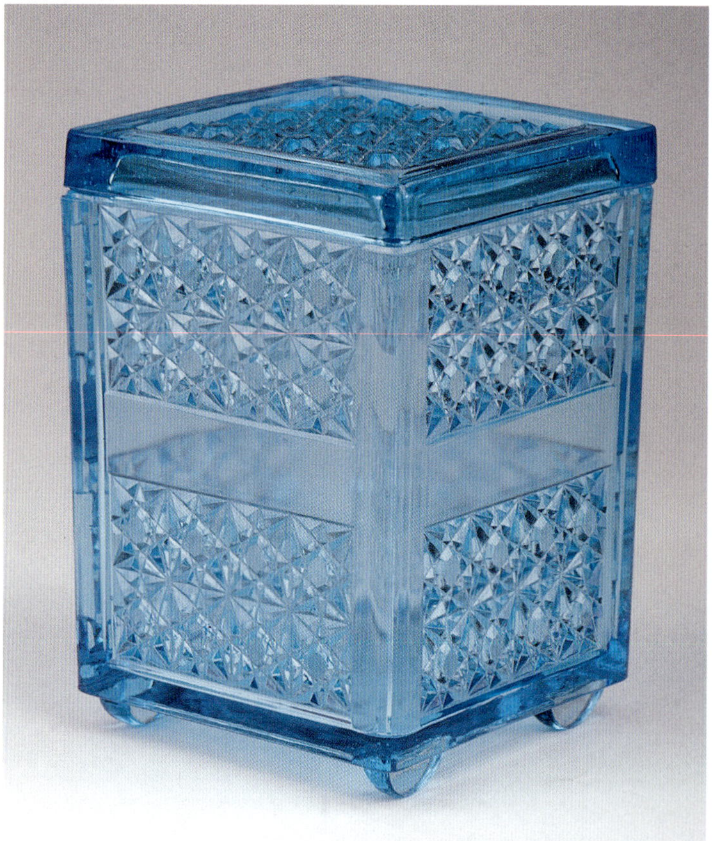

Safe in a daisy and button pattern. 5 1/2" high. Blue, $165-195.

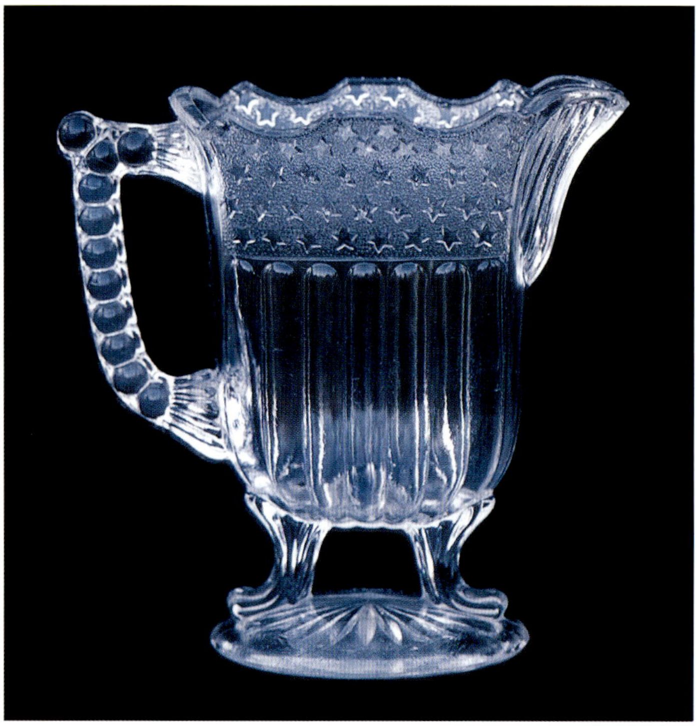

American Shield cream pitcher from a novelty table set, circa 1876. 5 1/4" high and 5 1/2" from handle to spout. $375-425.

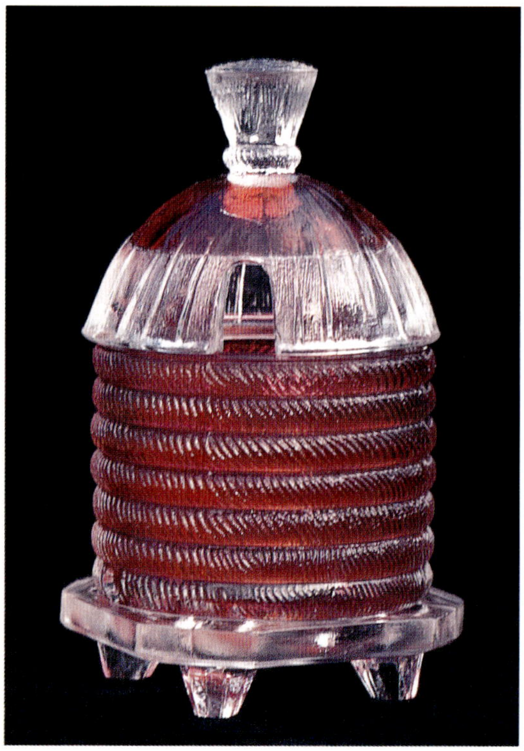

Beehive mustard and cover made by the Co-operative Flint Glass Company, circa late 1890s. 4 3/4" high and 2 1/2" diameter. Ruby Stain, $145-165.

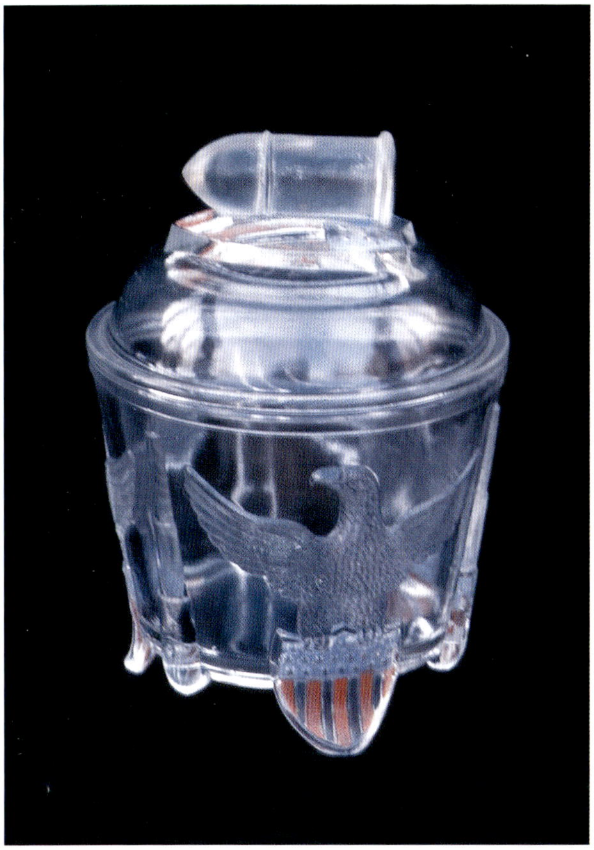

Bullet covered sugar bowl from a novelty table set, circa 1898. 6" high and 4 1/2" diameter. $300-350.

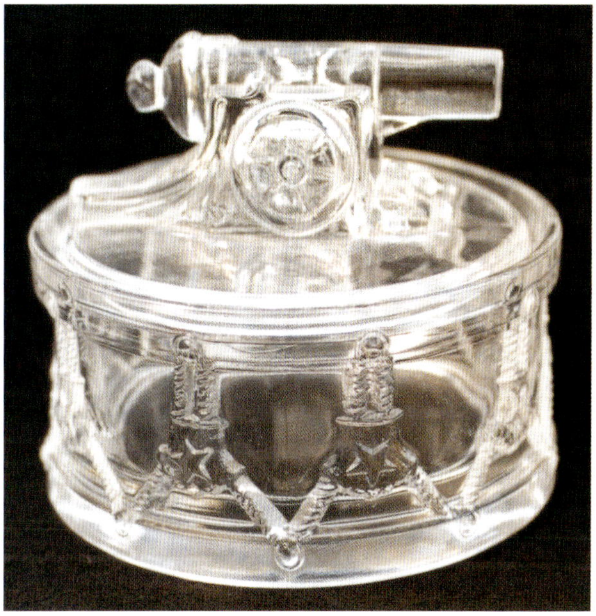

Musique container by Portieux, commonly called Cannon on a Drum, circa 1933. 3 1/4" high. Clear, $60-85.

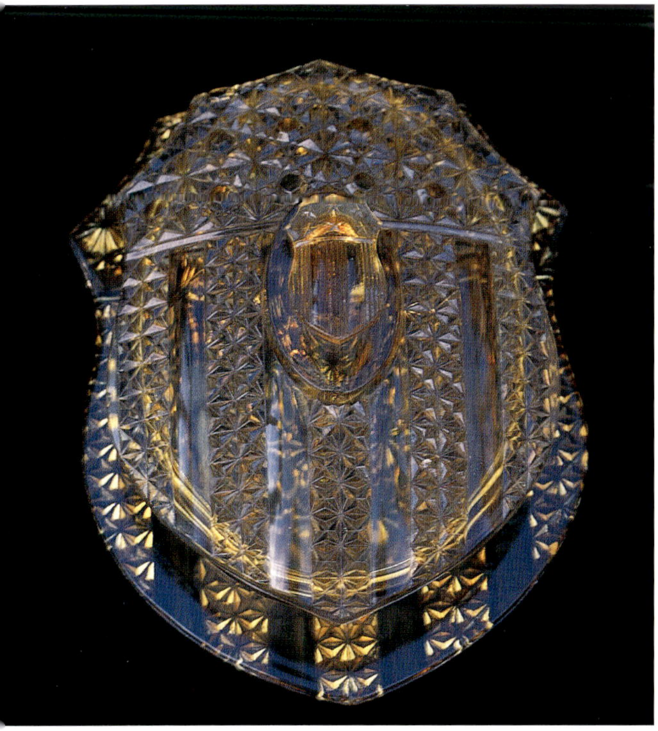

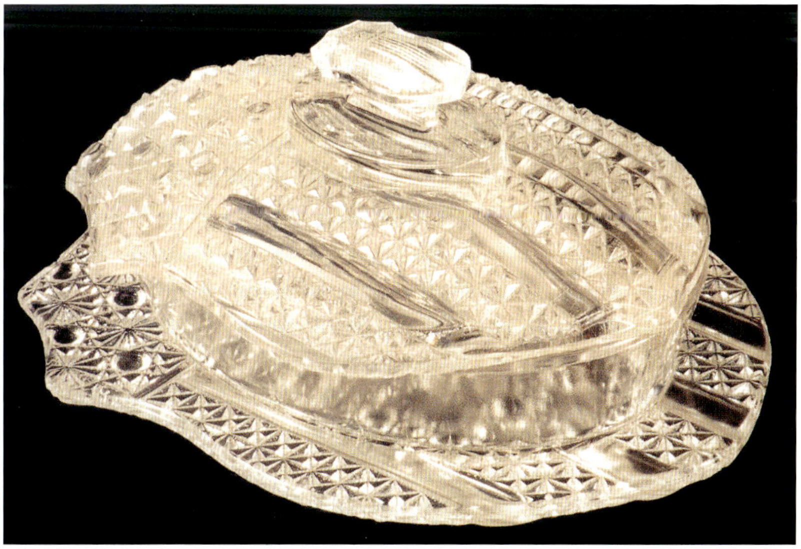

Banner butter dish made by Bryce Brothers, circa 1876. 7 1/2" long and 5 5/8" wide. Clear, $185-200. Amber, $300-350.

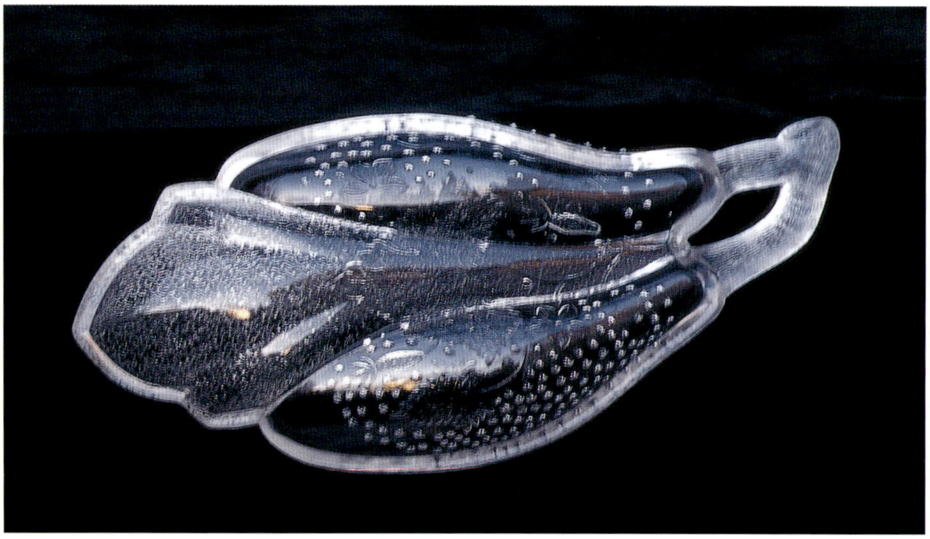

Derigo Pear pickle dish by the Portland Glass Company, circa 1870. 9 1/2" long. $60-75.

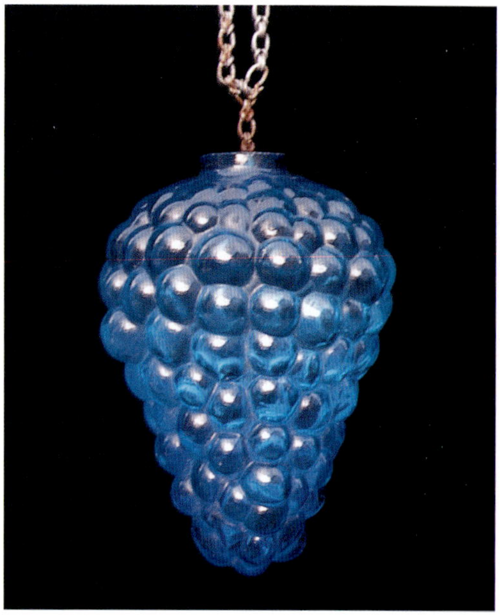

Hanging Bunch of Grapes, mold blown flint, circa 1880. 6" high and 5" wide. Sapphire, $85-100.

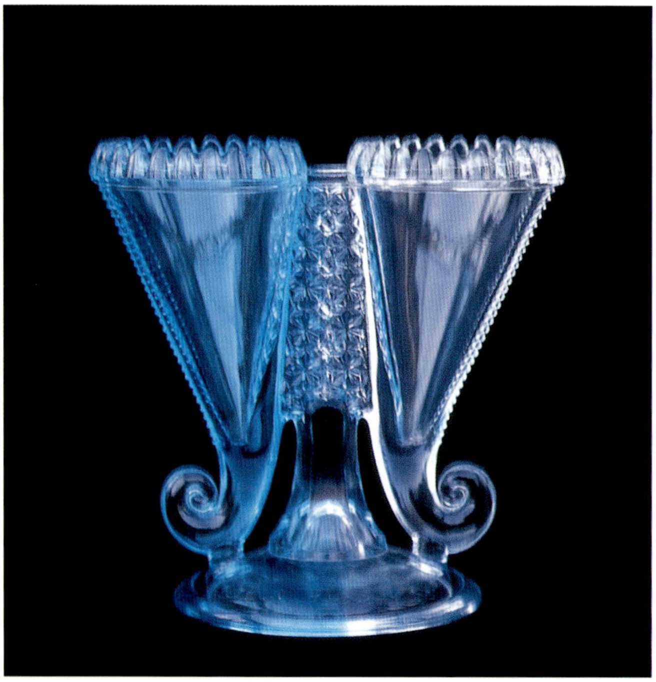

Twin Cornucopia vase made by Bryce, Higbee and Company, circa 1887. 5 1/2" high and 6" wide. $145-165.

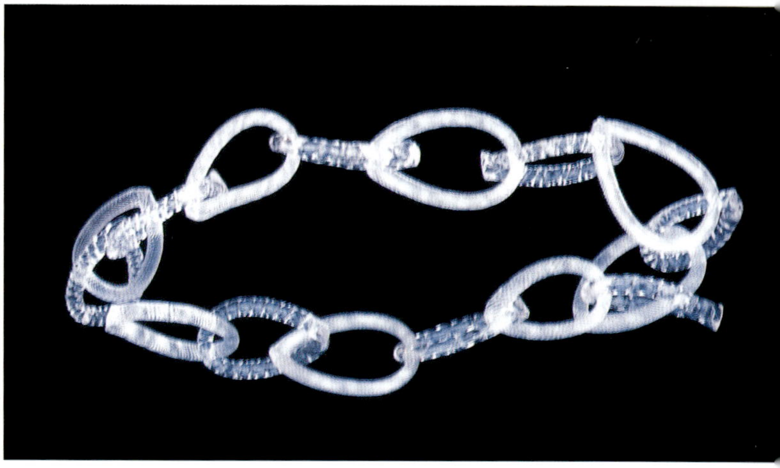

Chain whimsy by the Sandwich Glass Company, circa 1874, each link is 2 1/4" as formed. Up to three feet, $70-85.

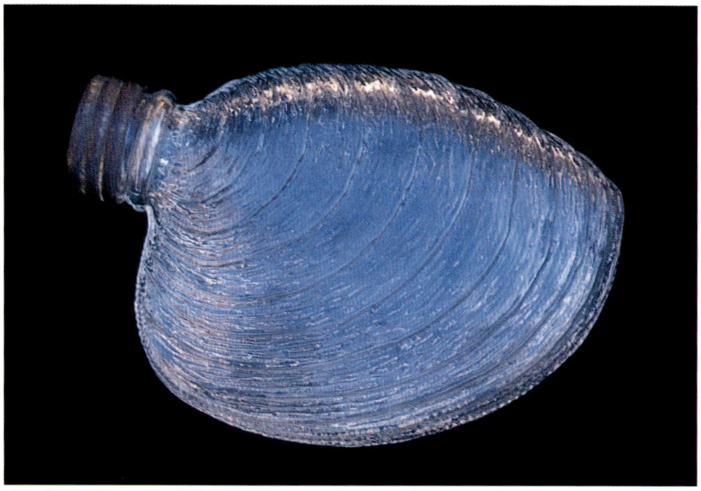

Clam Shell bottle patented by William T Murphy in 1892. 5" long. $145-165.

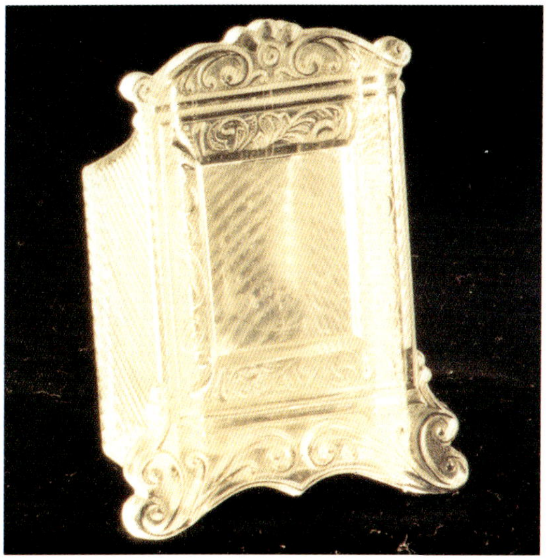

Picture Frame match holder made by the National Glass Company at their Indiana Tumbler and Goblet Glass Works, circa early 1900s. 3 1/2" high and 2 5/8" wide. $100-125.

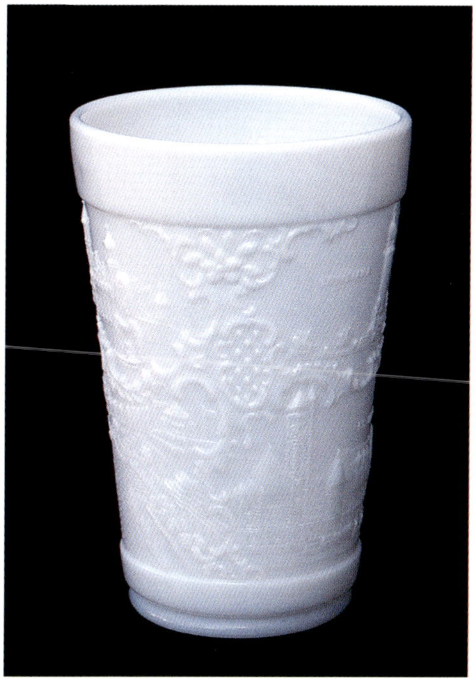

Louisiana Purchase Exposition 1904 tumbler. 5" high and 3 1/4" diameter. Opal, $50-60.

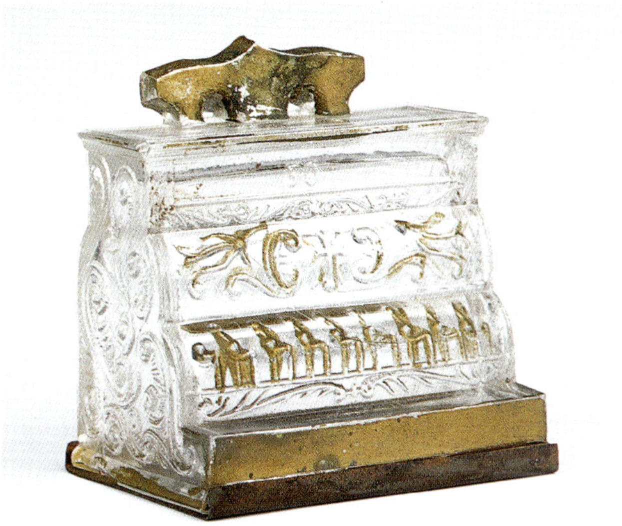

Cash Register candy container. 2 3/4" high and 2 1/2" wide. $1,900-2,100.

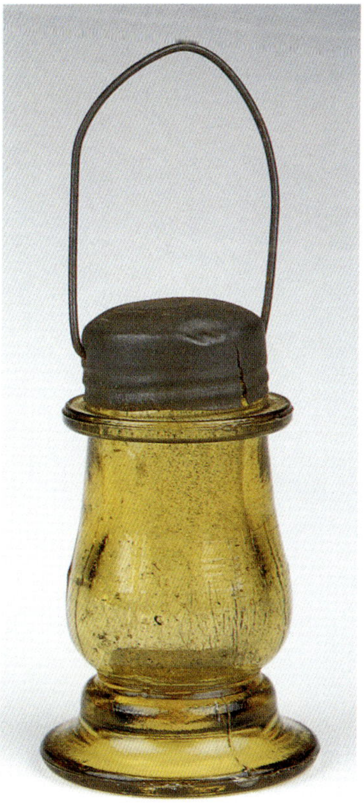

Lantern candy container. 3 1/2" high. Amber, $70-85.

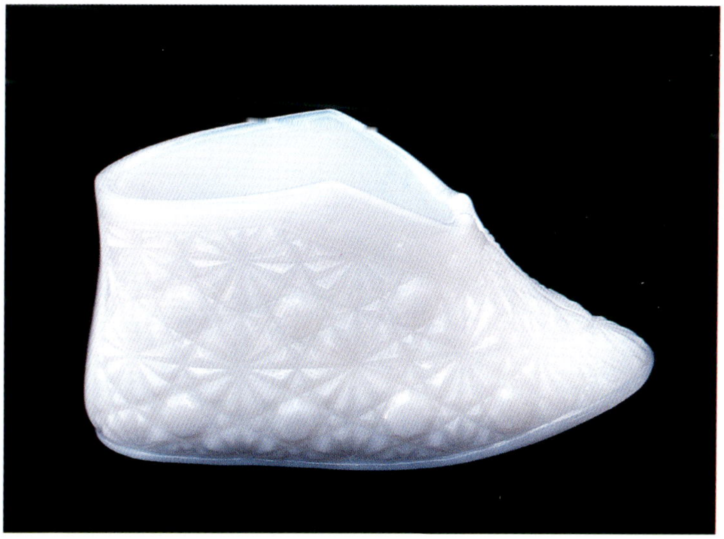

Baby Bootee in the daisy and button pattern made by the Fenton Glass Company, circa 1910. 4 3/8" long and 2" wide. Opal, $70-80.

Centennial Shoe made by Gillinder and Company, circa 1876. 6" long. Clear, $60-85.

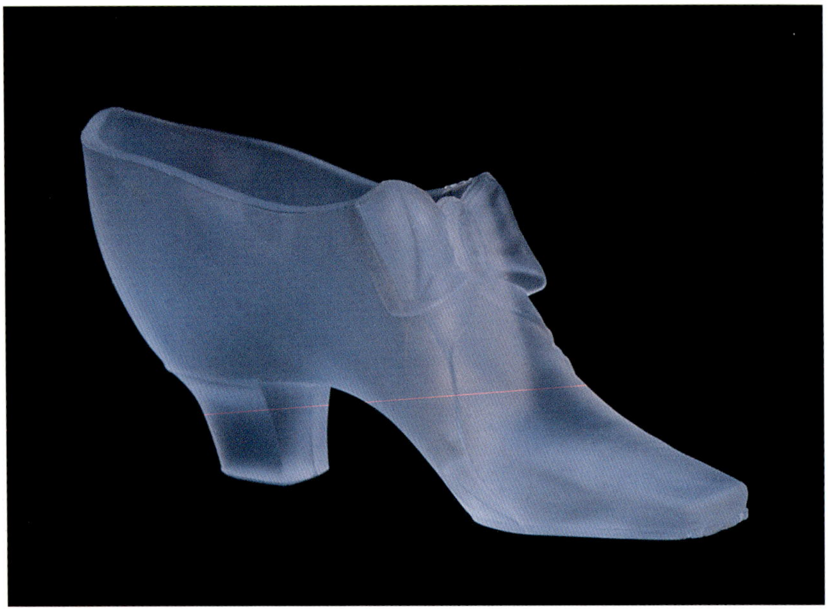

Shoe, 5" long. Blue opaque, $115-130.

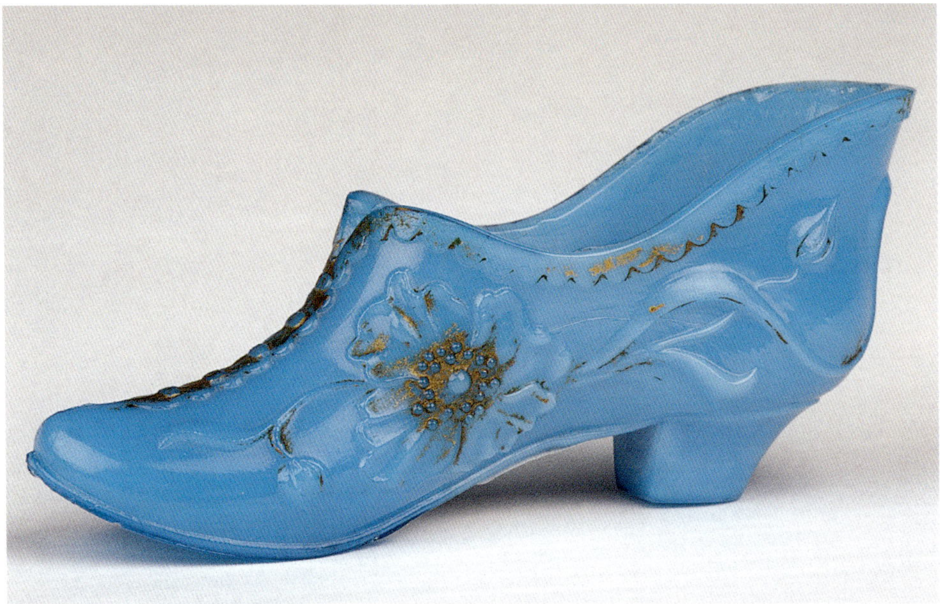

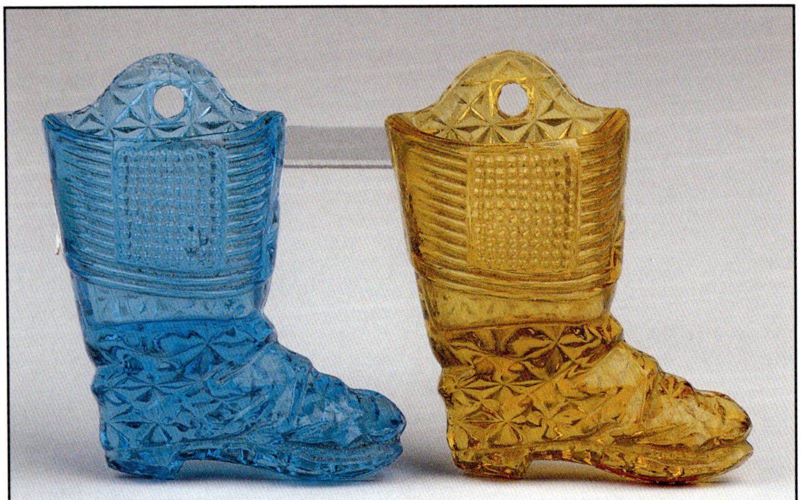

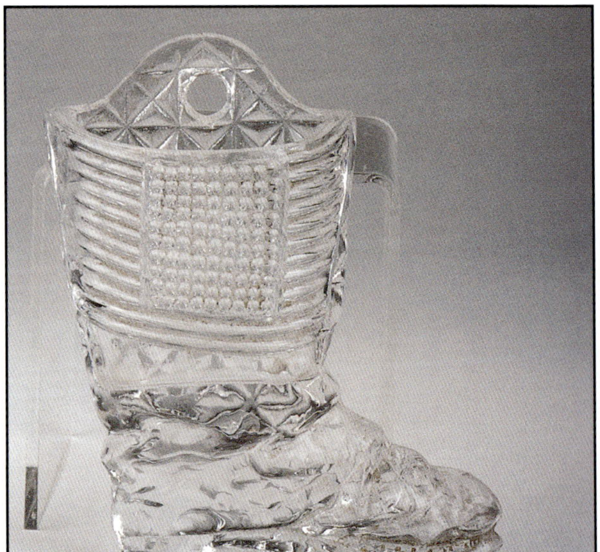

Tramp match safe made by the Bryce, Higbee & Company, circa 1880s. 4 1/2" long. Clear, $40-50. Amber, $50-65. Blue, $50-65.

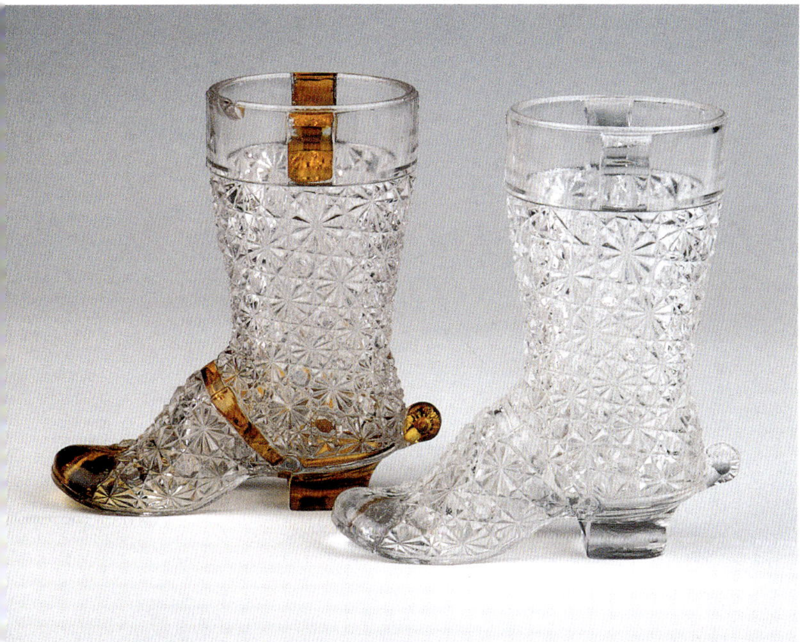

Boot with Spur in the daisy and button pattern, circa 1880s. 5 3/4" high. Clear, $80-95. Clear with amber stain, $220-250.

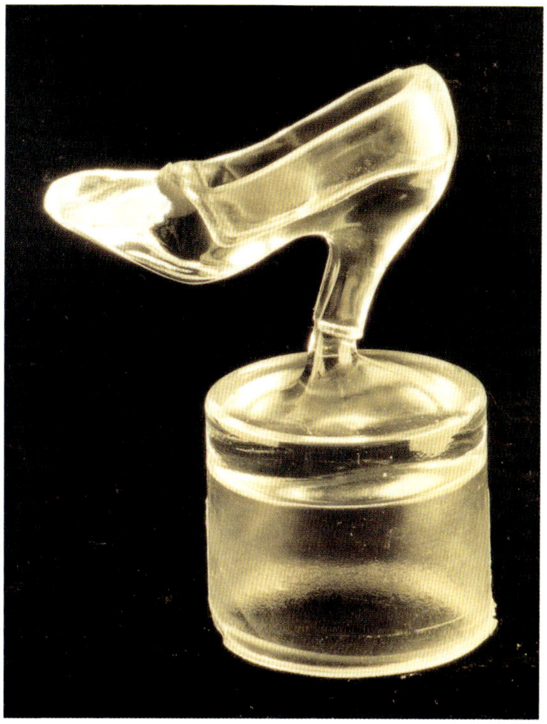

Shoe by the Tiffin Glass Company. 3 1/2" long. Clear, $55-75. Probably made in colors.

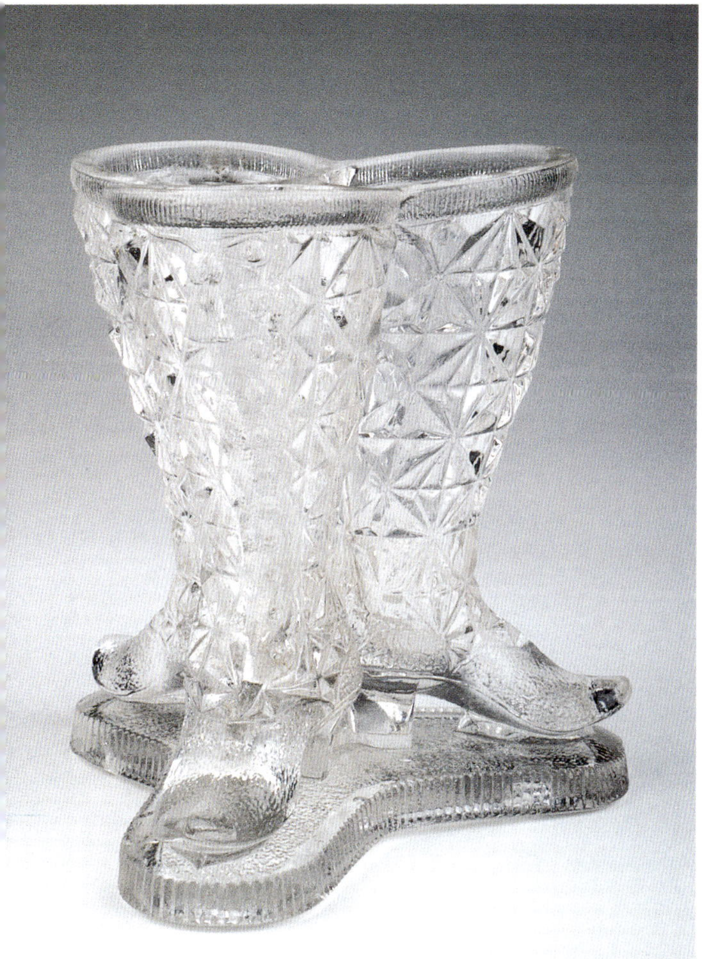

Three Boot match holder made by the Bellaire Goblet Company, circa 1887. 4 3/4" high. Clear, $275-325. Colors, $425-600.

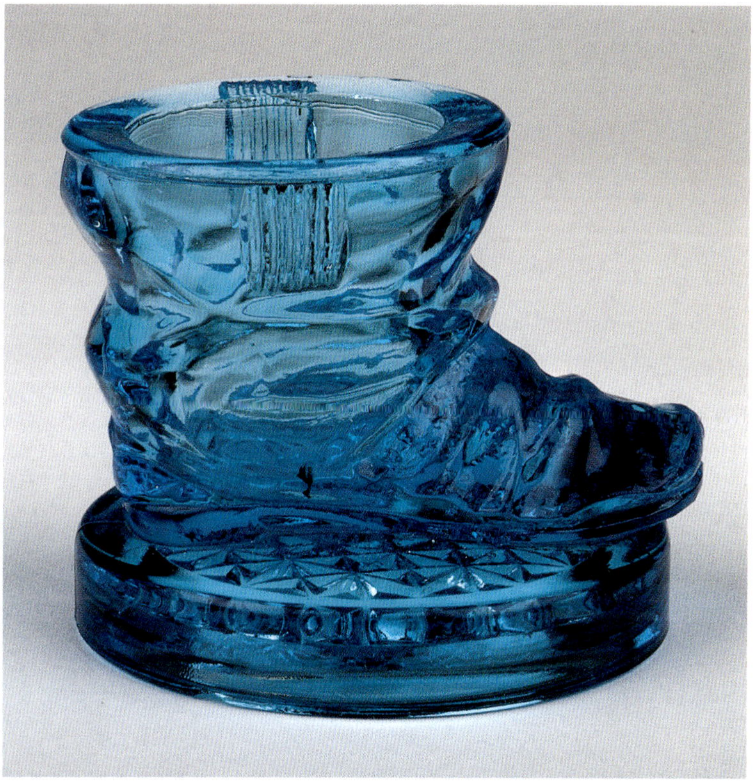

Utility Boot match or toothpick holder, when a cover is added it becomes an ink well. It is advertised both ways in a Bryce-Higbee Glass Company illustration, circa 1887. 2 7/8" high. Blue, $100-135.

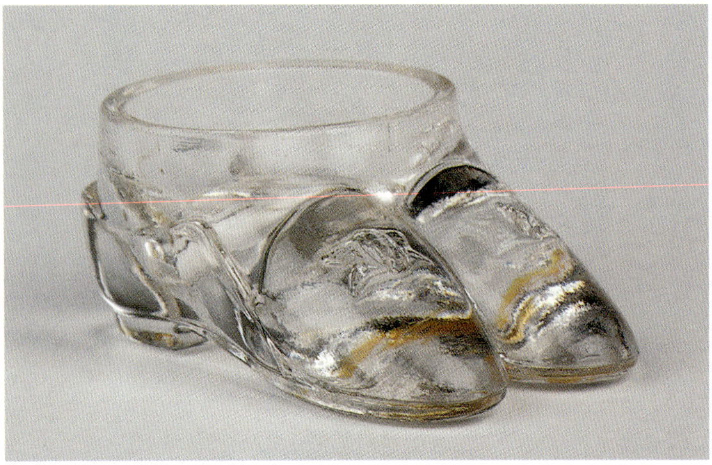

Pair of Shoes saltcellar, maker unknown. 2 3/4" long and 2" wide. Clear, $50-65.

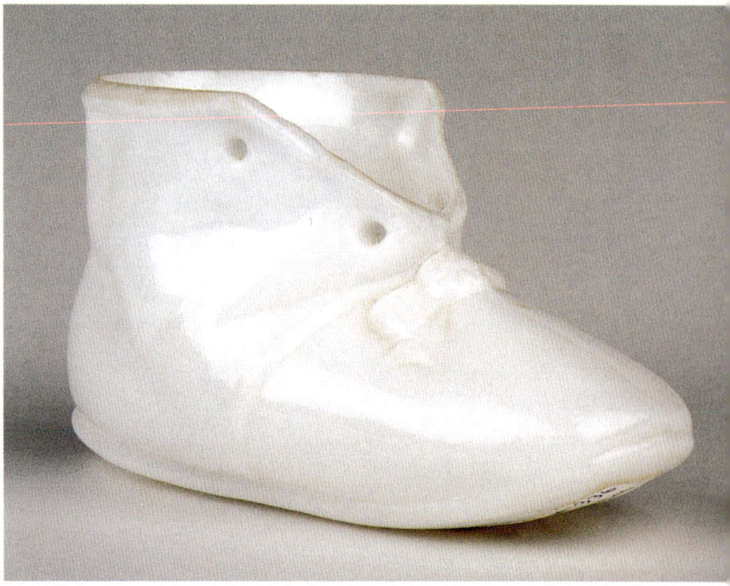

Baby Shoe, age questionable. Opal, $30-40.

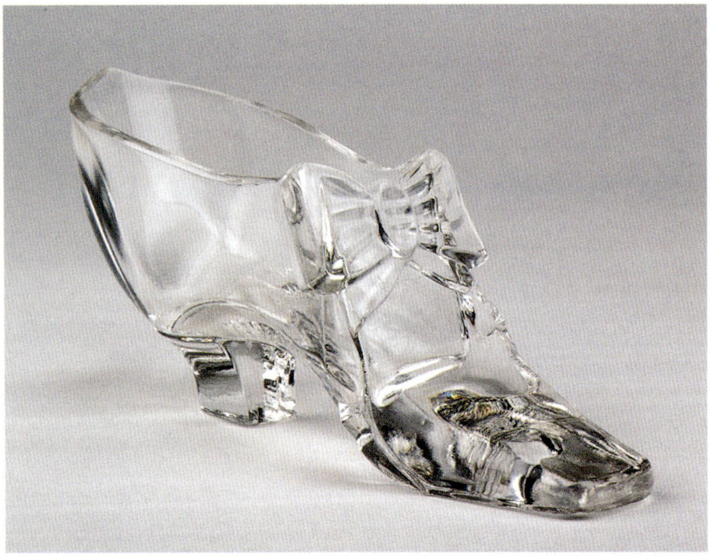

Shoe, *Gillinder & Sons Centennial Exhibition 1876*. 5 1/2" long. $45-55.

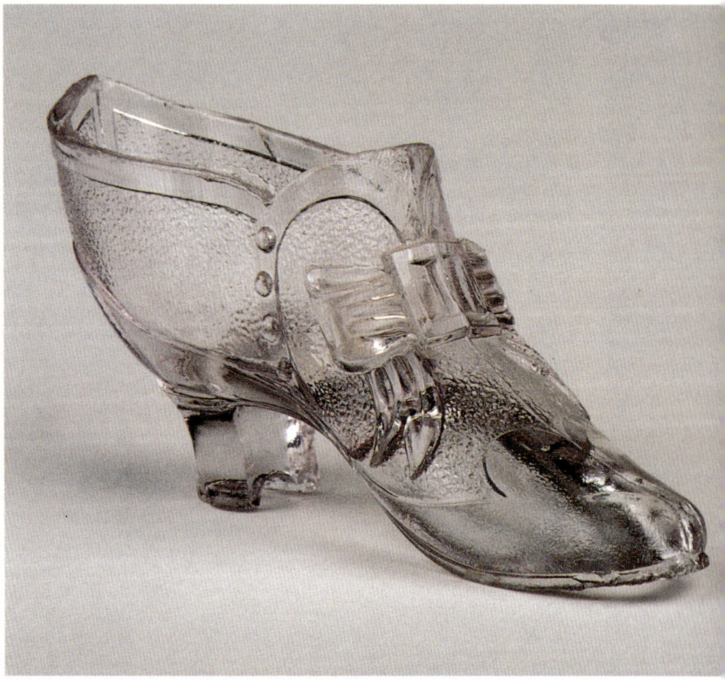

Shoe, note the design with buttons and a different type of bow. Clear, $85-110.

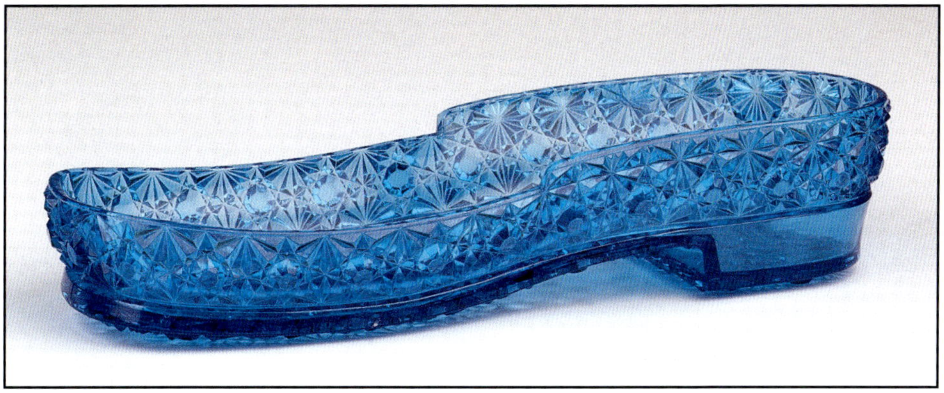

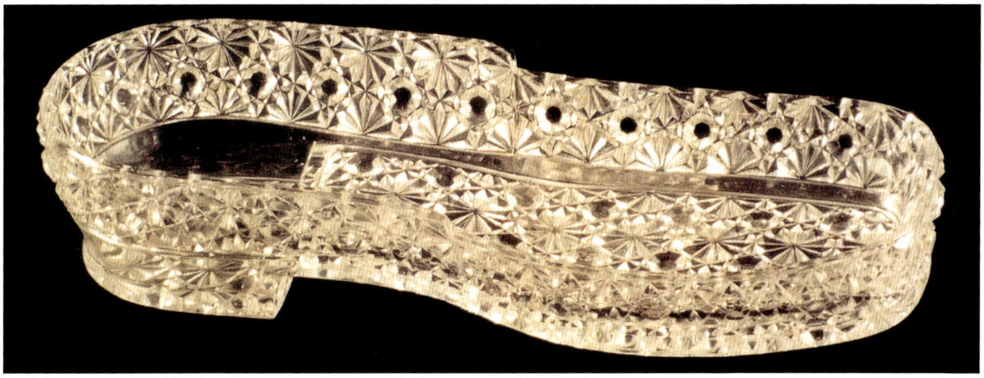

Shoe celery in the daisy and button pattern made by Hobbs, Brockunier and Company, circa 1884. 11 7/8" long and 4 5/8" wide. Clear, $125-150. Blue, $200-250.

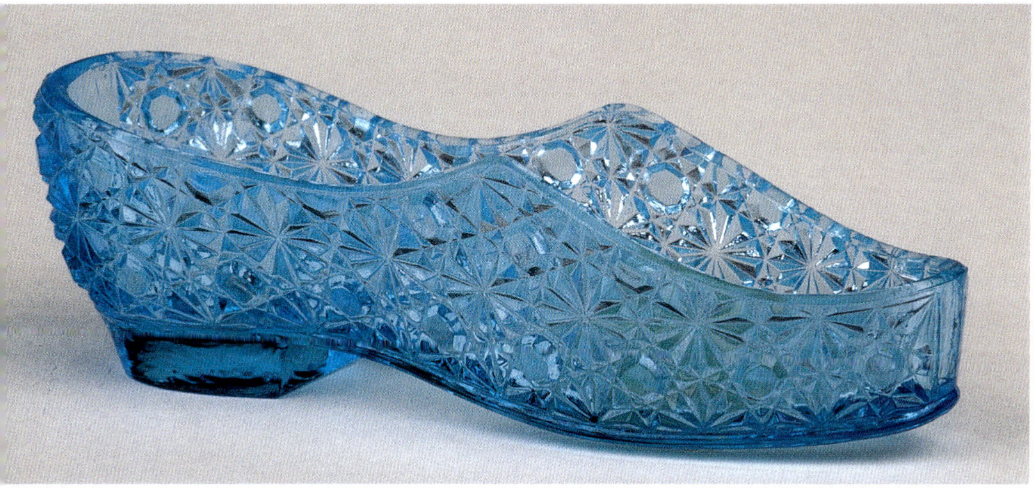

Shoe in the daisy and button pattern made by Bryce Brothers, circa 1886. 4 1/2" long. Blue, $65-85.

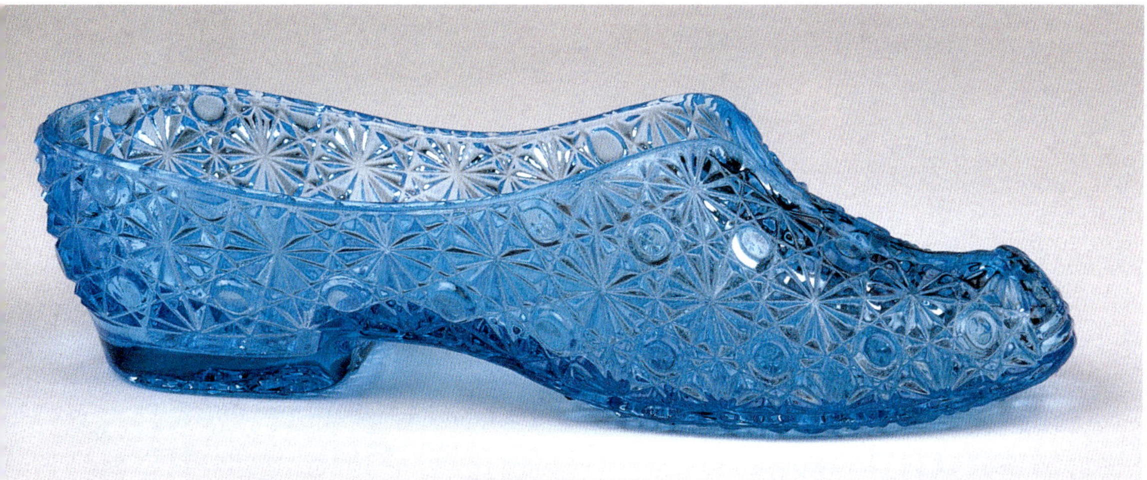

Shoe in the daisy and button pattern made by Bryce Brothers, with *Pat'd Oct. 19, 1886.* Blue, $65-85.

Shoe on a Tray, the shoe is in the daisy and button pattern and the tray is in the fishscale pattern. Made by Bryce Brothers, *PAT'D OCT 19 1886*. 5 3/8" long. Amber, $150-175.

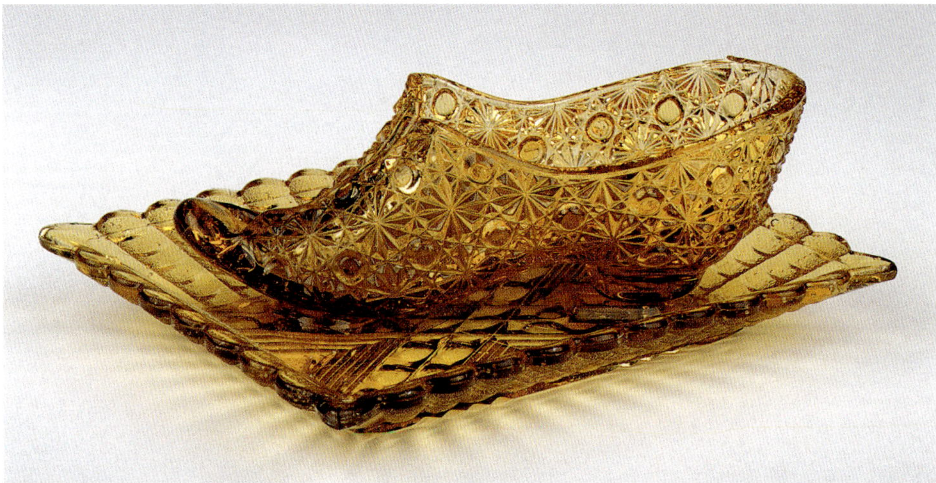

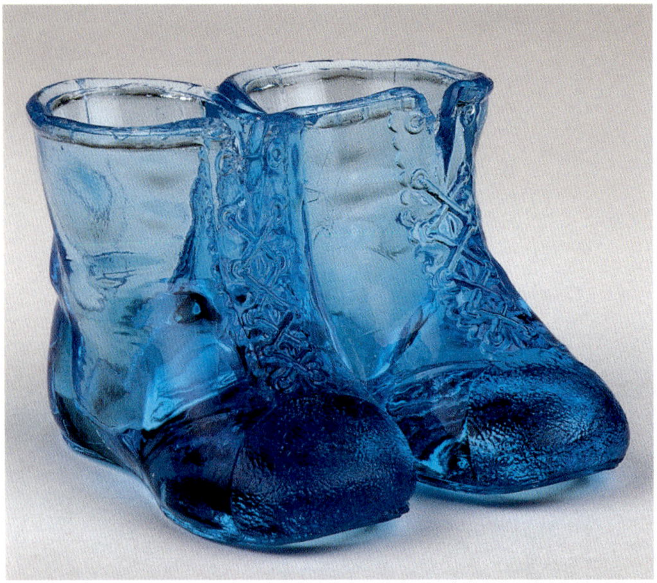

Double Shoe made by King, Son and Company, circa 1880s. 3 1/8" long. Blue, $125-150.

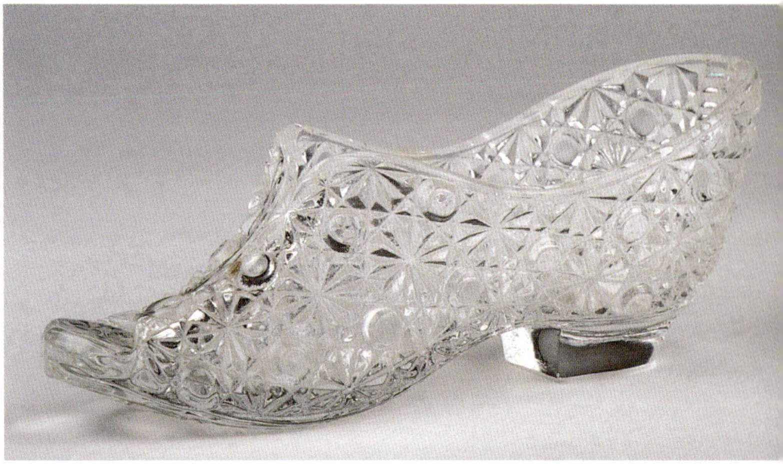

Shoe in the daisy and button pattern, circa 1880s. 4 7/8" long. Clear, $45-65.

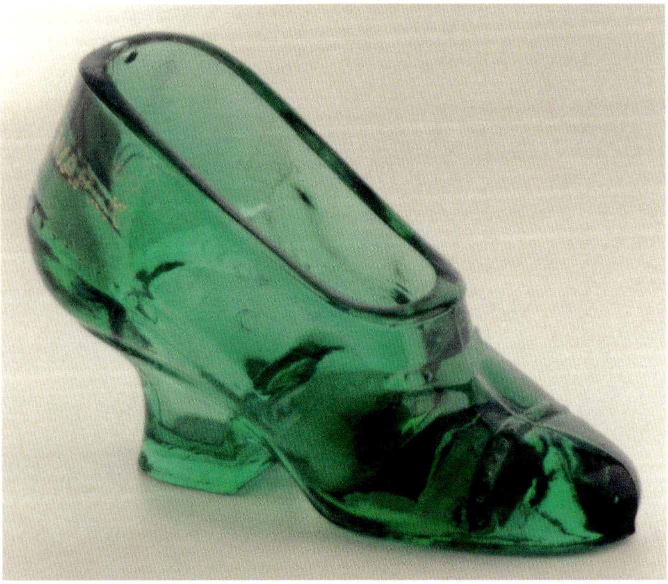

Slipper made by the United States Glass Company. 4 1/2" long and 1 7/8" wide. Green, $35-50.

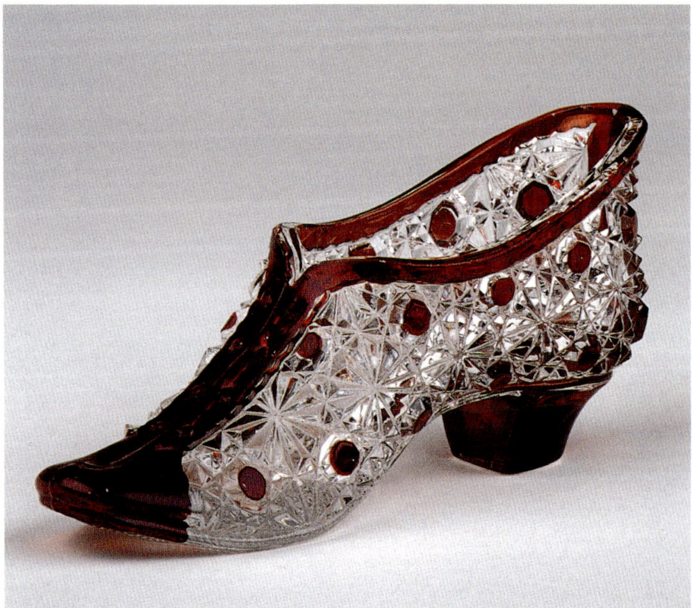

Shoe by the United States Glass Company at their factory D, circa 1891. Original made by Geo. Duncan and Sons, *PAT'D OCT 19/86*. Ruby Stain, $120-145.

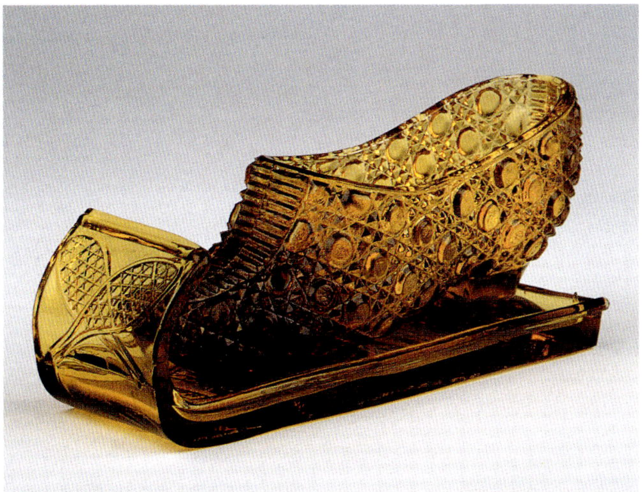

Shoe on a Toboggan in the cane pattern, circa 1880s. 5 1/2" long. Amber, $165-185.

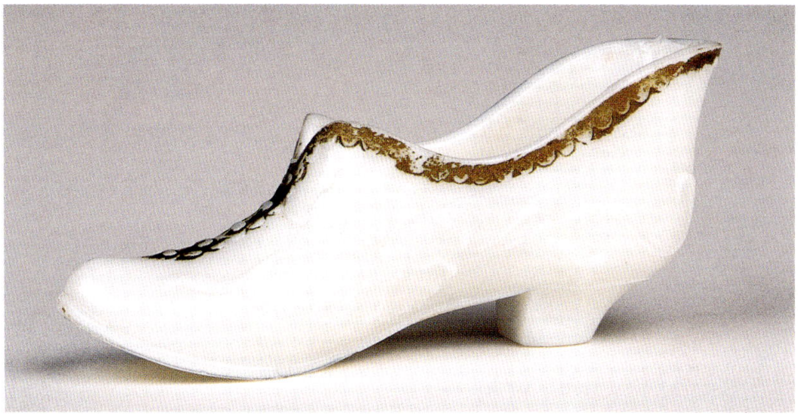

Shoe, opal with vine decoration and gold trim, 5 1/4" long. As shown, $70-85.

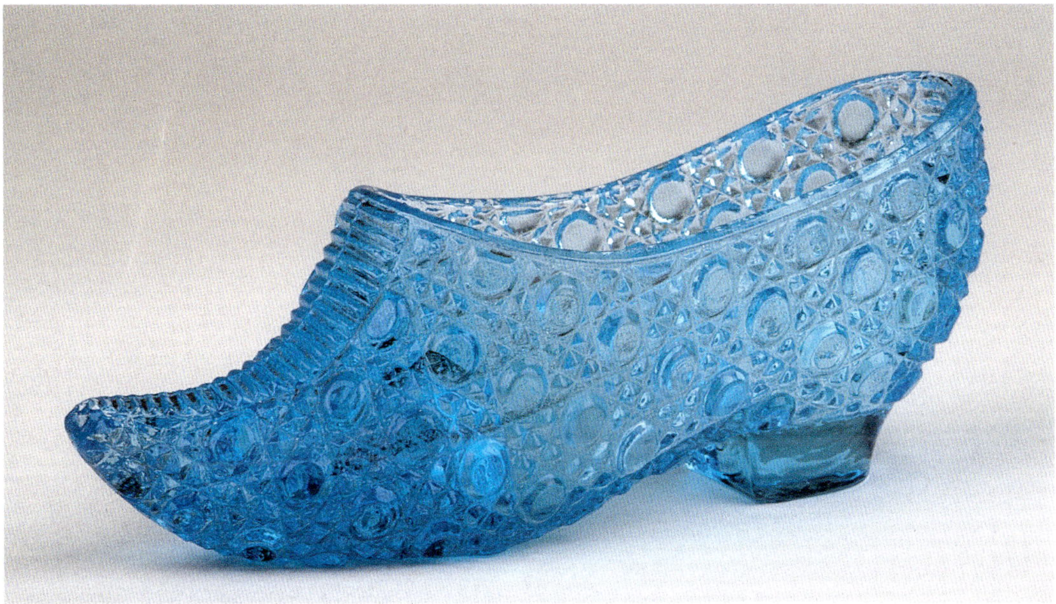

Shoe in the cane pattern made by Bryce Brothers, circa 1890. Blue, $75-95.

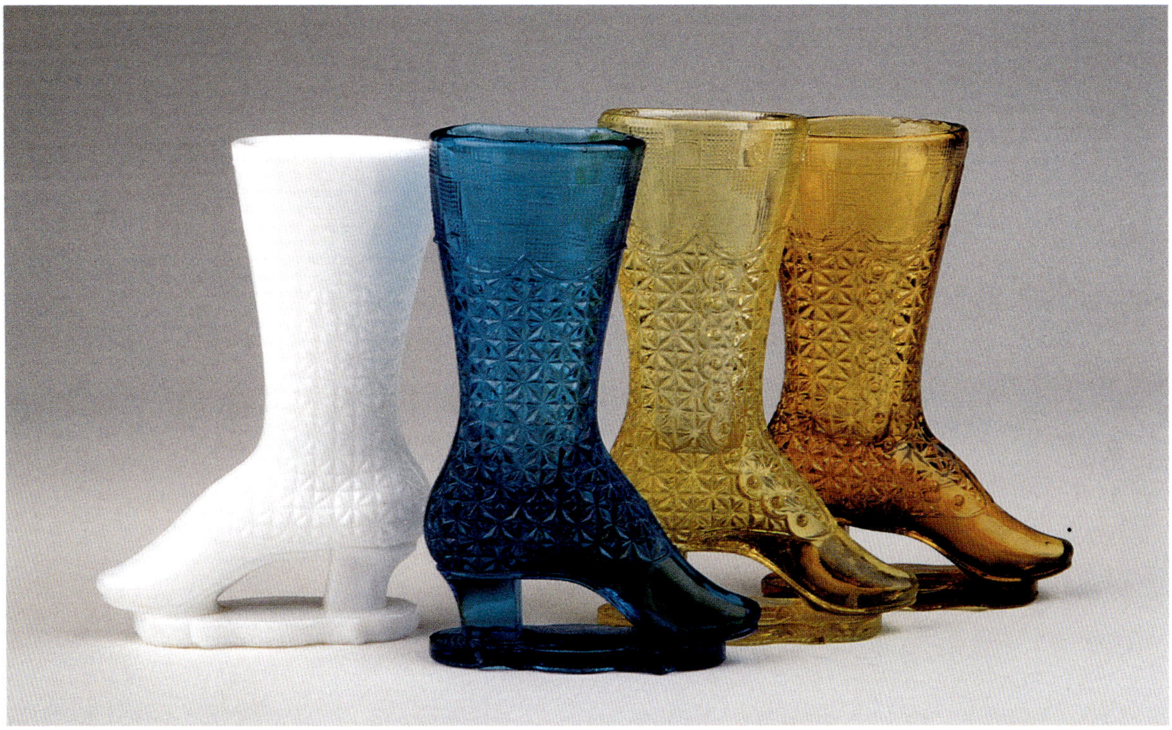

Shoe in the fine cut pattern made by the Bellaire Goblet Company, B&H on the bottom, 5 1/2" high. It was made in both left and right shoes. Amber, $65-85. vaseline, $85-110. Blue, $85-110. Opal, $95-125.

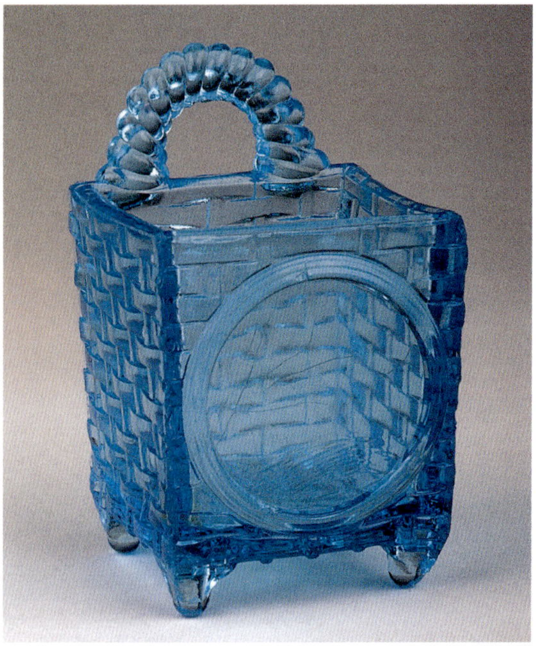

Wall Pocket match holder made by Bryce Brothers, circa 1888. 2 1/2" high and 2 1/4" wide. Blue, $80-100.

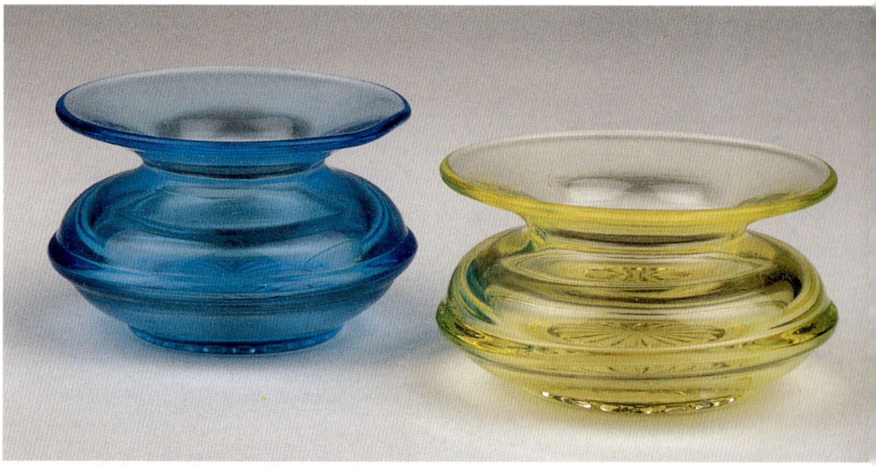

Spittoon of unknown origin collected as a toothpick holder, 1 1/2" high and 3" wide. Blue, $80-100. Canary, $80-100.

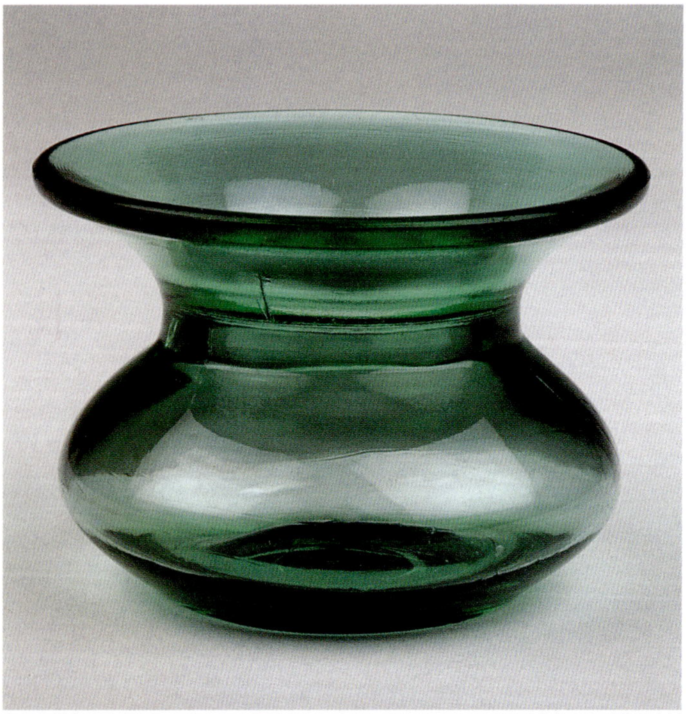

Spittoon Toothpick or match holder. Green, $55-70.

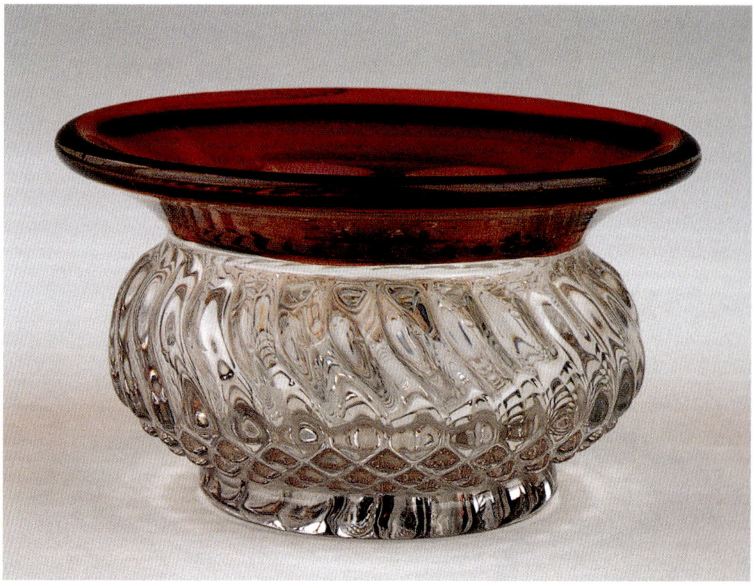

Spittoon toothpick holder in the Jersey Swirl pattern made by the Windsor Glass Company, 1 5/8" high and 2 3/8" wide. Ruby Stain, $85-125.

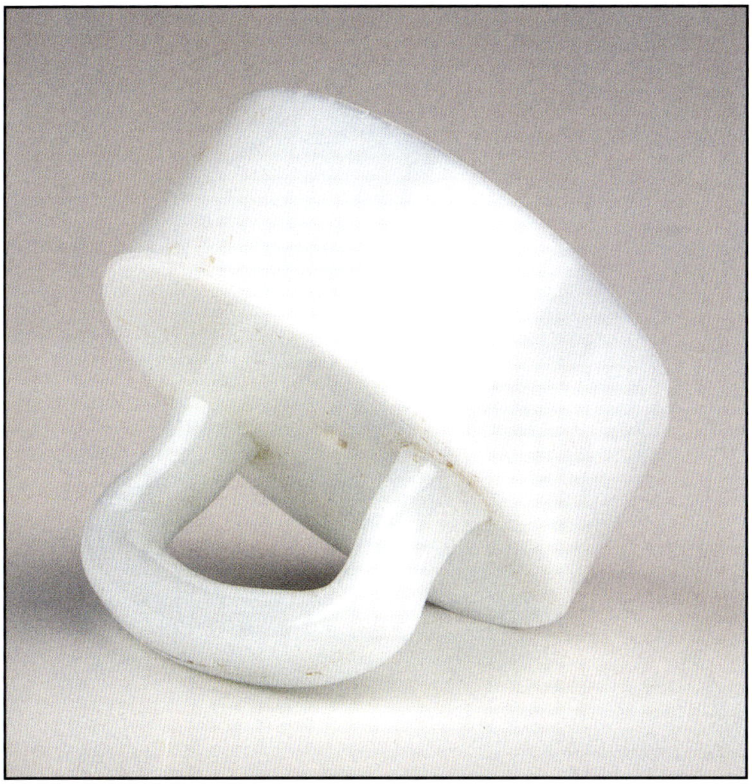

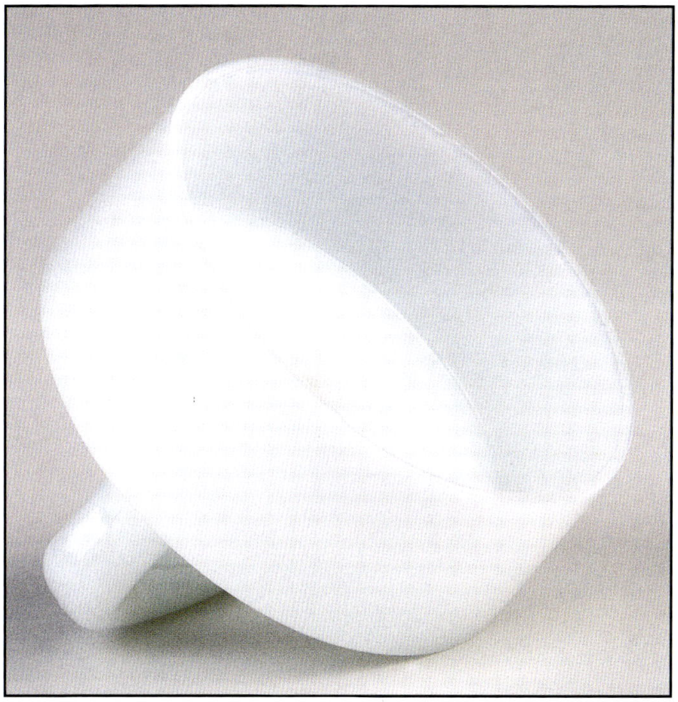

Cookie Cutter, *PAT APL FOR*. 3" diameter. Opal, $120-135.

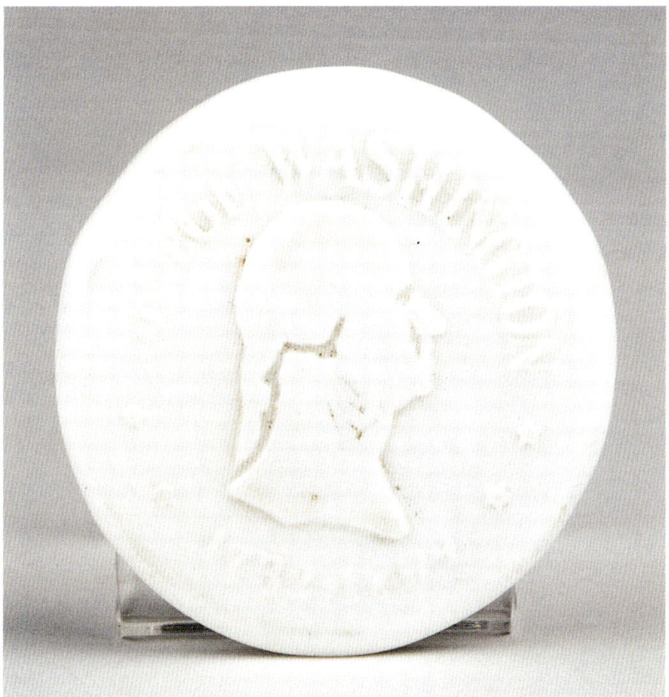

Medallion, *Washington Memorial 1732-1799*. 2 7/8" diameter. Opal, $120-140.

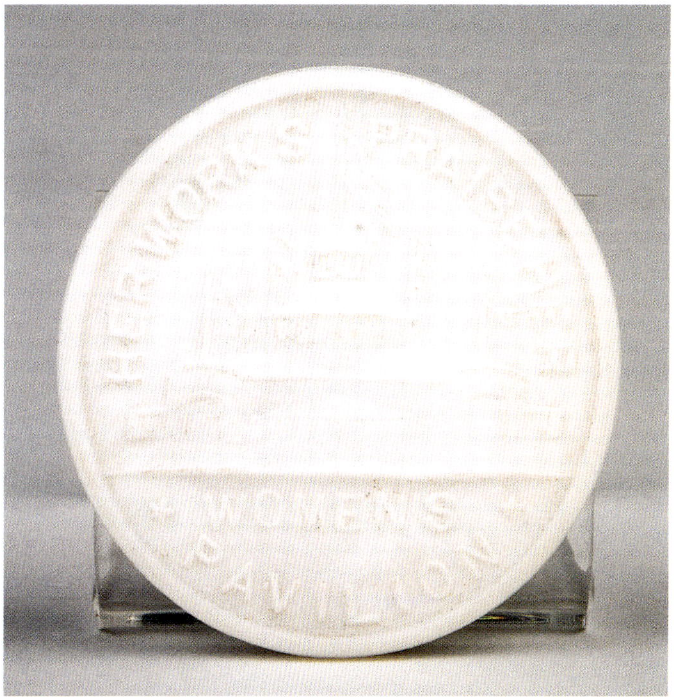

Medallion, Eagle with *1776-1876. America Celebration*. The reverse shows the Woman's Pavilion: *Her Works Praise Her*. 2 1/4" diameter. Opal, $190-225.

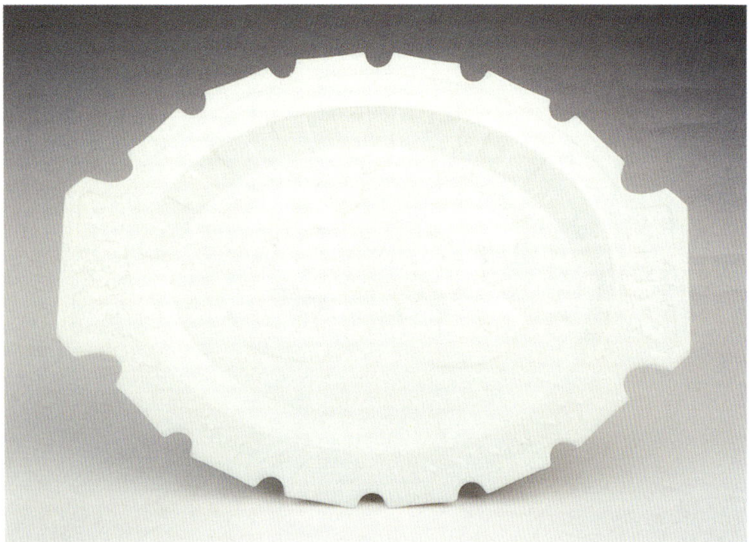

Blaine-Logan platter, a political item of 1884. 13 1/8" long. Opal, $1,450-1,550.

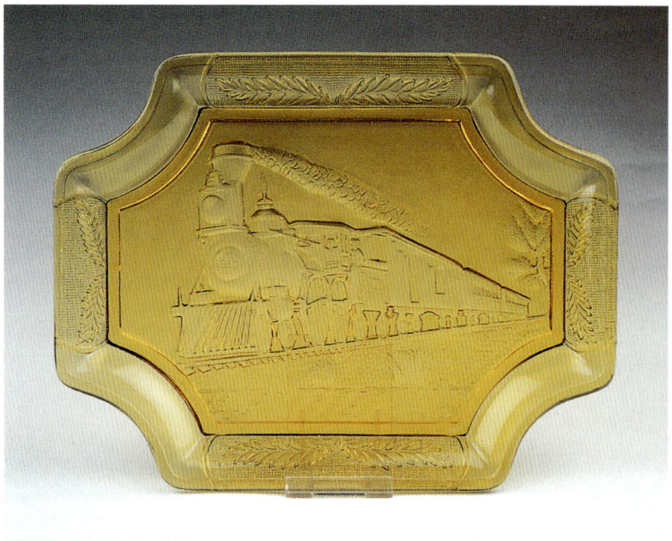

Train or Railroad platter made by the Canton Glass Company. This was made at a factory at Beaver Falls, Pennsylvania, at a time when the Canton, Ohio, factory had been destroyed by fire and production continued at this glass works. The platter is 12" long. Amber, $290-325.

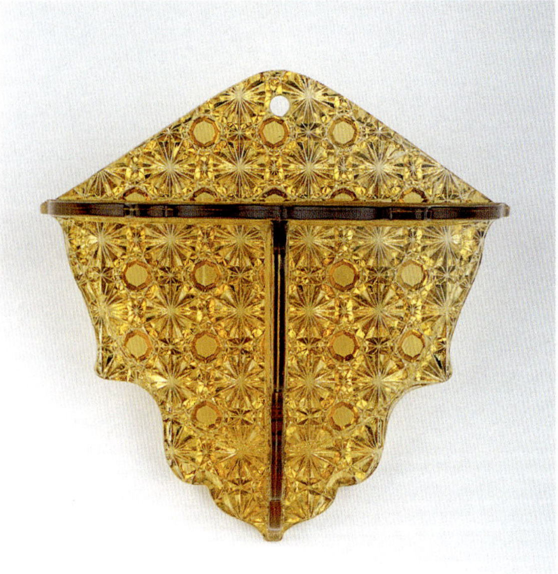

Wall Shelf in the daisy and button pattern. This example has several inches of glass missing from the top. It was cut down to eliminate the breakage and then redrilled. 7 1/2" wide. Amber, $75-110 as shown.

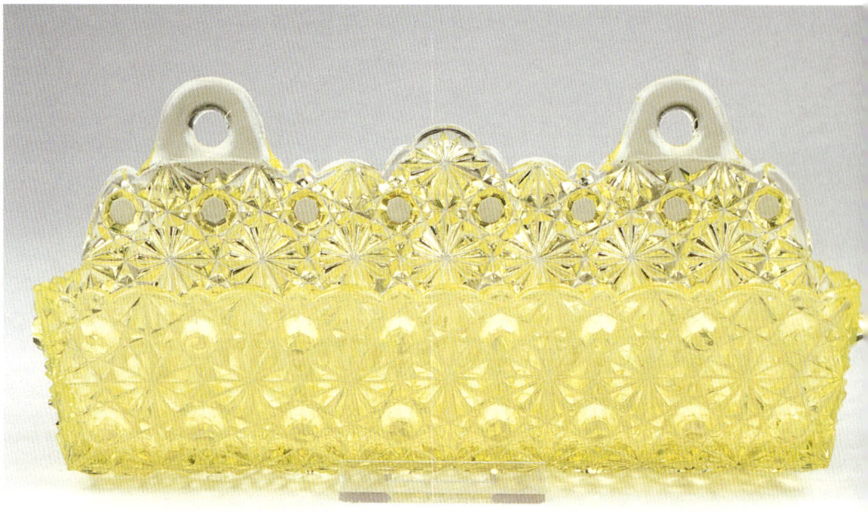

Wall Comb Tray in the daisy and button pattern. 8 3/4" long. vaseline, $250-275.

Oval Basket toothpick holder made by Adams and Company, circa 1890, and continued by the United States Glass Company in 1891. 2 3/4" high and 2 1/4" wide. Clear, $40-50. Amber, $50-60. Blue, $60-70. Canary, $60-70.

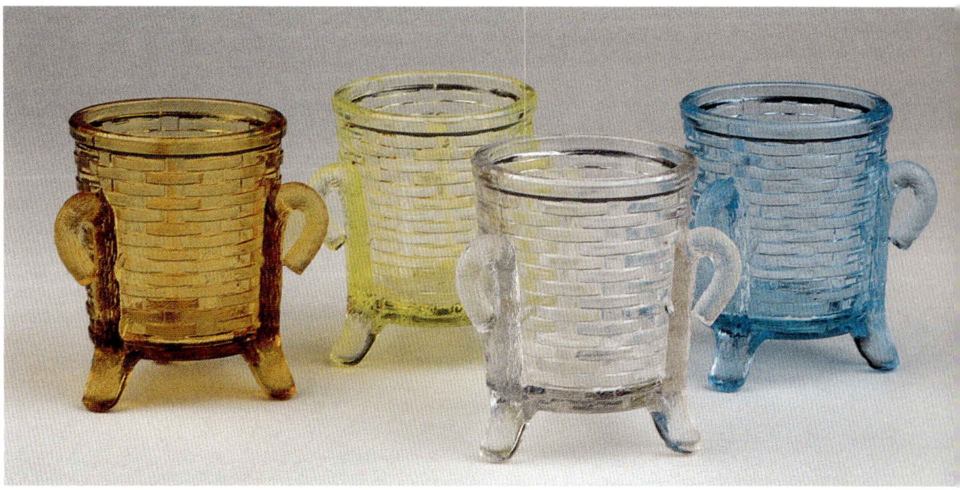

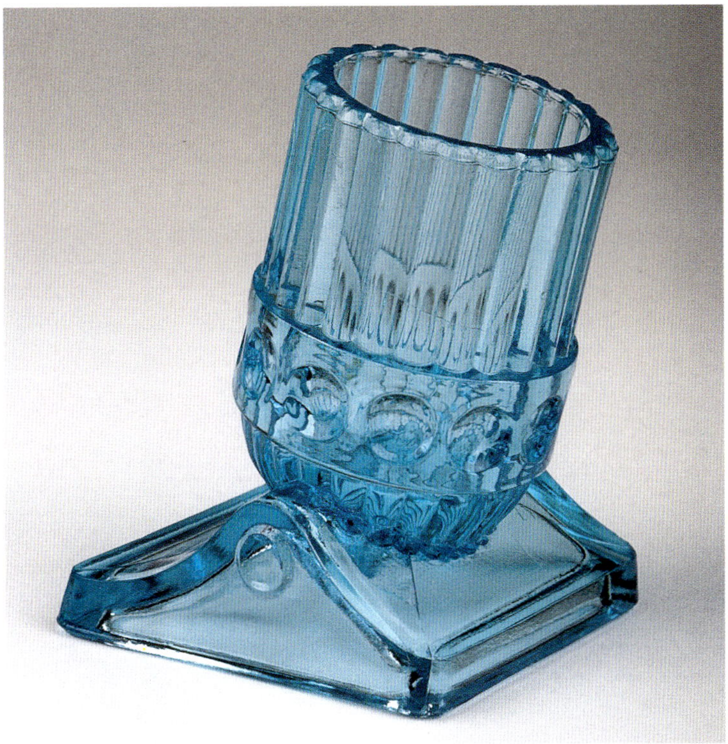

Gatling Gun toothpick or match holder. 2 7/8" high and 1 5/8" wide. Blue, $65-80.

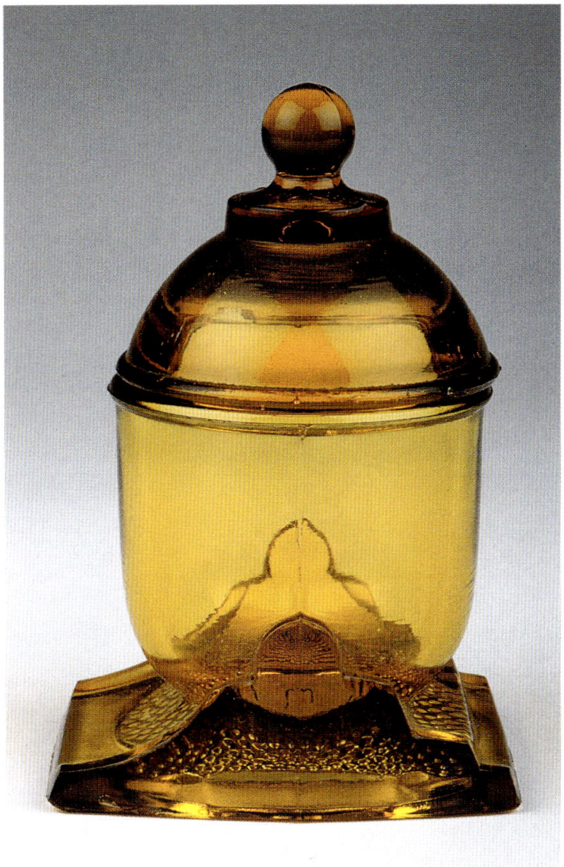

Mortar mustard container. 2 1/2" high and 2 1/2" wide. Amber, $55-75.

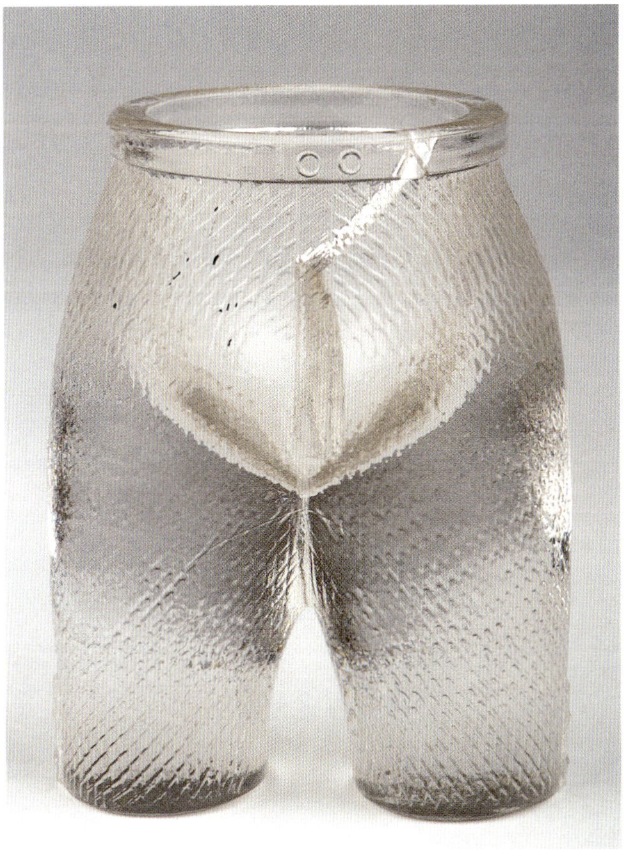

Drawers toothpick holder made by the Findlay Flint Glass Company, circa 1890. 2 7/8" high and 2 1/4" wide. Clear, $100-125.

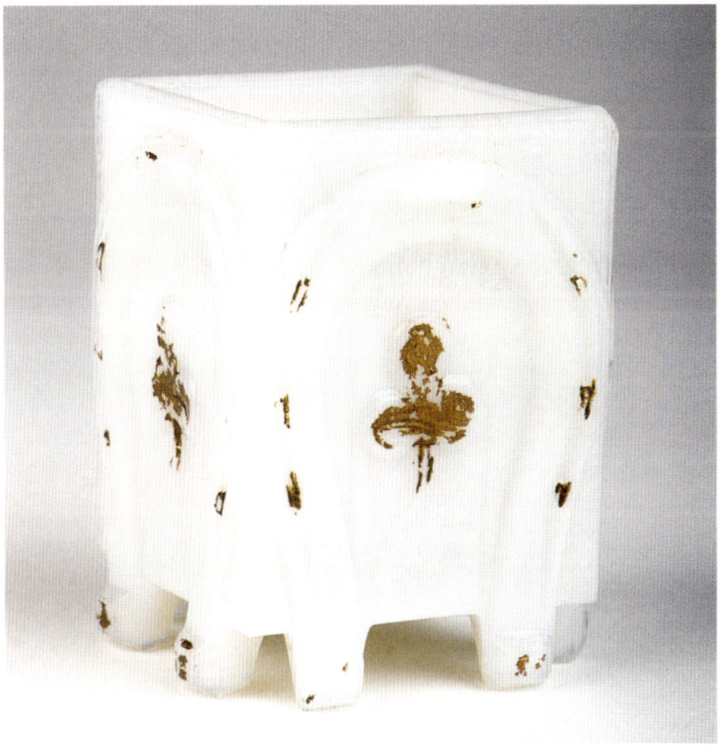

Horseshoe with Clover toothpick holder. It was illustrated in the Lyons Brothers catalog of 1906. 2 1/4" high and 1 3/4" wide. Opal decorated, $100-125.

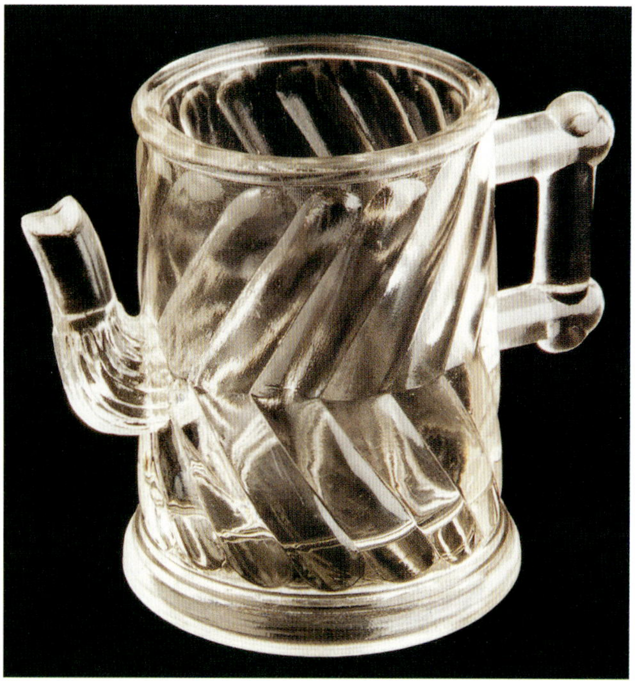

Miller toothpick holder or mustard jar made by the Findlay Flint Glass Company, circa 1891. 2 3/4" high and 2" wide. Clear, $350-380.

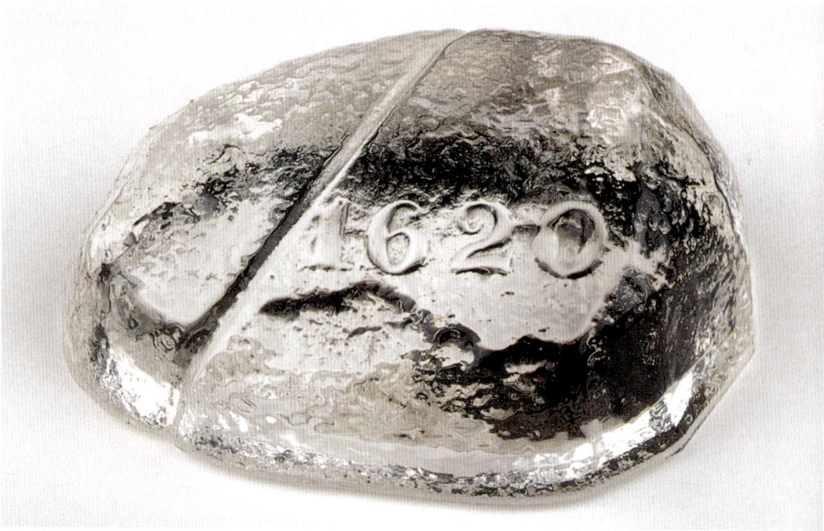

Plymouth Rock paperweight *1620* believed to be the product of the Bellaire Goblet Company, circa 1882 (see text). $90-120.

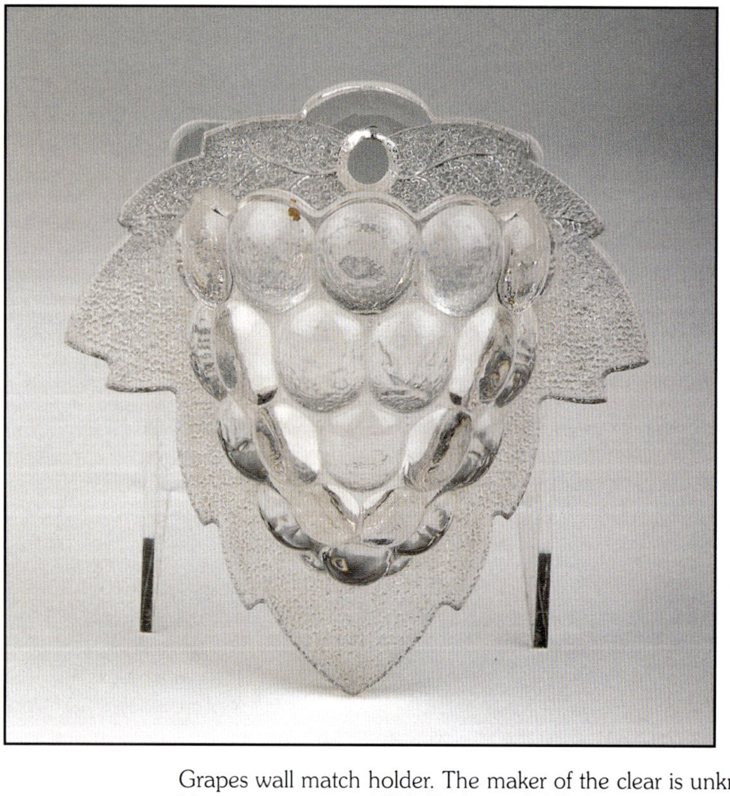

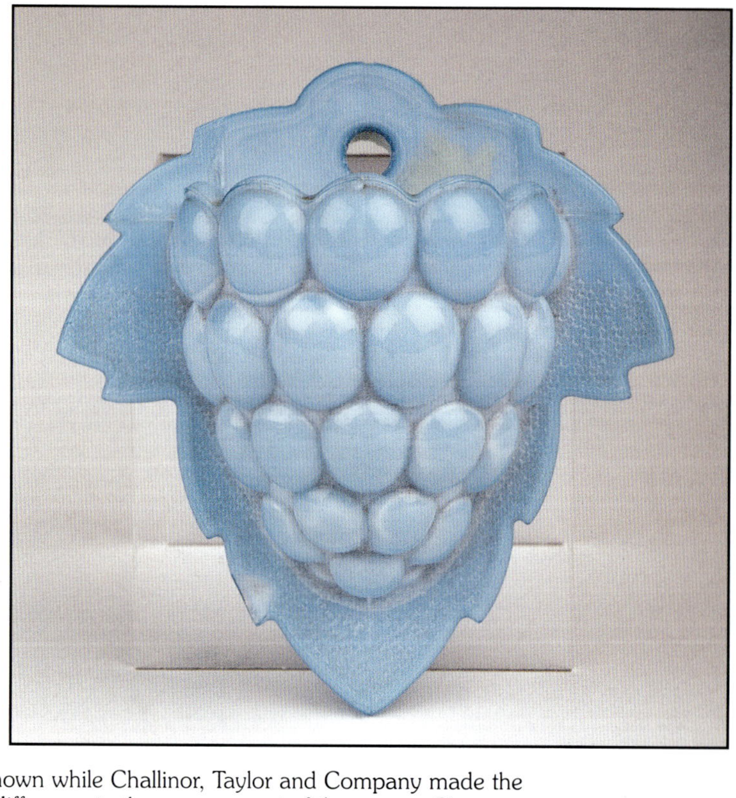

Grapes wall match holder. The maker of the clear is unknown while Challinor, Taylor and Company made the blue opaque, circa 1891. Both are 4 1/2" high. Note the difference in the arrangement of the grapes. Clear, $50-70. Blue opaque, $90-125.

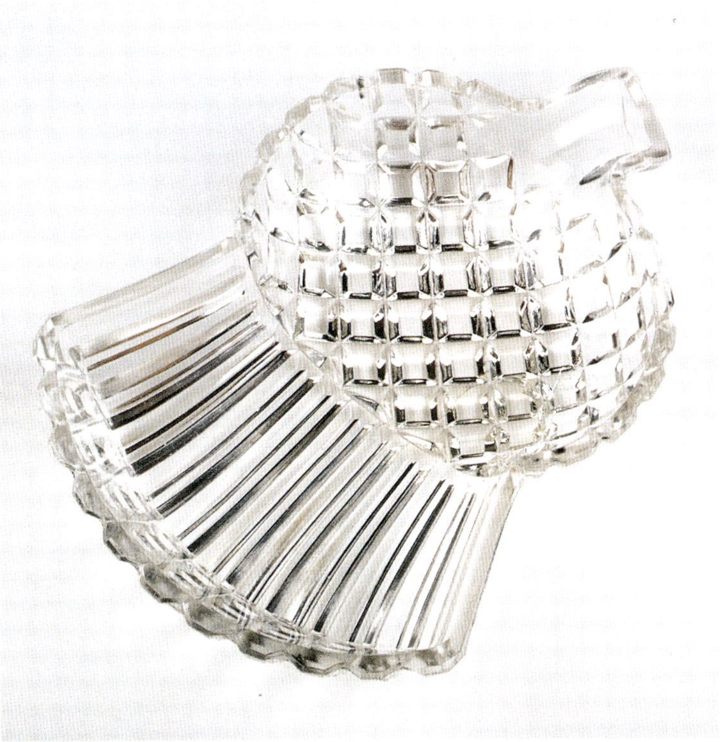

Thistle pickle made by the Dalzell, Gilmore & Leighton Company, circa 1898. This is documented by a Dalzell, Gilmore & Leighton catalog of the late 1890s. 8" long. Reproduced by the National Glass Company at their #9 glass works from the original mold. Clear, $65-85.

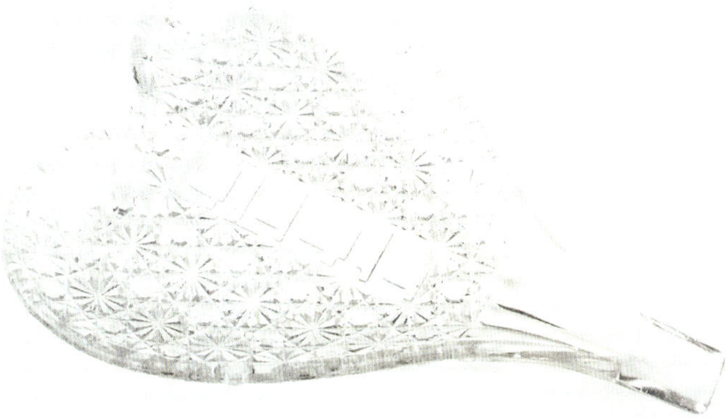

Lillie daisy and button pattern pickle dish made by the Co-operative Flint Glass Company, circa 1880s. 8 5/8" long. Clear, $65-80.

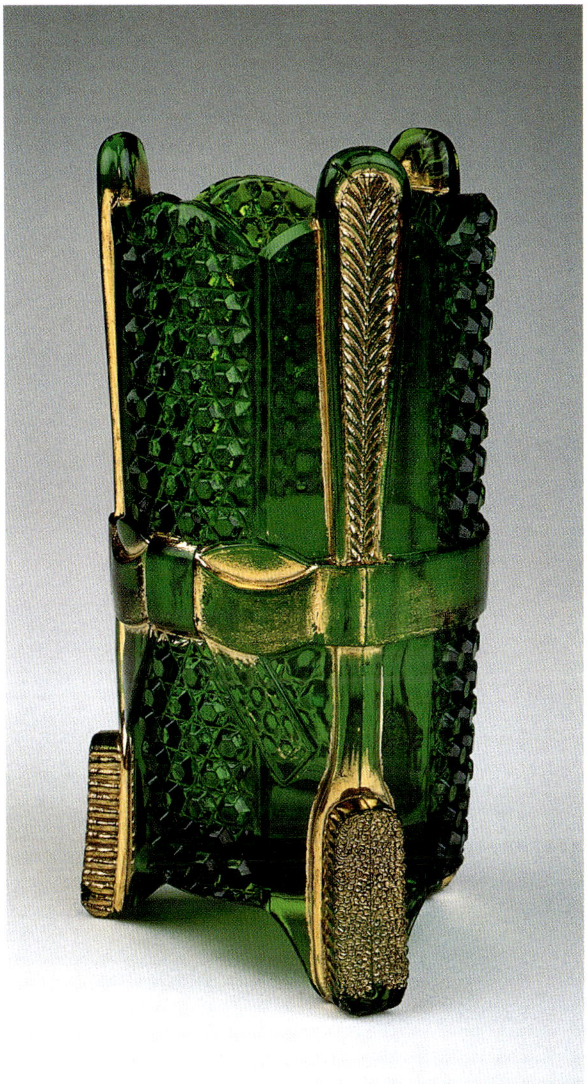

Toothbrush holder made by the United States Glass Company. 4 3/4" high. Green with gold, $175-200.

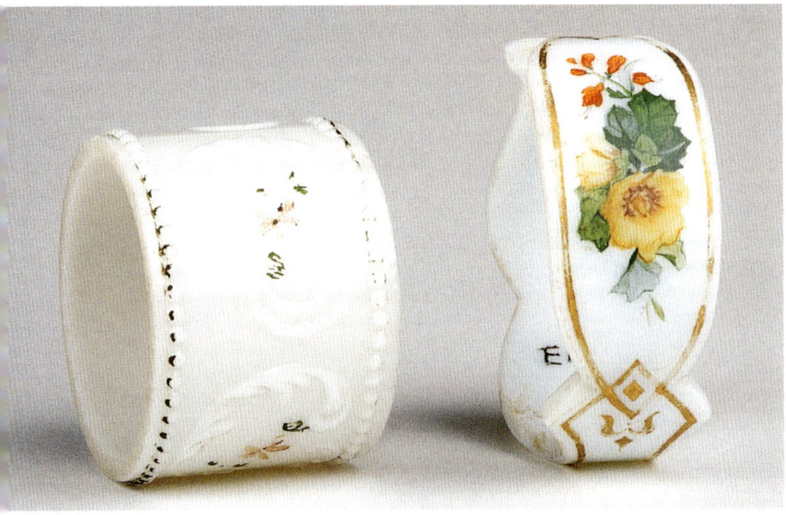

Napkin Rings. 2 1/2" diameter and 2" diameter. Opal decorated, $130-145.

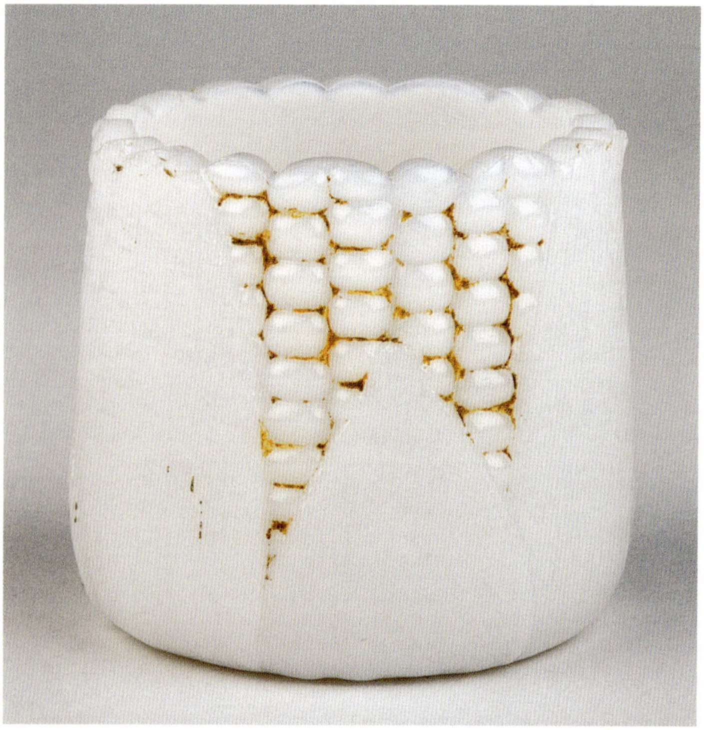

Corn with Husks toothpick holder. 2" high and 2 1/4" wide. Opal decorated, $80-90.

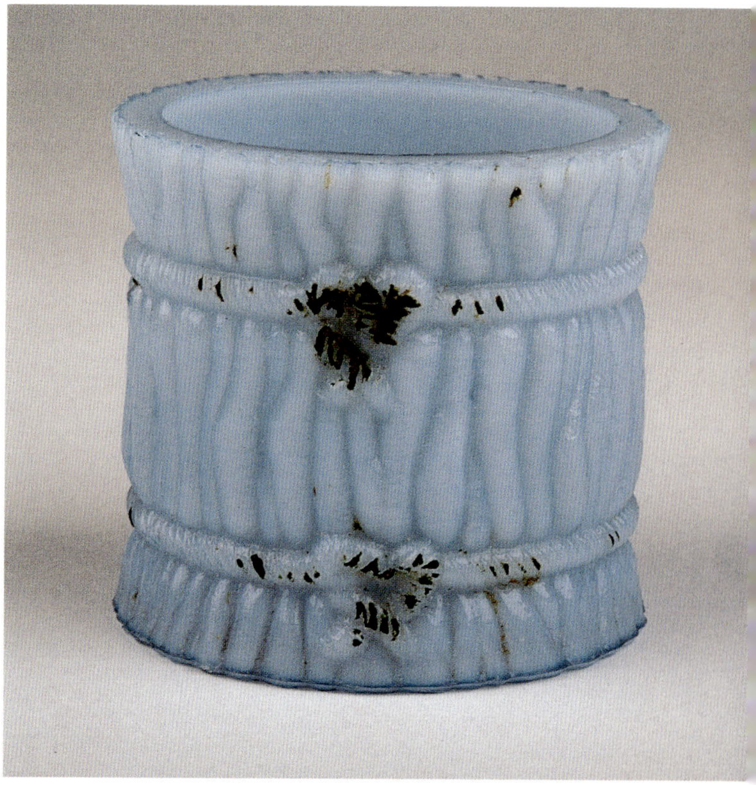

Fiber Bundle toothpick holder made by the Eagle Glass Company, circa 1897. 2" high and 2 1/8" wide. Blue opaque, $60-70.

Jardinière, two piece, made for the Pan American Exposition of 1901. 6" high. $220-240.

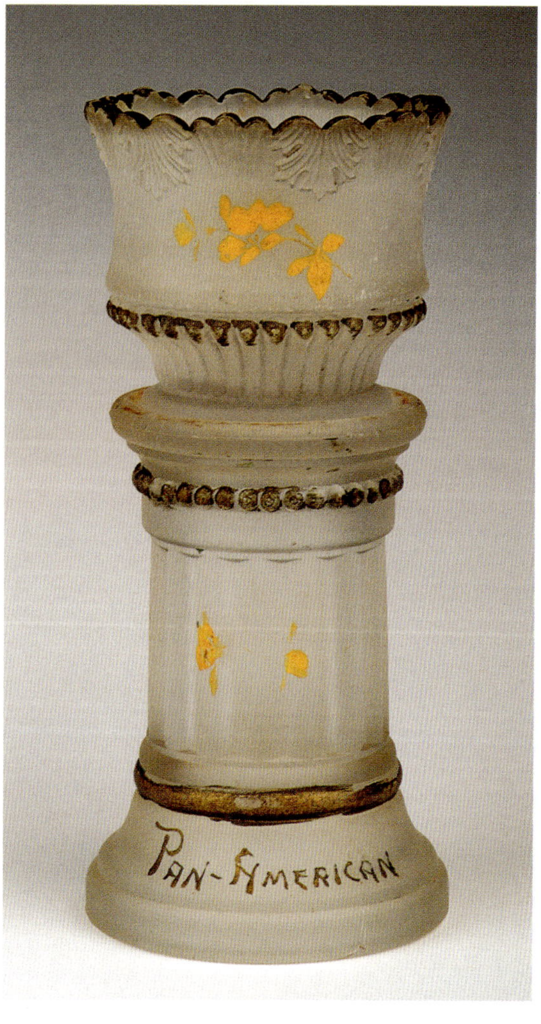

Wall match holder made in the cane pattern. vaseline, $150-175.

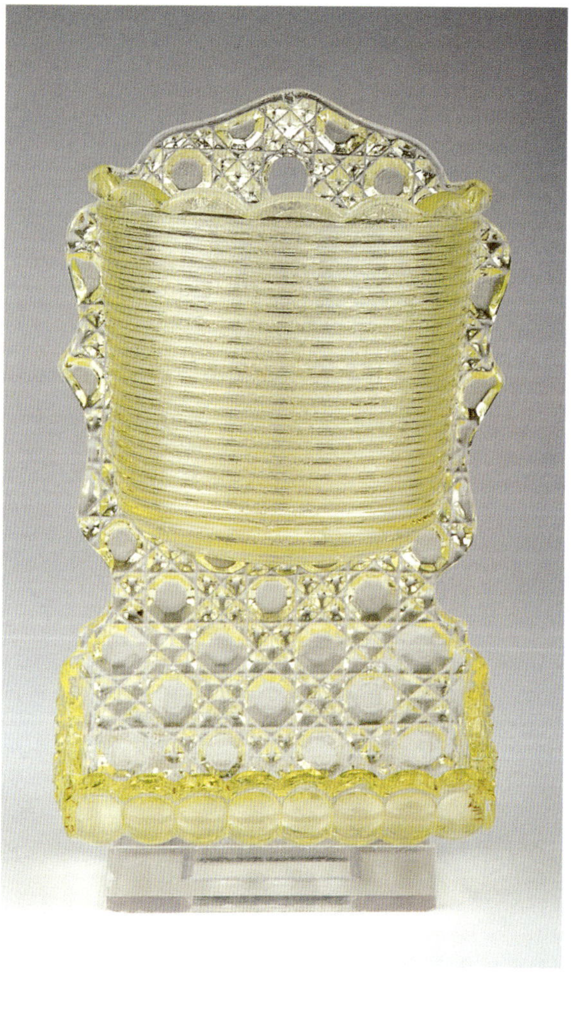

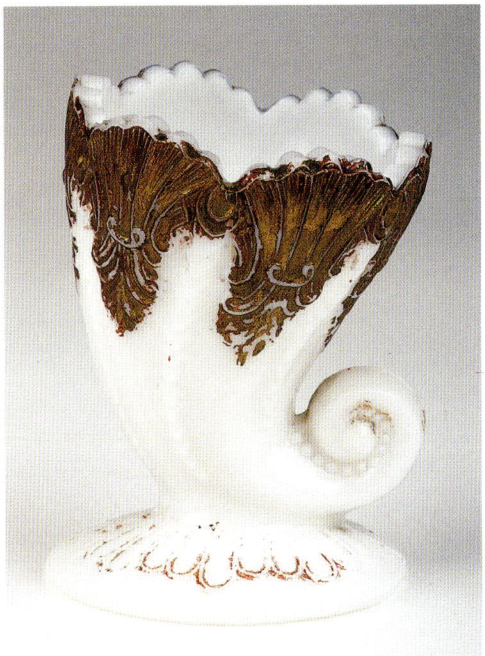

Cornucopia vase, maker unknown. Decorated opal, $55-75.

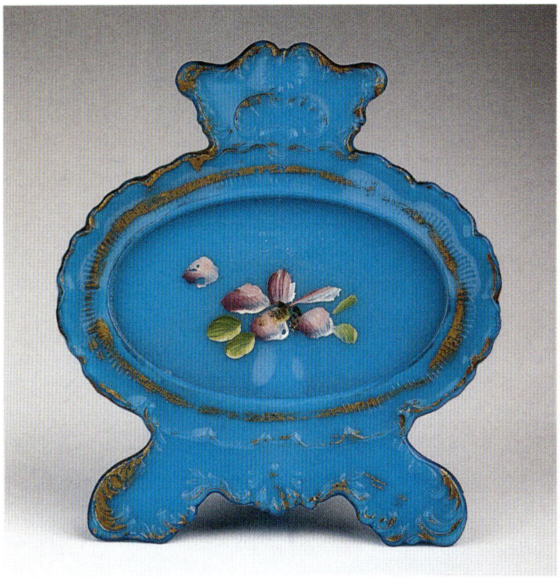

Easter Easel made by the Dithridge and Company, circa 1890s. 7 1/4" high. Blue opaque, $120-135.

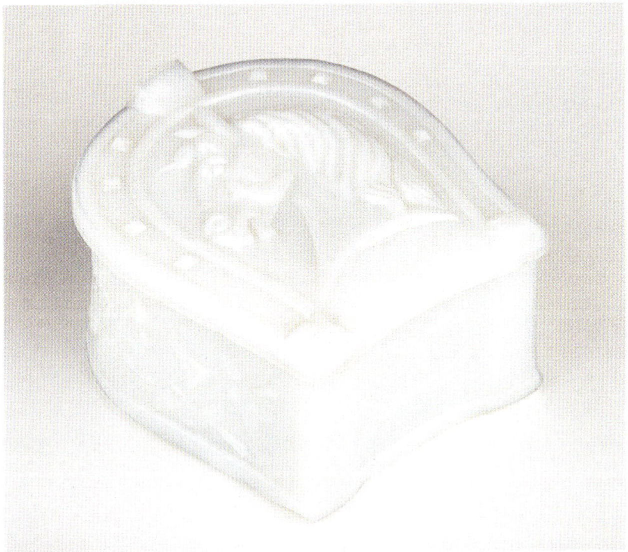

Horseshoe box with a horse head on the lid, reported to have been made by the Sandwich Glass Company. 3 1/2" wide. Opal, $345-360.

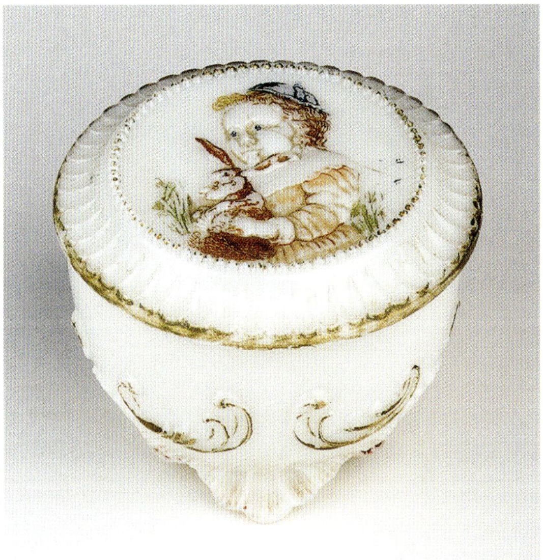

Powder box with a girl on the lid. 3 1/4" high and 4 1/4" wide. Opal, $625-675.

Horseshoe saltcellar. 3" long. Opal decorated, $50-70.

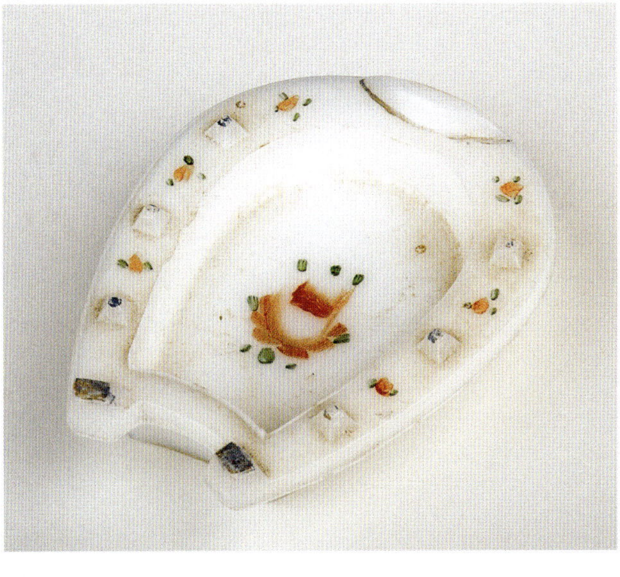

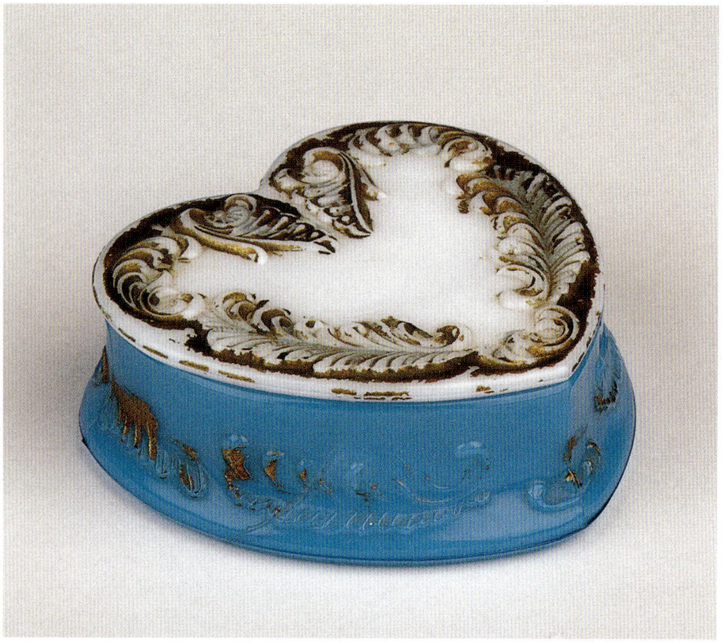

Heart Jewel Box covered dish made by McKee and Brothers, circa 1897. 3 1/2" diameter. This is a married piece. The values given are for matching tops and bases. Opal, $75-85. Blue opaque, $90-100.

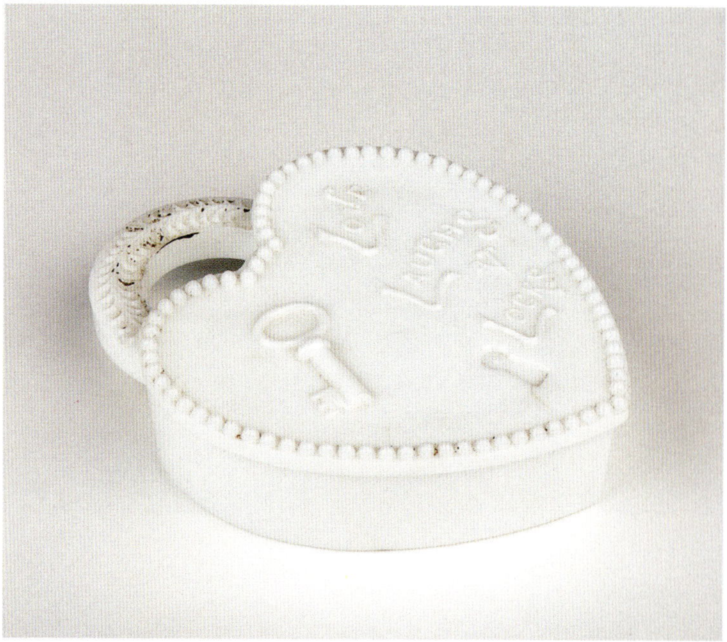

Lock Box covered dish made by McKee and Brothers, circa 1897. 4 3/4" high. Opal, $110-125.

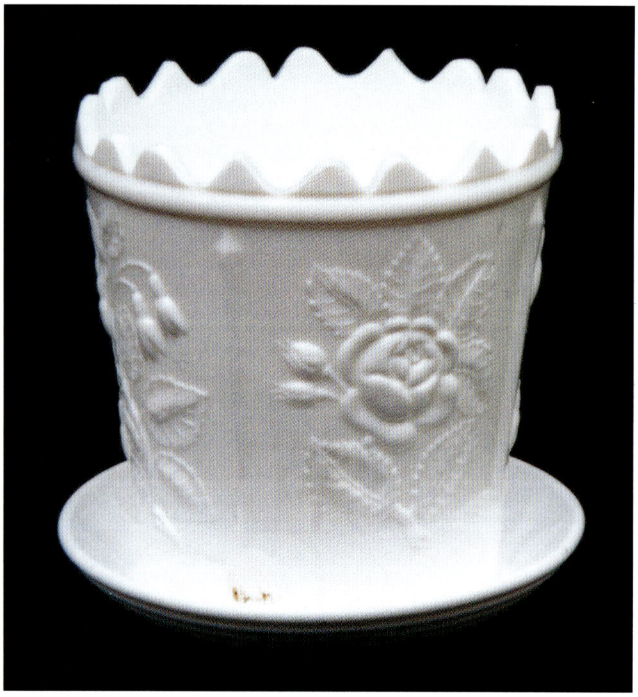

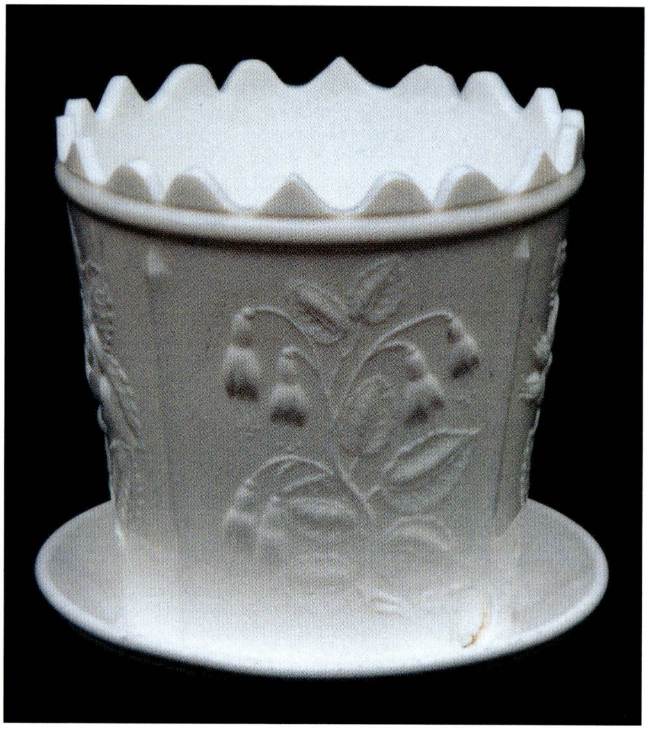

Russell Flower pot patented by William Russell on Nov 6, 1877, patent # 196,937, and made by the Model Flint Glass Company at Findlay, Ohio, circa 1889. Can be found in dark amber, steel blue, and opal. Opal, $1,800-2,500.

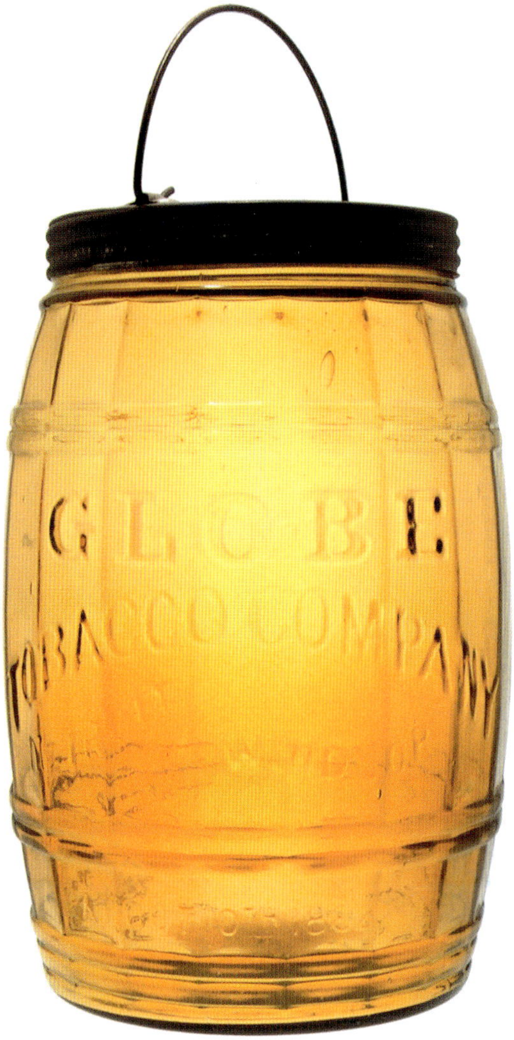

Globe Tobacco Jar made by the Hemingray Glass Company. Various shades of amber, $275-300 for this item shown.

Paperweight, *E L Packer Lumber Pittsburgh, Pa.*, 3 3/4" high and 2 1/4" wide. Blue, $170-210.

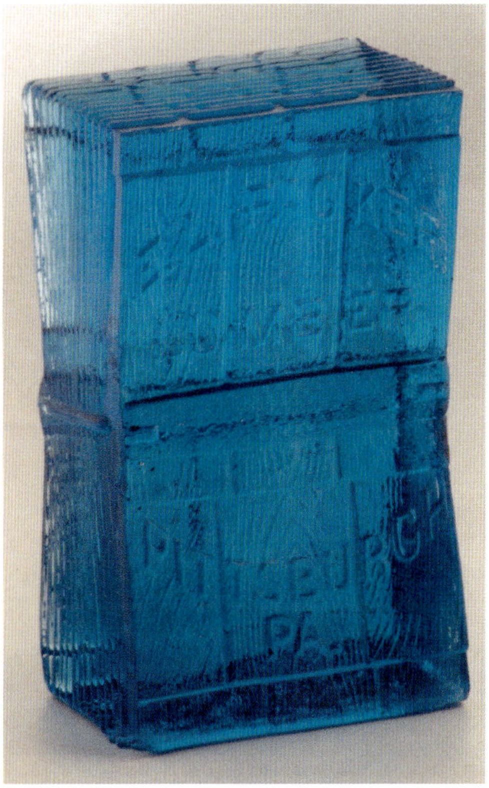

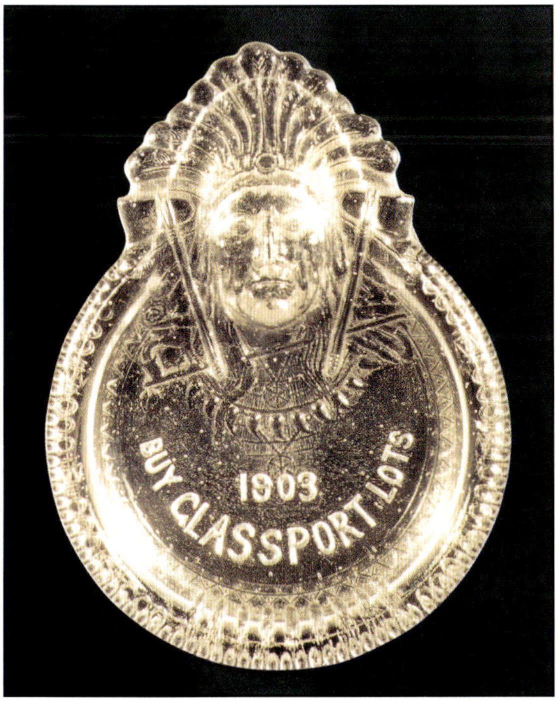

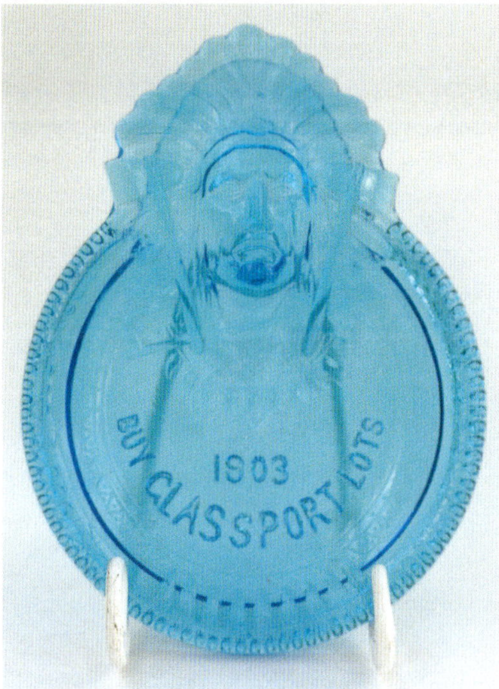

Glassport Paperweight made by the United States Glass Company to advertise their Glassport factory products, circa 1903. 5 1/2" high and 4 1/4" wide. Clear, $65-90. Blue, $175-200.

Bibliography

Books

Bredehoft, Neila & Tom. *Victorian Novelties & Figurals.* St. Louisville, Ohio: Geo. Duncan & Sons. Cherry Hill Publications, 1989.

Bredehoft & Sanford. *Findlay Flint Glass Co.* St. Louisville, Ohio: Cherry Hill Publications, 1994.

_____. *Columbia Glass Co.* DeLeon Springs, Florida: Researched Glass Facts, 1997.

_____. *Glass Toothpick Holders.* Paducah, Kentucky: Collector Books, 1999.

Ferson, Regis F. & Mary F. *Yesterdays Milk Glass Today.* Greensburg, Pennsylvania: Chas. H. Henry Printing Co., 1981.

Lucas, Robert I. *Tarentum Pattern Glass.* Tarentum, Pennsylvania: Privately Published, 1981.

Sanford, Jo & Bob. *The Bonita Glass Co.* DeLeon Springs, Florida: Researched Glass Facts, 1997.

_____. *The Canton Glass Co.* DeLeon Springs, Florida: Researched Glass Facts, 1999.

_____. *Glass Tableware-The Factories and The Men.* DeLeon Springs, Florida: Researched Glass Facts, 2000.

Smith, Don. *Findlay Pattern Glass.* Findlay, Ohio: Privately Published, 1970.

Stout, Sandra McPhee. *The Complete Book of McKee Glass.* North Kansas City, Missouri: Trojan Press, Inc., 1972.

Welker, John W. & Elizabeth F. *Pressed Glass in America.* Boyertown, Pennsylvania: Antique Acres Press, 1985.

Yalom, Libby. *Shoes of Glass, 2.* Marietta, Ohio: The Glass Press, 1998.

Factory Catalogs

Adams & Co.
Bellaire Goblet Co.
Central Glass Co.
Co-operative Flint Glass Co.
Dalzell, Gilmore & Leighton
Hobbs, Brockunier & Co.
King, Son & Co.
McKee & Brothers
National Glass Co.
O'Hara Glass Co.

Jobbers' Catalogs

Baltimore Bargain House
Butler Brothers
Lovell, F. H. & Co.
Lyon Brothers
Ogden, Merrill & Greer
Pitkin & Brooks
Spelman Brothers
T. M. Roberts
Wallace & Co.

Trade Journals

American Glassworker, various issues.
China, Glass & Lamps, various issues.
Crockery & Glass Journal, various issues.
Pottery & Glassware Salesman, various issues.